Criminalizing Intimate Image Abuse

Criminalizing Intimate Image Abuse

A Comparative Perspective

Edited by

GIAN MARCO CALETTI
KOLIS SUMMERER

OXFORD
UNIVERSITY PRESS

OXFORD
UNIVERSITY PRESS

Great Clarendon Street, Oxford, OX2 6DP,
United Kingdom

Oxford University Press is a department of the University of Oxford.
It furthers the University's objective of excellence in research, scholarship,
and education by publishing worldwide. Oxford is a registered trade mark of
Oxford University Press in the UK and in certain other countries

First Edition published in 2024

Published in the United States of America by Oxford University Press
198 Madison Avenue, New York, NY 10016, United States of America

British Library Cataloguing in Publication Data

Data available

Library of Congress Control Number: 2023948186

ISBN 978–0–19–887781–3

DOI: 10.1093/oso/9780198877813.001.0001

To our girls,
Vera, Agata (KS)
and Francesca (GMC)

Foreword

*Professor Dr John AE Vervaele**

Image-based sexual abuse has become an increasing and even endemic phenomenon in our digital societies. As the use of Internet-enabled devices, social media, and technology proliferates, it has become very easy to create these images, to share them, and even to reach out to an infinite audience. Many of these images have been created in the specific context of intimacy or privacy, even auto-produced by the victim and shared with their partner by sexting. Although these images were intended to remain private, they have been further disclosed by a perpetrator to a wider public, by 'cyberflashing', distribution on social media, or posting on the Internet by a second circle of perpetrators. This reality is not limited to vulnerable victims, such as children, but has become common practice between adults. Most of the victims are women, although this is by no means exclusively so. This phenomenon is therefore also part of digital forms of gender-based violence against women. All these acts are perpetrated without the explicit or affirmative consent of the victim. Non-consensual disclosure converts these images into 'pornography', which can also be 'revenge porn' and result in sextortion, depending on the specific motives of the perpetrators in question.

Given the devastating harm that this entails for the victims and society, affecting legal interests such as privacy and intimacy, sexual identity, autonomy and privacy, moral freedom, and leading in some cases to the suicide of the victim, it has become clear that the existing criminal law framework, aiming at protecting privacy and combating the sexual exploitation of children and child pornography as well as violence against women or cybercrime, falls short when it comes to this specific reality. The same can be said of the existing international legal framework, such as for instance the Inter-American Convention on the Prevention, Punishment, and Eradication of Violence against Women (Convention of Belém do Pará) of the Organization of American States (OAS) of 1994, the 2001 Budapest Convention on cybercrime of the Council of Europe, the Council of Europe Convention on preventing and combating violence against women and domestic violence (Istanbul Convention) of 2011, and the EU Directive of 2011 on combating the sexual abuse and sexual exploitation of children and child pornography. Even when Expert Groups make specific recommendations, such as for instance the Council of Europe Expert Group on Action against Violence against Women and Domestic

* Professor at the College of Europe, Bruges; Emeritus Professor of Economic and European Criminal Law, Utrecht University, President of the International Association of Penal Law (AIDP-IAPL).

Violence (GREVIO) which offers a General Recommendation (no 1) on the digital dimension of violence against women laid down in the Istanbul Convention, protection gaps remain. The lack of sufficient and adequate criminal law protection in relation to this harmful conduct also triggers the positive obligations of states under the existing human rights instruments, as confirmed by the European Court of Human Rights in the case of *Buturugă v Romania*.

When considering an appropriate criminal law solution as part of a general policy to prevent, protect, and repress, considerable problems do arise. First of all, there is no clear typology or conceptual definition of the phenomenon, which is also illustrated by the variety of definitions involved. Second, adults have a right to sexual freedom and identity and criminal law should not intervene as a moral agent in the essence of sexual freedom. Third, the non-consensual use of sexual images is also a difficult issue as the lack of consensus is in many cases not related to the production of these images and even not to their disclosure in an intimate setting, but to their further or extended disclosure. Must those who further disclose or distribute always ask for affirmative consensus or can this consensus also be deduced from the facts in the intimate setting? Does the behaviour of the victim play a role in this, or would this always result in victim blaming? And what type of legal interest should be protected by criminal law? Should the criminal law intervention aim at protecting sexual privacy as such?

In the light of all these challenges and legal developments this comparative criminal law study under the leadership of Gian Marco Caletti andKolis Summerer fills a real gap by providing us with an insight into (1) the conceptual and theoretical issues; (2) the criminal law responses at the national level; (3) the functions of criminal law and its limitations; and (4) a more coordinated policy of prevention, protection, and repression, including forms of restorative and transformative justice. As the reader will understand from these four dimensions, this edited volume offers a highly interesting and very valuable analysis of the state of the art and the challenges to be overcome. The contributors are key experts in the field, and the countries selected for the comparative analysis illustrate perfectly the divergence of the actual approaches in relation to *actus reus*, *mens rea*, and legal interests, with their respective pros and cons.

The edited volume clearly underpins the need for new legislative criminal law solutions, but leaving food for thought when it comes to the choices to be made by the criminal law legislator. In my opinion the legislator should in that case not be limited to the national level, but also include new international suppression treaties.

For all of these reasons I highly recommend this richly edited volume to scholars, legislators, and practitioners alike.

Foreword: Law in the Service of Privacy and Autonomy

*Stephen J Schulhofer***

Not so long ago, law (and the male-dominated societies it reflected) conceived of sexual abuse as strictly and doubly physical. Except when involving minors, a sexual offence typically required proof that the perpetrator had intruded on the physical body of another person, and had done so using substantial physical force. With a better understanding of sexual harm, protection now extends not only to physical safety but also to sexual autonomy, the right to choose freely whether, when, and with whom to be sexually intimate.[1] Yet vestiges of the older view persist in corners of the law and in common social assumptions,[2] underscoring the continuing need for energetic reform.

Initial reforms reoriented protection for the physical body, centring the criminal offence on *unwanted* contact, whether forcible or not. But more broadly, devastating harm results even without unwanted contact, when intimate images are taken or distributed without consent.

Which kinds of images should the law protect? How can we distinguish egregious violations from misconduct warranting milder sanctions or no state intervention? When is consent absent? Is this the same question as in cases of sexual contact, or should distributing a sexual image require a different kind of permission?

This volume provides an invaluable resource for tackling these issues. Comparative law is especially helpful in suggesting *possibilities*, less so for the merits of *particular solutions*. Answers that make sense for one nation may not be wise for another. In particular, in criminal justice the US is truly exceptional, and not always in a good way. Five distinctive features make new sexual offences especially problematic for the United States: its criminal law is exceptionally decentralized, populist, discretionary, punitive, and racially fraught, all to an extreme degree.

Decentralized: Enforcement in American states is controlled by District Attorneys (DAs) in each county, of which the US has over 3,000. American

** Robert B McKay Professor of Law Emeritus, New York University School of Law.

[1] See Stephen J Schulhofer, *Unwanted Sex* (Harvard University Press 1998).

[2] Many American states still require proof of physical force as a prerequisite to conviction for rape or sexual assault. See Stephen J Schulhofer, 'What Does "Consent" Mean?' in Tatjana Hörnle (ed), *Sexual Assault* (OUP 2023) 53.

DAs have complete independence in making enforcement decisions for their jurisdiction.

Populist: More significant than the jury is the fact that these DAs are elected. They are responsible to public opinion in their particular county, be it urban or rural, affluent or poor, permissive or prudish. And American DAs seldom have the kind of systematic training taken for granted in Europe.

Discretionary: Vast discretion is presupposed. The resources that counties allocate typically are insufficient to prosecute even half the known offences, even less for misdemeanours. Selectivity is imperative but opaque and largely unguided by rules. Among cases singled out for prosecution, 90 per cent are resolved by plea bargaining, adding further opacity and discretion.

Punitive: For sexual offences, the well-known severity of American punishments is compounded by America's distinctive manner of registering persons convicted. Unlike virtually every other country on earth—and to an extent inconceivable in Europe—America allows unrestricted public access to its online sex-offence registries, which can extend even to juveniles and misdemeanours, exposing registrants to potentially insuperable obstacles to education, employment, and decent housing. In the United States, conviction for a sexual felony, and often even for a misdemeanour, can carry life-shattering consequences.

Racial inequity. All Western nations struggle to ensure equity across racial and ethnic lines. But the United States is in a class by itself. Following the abolition of slavery (only in 1865), Southern states and many others instituted regimes of legally enforced apartheid—dismantled only slowly, piecemeal, and starting only in the 1950s and 1960s. That legacy persists in multiple forms, especially for the 12–14 per cent of the current US population descended from people once enslaved in the Southern states. Notoriously, these African-Americans represent a disproportionate share of people who are prosecuted, likewise a disproportionate share of victims. Even absent overt racism, subconscious bias powerfully shapes the application of American criminal law.

With this extraordinarily decentralized, populist, discretionary, punitive, and racially fraught system, the United States has an engine of potentially intolerable inconsistency and severity. The usual requirements of clarity, parsimony, and proportionality become especially imperative. Balances that can be workable for some countries are not always prudent for the United States.

Similarly, there are limits on the utility of an international convention setting global standards.[3] A convention that can win US support may be too weak from a European perspective. Either way, the United States—a crucial partner in the

[3] For discussion of related pitfalls in the context of regulating government surveillance, see Stephen J Schulhofer, 'A Transatlantic Privacy Pact?: A Skeptical View' in David D Cole, Federico Fabbrini, and Stephen Schulhofer (eds), *Surveillance, Privacy and Transatlantic Relations* (Hart Publishing 2017) 173.

effort—does not ratify such conventions without formal reservations that can nullify their binding effect at the state level.[4]

Given these operational realities, the already-apparent challenges of delineating an image-abuse offence become exceptionally daunting. Defining consent is just one example.

Certainly, consent must be *affirmative*, in the sense that it must be present; prosecutors should not need to prove that the aggrieved person objected. Affirmative consent becomes debatable, however, if it requires someone to obtain explicit permission for each step of a sexual advance. Explicit permission is a valuable safeguard against the grave injury of false positives—unwanted intrusions inflicted by mistakenly interpreting ambiguous behaviour as consent. But many consider this sort of affirmative consent too burdensome in the context of free-flowing physical interaction. Reformers concerned about over-breadth push for a more flexible (but more dangerous) concept of *contextual consent*, signalled by the totality of a person's behaviour under all the circumstances.[5]

Consent for taking and distributing sexual images arguably does not require that flexibility. The conduct is typically less spontaneous, and the interest potentially burdened by a demanding standard is not sexual intimacy, a fundamental human need, but only the interest in taking and sharing images of it. Requiring explicit permission therefore makes even more sense than it already does for sexual contact and penetration. But the first step, taking the image, can likewise be embedded in a free-flowing, mutually desired encounter. Screenshots may not be central to sexual gratification for most people, but they can be a component of pleasure for many.

The privacy frame is relatively one-directional: the more privacy the better. This risks over-simplification because sexual autonomy is both negative and positive: freedom from unwanted intimacy and freedom to pursue mutually desired intimacy.[6] As in BDSM,[7] the law must hesitate to devalue or chill less common forms of sexual fulfilment. For taking a sexual image, the contextual-consent standard therefore may still deserve consideration, even though spontaneity can be less central than it is for physical contact.

[4] See, eg, <https://treaties.un.org/Pages/ViewDetails.aspx?src=IND&mtdsg_no=XVIII-12-a&chapter=18#EndDec> (stipulating on ratification of the Palermo Protocol for prevention of human trafficking that the United States 'reserves the right to assume obligations under this Protocol in a manner consistent with its fundamental principles of federalism . . .').

[5] eg American Law Institute, Model Penal Code Article 213, §213.0(2)(e)(ii) (Official Statutory Text Sept 2022) ('Consent may be express or it may be inferred from behavior—both action and inaction—in the context of all the circumstances'). I was the Reporter for this revision of the MPC but did not concur in this formulation. See Schulhofer (n 2) 56–57, 63.

[6] Schulhofer (n 1).

[7] The term is an acronym for practices involving 'bondage, discipline (or domination), sadism (or submission), and masochism'. See *Oxford English Dictionary* (Draft Additions, June 2013) <http://www.oed.com/view/Entry/14168#eid289098363> accessed 10 October 2023.

Distribution is another matter. Here too, spontaneity remains a factor; on-the-spot decisions to post or share sexual imagery probably occur more often and more seamlessly than older generations might imagine. And we can readily understand that for some, sharing an encounter within a small circle or even publicly, either in real time or later, can enhance sexual pleasure or even be its prerequisite; exhibitionism is a familiar sexual preference. That said, spontaneity is far less common in decisions to distribute than it is for physical contact or for initially taking the image. And the grave potential for harm in *unwanted* distribution reinforces the case for a robust requirement of explicit permission.

These issues and many more are carefully appraised in the pages that follow. The editors, Gian Marco Caletti and Kolis Summerer, deserve our gratitude for inspiring and curating this timely, much-needed volume.

Acknowledgements

A collection of this sort does not come into existence without the involvement of a great number of people.

The volume brings together an impressive range of prominent scholars and it is to them that, firstly, we would like to express our gratitude. We are glad and proud that they participated with enthusiasm, commitment, and excellence in this project. Their diligence in meeting deadlines and constructive approach to engaging with our editorial comments has been greatly appreciated. The acknowledgement is also owed to Professor Stephen Schulhofer and Professor John Vervaele for immediately recognizing the importance of a collection on this topic and agreeing to write two authoritative presentations.

We are particularly indebted to Clare McGlynn and Mike Vitiello, who supported our work on this project with many suggestions and insights.

To some extent, this volume constitutes the culmination of the research project 'Creep—Criminalizing Revenge Porn', the framework within which we conducted our research on the topic of the collection. We are both grateful to the Free University of Bozen/Bolzano for giving financial support to this research, which we have pursued for four years with interest and passion.

We would also like to express our gratitude to Professor Stefano Canestrari for his relentless support and for having instilled in us a passion for scientific research, attention to detail, and interest in the multidisciplinary nature of law's problems.

Sincere thanks are due to Paolo Beccari, a PhD student at the University of Bologna, who worked with us in the editing of the chapters His effort was extremely helpful and well beyond the call of duty.

Finally, we would like to thank the publishing house for believing in our project. In particular, we are grateful to Fiona Briden, whose advice has encouraged us to improve the collection, and to Matthew Williams, project editor, who has given great support.

Gian Marco Caletti and Kolis Summerer,
Bologna-Bolzano,
March 2023.

Contents

IV. REGIONAL REPORTS ON INTIMATE IMAGE ABUSE FROM LATIN AMERICA AND ASIA

VII. LAW ENFORCEMENT, PREVENTION, AND ALTERNATIVE JUSTICE STRATEGIES

List of Contributors

Moira Aikenhead's research focuses on criminal justice responses to technology-facilitated gender violence, applying feminist critique and analysis to legislation, jurisprudence, and policy targeting these rapidly evolving forms of violence. She has published on the topics of non-consensual distribution of images, voyeurism, consent, and privacy. Dr Aikenhead is a member of the Women's Legal Education and Action Fund's Technology-Facilitated Violence Advisory Committee. She has contributed to policy papers and interveners' facta for Supreme Court of Canada decisions related to technology-facilitated violence. She has taught courses on the law of evidence, sentencing, legal research and writing, and tort law at the University of Victoria Faculty of Law and Peter A. Allard School of Law in British Columbia, Canada.

Jane Bailey is a Full Professor of Law at the University of Ottawa. She teaches Cyberfeminism, Technoprudence, and Contracts. She and Valerie Steeves co-lead the eQuality Project, a seven-year SSHRC-funded partnership initiative focused on young people's experiences with privacy and equality in digitally networked environments. Jane leads the project stream on tech-facilitated violence. Among her proudest professional achievements are co-leading the eGirls Project and appearing as lead counsel for an intervenor before the Supreme Court of Canada in two voyeurism cases. She, Nicola Henry, and Asher Flynn co-edited *Emerald International Handbook on Technology-facilitated Violence and Abuse*, a 2021 open-access publication.

Elena Cama is a Postdoctoral Researcher at the Centre for Social Research in Health at the University of New South Wales, Sydney. She is a mixed-methods researcher with a background in criminology, social science, and public health. Her research has focused on sexual harms experienced in a range of contexts, including those facilitated via dating and hook-up apps, in the context of using taxi and rideshare services, in the night-time economy, and in higher education settings.

Manuel Cancio Meliá is a Full Professor of Criminal Law at the Universidad Autónoma de Madrid. He is Research Fellow of the German Academic Exchange Service, the Max-Planck-Gesellschaft, and Alexander von-Humboldt Fellowship. He has been awarded eight Dr honoris causa degrees by Latin American universities. Manuel has been a member and secretary of the Criminal Law Section of the Spanish Royal Academy for Jurisprudence and Legislation since 2005, and a member of the Criminal Law Section of the Spanish General Codification Commission since 2015. He served as a member and Vice President of the Georg Forster Selection Committee of the Humboldt Foundation 2014–2022. Among his works are monographs on victim's behaviour relevance in criminal law and causation, terrorism offences, and the so-called 'enemy criminal law'. Some of these works have been published in many countries of Europe, the Americas, as well as China.

Danielle Keats Citron is the Jefferson Scholars Foundation Schenck Distinguished Professor in Law and Caddell & Chapman Professor of Law at the University of Virginia School of Law. A 2019 MacArthur Fellow, Danielle is the author of *The Fight for Privacy: Protecting Dignity, Identity, and Love in the Digital Age* (Penguin 2022) and *Hate Crimes in Cyberspace* (Harvard University Press 2014). She serves as Vice President of the Cyber Civil Rights Initiative.

María Camila Correa Flórez is Professor and Coordinator of the Criminal Law Area of the Faculty of Law of the Universidad del Rosario, Bogotá (Colombia). She is a member of the research line on gender and law of the same Faculty, Co-Coordinator of the Observatory of the Especial Jurisdiction for Peace (ObservadorvaJEP), adherent member of the ALAS Network, Co-Editor of the *Journal Ius Género América Latina (IGAL)*, and Researcher allied with the Center for Constitutional Studies of the Supreme Court of Justice of the Nation (Mexico). María Camila holds a PhD in Law from the Universidad Autónoma de Madrid, a master's degree in European Union Law from the Universidad Autónoma de Madrid, and a master's degree in Criminal Law from the Universidad de Sevilla, Spain.

Thomas Crofts is a Professor in the School of Law and Department of Social and Behavioural Sciences at City University of Hong Kong, Associate Dean for Research and International Affairs, and Co-Director of the Centre for Public Policy and Law. His research interests are criminalization and criminal responsibility, comparative criminal law, and criminal law reform. Recent research projects explore the practices, motivations, and consequences of sexting by young people (funded by the Australian Institute of Criminology) and the legal responses to intimate image abuse (funded by the Hong Kong Research Grants Council).

Suzie Dunn is an Assistant Professor on Law and Technology at Dalhousie's Schulich School of Law. Her research centres on the intersections of equality, technology, and the law, with a specific focus on technology-facilitated violence, deepfakes, and impersonation in digital spaces. She currently sits on the Women's Legal Education and Action Fund's Technology Facilitated Violence Project Committee, is an associate member of the Centre for Law Technology and Society, and is a Senior Fellow at the Centre for International Governance Innovation where she is supporting a global survey of people's experiences with technology-facilitated violence.

Maria Elósegui is currently a Judge at the European Court of Human Rights in Strasbourg since March 2018 for a mandate of nine years. Previously, she was a Professor of Philosophy of Law at the Faculty of Law of the University of Zaragoza, where she taught for more than thirty years. She holds a PhD in both Law and Philosophy and has been a Research Fellow at the University of Glasgow, Researcher at the University of Saint Louis in Brussels, and Humboldt Researcher at the Faculty of Law of the Christian Albrechts University of Kiel, Schleswig-Holstein (Germany). Maria has been a Visiting Professor at the Max Planck Institute of International Law in Heidelberg (Germany), University of UCLA (Los Angeles), University of Chicago, University of Toronto, Laval University of Quebec, and the Institute of Human Rights in Berlin. She has published more than seventy articles and about thirty chapters on human rights and anti-discrimination law based on race, gender, and on legal argumentation, as well as several monographs.

Asher Flynn is an Associate Professor of Criminology in the School of Social Sciences at Monash University, Editor-in-Chief of the *Journal of Criminology*, and a Chief Investigator on the Australian Research Council Centre of Excellence—the Centre for the Elimination of Violence Against Women. She is an award winning, leading international researcher in policy and prevention concerning gendered and sexual violence, and artificial intelligent and technology-facilitated abuse. Asher has been awarded over $40 million in funding for her work and published eight books and approximately eighty chapters, articles, and reports in these fields.

Mary Anne Franks is the Eugene L and Barbara A Bernard Professor in Intellectual Property, Technology, and Civil Rights Law at George Washington Law School. She is also the President and Legislative & Tech Policy Director of the non-profit organization Cyber Civil Rights Initiative and the drafter of the first US model criminal statute on non-consensual pornography. Mary Anne is the author of *The Cult of the Constitution: Our Deadly Devotion to Guns and Free Speech* (Stanford University Press 2019). She earned her JD from Harvard Law School and her DPhil and MPhil from Oxford University, where she studied as a Rhodes Scholar.

Aya Gruber is a Professor at the University of Southern California Gould School of Law and an expert on criminal law and violence against women. Before academia, she was a Public Defender in Washington DC and Miami. Her widely read scholarship has been featured in publications including the *New York Times*, *Slate*, *The Guardian*, and the Harvard Law Review. Aya is the author of *The Feminist War on Crime* (University of California Press 2022), which PEN America called 'an exciting and brave book that tackles the cause and effect between gender-based violence, mass incarceration, and a broken legal system'. Aya's forthcoming *Stanford Law Review* article, 'Sex Exceptionalism in Criminal Law', explores the origins of sex crimes' unique status in American law.

Margareth Helfer is Associate Professor of Italian Criminal Law, Criminal Procedure, and Comparative Criminal Law at the University of Innsbruck, Austria. She is also Vice Director of the Institute of Italian Law and Coordinator of the joint PhD programme between the Universities of Innsbruck and Padova, Italy. She regularly teaches Comparative Criminal Law and Economic Crimes at the Universities of Padova and Vaduz, Liechtenstein. Margareth has published numerous works in the areas of child pornography, participation in crime, the statute of limitations, and self-responsibility.

Nicola Henry is a Professor and Australian Research Council Future Fellow in the Social Equity Research Centre at RMIT University in Melbourne, Australia. Her research investigates the prevalence, nature, and impacts of sexual violence, technology-facilitated abuse, and image-based abuse, including the legal and non-legal responses to these harms. Nicola's books include *Image-based Sexual Abuse: A Study on the Causes and Consequences of Non-Consensual Nude or Sexual Imagery* (Routledge 2021); *The Emerald International Handbook of Technology-Facilitated Violence and Abuse* (Emerald Group Publishing Limited 2021); *Sexual Violence in a Digital Age* (Palgrave Macmillan 2017); *Rape Justice: Beyond the Criminal Law* (Palgrave Macmillan 2015); *Preventing Sexual Violence: Interdisciplinary Approaches to Overcoming a Rape Culture* (Palgrave Macmillan 2014); and *War and Rape: Law, Memory, and Justice* (Routledge 2010).

Clare McGlynn is a Professor of Law at Durham University. She an expert on laws relating to sexual violence, pornography, and image-based sexual abuse, working closely with politicians, policy makers, and survivors to introduce new criminal laws on intimate image abuse and extreme pornography. Together with Erika Rackley, Clare developed the concept of image-based sexual abuse to develop a better understanding and response to these abuses. She is a co-author of the recently published books *Cyberflashing: Recognising Harms, Reforming Laws* (Bristol University Press 2021) and *Image-Based Sexual Abuse: A Study on the Causes and Consequences of Non-consensual Imagery* (Routledge 2021).

Yoshifumi Okada is a Professor at the School of Law and Head of the Imamura Institute of Legal Studies at Senshu University, Tokyo (Japan). He is interested in the role of criminal law in the information society. His research focuses on criminal justice responses to cybercrime, including illegal online activities such as defamation and piracy. Yoshifumi's recent publications include 'Current Status and Issues of Welfare Crimes Caused by the Internet' ((2020) 679 Seishonen Mondai 26) and 'Trends in Legal Revisions Against Online Insults' ((2022) 76 Senshu University Imamura Institute of Legal Studies Report 1).

Johanna Rinceanu is a Senior Researcher at the Max Planck Institute for the Study of Crime, Security and Law in Freiburg, Germany. Her research focuses are criminal procedure, comparative law, internet regulation, and human rights law. She studied Law at the University of Freiburg (1993–1998) and at the George Washington University Law School in Washington DC (1998–1999). Johanna earned her doctorate in 2007 at the Humboldt-Universität zu Berlin. She has been a Lecturer at the University of Freiburg since the 2007/2008 winter semester. She has had more than fifty papers published in English, German, Italian, Portuguese, Romanian, and Turkish.

Domenico Rosani is Assistant Professor of Criminal Law and Criminal Procedure at the Willem Pompe Institute for Criminal Law and Criminology, University of Utrecht, the Netherlands. Previously, he worked at the University of Innsbruck, Austria, and at the EU Fundamental Rights Agency in Vienna. His research especially focuses on the interaction between criminal law, human rights, and children's rights. In these fields, Domenico has served as a consultant for the Council of Europe's Lanzarote Committee, monitoring the Convention on Protection of Children against Sexual Exploitation and Sexual Abuse.

Anja Schmidt currently represents the professorship for Criminal Law, Criminal Procedure Law, Philosophy of Law and Comparative Law at the Goethe-University in Frankfurt am Main. She is the principal investigator of the research project 'Pornography and Sexual Autonomy', funded by the Deutsche Forschunsgemeinschaft at the Martin Luther University of Halle-Wittenberg. In this project, she has developed a fundamental critique of the German criminal law on pornography on the standard of the right to sexual autonomy including the incomplete and unsystematic regulation of abuse of sexual images. Her research focuses on criminal law, criminal procedure law, the foundations of law, and gender studies.

Adrian J. Scott is a Reader (Associate Professor) at Goldsmiths, University of London, where he is Co-Director of the Forensic Psychology Unit and of an accredited MSc programme in Forensic Psychology. Adrian is a chartered psychologist with Associate Fellow status within the British Psychological Society. He has a broad interest in forensic psychology, specializing in the areas of non-consensual image sharing, stalking, investigative interviewing, and eyewitness testimony.

Michael Vitiello is a Distinguished Professor of Law at McGeorge School of Law, University of the Pacific. He is a recognized expert on criminal law, sentencing policy, and marijuana law. He has been a member of the American Law Institute since 2002. In 1977, Michael began his teaching career at Loyola New Orleans School of Law. He has also taught at Tulane Law School, the University of Mississippi Law Center, the University of Salzburg, Queen's College in London, and the University of Parma. He is the author or co-author of seventeen books. New York University Press will publish his book *The Victims' Rights Movement: What It Gets Right and What It Gets Wrong* in June 2023.

Thomas Weigend received his doctoral degree in Law and his habilitation at the University of Freiburg. He taught Criminal Law and Criminal Procedure at the University of Cologne Faculty of Law from 1986 to 2016. Thomas has published seven books and many articles in German and foreign journals. His main research interests are in criminal law theory, (comparative) criminal procedure, criminal policy, and international criminal law. He has taught as a visiting professor at Tokyo University, New York University, University of Bologna, Peking University, and several others.

1

Criminalizing Intimate Image Abuse

An Introduction

Gian Marco Caletti and Kolis Summerer

I. The Modern Ubiquity of Sexual Images

According to the legend, Lady Godiva took pity on the people of Coventry, who were suffering under her husband's oppressive taxation. Despite her repeated appeals, her husband obstinately refused to reduce the taxes. At last, weary of her pleas, the Lord said he would meet her request if she would ride naked on a horse through the streets of the town. In the Lord's provocation, exposing herself naked to the people of Coventry was the worst form of humiliation, the one his wife would never accept to support the cause of the people. Instead, Lady Godiva took him literally, and after issuing a proclamation that all persons should stay indoors and shut their windows, she rode through the town, clothed only in her long hair. Only one person in the whole of Coventry, a tailor known as 'Peeping Tom', disobeyed the proclamation in what afterwards became the most famous instance of voyeurism.

While only a curious tailor dared to observe Lady Godiva's nudity, in contemporary societies the abuse of intimate or sexual imagery has become one of the most relevant concerns. As Danielle Citron points out in the second chapter of this collection, the non-consensual taking and exploitation of intimate images is endemic. Perpetrators secretly videotape people in hotel rooms, public bathrooms, and bedrooms; they photograph people up their skirts and down their blouses;

Gian Marco Caletti and Kolis Summerer, *Criminalizing Intimate Image Abuse* In: *Criminalizing Intimate Image Abuse*. Edited by: Gian Marco Caletti and Kolis Summerer, Oxford University Press.
DOI: 10.1093/oso/9780198877813.003.0001

they trick minors into sharing sexual images and threaten to release those images unless more are provided; they use deepfake technology to transform faces into pornography. Furthermore, above anything else, they disseminate these images, reaching millions of people.

This is not entirely surprising: from the beginning, new technologies have been used to extend rape culture into the digital dimension, to facilitate traditional forms of sexual violence, or create new types of abuse. In Chapter 3 in this volume, Jane Bailey and Suzie Dunn frame the intimate image abuse in the context of 'technology-facilitated gender-based violence'[1]—a label which has also been recently applied, to some extent, to certain forms of intimate image abuse by the European Court of Human Rights (ECtHR) (see Chapter 4 in this volume by the ECtHR judge Maria Elósegui).

It is also not surprising that criminal law has been invoked as one of the solutions to the problem: the harm experienced by victims of intimate image violence is particularly serious and involves diverse legal interests. Nevertheless, the criminal law role and limits in responding to intimate image abuse are still unclear. Criminalizing intimate image abuse, indeed, raises multiple legal issues and presents a challenge for traditional institutions of law and justice. The nature of this phenomenon requires coping with all the traditional complexities of regulating privacy, sexual offences, and cybercrimes, together with the social and cultural issue of what may be considered 'intimate', 'private', or indeed 'sexual'.

In addition, the harm triggered by intimate image abuse is multi-dimensional and can be usefully understood through multiple theoretical lenses. As a result, the phenomenon has been addressed from many viewpoints: privacy, new technologies, gender-based violence, human rights, non-consensual sexual offences, domestic and partner violence, harassment, pornography regulation, child sexual abuse material, and victim centred justice.

The effort to integrate different perspectives and types of methodology represents one of the main challenges of this book, which essentially aims to establish conceptual and theoretical frameworks to address the legal responses to intimate image abuse.

The volume emerged from an international symposium held at the Free University of Bolzano (Italy) in 2022 to mark the conclusion of a research project on the criminalization of 'revenge porn'. The symposium aimed at comparing the approach of Anglo-American and continental European laws to non-consensual

[1] See also Nicola Henry and Anastasia Powell, 'Technology-Facilitated Sexual Violence: A Literature Review of Empirical Research' (2016) 19 Trauma, Violence and Abuse 195; Suzie Dunn, 'Is it Actually Violence? Framing Technology-Facilitated Abuse as Violence' in Jane Bailey, Asher Flynn and Nicola Henry (eds), *The Emerald International Handbook of Technology-Facilitated Violence and Abuse* (Emerald Publishing 2021); Jane Bailey and Carissima Mathen, 'Technology-facilitated Violence against Women and Girls: Assessing the Canadian Criminal Law Response' (2019) 97(3) Canadian Bar Review 664.

pornography and related phenomena, offering a systematic and comprehensive analysis from all the mentioned viewpoints. This comparison has shed light on many issues of open debate and has led us to broaden the questions to be dealt with as well as the legal traditions to be brought into play (the experiences of Japan and many Countries of Latin America are analysed in the volume; see Part IV for regional reports).

In this introduction, we highlight some of the cross-cutting issues which emerge throughout the volume. In doing so, we also try to describe the structure of the volume, touching on the issues of concern that are unique to each of its parts.

II. Foundations of the Criminalization

The criminalization of intimate image abuse seems to have taken place rather rapidly in many countries. Almost all Western legal systems regulate it specifically, as do numerous Asian countries. As María Camila Correa Flórez's highlights (see Chapter 11 in this volume), even in Latin America more and more countries are carefully considering the need to criminalize intimate image abuse, encouraged by an international convention in defence of women rights (the Belém Do Pará Convention).

Given this undeniable international trend, it is important to emphasize that such criminalization has been approached suspiciously.

In the first place, a markedly paternalistic attitude has emerged in society: in creating images, or accepting to do so, the victims deserved what happened as they naively exposed themselves to an obvious and serious danger of images' dissemination.[2] This victim blaming narrative is the result of society's bias not to recognize the wrongdoing of some online conduct, to trivialize them, and to minimize their harm. 'Digital dualism'—to borrow the brilliant expression utilized in the chapter by Jane Bailey and Suzie Dunn—treats the *online* world as compartmentally sealed from the *offline* world and creates a false binary used by some to distinguish what happens *offline* as *real* whereas what happens *online* as trivial, *unreal*, easy to avoid, or even imaginary.

Digital dualism later translated into consistent criminal policy responses. As Maria Elósegui stressed in her chapter, this failure is also highlighted by the GREVIO[3] and is reflected in the jurisprudence of the ECtHR. In particular, GREVIO recently pointed out the difficulty for legislators and legal authorities to adequately reflect new phenomena of abuse and violence performed online or

[2] See, eg, Clay Calvert, 'Revenge Porn and Freedom of Expression: Legislative Pushback to an Online Weapon of Emotional and Reputational Destruction' (2014) 24 Fordham Intellectual Property Media and Entertainment Law Journal, 673–702.

[3] The acronym stands for 'Group of Experts on action against Violence against Women and Domestic Violence'.

through technology in prevention and sanction policies. This new dimension of violence against women, exactly as in the case of digital stalking as a new form of harassment, is not included in all relevant pieces of legislation or in social policies. On the other hand, in *Volodina v Russia* (No 2),[4] the ECtHR recognized that online violence, or 'cyberviolence', is closely linked with *offline* (or '*real* life') violence and falls to be considered as another facet of the complex phenomenon of gendered violence.

As well as society's victim blaming attitudes towards intimate image abuse, the resistance to criminalize the phenomenon depended on legal historical reasons.

In the second half of the twentieth century, legal systems managed to eliminate many traditional sexual offences based on the protection of moral values (eg adultery, homosexual intercourse). The trend marked the gradual—and painfully slow—transition from a moralizing criminal law to a liberal criminal law, guided by the harm principle and the concepts of sexual autonomy, choice, and sexual privacy—the latter understood as the right of citizens not to have intrusions into choices voluntarily made 'in the bedroom'.[5]

One of the main fields of this evolution was pornography,[6] also due, as is well known, to the lack of agreement in the feminist scholarship in arguments for its prohibition (or restriction)[7]. The only sexual images relevant to criminal law remained for decades those depicting children, which are the result of child abuse that threatens to impair the minor's life development.[8] It seems no coincidence that today there is a tendency to abandon the old term 'child pornography' in favour of the new terminology 'child sexual abuse material'.[9]

This scenario is being strongly challenged today given that new technologies are radically changing the relationship between (criminal) law and sexual images.

On the one hand, the mass fruition of pornography enabled by the Internet has reignited the debate about its harmful nature. Feminist movements have resumed denouncing the misogyny of mainstream pornography, considering it an institution of gender inequality which raises not only moral but also legal issues.[10] From

[4] *Volodina v Russia* (No 2) App no 40419/19 (ECHR, 14 September 2021).

[5] *Lawrence v Texas* 539 US 558 (2003).

[6] On this point, eg, the liberal reflections of Joel Feinberg are well known: see Joel Feinberg, 'Pornography and the Criminal Law' (1979) 40 University of Pittsburgh Law Review 567.

[7] Unlike rape law. See recently, Clare McGlynn and Vanessa Munro, 'Rethinking Rape Law: An Introduction' in Clare McGlynn and Vanessa Munro (eds), *Rethinking Rape Law* (Routledge 2010) 1, 3. However, Catharine MacKinnon's stance against pornography is well known: see Catharine MacKinnon, *Feminism Unmodified* (Harvard University Press 1988) 197.

[8] For an attempt to conceptualize the harm of child pornography as exploitation, see Suzanne Ost, *Child Pornography and Sexual Grooming: Legal and Societal Responses* (Cambridge University Press 2009) 139 ff.

[9] See, for instance, the explanation of the reasons for this choice of terminology on the RAINN (the American Rape, Abuse and Incest National Network) website, <https://www.rainn.org/news/what-child-sexual-abuse-material-csam> accessed 19 October 2023.

[10] See, eg, the contributions in Lynn Comella and Shira Tarrant (eds), *New Views on Pornography: Sexuality, Policy and Law* (Lynn eds 2015) (hereafter Comella and Tarrant (eds), *New Views on Pornography*).

this point of view, the focus has shifted to excessive and extreme pornography, which is beginning to be seen as harmful, especially to young people.[11]

On the other hand, smartphones make many forms of private or domestic pornography possible. This calls into question the prevailing liberal approach of criminal law to pornography, since new and recent forms of abuses can be very damaging to sexual privacy and, to some extent, bodily integrity. As clearly explained by Anja Schmidt's (see Chapter 6 in this volume), the demands for criminalization of intimate image abuse are not based on a general interest, but on the very serious harm suffered by specific victims. As Schmidt contends, developing the thesis of prominent Anglo-American scholars, intimate image abuse infringes not only the right to one's own image, but also the right to sexual autonomy in its non-physical dimension.

Reading the various contributions in this collection, it is possible to observe a significant expansion of the concept of sexual privacy requiring criminal protection. It no longer just calls for freedom from interference on how to experience sexuality but implies that such choices and activities remain private, without being recorded, publicly displayed, or in any way exploited. In other words, the shift has been from the right to make personal choices 'in the bedroom' to the right to be (also) 'virtually clothed'.[12]

According to Danielle Citron (see Chapter 2 in this volume), conceptualizing intimate-image abuse as a violation of intimate privacy enables us to understand its significance for individuals, groups, and society. It enables us to perceive the entirety of the wrongs at hand and the inflicted harms. Moreover, it frames it in a broader phenomenon revealing the powerful actors piercing the boundaries around intimate life for profit and power.[13]

However, the chapters in this volume reveal that resistance to broadening the framework of sexual offences occurred mainly in continental Europe. In particular, the chapters by Anja Schmidt and Manuel Cancio Meliá (see Chapters 6 and 10 in this volume) highlight the concern of European legal scholarship not to deny the traditional liberal approach to pornography. Later in this introduction, we analyse the practical consequences of this situation, which seems on the verge of definitively changing (see Section III below).

To some extent, this difference can also be attributed to the great effort of the Anglo-American scholarship, who has conducted remarkable empirical studies on

[11] Clare McGlynn and Ian Ward, 'Pornography, Pragmatism' 2009 36(3) Journal of Law and Society 327. See also the debate in Alisdair A Gillespie, *Cybercrime. Key, Issues and Debate* (Routledge 2016) 203 ff.

[12] Borrowing Peter W Cooper's expression in 'The Right to Be Virtually Clothed' (2016) 91 Washington Law Review 817.

[13] See further Danielle K Citron, *The Fight for Privacy: Protecting Dignity, Identity, and Love in the Digital Age* (W W Norton 2022).

victim-survivors of intimate image abuse and clearly emphasized the foundations of its criminalization.[14]

On a closer look, however, the specific criminalization of intimate image abuse conduct is by no means irreconcilable with a liberal criminal law perspective. Rather, it seems perfectly consistent with its theoretical foundations.[15]

The abandonment of morality as a protected legal interest, and the consequent reduction in the number of sex crimes in the last century, was justified on the principle of sexual autonomy. In other words: as long as sexual conduct represents a free choice of the individuals involved, it cannot be penalized with criminal sanctions. Nonetheless, the counterweight of this perspective is that if an act occurs without the consent of a person, it represents a violation of their sexual autonomy.[16]

This shift took a long time to become well established, as exemplified by the slow and travailed process which has led the crimes of rape and sexual assault to be emancipated from the concepts of force and violence.[17] According to a feminist perspective, behind the liberal veneer and the failure to protect sexual autonomy, the concern to safeguard male heterosexual dominance can be glimpsed (on this point, see Anja Schmidt chapter in this volume).

This idea now seems to be accepted with regard to physical sexuality, in which consent makes the 'difference between pleasure and crime' (to quote the title of Thomas Weigend's chapter in this collection). The same function cannot be denied to consent in the digital dimension, unless a paternalistic (and therefore anti-liberal) approach is adopted. Not recognizing this function of consent means, in the end, blaming those who, even if very young, decide to experience their sexuality through new technologies, 'sexting' for example.[18] In this field, therefore, criminal law must avoid any moralistic attitude, trying to achieve a balance between (positive) sexual autonomy and the protection of sexual privacy. Conversely, as it has been pointed out, the demand for effective protection of (negative) sexual autonomy does not represent a step back towards moralization.

In digital sexual contacts, moreover, it seems easier to draw a line between what is consensual and what is not. That is why, in this area, the paradigm of affirmative

[14] Many scholars immediately emphasized the seriousness of the harm caused by different forms of intimate image abuse (IIA). For a recent and very well researched analysis, see Nicola Henry and others, *Image-based Sexual Abuse: The Causes and Consequences of Non-Consensual Nude or Sexual Imagery* (Routledge 2020) (hereafter Henry and others, *Image-based Sexual Abuse*).

[15] On this relationship, see Stuart P Green, *Criminalizing Sex. A Unified Liberal Theory* (OUP 2020).

[16] The importance of sexual autonomy and its connection with the absence of consent is systematically highlighted by the milestone work of Stephen J Schulhofer, *Unwanted sex. The Culture of Intimidation and the Failure of Law* (Harvard University Press 1998).

[17] And has not yet concluded. See, for further references, Gian Marco Caletti, 'Coercion by Violence and its Changing Meaning in Action. The Experience of Italy, in Elisa Hoven and Thomas Weigend (eds), *Consent in Sexual Relationships. Comparative Perspectives* (Nomos 2022) 25 (hereafter Hoven and Weigend (eds), *Consent*).

[18] See Michael Salter, Thomas Crofts, and Murray Lee, 'Beyond Criminalisation and Responsibilisation: Sexting, Gender and Young People' (2013) 24 Current Issues in Criminal Justice 301.

consent (ie the incrimination of all sexual interactions that are not preceded by verbally expressed consent)[19] begins to be viewed as the right standard for the wording of the offence.[20] While the progressive nature of the physical sexual relationship makes the application of the 'yes means yes' paradigm extremely controversial, as Stephen Schulhofer (see the Foreword) and Thomas Weigend (see Chapter 13 in this volume) recognize in their contributions, with regard to the dissemination of sexual images, strong arguments exist in favour of demanding that a person explicitly asks for the other person's consent.

A liberal approach must, furthermore, be used to respond to the phenomenon of 'sexting' among adolescents. As mentioned, child pornography has long been the only form of pornography sanctioned by criminal law, even in case of mere possession. However, the traditional system of child pornography offences is challenged by the possibility for young people to create sexual imagery voluntarily using their smartphones and to share them with their partner. Margareth Helfer and Domenico Rosani explore the role of criminal law in this field advocating for an exemption from criminal liability based on the harm principle (see Chapter 8 in this volume).

III. What's in a Name? From 'Revenge Porn' to 'Intimate Image Abuse'

Terminologies frame options for law reform, as well as playing an undeniably expressive role in the public debate. This is not a figure of speech: in Italy, for instance, the prevalence of the term 'revenge porn' has led to a narrow criminalization, which, against our institutional advice,[21] ends in targeting only those who disseminate sexual imagery created in a sentimental context and with a vengeful purpose.[22]

The Italian experience is part of a well-defined trend. At first, the phenomenon was framed under the controversial neologism 'revenge porn', which as is known

[19] There are many possible declinations of affirmative consent, as illustrated in Aya Gruber, 'Consent Confusion' (2016) 38(2) Cardozo Law Review 415, especially 431 ff (hereafter Gruber 'Consent Confusion').

[20] See the arguments in Gian Marco Caletti, 'Can Affirmative Consent Save "Revenge Porn" Laws? Lessons from the Italian Criminalization of Non-Consensual Pornography' (2021) 25(3) Virginia Journal of Law and Technology 112, 143 ff. (hereafter Caletti, 'Affirmative Consent'), but see also Henry and others, *Image-based Sexual Abuse* (n 14), 161 f.

[21] See Gian Marco Caletti and Kolis Summerer, 'Libertà e riservatezza sessuale ai tempi di internet: il caso del revenge porn' (2020) 1 Indice Penale 8, 12.

[22] See Caletti, 'Affirmative Consent' (n 20) 150. On the first practical examples in the case law, see Paolo Beccari, 'Le prime difficoltà applicative della nuova fattispecie di "revenge porn" in caso di diffusione di materiale da parte di soggetti estranei al rapporto sessuale (2022) <https://www.sistemapenale.it/it/sentenza/tribunale-reggio-emilia-2021-528-revenge-porn-video-bagni-discoteca> accessed 19 October 2023.

indicates the revenge of one of the partners of a couple through the dissemination of sexual images created in the past.[23] In many jurisdictions, specific criminalization has been rushed due to the proliferation of some tragic non-consensual pornography cases, often without sufficient criminological investigation. Haste has led the legislative response to be fragmentary and typically to focus only on the practices of vengeful ex-partners, as proved by the widespread use in the wording of the offence of the further (or specific) intent to cause harm to the victim (see also Section IV below).

Recently, the debate and reflection on the legal answers to this problem started to seem well grounded and commonly supported, at least at the scholarship level. Therefore, despite the need for a better understanding of some aspects of the problem, some landmarks on terminology appear to be established.

The term 'revenge porn' has been criticized from many angles since the first studies that raised the need to criminalize the abuse of intimate images.[24] The conduct of disseminating sexual images is now predominantly referred to by the acronym 'NCDII', which stands for 'non-consensual distribution of intimate images'. The terminology is neutral and does not assume victim blaming logic: non-consensual distribution is not limited to the context of a former intimate partnership, nor is the motive for such behaviour exclusively 'revenge'. Moreover, it does not contain any references to the word 'pornography', which could fuel blame on the victim. This kind of conduct is the most well-known—and in some respects probably the most serious—iteration of 'IBSA' ('image-based sexual abuse').

This last terminology was proposed by Clare McGlynn and Erika Rackley to emphasize that the phenomenon is not limited to cases of dissemination of images, but that there are many different forms of abuse based on 'nudes'.[25] Other forms of IBSA, aside from NCDII, include voyeurism; coercing a person to create or share nude or sexual images; non-consensually filming a person who is nude or engaged in sexual activity without their consent; filming sexual assault; creating false 'deepfake' sexual images of another person; threatening to share sexual images online ('sextortion') in exchange for money, other images, or sexual intercourses; using images for other means such as impersonating that person or creating fake online dating or sexual service profiles.

Alongside IBSA there is the group of conducts that can be qualified from a perspective that emphasizes both the technological tool and gendered violence as

[23] For cases, psychological aspects, and motivations of 'revenge porn' specifically, see Matthew Hall and Jeff Hearn, *Revenge Pornography. Gender, Sexualities and Motivations* (Routledge 2018).

[24] See, eg, Danielle K Citron and Mary Anne Franks, 'Criminalizing Revenge Porn' (2014) 49 Wake Forest Law Review 345, especially 346; Clare McGlynn and Erika Rackley, 'Image-based Sexual Abuse' (2017) 37(3) Oxford Journal of Legal Studies 534, 535 (hereafter McGlynn and Rackley, 'Image-based Sexual Abuse'); Nicola Henry and Anastasia Powell, 'Sexual Violence in the Digital Age: The Scope and Limits of Criminal Law' (2016) 25(4) Social and Legal Studies 397, 400.

[25] McGlynn and Rackley, 'Image-based Sexual Abuse' (n 24).

'technology-facilitated gender-based violence'. As Jane Bailey and Suzie Dunn rationalize in their chapter, 'TFGBV' constitutes a wide array of harms facilitated by digital means, ranging from sexual harassment, sexualized doxing, to sexual extortion. The two groups have numerous behaviours in common since many sexualized forms of TFGBV fit within image-based sexual abuse (IBSA), but their chapter also explores some of the more novel forms of sexual violence that have emerged in the digital sphere, such as sexual harassment in the metasphere, which are not part of 'IBSA'.

In any case, 'IBSA' was later consolidated by the publication of an important book on its causes and consequences and, currently, is without any doubt the most widely used expression.[26]

Why then remove an 'S'? Why introduce a new term like 'Intimate Image Abuse' as we do with the title of this collection? In naming the book, we do not wish to question the preponderance of 'IBSA', considered as a balanced and effective terminology with the merit of focusing attention on a plurality of conducts. There are two reasons for our choice, both traceable in this volume.

As already noted, this volume aims to compare—for the first time—the various solutions developed in different legal systems. More than ten countries are represented, each with their own approach to the issues covered in the collection. Apart from already-mentioned insights into Japanese and Latin American legislation (see Part IV of the volume), the comparison is mainly between the Anglo-American criminalization pattern and that of continental Europe—legal traditions which have always looked at each other with increasing interest and have great influence on the legal cultures of many other countries.[27]

Part III of this volume is devoted to legal comparison in the strict sense. In the criminalization of intimate image abuse, two paradigms with substantial differences have emerged. The Anglo-American pattern brings non-consensual distribution of images closer to other sexual offences, recognizing the particular seriousness of the offence due to the *sexual* content of the images. The European model, on the other hand, punishes distributive conducts in the context of offences which protect privacy and intimacy as a whole.

The two models have very different practical implications, highlighted in the chapters by Mary Anne Franks and Manuel Cancio Meliá (Chapters 9 and 10). The main one is that European states criminalize any distribution of intimate images, that is, not just *sexual* images, but with lower penalties, typical of crimes against privacy and non-sexual offences. Anglo-American systems, on the other hand,

[26] Henry and others, *Image-based Sexual Abuse* (n 14).

[27] The area of sexual offences is one of the fields most involved in this comparative perspective, as evidenced by some recent comparative collections such as Tatjana Hörnle (eds), *Sexual Assault. Law Reform in a Comparative Perspective* (OUP 2023); Hoven and Weigend (eds), *Consent* (n 17).

have introduced narrower offences, limited to images with sexual content, but with extremely harsher penalties, comparable to those of traditional sexual offences.[28]

Curiously, neither of the two systems seem to be satisfied with their regulatory framework.

According to Thomas Crofts (see Chapter 7 in this volume), many Anglo-American jurisdictions perceive the limitation to sexual images as a loophole in the application of their offences and are considering extending the object of criminalized conduct to include 'intimate' images. This is undoubtedly related to the difficulty in defining what *sexual* is.

The opposite European trend is even more evident and tangible. As Manuel Cancio Meliá shows (see Chapter 10 in this volume), Italy first deviated from the German and Spanish pattern by introducing a specific offence modelled on the dissemination of 'sexually explicit images'. Moreover, the EU Commission proposed a directive which, if approved, would oblige Member States to criminalize the dissemination of images depicting 'sexual activities'. These are the reasons that drive the author to argue that there is no longer a single pattern of criminalization in Continental Europe.

It seems possible that the ECtHR case law, which recently qualified intimate image abuse as a form of sexualized violence (see Chapter 4 in this volume by Maria Elósegui) contributed to this new legal attitude.

The challenge legal systems are going to face, therefore, is to find a balance in the criminalization of sexual and intimate images, tailoring distinct punitive responses, proportionate to the different seriousness. Furthermore, it is crucial to consider the context of violence between partners, where experience shows an increase in abuse through images that do not have intimate content. In her chapter on Canadian case law in the field of domestic violence, Moira Aikenhead examines the prevalence of image-based abuse and several interesting cases.

We believe that behaviours involving nudes or images of sexual activity are significantly more serious. Quoting Jean-Paul Sartre, Danielle Citron connects the experience of 'pure shame' to the experience of having someone see us undress without our permission (see Chapter 2 in this volume). According to the existentialist philosopher, pure shame consists in awareness that others are seeing us as objects that can be violated, rather than as human beings who deserve respect. It is no coincidence that Lady Godiva's husband asked her to show herself without clothes in front of her people, to test to what extent she was willing to humiliate herself for them. Speaking more concretely, the cases analysed by Moira Aikenhead in her chapter demonstrate the greater seriousness of abuse perpetrated on sexual and not merely intimate images.

[28] For instance, Moira Aikenhead's casuistic analysis (Chapter 16 in this volume) highlights how in Canada perpetrators can be punished with a ban on the use of the Internet for a number of years. This would be an absolute novelty on the European scene.

As argued by Aya Gruber in this volume, even within the same anti-revenge-porn narrative, women's sexuality and nudity risks remaining taboo, stigmatizing, and conveying the idea that posting nude pictures is necessarily devastating. This happens—in the author's opinion—because concentrating on posters to the exclusion of the harm-causing viewers reinforces the message that public sexuality is so predictably and inevitably stigmatizing that women must avoid it all costs. The argument is interesting and evocative. Nevertheless, we cannot fail to recognize that, in this historical period, the victims depicted in disseminated sexual images are still subject to all societal reprehensions. Aya Gruber's advocacy on the need to change the social, familial, and employment practices that devastate women whose nude image becomes public for any reason is important. However, at present, criminalizing certain abuses does not seem to be an alternative.

In the light of all these considerations—and many more could be made—a ladder approach, such as the one Thomas Crofts proposes (see Chapter 7) appears appropriate for dealing with the diverse nature of abused images.

IV. The Theoretical and Practical Limits of Criminalization

Criminalising Intimate Image Abuse is also, if not primarily (especially in some of its parts), a book about criminalization of new behaviours. After all, the area of sexual crimes has long been a test case and frontier for criminalization issues.

As already stressed, new technological achievements have merged with old social attitudes, giving rise to new opportunities for highly harmful abuse of victims. Consequently, while it is important to recognize the harm and the wrongdoing associated with intimate image abuse (IIA), it is equally important to recognize and thematize the limits that criminalization encounters, both from a theoretical and practical point of view.

Another of the aims of this volume, therefore, is to establish these limits, seeking effective victim protection strategies, whilst ensuring respect of the principles of criminal law. The chapters in the collection adopt different stances, fuelling an internal debate on the role and functions of criminalization in the field under investigation, while the last part of the book focuses on the search for complementary solutions to the use of criminal justice which can compensate for its ontological deficiencies (see Part V).

As already mentioned, the first issue concerns the breadth or narrowness of criminal offences. In this volume, Thomas Crofts brilliantly highlights that, although, many jurisdictions have created offences to address invasions of a person's sexual autonomy using new technologies, as research unpacks the harms resulting from new ways of abuse, legal systems are re-evaluating whether the offences created to capture intimate image abuse are adequate and coherent. A concern with these early approaches is that offences tended to be created in an ad hoc and patchy way. The result was that offence elements were designed with a specific wrong in mind leading to a lack of coherency between offences, undesirable gaps, limitations, and inconsistent application.

More generally, as Thomas Crofts contends, while there seems to be a general understanding about the core types of behaviour that should be subject to criminal sanction, debate continues around the *periphery* of the elements of established offences. This includes questions such as how far the definition of intimate images should extend (see Section III above), what sort of behaviours should be criminalized, what defences should be available, and what mental states are the most appropriate for these offences.

The latter is, as already mentioned, a point of extensive debate within the volume. The majority of the contributors agree in criticizing jurisdictions whose criminal laws focus on the perpetrator's intent rather than the victim's lack of consent (see eg Chapter 9 by Mary Anne Franks). This allegedly misdirected focus entails these laws being applied only to situations in which the perpetrator is motivated by the purpose to harm the victim. However, as these contributors contend, many perpetrators of this abuse have other motives: voyeurism, profit, a desire for social status, or some other motive that disregards the humanity of the victim. According to Mary Anne Franks, requiring an intent to harm treats non-consensual pornography as a form of harassment, which it only *sometimes* is, rather than a privacy violation, which it *always* is.[29]

There are also those, such as Aya Gruber in this volume (see Chapter 5), who argue that such a perspective broadens the scope of criminal law too far. In her opinion, changing the name from 'revenge porn' to 'non-consensual intimate images distribution', thus dropping out the 'revenge', signifies that the law does not concern itself with the motive behind the distribution: those with bad motives, no motives, or benign motives are *equally* guilty.

The search for the limits of the IIA merges to a large extent with the discourse on the functions and purposes to be attributed to criminal law. Gruber suggests a 'neofeminist approach' which continues to focus on gender-based harms but is sceptical of the carceral system. In this view, feminists should look at criminalization as a very last resort, to be tried only if everything else has failed. To a European reader, Gruber's position certainly seems acceptable in many respects but also influenced by the US context, which she describes as 'a world of racialized overpolicing and over-imprisonment'.

[29] In contrast, cyberflashing, that is, sending one's own sexual image to another person who did not want to receive it, does not constitute a violation of privacy, as the person depicted decided to send their own image, but rather precisely constitutes a form of harassment. On this topic, see Clare McGlynn and Kelly Johnson, *Cyberflashing: Recognising Harms, Reforming Laws* (Bristol University Press 2021). Some examples of prolonged image abuse for the purpose of harassment are described in Danielle K Citron, *Hate Crimes in Cyberspace* (Harvard University Press 2014)

One of the merits of this approach is to emphasize that serious harm does not automatically warrant criminalization. As many of the authors in this volume note (see, among others, Crofts and Vitiello), criminal law strongly demands for the culpability of the perpetrator to be established.[30] This does not necessarily imply a requirement of further intent in the formulation of laws, which indeed seems inappropriate in the light of phenomenal reality, but that punishing a defendant, even when harm occurs, is unacceptable when the defendant lacks a culpable mind.[31] Abandoning that commitment risks violating one of the most fundamental principles of criminal law.[32]

This investigation inevitably triggers victim blaming dynamics. As Michael Vitiello's chapter insightfully and systematically explains, tracing the defendant's beliefs about a victim's consent requires in-depth scanning of the victim's behaviour. As underlined earlier, certain dynamics seem less complicated and opaque in digital sexuality than in traditional sexuality and drawing some lines is easier. Nonetheless, as Vitiello wittily demonstrates, some ambiguities can also occur in relation to the consent to the creation and distribution of sexual images.

Offences must therefore be designed so that they capture behaviours sufficiently culpable to be deserving of criminalization without bringing less culpable conducts within the reach of criminal law. For instance, a particularly strong culpability test is necessary when assessing the liability of second distributors, those who distribute images that have already been disclosed in the first instance.[33] Such persons may be unaware (or unsure) of the images' origins or the absence of consent to disclosure.

Another challenge is to create offences that are wide enough to deal with behaviours already identified as harmful and emerging behaviours that may not yet have been recognized as harmful. One example is the so-called 'deepfake', which has only recently been acknowledged as potentially harmful to victims.[34] Nevertheless, criminal laws cannot be overly broad and indefinite as this clashes with the principle of legality and its various declinations.[35]

These are just some of the many limits that criminal law faces in protecting victims of sexual abuse.[36] Other limitations do not stem from fundamental principles,

[30] Among many references, see Thomas Weigend, 'Subjective Elements of Criminal Liability' in Markus Dubber and Tatjana Hörnle (eds), *The Oxford Handbook of Criminal Law* (OUP 2014) 493.

[31] In this case, a form of strict liability occurs. See Andrew Ashworth, 'Strict Criminal Liability and Imprisonable Offences' (2010) 45 Irish Jurist 1, 5.

[32] This is because, as has been pointed out for many years, it is legitimate and fair to convict a person when that person 'has the capacity and a fair opportunity or chance to adjust his behaviour to the law'. Herbert LA Hart, *Punishment and Responsibility* (OUP 1968) 181.

[33] On the problem of second distributors and the original Italian solution, see more extensively Caletti, 'Affirmative Consent' (n 20) 168.

[34] On 'deepfake' sexual images, see Mary Anne Franks and Ari Ezra Waldman, 'Sex, Lies, and Videotape: Deep Fakes and Free Speech Delusions' (2019) 78 Maryland Law Review 892.

[35] On which, see Jeremy Horder, *Ashworth's Principles of Criminal Law* (9th edn, OUP 2019).

[36] For more reflections on criminalization, see the contributions in Antony Duff and others (eds), *Criminalization. The Political Morality of the Criminal Law* (OUP 2014).

as in the aforementioned case, but from practical challenges. Commenting on the case law of the ECtHR, which also assesses concrete law enforcement by Member States, Maria Elósegui points out multiple problems in this volume (see Chapter 4). From the point of view of the criminal investigation of IIA cases, she emphasizes that, on the one hand, significant obstacles arise from the lack of preparation of the police to deal with these new types of crime related to the use of digital tools in the context of domestic violence; on the other hand, the reluctance in recognizing new forms of abuse as a crime is connected with stereotypes and sexist attitudes which are still widespread even among the authorities expected to investigate and prosecute them. In this volume (see Chapter 15), Nicola Henry calls this 'institutional betrayal'.

The lack of efficient investigation is also related to evidentiary problems: while physical violence against women, although persistent and not always prosecuted in many geographical settings within the Council of Europe Member States, leaves an evidence, the traceability of digital harassment is more complicated, since it is often more anonymized or diluted among several actors.

As Clare McGlynn clearly affirms in her chapter (see Chapter 17), all these law enforcement failures make it necessary to look closely at victims' perspective to develop complementary strategies to criminalization, which meet their needs without subjecting them to the problems of traditional criminal justice (see Section V below).

Another issue that traverses many chapters of this volume is the potential educational function of the criminalization of IIA. In recent decades, it has often been argued, in feminist scholarship, that rape reforms should also pursue educational purposes, promoting the adoption of different behavioural patterns in society—such as more communicative approaches between sexual partners (eg 'only yes means yes').[37] Given the sexualized context of the new incriminations concerning image abuse, this possible function has also been invoked for criminal law.

Many of the contributors recognize that the primary advantage of using criminal law in this field is its deterrent effect (see eg, Crofts and Franks). Criminal law is, of course, not the only means that can be adopted to deter harmful conducts. Furthermore, it may not be able to produce, or provide in a timely fashion, the result that a victim of intimate image abuse desires—which in most cases is the withdrawal or removal of images from the Internet. Nonetheless, while non-criminal remedies can also be useful to victims, the immediate and often irreparable nature of the harm of IIA requires the maximum deterrence potential of criminal law.[38]

[37] On this point, see the critical overview in Gruber 'Consent Confusion' (n 19) 440 ff.

[38] On this specific issue, see also Alexa Dodge, 'Nudes are Forever: Judicial Interpretations of Digital Technology's Impact on "Revenge Porn"' (2019) 34(1) Canadian Journal of Law and Society 121. The author notes that, as sexual photos are seen as lasting 'forever', these perceptions have substantive impacts on legal rationales and especially on Canadian sentencing decisions, with the affordances of digital technology being treated as justifying harsher sentences to denounce and deter the non-consensual distribution of images.

On the contrary, most authors, especially criminal law scholars, are very cautious in recognizing further purposes, specifically educational ones, to criminalization. Cancio Meliá, for example, categorically excludes the possibility that criminal law can be used to modify sexual morality, given that it is a 'social event' to be well grounded within current social attitudes (see Chapter 10).

However, an 'expressive' role for the new criminalization seems undeniable. In this case, it is not a question of changing sexual morality through the wording of an offence, but, once the wrong of the IIA has been framed in violations of privacy and sexual autonomy, to recognize the symbolic value of a new criminalization. Criminal prohibition is one of the most powerful and effective ways for society to acknowledge and condemn serious wrongdoing.[39] As Thomas Crofts highlights, this function of cultural orientation is particularly important where new technologies present opportunities and challenges which bring about significant social and cultural changes requiring new codes and manners. The moral force of the criminal law, closely linked to its deterrent function, is greater when it comes to approaching entirely new phenomena and contexts, such as that of digital sexuality, where social attitudes are quickly shaping and abandoning digital dualism.

In any case, it is worth recalling that, as Cancio Meliá underlines, criminalization must not be guided by moral panic.[40] The rapid and non-thoughtful reaction to (real or supposed) problem areas that appear in the media, especially in extreme cases, is a main characteristic of 'penal populism' or purely symbolic criminal law. In some cases, the risk is to deviate towards forms of 'criminal law of the enemy' (on this problem, see also Helfer and Rosani in this volume); in other cases, the risk is to create offences with clear loopholes—as indeed happened in the case of several anti-revenge porn regulations. As Cancio Meliá warns, the chasing of the media-hyped emergence of various new harmful and potentially criminalizable case constellations, often on the basis of particularly striking individual cases, leads the lawmaker (and theoretical discussion) to fragmentary consideration on the possible scope of regulation and, sometimes, to a counterproductive criminal law coverage of relevant behaviour from various perspectives. A scholarly analysis should become a useful tool for possible criminalization and should aim to prevent these two possible outcomes—unfair and ultra-punitive rules, ineffective and

[39] The literature on this subject is, as is well known, extensive. We refer here only to a few cornerstones such as Joel Feinberg, 'The Expressive Function of Punishment, in Joel Feinberg, *Doing and Deserving: Essays in the Theory of Responsibility* (Princeton University Press 1970); Andrew von Hirsch, *Censure and Sanctions* (OUP 1993); Anthony R Duff, *Punishment, Communication and Community* (OUP 2001). More recently, and not only regarding criminal law, see Richard H McAdams, *The Expressive Powers of Law: Theories and Limits* (Harvard University Press 2017).

[40] The concept of moral panic is an example of sociological criticism. See, among others, Chas Critcher, *Moral Panics and the Media* (Open University Press 2003). There has undoubtedly also been a moral panic phenomenon with regard to the subject of this volume, often distracting from critical questions about how to adapt norms of privacy and consent for new media. On this issue, evident even from its title, see Amy A Hasinoff, *Sexting Panic. Rethinking Criminalization, Privacy, and Consent* (University of Illinois Press 2015).

merely symbolic offences. We hope that the valuable contributions to this volume will also serve this function.

V. The Needs of the Victim-Survivors. Prevention, Remediation, Alternative Strategies

Once the criminalization of IIA and its limits (theoretical and practical) have been established, the analysis must focus on other viable strategies, complementary or alternative to criminal justice, as effective safeguards for victims. Bailey and Dunn in this volume recall that approaches to tackling IIA require, as well as the other forms of 'TFGBV', a multi-disciplinary, victim-survivor-centred approach.

Part VI of this volume thus shifts the focus to the perspective of the victim-survivors, examining the law 'in action' in Canada and Australia, which were among the first countries to criminalize intimate image abuse and, therefore, already have case law.

The first chapter by Nicola Henry (see Chapter 15) focuses on justice responses to image-based sexual abuse, drawing on semi-structured, qualitative interviews with twenty-five Australian victim-survivors. We believe that this kind of empirical research is highly revealing. In fact, despite the significant reforms and the new IIA laws, as well as continuous public attention to this issue over the past decade, little is known about the experiences of victim-survivors and how they navigate complex reporting pathways and justice processes.

One of the most significant—but not surprising—results of Henry's investigation is that most participants thought there was 'no point' in reporting their experiences. Even in this respect, IIA has similarities with traditional sexual offences known to be characterized by a relevant 'dark figure'. As explained by the author, among the factors which consolidate this belief there is a negative perception of police, accused of not taking reports seriously. According to Henry's study, in many cases, this prejudice is based on previous experiences in which police had advised victim-survivors that there was nothing they could do and provided unhelpful advice, or expressed victim-blaming attitudes, such as admonishing them for sharing their intimate images or even having photos on their own social media.

These findings that highlight the reluctance of victim-survivors to engage in criminal justice are consistent with previous research by Clare McGlynn into sexual violence victims,[41] which are the empirical foundations for her new study in this volume (see Chapter 17). In this chapter, McGlynn broadens the spectrum of enquiry by addressing alternative strategies for facing intimate image abuse. With criminal justice systems largely failing victims of these forms of abuse, many

[41] Clare McGlynn and Nicole Westmarland, 'Kaleidoscopic Justice: Sexual Violence and Victim-Survivors' Perceptions of Justice' (2019) 28(2) Social and Legal Studies 179.

survivors are searching for alternative ways to secure a sense of justice. This ensues because, as Nicola Henry also emphasizes, although victim-survivors differ in their views on what justice entails, most participants in her interviews indicated that recognition of the harm was crucial. This is probably because these victim-survivors realized that the recognition of the nature of their experience and the understanding of the significance of the harm caused is the first fundamental step in the perspective of prevention and the education of perpetrators and society more generally. Moreover, as we have just observed, the expressive function of the law undoubtedly helps in this regard.[42]

McGlynn's chapter examines victim-survivors' transforming perspectives on what justice means to them and the opportunities for redress beyond conventional criminal justice systems. She develops the concept of 'kaleidoscopic justice' to reflect their perceptions of justice as being a 'continually shifting pattern, constantly refracted through new circumstances, experiences and understandings [with] multiple beginnings and possible endings'. The possibilities of restorative and transformative justice in this area are investigated, moving beyond formal mechanisms and relationships with the state, to develop more informal, community-based approaches.

The importance of a whole-of-community approach is underscored additionally by the experiences of Australian victim-survivors of image-based sexual abuse. The aim of these innovative ways of seeking justice is to heal a damaged relationship, not (only) between the victim and offender but also between the latter and their community. As Nicola Henry concludes, this broader approach includes, aside from criminal offences and their expressive function, policies of prevention education, well-resourced victim support services, police training, as well as greater action and transparency from the digital platforms and mobile applications that encourage, support, or otherwise host non-consensual imagery with little to no consequences. And it is not by chance that this volume addresses some of these issues in the final part.

Chapter 16 by Moira Aikenhead considers Canadian case law on intimate image abuse related to partner violence. The chapter reveals that IIA, in particular so-called 'sextortion', is playing an increasing role in abusive relationships. The fact that harmful images may be easily digitally captured and disseminated to a wide online audience is being exploited as a powerful tool of dominance and control. By shedding light on these patterns, the author identifies both strengths and weaknesses of the Canadian criminal justice approach to intimate image abuse, resulting in an extremely interesting comparative perspective. For example, attention is paid

[42] In Australia it has been suggested that often not only are the authors of IIA unaware of the criminal relevance of their conduct, but, in the past, before the introduction of the crime, even police officers showed total disinterest in victims when receiving complaints: see Michael Salter and Thomas Crofts, 'Responding to Revenge Porn: Challenges to Online Legal Impunity' in Comella and Tarrant (eds), *New Views on Pornography* (n 10) 233.

to the evidentiary problems which, in the area under investigation, are more than one might expect.

Observing the case law makes it possible to confirm that the non-consensual sharing of intimate images and threats to disseminate images are highly gendered activities that are primarily committed by males and disproportionately target women (and also, according to Bailey and Dunn, minorities and marginalized people; see Chapter 2 in this volume). Nevertheless, based on the data collected within the framework of our research project,[43] we think it would be criminologically interesting to discuss male victimization too. Digital tools eliminate both the physical differences that underlie many traditional sexual offences, as well as the shame of showing themselves naked or engaged in sexual acts that can be felt by most men. There is also reason to believe that, in the case of male victims, the dark figure of crime may be even larger. In light of these considerations, a possible trajectory for future research may be to consider whether cases involving men require different criminal justice responses.

As just noted, looking closely at the victims' experiences revealed the importance of a community approach to some of their needs. The final part of this volume, in addition to Clare McGlynn's chapter, contains two other insights in this direction.

The first insight, by Johanna Rinceanu (see Chapter 18 in this volume), addresses the issue of content moderation policies by Internet Service Providers. It is self-evident that criminalization alone is not sufficient to counteract the harm suffered by victims. The removal of images posted online is what victim-survivors are most interested in, and in the absence of legislative provisions, the cooperation of Internet platforms in this sense is not always effective. Rinceanu starts with an analysis of the German law (NetzDG) and, to some extent, its successor, the European Digital Services Act (DSA). According to her, it is highly questionable that both acts represent adequate means of combating hate and incitement on the Internet. As she warns, the human rights of various actors in the digital space can be at risk and users should fear for their freedom of expression, freedom of information, and freedom of artistic expression. In fact, NetzDG and DSA could push Internet Service Providers towards 'over-blocking' and 'over-filtering', and to some extent toward 'over-reporting', making Internet Service Providers private guardians of opinion against their own will.

These few considerations are enough to understand how delicate and complex the issue is and, specifically, how many conflicting interests are on the ground and must be balanced by law. However, it is worth emphasizing that this volume shows how the discussion on the legal framework on the moderation of user-uploaded content is increasing, with significant regulatory implications as well. In addition

[43] Antonella Brighi and others, 'Prevalence and Risk Factors for Nonconsensual Distribution of Intimate Images among Italian Young Adults: Implications for Prevention and Intervention' (2023) 23(4) International Journal of Clinical and Health Psychology 100414.

to the just-mentioned German law, it is interesting to consider the example of Japan, where the anti-revenge porn law contains an exception to Providers' responsibility exemption precisely in relation to the problem of sexual image sharing (see Yoshifumi Okada's chapter in this volume).

If it is very problematic to appoint ISPs as private guardians of the 'digital community', and it seems appropriate to reflect on the role the community itself can play in preventing IIA and limiting its effects. Along these lines, the last chapter of the volume by Asher Flynn, Elena Cama, and Adrian Scott explores barriers and facilitators to bystander intervention in IIA contexts. This chapter is based on the results of an empirical research conducted in Australia, utilizing data from thirty-five in-person focus groups with 219 participants in four Australian States. This perspective brings into focus, more than ever, the importance of the development of education campaigns around harms and consequences of IIA, alongside prevention and education on how bystanders can safely and effectively intervene and/or support victims when witnessing IIA.

This last chapter, thanks to its multidisciplinarity, further enhances the diverse range of perspectives through which this volume examines IIA. Our hope, as editors, is to offer the reader a tool to capture, through the many different lenses employed, the complexity and the fascinating challenges posed by the topic addressed, while at the same time establishing conceptual and theoretical frameworks to guide future legal responses.

Bibliography

Ashworth A, 'Strict Criminal Liability and Imprisonable Offences' (2010) 45 Irish Jurist 1

Bailey J and Mathen C, 'Technology-facilitated Violence against Women and Girls: Assessing the Canadian Criminal Law Response' (2019) 97(3) Canadian Bar Review 664

Beccari P, 'Le prime difficoltà applicative della nuova fattispecie di "revenge porn" in caso di diffusione di materiale da parte di soggetti estranei al rapporto sessuale' (2022) Sistema penale

Brighi A and others, 'Prevalence and Risk Factors for Nonconsensual Distribution of Intimate Images among Italian Young Adults: Implications for Prevention and Intervention' (2023) 23(4) International Journal of Clinical and Health Psychology 100414

Caletti GM, 'Can Affirmative Consent Save "Revenge Porn" Laws? Lessons from the Italian Criminalization of Non-Consensual Pornography' (2021) 25(3) Virginia Journal of Law and Technology 112

Caletti GM and Summerer K, 'Libertà e riservatezza sessuale ai tempi di internet: il caso del revenge porn' (2020) 1 Indice Penale 8, 12

Calvert C, 'Revenge Porn and Freedom of Expression: Legislative Pushback to an Online Weapon of Emotional and Reputational Destruction' (2014) 24 Fordham Intellectual Property Media and Entertainment Law Journal, 673

Citron DK, *Hate Crimes in Cyberspace* (Harvard University Press 2014)

Citron DK and Franks MA, 'Criminalizing Revenge Porn' (2014) 49 Wake Forest Law Review 345

Citron DK, *The Fight for Privacy: Protecting Dignity, Identity, and Love in the Digital Age* (W W Norton 2022)

Comella L and Tarrant S (eds), *New Views on Pornography: Sexuality, Policy and Law* (Lynn eds 2015)

Cooper PW, 'The Right to Be Virtually Clothed' (2016) 91 Washington Law Review 817

Critcher C, *Moral Panics and the Media* (Open University Press 2003)

Dodge A, 'Nudes are Forever: Judicial Interpretations of Digital Technology's Impact on "Revenge Porn"' (2019) 34(1) Canadian Journal of Law and Society 121

Duff AR, *Punishment, Communication and Community* (OUP 2001)

Duff AR and others (eds), *Criminalization. The Political Morality of the Criminal Law* (OUP 2014)

Dunn S, 'Is it Actually Violence? Framing Technology-Facilitated Abuse as Violence' in J Bailey, A Flynn, and N Henry (eds) *The Emerald International Handbook of Technology-Facilitated Violence and Abuse* (Emerald Publishing 2021)

Feinberg J, 'The Expressive Function of Punishment' in J Feinberg (ed), *Doing and Deserving: Essays in the Theory of Responsibility* (Princeton University Press 1970)

Feinberg J, 'Pornography and the Criminal Law' (1979) 40 University of Pittsburgh Law Review 567

Franks MA and Waldman AE, 'Sex, Lies, and Videotape: Deep Fakes and Free Speech Delusions' (2019) 78 Maryland Law Review 892

Gillespie AA, *Cybercrime. Key, Issues and Debate* (Routledge 2016)

Green SP, *Criminalizing Sex: A Unified Liberal Theory* (OUP 2020)

Gruber A, 'Consent Confusion' (2016) 38 Cardozo Law Review 415

Hall M and Hearn J, *Revenge Pornography. Gender, Sexualities and Motivations* (Routledge 2018)

Hart HLA, *Punishment and Responsibility* (OUP 1968)

Hasinoff AA, *Sexting Panic: Rethinking Criminalization, Privacy, and Consent* (University of Illinois Press 2015)

Henry N and Powell A, 'Sexual Violence in the Digital Age: The Scope and Limits of Criminal Law' (2016) 25(4) Social and Legal Studies 397

Henry N and others, *Image-based Sexual Abuse: The Causes and Consequences of Non-Consensual Nude or Sexual Imagery* (Routledge 2020)

Horder J, *Ashworth's Principles of Criminal Law* (9th edn, OUP 2019)

Hörnle T (eds), *Sexual Assault. Law Reform in a Comparative Perspective* (OUP 2023)

MacKinnon C, *Feminism Unmodified* (Harvard University Press 1988)

McAdams RH, *The Expressive Powers of Law: Theories and Limits* (Harvard University Press 2017)

McGlynn C and Ward I, 'Pornography, Pragmatism' (2009) 36(3) Journal of Law and Society 327.

McGlynn C and Munro V, 'Rethinking Rape Law: an Introduction' in C McGlynn and V Munro (eds), *Rethinking Rape Law* (Routledge 2010)

McGlynn C and Rackley E, 'Image-based Sexual Abuse' (2017) 37(3) Oxford Journal of Legal Studies 534

McGlynn C and Westmarland N, 'Kaleidoscopic Justice: Sexual Violence and Victim-Survivors' Perceptions of Justice' (2019) 28(2) Social and Legal Studies 179

McGlynn C and Johnson K, *Cyberflashing: Recognising Harms, Reforming Laws* (Bristol University Press 2021)

Ost S, *Child Pornography and Sexual Grooming: Legal and Societal Responses* (Cambridge University Press 2009)

Salter M, Crofts T, and Lee M, 'Beyond Criminalisation and Responsibilisation: Sexting, Gender and Young People' (2013) 24 Current Issues in Criminal Justice 301

Salter M and Crofts T, 'Responding to Revenge Porn: Challenges to Online Legal Impunity' in L Comella and S Tarrant (eds), *New Views on Pornography: Sexuality, Policy and Law* (Lynn eds 2015)

Schulhofer SJ, *Unwanted Sex: The Culture of Intimidation and the Failure of Law* (Harvard University Press 1998)

von Hirsch A, *Censure and Sanctions* (OUP 1993)

Weigend T, 'Subjective Elements of Criminal Liability' in M Dubber and T Hörnle (eds), *The Oxford Handbook of Criminal Law* (OUP 2014)

Weigend T and Hoven E (eds), *Consent in Sexual Relationships. Comparative Perspectives* (Nomos 2022)

PART I

INTRODUCTORY SECTION: THE THEORETICAL FRAMEWORK OF INTIMATE IMAGE ABUSE AND ITS CRIMINALIZATION

2

Intimate Image Abuse

Intimate Privacy Violation

*Danielle Keats Citron**

I. Introduction

The non-consensual taking and exploitation of intimate images is widespread and devastating. Culture to culture, country to country, the abuse follows a familiar playbook.[1] Whether strangers or confidantes, acquaintances or lovers, people record, fabricate, extort, share, or publicly disclose others' intimate images without permission.[2]

Consider a few ways that individuals abuse intimate imagery. Perpetrators secretly videotape people in hotel rooms, public bathrooms, and bedrooms.[3] They insinuate themselves into the right spot and photograph people up their skirts and down their blouses.[4] Perpetrators trick people, often minors, into sharing intimate images and threaten to release those images unless more—far more—are provided.[5] They use machine learning techniques like deepfake technology to swap

* I am grateful to Gian Marco Caletti for working with me on these issues and to Billi Jo Morningstar for her help reviewing and editing this chapter.

1 Danielle Keats Citron, *The Fight for Privacy: Protecting Dignity, Identity, and Love in the Digital Age* (W W Norton 2022) 28–47 (hereafter Citron, *Fight for Privacy*).

2 Danielle Keats Citron, 'Sexual Privacy' (2019) 128 Yale Law Journal 1870 (hereafter Citron, 'Sexual Privacy').

3 Citron, *Fight for Privacy* (n 1) 28–33.

4 ibid 29–30.

5 ibid 1915–17.

Danielle Keats Citron, *Intimate Image Abuse* In: *Criminalizing Intimate Image Abuse*. Edited by: Gian Marco Caletti and Kolis Summerer, Oxford University Press. © Oxford University Press 2024. DOI: 10.1093/oso/9780198877813.003.0002

people's faces into pornography.[6] Fancy technology, however, isn't needed to fabricate intimate images; photoshop can also do the trick. Real or fabricated intimate images are shared in texts, emails, or online.

Perpetrators pressure and cajole; they manipulate and lie.[7] They never ask for permission, nor would they get it.[8] No matter the tactics, the result is the non-consensual taking, faking, extorting, or disclosure of images of people's naked or partially undressed bodies.[9]

Name a geographic region, and stories abound about the non-consensual exploitation of intimate images.[10] Victims are predominantly female, non-white, LGBTQ +, or disabled. Often victims are, or are perceived to be, members of more than one vulnerable group.[11] The harm is profound—targeted individuals, their families, communities, and society suffer grievous losses.[12]

In 2018, hidden cameras in women's bathroom stalls in South Korea were so prevalent that women and girls brought kits with silicone to fill holes in doors (and thus block hidden cameras) and masks to hide their faces.[13] That year, perpetrators hid cameras up people's skirts at concerts, on public transportation, or in grocery aisles in the United Kingdom; they posted exes' nude photos on websites hosted in the United States.[14] The abuse escalated at a rapid clip reaching more and more vulnerable people each year and in more destructive ways.[15]

Academics, advocates, and policy makers often refer to these practices as 'intimate-image abuse' or 'image-based sexual abuse'. Scholars in Australia, Italy, New Zealand, and the United Kingdom have made a conscious decision to adopt this framing.[16] The United Kingdom spearheaded a reform commission regarding the criminalization of 'intimate image abuse'.[17] Advocates and policy makers in South Korea refer to the problem as 'digital sex crime content'.[18]

[6] Robert Chesney and Danielle Keats Citron, 'Deep Fakes: Looming Challenge for Democracy, National Security, and Privacy' (2019) 107 California Law Review 1753 (hereafter Chesney and Citron, 'Deep Fakes').

[7] Citron, *Fight for Privacy* (n 1) 31–32.

[8] ibid 39.

[9] ibid.

[10] ibid 28.

[11] ibid 39–40.

[12] ibid 41–43.

[13] ibid 28, 200–01.

[14] ibid 29–37, 196–97.

[15] ibid.

[16] Nicola Henry and others, *Image-based Sexual Abuse: A Study on the Causes and Consequences of Non-Consensual Nude or Sexual Imagery* (Routledge 2020).

[17] Law Commission Reforming the Law, *Intimate Image Abuse: A Final Report* (Law Com No 407, 2022) <https://www.lawcom.gov.uk/project/taking-making-and-sharing-intimate-images-without-consent/#related> accessed 22 November 2022.

[18] Interview with Won-Mo Lee, Commissioner of South Korea's Digital Sex Crime Content Commission (Washington DC, 21 September 2022). As the Commissioner explained to me during our meeting, the Commission has shifted from referring to the abuse as 'digital sex crime information' to 'digital sex crime content'. The goal was to ensure that the name of their office and endeavours captured evolving forms of intimate image abuse.

Intimate-image abuse and image-based sexual abuse are helpful short-hands. I use those terms along with others, such as non-consensual pornography, in interviews. But none fully capture the wrongs and harms at hand. Image-based sexual abuse is part of a broader phenomenon: the violation of *intimate privacy*. Intimate privacy violations include, but are not limited to, the non-consensual exploitation of intimate images. Individuals, companies, and governments invade intimate privacy by obtaining access to, and information about, our bodies, health, sexual activities, gender, and close relationships. Unwanted access to and information about our intimate lives—including but not limited to intimate images—isn't something that we want, expect, or deserve, yet it continues apace.

As this chapter explores, intimate privacy is the connective tissue linking non-consensual intimate imagery to other ways that intimate life is under surveillance. Intimate privacy helps us appreciate the fullness of the stakes. It brings in view the powerful actors piercing the boundaries around intimate life for profit and power. Describing image-based sexual abuse as violations of intimate privacy helps us appreciate the breadth of the wrongs and harms at hand. Intimate privacy provides us with an effective lens to chart a way forward.

II. The Concept of Intimate Privacy

Let me set the stage by defining intimate privacy and providing illustrations. I will then sketch out the values that intimate privacy secures, including the ability to develop authentic identities, to enjoy self- and social respect, to form and maintain close relationships, and to lay the groundwork for equal opportunity.

Intimate privacy refers to the physical and digital boundaries around intimate life. It involves the extent to which others have physical access to, and information about, our bodies; health; sexual orientation, gender, and sexual activities; innermost thoughts and fantasies (which we document in our browsing, reading, searches, texts, and emails); and close relationships. The concept is both descriptive and normative. As a descriptive matter, it concerns the intimate privacy that we expect, want, and may (or may not) enjoy. Crucially—and here is the normative point—it is the intimate privacy that every one of us *deserves* to flourish, to engage as citizens, and to feel that we belong.[19]

Every day, everywhere, people engage in vast and sundry activities, on- and offline, on the street and at home, in their inboxes and on their apps, expecting, hoping, and deserving intimate privacy. They undress in public bathrooms, gym locker rooms, and hotel bedrooms on the assumption that no one is recording them. They send emails and texts to close friends, revealing their hopes, fantasies,

[19] Citron, *Fight for Privacy* (n 1) x-xviii, 2–8.

past traumas, and intimate images. They expect that their confidences will be treated with care and discretion. They expect that messaging services will secure their communications from outsiders.[20]

All day long, all over the globe, people tell apps, search engines, and smartwatches about their menstrual cycles, drug prescriptions, health conditions, and desires. They search adult sites and watch videos. They talk to digital assistants on their mobile phones and personal devices in their homes. They assume that their intimate data is being used to help them, to make their lives easier, cheaper, and more fun. This is what companies tell them when they sign up for their services and purchase their devices. They expect that their intimate information will be treated with care. They assume that their intimate privacy is being protected.[21]

The women and girls of South Korea, as discussed in the introduction, neither wanted nor expected strangers to hide video cameras in public bathrooms; they neither wanted nor expected that videos of them urinating would be uploaded to websites. They expected, wanted, and deserved intimate privacy.[22] Individuals in the United Kingdom neither expected nor wanted concertgoers or people sitting next to them on the bus to take photos up their skirts. They expected and deserved intimate privacy; no one should have been sneaking under their clothing and photographing their crotches.[23]

The hundreds of millions of Americans using dating, period-tracking, and health apps and devices do not want their intimate data to be shared with advertisers, data brokers, or government agencies; they do not want their intimate privacy violated. They do not want, nor do they expect, that their intimate data will be used to raise life insurance premiums or deny them interviews or promotions.[24] They do not want insurance companies, third-party hiring companies, or law enforcement to buy dossiers about them from data brokers; dossiers that reveal intimate aspects of their lives, including whether they have been raped, bought sex toys, visited adult sites, or are LGBTQ + individuals.[25] They want their intimate privacy to be respected, but alas, what they want and expect isn't being honoured. Intimate privacy should be ours and regrettably—especially in the United States—it is not.

What does all of this do to our ability to develop, to love, and to engage with others? Let me explain intimate privacy's importance to self-development, dignity, intimacy, and democratic engagement.

We need intimate privacy to figure out who we are and who we want to become. Our bodies are our first port of call in the journey of self-exploration. We come to know ourselves—what we want, who we are, what hurts us, what pleasures

[20] ibid 2–9.
[21] ibid.
[22] ibid 200–03.
[23] ibid 28–37.
[24] ibid 17–24.
[25] ibid 11–14.

us—through our bodies.[26] We gain a sense of self-worth when we feel in 'possession and control' of our bodies.[27] Feminist philosopher and phenomenologist Iris Marion Young has explained that the privacy we enjoy with our bodies in crucial spaces like our homes enables us to let down our guard so we can develop authentic identities.[28]

When given the chance to retreat to on- and offline spaces either alone or with people we trust, to reveal our bodies and thoughts to others without the fear of being judged or ridiculed, we feel at ease. That feeling of ease enables us to play with our identities, experiment with ideas, and imagine the selves we want to become.[29] We need psychic and physical space, away from unwanted observers, to develop ourselves, our thoughts, and our beliefs.[30]

The ability to reveal our bodies, gender, or sexual orientation on our own terms is crucial to self-development. With intimate privacy, we can search LGBTQ + sites or view adult videos without worrying that our sexual orientation will be shared with advertisers, marketers, and data brokers.[31] We can explore our gender in dressing rooms or closets, trying on clothing, without worrying that hidden cameras are recording our emerging sense of self without our permission.[32]

Intimate privacy is crucial for both self-respect and social respect. When we can determine who sees us naked, hears our thoughts, or knows our health conditions (and who doesn't), we are able to see ourselves as in charge of our own lives.[33] Unwanted exposure of aspects of our intimate lives can trigger feelings of humiliation. In *Being and Nothingness: An Essay on Phenomenological Ontology*, existentialist philosopher Jean-Paul Sartre talked about the phenomenon of 'pure shame', which he distinguished from the notion that one feels ashamed when others find out that we have harmed another.[34] Pure shame is our awareness that others are seeing us as *objects* that can be violated, rather than as human beings deserving respect. Sartre connected the experience of pure shame to the experience of having someone see us undress without our permission. When we wear clothing, he explained, we are claiming the right to be seen without being seen as an object.[35] When we are stripped of our clothing without permission, when we are photographed in the bathroom or bedroom without permission, we are seen as just our

[26] ibid 114.
[27] ibid.
[28] Iris Marion Young, *On the Female Body Experience: Throwing Like a Girl and Other Essays* (OUP 2005).
[29] Julie Cohen, *Configuring the Networked Self* (Yale University Press 2010).
[30] Citron, *Fight for Privacy* (n 1) 114.
[31] ibid 113–15.
[32] Citron, 'Sexual Privacy' (n 2).
[33] Citron, *Fight for Privacy* (n 1) 114.
[34] Jean-Paul Sartre, *Being and Nothingness: A Phenomenological Essay on Ontology* (Hazel E Barnes tr, Washington Square Press 1956) 384.
[35] ibid.

genitals, breasts, or buttocks, not as whole, fully integrated people. Our body parts are all that people know about us.

Now for the importance of intimate privacy for the formation of close relationships. Close relationships are key to human flourishing, and they require intimate privacy to form and deepen. Legal scholar Charles Fried said it best long ago: privacy is the oxygen for love.[36] Social psychologists explain that close relationships develop through a process in which partners reveal themselves to each other.[37] We make ourselves vulnerable to partners, and they to us, and through that process, we come to trust one another. Key to mutual vulnerability is trust. We only peel back those layers and express ourselves truly when we trust others to be discreet. We share our deepest secrets, thoughts, and experiences with one another because we believe that our partners will treat our confidences as we hope and expect rather than as we fear.[38]

To be sure, confidentiality and seclusion do not always operate in 'intimacy-enabling, respect-securing, and autonomy-facilitating ways'.[39] The powerful often invoke their own 'privacy' to conceal their violations of intimate privacy of the vulnerable. That was the story of the sexual harassment and assault cases revealed in the #MeToo movement. Recall that television host Matt Lauer had a button installed on his desk so that he could lock his office door when female staff members entered, enabling him to initiate inappropriate contact knowing no one could see.[40] Comedian Louis CK masturbated in front of shocked and scared female comedians behind locked doors.[41] Film director Harvey Weinstein had employees protect his hotel rooms and office from entry except for female actresses whom he groped and raped.[42] Harassers and rapists have eviscerated women's intimate privacy while protecting their own privacy; they have forced women to reveal their naked bodies in settings that kept their abuse a secret.[43]

The regrettable legacy of invoking privacy to conceal intimate privacy violations does not undermine the significance of intimate privacy. Powerful men have

[36] Charles Fried, *An Anatomy of Values* (Harvard University Press 1970) 140.

[37] John Holmes and John K Rempel, 'Trust in Close Relationships' in Clyde Hendrick (ed), *Close Relationships: A Sourcebook* (Sage Publications 1989).

[38] Irwin Altman and Dalmas A Taylor, *Social Penetration: The Development of Interpersonal Relationships* (Holt, Reinhart and Winston 1973).

[39] Citron, *Fight for Privacy* (n 1) 117.

[40] Erik Wemple, 'Just How Did Matt Lauer's Desk Button Work?' *Washington Post* (Washington DC, 11 May 2018) <https://www.washingtonpost.com/blogs/erik-wemple/wp/2018/05/11/just-how-did-matt-lauers-famous-desk-button-work/> accessed 22 November 2022.

[41] Camila Domonoske, 'Multiple Women Say Louis C.K. Masturbated in Front of Them' *National Public Radio* (Washington DC, 9 November 2017) <https://www.npr.org/sections/thetwo-way/2017/11/09/563116374/multiple-women-say-louis-c-k-masturbated-in-front-of-them-new-york-times-reports> accessed 22 November 2022.

[42] Jodi Kantor and Megan Twohey, 'Harvey Weinstein Paid Off Sexual Harassment Accusers for Decades' *New York Times* (New York City, 5 October 2017) <https://www.nytimes.com/2017/10/05/us/harvey-weinstein-harassment-allegations.html> accessed 22 November 2022.

[43] Citron, *Fight for Privacy* (n 1) 118.

long invoked privacy in service of the denial of women's intimate privacy and in furtherance of their subordination. We should not protect a man's privacy if he is trying to conceal his violation of another's intimate privacy. The history of male abuse of women's intimate privacy does not diminish the significance of intimate privacy to enable autonomy, dignity, and companionship.[44] Instead, it gives us urgent reason to protect intimate privacy for everyone.[45] As feminist privacy scholar Anita L Allen powerfully argued in her foundational book *Uneasy Access: Privacy for Women in a Free Society*, the fact that women have no intimate privacy does not undermine their entitlement to it.[46]

Everyone needs intimate privacy to develop authentic identities, to enjoy respect, and to forge close relationships. But members of traditionally subordinated groups are more likely to face intimate privacy violations and to suffer more profound injuries than people from privileged groups.[47] Due to invidious cultural and social attitudes, the naked bodies of women and people from historically disadvantaged groups are often viewed as disgusting and shameful. Their predicaments are often viewed as their fault. Violations of intimate privacy result in the denial of crucial opportunities, including the ability to get and keep jobs, to be free from physical and emotional harm, to enjoy the esteem of others, and to feel like they have control over their lives.[48] Intimate privacy and equality are inextricably linked. Far too often, when women, LGBTQ + individuals, disabled individuals, and non-whites experience intimate privacy violations, their intimate data is counted against them. Grace, reprieve, and forgiveness are not theirs to enjoy.

To circle back to where we began, when individuals exploit people's intimate images, victims suffer a blow to their self-development, human dignity, capacity to love, and equality of opportunity. No matter the strategy, perpetrators make it impossible for victims to feel safe, to feel in charge of their destinies, to be seen as subjects and not objects, and to feel free to let their guard down and fall in love.

Peddling image-based intimate privacy violations are big business. When I was writing *Hate Crimes in Cyberspace* in 2013, which tackled the problem of cyberstalking, my research assistants and I found forty sites devoted to non-consensual intimate images. By 2017, researchers found that the number had grown to 2,000. By 2020, there were *9,500* sites.[49] Sites earn money by charging subscribers monthly fees, collecting ad revenues from people's clicks, or collecting personal data, which they sell. In 2018, the Candid Forum had more than 200,000 subscribers paying $19.99 a month to view upskirt and downblouse photos from all over the world.

[44] Anita Allen, *Uneasy Access: Privacy for Women in a Free Society* (Rowman & Littlefield 1988) 180 (hereafter Allen, *Uneasy Access*).

[45] ibid.

[46] Allen, *Uneasy Access* (n 44) 180.

[47] Citron, *Fight for Privacy* (n 1) 43–47.

[48] ibid.

[49] ibid 71–72.

In 2017, another site, The Candid Board (original, they are not), had a similar fee structure for 180,000 members. In 2015, an upskirt photo site with 70 million daily page views was estimated to be worth 100 million dollars.[50] These small sites are pulling in big money and using subscribers to supply the intimate images. It is a racket, and one that exacts profound costs to intimate privacy.

The fact is that men and women share intimate images with one another all the time, but these sites predominantly feature nude or sexually explicit photos of women, girls, or LGBTQ + individuals. Of the thousands of sites specializing in non-consensual intimate imagery, 98 per cent of the photos are of women, and not because women take more nude selfies than men. As law professor and Cyber Civil Rights Initiative (CCRI) President Mary Anne Franks put it, 'Men send more nude photos than women do[, but] revenge porn sites don't traffic in men's pictures'.[51]

III. Array of Intimate Privacy Violations

Intimate image-based abuse is a violation of intimate privacy, but intimate privacy is invaded in countless other ways. Individuals, companies, and governments are responsible for the abuse.

First let's consider the breadth of intimate privacy violations committed by individuals. Individual privacy invaders (often former domestic partners or lovers) hijack devices in people's homes so they can monitor activities and conversations. They install cyberstalking apps on people's phones. Cyberstalking apps secretly upload a phone's activities in real time to their servers. Perpetrators gain access to victims' texts, calls, voicemails, searches, social media activities, and locations—nothing is sacred or out of reach. From anywhere, perpetrators can activate an infected phone's mic to listen to conversations within 15 feet of the phone. Victims are never free from unwanted monitoring.[52]

Upon discovering or suspecting that partners have been tracking their mobile phone activity, movements, and conversations, victims internalize the notion that on- and offline spaces are not their own. Their self-expression is chilled. Victims get rid of their phones, stop using social media, and withdraw from friendships. They fear that their homes and workplaces are not safe from unwanted monitoring.[53]

Abusers also use the data that they obtain from victims' phones to terrorize and attack victims. Physical harm is a serious peril when abusers have access to victims' whereabouts. In one case, a woman fled her abuser with whom she was living in Kansas. Because the woman's abuser had installed a cyberstalking app on her

[50] ibid 72.
[51] ibid xvi.
[52] ibid 34. I have written extensively about cyberstalking apps: Danielle Keats Citron, 'Spying Inc.' (2015) 72 Washington and Lee Law Review 1243 (hereafter Citron, 'Spying Inc.').
[53] Citron, 'Spying Inc.' (n 52) 1258.

phone, he knew that she had moved to Illinois. The man tracked the woman to a shelter and then to a friend's home where he assaulted her. In another case, a woman tried to escape her abusive husband, but because he had installed a cyberstalking app on her phone, he was able to find her and her children. After tracking them down, the man murdered his two children.[54]

Individuals aren't the only ones spying on us. All day long, companies invade our intimate privacy. At times, intimate images are involved; at other times, they are not. Companies collect, share, and sell information about people's intimate lives in ways that they hardly expect and certainly do not want.

Monsignor Jeffrey Burrill served as a parish priest before taking on the role of associate general secretary at the US Conference of Catholic Bishops in 2016. In 2021, the Catholic news site, *The Pillar*, ran a story claiming that Burrill was gay because, the site claimed, Burrill had been using the gay dating app Grindr. The reporter explained that a 'mobile device correlated to Burrill emitted signals from Entourage, which bills itself as Las Vegas' "gay bathhouse"'.[55] Just before the story broke, Burrill submitted his resignation. As Father Thomas Berg told the news site, the use of hookup apps is 'inconsistent with clerical obligations to continence and chastity'.[56]

How did the reporter discover that Burrill had been using the gay hookup app and had visited a gay bathhouse? The reporter did not meet Burrill on the app, but rather obtained information based on the data that Grindr collects from its users and shares with advertising networks (that in turn share with data brokers). According to story, 'the data was obtained from a data vendor' which was not named.[57]

As Grindr and other dating apps tell users in their privacy policies, apps share subscribers' profiles and 'anonymized' location data with third parties. Those third parties include advertisers and marketers that sell information to data brokers.[58] What surely happened is that Grindr sold Burrill's 'anonymized' location data and mobile advertising ID to advertising networks; the information was then sold to a data broker; the data broker sold the information to the news site, enabling the reporter to out the priest as gay. 'Somewhere along the line, Burrill's mobile advertising ID was relinked to his full name, address, and other personally identifiable information, something data brokers specialize in'.[59] The reporter explained that he correlated a unique mobile device to Burrill when the mobile ID number was used at his residence, family lake house, and meetings that he attended.[60]

54 ibid 1257.

55 'Pillar Investigates: USCCB Gen Sec Burrill Resigns After Sexual Misconduct Allegations' (*The Pillar*, 20 July 2021) <https://www.pillarcatholic.com/pillar-investigates-usccb-gen-sec/> accessed 22 November 2022 (hereafter 'Pillar Investigates').

56 ibid.

57 ibid.

58 Citron, *Fight for Privacy* (n 1) 11–13, 97–99.

59 ibid 11.

60 'Pillar Investigates' (n 55).

Grindr isn't exceptional. Nearly every app and service collects, uses, and shares an enormous amount of our intimate data. Our health, sexual activities, sexual orientation, movements, reading habits, browsing, and searches are being collected, stored, used, and shared with advertisers, marketers, and data brokers. Overcollection is the business model.[61] More than 84 per cent of period-tracking apps are selling people's intimate data to third parties, including advertisers, marketers, and data brokers.[62] US law enforcement spends hundreds of millions of dollars purchasing access to data-broker dossiers.[63]

In the United States, if a company has a privacy policy and does not lie about its data handling practices, then the exploitation of intimate data is perfectly legal.[64] As Professor Woodrow Hartzog explains, privacy policies are drafted to protect companies; they are not privacy guarantees for users. 'Privacy policies in fact end up being *antiprivacy* policies', he notes.[65] In the aftermath of *Dobbs v Jackson Women's Health*, which struck down the constitutional right to reproductive liberty and paved the way for states to criminalize abortions, the profligate collection and sale of intimate data can now result in the prosecution of individuals exercising their reproductive freedom.[66]

People do not want data about their health conditions, abortions, or sexual activities to be sold to advertisers, marketers, and data brokers (and then on to law enforcement), but that is what is happening, with scant legal limits in the United States.[67] The General Data Protection Regulation (GDPR) in the European Union and the United Kingdom offers a bit more protection, but not as much as one might think. Under the GDPR, to share subscribers' intimate data, companies need to get people's express permission or have another legitimate reason to process and share it.[68]

Governments also exploit intimate data in unwanted and unexpected ways. In the United States, state Medicaid rules require social workers to ask poor pregnant individuals about their history with abortion, miscarriage, rape, domestic abuse, or school expulsion. Answering those questions are a prerequisite to obtaining

[61] Citron, *Fight for Privacy* (n 1) 5–17.

[62] '84% of Period Tracker Apps Share Data with Third Parties' (*Orcha*, 21 July 2022) <https://orchahealth.com/84-of-period-tracker-apps-share-data-with-third-parties/#:~:text=A%20research%20team%20at%20ORCHA,apps%20and%20revealed%20significant%20flaws> accessed 22 November 2022.

[63] Citron, *Fight for Privacy* (n 1) 13–14.

[64] ibid 4–6.

[65] ibid 5.

[66] Danielle Keats Citron, 'The End of Roe Means We Need a New Civil Right to Intimate Privacy' *Slate* (New York City, 27 June 2022) <https://slate.com/technology/2022/06/end-roe-civil-right-intimate-privacy-data.html> accessed 22 November 2022.

[67] Danielle Keats Citron, 'A New Compact for Sexual Privacy' (2021) 62 William and Mary Law Review 1763.

[68] Citron, *Fight for Privacy* (n 1) 4, 99.

state-funded medical care.[69] Wealthy women with private insurance do not have to answer any such questions for the state.

State agencies are the tip of the government data exploitation iceberg. In 2017, the Department of Justice (DOJ) showed to members of the press 375 text messages exchanged between two FBI officials, exceeding the bounds of federal law, propriety, and basic humanity. On 12 December 2017, DOJ spokeswoman Sarah Isgur Flores invited select reporters to her office after hours to view text messages exchanged between Lisa Page, special counsel to the FBI's deputy director, and Peter Strzok, deputy assistant director of the FBI's Counterintelligence Division. Reporters were only allowed to view the texts; they were told that they could not report that the DOJ let them see the texts. Page and Strzok had served on the teams that investigated Hillary Clinton's use of a private email service and Donald Trump campaign officials' ties to Russia. During some of that time, they had an extramarital affair. In their texts, they discussed work, their kids, and their health. They also talked about politics and the Trump campaign.[70]

In ordinary times, Page and Strzok's texts would have remained between them. No one would have retrieved them from the FBI's electronic storage system. The federal Privacy Act of 1974 protects the confidentiality of agency records about US persons, including federal employees like Page and Strzok. Agency records can only be shared with a person's written permission or for a routine use like paying federal employees.[71]

Despite the Privacy Act's protections, the DOJ showed the press those texts (without Page's or Strzok's permission). President Trump tweeted about the text message and Page and Strzok's affair countless times. Trump described Page and Strzok as treasonous, sick lovers and called for their firing.[72]

The fallout from the DOJ's and the President's exploitation of Page's and Strzok's texts and affair was profound. Both have been attacked by cybermobs bent on terrorizing them. Online searches of their names are filled with news of their affair and texts. Strzok was fired from the FBI; he has not been able to find full-time employment despite the fact that he was considered one of the best counterintelligence agents in the country. Page has got a job in the private sector, but it does not provide the kind of compensation that someone at her level would otherwise earn. The governmental privacy violations deprived both Page and Strzok of jobs that they loved, destroyed their anonymity, and radically changed the arc of their lives.[73]

[69] ibid 58–60. For a brilliant work on the denial of privacy to pregnant individuals, see the scholarship of Dr Khiara Bridges, including her books *Reproducing Race* and *The Poverty of Privacy Rights*.

[70] Danielle Keats Citron, 'Presidential Privacy Violations' (2022) 5 University of Illinois Law Review 1919–22 (hereafter Citron, 'Presidential Privacy').

[71] Citron, 'Presidential Privacy' (n 70) 1935–36.

[72] Citron, *Fight for Privacy* (n 1) 52–53.

[73] ibid 53–54, 207–08.

Seeing these wrongs together helps us understand the broader stakes for identity development, human dignity, and love. We can better appreciate that the risks to intimate privacy come from individuals, companies, and governments. We can see that intimate image-based abuse is one way that our intimate privacy is exploited, but it is not the only way.

IV. A Civil Right to Intimate Privacy

Intimate privacy violations are all around us. The harm to individuals, groups, and society at large is clear and profound. Because women, non-whites, sexual and gender minorities, and disabled individuals suffer the brunt of the damage, inequality is a direct result of intimate privacy violations.[74] As I have argued in my work, intimate privacy is a moral right, a human right, and a civil right that everyone deserves to flourish, grow, and engage as citizens. Because intimate privacy is more often denied to the most vulnerable, we need special protections against its discriminatory denial.[75]

We need to secure intimate privacy for this generation and the next and the one thereafter. Industry, individuals, and governments will not protect intimate privacy on their own. Without law's intervention, companies will continue to collect, use, and share intimate data because it generates profits and dividends for shareholders.[76] Individual perpetrators have few reasons to stop violating intimate privacy. They face little to no penalties. To the extent that criminal sanctions exist in the United States and elsewhere, intimate privacy violations are treated with light penalties (some akin to traffic tickets).[77] Law enforcers often do not want to spend the energy pursuing such cases; officers tend to trivialize the problem, sending victims away with comments like 'boys will be boys'.[78] In the United States, where countless sites devoted to intimate privacy violations are hosted, federal law provides a broad shield from liability for user-generated content.[79] Even when sites solicit, encourage, or deliberately keep up intimate privacy violations and profit from them, they cannot be sued for the damage that they enable.[80] There are no deep pockets to sue. There is too little justice and too few restrictions.[81]

[74] ibid.
[75] ibid.
[76] ibid.
[77] ibid 94–96.
[78] ibid 76–80.
[79] Danielle Keats Citron, 'How to Fix Section 230' Boston University Law Review (forthcoming) <https://papers.ssrn.com/sol3/papers.cfm?abstract_id=4054906> accessed 22 November 2022 (hereafter Citron, 'How to Fix Section 230').
[80] Citron, 'How to Fix Section 230' (n 79) 9–13.
[81] Citron, *Fight for Privacy* (n 1) 84–90.

Law should treat intimate privacy as a fundamental human and civil right. Civil rights are legally protected rights the protection of which are essential for human beings to flourish, enjoy respect, and feel that they belong. When you say something is a civil right, it means that it cannot be denied or traded away without a good reason.[82] If law recognized intimate privacy as a fundamental human and civil right, as it should, it would not be good enough for companies to justify their data practices on the grounds that the exploitation of intimate data makes their work more profitable or efficient. Individual perpetrators could not justify their actions by saying that they did not mean to hurt the other person, that it was just silly showing off (as many do say when they are explaining why they violated someone's intimate privacy). Companies, individuals, and governments would need a darn good reason to jeopardize intimate privacy because human flourishing and equality are on the line.[83] Critically, a civil right to intimate privacy would acknowledge the unique harms suffered by women and minorities and the corrosive impact that discriminatory attitudes have on their careers, psyches, education, and more.[84]

The Congress and state lawmakers would have to recognize a civil right to intimate privacy. That right, enshrined in federal and state law, would then have the democratic imprimatur of the people. State courts might find that their state constitutions secure protection for intimate privacy. It is hard to imagine that the Supreme Court would find a right to intimate privacy embedded in the US Constitution in the wake of *Dobbs*. After fifty years of precedent, individuals have lost their constitutionally secured right to reproductive autonomy. We need to look to lawmakers to protect reproductive freedom and intimate privacy.

A civil rights approach would have practical and expressive pay off. Under modern civil rights laws in the United States, entities with power over important rights have obligations to act as the guardians of those rights.[85] Individuals and entities with power over our intimate privacy should be viewed as guardians of our intimate data. Anyone handling intimate data would have to act as the caretaker of that data, not as an exploiter of that data.[86] When it comes to section 230 of the Communications Decency Act of 1996, sites could enjoy the immunity only if they fulfilled a duty of care to tackle intimate privacy violations, one that would include having processes to respond to complaints about privacy violations and taking down content amounting to IP violations[87] (also,

[82] ibid 106, 108–10, 119–20.

[83] ibid 121–22.

[84] ibid 119–20.

[85] ibid 148–49.

[86] ibid.

[87] As currently interpreted, section 230 provides a broad immunity to platforms for hosting information provided by someone else, including non-consensual intimate imagery. This legal shield is afforded to sites that encourage, solicit, or keep up non-consensual intimate images. It is extended to sites that fail to remove non-consensual intimate imagery. See generally Citron, 'How to Fix Section 230' (n 79).

sites trafficking in intimate privacy violations should not enjoy immunity at all).[88] Companies handling intimate data should have duties of care, loyalty, and non-discrimination. That might mean not collecting, and definitely not selling, intimate data to third parties, period, the end.[89] A civil right to intimate privacy would suggest a new approach for individual violations of intimate privacy. Rather than treating violations as distinct crimes—such as video voyeurism and non-consensual posting of intimate images—violations of intimate privacy should be treated as such, variations on a vicious theme. We would need a comprehensive legislative approach to intimate privacy so we could see the wrongs and harms in their fullness and scope.

Beyond the practical, the recognition of a civil right to intimate privacy would have expressive power. A civil rights approach gives us the vocabulary to understand its centrality to human flourishing. It would tell victims that their intimate privacy and intimate expression matter, that they matter, and that the law sees and redresses the structural damage to vulnerable groups. It would say to companies that they should design products and services with duties of care in mind, so less intimate information is collected and exploited, so that intimate privacy is prioritized rather than destroyed or ignored.[90]

As we wait for reform, we need companies to step up and address intimate privacy violations. We need companies to hire diverse staff so that they can spot issues before they build violations of intimate privacy into their products and services. They should take opportunities to educate users about their policies against intimate privacy violations. We do not have to wait for them to do it: we can and should bring moral suasion to bear to nudge them in that direction.[91]

V. Conclusion

Although I have laid out a broad overview of the kind of reforms that are needed, I want to end where I began. The first step in any reform agenda must be a proper conceptualization of the problem. Intimate privacy is the foundational right at issue. Intimate-image abuse is a violation of intimate privacy. Everyone deserves intimate privacy to create a life of meaning, respect, and love. Violations of intimate privacy undermine human flourishing, democratic engagement, and equal opportunity.

Conceptualizing intimate-image abuse as a violation of intimate privacy enables us to understand its significance for individuals, groups, and society. It lets

[88] ibid 35–43.
[89] Citron, *Fight for Privacy* (n 1) 156–65.
[90] ibid 120.
[91] ibid 178–79, 210.

us see the fullness of the wrongs at hand and the harms inflicted. It helps us appreciate the legal significance and moral resonance. It helps us change the social meaning of the practice, from just 'boys being boys' to a moral reckoning that implicates not only individual privacy invaders but also corporate and government spies. It would say that the stakes are too high for law enforcers to sit on their hands; for lawmakers to put off reforms to section 230, which allows sites to encourage, solicit, and profit from intimate privacy violations; and for companies to do anything less that acting proactively to prevent and mitigate the damage from intimate privacy violations.

With the right conceptual apparatus—intimate privacy—lawmakers might wake from their slumber to protect victims in a comprehensive manner and to train law enforcement officers about the exploitation of intimate images. The public might get the message that the erosion of intimate privacy is neither inevitable nor acceptable. Victims might see themselves as wronged, rather than blaming themselves, and they might bring the fight for intimate privacy to lawmakers. Some potential perpetrators might see intimate privacy violations as wrongful and damaging. My greatest hope is that intimate privacy and its protection will become the moral law within us.

Bibliography

Allen A, *Uneasy Access: Privacy for Women in a Free Society* (Rowman & Littlefield 1988)

Altman I, and Taylor DA, *Social Penetration: The Development of Interpersonal Relationships* (Holt, Reinhart and Winston 1973)

Chesney R, and Citron DK, 'Deep Fakes: Looming Challenge for Democracy, National Security, and Privacy' (2019) 107 California Law Review 1753

Citron DK, 'Spying Inc.' (2015) 72 Washington and Lee Law Review 1243

Citron DK, 'Sexual Privacy' (2019) 128 Yale Law Journal 1870

Citron DK, 'A New Compact for Sexual Privacy' (2021) 62 William and Mary Law Review 1763

Citron DK, 'Presidential Privacy Violations' (2022) 5 University of Illinois Law Review 1919–22

Citron DK, *The Fight for Privacy: Protecting Dignity, Identity, and Love in the Digital Age* (W W Norton 2022)

Citron DK, 'How to Fix Section 230' Boston University Law Review (forthcoming)

Cohen J, *Configuring the Networked Self* (Yale University Press 2010)

Fried C, *An Anatomy of Values* (Harvard University Press 1970)

Henry N and others, *Image-based Sexual Abuse: A Study on the Causes and Consequences of Non-Consensual Nude or Sexual Imagery* (Routledge 2020)

Holmes J and Rempel JK, 'Trust in Close Relationships' in C Hendrick (ed), *Close Relationships: A Sourcebook* (Sage Publications 1989)

Sartre JP, *Being and Nothingness: A Phenomenological Essay on Ontology* (Hazel E Barnes tr, Washington Square Press 1956)

Young IM, *On the Female Body Experience: Throwing Like a Girl and Other Essays* (OUP 2005)

3

Recurring Themes in Tech-Facilitated Sexual Violence Over Time

The More Things Change, the More They Stay the Same

Jane Bailey and Suzie Dunn

I. Introduction

Technology-facilitated gender-based violence (TFGBV) constitutes a wide-array of harms facilitated by digital means, ranging from sexual harassment, sexualized doxing, and sexual extortion (often for purposes of financial abuse).[1] These digital attacks against cis and transgender women, girls, and gender-diverse people are often sexualized or gendered in nature, such as threats of sexual violence, posts of their sexualized images without consent,[2] and demeaning sexist or transphobic commentary used to reinforce patriarchal expectations of women and gender-diverse people.[3] TFGBV is gaining increasing attention as more people are

[1] Suzie Dunn, *Technology-Facilitated Gender-based Violence-An Overview* (Centre for International Governance Innovation: Supporting a Safer Internet Paper No 1 2021) (hereafter Dunn, 'Technology-Facilitated Gender-based Violence-An Overview'). With respect to sextortion and financial abuse, seeRoberta Liggett O'Malley and Karen Holt, 'Cyber Sextortion—An Exploratory Analysis of Different Perpetrators Engaging in a Similar Crime' (2022) 37(1–2) Journal of Interpersonal Violence 258.

[2] Danielle Citron, 'Sexual Privacy' (2019) 128 Yale Law Journal 1870 (hereafter Citron, 'Sexual Privacy').

[3] Sharon Goulds and others, *Free to be Online? Girls' and Young Women's Experiences of Online Harassment* (Plan International 2020).

Jane Bailey and Suzie Dunn, *Recurring Themes in Tech-Facilitated Sexual Violence Over Time* In: *Criminalizing Intimate Image Abuse*. Edited by: Gian Marco Caletti and Kolis Summerer, Oxford University Press.
DOI: 10.1093/oso/9780198877813.003.0003

impacted by it and was recently recognized by the United Nations as a serious form of gender-based violence (GBV).[4]

Many sexualized forms of TFGBV fit within what Clare McGlynn and Erika Rackley termed image-based sexual abuse (IBSA).[5] IBSA has a variety of subsets including the non-consensual distribution of intimate images (NCDII), voyeurism, livestreaming sexual assaults, creepshots, and deepfakes,[6] but technology-facilitated sexual violence (TFSV) goes far beyond the non-consensual taking and sharing of sexual images. Online apps are used to facilitate sexual assault,[7] and malicious sexualized online impersonation that has led to physical violence.[8] Journalists and activists are sexually targeted for speaking out about gender-discrimination,[9] and sexual harassment and threats occur via all forms of digital technology.[10] These harms are further exacerbated for women and gender-diverse people with intersecting marginalized identity factors who often have racist,[11] ableist,[12] homophobic,[13] xenophobic,[14] and

[4] Dubravka Šimonović, *Report of the Special Rapporteur on Violence against Women, Its Causes and Consequences on online violence against women and girls from a human rights perspective* (UN Human Rights Council 2018); United Nations 67th Commission on the Status of Women, *Agreed Conclusions: Innovation and Technological Change, and the Education in the Digital Age for Achieving Gender Equality and the Empowerment of All Women and Girls* (UN Commission on the Status of Women 2023).

[5] Clare McGlynn and Erika Rackley, 'Image-based Sexual Abuse' (2017) 37(3) Oxford Journal of Legal Studies 534.

[6] Kristen Thomasen and Suzie Dunn, 'Reasonable Expectations of Privacy in the Era of Drones and Deepfakes: Examining the Supreme Court of Canada's Decision in R v Jarvis' in Jane Bailey and others (eds), *The Emerald International Handbook of Technology-Facilitated Violence* (Emerald Publishing 2021) (hereafter Thomasen and Dunn, 'Reasonable Expectations of Privacy in the Era of Drones and Deepfakes').

[7] Amanda Turnbull, 'Onlife Harms: Uber and Sexual Violence' (2022) 19(2) Canadian Journal of Law and Technology 279; Brian Edwards and others, *Addressing Rape in Four Minutes or Less: Dating App Reps Left Unprepared to Respond to Assault Victims* (ProPublica 2021).

[8] *R v JTB* [2018] ONSC 2422; Carrie Goldberg, *Nobody's Victim: Fighting Psychos, Stalkers, Pervs, and Trolls* (Penguin Publishing Group 2019).

[9] Julie Posetti and others, *The Chilling: Global Trends on Violence against Women Journalists* (United Nations Educational, Scientific and Cultural Organization 2021) (hereafter Posetti and others, 'The Chilling'); Mardiya Sib Yahaya and Neema Iyer, *(In)Visible: The Digital Threats Muslim Women Human Rights Defenders Face in the Greater Horn of Africa* (Pollicy 2022); Mariana Palumbo and Delfina Schenone Sienra, *EROTICS Global Survey 2017: Sexuality, Rights and Internet Regulations* (Association of Progressive Communication 2017).

[10] Suzie Dunn and others, *Supporting Safer Digital Spaces: An International Examination of Gender, Sexual Orientation, and Technology-facilitated Violence* (Centre for International Governance Innovation, forthcoming 2023) (hereafter Dunn and others, *Supporting Safer Digital Spaces*).

[11] Chrissy Thompson and Mark A Wood, 'A Media Archaeology of the Creepshot' (2018) 18(4) Feminist Media Studies 560; Moya Bailey, *Misogynoir Transformed: Black Women's Digital Resistance* (New York University Press 2021).

[12] Erin Pritchard, 'The Intersection of Disability and Gender with Online Harassment' (National Sexual Violence Resource Centre, 6 April 2022). <https://www.nsvrc.org/blogs/intersection-disability-and-gender-online-harassment> accessed 22 March 2023.

[13] Ari Ezra Waldman, 'Law, Privacy, and Online Dating: "Revenge Porn" in Gay Online Communities' (2019) 44(4) Law and Social Inquiry 987–1018.

[14] Yee Man Louie, 'Technology-facilitated Domestic Abuse and Culturally and Linguistically Diverse Women in Victoria, Australia' in Jane Bailey and others (eds), *The Emerald International Handbook*

transphobic[15] commentary intertwined with the sexual and gendered attacks against them.

TFGBV victims/survivors are often blamed for their own victimization, chastised for taking nude or sexual images of themselves in the first place, having public-facing online profiles where men can see them, stepping outside of limited sexist gender roles,[16] or for speaking out about feminism, trans rights, and other equality issues online.[17] This was clearly demonstrated in some of the earliest cases of 'revenge porn' websites and social media groups, where the owners, contributors, and users of those sites mocked the women in the images and blamed them for having taken the pictures in the first place.[18] This was despite the fact that the images were posted online without their consent and many of the images were taken without consent or were stolen from women's devices.[19] This victim-blaming narrative, along with the normalization of sexual violence against women and gender-marginalized people, continues in other digital spheres.[20]

While the ease and scope of transmission, sense of anonymity, and non-physical digital component in TFGBV differentiate it in many ways from non-tech facilitated GBV, systemically so much remains the same.[21] These include all-too familiar themes that involve questioning whether the harms of such violence are 'real', blaming the victim, and failing to acknowledge this violence as a product of structural and systemic discrimination.[22] This chapter will explore some of the more novel forms of sexual violence that have emerged, such as sexual harassment in the metasphere, and link them back to previous forms of sexual violence in digital

of Technology-Facilitated Violence and Abuse (Emerald Publishing 2021); Nicola Henry and others, *Image-based Sexual Abuse—A Study on the Causes and Consequences of Non-Consensual Nude or Sexual Imagery* (Routledge 2020).

[15] Abigail Curlew and Jeffery Monaghan, 'Stalking "Lolcows" and "Ratkings": DIY Gender Policing, Far-Right Digilantes, and Anti-Transgender Violence' in Joseph McQuade, Tiffany Kwok, and James Cho (eds), *Disinformation and Digital Democracies in the 21st Century* (NATO Association 2019).

[16] Azmina Dhrodia, *Toxic Twitter: Violence and Abuse against Women Online* (Amnesty International 2018); Sarai Chisala-Tempelhoff and Monica Twesiime Kirya, 'Gender, Law, and Revenge Porn in Sub-Saharan Africa: A Review of Malawi and Uganda' (2016) 2(1) Palgrave Communications 1–9.

[17] Posetti and others, 'The Chilling' (n 9).

[18] Jordan Fairbairn, 'Rape Threats and Revenge Porn- Defining Sexual Violence in the Digital Age' in Jane Bailey and Valerie Steeves (eds), *eGirls, eCitizens* (University of Ottawa Press 2015); Jared Keller, 'Nude photo scandal exposes marines' culture of misogyny' (*Newsweek*, 16 March 2017) <https://www.newsweek.com/nude-photo-scandal-exposes-marines-culture-misogyny-569104> accessed 22 March 2023.

[19] Danielle Keats Citron, *The Fight for Privacy: Protecting Dignity, Identity, and Love in the Digital Age* (WW Norton Company 2022) (hereafter Citron, *Fight for Privacy).*

[20] Lisa Sugiura and April Smith, 'Victim Blaming, Responsibilization and Resilience in Online Sexual Abuse and Harassment' in Jacki Tapley and Pamela Davies (eds), *Victimology: Research, Policy and Activism* (Palgrave Macmillan 2020).

[21] Abdul Aziz, *Online Violence against Women in Asia: A Multicounty Study* (United Nations Women 2020).

[22] Jane Bailey and others, 'AI and Technology-Facilitated Violence and Abuse' in Martin-Bariteau and Teresa Scassa (eds), *Artificial Intelligence and the Law in Canada* (LexisNexis Canada 2021).

spaces and the historic lack of support for victims/survivors of all forms of sexual violence.

This chapter pursues its analysis in four parts. First, we define TFGBV, with reference to concerns that a lack of direct physicality can lead to online attacks being treated as somehow less 'real' or less worthy of being categorized as 'violence'. Second, we offer examples of TFGBV from the past, and present, as well as looking to the future. While acknowledging certain fundamental shifts, we also highlight the re-emergence of familiar themes relating to sexual violence. Third, we briefly overview the deficiencies in support for targets of TFGBV. Fourth, we focus on a particular deficiency with respect to TFGBV—the generalized focus on individual perpetrators rather than on systemic drivers and the roles and responsibilities of industry players and states in shaping the digital environment in ways that not only perpetuate but also perpetrate violence for profit.

II. Is it *Really* Violence?

TFGBV is a complex and contested term, as the terminology for this type of violence has been developing and evolving over the last two decades.[23] This section examines and details our interpretation of the term and explains why we choose to use this specific terminology over other terminology that has been used in the past.

First, we use the word 'technology' to encompass a range of modern technologies that are used to communicate information. The term 'technology' in the grander sense is broad enough to cover all sorts of non-digital tools.[24] However, in the context of TFGBV, our definition of 'technology' is limited to digital technologies that communicate information like cell phones, texting, apps, and artificial intelligence (AI), although the pace of technological change means the precise content of this category is constantly subject to change and the concept of technology in TFGBV will expand.[25] We prefer the prefix 'technology' over the prefixes 'cyber' or 'online' as it is a more encompassing term.[26] Many technologies are not Internet enabled, such as text messaging, GPS tracking, or hidden cameras, but are commonly used to facilitate TFGBV. Thus, the term technology is preferred as it captures a broader range of technologies used to facilitate TFGBV.

[23] Suzie Dunn and others, 'Is it Actually Violence? Framing Technology-Facilitated Abuse as Violence' in Jane Bailey, Asher Flynn, and Nicola Henry (eds), *The Emerald International Handbook of Technology-Facilitated Violence and Abuse* (Emerald Publishing 2021) (hereafter Dunn and others, 'Is it Actually Violence?').

[24] La Shun L Carroll, 'A Comprehensive Definition of Technology from an Ethnological Perspective' [2017] Social Sciences 126.

[25] Thomasen and Dunn, 'Reasonable Expectations of Privacy in the Era of Drones and Deepfakes' (n 6).

[26] Dunn, 'Technology-Facilitated Gender-based Violence-An Overview' (n 1).

Second, we use the term 'gender-based' to be inclusive of all people whose sex and gender-identities are systemically marginalized. This includes cis and trans women and girls, and non-binary, agender, and gender variant individuals. Definitions of gender-based violence originate in the advocacy and research based on violence against cis women and girls.[27] There is a long and rich history of feminist advocacy to have violence against women and girls recognized and the gendered-marginalization of women and girls taken seriously.[28] A broader concept of gender-marginalization was introduced through the work of LGBTQ + advocacy and research.[29] Non-binary and transgender conceptions of gender entered feminist discourse and challenged the ways that many feminists overlooked and outright rejected the inclusion of transgender and non-binary people in conversations about gender and GBV.[30] It became clear to many gender-equality and anti-violence advocates and researchers that the sole focus on cis women and girls was not expansive enough to include all forms of gender-based harms and reinforced problematic gender binaries that exclude many gender-marginalized people who are also at significant risk of GBV, but do not fit neatly in problematic binary concepts of gender.[31] It took decades of advocacy by the LGTBQ + community to expand this terminology to become more inclusive of all gender-marginalized people and recognize transgender women as women, although there continues to be resistance about this inclusivity from particular communities, including some feminist communities. We recognize the essential work done by the LGBTQ + community and prefer the more inclusive term 'gender-based violence' over 'violence against women and girls'.

Third, our approach to 'violence' is rooted in the history of feminist anti-violence advocacy to define the concept of violence using a human-rights and feminist-based approach. We recognize the term 'violence' has different meanings, depending on the context.[32] Some definitions of sexual violence are limited to

[27] Marsha Freeman and others, *The UN Convention on the Elimination of All Forms of Discrimination against Women: A Commentary* (OUP 2012).

[28] Elizabeth Sheehy, *Sexual Assault in Canada: Law, Legal Practice and Women's Activism* (University of Ottawa Press 2012); Constance Backhouse, *Carnal Crimes: Sexual Assault Law in Canada, 1900–1975* (Osgoode Society for Canadian Legal History 2008); Holly Johnson, 'Preventing Violence against Women- Progress and Challenges' (2007) 1 IPC Review.

[29] Judith Butler, *Gender Trouble* (Routledge 1990).

[30] Viviane Namaste, *Oversight: Critical Reflections on Feminist Research and Politics* (Women's Press 2015); Judith Butler, *Gender Trouble: Feminism and the Subversion of Identity* (Routledge 1990).

[31] Alicia Gill, 'Survivor-Centered Research: Towards an Intersectional Gender-based Violence Movement' (2018) 33(8) Journal of Family Violence 559; Andrea Wirtz and others, 'Gender-based Violence against Transgender People in the United States: A Call for Research and Programming' (2018) 21(2) Trauma, Violence and Abuse 227; Women's Legal Education and Action Fund, *Mission and Vision* (2023); Brooke Taylor, 'Trans Women Often Excluded from Conversation on Violence against Women' (*CTV News*, 23 March 2021); Sean Arayasirikul and others, 'A Global Cautionary Tale: Discrimination and Violence against Trans Women Worsen Despite Investments in Public Resources and Improvements in Health Insurance Access and Utilization of Health Care' (2022) 21 International Journal for Equity in Health 32.

[32] Diane Follingstad and M Jill Rogers, 'Validity Concerns in the Measurement of Women's and Men's Report of Intimate Partner Violence' (2013) 69(3) Sex Roles 149.

physical violence[33] and others include psychological harm and coercive control.[34] Physical forms of violence, including domestic violence and sexual assault were two of the earliest recognized forms of what is now known as GBV.[35] However, the definition of violence has evolved beyond solely physical violence towards a continuum of violence approach that also includes sexual, emotional, and psychological harms,[36] including non-physical harms like sexual harassment and coercive control.[37] As the concept of violence has evolved, TFV is now recognized by some as a form of GBV in the international arena.[38] We adopt this more expansive approach to the concept of violence, which better recognizes the severity of the harms TFGBV victims/survivors experience.

As technology, social norms, and laws evolve, individuals, societies, governments, companies, and institutions all have responsibilities for working to address TFGBV's pernicious harms.

III. Technology-Facilitated Sexual Violence: Past, Present, and Future

In 1993 Village Voice journalist Julian Dibbell wrote about a 'rape in cyberspace'.[39] In what was then a state-of-the-art fully text-based online space called LambdaMOO, the real space operator(s) of a virtual character named Mr Bungle controlled the text describing the conduct of other characters using a computer program to make it appear that female and non-binary characters had willingly

[33] For example, the sexual assault provision in the Canadian Criminal Code: Criminal Code RSC 1985 cl C-46 s 271, 272; Statistics Canada, 'A Comprehensive Protrait of Police-Reported Crime in Canada 2021' (2 August 2022).

[34] Dunn, 'Is it Actually Violence?' (n 23).

[35] Mahnaz Afkhami and others, *Feminist Advocacy, Family Law and Violence against Women: International Perspectives* (Routledge 2019); Jan Hagen and Judy Postmus, *Violence against Women: Synthesis of Research for Advocacy Organizations* (National Institute for Justice 2000).

[36] Liz Kelly, 'The continuum of Sexual Violence' in Jalna Hanmer and Mary Maynard (eds), *Women, Violence, and Social Control* (Macmillan Press 1987) 36–40.

[37] Constance Backhouse and Leah Cohen, *The Secret Oppression: Sexual Harassment of Working Women* (Macmillan of Canada 1978); Carmen Gill and Mary Aspinall, *Understanding Coercive Control in the Context of Intimate Partner Violence in Canada: How to Address the Issue Through the Criminal Justice System* (Office of the Federal Ombudsman for Victims of Crime, Department of Justice Canada 2020).

[38] United Nations, *A/HRC/38/47 Report of the Special Rapporteur on violence against women, its causes and consequences on online violence against women and girls from a human rights perspective* (HRC 2018); United Nations 67th Commission on the Status of Women, *Agreed Conclusions: Innovation and Technological Change, and the Education in the Digital Age for Achieving Gender Equality and the Empowerment of All Women and Girls* (UN Commission on the Status of Women 2023).

[39] Julian Dibbell, 'A Rape in Cyberspace; How an Evil Clown, a Haitian Trickster Spirit, Two Wizards, and a Cast of Dozens Turned a Database into a Society' (*Village Voice*, 23 December 1993) <http://www.juliandibbell.com/texts/bungle_vv.html> accessed 22 March 2023 (hereafter Dibbell, 'A Rape in Cyberspace'). Our analysis of Dibbell's piece draws upon Jane Bailey and Adrienne Telford, 'What's So Cyber About It? Reflections on Cyberfeminism's Contribution to Legal Studies' (2007) 19(2) Canadian Journal of Women and the Law 243.

participated in their own sexual violation. While no one operating characters in LambdaMOO had been physically violated, Dibbell acknowledged that these word-based sexual assaults had very real effects. For example, while calling for community redress in this otherwise rather libertarian online community, 'posttraumatic tears were streaming down' the face of the Seattle woman who operated one of the victimized characters. Dibbell noted the parallels between the gendered realities of 'virtual' and 'real' space, stating:

> and thus the woman in Seattle who had written herself the character called legba, with a view perhaps to tasting in imagination a deity's freedom from the burdens of the gendered flesh, got to read similarly constructed sentences in which legba, messenger of the gods, lord of crossroads and communications, suffered a brand of degradation all-too-customarily reserved for the embodied female.[40]

Later research by Dibbell revealed that Mr Bungle originated from an IP address at a New York University dorm, and that the young man who typed out the violent text 'was surrounded by friends and acquaintances who had been calling out suggestions'.[41]

Some questioned whether the term 'rape' ought to have been used in relation to these events in LambdaMOO. Since no physical touching was involved, some argued that the use of that term trivialized 'real' rape and sexual assault.[42] Such criticisms share much in common with longstanding analyses that minimize as less 'harmful' sexual violence that does not result in extreme physical injury, sometimes mischaracterized as 'non-violent rape'.[43] These analyses frame the harms of sexual violence according to a heterosexual male-defined conception of violence, with insufficient regard for the emotional and psychological harms of sexual violence.[44] This conception ignores the use of unequal power, including societal male dominance, to cause sexual harms and fails to recognize the various forms of violence along the sexual violence continuum.[45] Presuming that extreme physical injury is either the only or the most important, indicator of violence leaves little space for meaningfully taking into account survivors' own understandings of the harms

[40] Dibbell, 'A Rape in Cyberspace' (n 39).

[41] Stephanie Buck, 'The "Rape in Cyber Space" From 25 Years Ago Posed Problems We Still Haven't Solved Today' (*Timeline*, 30 October 2017) <https://timeline.com/rape-in-cyberspace-lambdamoo-da9cf0c74e9e> accessed 22 March 2023 (hereafter Buck, 'The "rape in cyber space" from 25 years ago posed problems we still haven't solved today').

[42] ibid.

[43] Lynn Hecht Schafran, 'Maiming the Soul: Judges, Sentencing and the Myth of the Nonviolent Rapist' (1993) 20 Fordham Urban Law Journal 439.

[44] Dunn, 'Is it Actually Violence?' (n 23).

[45] Liz Kelly, 'The Continuum of Sexual Violence' in Jalna Hanmer and Mary Maynard (eds), *Women, Violence, and Social Control* (Macmillan Press 1987); Karen Boyel, 'What's in a Name? Theorising the Inter-relationships of Gender and Violence' (2019) 20(1) Feminist Theory 19.

they have suffered and the larger systemic impacts these forms of violence have on gender-marginalized people.

The trivialization of non-physical violence has also to some extent been reflected in the context of digital sexual harassment[46] and NCDII, and layered together with victim blaming rhetoric, sometimes leaves survivors doubting whether they have actually experienced violence.[47] 'Digital dualism', which treats the 'online' world as compartmentally sealed from the 'offline' world, creates a false binary that is then used by some to distinguish what happens 'offline' as *real* whereas what happens 'online' as trivial, *un*real, easy to avoid, or even imaginary.[48] Once cast as 'unreal' or 'trivial', experiences of TFV in forms such as NCDII or digital sexual harassment are more easily dismissed as events that individual targets are responsible for dealing with. This leads to all-too-familiar victim-blaming logics that yield advice to survivors that they should just stay offline, not take or share images of themselves, stop thinking of themselves as victims, and learn to distinguish between the *real* world and the online world, notwithstanding the very intimate ways in which physical and digital experiences are intertwined in their lives.[49] This intertwining is particularly pronounced for women targeted by rape threats online, a tactic frequently directed at women writers and journalists whose work challenges discriminatory norms and stereotypes, sometimes leading them to withdraw from social media in order to protect the safety of themselves and their families.[50]

In parallel with historic trends, the negative impact of sexualized violence such as NCDII[51] and the gaslighting rhetoric that accompanies it are unevenly born by women, girls, and gender-marginalized people. The targeting of members of these communities also often involves deployment of intersecting forms of discrimination such as misogyny, racism,[52] homophobia, transphobia,[53] classism,

[46] Danielle Keats Citron, *Hate Crimes in Cyberspace* (Harvard University Press 2014).

[47] Chandell Gosse, '"Not the Real World": Exploring Experiences of Online Abuse, Digital Dualism, and Ontological Labor' in Jane Bailey, Asher Flynn, and Nicola Henry (eds), *The Emerald International Handbook of Technology-Facilitated Violence and Abuse* (Emerald Publishing 2021).

[48] ibid.

[49] ibid.

[50] Jessica Valenti, 'Insults and Rape Threats. Writers Shouldn't Have to Deal with This' (*The Guardian*, 14 April 2016) <https://www.theguardian.com/commentisfree/2016/apr/14/insults-rape-threats-writers-online-harassment> accessed 22 March 2023.

[51] The devastating impacts of NCDII on targets' mental health include trust issues, PTSD, anxiety, depression, suicidal thoughts, and other mental health effects similar to those suffered by sexual assault survivors: Samantha Bates, 'Revenge Porn and Mental Health: A Qualitative Analysis of the Mental Health Effects of Revenge Porn on Female Survivors' (2017) 12(1) Feminist Criminology 22.

[52] A 2018 study showed that 96 per cent of publicly available deepfakes were sexual deepfakes using images 'exclusively of women without their consent' and that South Korean women were disproportionately targeted: Suzie Dunn, 'Identity Manipulation: Responding to Advances in Artificial Intelligence and Robotics' (Conference paper delivered at the WeRobot Conference, Ottawa, 4 April 2020) 10 (unpublished) citing Henry Ajder and others, 'The State of Deepfakes: Landscape, Threats, and Impact' (*Tracer Newsletter*, 29 November 2019) <https://medium.com/deeptrace/mapping-the-deepfake-landscape-27cb809e98bc> accessed 22 March 2023 (hereafter Ajder and others, 'The State of Deepfakes').

[53] Dunn and others, *Supporting Safer Digital Spaces* (n 10).

colonialism, and ableism,[54] and preys on 'pre-existing structural prejudices that seek to control and constrain expressions of sexuality and gender according to discriminatory myths, norms, and stereotypes in order to shame members of these communities with respect to gender and sexual expression.[55]

The very graphic interplay between physical and digital experiences and disparate impacts on equality-seeking communities is evident in the context of doxing—the release of personal information online about a person without their consent, which can and often does include the non-consensual release of images.[56] For example, non-consensual release of the former names and pre-transition photos of trans people on transphobic websites draws on and perpetuates systemic transphobia, aiming to silence, humiliate, and shame trans people, as well as exposing them to the risk of physical violence.[57] Similarly, doxing that includes release of the names, addresses, places of work, and phone numbers of both cis and trans women, in combination with false invitations to engage in sexual activity, puts them at risk of physical sexual violence.[58]

Unfortunately (though perhaps unsurprisingly), current indications suggest that technologies and platforms of the future are poised to re-entrench, if not to deepen, the problematic patterns of the past and present. We begin with the so-called 'metaverse', a 'vague and complex' term that 'doesn't really refer to any one specific type of technology, but rather a broad (and often speculative) shift in how we interact with technology'.[59] While some, like Mark Zuckerberg of Meta (the parent company of Facebook and Instagram), seem to suggest that the metaverse is the future of the Internet, others see it as just a video game or even 'a deeply uncomfortable, worse version of Zoom'.[60] For its part, Meta is focused on creating a virtual reality (VR) social platform (Horizon Worlds) and a VR app for hosting

[54] Nasreen Rajani, '"I Bet You Don't Get What We Get": An Intersectional Analysis of Technology-Facilitated Violence Experienced by Racialized Women Anti-Violence Online Activists in Canada' (2022) 19(2) Canadian Journal of Law and Technology 217.

[55] Jane Bailey and Jasmine Dong, 'Toward Survivor-Centred Outcomes for Targets of Privacy-Invasive TFVA: Assessing the Equality-Affirming Impact of Jarvis' in Christopher Hunt and Robert Diab (eds), *The Last Frontier: Digital Privacy and the Charter* (Thomson Reuters Press 2021) 125, citing Dunn, 'Technology-Facilitated Gender-based Violence: An Overview' (n 1) 6.

[56] Nicola Henry and others, *Image-based Sexual Abuse—A Study on the Causes and Consequences of Non-Consensual Nude or Sexual Imagery* (Routledge 2020).

[57] Abigail Curlew, 'Vigiliantism & Transmisogyny: Digital Violence against Women and Hate Motivated Violence' (*The Learning Network*, 2020) <https://gbvlearningnetwork.ca/webinars/recorded-webinars/2020/webinar-2020-4.html> accessed 3 October 2023; Florence Ashley, 'Trans People Under Attack' (*The McGill Daily*, 12 November 2018) <https://www.mcgilldaily.com/2018/11/trans-people-under-attack> accessed 22 March 2023.

[58] Citron, 'Sexual Privacy' (n 2); Dunn, 'Technology-Facilitated Gender-based Violence: An Overview' (n 1)

[59] Eric Ravenscraft, 'What is the Metaverse, Exactly?' (*Wired*, 25 April 2022) <https://www.wired.com/story/what-is-the-metaverse/> accessed 22 March 2023 (hereafter Ravenscraft, 'What is the Metaverse, Exactly?').

[60] ibid.

livestream events on the metaverse (Horizon Venue),[61] while others are enabling users to generate video games.[62]

Whatever the exact future of 'the' metaverse, early reports suggest it/they will only further embed all-too-familiar sexual violence patterns and scripts, with the multisensory experience of VR facilitating deeply daunting experiences of such violence,[63] and facilitating non-consensual 'sex' with 3D avatars of ex-partners and celebrities.[64] None of this comes as a surprise in light of longstanding reports of sexual harassment, verbal abuse, racial slurs,[65] and invasion of personal space in VR and non-VR environments where minimal content moderation has been associated with allowing attacks on avatars that look or sound female or femme to thrive.[66] These patterns were already well-reflected in much earlier forms of abuse in online environments, which included creating false profiles on social media, non-consensual uploading of sexual images on 'revenge porn' sites, and launching personalized attacks on message boards, practices that Mary Anne Franks compellingly argued in 2009 made 'their targets into unwilling avatars'.[67]

Considerable press has been devoted to such experiences on Meta-owned platforms, including Horizon Worlds and Population One, where participants use VR headsets and hand controllers and rely on avatars to communicate and engage with others. SumOfUs' 2022 analysis reported instances of 'virtual groping and gang-rape, and sexual, homophobic and racist comments', as well as inadequate violation reporting and response mechanisms on Facebook metaverse platforms.[68] One woman gamer reported seeing sexual assault and harassment happen in the VR

[61] SumOfUs, 'Metaverse: Another Cesspool of Toxic Content' (*SumOfUs*, May 2022) <https://www.sumofus.org/images/Metaverse_report_May_2022.pdf> accessed 22 March 2023 5 (hereafter SumOfUs, 'Metaverse').

[62] Ravenscraft 'What is the Metaverse, Exactly?' (n 59).

[63] Trang Le, 'Sexual Assault in the Metaverse is Part of a Bigger Problem that Technology Alone Won't Solve' (*Lens*, 22 July 2022) <https://lens.monash.edu/@politics-society/2022/07/22/1384871/sexual-assault-in-the-metaverse-theres-nothing-virtual-about-it> accessed 22 March 2023. These experiences can include users wearing haptic clothing that 'relays sensations through buzzes and vibrations': Sheera Frankel and Kellen Browning, 'The Metaverse's Dark Side: Here Come Harassment and Assaults' (*New York Times*, 30 December 2021) <https://www.nytimes.com/2021/12/30/technology/metaverse-harassment-assaults.html> accessed 22 March 2023 (hereafter Frankel and Browning, 'The Metaverse's Dark Side).

[64] Samantha Cole and Emanual Malberg, '"They Can't Stop Us": People are Having Sex with 3D Avatars of Their Exes and Celebrities' (*Vice*, 19 November 2019) <https://www.vice.com/en/article/j5yzpk/they-cant-stop-us-people-are-having-sex-with-3d-avatars-of-their-exes-and-celebrities> accessed 22 March 2023.

[65] Lisa Nakamura, 'Gender and Race in the Gaming World' in Mark Graham and William Dutton (eds), *Society and the Internet: How Networks of Information and Communications are Changing Our Lives* (2nd edn, OUP 2019) 127–45.

[66] Frankel and Browning, 'The Metaverse's Dark Side (n 63).

[67] Mary Anne Franks, 'Unwilling Avatars: Idealism and Discrimination in Cyberspace' (2011) 20 Columbia Journal of Gender and Law 224.

[68] ibid 2.

game Population One 'two to three times per week, if not more'.[69] Meta responded to a complaint by a Horizon Worlds beta tester that her 'avatar had been groped by a stranger' by pointing out that she had failed to use adequate personal safety features[70]—the digital equivalent to the victim-blaming and responsibilization logics reflected in longstanding admonitions about how women should behave so as to avoid sexual assault.[71]

Concerns that future technologies may well perpetuate or even deepen the longstanding problem of sexual violence extend well beyond the so-called metaverse. For example, AI technologies are being used to create 'fake' images or videos of people in which digital maps of one person's face are superimposed over the face of another person in a video, making it appear that the person whose face was superimposed was actually engaged in the activity depicted in the video.[72] While deepfake technology can and is used for a variety of purposes, a 2019 Deeptrace Labs report showed that 96 per cent of all deepfake videos were non-consensual, pornographic videos, and of those, 99 per cent were of women,[73] with South Korean and US women celebrities being particularly likely to be targeted.[74] Art-generating AI apps appear poised to repeat similar outcomes by converting actual photos of women into hyper-realistic nude and/or hyper-sexualized images and avatars.[75]

We now turn from reflecting on the disturbing continuity of familiar systemic drivers of sexual violence and the trivialization, victim-blaming, gaslighting rhetoric surrounding them to assess the (in)adequacy of support for victims/survivors of these attacks.

[69] Frankel and Browning, 'The Metaverse's Dark Side (n 63).

[70] SumOfUs, 'Metaverse' (n 61).

[71] Jane Bailey and Carissima Mathen, 'Technology-facilitated Violence against Women and Girls: Assessing the Canadian Criminal Law Response' (2019) 97(3) Canadian Bar Review 664, 694 (hereafter Bailey and Mathen, 'Technology-Facilitated Violence against Women and Girls). Of course, the latter of these admonitions defies logic in another way, since most survivors of sexual violence are attacked by someone they know: Canadian Women's Foundation, 'The Facts About Sexual Assault and Harassment' (*Canadian Women's Foundation,* 2019) <https://canadianwomen.org/the-facts/sexual-assault-harassment/> accessed 22 March 2023, citing Adam Cotter and Laura Savage, 'Gender-based Violence and Unwanted Sexual Behaviour in Canada, 2018: Initial Findings from the Survey of Safety in Public and Private Spaces' (*Statistics Canada*, 5 December 2019) <https://www150.statcan.gc.ca/n1/pub/85-002-x/2019001/article/00017-eng.htm> accessed 22 March 2023.

[72] Citron, 'Sexual Privacy' (n 2); Thomasen and Dunn, 'Reasonable Expectations of Privacy in the Era of Drones and Deepfakes' (n 6).

[73] Ajder and others, 'The State of Deepfakes' (n 52); Thomasen and Dunn, 'Reasonable Expectations of Privacy in the Era of Drones and Deepfakes' (n 6).

[74] Suzie Dunn, 'Women, Not Politicians, Are Targeted Most Often by Deepfake Videos' (*Centre for International Governance Innovation*, 3 March 2021) <https://www.cigionline.org/articles/women-not-politicians-are-targeted-most-often-deepfake-videos/> accessed 22 March 2023.

[75] Haje Jan Kamps, 'Updated: It's Way Too Easy to Trick Lensa AI into Making NSFW Images' (*TechCrunch*, 6 December 2022) <https://techcrunch.com/2022/12/06/lensa-goes-nsfw/> accessed 22 March 2023.

IV. Deficient Support for Targets of TFV

As the issue of TFGBV gained public attention, some law and policy makers began to recognize the harms caused by these behaviours, particularly following public outrage around upsetting examples of TFGBV and their consequences.[76] However, change has been slow in many regions. As technologies like digital cameras and the Internet have been adopted as tools for committing sexual violence and the public has become more aware of this abuse, legal, technical, and social supports have lagged behind the needs of victims/survivors. In some countries, existing laws, such as harassment and extortion have been applied to TFGBV,[77] and over time some legal gaps have been filled in certain countries by introducing laws against specific TFGBV offences like child sexual abuse materials,[78] voyeurism,[79] and NCDII.[80] These laws have allowed some victims/survivors to find legal redress in some countries, but more legal gaps remain. For example, even in those countries that have introduced legislation, law enforcement continues to struggle with adequately enforcing existing laws.[81]

TFGBV victims/survivors can get caught-up in the conceptualization of the online and offline divide, with some actors in the legal system downplaying or minimizing the experiences of victims/survivors of TFGBV because they did not occur 'in real life'.[82] Additional barriers are caused as some police officers, lawyers, and judges may not be properly trained to collect and interpret digital evidence,[83] and may hold victim-blaming perspectives related to sexual and gender-based crimes like NCDII.[84] Further, because of historically problematic relationships between law enforcement and certain marginalized communities, going to law enforcement

[76] Dunn and others, *Supporting Safer Digital Spaces* (n 10).

[77] Michelle Bordachar and others, *Non-Consensual Intimate Image Distribution: The Legal Landscape in Kenya, Chile, and South Africa* (Centre for International Governance Innovation 2021); Bailey and Mathen, 'Technology-Facilitated Violence against Women and Girls' (n 71).

[78] For example child pornography laws were introduced in Canada in 1993. Criminal Code, RSC, 1985, c C-46, s 163.1; International Centre for Missing and Exploited Children, 'Child Sexual Abuse Material: Model Legislation and Global Review' (9th edn, 2018).

[79] Department of Justice, 'Voyeurism as a Criminal Offence: A Consultation Paper' (2002); Criminal Code RSC 1985 cl C-46 s 162

[80] The Philippines was the first country to introduce a law addressing NDCII in 2009. See: Anastasia Powell and Nicola Henry, *Sexual Violence in a Digital Age* (Palgrave MacMillan 2017) 204; Mary Anne Franks, 'Drafting an Effective "Revenge Porn" Law: A Guide for Legislators' (17 August 2015) <https://ssrn.com/abstract=2468823> accessed 3 October 2023 (hereafter Franks, 'Drafting an Effective "Revenge Porn" Law').

[81] Alexa Dodge and others, '"This Isn't Your Father's Police Force"— Digital Evidence in Sexual Assault Investigations' (2019) 52(4) Australian and New Zealand Journal of Criminology 499 (hereafter Dodge and others, 'This Isn't Your Father's Police Force').

[82] NORC at the University of Chicago and the International Center for Research on Women, 'Technology-facilitated Gender-based Violence in Asia: India' [2022]

[83] Suzie Dunn and Moira Aikenhead, 'On the Internet, Nobody Knows You are a Dog: Contested Authorship of Digital Evidence in Cases of Gender-based Violence' (2022) 19(2) Canadian Journal of Learning and Technology 371.

[84] Alexa Dodge and others, 'This Isn't Your Father's Police Force' (n 84).

may not be a legitimate choice for some survivors/victims. For example, this may be true for members of racialized communities that have experienced historic and ongoing police brutality and discrimination against members of their communities,[85] fear social repercussions for reporting to the police,[86] or have legitimate distrust in the effectiveness of the criminal justice system.[87] As an additional barrier, existing laws such as child pornography and obscenity laws have even been used against people who have taken consensual sexual images of themselves or have had their images of themselves labelled as obscene when they were shared without consent.[88]

Other avenues for support, such as civil society organizations or government-led administrative bodies that provide support for TFGBV victims/survivors[89] are still few and far between. There is a growing number of organizations that support TFGBV victims/survivors,[90] but many civil society organizations that address sexual violence are often underfunded and lack the technical training to provide adequate support.[91] As such, TFGBV victims/survivors continue to lack meaningful supports, even in the community. The lack of support is further exacerbated by social media companies' failure to adequately address TFGBV. Many platforms are not financially incentivized to fully address many of the concerns victims/survivors have with their current content moderation practices.[92] Although some social media companies include rules and regulations in their terms of service that forbid several forms of TFSV,[93] Cynthia Khoo notes that the measures in place vary widely from platform to platform and often do not take a feminist and survivor-centred approach.[94] Even where companies have rules in place, many survivors complain action is not always taken on reported content and that little explanation

[85] Nnennaya Amuchie, '"The Forgotten Victims" How Racialized Gender Stereotypes Lead to Police Violence against Black Women and Girls: Incorporating an Analysis of Police Violence into Feminist Jurisprudence and Community Activism' (2016) 14(3) Seattle Journal for Social Justice 617–67, 619–20.

[86] Donald Flywell Malanga, *Tackling Gender-based Cyber Violence against Women and Girls in Malawi Amidst the COVID-19 Pandemic* (Association for Progressive Communication 2020).

[87] Anja Kovacs, Richa Kaul Padte, and Shobha SV, '"Don't Let it Stand!" An Exploratory Study of Women and Verbal Online Abuse in India' (2013) Internet Democracy Project.

[88] Dunn and others, *Supporting Safer Digital Spaces* (n 10).

[89] Pam Hrick, 'The Potential of Centralized and Statutorily Empowered Bodies to Advance a Survivor-Centered Approach to Technology-Facilitated Violence against Women' in Jane Bailey, Asher Flynn, and Nicola Henry (eds), *The Emerald Handbook of Technology-Facilitated Violence and Abuse* (Emerald Publishing 2021).

[90] For examples of some existing organizations, see 'Latin America in a Glimpse' (*Derechos Digitales & Association for Progressive Communications* 2017); 'Technology Safety' (*British Columbia Society of Transition Houses* 2022).

[91] Citron, *Fight for Privacy* (n 19); Cynthia Khoo, 'Deplatforming Misogyny: Report on Platform Liability for Technology-Facilitated Gender-based Violence' (*Women's Legal Education and Action Fund* 2021) <https://www.leaf.ca/wp-content/uploads/2021/04/Full-Report-Deplatforming-Misogyny.pdf> accessed 22 March 2023 (hereafter Khoo, 'Deplatforming Misogyny').

[92] Tarleton Gillespie, *Custodians of the Internet: Platforms, Content Moderation, and the Hidden Decisions that Shape Social Media* (Yale University Press 2018).

[93] Robyn Caplan, 'Content or Context Moderation? Artisanal, Community-Reliant, and Industrial Approaches' (*Data Society* 2018) 1.

[94] Khoo, 'Deplatforming Misogyny' (n 91)

is provided.[95] Algorithms or overworked content moderators are often making decisions, and there are few avenues for appeal or explanation once a decision has been made.[96]

Approaches to ending TFGBV require a multi-disciplinary, victim/survivor-centred approach. This includes the introduction and implementation of human-rights based laws, the development and support of civil society organizations, and significant improvements to content moderation policies.

V. Expanding Beyond Individual Bad Actors: Addressing Structural and Systemic Drivers and State and Corporate Perpetrators

As Section IV indicates, support for TFGBV victims/survivors is profoundly inadequate, although there has been movement towards improving reactive legal responses against individual abusers over the past several years. That lack of support represents a continuation of a longstanding pattern of inadequately supporting sexual violence victims/survivors that long predated the advent of digital technologies.[97] Improving TFGBV victims/survivors' access to remedies against their individual abusers should they choose to do so could play an important role in development of more survivor-centred outcomes.[98] However, deficiencies in the availability of reactive, individual responses represent only a fraction of the problem. To develop meaningful, robust approaches to TFGBV (and to GBV more generally), we must also focus on proactive approaches aimed at systemic and structural drivers as well as state and corporate actors that both perpetuate and perpetrate abuse.[99]

As Black, Indigenous, and people of colour (BIPOC) feminist scholars and activists have long made clear, treating violence only (or even primarily) as an individual interpersonal act is particularly exclusionary and dangerous for members of equality-seeking communities affected by multiple axes of oppression, such as sexism, racism, homophobia, transphobia, colonialism, and ableism. As Yasmin

[95] Amnesty International, "#ToxicTwitter" (2018).

[96] Sarah T Roberts, *Behind the Screen: Content Moderation in the Shadows of Social Media* (Yale University Press 2019).

[97] Elaine Craig, *Putting Trials on Trial* (McGill-Queen's University Press 2018).

[98] For a discussion of the elements of a survivor-centred approach to TFV, see: Pam Hrick, 'The Potential of Centralized and Statutorily Empowered Bodies to Advance a Survivor-Centered Approach to Technology-Facilitated Violence against Women' in Jane Bailey, Asher Flynn, and Nicola Henry (eds), *The Emerald International Handbook of Technology-Facilitated Violence and Abuse* (Emerald Publishing 2021) 595–614.

[99] Jane Bailey and Jacquie Burkell, 'Tech-facilitated Violence: Thinking Structurally and Intersectionally' (2021) 5(3) Journal of Gender Based Violence 531 (hereafter Bailey and Burkell, 'Tech-facilitated Violence'); Jane Bailey and others, 'AI and Technology-Facilitated Violence and Abuse' in Florian Martin-Bariteau and Teresa Scassa (eds), *AI and the Law in Canada* (Lexis Nexis 2021).

Jiwani has demonstrated, individualized understandings of violence result in structural oppressions being 'erased, trivialized, or contained within categories that evacuate the violation of [structural] violence',[100] making 'structured and systemic social problems appear random, unpatterned and individualized'.[101] The individualized approach obfuscates the disparate targeting of members of equality-seeking communities (especially those affected by multiple axes of oppression), burying the need for responses tailored to the realities, needs, and aspirations of members of those communities. Further, as Kimberle Crenshaw has demonstrated, it also routinely results in 'solutions' that are not only ineffective for, but are potentially dangerous to members of multiple marginalized communities.[102] As a result, opportunities to identify systems and behaviours beyond those of individual perpetrators that need to be redressed are missed, often leading to 'solutions' that emphasize responses by state-based entities, entities that many members of BIPOC and other multiply marginalized communities have come to fear due to long histories of state-enacted oppression and violence.[103]

These are also essential to developing meaningful responses to TFGBV. If, for example, all or even most of our attention is focused on criminal legal remedies against individual bad actors, we leave untouched state and corporate actors, collectives, and systems and their intersections. We may fail to see, for example, the connection between the surveillance capitalism business model that currently drives our digital environment[104] and multiple forms of violence against cis and trans women, girls, and members of other equality-seeking communities.[105] Included among these forms are corporate entities profiting both directly by creating and disseminating NCDII, and other forms of sexual violence online (eg video games embedding sexist, racist, and otherwise violent discourses and AI chatbots perpetrating sexual harassment),[106] and indirectly by promoting sexually violent content through algorithms designed to maximize the number of users of their platforms, and the amount of time users spend there.[107]

[100] Yasmin Jiwani, *Discourses of Denial: Mediations of Race, Gender and Violence* (UBC Press 2006) xi–xii.

[101] Yasmin Jiwani, Helene Berman, and Ann Cameron, 'Violence Prevention and the Canadian Girl Child' (2010) 1(2) International Journal of Child, Youth and Family Studies 134–56.

[102] Kimberle Crenshaw, 'Mapping the Margins: Intersectionality, Identity Politics, and Violence against Women of Color' (1991) 43(6) Stanford Law Review 1241–99.

[103] ibid.

[104] Shoshana Zuboff, *The Age of Surveillance Capitalism: The Fight for a Human Future at the New Frontier of Power* (PublicAffairs 2019).

[105] This includes the structural violence of digital colonialism: Ruha Benjamin, *Race After Technology: Abolitionist Tools for the New Jim Code* (MA Polity Press 2019) (hereafter Benjamin, *Race After Technology*). With respect to AI chatbots and sexual harassment, see Samantha Cole, '"My AI is Sexually Harassing Me": Replika Users Say the Chatbot Has Gotten Way to Horny' *Motherboard: Tech by Vice* (12 January 2023) <https://www.vice.com/en/article/z34d43/my-ai-is-sexually-harassing-me-replika-chatbot-nudes> accessed 22 March 2023.

[106] Bailey and Burkell, 'Tech-facilitated Violence' (n 99).

[107] Khoo, 'Deplatforming Misogyny' (n 91).

The work of BIPOC feminist and other anti-oppression scholars and activists is forcing the need to address structural and systemic violence and the corporate and state roles in such violence onto the policy agenda. From criticisms of corporate immunity models,[108] to exposés of the discriminatory sexualized tropes being re-entrenched through algorithmically generated search results[109] and associated demands for corporate regulation to improve transparency and accountability,[110] to calls for improved anti-oppression education and community support networks,[111] to demands that police stop using facial recognition technology,[112] to the naming and documentation of digital colonialism and its global manifestations,[113] the case for situating TFGBV in its broader systemic context is increasingly difficult to deny or avoid. And yet, we remain conscious of and concerned about the fact that the case for addressing structural and systemic violence is part of a longstanding anti-oppression critique of the societal conception and treatment of violence that is still, to some extent, struggling to be recognized and centred.

VI. Conclusion

TFSV and other forms of TFGBV violate the human rights of the cis and trans women and girls, and other gender-marginalized people who it disproportionately negatively harms. These harms are magnified for community members multiply marginalized by intersecting oppressions including racism, colonialism, ableism, transphobia, and homophobia. As a seemingly ever-evolving array of digital technologies enables a growing diversity of forms of gender-based and sexual violence, long-familiar tropes and systemic patterns continue to proliferate. From now-basic technologies like text-based 'online worlds' and social media platforms to emerging systems like the 'metaverse', AI-enabled deepfake and art-generating technologies, and chatbot sexual harassers, community members who have historically been most targeted by sexual and other forms of GBV are now the 'unwilling avatars'[114] of technology-facilitated instantiations of these longstanding forms of violence. As established systemic patterns of victimization are further entrenched, so too are victim-blaming, violence-normalizing tropes that refuse to recognize non-physical violence as violence, mischaracterize gender-based and sexual violence

[108] Danielle Citron, 'How to Fix Section 230' Boston University Law Review 2022 (forthcoming 2022).

[109] Safiya Umoja Noble, *Algorithms of Oppression: How Search Engines Reinforce Racism* (New York University Press 2018).

[110] Khoo, 'Deplatforming Misogyny' (n 91).

[111] Bailey and Burkell, 'Tech-facilitated Violence' (n 99).

[112] Kate Robertson, Cynthia Khoo, and Yolanda Song, 'To Surveil and Predict: A Human Rights Analysis of Algorithmic Policing in Canada' (Citizen Lab 2020).

[113] Benjamin, *Race After Technology* (n 105); Olufunmilayo B Arewa, *Disrupting Africa: Technology, Law and Development* (Cambridge University Press 2021).

[114] Franks, 'Drafting an Effective "Revenge Porn" Law' (n 80).

solely as acts of individual bad actors, and obfuscate systemic and structural forms of violence perpetuated and perpetrated collectively, including through corporate and state entities. And just like with non-technology facilitated violence, the stubborn intransigence of these tropes in relation to TFGBV self-servingly undermines the prospects for much-needed, well-resourced, survivor-centred community-based systems of support for victims/survivors, and legal reforms aimed at meaningfully addressing gendered forms of violence. Unless and until these patterns are disrupted, it seems likely that although digital technologies will change, the disproportionate, human-rights-undermining targeting of cis and trans women and girls and other gender-marginalized people will remain frustratingly the same.

Bibliography

Aboulez N and others, *The Chilling: Global Trends on Violence against Women Journalists* (United Nations Educational, Scientific and Cultural Organization 2021)

Afkhami M, Ertürk Y, and Mayer AE, *Feminist Advocacy, Family Law and Violence against Women: International Perspectives* (Routledge 2019)

Aikenhead M and Dunn S, 'On the Internet, Nobody Knows You are a Dog: Contested Authorship of Digital Evidence in Cases of Gender-based Violence' (2022) 19(2) Canadian Journal of Learning and Technology 371

Amuchie N, '"The Forgotten Victims" How Racialized Gender Stereotypes Lead to Police Violence against Black Women and Girls: Incorporating an Analysis of Police Violence into Feminist Jurisprudence and Community Activism' (2016) 14(3) Seattle Journal for Social Justice 617

Arayasirikul S and others, 'A Global Cautionary Tale: Discrimination and Violence against Trans Women Worsen Despite Investments in Public Resources and Improvements in Health Insurance Access and Utilization of Health Care' (2022) 21(32) International Journal for Equity in Health 1

Arewa OB, *Disrupting Africa: Technology, Law and Development* (Cambridge University Press 2021)

Aspinall M and Gill C, *Understanding Coercive Control in the Context of Intimate Partner Violence in Canada: How to Address the Issue Through the Criminal Justice System* (Office of the Federal Ombudsman for Victims of Crime, Department of Justice Canada 2020)

Aziz A, *Online Violence against Women in Asia: A Multicounty Study* (United Nations Women 2020)

Backhouse C and Cohen L, *The Secret Oppression: Sexual Harassment of Working Women* (Macmillan of Canada 1978)

Backhouse C, *Carnal Crimes: Sexual Assault Law in Canada, 1900–1975* (Osgoode Society for Canadian Legal History 2008)

Bailey M, *Misogynoir Transformed: Black Women's Digital Resistance* (New York University Press 2021)

Bailey J and others, 'AI and Technology-Facilitated Violence and Abuse' in M Bariteau and T Scassa (eds), *Artificial Intelligence and the Law in* Canada (LexisNexis Canada 2021)

Bailey J and Dong J, 'Toward Survivor-Centred Outcomes for Targets of Privacy-Invasive TFVA: Assessing the Equality-Affirming Impact of Jarvis' in C Hunt and R Diab (eds), *The Last Frontier: Digital Privacy and the Charter* (Thomson Reuters Press 2021)

Bailey J and Mathen C, 'Technology-facilitated Violence against Women and Girls: Assessing the Canadian Criminal Law Response' (2019) 97(3) Canadian Bar Review 664

Bailey J and Telford A, 'What's So Cyber About It? Reflections on Cyberfeminism's Contribution to Legal Studies' (2007) 19(2) Canadian Journal of Women and the Law 243

Ballucci A and others, '"This Isn't Your Father's Police Force": Digital Evidence in Sexual Assault Investigations' (2019) 52(4) Australian and New Zealand Journal of Criminology 499

Bates S, 'Revenge Porn and Mental Health: A Qualitative Analysis of the Mental Health Effects of Revenge Porn on Female Survivors' (2017) 12(1) Feminist Criminology 22

Benjamin R, *Race After Technology: Abolitionist Tools for the New Jim Code* (MA Polity Press 2019)

Bordachar M and others, *Non-Consensual Intimate Image Distribution: The Legal Landscape in Kenya, Chile, and South Africa* (Centre for International Governance Innovation 2021)

Boyel K, 'What's In a name? Theorising the Inter-relationships of Gender and Violence' (2019) 20(1) Feminist Theory 19

Butler J, *Gender Trouble: Feminism and the Subversion of Identity* (Routledge 1990)

Caplan R, *Content or Context Moderation? Artisanal, Community-Reliant, and Industrial* Approaches (Data Society 2018)

Carroll L and Shun L, 'A Comprehensive Definition of Technology from an Ethnological Perspective' [2017] Social Sciences 126

Chisala-Tempelhoff S and Kirya MT, 'Gender, Law, and Revenge Porn in Sub-Saharan Africa: A Review of Malawi and Uganda' (2016) 2(1) Palgrave Communications 1–9

Citron D, *Hate Crimes in Cyberspace* (Harvard University Press 2014)

Citron D, 'How to Fix Section 230' Boston University Law Review (forthcoming 2022) 1

Citron D, 'Sexual Privacy' (2019) 128(7) Yale Law Journal 1870

Citron D, *The Fight for Privacy* (WW Norton Company 2022)

Corr A and others, *Free to be Online? Girls' and Young Women's Experiences of Online Harassment* (Plan International 2020)

Cousins K and others, *Addressing Rape in Four Minutes or Less: Dating App Reps Left Unprepared to Respond to Assault Victims* (ProPublica 2021)

Curlew A and Monaghan J, 'Stalking "Lolcows" and "Ratkings": DIY Gender Policing, Far-Right Digilantes, and Anti-Transgender Violence' in J McQuade, T Kwok, and J Cho (eds), *Disinformation and Digital Democracies in the 21st Century* (NATO Association 2019)

Dhrodia A, *Toxic Twitter: Violence and Abuse against Women Online* (Amnesty International 2018)

Dunn S, 'Identity Manipulation: Responding to Advances in Artificial Intelligence and Robotics' (Conference paper delivered at the WeRobot Conference, Ottawa, 4 April 2020) (unpublished)

Dunn S, 'Is it Actually Violence? Framing Technology-Facilitated Abuse as Violence' in J Bailey, A Flynn, and N Henry (eds) *The Emerald International Handbook of Technology-Facilitated Violence and Abuse* (Emerald Publishing 2021)

Dunn S, *Technology-Facilitated Gender-based Violence-An Overview* (Centre for International Governance Innovation: Supporting a Safer Internet Paper No 1, 2020)

Dunn S and Thomasen K, 'Reasonable Expectations of Privacy in the Era of Drones and Deepfakes: Examining the Supreme Court of Canada's Decision in R v Jarvis' in J Bailey, F Ahser, and N Henry (eds), *The Emerald International Handbook of Technology-Facilitated Violence* (Emerald Publishing 2021)

Dunn S, Vaillancourt T, and Brittain H, *Supporting Safer Digital Spaces: An International Examination of Gender, Sexual Orientation, and Technology-facilitated Violence* (Centre for International Governance Innovation, forthcoming 2023)

Fairbairn J, 'Rape Threats and Revenge Porn- Defining Sexual Violence in the Digital Age' in J Bailey and V Steeves (eds), *eGirls, eCitizens* (University of Ottawa Press 2015)

Flynn A and others, *Image-based Sexual Abuse—A Study on the Causes and Consequences of Non-consensual Nude or Sexual Imagery* (Routledge 2022)

Flynn, A, Henry, N, Johnson, K, McGlynn, C, Powell, A, and Scott, AJ, *Image-Based Sexual Abuse- A Study on the Causes and Consequences of Non-Consensual Nude or Sexual Imagery* (Routledge 2020)

Follingstad D and Rogers J, 'Validity Concerns in the Measurement of Women's and Men's Report of Intimate Partner Violence' (2013) 69(3) Sex Roles 149

Franks MA, 'Drafting an Effective "Revenge Porn" Law: A Guide for Legislators' (17 August 2015) <https://ssrn.com/abstract=2468823> accessed 3 October 2023

Franks MA, 'Unwilling Avatars: Idealism and discrimination in cyberspace' (2011) 20 Columbia Journal of Gender and Law 224

Freeman M and others, *The UN Convention on the Elimination of All Forms of Discrimination against Women: A Commentary* (OUP 2012)

Gill A, 'Survivor-Centered Research: Towards an Intersectional Gender-based Violence Movement' (2018) 33(8) Journal of Family Violence 559

Gillespie T, *Custodians of the Internet: Platforms, Content Moderation, and the Hidden Decisions that Shape Social Media* (Yale University Press 2018)

Glass N and others, 'Gender-based Violence against Transgender People in the United States: A Call for Research and Programming' (2020) 21(2) Trauma, Violence and Abuse 227

Goldberg C, *Nobody's Victim: Fighting Psychos, Stalkers, Pervs, and Trolls* (Penguin Publishing Group 2019)

Gosse C, ' "Not the Real World": Exploring Experiences of Online Abuse, Digital Dualism, and Ontological Labor' in J Bailey, A Flynn, and N Henry (eds), *The Emerald International Handbook of Technology-Facilitated Violence and Abuse* (Emerald Publishing 2021)

Hagen J and Postmus J, *Violence against Women: Synthesis of Research for Advocacy Organizations* (National Institute for Justice 2000)

Henry N and Powell A, *Sexual Violence in a Digital Age* (Palgrave MacMillan 2017)

Hrick P, 'The Potential of Centralized and Statutorily Empowered Bodies to Advance a Survivor-Centered Approach to Technology-Facilitated Violence against Women' in J Bailey, A Flynn, and N Henry (eds), *The Emerald Handbook of Technology-Facilitated Violence and Abuse* (Emerald Publishing 2021)

Iyer N and Yahaya MS, *(In)Visible: The Digital Threats Muslim Women Human Rights Defenders Face in the Greater Horn of Africa* (Pollicy 2022)

Johnson H, 'Preventing Violence against Women- Progress and Challenges' (2007) 1 IPC Review 69

Kelly L, 'The Continuum of Sexual Violence' in J Hanmer and M Maynard (eds), *Women, Violence, and Social Control* (Macmillan Press 1987)

Khoo C, Robertson K, and Song Y, *To Surveil and Predict: A Human Rights Analysis of Algorithmic Policing in Canada* (Citizen Lab 2020)

Kovacs A, Padte RK, and Shobha SV, '"Don't Let it Stand!" An Exploratory Study of Women and Verbal Online Abuse in India' (2013) Internet Democracy Project 1

Liggett O'Malley R and Holt K, 'Cyber Sextortion- An Exploratory Analysis of Different Perpetrators Engaging in a Similar Crime' (2022) 37(1–2) Journal of Interpersonal Violence 258

Louie YM, 'Technology-facilitated Domestic Abuse and Culturally and Linguistically Diverse Women in Victoria, Australia' in J Bailey, F Ahser, and N Henry (eds), *The*

Emerald International Handbook of Technology-Facilitated Violence and Abuse (Emerald Publishing 2021)

Malanga DF, *Tackling Gender-based Cyber Violence against Women and Girls in Malawi Amidst the COVID-19 Pandemic* (Association for Progressive Communications 2020)

McGlynn C and Rackley E, 'Image-based Sexual Abuse' (2017) 37(3) Oxford Journal of Legal Studies 534

Nakamura L, 'Gender and Race in the Gaming World' in M Graham and WH Dutton (eds), *Society and the Internet: How Networks of Information and Communications are Changing Our Lives* (2nd edn, OUP 2019)

Namaste V, *Oversight: Critical Reflections on Feminist Research and Politics* (Women's Press 2015)

Noble SU, *Algorithms of Oppression: How Search Engines Reinforce Racism* (New York University Press 2018)

Palumbo M and Sienra DS, *EROTICS Global Survey 2017: Sexuality, Rights and Internet Regulations* (Association of Progressive Communication 2017)

Pritchard E, 'The Intersection of Disability and Gender with Online Harassment' (National Sexual Violence Resource Centre 6 April 2022) <https://www.nsvrc.org/blogs/intersection-disability-and-gender-online-harassment> accessed 22 March 2023

Rajani N, '"I Bet You Don't Get What We Get": An Intersectional Analysis of Technology-Facilitated Violence Experienced by Racialized Women Anti-Violence Online Activists in Canada' (2022) 19(2) Canadian Journal of Learning and Technology 217

Roberts ST, *Behind the Screen: Content Moderation in the Shadows of Social Media* (Yale University Press 2019)

Schafran LH, 'Maiming the Soul: Judges, Sentencing and the Myth of the Nonviolent Rapist' (1993) 20 Fordham Urban Law Journal 439

Sheehy E, *Sexual Assault in Canada: Law, Legal Practice and Women's Activism* (University of Ottawa Press 2012)

Šimonović D, *Report of the Special Rapporteur on Violence against Women, Its Causes and Consequences on online violence against women and girls from a human rights perspective* (UN Human Rights Council 2018)

Smith A and Sugiura L, 'Victim Blaming, Responsibilization and Resilience in Online Sexual Abuse and Harassment' in J Tapley and P Davies (eds), *Victimology: Research, Policy and Activism* (Palgrave Macmillan 2020)

Turnbull A, 'Onlife Harms: Uber and Sexual Violence' (2022) 19(2) Canadian Journal of Law and Technology 277

Thompson C and Wood MA, 'A Media Archaeology of the Creepshot' (2018) 18(4) Feminist Media Studies 560

Waldman AE, 'Law, Privacy, and Online Dating: "Revenge Porn" in Gay Online Communities' (2019) 44(4) Law and Social Inquiry 987

Zuboff S, *The Age of Surveillance Capitalism: The Fight for a Human Future at the New Frontier of Power* (PublicAffairs 2019)

4

The Case Law of the European Court of Human Rights on Violence against Women and the Intimate Image Abuse

*María Elósegui**

* The author would like to thank her criminal law research team at the University of Zaragoza for the exchanges on this matter. The coordinator of the group, Miguel Ángel Boldova, Full Professor of Criminal Law, deserves her special gratitude.

María Elósegui, *The Case Law of the European Court of Human Rights on Violence against Women and the Intimate Image Abuse* In: *Criminalizing Intimate Image Abuse.* Edited by: Gian Marco Caletti and Kolis Summerer, Oxford University Press.
 DOI: 10.1093/oso/9780198877813.003.0004

I. Introduction

My contribution to this collective work will focus on a specific aspect: namely, the recent jurisprudence of the European Court of Human Rights (ECtHR) on the issue of the dissemination of intimate images by partners or ex-partners as a form of revenge or in an attempt to maintain the dominance of men over women.[1] I will deal expressly with the jurisprudence of the ECtHR in the context of the use of images, or other means of control by men through digital devices, to exercise domination over women, usually in the context of domestic violence or gender violence. In the national arena, judges can face some difficulties when adjudicating on criminal cases in this area. These problems increase when acting as a judge in an international organization, where it is not possible to obtain direct evidence in relation to the acts complained of, and it is the actions of the national courts against which the claim is filed that must be examined. I was part of the composition of judges of the ECtHR who handed down *Volodina v Russia*[2] and *Volodina v Russia* (No 2),[3] two of the Court's first judgments on cyberviolence. Therefore, the analysis of these cases will be made with the benefit of the experience of being involved in the creation of that jurisprudence (along with the other judges and the support of the Court's lawyers).[4]

II. The Context of the United Nations: The 2015 Report by the UNESCO-ITU Broadband Commission for Digital Development's Working Group on Broadband and Gender

In its ruling in *Volodina v Russia* (No 2), the ECtHR cited this report as one of the first documents in which the concept of cyberviolence against women was elaborated. This notion is sometimes difficult to define as various behaviours are intermingled. The English term 'stalking' comes from the world of hunting, which is, stalking animals. It was first used in the legal world in the United States in the 1990s and was applied to what we understand today as harassment or online bullying. In its literal sense, harassment or surveillance of a person can be physical. However,

[1] See, eg, Gian Marco Caletti, 'Can Affirmative Consent Save "Revenge Porn" Laws? Lessons from the Italian Criminalization of Non-Consensual Pornography' (2021) 25 Virginia Journal of Law and Technology 3, 116 (hereafter Caletti, 'Affirmative Consent'): 'In 2019, following general dramatic cases, Italy introduced a new law criminalizing so-called "revenge porn", that is, the disclosure of intimate images by an ex-partner.'

[2] *Volodina v Russia* App no 4126/17 (ECHR, 9 July 2019) (hereafter *Volodina v Russia*).

[3] *Volodina v Russia* (No 2) App no 40419/19 (ECHR, 14 September 2021) (hereafter *Volodina v Russia* (No 2)).

[4] I should clarify that all the information provided in this chapter is public and can be found in the ECtHR judgments. Matters relating to the deliberations are not disclosed as judges are bound by their ethical oath of confidentiality. Otherwise, the chapter reflects my own research and academic freedom as a university professor.

in the legal context, the intimidation of one person by another on social networks has been framed within these behaviours. Behaviours, such as harassment and surveillance, and subsequent disclosure of intimate data without the subject's consent are regulated in both civil and criminal law. With the development of technology, the right to privacy of correspondence has been expanded exponentially to mean all types of digital communication between private parties such as emails or the use of social networks. These types of cyberviolence can, and do, occur between people regardless of their sex. However, it typically occurs in a situation of sexual harassment of men towards women, which has specific characteristics.

There are of course many other types of digital sexual harassment that include, for example, mature men with minors or between minors or young people themselves.[5] However, for the purposes of this chapter, I focus on cyberviolence against women, carried out by a male current or ex-partner. The 2015 report by the UNESCO-ITU Broadband Commission for Digital Development's Working group on Broadband and Gender, 'Cyberviolence against Women and Girls: A World-wide Wake-up Call', observes that 'violence online and offline, or "physical" violence against women and girls (VAWG) and "cyber" VAWG, feed into each other' and that 'abuse may be confined to networked technologies or may be supplemented with offline harassment including vandalism, phone calls and physical assault'.[6]

The ECtHR has in a way made this definition its own by introducing it into its jurisprudence in the case of *Volodina v Russia* (No 2). The applicant in the *Volodina* cases was subjected to all of the types of violence included in this description. The applicant's ex-partner harassed her by sending threatening mobile phone messages, he physically stole her phone and shared her photos, used physical violence, pushing, hitting, and throwing her to the ground. The applicant's ex-partner impersonated her by using her digital name and identity to send false messages to her contacts and blocked her social network passwords. The applicant was subjected to both offline harassment and online cyberbullying.

The judgment in *Volodina v Russia* (No 2) describes the categories of cyberviolence as set out in the UNESCO report:

> Forms of cyber VAWG fall into six broad categories which include 'hacking', 'impersonation' (the use of technology to assume the identity of the victim in order to embarrass or shame her, e.g., by sending offensive emails from the victim's email account), 'surveillance/tracking' (stalking and monitoring a victim's activities either in real-time or historically; e.g., GPS tracking), 'harassment/spamming' (the

[5] See the discussion and the bibliography quoted in Caletti, 'Affirmative Consent' (n 1) 126, note 56.

[6] UNESCO-ITU Broadband Commission for Digital Development's Working group on Broadband and Gender, 'Cyberviolence against Women and Girls: A World-wide Wake-up Call' (2015) (hereafter UNESCO 'Cyberviolence against Women and Girls').

use of technology to continuously contact, annoy, threaten, and/or or scare the victim), 'recruitment' (luring potential victims into violent situations), and 'malicious distribution' (manipulating and distributing defamatory and illegal materials related to the victim; e.g., threatening to or leaking intimate photos/video). In addition, some terminology is particular to cyber VAWG: thus, 'revenge porn' consists of an individual posting intimate photographs of another individual online with the aim of publicly shaming and humiliating that person, and even inflicting real damage on the target's 'real- world' life, such as getting them fired from their job.[7]

A. Anonymity

The 2015 report by the United Nations Broadband Commission for Digital Development's Working group on Broadband and Gender, 'Cyberviolence against Women and Girls: A World-wide Wake-up Call', describes five characteristics that distinguish cyber VAWG: 'anonymity' (abusive person can remain unknown to victim), 'action at a distance' (abuse can be done without physical contact and from anywhere), 'automation' (abusive actions using technologies require less time and effort), 'accessibility' (variety and affordability of many technologies make them readily accessible to perpetrators), and 'propagation and perpetuity' (texts and images multiply and exist for a long time or indefinitely).[8]

As regards anonymity, in the case of *Volodina v Russia* (No 2), the applicant's ex-partner had used a friend's IP address registered in Azerbaijan. The victim knew that the origin of the cyberbullying was her ex-partner. After much reluctance to carry out the investigation, the police managed to trace the origins of the fake profiles and located the person whose IP address had been used. However, it took the police two years to initiate the process and the victim had not received any information about it until she filed her claim before the Strasbourg Court. She was represented before the ECtHR by a lawyer specializing in cyberviolence against women, Ms Vanessa Kogan, Director of the Stitching Justice Initiative, a human rights organization based in Utrecht.[9]

If the case had not reached the ECtHR, the victim might never have been informed of the outcome of the investigation. In fact, she only knew of the police's decision to close the criminal case when she became aware of the investigation's existence from the government's Action Plan submitted to the Committee of Ministers in the framework of execution of the *Volodina* group of cases.[10] In

[7] *Volodina v Russia* (No 2) (n 3) § 22.
[8] UNESCO 'Cyberviolence against Women and Girls' (n 6) 23.
[9] *Volodina v Russia* (No 2) (n 3) § 2.
[10] ibid § 21.

addition, despite the fact that the owner of the Azerbaijani phone number which had been used to create the fake profile had been identified and questioned, the investigator of the case, in a flagrant contradiction, suspended the procedure alleging that the perpetrator had not been identified.[11] On 14 October 2020, it was established with certainty that it had been the applicant's ex-partner who, in February and March 2018

> had created fake profiles on VKontakte in the applicant's name and had published nude photos of her without her consent. The published photos had been found on his phone during an inspection. On October 13, 2010, S. [the applicant's ex-partner] had filed a motion to discontinue the proceedings because the limitation period had expired. The motion had been granted: as the offence under Article 137 was of lesser gravity, the two-year period of limitation had expired in March 2020.[12]

This shows the inadequacy of the classification of this type of crime to which, especially from the perspective of authorities such as the police, prosecutors, and judges without adequate training in gender perspective, no seriousness is attributed. Hence, for example, GREVIO's insistence on training all legal operators and digital media companies in these matters.[13]

B. Propagation and Perpetuity

Another of the big problems with cyberbullying is that data can remain on the Internet for long periods, or indefinitely, and due to the number of intermediaries involved, companies, servers, platforms, data search engines, with diluted legal responsibilities it is difficult to have data removed.[14]

Aside from this, problems of direct or indirect criminal responsibility are also raised. For example, under the Spanish legal model, until recently only the first distributor was penalized and the second distributor was excluded from the criminal sphere.[15]

[11] ibid § 18.

[12] ibid § 20.

[13] GREVIO General Recommendation No 1 on the digital dimension of violence against women (adopted on 20 October 2021) GREVIO (2021) 20, § 51 (hereafter GREVIO General Recommendation No 1).

[14] See Alexa Dodge, 'Nudes are Forever: Judicial Interpretations of Digital Technology's Impact on "Revenge Porn"' (2019) 34(1) Canadian Journal of Law and Society 121, 128–33.

[15] See the new Spanish Criminal Code, Art 172 *ter*, 1 and 5. Ley Orgánica 10/2022 of reform of the Criminal Code.

C. Lack of Informed Consent of the Victim to Disseminate Her Image on Social Media

Another important point raised in these international instruments is the lack of consent in the dissemination of these images. The Report of the UN Human Rights Rapporteur on violence against women defines this new form of so called 'revenge porn' as 'the non-consensual online dissemination of intimate images, obtained with or without consent, with the purpose of shaming, stigmatizing or harming the victim'.[16]

However, the term 'revenge porn' may not be the most appropriate way to describe this phenomenon. On this point, I agree with the proposals given by Professor Caletti in his previously mentioned article. According to Caletti, the concept of the lack of the victim's explicit consent should be included in the crime. He proposes using the expression 'non-consensual pornography', following the proposals of Daniele Keats Citron and Mary Anne Franks.[17] Some legislation on this issue sets out that if there is no explicit refusal, tacit consent is assumed for the dissemination of sexual information.[18] This in turn raises questions such as whether the intimate sexual images were made with the consent of the victim or whether the victim was forced to make them by her partner with the promise that they were only for their use.[19] On other occasions, disseminated images are not real but are montages made by the harasser with forged photos, in which case it is impossible that there was any consent, not even implicit consent.

In Spain, the phenomenon of the rape of a woman by several men being recorded and uploaded to social networks has spread among young people, and there have been several convictions in this regard.[20] This type of phenomenon does not exactly fit with the concept of 'revenge porn' as the videos have not been made in the context of a couple, but rather by a group of strangers. Nor is it revenge

[16] Report of the Special Rapporteur on violence against women, its causes and consequences on online violence against women and girls from a human rights perspective, A/HRC/38/47, § 41; see also *Volodina v Russia* (No 2) (n 3) § 23.

[17] Danielle Keats Citron and Mary Anne Franks, 'Criminalizing Revenge Porn' (2014) 49 Wake Forest Law Review 346 cited in Caletti 'Affirmative Consent' (n 1) 124, notes 39, 43.

[18] Caletti, 'Affirmative Consent' (n 1) 116, 164. See also Gian Marco Caletti, '"Revenge porn" e tutela penale. Prime riflessioni sulla criminalizzazione specifica della pornografia non consensuale alla luce delle esperienze angloamericane (2018) 3 Diritto penale contemporaneo—Rivista Trimestrale 63. About minors, see 85–86.

[19] See Alisdair Gillespie, '"Trust Me, It's Only For Me": "Revenge Porn" and the Criminal Law' (2015) 11 Criminal Law Review 866, 873–75.

[20] Miguel Ángel Boldova Pasamar, 'Presente y futuro de los delitos sexuales a la luz de la Sentencia del Tribunal Supremo 344/2019, de 4 de julio, en el conocido caso de "la Manada"' (*The present and future of sexual crimes in light of Supreme Court Judgment 344/2019, of July 4, in the so-called 'caso de la Manada'*), *Diario la Ley*, No 9500, 2019. According to the author: 'In the aforementioned sentence, a before and after was marked in the jurisprudence on sexual crimes. Although the central discussion was reduced to whether the facts should be classified as sexual abuse or rape, the interest of the sentence extends to the unity and plurality of actions, aggravating circumstances, authorship and participation, as well as the criminal framework. applicable to cases of gang rapes.'

following the break-up of a relationship because a relationship never existed. These cases support the opinions of authors such as Clare McGlynn and Erika Rackley regarding the inappropriateness of using the term 'pornography' to describe these situations.[21] The group of five young Spanish men who called themselves 'la manada (herd)', and who are now in prison, sent videos of a rape via WhatsApp to their group of friends. These recordings were made available to the judges as the mobiles had been located by the police. The men were sentenced to nine years in prison for continued sexual abuse. This type of rape is sometimes recorded when victims are drunk or drugged and are therefore not even aware of the existence of the recordings.

III. The Context of the Council of Europe: The 'Istanbul Convention'

A. The Istanbul Convention

The Council of Europe Convention on preventing and combating violence against women and domestic violence of 11 May 2011 is the first instrument of the Council of Europe in which the issue of harassment of women through digital media in the field of relationships is explicitly introduced.[22] The purposes of the Convention include: to 'protect women against all forms of violence, and prevent, prosecute and eliminate violence against women and domestic violence' (Article 1(1)(a)); 'design a comprehensive framework, policies and measures for the protection of and assistance to all victims of violence against women and domestic violence'(Article 1(1)(c)); and 'provide support and assistance to organizations and law enforcement agencies to effectively co-operate in order to adopt an integrated approach to eliminating violence against women and domestic violence' (Article 1(1)(e)). This convention was born following several Recommendations of the Committee of Ministers to protect women against violence in general, and against domestic violence in particular, including recommendations on the protection of women against violence, on gender equality standards and mechanisms, and on the role of women and men in prevention and resolution in peace building.[23] In addition to the Istanbul Convention there are other treaties such as the Convention on

[21] Clare McGlynn and Erika Rackley, 'Image-based Sexual Abuse' (2017) 37 Oxford Journal of Legal Studies 53.

[22] Council of Europe Convention on preventing and combating violence against women and domestic violence (opened for signature 11 May 2011, entered into force 1 August 2014) CETS No 210. (hereafter 'the Istanbul Convention').

[23] Council of Europe Committee of Ministers Recommendation (Rec (2002)5 on the protection of women against violence; Recommendation CM/Rec(2007)17 on gender equality standards and mechanisms; and Recommendation CM/Rec(2010)10 on the role of women and men in prevention and resolution in peace building.

Cybercrime of the Council of Europe (the 'Budapest Convention')[24] and soft-law such as the non-binding Recommendation CM/Rec(2019)1 of the Committee of Ministers to member states on preventing and combating sexism.[25]

B. The Definition of Violence against Women Including Psychological and Digital Violence

Violence against women is defined in Article 3(a) of the Istanbul Convention as 'a violation of human rights and a form of discrimination against women and shall mean all acts of gender-based violence that result in, or are likely to result in, physical, sexual, psychological or economic harm or suffering to women, including threats of such acts, coercion or arbitrary deprivation of liberty, whether occurring in public or in private life'. This definition includes psychological harassment.[26] The fact that the use of new digital media for harassment and coercion does not require physical proximity or bodily contact sets it aside from other forms of harassment. From a legal point of view, its regulation raises many problems because it is very difficult to define its terms. For example, Suzan van der Aa, an academic expert on stalking from the University of Tilburg in the Netherlands, explores how the EU countries which have begun to regulate the criminal prosecution of this phenomenon have formulated it in very different ways, sometimes with great ambiguities in its classification.[27]

Domestic violence includes violence by a man against a woman during a legal marriage, as well as during a relationship with an intimate partner, or violence by an ex-partner. In practice, in the legal sphere, what we find are situations of violence that start while a couple is living together and continue when they separate. My experience from the ECtHR, shows that men begin by using physical violence within a relationship and when the woman decides to leave them, they

[24] Budapest Convention on Cybercrime of the Council of Europe (opened for signature 23 November 2001, entered into force 1 July 2004) ETS No 185. See also the Council of Europe Parliamentary Assembly Recommendation 2098 (2017) on ending cyberdiscrimination and online hate, available at <https://pace.coe.int/en/files/23457#trace-6> accessed 28 December 2022 and Council of Europe (2017), Parliamentary Assembly Resolution on putting an end to sexual violence and harassment of women in public space, available at <https://pace.coe.int/en/files/23977> accessed 28 December 2022.

[25] Council of Europe Committee of Ministers Recommendation (CM/Rec(2019)1) on preventing and combating sexism <https://rm.coe.int/cm-rec-2019-1e-sexism/1680a217ca#:~:text=1.,2> a 28 December 2022.

[26] Most of the research has taken place in the United States. As such, this article, based on research undertaken in Germany could be useful. Harald Dressing, Christine Kuehner, and Peter Gass, 'Lifetime Prevalence and Impact of Stalking in a European Population. Epidemiological Data from a Middle-sized German City' (2005) 187 British Journal of Psychiatry 168, also published online by Cambridge University Press, 2 January 2018 <https://www.cambridge.org/core/journals/the-british-journal-of-psychiatry/article/lifetime-prevalence-and-impact-of-stalking-in-a-european- population/221E3997 3D60A18766490C6B4CBCAC81> accessed 28 January 2023.

[27] Suzan van der Aa, 'New Trends in the Criminalization of Stalking in the EU Member States' (2018) 24 European Journal on Criminal Policy and Research 315–33.

continue with other types of violence at a distance, using digital techniques. Of course, digital violence among young people who have not become couples is also widespread today.[28] While this sometimes occurs within a friendship group, it can also happen in the context of strangers in youth leisure situations. In some of these contexts, we are talking about people known by the victims, not external predators.

Most of the applications to the ECtHR regarding violence against women in the domestic sphere have been filed by previously married women after their divorce or separation. However, it must not be forgotten that applications are also received from an accused or convicted harasser, alleging a lack of procedural guarantees in the domestic proceedings that have convicted them. These cases are considered on an individual basis as a fair and lawful trial must also be guaranteed to defendants. A large number of these applications are rejected by a single judge once it has been verified that the national courts and other authorities have acted correctly. In these cases, the applicant is informed of the outcome directly in a letter addressed to them or their lawyer. The only record of this remains at the ECtHR and only the applicant can make use of that information. In other cases, as is the usual procedure in the ECtHR, an application may be declared inadmissible by a formation of three judges or a Chamber of seven judges through a decision of inadmissibility or a judgment of admissibility and/or violation of the European Convention on Human Rights. There have been multiple cases before the ECtHR related to sexual crimes filed by the aggressors and resolved through a decision or judgment of the Court. However, there is still no case law raised by applicants involved in cyberbullying or cyberstalking between adults and minors, or between young people themselves.

C. The Problem of Distinguishing between Public and Private Spheres with New Technologies

The other difficulty is to distinguish among public and private spheres applied to stalking. The fight against violence against women took a big step forward when penal codes began to reflect that a husband or male partner did not have the right to force a wife or woman to have non-consensual sexual relations or certain forms of sex within a relationship. Previously (although this remains the case in some geographical areas of the Council of Europe), authorities considered that what

[28] From my research group, see Miguel Ángel Boldova Pasamar, 'Menores de edad penalmente responsables de delitos sexuales' ('Minors criminally responsible for sexual crimes'), in *Un modelo integral de Derecho penal: Libro homenaje a la profesora Mirentxu Corcoy Bidasolo* (*A comprehensive model of criminal law: Tribute book to Professor Mirentxu Corcoy Bidasolo*) coordinated by Vicente Valiente Ivañez, Guillermo Ramírez Martín; Víctor Gómez Martín (dir), Carolina Bolea Bardón (dir), José Ignacio Gallego Soler (dir), Juan Carlos Hortal Ibarra (dir), Ujala Joshi Jubert (dir), vol 2, 2022, 1023–36.

belonged within the sphere of the couple was a private world in which the state should not interfere. Over time, this mentality evolved, crimes related to conjugal violence were regulated, and rape within marriage was considered a criminal offence. Once this step was taken, it became possible to prove this violence when physical injuries were present.

Now, with new technologies, persecution of a victim is carried out from outside, rather than inside the home, by pirating social networks and invading privacy in different ways. The Court has reiterated in much of its jurisprudence that: 'the concept of private life includes a person's physical and psychological integrity which the States have a duty to protect, even if the danger comes from private individuals'.[29]

The ECtHR has categorized the acts of cyberviolence and cyberharassment as forms of violence against women.[30] The terms cyberstalking or cybersurveillance are also used.

D. Gender-based Violence against Women and Stalking

The Istanbul Convention addresses violence against women insofar as a woman is persecuted because she is a woman (Article 3(c) defines 'gender-based violence against women'). This clear premise has unquestionably given rise to many academic discussions, which are, however, not the subject of this chapter. The Istanbul Convention presupposes that part of this violence is built on prejudice based on the idea of the inferiority of women or on the stereotyped roles assigned to women and men.[31]

Articles 33 and 34 of the Istanbul Convention introduce, in a novel way, the idea of psychological violence and the notion of stalking. The concepts are interlinked:

> Article 33 – Psychological violence
> Parties shall take the necessary legislative or other measures to ensure that the intentional conduct of seriously impairing a person's psychological integrity through coercion or threats is criminalised.
>
> Article 34 – Stalking
> Parties shall take the necessary legislative or other measures to ensure that the intentional conduct of repeatedly engaging in threatening conduct directed at another person, causing her or him to fear for her or his safety, is criminalised.

In the context of stalking, it is also possible to have sexual harassment, as defined in Article 40 of the Istanbul Convention: 'Parties shall take the necessary legislative or

29 *Volodina v Russia* (No 2) (n 3) § 47.
30 *KU v Finland* App no 2872/02 (ECHR, 2 December 2008) § 41.
31 The Istanbul Convention (n 22), Art 12(1).

other measures to ensure that any form of unwanted verbal, non-verbal or physical conduct of a sexual nature with the purpose or effect of violating the dignity of a person, in particular when creating an intimidating, hostile, degrading, humiliating or offensive environment, is subject to criminal or other legal sanction.'

E. The Creation of GREVIO and its Recommendations

The Istanbul Convention created the Group of experts on action against violence against women and domestic violence (known as 'GREVIO') to monitor the implementation of the Convention.[32] The group of experts consists of between ten and fifteen experts of different nationalities from countries party to the Istanbul Convention. Among its functions is that of adopting general recommendations. While these recommendations are not legally binding, they are an important guide for the member states of the Council of Europe.

On 20 October 2021, GREVIO adopted its first general recommendation, General Recommendation No 1 on the digital dimension of violence against women.[33] In this recommendation, the group of experts highlighted how the perception of women as inferior can be present in all aspects of women's lives; in their family lives, their work relationships, their social life, and on social platforms. Paragraph 10 of this recommendation states:

> For many years now, women's and girls' experiences of gender-based violence against women in these and other settings have been amplified or facilitated by technology, in particular the technology used in online and digital environments. Information and communication technology (ICT) has enabled the perpetration of violence against women on a scale previously unknown.

As reflected in this recommendation, there is verbal violence against men on social networks too, but a distinctive characteristic is that digital violence against women has many more sexual connotations. This new type of violence leads to the sharing of women's private information with a large number of people online. This in turn leads to damage to reputation, with a great psychological burden. Women and girls feel continually exposed to the eyes of strangers or worse still, people within their own environment. In relation to intimate relationships or ex-partners, the desire for dominance prevails, but in other areas, such as that of young people, the exposure of the body is treated in a frivolous and superficial way, and sexual bullying among the young generation has some peculiar characteristics. Everything is seen as a game, just another diversion, as if the fact of being virtual

[32] ibid Art 66.

[33] GREVIO General Recommendation No 1 (n 13).

does not affect people's real lives. Personal images, or what was written for a single recipient, become open in the public domain without the consent or knowledge of the person involved.[34] The sense of intimacy and privacy has been lost, especially with the phenomenon of sexting.[35]

GREVIO points out the difficulty for legislators and legal authorities to adequately reflect this new phenomenon of abuse and harm of violence performed online or through technology in prevention and sanction policies.[36] In particular, this new dimension of violence against women, digital stalking as a new form of harassment, is not included in all relevant pieces of legislation or in social policies. This failure highlighted by GREVIO is also reflected in the jurisprudence of the ECtHR. While physical violence against women, although persistent and not always prosecuted in many geographical settings within the Council of Europe member states, leaves a trace, the traceability of digital harassment is more complicated; it is often more anonymized or diluted among several actors.

The digital dimension of violence requires specific regulation, but within a holistic context of gender violence and not in isolated norms that prevent one from seeing the full picture of a violent situation.[37] This lack of global vision with regards to this phenomenon is evidenced in a paradigmatic way in the two *Volodina* judgments.

[34] See Feona Attwood, *Mainstreaming Sex: The Sexualization of Western Culture* (Bloomsbury Publishing 2009).

[35] See Alisdair A Gillespie, 'Adolescents, Sexting and Human Rights' (2013) 13 Human Rights Law Review 623–43. This very significant article on this matter looks at the phenomenon in relation to England. Gillespie proposes distinguishing among different situations and using education to advise on risks, rather than criminalizing everything (see 642–43).

[36] GREVIO General Recommendation No 1 (n 13) §§ 16, 28.

[37] GREVIO General Recommendation No 1 (n 13) § 18; I share this idea with Anna María Maugen 'El 'stalking' en el derecho comparado: la obligación de incriminación de la Convención de Estambul y técnicas de tipificación' ('Stalking in Comparative Law: The Obligation to Incriminate the Istanbul Convention and Criminalization Techniques') (2016) 38 Revista Penal 226–43. In order to deal with the delicate criminal phenomenon of stalking, all legal systems feel the need to introduce an ad hoc regulation due to extra-criminal tools such as pre-existing criminal instruments, being incapable of covering it. This need has been determined by the obligation of incrimination contained in the Istanbul Convention, Art 34. A comparative analysis reveals the difficulty of typifying this phenomenon in a legislative formula that, on the one hand, is compatible with the constitutional principle of legality and, on the other, is capable of criminalizing the variety of behavioural types in which it manifests itself. In particular the greatest difficulty encountered by lawyers is the identification of the typical threshold coinciding with an effective offence of the protected objects, precisely because of the fact that very often the individual conduct is in itself completely legitimate and socially appropriate, but their character offensive comes only from obsessive and stubborn repetition, making them eligible to offend the victim's freedom of self-determination, their tranquillity, and their mental and physical health, in addition to the associated risk of violence. In any case, the fight against stalking or harassment, in particular, and against gender violence in general, requires a strong cultural and legislative commitment, which should be aimed at the prevention and elimination of inequality between men and women that the Istanbul Convention demands by imposing specific obligations. In this regard, the Spanish experience is very interesting.

GREVIO, coinciding with what was pointed out by the UNESCO group, highlights the extent of this phenomenon and the number of actors involved in paragraph 23 of its Recommendation No 1:

> GREVIO's understanding of the concept of violence against women in its digital dimension encompasses both online aspects (activities performed and data available on the internet, including internet intermediaries on the surface web as well as the dark web) and technology-facilitated (activities carried out with the use of technology and communication equipment, including hardware and software) harmful behaviour perpetrated against women and girls. Internet intermediaries refer to entities that facilitate interactions on the Internet between natural and legal persons by offering and performing a variety of functions and services and include Internet service providers (ISPs), search engines and social media platforms. Technological tools which may be misused by abusers to stalk, harass, surveil, and control victims include smartphones, cameras and other recording equipment, global positioning systems (GPS) or satellite navigators, other internet-connected devices such as smart watches, fitness trackers and smart home devices as well as software such as spyware or other mobile applications that may facilitate violence.

IV. The Case Law of the ECtHR: The Two *Volodina* Judgments

The case of *Buturuga v Romania*[38] 'saw the first explicit recognition of cyberviolence by the European Court of Human Rights. It concerned allegations of domestic violence and of violations of the confidentiality of electronic correspondence by the former husband of the applicant who complained of shortcomings in the system for protecting victims of this type of violence.'[39]

In that context, *Volodina v Russia* (No 2) is one of the first ECtHR cases that deals with 'cyberviolence', which the Court described as 'an individual posting intimate photographs of another individual online with the aim of publicly shaming and humiliating that person, and even inflicting real damage on the target's "real-world" life'.[40] *Volodina v Russia* (No 2) deals specifically with the use of digital devices to disseminate pictures (intimate images) of a woman, normally with sexual content, through social networking to people who already know the victim. This is a common feature of the behaviour of men engaging in 'revenge porn'.

The *Volodina* judgments are particularly illustrative of the process that usually occurs in cases of stalking or harassment through digital media. Typically this

[38] *Buturuga v Romania* App no 56867/15 (ECHR, 11 February 2020).
[39] GREVIO General Recommendation No 1 (n 13) § 20.
[40] *Volodina v Russia* (No 2) (n 3) § 22.

occurs in parallel with, or following, the use of physical violence, verbal aggression, and coercion within the context of an intimate-partner relationship. The usual pattern is that when a woman reports these previous incidents of violence, aggression, or coercion, the authorities, including police, prosecutors, and judges dismiss them as unimportant. This case is paradigmatic of the description that GREVIO gives in paragraph 25 of its Recommendation No 1. In *Volodina v Russia* (No 2) all of these elements are present: the applicant (victim) suffered physical violence that is detailed in her first application to the Court, to which digital harassment was added. Her ex-partner monitored her and her movements, both physically (stalking her on her own street) and digitally (placing a GPS on her to follow her, kidnapping her, and physically assaulting her when she managed to escape).

In *Volodina v Russia*, the ECtHR examined several acts of violence perpetrated by Ms Volodina's former partner, an Azerbaijani national from whom she had separated in 2015, including physical assault, threats, and kidnapping. The Court held that Ms Volodina had been both physically and psychologically ill-treated by her former partner and that the authorities had failed to comply with their obligations under the Convention to protect her from his abuse. It concluded that the existing legal framework had been deficient in several important respects and found a violation of Article 3 of the Convention in respect of ill-treatment and of Article 14 of the Convention, taken in conjunction with Article 3, in respect of the Russian authorities' failure to create conditions of substantive gender equality.

In the case of *Volodina v Russia* the ECtHR found the authorities had failed to recognize the severity of the harassment, both online and offline, that Ms Volodina had suffered, despite her multiple complaints to them and the risk to her life. The harassment was so severe that, fearing for her safety, Ms Volodina obtained a legal change of name so that her ex-partner would not be able to find her and track her movements. Once Ms Volodina had decided that she did not want to continue the relationship, her ex-partner used digital means to punish, silence, devalue, and traumatize her. He stole her mobile phone, he hacked into her account on a Russian social media platform and uploaded intimate photos, as well as adding classmates of her 12-year-old son and her son's teacher as friends. This behaviour had the aim of humiliating her in the eyes of her closest entourage, and increasing her fear, anxiety, and gradual isolation from friends and family. Having fled to another city to escape her ex-partner, the victim published her curriculum vitae (CV) on job-hunting websites. This seems to have enabled her ex-partner to locate her. He appeared in front of her house and made threatening calls to her mobile phone (physical stalking, but preceded by espionage on the networks).[41]

[41] *Volodina v Russia* (n 2) §§ 13–39.

A. The Facts of *Volodina v Russia* (No 2) and the Lack of Effective Investigation

Coming back to the judgment of *Volodina v Russia* (No 2), in addition to the described physical attacks, the applicant's ex-partner downloaded a stash of her intimate photographs onto his phone and created fake profiles on social media, populating them with sexually explicit content. Moreover, he hacked into one of her social media platforms, replacing her invented name with her real one, adding her personal details, a photograph of her passport, and uploading her intimate photographs. He also added classmates of her 12-year-old son and his class teacher as friends, as well as changing her password so that she could not log in. Furthermore, he hacked into her email account and sent obscene messages to her contacts. He also sent her death threats on social media.

From the perspective of the criminal investigation of such cases, the problem arises, on the one hand, from the lack of police preparation for dealing with these new types of crimes related to the use of digital tools in the context of domestic violence, and, on the other hand, the lack of will in recognizing them as crimes, the result of stereotypical and sexist attitudes of the very authorities responsible for investigating and prosecuting them.

In fact, while monitoring the implementation of the Istanbul Convention, GREVIO has discovered that the digital dimension of VAWG is often being overlooked in domestic laws and policies even though the Convention on Cybercrime of the Council of Europe (known as the 'Budapest Convention') 'offers a comprehensive set of legally binding standards to criminalise aspects of cyberviolence, secure evidence and engage in cross-border and international co-operation to investigate and also prosecute online violence against women'.[42]

One of the problems, in these cases, is the lack of efficient investigation. The applicant's file had moved around different police jurisdictions due to their inability to find the applicant's ex-partner, with the Ulyanovsk police declining to institute proceedings in November 2016 on the ground that the information had been made public on social media rather than in the media—a formalistic approach. After declining various times to open a criminal case, the Ulyanovsk police finally opened one in March 2018. They interviewed the applicant, her family members, and her former partner, as well as examining their mobile phones; they obtained logs of phone communications from mobile providers, received information from the company operating the social media site, and talked to social media experts.

The applicant asked the investigator to seek an order which would prevent her former partner from using the Internet, contacting her by any means including via

[42] GREVIO Recommendation No 1 (n 13) § 19.

social media, email, or Internet messengers, and approaching her or her family. The investigator refused her request on the basis that this action could only be applied in exceptional cases.

In January 2019, the police suspended the investigation into the fake social media profiles. They established that two fake profiles had been created using IP addresses and phone numbers registered in Azerbaijan and that, according to the applicant's ex-partner's billing information from his phone and the police database, he had been in Russia. The applicant applied for judicial review of the investigators' decisions, complaining, among other things, that the fake profiles created in 2016 had not been investigated. The application was ultimately rejected by the Ulyanovsk Regional Court.

Subsequently, in October 2019, the owner of the telephone number registered in Azerbaijan used for the fake social media accounts was established and questioned. The applicant was not informed of this development. Finally, in October 2020, the police closed the criminal case based on the fact that the limitation period had expired, despite the police having established that in February and March 2018 the applicant's former partner had created fake social media profiles and published nude photos of her without her consent. The decision was not communicated to the applicant. The online harassment suffered by the applicant went on for at least three years.

B. The Complaints before the ECtHR in *Volodina v Russia* (No 2)

The applicant complained, first, that the Russian authorities had failed to protect her from repeated acts of cyberviolence—publication of her intimate photographs without consent, impersonation through the creation of fake social-media profiles, and tracking her with the use of a GPS device)—committed by her former partner for at least three years and second, that the authorities had failed to conduct an effective investigation into these acts.

The Court affirmed that the acts of cyberharassment, revenge porn, and malicious impersonation had been categorized as forms of violence against women and children 'capable of undermining their physical and psychological integrity in view of their vulnerability'.[43] The main question was whether the authorities, once they had become aware of the interference with the applicant's rights under Article 8 of the Convention (right to respect for private and family life), had discharged their obligations under that Article to take sufficient measures to put an end to that interference and prevent it from recurring. In order to analyse this point, the Court undertook a double analysis or a double step test, considering: (a) whether

[43] *Volodina v Russia* (No 2) (n 3) § 48.

the respondent state had put in place an adequate legal framework providing the applicant with protection against the acts of cyberviolence and (b) the manner in which the authorities had conducted the investigation into the applicant's reports.

(a) Whether the respondent state had put in place an adequate legal framework providing the applicant with protection against the acts of Cyberviolence.

It was not necessary for the Court to revisit the general finding in the first *Volodina* case as to the existing domestic legal framework. The scope of the second inquiry was more limited. It had to determine whether the manner in which the private-life legislation had been applied in the applicant's case had given rise to a violation of the Convention.

The Court found that the existing framework, both in civil and criminal law and in light of the state's margin of appreciation in choosing legal means to ensure compliance with the Convention, had equipped the authorities with the legal tools for investigating the acts of cyberviolence of which the applicant had been the victim. The domestic authorities had accepted that the acts in question had the requisite elements of prosecutable offences under the Criminal Code. Furthermore, the acts had been sufficiently serious to require a criminal-law response on their part.

The Russian state did not provide victims of domestic violence with any measures of protection resembling immediate 'restraining' or 'protection' orders capable of forestalling the recurrence of domestic violence. Furthermore, the respondent government had not identified any effective remedies that the authorities could have used to ensure the applicant's protection against recurrent acts of cyberviolence. For instance, the applicant's petition for an order, under criminal law, prohibiting certain conduct, had been refused by the investigator, who had had full discretion in this matter, as had her application for judicial review without an independent scrutiny of the substantive grounds of the investigator's refusal.

The authorities had not considered at any point in time what could and should have been done to protect the applicant from recurrent online violence. As it had in *Volodina v Russia*, the Court held that the authorities' response to the known risk of recurrent violence on the part of the applicant's ex-partner had been manifestly inadequate and that, through their inaction and failure to take measures of deterrence, they had allowed him to continue threatening, harassing, and assaulting her without hindrance and with impunity.

(b) As to the manner in which the authorities had conducted an investigation into the applicant's reports

According to the ECtHR, the investigation had been opened late; almost two years after the applicant had first reported the fake profiles to the police. Before that, the police had sought to dispose hastily of the matter on formal grounds instead of making a serious and genuine attempt to establish the circumstances of the applicant's malicious impersonation on social media.

The police should have acted promptly and in good faith to secure forensic evidence of the alleged offences, such as the identification of phone numbers and Internet addresses which had been used to create the fake profiles and upload the applicant's photos. This had not been done, however, until two years later, resulting in loss of time and undermining the authorities' ability to secure evidence relating to the acts of cyberviolence.

The ECtHR's conclusion that there had been a violation of Article 8 of the European Convention of Human Rights was unanimous. Although the existing framework equipped the authorities with legal tools to prosecute the acts of cyberviolence of which the applicant was a victim, the manner in which they had actually handled the matter—notably a reluctance to open a criminal case and the slow pace of the investigation resulting in the perpetrator's impunity—disclosed a failure to discharge their positive obligations under Article 8 of the Convention.[44]

I would like to add some final thoughts about the obligations of the authorities when undertaking a risk assessment and the credibility of victims of gender violence. In this sense, much of the ECtHR case law has developed in cases such as *Opuz v Turkey*[45] and *Talpis v Italy*.[46] But even in this area there are many problems regarding proof and victims' credibility at the time of a risk assessment. While the Court has elaborated the *Osman* test[47] to take into account the special features of domestic violence, it is obvious that problems remain. In *Kurt v. Austria*[48]— a case dealing with the murder of a child by his father against the background of a long history of domestic violence—the majority of the Grand Chamber of the Court concluded that Austria had not failed in its positive obligations of protection because the risk had been unforeseeable. However, the Grand Chamber was divided and seven judges, including myself, gave a dissenting opinion, considering that the Austrian authorities had failed to undertake a comprehensive risk assessment, and had not correctly interpreted the alarm signals reported to the police by the applicant on multiple occasions. While this case does not deal with cyberharassment or violence, I note it here because of the similarities in the problems related to risk assessment and the prevention of domestic violence.

[44] See Róisin Á Costello, 'Volodina v Russia (no. 2): Intimate Images, Domestic Violence and the Positive Obligations of Member States under Article 8 ECHR Case Notes' (2021) 4(7) European Data Protection Law Review 614.

[45] *Opuz v Turkey* App no 33401/02 (ECHR, 9 June 2009).

[46] *Talpis v Italy* App no 41237/14 (ECHR, 2 March 2017).

[47] *Osman v UK* App no 23452/94 (ECHR, 28 October 1998).

[48] *Kurt v Austria* App no 62903/15 (ECHR, 15 June 2021).

V. Conclusion

Further efforts are needed to clarify the concept of cyberstalking and to fulfil GREVIO's General Recommendation No 1 on the prevention, protection, and persecution of the digital harassment against women. While education on mutual respect among men and women is perhaps the most pressing task, crimes must, nevertheless, be properly prosecuted. In order to do that, legislation must be clear, but it must also be implemented. In the analysed *Volodina* cases, we have seen that while there was a sufficient legal framework, it was not applied. There is still much to be done to comply with the recommendations made by GREVIO in its recommendation to 'ensure that victims of violence against women perpetrated in the digital sphere have effective access to criminal justice systems and that the authorities adequately respond to such cases, including by applying criminal law and, as appropriate, ex officio prosecution'.[49] In the *Volodina* cases there was a lack of urgency regarding barring orders and protection orders against violence perpetrated online or via ICT. Moreover, there was no effective investigation against the perpetrator of violence and the authorities did not take the victim's complaints, or the real risk to her seriously. All in all, 'the Court has recognized that online violence, or cyberviolence, is closely linked with offline, or "real life", violence and falls to be considered as another facet of the complex phenomenon of domestic violence'.[50]

Bibliography

Attwood F, *Mainstreaming sex: The Sexualization of Western Culture* (Bloomsbury Publishing 2009)

Boldova Pasamar MA, 'Menores de edad penalmente responsables de delitos sexuales' in Valiente Ivañez and others (eds), *Un modelo integral de Derecho penal: Libro homenaje a la profesora Mirentxu Corcoy Bidasolo* vol 2 (Boletín Oficial del Estado 2022)

Caletti GM, '"Revenge porn" e tutela penale. Prime riflessioni sulla criminalizzazione specifica della pornografia non consensuale alla luce delle esperienze angloamericane (2018) 3 Diritto penale contemporaneo—Rivista Trimestrale 63

Caletti GM, 'Can Affirmative Consent Save "Revenge Porn" Laws? Lessons from the Italian Criminalization of Non-Consensual Pornography' (2021) 25(3) Virginia Journal of Law and Technology 116

Citron DK and Franks MA, 'Criminalizing Revenge Porn' (2014) 49 Wake Forest Law Review 346

Costello RÁ, 'Volodina v Russia (no. 2): Intimate Images, Domestic Violence and the Positive Obligations of Member States under Article 8 ECHR Case Notes' (2021) 4(7) European Data Protection Law Review 614

Dodge A, 'Nudes are Forever: Judicial Interpretations of Digital Technology's Impact on "Revenge Porn"' (2019) 34(1) Canadian Journal of Law and Society 121–43

[49] GREVIO General Recommendation No 1 (n 14) §55 (d).

[50] *Volodina v Russia* (No 2) (n 3) § 49.

Dressing H, Kuehner C, and Gass P, 'Lifetime Prevalence and Impact of Stalking in a European Population. Epidemiological Data from a Middle-sized German City' (2005) 187 British Journal of Psychiatry 168

Gillespie AA, 'Adolescents, Sexting and Human Rights' (2013) 13(4) Human Rights Law Review 623–43

Gillespie AA, '"Trust Me, It's Only For Me": "Revenge Porn" and the Criminal Law' (2015) 11 Criminal Law Review 866

McGlynn C and Rackley E, 'Image-based Sexual Abuse' (2017) 37 Oxford Journal of Legal Studies 53

van der Aa S, 'New Trends in the Criminalization of Stalking in the EU Member States' (2018) 24 European Journal on Criminal Policy and Research 315–33

5

Cautions against Criminalization

Aya Gruber

I. Introduction

For decades, certain crimes have captured the American public's imagination. Crime stories often find their origins in conservative politics and racial constructions of criminality, but they can also be manifestations of advocates' sincere efforts to expose long-tolerated or little known exploitations of the vulnerable by the powerful.[1] Alternately celebrated as democracy in its purest form or decried as a moral panic, high-profile crime preoccupations can embody progressive and regressive sentiments.[2] Regardless of their genesis, because media and public attention tend to flatten analysis, crime stories often involve 'innocent', white, and non-poor victims who suffer at the hands of intentionally evil, irredeemable, and privileged bad actors.[3] Such spectacular narratives cement inaccurate presumptions about the causes of crime, the magnitude of offending, and the gravity of the harm.[4]

[1] William J Stuntz, 'The Pathological Politics of Criminal Law' (2001) 100 Michigan Law Review 505, 533 (hereafter Stuntz, 'Pathological Politics').

[2] Craig Reinarman and Harry G Levine, 'Crack in Context: Politics and Media in the Making of a Drug Scare (1989) 16 Contemporary Drug Problems Journal 535 (hereafter Reinarman and Levine, 'Crack in Context').

[3] Elayne Rapping, 'Television, Melodrama, and the Rise of the Victims' Rights Movement' (2000) 43 New York Law School Law Review 665, 680; Lynne Henderson, 'Co-Opting Compassion: The Federal Victim's Rights Amendment' (1998) 10 St Thomas Law Review 579, 584.

[4] Roger N Lancaster, *Sex Panic and the Punitive State* (University of California Press 2011) 26 (hereafter Lancaster, *Sex Panic*).

Aya Gruber, *Cautions against Criminalization* In: *Criminalizing Intimate Image Abuse*. Edited by: Gian Marco Caletti and Kolis Summerer, Oxford University Press. © Oxford University Press 2024. DOI: 10.1093/oso/9780198877813.003.0005

In recent years, 'revenge porn', as it is called in media circles, or 'non-consensual intimate image distribution' and 'intimate image sexual abuse' in legal-speak, has enthralled the populace, attained broad press and social media coverage, including a trending Netflix documentary, and rapidly engendered a slew of new criminal prohibitions.[5] The Netflix revenge-porn documentary, for example, has as its main protagonist a young, thin, attractive, and college-educated white woman who was utterly devastated when a hacker obtained the secret topless photos she took only for herself. That hacker uploaded the photos to a revenge-porn site run by a gleeful, powerful, and unrepentant misogynist, Hunter Moore.[6] Responding to this and similar stories, states have passed revenge-porn laws at a rapid pace. The pattern is all too familiar. Awash with information about evil criminals running amok and ruined victims with nowhere to turn, powerful influencers and policy makers have long endorsed expansive criminal laws, which enjoy widespread popular support. Rachel Barkow remarks that 'criminal justice policy in the United States is set largely based on emotions and the gut reactions of lay people. We have been doing this for decades, with the public and politicians reacting to stories or panics about crime with ill-informed laws and punitive policies.'[7]

This pattern of basing policy on punitive impulses is in many ways quintessentially American, and it helped propel the United States to a contemptable status of the most carceral nation on earth.[8] One European scholar observed: 'The international consensus that imprisonment should be used as only a last resort has never been questioned in Europe, with few exceptions and periods of crime policy, whereas incapacitation and deterrence flourished in the US from the mid-1970s until recently.'[9] Still, it is worth noting that western Europe too saw incarceration rates rise precipitously between the mid-1980s and the early 2000s, and in many European countries, the incarceration rate remains far higher today than during the 1980s and 1990s.[10] Just as the US prison system disproportionately locks away people of colour, western European prisons disproportionately incarcerate foreigners and migrants.[11] Thus, European lawmakers also risk hastily passing

[5] 'The Most Hated Man on the Internet' (*Netflix* 2022) <https://www.netflix.com/title/81387065?source=35> accessed 9 March 2023 (hereafter 'The Most Hated Man'). For a list of revenge-porn statutes, see Nicole Prebeck, 'State Revenge Porn Laws', *FindLaw* (8 December 2022) <https://www.findlaw.com/criminal/criminal-charges/revenge-porn-laws-by-state.html> accessed 9 March 2023; Cyber Civ Rights Initiative, 'Nonconsensual Pornography Laws' (2023) <https://www.cybercivilrights.org/nonconsensual-pornography-laws/> accessed 9 March 2023.

[6] 'The Most Hated Man' (n 5).

[7] Rachel Elise Barkow, *Prisoners of Politics* (Harvard University Press 2021) (hereafter Barkow, *Prisoners of Politics*); Sara Sun Beale, 'The News Media's Influence on Criminal Justice Policy: How Market-Driven News Promotes Punitiveness' (2006) 48 William and Mary Law Review 397.

[8] Barkow, *Prisoners of Politics* (n 5).

[9] Frieder Duenkel, 'European Penology: The Rise and Fall of Prison Population Rates in Europe in Times of Migrant Crises and Terrorism' (2017) 14 European Journal of Criminology 629, 630.

[10] ibid 633–36.

[11] ibid 635.

problematic criminal laws under public pressure, especially pressure from activists who equate incarceration with gender justice.

As so-called revenge pornographers have taken on the mantle of the public's 'most hated man', the calls to seek official revenge on them have amplified in number, intensity, and influence.[12] Here, I direct some cautions to those who make and heed such calls. As intuitive are the ideas that harms must be criminalized and the failure to criminalize gendered harms is sexism manifest, we have amassed a wealth of information that complicates and often counters these ideas. First, the public's and state's identification of conduct that warrants criminalization, much less the media's publicization of such conduct, does not occur in a vacuum of moral and legal objectivity. Many values, presumptions, and biases underlie people's identification of what *is* criminal and who is responsible for the criminal conduct. For decades in the United States, the trend has been to understand most of society's ills as products of evil individuals' intentional behaviour.[13] Such individuals, the argument goes, can be stopped only by incarceration, which they also deserve. Over time, this reasoning has become an impulse, such that when people hear a story of suffering, they immediately look for the bad person to imprison.[14]

Second, this focus on individual criminality, on balance, serves to deflect attention away from the structures, legal arrangements, and social forces that underlie social problems and to relieve the state and powerful entities of the obligation to address them. In fact, the insistence that individual evil actors are the primary cause of societal harms was part of a distinct conservative strategy in the 1980s and 1990s to instil neoliberal ethics and minimize the government's role in preventing and addressing social ills.[15] And since that time, the public has quite consistently supported newer and harsher criminal law programmes, believing that criminal law alone 'sends a message' and holds bad people accountable. However, the very pathologies of the penal system render it a particularly poor vehicle for sending any moral message—no less a feminist antiviolence and egalitarian message. People ensnared by the carceral web hear a message about dominance, indeed, masculinist dominance. The message is that domination, control, and the infliction of pain are *empowerment* and the key to status.[16] Moreover, criminal laws do more than just send messages—they operate within a law-enforcement

[12] 'The Most Hated Man' (n 5).

[13] Bernard E Harcourt, 'Neoliberal Penality: A Brief Genealogy' (2010) 14 Theoretical Criminology 74.

[14] Aya Gruber 'Race to Incarcerate: Punitive Impulse and the Bid to Repeal Stand Your Ground' (2014) 68 University of Miami Law Review 961, 967 (hereafter Gruber, 'Race to Incarcerate').

[15] Aya Gruber, *The Feminist War on Crime: The Unexpected Role of Women's Liberation in Mass Incarceration* (University of California Press 2020) 64–68 (hereafter Gruber, *The Feminist War on Crime*); Marie Gottschalk, *The Prison and the Gallows, The Politics of Mass Incarceration in America* (Cambridge University Press 2006).

[16] Bernard E Harcourt, 'Joel Feinberg on Crime and Punishment: Exploring the Relationship between the Moral Limits of the Criminal Law and the Expressive Function of Punishment' (2001) 5 Buffalo Criminal Law Review 145, 168.

system with a condemnable history and present.[17] Critical race theorists observe that minoritized and disempowered groups have always shouldered the burdens of carceral message-sending.[18] Indeed, in some accounts, the American policing and prison system's primary *function* is to maintain economic and racial hierarchy.[19]

Expanding on these thoughts and others below, I advance caution against following the lead of the American states that jumped on the bandwagon of criminalizing intimate image distribution, just as they jumped on the bandwagon of most media-driven criminalization proposals.[20] I conclude by urging criminalization proponents to engage in earnest with mass incarceration and grapple with the fact that their new criminal laws expand an inhumane system that inflicts pain disproportionately on poor people of colour.

II. Caution 1: The American Punitive Impulse is Strong

Few principles seem more universal than wrongdoers must be held accountable. Yet for decades, scholars have warned against using simple retribution to justify carceral institutions that have complex and often quite nefarious operations and origins. Demanding accountability begs the questions of what constitutes wrongdoing, who is a wrongdoer, and what accountability looks like. Thus, 'criminals deserve punishment' mostly serves as a political soundbite that justifies practices that thoughtful retributivists reject.[21] There were periods in US history when law and society treated crime as a social disease and those associated with it as people in need of resources or rehabilitation.[22] Of course, penal policy during these moments was no panacea, and plenty of painful detention proceeded under the banner of treatment. The point is that America's punitive paradigm did not always exist, and the penal sanction was not always the presumptively superior technology of social policy.

[17] Duncan Kennedy, 'Sexual Abuse, Sexy Dressing and the Eroticization of Domination' (1992) 26 New England Law Review 1309, 1338.

[18] Michelle Alexander, *The New Jim Crow: Mass Incarceration in the Age of Colorblindness* (New Press 2012) (hereafter Alexander, *The New Jim Crown*).

[19] Paul Butler, 'The System is Working the Way it is Supposed To: The Limits of Criminal Justice Reform' (2016) 104 Georgetown Law Journal 1419 (hereafter Butler, 'The System is Working').

[20] These cautions are condensed versions of previous in-depth analyses of feminist and other progressive reformers' contribution to mass incarceration that appear in several articles and my 2020 book. See Gruber, *The Feminist War on Crime* (n 15); see also Gruber, 'Race to Incarcerate' (n 14); Aya Gruber, 'Sex Exceptionalism in Criminal Law' (forthcoming 2023) 75 Stanford Law Review 755 (hereafter Gruber, 'Sex Exceptionalism'); Aya Gruber, 'Sex Wars as Proxy Wars' (2019) 5 Critical Analysis of Law 1; Aya Gruber, 'Consent Confusion' (2017) 38 Cardozo Law Review 415; Aya Gruber, 'When Theory Met Practice: Distributional Analysis of Race and Gender in Criminal Law' (2015) 83 Fordham Law Review 3211.

[21] Kyron Huigens, 'What is and is Not Pathological in Criminal Law' (2002) 101 Michigan Law Review 811, 812.

[22] Jonathan Simon, 'Crime, Community, and Criminal Justice' (2002) 90 California Law Review 1415.

It was in the late twentieth century that criminal law solidified as the default method of addressing harm and the politically acceptable form of state governance. This shift, though complex and multifactored in origin, stemmed in large part from a specific neoliberal political and economic project that reframed social problems as individual choices. Criminalization and tough-on-crime rhetoric were integral to the United States' economic and political shift towards neoliberalism—'a political project to re-establish the conditions for capital accumulation and to restore the power of economic elites'.[23] President Ronald Reagan deftly exploited the crime issue to recast poverty, inequality, and marginalization as products of bad individuals.[24] The war on crime allowed small-state politicians to decry welfare 'handouts' and claim to be tackling the country's pressing problems. Conservatives maintained the appearance of a Nozickian minimal night-watchman state by confining criminal hyper-governance to minorities and the poor—the groups with the least political power. In fact, as Marxist theorists observe, this expansive penal authority was an effective mechanism for managing the denizens of surplus labour in an era of increasing automation and migration of corporate production overseas.[25]

Neoliberal narratives of crime became so powerful and entrenched over time that the carceral default became a near universal and reflexive impulse. Today, people across the ideological spectrum embrace severe punishment of the person they identify as producing what they consider a significant harm. Because the impulse arose from politics and culture more than rising crime, it endures in places with high and low crime rates and in times of increasing crime and precipitous crime decline.[26] It has endured in modern times, despite that the 'New Jim Crow' critique of the racialized carceral state has gained widespread attention and 'criminal justice reform' has become a bipartisan issue.[27] Today, there is widespread awareness that American tough-on-crime ideologies produced the world's largest carceral system and transformed marginalized neighbourhoods into demilitarized zones with roving squads of police combatants.[28] On a macro-level, progressives, including feminists, critique this sorry state. They condemn sentences as too high,

[23] David Harvey, *A Brief history of Neoliberalism* (Oxford Academic 2005) 19; Gruber, *The Feminist War on Crime* (n 15) 64–66.

[24] Ronald W Reagan, 'Remarks at the Annual Conference of the National Sheriff's Association in Hartford, Connecticut' Ronald Reagan Presidential Library and Museum Archives (20 June 1984) <http://www.reaganlibrary.gov/archives/speech/remarks-annual-conference-national-sheriffs-association-hartford-connecticut> <https://perma.cc/SU8G-V6A4> accessed 9 October 2023.

[25] Ahmed White, 'Capitalism, Social Marginality, and the Rule of Law's Uncertain Fate in Modern Society' (2005) 37 Arizona State Law Journal 759 (hereafter White, 'Modern Society'); Loïc Wacquant, 'From Slavery to Mass Incarceration' (2002) 13 New Left Review 42 (Wacquant, 'Mass Incarceration').

[26] Scott Boggess and John Bound, 'Did Criminal Activity Increase During the 1980's? Comparisons Across Data Sources' (National Bureau of Economic Research Working Paper No 4431, 1993) <https://www.nber.org/papers/w4431> accessed 9 October 2023.

Reinarman and Levine, 'Crack in Context' (n 2); Alexander, *The New Jim Crown* (n 18).

[27] Alexander, *The New Jim Crown* (n 18).

[28] Radley Balko, *Rise of the Warrior Cop: The Militarization of America's Police Forces* (Hachette 2013).

juvenile dispositions as too harsh, and police as too abusive. Many seek to limit—even abolish—the penal system.

The punitive impulse, however, is not an ideology. Progressives who philosophically reject punitive ideology nonetheless endorse penal severity for individuals who commit 'under-punished' crimes that reflect and reinforce regressive values, such as sex, environmental, and corporate crimes. Thus, for many feminists, the natural way to tackle technology-enabled sexual misconduct is criminally punishing the individual users of tech. Perhaps in certain contexts, the anti-subordination benefits borne by new criminal law regimes outweigh the drawbacks, including the drawback of broadening painful and racially discriminatory carceral authority. Nevertheless, the problem is not that feminists sometimes support criminalization but the regularity with which they instinctively presume that criminal law *must* be the response to harm and holds more promise than peril.

Policy makers' intuitive and non-critical embrace of criminal law, even for progressive reasons, has proven time and again to harm the most subordinated people.[29] Indeed, the punitive impulse transmogrifies progressives' anti-authoritarian and anti-subordination energy into passionate support for state-centric carceral intervention. Because punishing 'bad guys'—especially sex offenders—has popular and political appeal, there is an ever-present risk of criminal-law advocacy taking over progressive social movements. The ensuing criminal law reforms, created in the name of fighting monstrous criminals *and* gender justice, are particularly difficult to reverse, even when evidence proves they are harmful to marginalized people, including women.[30]

III. Caution 2: Reformers, Including Feminists, Should Adopt an Ethic of Responsibility

Given the punitive impulse's carceral, neoliberal, and discriminatory origins and costly manifestation (caging human beings), progressive reformers should resist it.[31] In my book, *The Feminist War on Crime*, I suggest a 'neofeminist approach' that focuses on gender-based harms but is sceptical of carceral remedies.[32] Under this approach, feminists predict as best as they can how their law reform proposals will operate in the world as it exists: a world of racialized over-policing and over-imprisonment. In the heat of an activist moment, feminists forget or ignore that the American carceral system originated and functions to serve a range of

[29] Aya Gruber, 'Equal Protection under the Carceral State' (2018) 112 Northwestern University Law Review 1.

[30] Lancaster, *Sex Panic* (n 3).

[31] White, 'Modern Society' (n 5); Wacquant, 'Mass Incarceration' (n 25); Butler, 'The System is Working' (n 19).

[32] Gruber, *The Feminist War on Crime* (n 15) ch 1–5.

hierarchy-preserving and state-aggrandizing disciplinary functions. Immersing oneself in the reality of the American penal state, rather than a constructed imaginary of its liberationist potential, should lead one to adopt the stance that criminalization is a last resort to be tried only after diligent study and when all else has failed.

Throughout history, feminist groups have clung to criminalization like a life raft in a sea of misogyny. It is understandable that reformers have gravitated towards the proposals most likely to be implemented in the status quo. Nevertheless, in every area where criminalization became the mainstream 'feminist' approach—domestic violence, rape, and sex work, among others—there were a variety of non-criminal paths not taken. To be sure, less powerful feminist groups, including socialist feminists and Black feminists, advocated for such paths, but their agendas fared far worse than mainstream criminalization agendas.[33] In recent times, the opportunities for feminists to pursue women's safety and empowerment without bolstering the penal state are more plentiful than ever, and yet activists continue to default to criminal law.

Prison abolitionists in the United States, many of whom are feminists of colour, criticize 'reformist reforms' that 'continue or expand the reach' of policing and prosecution and favour 'abolitionists steps' that 'chip away' at the penal state.[34] Black feminist scholars have questioned the potential of piecemeal reforms to change penal institutions that were born of and are presently infused with racial and other forms of discrimination'.[35] However, one need not adopt such strong positions against incremental and internal reform to question feminist criminalization reforms, because simply, *they do not change the system*. Feminists create new offences, more expansive policing, tougher prosecutorial policies, and lengthier sentences within the system *as it exists*. Like other tough-on-crime proponents, they adopt backward-looking justifications, rehashing the details of the horrible crimes or troubling statistics that provoked their efforts. But before activating the penal machine and all that comes with it, reformers should at least *think about* how their newly minted penal regime affects everyone it touches, not just the punishment-demanding victims highlighted in activist discourse.

Critical feminist scholars call this an 'ethic of responsibility'.[36] Scholars of 'governance feminism' observe that feminists' move to the centre of state governance in recent decades has created new obligations that were not present when

[33] ibid.

[34] Critical Resistance, 'Reformist Reforms vs Abolitionist Steps in Policing' (Critical Resistance nd)> <https://static1.squarespace.com/static/59ead8f9692ebee25b72f17f/t/5b65cd58758d46d34254f22c/1533398363539/CR_NoCops_reform_vs_abolition_CRside.pdf> <https://perma.cc/YN2Q-JYFZ> accessed 9 October 2023.

[35] Angela Y Davis, *Are Prisons Obsolete?* (Seven Stories 2011); Mariame Kaba and Andrea J Ritchie, *No More Police: A Case for Abolition* (New Press 2022).

[36] Janet Halley and others, *Governance Feminism: An Introduction* (University of Minnesota Press 2018) xiv.

feminists shouted their demands from the margins.[37] Drawing from Max Weber, governance-feminism scholars assert: 'To engage governance is to make use of force; to do so responsibly is to acknowledge that this is so.'[38] Thus, 'politics can be fully responsible only if one is willing to look down and behold the blood on one's own hands'.[39] Mindy Jane Roseman and Alice Miller similarly advocate a 'politics of accountability' where feminists factor in 'the material deprivations [penal law] entails: the intentional infliction of pain, at a minimum'.[40]

Spectacular narratives of egregious behaviour predictably spark punitive impulses. The public then demands new laws to remedy a 'weak' criminal system, even when existing criminal law covers the behaviour.[41] William Stuntz points to the example of carjacking in the 1990s:

> In 1992, a Maryland woman and her one-year-old daughter had their car hijacked; the mother was killed in the course of the theft. The story made national headlines and created the (mistaken) impression that these 'carjacking' cases were common. The public demanded that politicians solve this new problem, notwithstanding that existing criminal laws—auto theft, robbery, assault, kidnapping, and homicide—already covered the relevant behavior.... [L]egislatures ... create[d] new crimes not to solve the problem, but to give voters the sense that they are doing something about it.[42]

In the case of ostensibly new misconduct like intimate image sharing, there is often a time gap during which prosecutors experiment with how to use their already vast penal authority against the new misconduct. Inevitably, there will be prosecutors who decline to use the existing laws to prosecute and judges who disallow such use, as well as defendants who win their cases. During that time gap, advocates and the public object that defendants are getting off on 'technicalities' and call for more prosecutorial 'tools'. Indeed, there is a time-worn argument that too many offenders are let off because of legal 'loopholes' and that criminal-favouring constitutional and evidentiary rules are to blame for these outrages. While such anti-process sentiments seem right-wing, feminist discourse is rife with claims about weak criminal laws and pro-defendant procedures that produce outrageous impunity.[43] Feminists regularly decry that convicted defendants receive sentences

[37] ibid.
[38] ibid.
[39] ibid xv.
[40] Alice M Miller and Mindy Jane Roseman, 'Introduction' in AM Miller and MJ Roseman (eds), *Beyond Virtue and Vice: Rethinking Human Rights and Criminal Law* (University of Pennsylvania Press 2019) 13.
[41] Stuntz, 'Pathological Politics' (n 1).
[42] ibid.
[43] Karen Engle, 'Anti-Impunity and the Turn to Criminal Law in Human Rights' (2015) 100 Cornell Law Review 1069.

they deem too lenient and even protest that certain defendants are allowed to present a defence at all.[44] Sometimes advocates trace impunity, not to the operation of the criminal system, but to external factors like 'under-reporting'.[45] But invariably, new and harsher criminal law is the demand.

As I watched the Netflix documentary, I heard plea after plea for new revenge-porn laws because such was necessary to put Hunter Moore in prison.[46] But at the time of the film, Moore was *already* serving time, having been convicted under the *existing* legal regime governing criminalizing hacking.[47] A similar hateful revenge pornographer was Kevin Bollaert who ran a scheme involving the sites UGotPosted.com and ChangeMyReputation.com, where victims whose photos were posted on the first site could pay Bollaert to remove them via the second.[48] In 2015, a jury convicted Bollaert of an array of identity theft and extortion crimes. After a lengthy sentencing hearing in which victims testified about their embarrassment and the hurtful reactions from bosses and loved ones, the judge sentenced the 28-year-old Bolleart to eighteen years of imprisonment.[49] This was the longest jail sentence ever handed down in San Diego County. (A 2011 California law required people convicted of non-violent offences to serve their time in county jails rather than state prisons.)[50]

Yet commentators still understood Bollaert's case as proof that we need *more* laws.[51] 'So what's next in the fight against revenge porn now that California is

[44] Victoria Nourse, 'Passion's Progress: Modern Law Reform and the Provocation Defense' (1997) 106 Yale Law Journal 1331.

[45] Andrew Van Dam, 'Less Than 1% of Rapes Lead to Felony Convictions. At Least 89% of Victims Face Emotional and Physical Consequences' *Washington Post* (6 October 2018) <https://www.washingtonpost.com/business/2018/10/06/less-than-percent-rapes-lead-felony-convictions-least-percent-victims-face-emotional-physical-consequences> accessed 9 October 2023.

[46] 'The Most Hated Man' (n 5).

[47] Abby Ohlheiser, 'Revenge Porn Purveyor Hunter Moore is Sentenced to Prison' *Washington Post* (3 December 2015) <https://www.washingtonpost.com/news/the-intersect/wp/2015/12/03/revenge-porn-purveyor-hunter-moore-is-sentenced-to-prison> accessed 9 October 2023.

[48] Scott Neuman, 'Owner Of "Revenge Porn" Site Sentenced to 18 Years in Jail' *NPR* (4 April 2015) <https://www.npr.org/sections/thetwo-way/2015/04/04/397509157/owner-of-revenge-porn-site-sentenced-to-18-years-in-jail> accessed 9 October 2023.

[49] ibid.

[50] Dana Littlefield, 'Jail Term in "Revenge Porn" Case is County's Longest', *San Diego Union-Tribune* (24 August 2016) <https://www.sandiegouniontribune.com/sdut-revenge-porn-jail-sentence-longest-realignment-2015apr11-story.html> accessed 9 October 2023. The change in California's prison structure was a consequence of a 2011 Supreme Court decision that California's quite horrific overcrowded prison system constituted cruel and unusual punishment: *Brown v Plata* 563 US 493. In response, the state essentially rearranged the deck chairs on the Titanic and passed a law diverting those convicted of non-violent crimes to a different carceral structure, county jail. Margo Schlanger, 'Plata v. Brown and Realignment: Jails, Prisons, Courts, and Politics' (2013) 48 Harvard Civil Rights-Civil Liberty Law Review 165. Because jails offer no programming or services for those with years-long sentences, Bolleart was in a uniquely deleterious situation. His legal team was able to convince a judge to split his time between the jail and state prison, which led to a very slight reduction in the actual time he would serve. That minor readjustment produced headlines that Bolleart's sentence had been reduced.

[51] Allie Conti, 'Will Giving Kevin Bollaert 18 Years in Prison Finally End Revenge Porn?' *Vice* (10 March 2023) <http://www.vice.com/en/article/dpwaek/is-giving-kevin-bollaert-18-years-enough-to-finally-end-revenge-porn-406> accessed 9 October 2023.

throwing the book at operators like Bollaert and the feds got Hunter Moore to plead guilty to charges that carry at least two years in jail?', one journalist queried. 'First, it's necessary for more states to pass laws'.[52] It is an all too familiar pattern that activists publicize the worst actors whose egregious misconduct is already criminalized and then propose broad legal regimes that sweep in less egregious and less empowered actors.[53] Activists focus on powerful abusers instead of the marginalized people who typically bear the burden of criminal law, even though powerful men can beat even the most draconian of systems.

In 2018, Congress passed the Allow States and Victims to Fight Online Sex Trafficking Act (FOSTA) amid high-profile allegations that the Backpage website, infamous for its open commercial-sex advertisements, was a major source of child sex trafficking.[54] Celebrities including Amy Schumer and Seth Meyers had released a pro-FOSTA PSA with more than a little QAnon-ness, warning that rapists can 'buy a child online for sex ... as easy as ordering a pizza'.[55] FOSTA made it a ten-year felony to own or operate a computer service 'with the intent to promote or facilitate the prostitution of another person'.[56] However, by the time the sweeping legislation was passed, the feds had already shut down Backpage and charged it with racketeering crimes. It was never a tenable thesis that sex trafficking, a highly criminalized and investigated enterprise, would mostly happen on the Clearnet and be as easy as ordering pizza. So FOSTA deterred not the exploitation of children, which happens underground, but open commercial-sex advertising.[57] Sex-worker organizations condemned the measure for endangering and further marginalizing people already in a precarious environment. A 2022 survey of sex workers' opinions about FOSTA reported: 'People are losing access to work and are less able to support themselves and their families [and experiencing] increased financial insecurity, increased exposure to violence, lack of access to community resources, inability to find work, and increased feelings of fear and anxiety'.[58]

Laser focused on people like Moore and Bolleart, we might imagine only their type will be prosecuted for non-consensual intimate image sharing. However, it

[52] ibid.

[53] For example, media driven federal sex-crime legislation disproportionately burdened the few groups, namely Native Americans, who fell within the federal government's limited jurisdiction. Jon M Sands, 'Re: Adam Walsh Child Protection and Safety Act of 2006, Pub L 109-248, Federal Public Defender District of Arizona (16 November 2006) 12–13 <https://perma.cc/CU6M-S358> accessed 9 October 2023.

[54] Allow States and Victims to Fight Online Sex Trafficking Act, 18 USCA § 2421A (hereafter FOSTA).

[55] 'PSA featuring Seth Meyers, Amy Schumer, Josh Charles, Tony Shalhoub and others—FOSTA-SESTA' <https://vimeo.com/249095210> accessed 9 October 2023.

[56] FOSTA (n 54).

[57] US Government Accountability Office (GAO), 'Sex Trafficking: Online Platforms and Federal Prosecutions' (2 January 2023) <https://www.gao.gov/assets/gao-21-385.pdf> accessed 9 October 2023.

[58] Danielle Blunt and Ariel Wolf, 'Erased: The impact of FOSTA-SESTA and the removal of Backpage on sex workers' (ATR no 14, 27 April 2020) 117–21 <https://hackinghustling.org/wp-content/uploads/2020/01/HackingHustling-Erased.pdf> accessed 9 October 2023.

is beyond Pollyannish to assume that broadly drawn criminal laws catch only the most egregious offenders. Laws operate within complex social and political contexts and through 'noisy' enforcement systems. Reformers have an ethical responsibility to attempt to get the lay of this land.[59] Activists' agitate for criminal law to address pre-identified bad actors without fully interrogating the nature and causes of the harm and the realities of the enforcement.[60] It is possible, though unlikely, that a detailed distributional analysis would reveal that the newly minted revenge-porn laws ensnare mostly the Moore-Bolleart types and spare less egregious, more marginalized actors. Even so, as Bentham argued centuries ago, there are costs *inherent* to punishment and the persistent possibility of less painful remedies.[61]

IV. Caution 3: Broad Criminalization Programmes Have Far-reaching Effects

Advocates' backward-looking focus frequently leads to over-broad criminalization proposals. With an eye trained on the past, reformers concentrate on the horrible and often disproportionally powerful men (ie Harvey Weinstein and Donald Trump) who have managed to escape liability, even if just for a while, and propose sweeping laws that they presume would have stopped them. Accordingly, they reserve little mental energy for the many not-as-bad actors whose conduct is also swept in. In constructing their proposals, reformers frequently seek the most expansive definitions to ensure that there are no 'loopholes' for bad actors to slip though. They then write off the costs of over-breadth by arguing that prosecutors will use their discretion to weed out all but the worst cases.

Take, for example, affirmative consent in rape law. Worried that laws that outlaw sex without consent are not pro-victim and permit the jury to scrutinize the complainant's state of mind during sex, anti-rape activists proposed an 'affirmative consent' standard that makes it a rape to engage in sexual activity with a person unless they communicate an 'affirmative' expression of consent. The problem is that the standard makes a lot of sexual activity that people actually engage in a felony. People in long-term relationships rarely express clear consent, and 'numerous studies have demonstrated that the preferred approach to signal consent for both women and men tends to be nonverbal instead of verbal'.[62] In fact, 'many men and

[59] Duncan Kennedy, 'Sexual Abuse, Sexy Dressing and the Eroticization of Domination' (1992) 26 New England Law Review 1309, 1338.

[60] ibid 258.

[61] Jeremy Bentham, *An Introduction to the Principles of Morals and Legislation* (OUP 1823).

[62] Ibid; Terry P Humphreys, 'Understanding Sexual Consent: An Empirical Investigation of the Normative Script for Young Heterosexual Adults' in Mark Cowling and Paul Reynolds (eds), *Making Sense of Sexual Consent* (1st edn, Routledge 2004) 209; David S Hall, 'Consent for Sexual Behavior in a College Student Population (1998) 1 Electronic Journal of Human Sexuality <http://www.ejhs.org/volume1/consent1.htm> accessed 9 October 2023.

women passively indicate their consent to sexual intercourse by not resisting, such as allowing themselves to be undressed by their partner, not saying no, or not stopping their partner's advances'.[63] Some proponents recognize this mismatch between affirmative consent and actual sexual practice. One opined: 'The Yes Means Yes law creates an equilibrium where too much counts as sexual assault. Bad as it is, that's a necessary change.'[64]

Unlike the above commentator, affirmative-consent proponents often admit that imprisoning ordinary actors to change culture is a serious cost. In turn, they defend the yes-mean-yes standard on the ground that it will mostly *not be enforced.*[65] Affirmative-consent proponents assert that prosecutors will go after 'real rapists'—those who intentionally force sex or have sex against a person's will—not those who simply did not get an affirmative yes.[66] Assuming the unlikely scenario that prosecutors dust off affirmative-consent law only for the worst actors,[67] one is left to wonder who those 'worst actors' are. Prosecutors' intuitive assessments of whether the defendant is 'a bad guy' and the complainant is a 'true' victim are often influenced more by racial and socioeconomic characteristics than by the nature of the event.[68]

Anti-revenge porn activists have championed extremely broad criminal prohibitions that portend to sweep in people nothing like the publicized bad actors. The Cyber Civil Rights Initiative (CCRI), a feminist think-tank and driving force behind cybersex criminalization, offers a 'model' law making it a crime to 'disclose an image of another, identifiable person whose intimate parts are exposed or who is engaged in a sexual act with knowledge of or reckless disregard for the fact that the person depicted did not consent to such disclosure'.[69] Adopting this definition, federal lawmakers proposed the Stopping Harmful Image Exploitation and Limiting Distribution (SHIELD) Act, which if passed would make such disclosure, even to a single other person, a five-year felony.[70]

63 Terry P Humphreys and Melanie M Brousseau, 'The Sexual Consent Scale—Revised: Development, Reliability, and Preliminary Validity' (2010) 47 Journal of Sex Research 421.

64 Ezra *Klein*, '"Yes Means Yes" is a Terrible Law, and I Completely Support It' *Vox* (13 October 2014) <https://www.vox.com/2014/10/13/6966847/yes-means-yes-is-a-terrible-bill-and-i-completely-support-it> accessed 9 October 2023.

65 Deborah Tuerkheimer, 'Affirmative Consent' (2016) 13 Ohio State Journal of Criminal Law 441, 464–68.

66 ibid.

67 National District Attorneys Association, 'National Sexual Assault Investigation and Prosecution Best Practices Guide' (Women Prosecutors Section, 3 January 2018) 15 <https://perma.cc/8UQF-U3AT> accessed 9 October 2023.

68 Robert W Hymes and others, 'Acquaintance Rape: The Effect of Race of Defendant and Race of Victim on White Juror Decisions' (1992) 133 Journal of Social Psychology 627; Gary D LaFree, 'The Effect of Sexual Stratification By Race on Official Reactions to Rape' (1980) 45 American Sociological Review 842; Nazgol Ghandnoosh, 'Race and Punishment: Racial Perceptions of Crime and Support for Punitive Policies' (The Sentencing Project, September 2014) <https://perma.cc/JK6Z-GRZZ> accessed 9 October 2023.

69 Cyber Civil Rights Initiative (CCRI), *Model State Law* (2021) <http://cybercivilrights.org/wp-content/uploads/2021/10/CCRI-Model-State-Law-for-NCP.pdf> accessed 9 October 2023.

70 SHIELD Act 2019, HR 2896 § 2(a), 116th Congress.

There is something telling about the name change from 'revenge porn' to 'non-consensual intimate images distribution'. Feminists championed the change because the word 'pornography' insults victims by suggesting that they somehow consented to public nudity. But 'revenge' also dropped out. Under the SHIELD Act, it matters not *why* the distribution occurred. Those with bad motives, no motives, or benign motives are equally guilty. Not only does the statutory regime lack motive, but it also lacks *intent*.[71] Although a matter of some interpretation, a recklessness standard generally allows defendants to be imprisoned even when they *honestly* believed the image sharing did not offend the subject (ie 'I didn't think my boyfriend would care so much'.). State laws go even further. Illinois's 2016 revenge-porn law, which was hailed as a breakthrough by CCRI leaders, makes it a three-year felony for a person to share an intimate image when they '*should have known* that the person in the image would not consent to the dissemination'.[72]

Moore and Bolleart were extreme actors whose intentional, even gleeful, behaviour harmed numerous victims. After the existing law caught up, imprisoned Moore and Bolleart, and shut down their sites, large-scale revenge porn sites continued to exist, but on the dark web and in the shadows.[73] To be sure, police departments in states that adopted broad intimate image laws received a slew of technological spying tools to investigate non-consensual image sharers—and everyone else.[74] Still, local police departments hardly have the capacity to take down overseas, dark-web operators. Thus, they target more 'ordinary' vengeful folks who commit their misconduct on the Clearnet—including vengeful women. The first person convicted under Virginia's revenge-porn law was 28-year-old Rachel Lynn Craig, who posted a nude photo of another woman on Facebook.[75] North Carolina's first defendant was 20-year-old Ashley Augustine who faced a felony for posting a picture of someone having sex.[76] Shortly after the passage of Illinois' law, police arrested a woman who had posted to Facebook topless pictures of a friend with whom she had a falling out.[77]

To be sure, these defendants are not sympathetic characters. All of them intentionally posted private nudes for the *purpose* of harassing, humiliating, and getting

[71] ibid.

[72] 720 Ill Comp Stat Ann 5/11-23.5. See also Idaho Code Ann § 18-6605; Minn Rev Stat § 617.261.

[73] Sarah Jeong, 'Revenge Porn Is Bad. Criminalizing It Is Worse' *Wired* (28 October 2013) <http:www.wired.com/2013/10/why-criminalizing-revenge-porn-is-a-bad-idea> accessed 9 October 2023 (hereafter Jeong, 'Revenge Porn Is Bad').

[74] Samantha Allen, 'She Posted Explicit Images of a Lifelong Friend' *Daily Beast* (13 April 2017) <http://www.thedailybeast.com/she-posted-explicit-images-of-a-lifelong-friend> accessed 9 October 2023 (hereafter Allen, 'Explicit Images').

[75] Associated Press, 'The First Person Charged Under Virginia's New 'Revenge Porn' Law Is a Woman' *Business Insider* (20 October 2014) <http://www.businessinsider.com/the-first-person-charged-under-virginias-new-revenge-porn-law-is-a-woman-2014-10> accessed 9 October 2023.

[76] Kendra Alleyne, 'Apex Woman is the First Charged under North Carolina's New "Revenge Porn" Law' *Campbell Law Observer* (14 April 2016) <campbelllawobserver.com/apex-woman-is-the-first-charged-under-north-carolinas-new-revenge-porn-law> accessed 9 October 2023.

[77] Allen, 'Explicit Images' (n 74).

revenge on the person they felt wronged them. But even if revenge-porn laws were limited to such ill-willed actors, which they are not, one could still question the wisdom of fating these vengeful women to lives as convicted *felons*, with all that entails. But in any case, many of the image-distribution laws do not restrict criminalization to those who disseminate images in order to harass, humiliate, or harm the victim. Instead, such broad laws, as the ACLU said of Arizona's felony law, apply equally to the abusive boyfriend and 'a bookseller who sells a history book containing an iconic image such as the Pulitzer Prize-winning photograph "Napalm Girl" …, [a] library lending a photo book about breast feeding to a new mother, a newspaper publishing pictures of abuse at the Abu Ghraib prison, or a newsweekly running a story about a local art show'.[78] Indeed, CCRI president Mary Anne Franks took the remarkable stance that 'limit[ing] revenge porn to situations in which the perpetrator acts with the intent to harm or harass his or her target [is] a very serious mistake that fundamentally misunderstands the nature of the abuse because most non-consensual porn cases *do not involve someone trying to harm the victim*'.[79]

Bethany Austin was another member of the initial cohort charged under Illinois' revenge-porn law. Before the drama arose, Austin shared an iCloud account with her fiancé. One day, she discovered intimate messages and images sent to him by another woman.[80] She broke off the engagement and ended their seven-year relationship. The fiancé told friends and family that Austin cancelled the wedding because she is 'crazy'. In response, Austin wrote a letter to family and friends with proof of the affair, including the intimate pictures (the defence argued that the other woman was essentially unrecognizable from the pictures).[81] After prosecutors charged her, Austin contested the constitutionality of the statute up to the Illinois Supreme Court. Devoting much of its opinion to the 'staggering' problem of revenge porn on the web, the mostly liberal court upheld the tough felony law as a proper exercise of state penal authority.[82] Today, Bethany Austin is a convicted felon.[83]

[78] American Civil Liberties Union (ACLU), 'First Amendment Lawsuit Challenges Arizona Criminal Law Banning Nude Images' (American Civil Liberties Union, 22 September 2014) <https://www.aclu.org/press-releases/first-amendment-lawsuit-challenges-arizona-criminal-law-banning-nude-images?redirect=free-speech%2Ffirst-amendment-lawsuit-challenges-arizona-criminal-law-banning-nude-images> accessed 9 October 2023. After the ACLU filed suit, Arizona's attorney general agreed not to enforce the law, and the legislature later amended it to require 'intent to harm, harass, intimidate, threaten or coerce'. Ariz Rev Stat § 13-1425 (2022).

[79] Deanna Paul, 'Is Revenge Porn Protected Speech? Lawyers Weigh in and Hope for a Supreme Court Ruling' *Washington Post* (26 December 2019) (quoting Mary Anne Franks) (internal quotations omitted, emphasis added) <http://www.washingtonpost.com/nation/2019/12/26/is-revenge-porn-protected-speech-supreme-court-may-soon-weigh> accessed 9 October 2023.

[80] ibid.

[81] ibid.

[82] *People v Austin* [2019] 155 NE 3d 439.

[83] Robert McCoppin, 'McHenry County Woman Found Guilty in "Revenge Porn" Case Following Ruling by Illinois Supreme Court' *Chicago Tribune* (27 April 2021) <http://www.chicagotribune.com/

These are the people convicted under revenge porn statutes who turn up in a simple Google search. Who are the others? Are they sexists? Are they women? Are they juveniles? Were they acting impulsively? Were they trying to harm? Perhaps not to Professor Franks, but to me, such questions matter. Moreover, there are all kinds of revenge-seeking behaviours we do not criminalize as felonies. In fact, one self-proclaimed feminist website invites women to post all manner of private things about their rotten exes as an act of feminist solidarity.[84] Why is it that out of all the ways people mistreat their exes—including by posting embarrassing but non-sexual images—only intimate image distribution has spurred public outrage and rapidly moved the slow machinery of politics? The answer is simple: the social preoccupation with sex and especially female sexuality.[85] Civil laws sometimes cover intentionally malicious non-sexual privacy invasions, but if the invasion is sexual, it is a *crime*, regardless of the defendant's intent to harm and the level of distress produced. Within the law and public discourse, women's sexuality and nudity are so taboo, potentially stigmatizing, and in need of covering from prying eyes that posting a woman's topless picture is *presumptively* horrific behaviour that traumatizes and devastates. All other malicious and privacy-violating exposures—revealing an ex's deepest secret, shaming someone for having committed a crime, humiliating someone because of long past behaviour—are, well, nothing.

This is not to deny that many women, in fact, feel more harmed by sexual privacy violations than non-sexual violations. But this is largely because of how society continues to treat women whose sexuality is public. Revenge-porn victims recount in heart-wrenching detail how a few naked pictures led to online abuse, social shunning, destruction of family relationships, loss of employment, and in extreme cases, forfeiture of parental rights. If the new criminal laws do in fact deter intimate image sharing, rather than driving it underground, some would-be victims will be spared this pain. However, even prescribing the death penalty for revenge porn would do little for the people whose pictures are *already on the Internet*.[86] These individuals are yet subject to all the societal reprehension directed towards anyone who is inappropriately sexual, such as women in the commercial sex industry or camming gay men. If anything, concentrating on the people who post the non-consensual nudes to the exclusion of all the people whose condemnatory and scandalized reactions produce such profound harm to victims reinforces the idea that for women, public sexuality is so inherently stigmatizing and degrading that they must avoid it at all costs.

news/breaking/ct-mchenry-county-revenge-porn-trial-20210426-kyuvx23wnjcitgdukaudofqzwe-story.html> accessed 9 October 2023. Austin received a probationary sentence.

84 Tracy Tegan, 'The Ex-Boyfriend List: Get your Ex Reported!' (Girl Power Girl Strong, 18 September 2022) <https://girlpowergirlstrong.com/the-ex-boyfriend-list> accessed 9 October 2023.

85 Gruber, 'Sex Exceptionalism' (n 20).

86 Jeong, 'Revenge Porn Is Bad' (n 73).

Advocates deride the use of the term 'pornography' for suggesting that the innocent women in the distributed images are really sex workers who 'asked for it'. To be sure, I also generally try to avoid using the stigmatizing terms 'pornography' and 'prostitution'. But I do so to destigmatize sex work and those involved in it. Anti-revenge-porn activists' rhetoric, by contrast, creates a strict divide between 'porn' women who willingly engaged in public sexuality and can be subject to firing and social abuse and innocent women who tried valiantly to keep their sexuality under wraps. Of course, sex workers are not automatically excluded as victims under the new image-distribution laws, but advocacy and discourse focuses on women whose nude pictures were taken secretly, hacked, or shared with a single person, not sex workers seeking to control the distribution of their work product.[87]

We find ourselves in a technological age where efforts to maintain digital privacy increasingly resemble fighting a rising tide. Instead of narrowly focusing on imprisoning the few image distributors who come within the purview of state authorities, advocates could seek to change the social, familial, and employment practices that devastate women whose nudes become public, willingly or not. For the most part, feminists have not concentrated their condemnation on the *employers* who fire employees after they discover public intimate pictures of them. In 2022, a New York City news station fired well-known meteorologist Erick Adame after an anonymous person posted online and sent to the station photos surreptitiously taken of Adame engaging in a sexual activity on a gay web-camming site.[88] Adame had been participating in camming for several years when the anonymous harasser published the photos in a clear effort to harm him. The effort paid off as the news station promptly fired Adame for violating a 'morals clause' in his contract.[89] Morals clauses, another legal intervention widely championed by feminists in the #MeToo era, allow companies to summarily fire those who they deem to have engaged in immoral—read sexual—behaviour that harms the company's reputation.[90]

Activists should have been outraged at a company firing a revenge-porn victim and thereby rewarding the person who intentionally set out to harm him. Yet, because Adame's history of gay camming rendered him an imperfect revenge-porn victim, the mood regarding his victimization was decidedly measured. Reporting on the firing, *The New York Times*, a paper that regularly features condemnatory coverage of revenge porn, characterized the situation as 'not clear cut'.[91] Adame's

[87] Robert Jackman, 'How the OnlyFans Leak Puts Porn Performers and Sex Workers in Danger' *Metro* (28 February 2020) <https://metro.co.uk/2020/02/28/onlyfans-leak-puts-porn-performers-sex-workers-danger-12320740/?ito = cbshare> accessed 9 October 2023.

[88] Liam Stack, 'Meteorologist Erick Adame's Firing Over Online Sex Prompts Backlash' *New York Times* (28 September 2022) <https://www.nytimes.com/2022/09/28/nyregion/erick-adame-ny-weatherman-fired-scandal.html> accessed 9 October 2023 (hereafter Stack, 'Online Sex Prompts').

[89] ibid.

[90] David E Fink and Sarah E Diamond, 'Morality Clauses in the Age of #MeToo and Time's Up' (2019) 34 Communications Law Journal 4.

[91] Stack 'Online Sex Prompts' (n 88).

status as a victim, it reported, was 'complicated by other factors, including his role as a television personality, an unusually public facing position'.[92] *The New York Times* was more willing than usual to blame the victim, quoting an expert who opined, 'there's the fact that there are things done in private and things done in public and [Adame] just misjudged the line between the two'.[93]

V. Conclusion

Now that the progressive critique of mass incarceration is familiar territory, feminist advocates of broadly drawn criminal laws cannot simply ignore it. Professor Franks and co-author Danielle Citron remark: 'While we share general concerns about over-criminalization and over-incarceration, rejecting the criminalization of serious harms is not the way to address those concerns.'[94] They go on to say: 'Only the shallowest of thinkers would suggest that the question whether non-consensual pornography should be criminalized—indeed, whether any conduct should be criminalized—should turn on something as contingent and arbitrary as the number of existing laws. Rather, the question of criminalization should be a question about the seriousness of the harm caused.'[95]

I disagree. That our books overflow with criminal laws and our prisons overflow with disproportionately marginalized people is not some contingent and arbitrary accident. Our mass-incarceration system has a history—one that includes enslavement, union-busting, and political imprisonment. Mass imprisonment did not arise from magical forces but from politics, ideologies, economic interests, and social conditions that scholars have studied in detail. The very idea Franks and Citron endorse—that identifying a 'serious' harm is the beginning and end of the criminalization question—is one such ideology. For *every* modern crime, some proponent identified a problem as 'serious' and championed penal law as the solution. The presumption that identifying 'serious' harms automatically warrants criminal law *created* the concerning problem of over-incarceration.

Many feminists recognize that criminal law carries grave human costs and often exacerbates problems, but they nonetheless support criminalizing gendered misconduct out of some sense that to do otherwise is unfair to women.[96] They maintain that the incarceration system, broken, racist, and ineffective though it may be, is not going away any time soon. Thus, failing to criminalize these new or newly

[92] ibid. It should be noted that the *New York Times* also makes its employees sign morals clauses.

[93] ibid.

[94] Daniele Keats Citron and Mary Anne Franks, 'Criminalizing Revenge Porn' (2014) Wake Forest Law Review 345, 362.

[95] ibid.

[96] Clare McGlynn, 'Challenging Anti-carceral Feminism: Criminalisation, Justice and Continuum Thinking' (2022) 93 Women's Studies International Forum 102614, at 6.

identified harms treats women as unimportant. One feminist argued that failing to criminalize intimate image distribution 'privilege[s] existing criminal offences' and denigrates 'women's experiences'.[97] Under this logic, creating the criminal law is *itself* gender justice, and it does not matter whether criminalization makes the problem better or worse or ends up harming more than helping vulnerable people.

Feminist activists could seize the opportunity to address these new or newly publicized harms in new and non-carceral ways.[98] Yet instead, they imagine that they can make limited intellectual insurgencies onto the terrain of American penal logic. However, if criminal law deters, satisfies victims, distributes fairly, and humanely resolves conflicts for the revenge-porn problem, there is little reason to doubt that it does so *for every problem*. Feminist proponents do not couple their efforts to expand the criminal law books with proposals for procedures to ensure that the execution of *their* laws will avoid the pathologies and discriminatory consequences of the current criminal system. In fact, when feminists tinker with process, it is usually to *reduce* defendants' protections and privilege prosecutors. Proponents do not seek to ensure that people convicted under *their* laws go to humane institutions instead of our overcrowded prisons rife with sexual and non-sexual violence. Proponents do not endeavour to spare *their* newly minted 'convicted sex offenders' from the social shunning, unemployability, and essentially civil death required by the US's draconian sex-offender management laws.

Those who wield legal power must own its costs. I am not asking feminist activists to balance the costs and benefits of criminalization the same way I do. I am simply asking reformers to take seriously the blood spilled when expanding one of the most condemned penal systems in the world.

Bibliography

Alexander M, *The New Jim Crow: Mass Incarceration in the Age of Colorblindness* (New Press 2012)

Balko R, *Rise of the Warrior Cop: The Militarization of America's Police Forces* (Hachette 2013)

Barkow RE, *Prisoners of Politics* (Harvard University Press 2021)

Beale SS, 'The News Media's Influence on Criminal Justice Policy: How Market-Driven News Promotes Punitiveness' (2006) 48 William and Mary Law Review 397

Beck B and Gruber A, 'Facts about Defunding Police Departments' *NY Daily News* (17 June 2020) <http://www.nydailynews.com/opinion/ny-oped-facts-about-defunding-police-departments-20200615-fvqkukbngbb2bko3tev5fq52oe-story.html> accessed 9 October 2023

Bentham J, *An Introduction to the Principles of Morals and Legislation* (OUP 1823)

[97] ibid.

[98] Hadar Dancig-Rosenberg, Anat Peleg and Roy Rosenberg, 'Post-Trauma and Post' (forthcoming 2023) University of Illinois Law Review (study finding that sexual assault survivors rated Facebook as better at addressing their needs than the criminal system); Danielle Sered, *Until We Reckon. Violence, Mass Incarceration, and a Road to Repair* (New Press 2022).

Berlant L, *The Queen of America Goes to Washington City* (Duke University Press 1997)
Blunt D and Wolf A, 'Erased: The Impact of FOSTA-SESTA and the Removal of Backpage on Sex Workers' (ATR no 14, 27 April 2020) 117–21 <https://hackinghustling.org/wp-content/uploads/2020/01/HackingHustling-Erased.pdf> accessed 9 October 2023
Boggess S and Bound J, 'Did Criminal Activity Increase During the 1980's? Comparisons Across Data Sources' (National Bureau of Economic Research Working Paper No 4431, 1993) <https://www.nber.org/papers/w4431> accessed 9 October 2023
Butler P, 'The System is Working the Way it is Supposed To: The Limits of Criminal Justice Reform' (2016) 104 Georgetown Law Journal 1419
Calabresi G, 'The Exclusionary Rule' (2003) 26 Harvard Journal of Law and Public Policy 111
Citron DK and Franks MA, 'Criminalizing Revenge Porn' (2014) Wake Forest Law Review 345, 362.
Dancig-Rosenberg H, Peleg A, and Rosenberg R, 'Post-Trauma and Post' (forthcoming 2023) University of Illinois Law Review
Davis AY, *Are Prisons Obsolete?* (Seven Stories 2011)
Duenkel F, 'European Penology: The Rise and Fall of Prison Population Rates in Europe in Times of Migrant Crises and Terrorism' (2017) 14 European Journal of Criminology 629, 630
Engle K, 'Anti-Impunity and the Turn to Criminal Law in Human Rights' (2015) 100 Cornell Law Review 1069
Esquirol J, 'Legal Latin Americanism' (2013) 16 Yale Human Rights and Development Law Journal 145
Fink DE and Diamond SE, 'Morality Clauses in the Age of #MeToo and Time's up' (2019) 34 Communications Law Journal 4
Ghandnoosh N, 'Race and Punishment: Racial Perceptions of Crime and Support for Punitive Policies' (The Sentencing Project, September 2014) <https://perma.cc/JK6Z-GRZZ> accessed 9 October 2023
Gottschalk M, *The Prison and the Gallows, The Politics of Mass Incarceration in America* (Cambridge University Press 2006)
Gruber A, 'Consent Confusion' (2017) 38 Cardozo Law Review 415
Gruber A, 'Equal Protection under the Carceral State' (2018) 112 Northwestern University Law Review 1
Gruber A, 'Race to Incarcerate: Punitive Impulse and the Bid to Repeal Stand Your Ground' (2014) 68 University of Miami Law Review 961, 967.
Gruber A, 'Sex Exceptionalism in Criminal Law' (2023) 75 Stanford Law Review 755
Gruber A, 'Sex Wars as Proxy Wars' (2019) 6 Critical Analysis of Law 1
Gruber A, *The Feminist War on Crime: The Unexpected Role of Women's Liberation in Mass Incarceration* (University of California Press 2020)
Gruber A, 'When Theory Met Practice: Distributional Analysis of Race and Gender in Criminal Law' (2015) 83 Fordham Law Review 3211
Hall DS, 'Consent for Sexual Behavior in a College Student Population' (1998) 1 Electronic Journal of Human Sexuality <http://www.ejhs.org/volume1/consent1.htm> accessed 9 October 2023
Halley J and others, *Governance Feminism: An Introduction* (University of Minnesota Press 2018)
Harcourt BE, 'Joel Feinberg on Crime and Punishment: Exploring the Relationship between the Moral Limits of the Criminal Law and The Expressive Function of Punishment' (2001) 5 Buffalo Criminal Law Review 145, 168
Harcourt BE, 'Neoliberal Penality: A Brief Genealogy' (2010) 14 Theoretical Criminology 74

Harvey D, *A Brief History of Neoliberalism* (Oxford Academic 2005)

Henderson L, 'Co-Opting Compassion: The Federal Victim's Rights Amendment' (1998) 10 St Thomas Law Review 579, 584

Herrington LH and others, 'Recommendations for Government Action, President's Task Force on Victims of Crime' (December 1982) 114 <https://perma.cc/FF4N-ESLQ> accessed 9 October 2023

Huigens K, 'What is and is Not Pathological in Criminal Law' (2002) 101 Michigan Law Review 811, 812

Humphreys TP, 'Understanding Sexual Consent: An Empirical Investigation of the Normative Script for Young Heterosexual Adults' in M Cowling and P Reynolds (eds), *Making Sense of Sexual Consent* (1st edn, Routledge 2004)

Humpreys TP and Brousseau MM, 'The Sexual Consent Scale—Revised: Development, Reliability, and Preliminary Validity' (2010) 47 Journal of Sex Research 420, 421

Hymes RW and others, 'Acquaintance Rape: The Effect of Race of Defendant and Race of Victim on White Juror Decisions' (1992) 133 Journal of Social Psychology 627

Kaba M and Ritchie AJ, *No More Police: A Case for Abolition* (New Press 2022)

Klein E, '"Yes Means Yes" is a Terrible Law, and I Completely Support It' *Vox* (13 October 2014) <https://www.vox.com/2014/10/13/6966847/yes-means-yes-is-a-terrible-bill-and-i-completely-support-it> accessed 9 October 2023

Kennedy D, 'Sexual Abuse, Sexy Dressing and the Eroticization of Domination' (1992) 26 New England Law Review 1309, 1338

LaFree GD, 'The Effect of Sexual Stratification by Race on Official Reactions to Rape' (1980) 45 American Sociological Review 842

Lancaster RN, *Sex Panic and the Punitive State* (University of California Press 2011) 26

Mathiesen T, 'The Politics of Abolition' (1986) 10 Contemporary Crises 81, 84–87

McGlynn C, 'Challenging anti-carceral feminism: Criminalisation, justice and continuum thinking' (2022) 93 Women's Studies International Forum 102614, at 6

McLeod AM, 'Prison Abolition and Grounded Justice' (2015) 62 UCLA Law Review 1156, 1202–06

Miller AM and Roseman MJ, 'Introduction' in AM Miller and MJ Roseman (eds), *Beyond Virtue and Vice: Rethinking Human Rights and Criminal Law* (University of Pennsylvania Press 2019) 13

Nourse V, 'Passion's Progress: Modern Law Reform and the Provocation Defense' (1997) 106 Yale Law Journal 1331

Packer HL, 'Two Models of the Criminal Process' (1964) 113 University of Pennsylvania Law Review 1

Rapping E, 'Television, Melodrama, and the Rise of the Victims' Rights Movement' (2000) 43 New York Law School Law Review 665, 680

Reagan RW, 'Remarks at the Annual Conference of the National Sheriff's Association in Hartford, Connecticut' Ronald Reagan Presidential Library and Museum Archives (20 June 1984) <http://www.reaganlibrary.gov/archives/speech/remarks-annual-conference-national-sheriffs-association-hartford-connecticut> <https://perma.cc/SU8G-V6A4> accessed 9 October 2023

Reinarman C and Levine H, 'Crack in Context: Politics and Media in the Making of a Drug Scare (1989) 16 Contemporary Drug Problems Journal 535

Schlanger M, 'Plata v. Brown and Realignment: Jails, Prisons, Courts, and Politics' (2013) 48 Harvard Civil Rights-Civil Liberties Law Review 165

Sered D, *Until We Reckon: Violence, Mass Incarceration, and a Road to Repair* (New Press 2022)

Simon J, 'Crime, Community, and Criminal Justice' (2002) 90 California Law Review 1415

Steffensmeier D, Ulmer J, and Kramer J, 'The Interaction of Race, Gender, and Age in Criminal Sentencing: The Punishment Cost of Being Young, Black, and Male' (1992) 36 Criminology 768

Stuntz WJ, 'The Pathological Politics of Criminal Law' (2001) 100 Michigan Law Review 505, 533

Taslitz AE, 'Respect and the Fourth Amendment' (2003) 94 Journal of Criminal Law and Criminology 15, 16

Tuerkheimer D, 'Affirmative Consent' (2016) 13 Ohio State Journal of Criminal Law 441, 464–68

Wacquant L, 'From Slavery to Mass Incarceration' (2002) 13 New Left Review 42

White A, 'Capitalism, Social Marginality, and the Rule of Law's Uncertain Fate in Modern Society' (2005) 37 Arizona State Law Journal 759

PART II

BEYOND REVENGE PORNOGRAPHY: FOUNDATIONS OF THE CRIMINALIZATION OF INTIMATE IMAGE ABUSE

6

The Abuse of Sexual Images between Liberal Criminal Law and the Protection of Sexual Autonomy

Anja Schmidt

I. Introduction

Gunter Schmidt, one of the most significant German sexual scientists, wrote in 2014:

> Two discourses determine today's sexual relations in Western industrial societies. One is the *liberal discourse* of the 1960s and 1970s—the 'sexual revolution'—which swept away sexual taboos that had long been disruptive in a democratic society of consumers. The other one is the *autonomy discourse* of the 1980s, which

Anja Schmidt, *The Abuse of Sexual Images between Liberal Criminal Law and the Protection of Sexual Autonomy*
In: *Criminalizing Intimate Image Abuse*. Edited by: Gian Marco Caletti and Kolis Summerer, Oxford University Press.
 DOI: 10.1093/oso/9780198877813.003.0006

> civilized the free 'deregulated' love market that liberalization had created, and controlled male dominance and male definitions in that market.[1]

The successive and successful implantation of the requirements of the legal protection of sexual autonomy was persistently pushed forward by protracted struggles of feminist and homosexual movements.

This quote touches all aspects which are connected to the legal regulation of sexuality in the last sixty years in Western societies. It highlights the step from the legal protection of a unified sexual morality towards a liberal regulation of sexuality. This paradigm shift was an important step towards sexual freedom, but it was closely linked to a market logic and to the maintenance of heterosexual male dominance in the sexual area. It has therefore been harshly criticized by homosexual and feminist movements, which have fought for a consistent legal protection of the equal right to sexual autonomy regardless of gender and sexual orientation.

These discourses on sexuality and its legal regulation have simultaneously been discourses on pornography and its legal regulation, due to the fact that pornography not only stages sexual fantasies but also mirrors and shapes sexual practice. Traditionally, criminal law on pornography protects against the perception of sexual content in order to preserve moral standards regarding sexuality. The sexual revolution liberalized criminal law on pornography; since then, adults have been allowed to produce and use pornographic content, except violent and child pornography. Technological progress allowed professional production of pornography in the 'adult entertainment industry' and easy private use of pornography through videotapes. However, the performers' rights and the misogynistic content of mainstream pornography remained relatively unnoticed. In particular, the women's movement has repeatedly denounced exploitative conditions in the porn industry and the promotion of misogynistic ideas of sexuality through pornographic content. At the same time, alternative, feminist, and queer pornography emerged, staging sexuality beyond exploitative and heterosexist gender stereotypes and, in this way, wishing to promote sexual autonomy. This development has been facilitated by digitalization. However, digitalization also facilitates the abusive production and use of sexual content through image-based sexual abuse, among others.

In this chapter, I will explain how the discourse around pornography has evolved from moralization, to liberalization, to a discourse of autonomy and how this affects legal regulation of sexual content. It especially focuses on the abuse of sexual images in this context as one of the most pressing problems of legal regulation of sexual content in today's world.

Firstly, the development of German criminal law on sexual offences is described as a paradigm shift from a moralizing to a liberal criminal law and the change from a liberal criminal law to the effective protection of sexual autonomy by law.

[1] Gunter Schmidt, *Das neue Der Die Das: Über die Modernisierung des Sexuellen* (4th edn, Psychosozial-Verlag 2014) 8 (translation and emphasis by the author).

Secondly, these considerations are concretized for the development of criminal law on pornography as part of criminal law on sexual offences. Thirdly, the way in which the abuse of sexual images infringes the right to sexual autonomy of the depicted person, although the body of this person is not touched, is explained. Finally, conclusions are drawn for a legal regulation of sexual images that effectively protects the right to sexual autonomy of the person depicted. The example of German law reveals developments and figures of argumentation that exemplify the development of the legal regulation of sexuality and sexual images in the Western world.

Below, I shall use the term *sexual content* as an umbrella term for all forms of sex-related presentation. This can be sexually explicit but also educational content. I use the term *obscene content* for content which, because of its relation to sexuality, violates prevailing sexual moral beliefs where only one sexual moral standard is socially recognized, as was the case in Western countries until well into the twentieth century. The term *pornography* refers, in particular, to sexually explicit content aimed at the arousal of a sexual stimulus. The terms *obscene* and *pornographic* have negative connotations because they are part of a tradition of excluding sexuality from private and public communication. The term *sexual content* is intended to provide a more neutral approach in order to be able to evaluate sexual content in a more diversified manner regarding its liberal-emancipatory potentials on the one hand and its harmful potentials on the other.

II. The Development of the Law on Sexual Offences in the Western World

Monika Frommel, an important German legal scientist, described the paradigm shift from a criminal law protecting a unified sexual moral to a liberal criminal law on sexual offences very concisely:

> Since the 1970s, an outdated and overly monistic sexual morality has been replaced for the first time by an individualized concept of sexuality.[2]

Traditionally, sexual offences law protected a unified sexual moral standard shaped by heterosexual and male dominance. Anything that contradicted the prevailing moral sexual standard was forbidden as obscene (in German 'unzüchtig'). For instance, sexual acts were restricted to marriage, in which the wife had to be submissive to the husband; homosexual acts of men were forbidden; and it was forbidden to produce, distribute, and consume obscene content.

[2] Monika Frommel, 'Vorbem. zu §§ 174 ff. §§ 174-184j StGB' in Urs Kindhäuser, Ulfrid Neumann and Hans-Ullrich Paeffgen (eds), *Strafgesetzbuch: Nomos-Kommentar* (5th edn, Nomos 2017) § 177 Rn 6 (translation by the author).

The liberal discourse led to the conviction of broader parts of society that the state and the law should not interfere with sexuality, it being a part of the private life of citizens. Sexuality should be an area in which each person should act according to their own sexual preferences and moral beliefs. In Germany, the 4th Criminal Law Reform Act (4. Gesetz zur Reform des Strafrechts vom 23. November 1973) came into force in 1974, and was intended to remove the concept of obscenity from sexual criminal law and to focus on the protection of individual sexual freedom. For instance, citizens should be able to freely decide whether they have sex outside of marriage or the sexual content they wish to use.

The guarantee of individual freedom in the sexual sphere was indeed an important step towards ensuring sexual autonomy because the freedom of acting according to one's own sexual preferences and moral ideas is an indispensable aspect of sexual autonomy. However, guaranteeing liberal freedom by law is not enough to ensure sexual autonomy. The reason is that liberalization has maintained the sexual area as a space of male and heterosexual dominance, but it does not effectively protect the conditions of sexual autonomy for all people by law. This can be illustrated by two paradigmatic examples. Only since 1994 have homosexual acts been treated the same as heterosexual acts in German criminal law[3] and until 1997, the rape of men and the rape of a wife by her husband was not punishable as a sexual act in the private sphere.[4] Thus, sexual liberty meant only the sexual freedom of heterosexual men.

The need for an effective legal guarantee of sexual autonomy for all people by law was strongly demanded by feminist and homosexual movements. Although there were also doubts as to whether the patriarchal state could guarantee sexual autonomy for all, the demands for the formal and material guarantee of equal sexual rights for everyone prevailed. Sexual autonomy is thus closely linked to a right to non-discrimination. It includes the right to sexual autonomy with respect for the sexual rights of other people, which is guaranteed regardless of their gender and sexual orientation. Sexual rights are closely linked to gender and sexual orientation because 'gender is sexual', as Catharine MacKinnon stated,[5] and I would like to add that sexuality is gender(ed). The guarantee of the right to sexual autonomy must counter the male and heterosexual dominance to ensure that all people enjoy the same conditions for an equal sexual life. As long as sexuality is gendered, the regulation of sexuality is also a question of gender justice.

It should be emphasized that the demand for effective protection of sexual autonomy does not represent a step back towards moralization. It is true that this concept requires state regulation of the private sphere, for example, by means of criminal prosecution of marital rape. However, this only serves to protect the conditions of sexual autonomy for each person and thus to enable individual moral

[3] With the 29. Strafrechtsänderungsgesetz—§§ 175, 182 StGB of 31 May 1994, BGBl. I 1994, 1168.

[4] Abolished by the 33. Strafrechtsänderungsgesetz of 1 July 1997, BGBl. I 1997, 1607.

[5] Catharine A MacKinnon, *Towards a Feminist Theory of the State* (1st edn, Harvard University Press 1989) 197 (hereafter MacKinnon, *Towards a Feminist Theory of the State*).

decisions in the area of sexuality for each person equally. This is not moralizing, but necessary to guarantee the right to sexual autonomy and the right to non-discrimination. Thus, legal regulation of the private sphere cannot be equated with moralizing regulation.

III. The Development of Liberal Criminal Law on Sexual Depictions

The evolution of criminal law on sexual offences from a moralizing to a liberal law to an effective protection of sexual rights is also reflected in the development of the regulation of sexual content.

A. Moralizing Criminal Law on Sexual Depictions

In a moralizing concept of the regulation of sexuality, sexual depictions were usually prohibited as obscene. Content showing sexuality in a way that contradicted prevailing moral concepts was considered obscene in this context. For instance, the 3rd International Convention for the Suppression of the Circulation of and Traffic in Obscene Publications of 12 September 1923[6] obligated the State parties to, among others, take all measures to discover, prosecute and punish any person engaged in making or producing or having in their possession obscene writings, drawings, prints, paintings, printed matter, pictures, posters, emblems, photographs, cinematographic films or any other obscene objects for the purposes of, or by way of, trade or for distribution or public exhibition. Therefore, the evaluation as obscene was linked to the subject matter of the depiction, i.e. it does not depend on the circumstances of the production of the content, but on the fact that its content is considered offensive.

This concept of obscene content aimed at excluding sexuality from private and public communication to protect prevailing moral concepts. Thus, the perception of sexual content which endangers prevailing sexual standards in a society should be prevented. It could thereby encompass many things regarding sexuality, such as images of a naked person or of sexual acts, or even information on contraceptive methods. For instance, the so-called German 'Lex Heinze' of 25 June 1900[7] extended the prohibition of obscene ('unzüchtige') writings to objects intended for lewd use, insofar as these were exhibited in places accessible to the public or

[6] Available at <https://treaties.un.org/doc/Treaties/1923/09/19230912%2006-01%20AM/Ch_VIII_03p.pdf> accessed 17 February 2023.

[7] Gesetz betreffend Änderungen und Ergänzungen des Strafgesetzbuches of 25 June 1900, RGBl 1900, 301.

were announced or advertised to the public. This included, among other things, objects intended for sexual intercourse, also for contraception, such as condoms, pessaries, or diaphragms, and was the result of a tradition of protecting a unified sexual moral standard by law.[8]

B. The Paradigm Shift to a Liberal Criminal Law on Sexual Depictions

Liberalization of criminal law on sexual offences led, in the field of sexual content, to the freedom to produce, distribute and consume sexual content of various kinds, for instance, sexual education content, literary sexual representations or sexually explicit images. Under this approach, the handling of sexual content may be prohibited only for certain high-level purposes, for example, to protect children from coming into contact with, and from being abused for the production of, sexual content. The liberal paradigm shift also became clear in the naming of problematic content. Some sexual content is described differently, for instance, as education on contraception and the prevention of sexually transmitted diseases, or sexual education material. Sexually explicit content aimed at arousing a sexual response is now more likely to be labelled as pornographic. For example, under art. 34 lit. c) of the Convention on the Rights of the Child of 20 November 1989, States are required to take all appropriate measures, including legislative, administrative, social, and educational measures, to protect children from exploitative use in pornographic performances and materials. The Council of Europe Convention on the Protection of Children against Sexual Exploitation and Sexual Abuse of 25 October 2007 (Lanzarote-Convention) requires in art 20 par. 1 that each convention party shall take the necessary legislative or other measures to ensure criminalization of producing, offering or making available, distributing or transmitting, and possessing child pornography, and, through information and communication technologies, knowingly obtaining access to child pornography and procuring child pornography for oneself or for another person.

The liberal concept is also linked with the evaluation of the subject of a representation. However, in contrast to a moralizing concept of law, the liberal concept is not about protecting prevailing moral concepts by banning certain content, but about protecting rights that are primarily endangered by the consumption of this content. In particular, it is asked whether the consumption of the content is dangerous for the development of minors or whether its imitation results in dangers for others, for instance, by imitating child pornography through sexual abuse. Therefore, under the liberal concept, adults are usually allowed to produce,

[8] Johannes AJ Brüggemann, *Entwicklung und Wandel des Sexualstrafrechts in der Geschichte unseres StGB* (1st edn, Nomos 2013) 412 ff.

distribute, and consume pornographic content, except violent and child pornography. In addition, minors are protected from access to pornography.

The more liberal handling of sexual content has been one important and indispensable step towards sexual autonomy because it helps to deal with sexuality communicatively by means of the media. In this way, for example, materials for education on sexuality, contraception, and the prevention of sexually transmitted diseases, which are an important prerequisite for sexual autonomy, become freely available. However, liberalization of the regulation of sexual content has also maintained free space for male and heterosexual dominance, just as the sexual revolution did in general. With the release of pornographic content for adults, the porn industry or 'adult entertainment industry' grew. In the 1970s, films like 'Deep Throat' (USA 1972) had great success in the US.[9] The advent of videotapes enabled undisturbed and frequent private consumption of pornography, thus fostering the so-called adult entertainment market and industry. Freely available mainstream pornography depicted primarily heterosexual sexuality, with men in the role of sexual subjects and women in the role of freely available sexual objects—'Man fucks woman. Subject verb object' as Catharine A MacKinnon pointedly put it.[10]

C. The Feminist Struggle for Sexual Autonomy Regarding Pornography

Feminist movements denounced in particular the misogyny of mainstream pornography and analysed pornography as 'a form of forced sex, a practice of sexual politics, an institution of gender inequality'; as well as rape and prostitution pornography 'institutionalizes the sexuality of male supremacy'.[11] MacKinnon considered pornography as a form of sexual and economic exploitation of women by men.[12] This, in her view, is not only the exploitation of porn actresses in the process of producing pornography, but also the effects of pornography: 'What pornography does, it does in the real world.'[13] What men see in pornography, they act out on women in the real world.[14] Together with anti-pornography activist Andrea Dworkin, she developed the Model Antipornography Civil Rights Ordinance which aimed to enable women to take direct civil action against pornography as a practice of sexual discrimination.

This position was heavily criticized, including by feminists. These conflicting feminist positions came to a head in the so-called 'feminist sex wars' that were waged

[9] In her autobiography 'Ordeal', the leading actress Linda Susan Boreman (Linda Lovelace) accused her then husband Chuck Traynor of having forced her to take part in the film.

[10] MacKinnon, *Towards a Feminist Theory of the State* (n 5) 124.

[11] ibid 197.

[12] ibid 195.

[13] Catharine A MacKinnon, *Only Words* (Harvard University Press 1996) 15.

[14] See, among others, ibid 20.

primarily in the 1980s and 1990s.[15] The feminist PorNO position was evaluated as a moralizing concept that would turn against marginalized groups, because it makes it impossible to produce and disseminate sexual images that stand for an autonomous sexuality of women and other marginalized groups. Nadine Strossen found that pornography was a way to address sexuality in the first place, to learn about the body and one's own sexual possibilities.[16] Ellen Willis also pleaded for distinguishing different qualities of pornography and considering it as a form of sexual fantasy.[17] Thus, it was disputed that pornography is a form of direct violence against women because it involves a staging of sexuality that reflects and can influence notions of sexuality but cannot control sexual actions according to the stimulus-response scheme.

In 1989 Linda Williams published her book '*Hard Core*' in which she pointed out that mainstream content is also staged, representing a thoroughly fragile male sexuality. This more neutral analysis of pornography became the starting point of porn studies which explore pornography as a phenomenon of popular culture.[18]

In the dissociation from the radical feminist movement, which, among other things, campaigned against pornography, the so-called sex-positive feminist movement developed, in the context of which women and queer people, amongst others, have been using technical progress to produce, distribute, and consume sexually explicit depictions to promote sexual practice beyond gender stereotypes. Since 2006, the Feminist Porn Award has been presented in North America, initiated by the Good for Her adult store in Toronto (Canada) which has existed since 1997.[19] The regular awarding of the European Feminist Porn Award PorYes followed in 2009.[20] It can be said that there is a thriving effort to produce and distribute non-discriminatory sexually explicit content, even if this is unlikely to challenge the dominance of traditional misogynistic pornography.

Both feminist positions focus on important aspects of sexual autonomy in the field of sexual content. The feminist movement against pornography (PorNO) highlights the negative impact of misogynist mainstream pornography on the ideas of sexuality, sexual behaviour, and aggressiveness, even if it cannot be assumed that pornography directly controls attitudes and behaviour. The misogyny of mainstream pornography and its impact on dominant gender role stereotypes

[15] See in detail, Lisa Duggan and Nan D Hunter (eds), *Sex Wars: Sexual Dissent and Political Culture* (10th anniversary edn, Routledge 2006).

[16] Nadine Strossen, *Defending Pornography: Free Speech, Sex, and the Fight for Women's Rights* (Reprint edn, New York University Press 2000) 161 ff.

[17] Ellen Willis, 'Feminism, Moralism and Pornography' in Ann Snitow, Christine Stansell, and Sharon Thompson (eds), *Powers of Desire: The Politics of Sexuality* (Monthly Review Press 1983) 462 ff.

[18] See Feona Attwood and Clarissa Smith, 'Porn Studies: An Introduction' (2014) Porn Studies 1.

[19] Good for Her, 'The Feminist Porn Award: How did it all start?' (Feminist Porn Awards, 13 March 2015) <https://www.feministpornawards.com/blog/the-feminist-porn-awards-how-did-it-all-start/> accessed 17 February 2023.

[20] PorYES und Freudenfluss Network, 'What is this all about?' <https://www.poryes.de/what-is-this-all-about/> accessed 17 February 2023.

and sexual practice are still the subject of empirical research today.[21] Moreover, feminist positions against pornography have shown that pornography production, distribution, and use is not only a moral or private issue, but also a legal one, because it affects the conditions of exercise of the right to equal sexual autonomy of pornography performers and consumers of all genders. The feminist pro-porn movement (PorYES) emphasizes the emancipatory potential of sexually explicit content that can enable women, men, and queer people to develop and practise ideas of sexuality beyond traditional heteronormative gender stereotypes and thus promote equal sexual autonomy and consensual safe sexual practice for all people, regardless of gender and sexual orientation.

D. New Opportunities and Challenges through Digitalization

The expansion of technical possibilities through digitalization brings with it new opportunities and challenges. Digitalization enables any person to produce, share, and consume sexual content in an easy way. It is now easier to find information on sexuality on the Internet and to produce, distribute, and consume sexual content of any kind. This applies to sex-positive content as well as misogynistic or other heteronormative content. Any person may produce sexual content by themselves with digital devices, which enable the production and distribution of amateur pornography on porn platforms on the Internet. The distribution of sexual content produced with little effort via porn platforms is likely to have pushed the traditional porn industry out of the market in the process.[22] This is also accompanied by many new opportunities for abuse.

One of the most pressing problems in this context is the misuse of content that depicts another person in a sexual context without their effective consent, the abuse of sexual images. The abuse of sexual images includes phenomena such as revenge porn, spy cam recordings of sexual acts, naked bodies or genitals, upskirting, downblousing, and sextortion. Such unauthorized content can be easily produced

[21] See, among others, Nicky Stanley and others, 'Pornography, Sexual Coercion and Abuse and Sexting in Young People's Intimate Relationships: A European Study' (2018) Journal of Interpersonal Violence 2919 ff; Paul J Wright, Robert S Tokunaga, and Ashley Kraus, 'A Meta-Analysis of Pornography Consumption and Actual Acts of Sexual Aggression in General Population Studies' (2016) Journal of Communication 183 ff; Gert M Hald, Neil N Malamuth, and Theis Lange, 'Pornography and Sexist Attitudes among Heterosexuals' (2013) Journal of Communication 638 ff; Gert M Hald, Neil M Malamuth, and Carlin Yuen, 'Pornography and Attitudes Supporting Violence against Women: Revisiting the Relationship in Nonexperimental Studies' (2010) Aggressive Behavior 14 ff; Jochen Peter and Patti M Valkenburg, 'Adolescents' Exposure to Sexually Explicit Internet Material and Notions of Women as Sex Objects: Assessing Causality and Underlying Processes' (2009) Journal of Communication 407 ff; Norbert Mundorf and others, 'Effects of Sexually Explicit Media' in Raymond W Preiss and others (eds), *Mass Media Effects Research: Advances through Meta-Analysis* (Lawrence Erlbaum Associates Publishers 2007).

[22] Revealing is the 2017 documentary: Ovidie, *Pornocracy: The New Sex Multinations* (Magneto Presse, Fatalitas Productions 2017).

by means of easy-to-use digital devices and distributed via porn platforms without the depicted person knowing about it. The unauthorized production and sharing of sexual content depicting another person is also a new form of cyberbullying and domestic violence.

E. New Concept of the Protection of Sexual Autonomy Regarding Sexual Content

The change to an effective protection of sexual autonomy in the context of handling of sexual content allows a diversified evaluation of the legal regulation of sexual content which is not only linked to an evaluation of the subject of the content. In addition to the traditional problems associated with pornography, the challenges resulting from digitalization also have to be taken into account.

There is the need for a diversified view on sex-related content that equally guarantees the right to produce and use sex-related content as an expression of the right to sexual self-determination and that protects against violations of the right to sexual self-determination, the right to one's own image etc, through the production and use of sex-related content. An effective protection of sexual autonomy when dealing with sexual content means the guarantee of the right to produce and use sexual content for different purposes, for instance to become sexually aroused, to learn something about sexuality, to entertain oneself, to communicate with others sexually or about sexuality, or to earn money. In the field of sexual content, sexual autonomy is closely related to the freedom of communication and economic freedom. However, sexual autonomy, like any right of freedom, is not guaranteed without limits, but is restricted by the sexual autonomy and other rights of freedom of others. Therefore, the freedom to produce, share, and consume sexual content can and must be restricted for various reasons.

Firstly, it may be legitimate to protect minors from accessing sexual content. This requires a diversified view of the content. For example, it is not reasonable to prevent access to materials that are age-appropriate for sexual education, while access to sexually explicit mainstream materials should be prohibited, especially if it could enhance pornography addiction and if it conveys misogynist gender-stereotypical or other discriminating notions of sexuality.

Secondly, it may be legitimate to prevent dangerous impacts on consumers when the consumption may lead to sexual violence. For this reason, conventionally, the handling of violent pornography and child pornography is prohibited. However, this presupposes assumptions on the effects of pornography consumption that are controversial, because no direct link can be established between pornography consumption and the use of sexual violence.

Thirdly, it is mandatory to prohibit the production, sharing, and consumption of content that portrays a person in a sexual manner without that person's effective consent. This reason allows bans on sexual content not because of its subject matter, but because of the circumstances of its production and use. That is why sexually explicit content is not always problematic. Adults are free to produce, share, and consume sexual content as long as it shows persons who gave their effective consent to this. However, it should be strictly forbidden to produce, share, and consume sexual content which depicts another person who has not effectively consented to this. In addition to image-based sexual abuse, this includes real child and violent pornography.

Fourthly, the circumstances of production are also relevant in the case of exploitation of porn actresses and actors. As both cases concern the provision of sexual services for remuneration, this aspect needs to be discussed in the context of prostitution and its legal regulation.

IV. Abuse of Sexual Images

These considerations raise many questions regarding pornography and its legal regulation: How does sexually explicit content influence attitudes towards and the practice of sexuality? What influences do sexual education and the promotion of pornography and media literacy have on the use of pornography? How can one determine whether or not a content promotes equal sexual autonomy and consensual sexual practice without discrimination? To whom may sexually explicit content be accessible, even when it depicts consensual self-determined sexuality? When is a porn actress or actor exploited and how can this be legally combated? In the context of this chapter, however, I would like to take a closer look at the unauthorized production, sharing, or use of images of a person who is depicted naked or in a sexual context without consent.

A. Sexual Privacy

Danielle Citron expanded the concept of privacy to include the realm of sexuality as sexual privacy. She states that:

> [S]exual privacy concerns the social norms governing the management of boundaries around intimate life. It involves the extent to which others have access to and information about people's naked bodies (notably the parts of the body associated with sex and gender); their sexual desires, fantasies, and thoughts;

> communications related to their sex, sexuality, and gender; and intimate activities (including, but not limited to, sexual intercourse).[23]

It constructs sexual privacy in parallel to, among other things, the boundaries we set to access personal data. Accordingly, unlike other types of privacy, sexual privacy has a special value, because it enables and protects sexual autonomy, identity development, and intimate relationships: 'With sexual privacy, individuals determine the contexts in which their naked bodies are seen, recorded, photographed, or exhibited. They can decide if and to what extent their intimate information will be revealed, published, or disclosed. They can choose to tell another person about their sexual orientation, gender, or sexual history.'[24]

In the context of German constitutional law, Dana-Sophia Valentiner and I concretized the right to free development of one's personality (Recht auf freie Entfaltung der Persönlichkeit) as a person's authority to dispose of content that reflects them in a sexual manner. In this construction, the right to sexual autonomy and the right to one's own image merge into each other. A person's authority to dispose of content that reflects them in a sexual manner is constructed similarly to the power of disposal over personal data in general. The inclusion of the right to sexual autonomy makes it possible to grasp why content that reproduces a person naked or in a sexual manner affects one's sexual autonomy in a specific way when this area of disposition is infringed without consent.[25]

Using the example of sexual harassment and the abuse of sexual images, Boris Burghardt, Leonie Steinl, and I pointed out that sexual autonomy has a non-physical dimension, that is, that persons are vulnerable in their sexual autonomy even if they are not physically touched. The reason for this is that sexual autonomy, like autonomy in general, is formed by social interaction and can thus also be violated by non-physical assaults, through any form of social interaction, such as words or the misuse of personal sex-related content. Therefore, the abuse of intimate images also violates the right to sexual autonomy. It violates the status of a person who should be able to determine for themselves how they appear sexually to others and it objectifies them sexually.[26] Since nude and sexual images of a person can also serve to express oneself sexually, Nicola Henry, Clare McGlynn, Asher

[23] Danielle K Citron, 'Sexual Privacy' (2019) 128 Yale Law Journal 1870 (hereafter Citron, 'Sexual Privacy'). See also Chapter 2 in this volume by the same author.

[24] Citron, 'Sexual Privacy' (n 23) 1882.

[25] See Dana-Sophia Valentiner, *Das Grundrecht auf sexuelle Selbstbestimmung: Zugleich eine gewährleistungsdogmatische Rekonstruktion des Rechts auf freie Entfaltung der Persönlichkeit* (Nomos 2021) 399 ff; Anja Schmidt, *'Missbrauchsdarstellungen' statt 'Kinderpornographie'? Rechtliche Expertise zur Ersetzung der Begriffe der Kinder- und Jugendpornographie in den §§ 184b, 184c StGB* (Erstellt für die Landtagsfraktion der FDP in Nordrhein-Westfalen 2022) 26 ff.

[26] See Boris Burghardt, Anja Schmidt, and Leonie Steinl, 'Der strafrechtliche Schutz der sexuellen Selbstbestimmung vor nicht-körperlich wirkenden Beeinträchtigungen' (2022) JuristenZeitung 503 ff.

Flynn, and others accurately designate the abuse of sexual images as 'breaches of an individual's fundamental rights to dignity and privacy, as well as their freedom of sexual expression and autonomy'.[27]

Moreover, all these concepts emphasize a relationship between sexual autonomy or sexual privacy and subordination, for instance, regarding gender, race, and sexual orientation. Accordingly, sexual privacy infringements have a more serious impact on women, sexual minorities, and non-whites.[28] Therefore, the right to non-discrimination also plays an important role in the evaluation of the abuse of sexual images.[29]

B. The Concept of Abuse of Sexual Images

A network of British, Australian, and New Zealand scholars, among others Nicola Henry, Clare McGlynn, and Asher Flynn, developed the concept of image-based sexual abuse.[30] Image-based sexual abuse in this framework includes non-consensual taking or sharing of nude or otherwise sexual images and threatening to share such images. Abusive behaviours cover the use of artificial intelligence and other manipulation techniques.[31] I agree with this definition, but I would like to add that child pornography depicting a real child in a sexual way[32] and depictions of real sexual assaults are also a form of abuse of sexual images. This is because in all these cases, the right of a person to decide for themselves whether or not they are portrayed in a sexual manner is violated.

The abuse of sexual images infringes the sexual privacy of a person as the right to sexual autonomy and the right to one's own image. This does not depend on whether what is shown is legal or not. Rather, it depends on the fact that the person depicted in a sexual context has not effectively consented to the production, sharing, or use of that content. If the content shows something illegal, such as the sexual abuse of a child or sexual assault on an adult, the infringement by making, sharing, and using the content is ancillary to the sexual abuse as such. This is because documenting the abuse or assault also violates the rights of the person

[27] Nicola Henry and others, *Image-based Sexual Abuse: A Study on the Causes and Consequences of Non-consensual Nude or Sexual Imagery* (Routledge 2021) 50 (hereafter Henry and others, *Image-based Sexual Abuse*).

[28] See Citron, 'Sexual Privacy' (n 23) 1890.

[29] See Burghardt, Schmidt, and Steinl, 'Sexuelle Selbstbestimmung' (n 26) 504.

[30] See especially Henry and others, *Image-based Sexual Abuse* (n 27).

[31] ibid 4 ff.

[32] Commonly defined as 'any representation, by whichever means, of a child engaged in real … explicit sexual activities or any representation of the sexual parts of a child for primarily sexual purposes', from Art 2(c) of the Optional protocol to the Convention on the Rights of the Child (CRC) on the sale of children, child prostitution and child pornography (2000); see also Art 20 p 2 of the Council of Europe Convention on the Protection of Children against Sexual Exploitation and Sexual Abuse (2007) CETS 201 (hereafter Lanzarote-Convention).

depicted due to the fact that the abuse is documented and made available to others. This is why these contents are also problematic per se.

This aspect not only concerns phenomena such as upskirting, downblousing, revenge porn, or spy cams in toilets, but also real child pornography which depicts sexual abuse and depictions of real sexual assaults. For this reason, bans on sexual content are allowed not because of its subject but because of the circumstances of its production and use. Children are not able to effectively consent to the production, sharing, and use of contents which depict them in a sexual manner, in order to protect their sexual privacy as a space for growing into sexual autonomy. Adults depicted in a situation of sexual assault are also unlikely to effectively consent to being depicted in an image recording. Content depicting sexual abuse or sexual assault infringes their right to sexual privacy in addition to the sexual abuse or sexual assault. Such content is not only problematic due to lack of consent, but also because they document sexual abuse or assault. This is the reason why so-called real child pornography or violent pornography are to be strictly forbidden. Therefore, the concept of image-based sexual abuse should be extended to depictions of sexual abuse of children and sexual assault of adults. Exceptions are conceivable for the sexting of minors for personal use, as they are allowed to perform sexual acts according to the national legal system.[33]

From this perspective, abuse of sexual images does not include cyberflashing with sexual content. It is true that cyberflashing also constitutes a violation of the right to sexual autonomy. However, in the case of cyberflashing with sexual content a person is confronted without consent and this is a form of sexual harassment. Sexual harassment can take different forms, for instance cyberflashing, catcalling, exhibitionism, or the presentation of sexual acts in front of others. In the case of sexual harassment, it is not a question of misuse of images that depict another person sexually, as their right of disposal over the images is not violated. Sexual harassment attempts to invade sexual privacy from the outside, whereas the abuse of sexual content is not only an invasion of sexual privacy, but it is also an impermissible access to information in this sphere.

I prefer the term *sexual images abuse* to *intimate images abuse* because it emphasizes the importance of these images and their abuse for the unfolding of that person through their sexuality. It also includes nude images or images of that person's genitals, even if they are not directly involved in sexual activity. The term intimate does seem better suited to capture content that shows, for example, naked genitals but no sexual interactions. Nevertheless, the unwanted sexualization of a person through the depiction of naked genitals is likely to be in the foreground

[33] See Lanzarote-Convention, art 20, para 3 (n 30) and Directive 2011/92/EU of the European Parliament and the Council on combating the sexual abuse and sexual exploitation of children and child pornography, and replacing Council Framework Decision 2004/68/JHA (2011), art 8, para 3.

here. The term sexual images emphasizes the connection of these contents to sexual autonomy.

C. The Impact on the Lives of the Victims

In their empirical research, the scholars who developed the concept of image-based sexual abuse showed how severe its consequences are for victims and that they hit marginalized groups harder. Although the body of the victims is not compromised by the abuse of sexual images, they experience it partly as if they had been sexually assaulted in a physical way.[34] The victims describe their experience as life-ruining social rupture which can affect everything. The experience is perceived as endlessly ongoing, because every-day victims fear that the images could be discovered by others. Abuse often leads to isolation of the person concerned, because they have lost confidence in social contacts. In some cases, they also begin to avoid the digital space, which deprives them of a space for communicative development.[35]

The scholars showed that the experiences of image-based sexual abuse clearly differed regarding intersections of marginalization, in particular in relation to sexuality, race, ethnicity, and indigeneity. Men and women were equally affected, although the 'dark figure' was not explored. However, the impacts of image-based sexual abuse were experienced differently according to gender.[36] These results are explained with a concept described in 1988 by Liz Kelly: the 'continuum of sexual violence'.[37] Accordingly, women experience a lot of different but interlinked acts of misogyny across their lifetime. Within this framework, 'the impacts and harms experienced in any one incident of sexual violence can connect with, or reinforce or amplify, the impacts of a lifetime of these experiences'.[38]

D. Urgent Necessity of Legal Protection

It is urgently necessary to legally protect victims of the abuse of sexual images as it is a severe violation of the person's right to dispose of content that reflects them in a sexual manner, which covers the right to sexual autonomy; communication rights, including the right to sexual self-expression; the right to one's own image; and the right to non-discrimination. These rights and their conditions must be guaranteed equally to allow everyone freedom of personal and sexual development. Criminal law should include comprehensive prohibitions on the abuse of sexual images

[34] See Henry and others, *Image-based Sexual Abuse* (n 27) 5.
[35] ibid 51 ff.
[36] ibid 34 ff.
[37] Liz Kelly, *Surviving Sexual Violence* (1st edn, John Wiley & Sons 2013) 76.
[38] Henry and others, *Image-based Sexual Abuse* (n 27) 38.

along the lines of existing prohibitions on real child pornography, which is a specific form of abuse of sexual images. Civil law should allow victims to take swift action against the abuse of sexual images, for example by claiming injunctive relief and damages. It should be noted that the traditional means of criminal and civil law are often too slow and ineffective to provide a remedy in the age of digitalization. Therefore, special forms of network regulation are also needed to protect victims, for example through obligations of Internet platforms to delete content or effective reporting procedures to enforce them through, for example, requests for account blocking.[39]

E. Wording

It is generally not advisable to use terms such as pornography or obscenity in connection with the legal regulation of sexual content. This is because they are part of a tradition that tried to suppress sexual content from private and public communication for moralizing reasons. However, this contradicts the idea of sexual autonomy. The problem is not so much that there is sexual content, but rather that it is abused.

In particular, the abuse of sexual images should not be named as pornography or obscene. With both terms, a content is negatively evaluated because it deals with something sexual. But addressing sexual issues is not problematic per se. It can be an expression of sexual autonomy for adults to produce sexually explicit or other sexual content of themselves and others if they agree, and to share it with others if the depicted persons consent. Sexual privacy or the right to sexual autonomy in connection with the right to one's own image is only violated if the person depicted naked or in a sexual manner has not effectively consented to the production, sharing, or use of that content. Furthermore, terms such as pornography and obscene do not consider these circumstances of the production and handling of sexual content. They describe that something sexual is depicted, or the way sexuality is depicted in them, but they do not express the serious violation of the personality rights of the person portrayed.

Therefore, I agree with the arguments of Nicola Henry, Clare McGlynn, Asher Flynn and others who choose the term image-based sexual abuse to address the problem associated with terms like revenge porn or non-consensual porn. In particular, the term porn is a misnomer as it 'misrecognises the harms of image-based sexual abuse and fails to capture the diversity of images, many of which are neither pornographic nor sexually explicit'.[40]

[39] On this topic, see also Chapter 17 in this volume.
[40] Henry and others, *Image-based Sexual Abuse* (n 27) 4.

V. Conclusion

Legal regulation of the handling of sexual content should be based on a diversified concept of sexual autonomy. The right to sexual autonomy includes the right to produce, share, and consume sexual content. This right guarantees the development of personality in the field of sexuality, which depends on communication about sexuality, and this right is limited by the sexual rights of others. Thus, it can be restricted to protect minors in their right to grow into sexual autonomy, to protect against the negative impact of the consumption of sexually explicit content for others, and to protect against exploitation especially in the production of sexually explicit content. The guiding principle of the law should be to ensure the conditions of consensual sexuality. In addition, it must be legally prohibited to make, share, or use content of another person in a sexual context, unless that person has effectively consented. This is a serious violation of their sexual privacy as the right to their own image in conjunction with their right to sexual autonomy. This concerns phenomena such as so-called real child pornography, revenge porn, and upskirting.

In the context of legal regulation of the unauthorized handling of sexual content depicting another person, terms such as pornography or obscene should be avoided due to the fact that they evaluate the way in which sexuality is depicted and do not concern the violation of a person's right to sexual autonomy and the right to one's own image being reproduced in a sexually related manner without their effective consent. There is a need for consistent and full legal protection against the abuse of sexual images, regardless of whether it is child pornography or the unauthorized reproduction of adults in a sexual context. In addition to criminal and civil law regulations, there is a particular need for legal protection regarding the dissemination of such content via the Internet, in particular via porn platforms.

Bibliography

Attwood F and Smith C, 'Porn Studies: An Introduction' (2014) 1(1–2) Porn Studies 1

Brüggemann JAJ, *Entwicklung und Wandel des Sexualstrafrechts in der Geschichte unseres StGB* (1st edn, Nomos 2013)

Burghardt B, Schmidt A, and Steinl L, 'Der strafrechtliche Schutz der sexuellen Selbstbestimmung vor nicht-körperlich wirkenden Beeinträchtigungen' (2022) 77 JuristenZeitung 502

Citron DK, 'Sexual Privacy' (2019) 128 Yale Law Journal 1870

Duggan L and Hunter ND (eds), *Sex wars: Sexual Dissent and Political Culture: 10th Anniversary Edition* (Routledge 2006)

Frommel M, 'Vorbem. zu §§ 174 ff. §§ 174-184j StGB' in U Kindhäuser, U Neumann, and HU Paeffgen (eds), *Strafgesetzbuch: Nomos-Kommentar* (5th edn, Nomos 2017)

Hald GM, Malamuth NM, and Yuen C, 'Pornography and Attitudes Supporting Violence against Women: Revisiting the Relationship in Nonexperimental Studies' (2010) 36 Aggressive Behavior 14

Hald GM, Malamuth NN, and Lange T, 'Pornography and Sexist Attitudes among Heterosexuals' (2013) 63 Journal of Communication 638

Henry N and others, *Image-based Sexual abuse: A Study on the Causes and Consequences of Non-consensual Nude or Sexual Imagery* (1st edn, Routledge 2021)

Kelly L, *Surviving Sexual Violence* (1st edn, John Wiley & Sons 2013)

MacKinnon CA, *Towards a Feminist Theory of the State* (1st edn, Harvard University Press 1989)

MacKinnon CA, *Only Words* (1st edn, Harvard University Press 1996)

Mundorf N and others, 'Effects of Sexually Explicit Media' in RW Preiss and others (eds), *Mass Media Effects Research. Advances through Meta-analysis* (Lawrence Erlbaum Associates Publishers 2007)

Peter J and Valkenburg PM, 'Adolescents' Exposure to Sexually Explicit Internet Material and Notions of Women as Sex Objects: Assessing Causality and Underlying Processes' (2009) 59 Journal of Communication 407

Schmidt A, *'Missbrauchsdarstellungen' statt 'Kinderpornographie'? Rechtliche Expertise zur Ersetzung der Begriffe der Kinder- und Jugendpornographie in den §§ 184b, 184c StGB* (Erstellt für die Landtagsfraktion der FDP in Nordrhein-Westfalen 2022)

Schmidt G, *Das neue Der Die Das: Über die Modernisierung des Sexuellen* (4th edn, Psychosozial-Verlag 2014)

Stanley N and others, 'Pornography, Sexual Coercion and Abuse and Sexting in Young People's Intimate Relationships: A European Study' (2018) 33 Journal of Interpersonal Violence 2919

Strossen N, *Defending Pornography: Free Speech, Sex, and the Fight for Women's Rights* (Reprint edn, New York University Press 2000)

Valentiner DS, *Das Grundrecht auf sexuelle Selbstbestimmung: Zugleich eine gewährleistungsdogmatische Rekonstruktion des Rechts auf freie Entfaltung der Persönlichkeit* (Nomos 2021)

Willis E, 'Feminism, Moralism and Pornography' in A Snitow, C Stansell, and S Thompson (eds), *Powers of Desire: The Politics of Sexuality* (Monthly Review Press 1983)

Wright PJ, Tokunaga RS, and Kraus A, 'A Meta-Analysis of Pornography Consumption and Actual Acts of Sexual Aggression in General Population Studies' (2016) 66(1) Journal of Communication 183

7
Refining the Contours of Intimate Image Abuse Offences

*Thomas Crofts**

I. Introduction

Many jurisdictions have created offences to address invasions of a person's sexual autonomy and dignity through the use of new technologies. However, as technological developments continue to outpace law, and research is unpacking the harms resulting from new ways of causing harm, jurisdictions are comparing notes and re-evaluating whether the offences created to capture intimate image-based abuse are adequate and coherent. While there is now a general understanding about the core types of behaviour that should be subject to criminal sanction, debate continues around the periphery of the elements of established offences. This includes questions such as how far the definition of intimate images should extend, what

* The research for this chapter was supported by a grant from the Research Grants Council of the Hong Kong Special Administrative Region, China (Project No 9043260).

Thomas Crofts, *Refining the Contours of Intimate Image Abuse Offences* In: *Criminalizing Intimate Image Abuse*.
Edited by: Gian Marco Caletti and Kolis Summerer, Oxford University Press.
DOI: 10.1093/oso/9780198877813.003.0007

sort of behaviours should be criminalized, what mental states are the most appropriate for these offences, and what defences should be available. This chapter contributes to that debate by comparatively considering some of the offences recently created in various jurisdictions and recommendations for reform proposed by the Law Commission for England and Wales in its 2022 Report.[1] The starting point of the chapter is an examination of why there should be a focus on both harm and culpability to ensure that the harm to the victim and culpability of the perpetrator are most adequately captured and reflected in any intimate image abuse offences. The chapter then explores how the physical, mental, and defence elements can be defined and balanced to ensure that there is neither over- nor under-criminalization of intimate image abuse.

II. The Need for a Criminal Law Response to Intimate Image Abuse

Initially, the harms associated with the creation and dissemination of intimate images tended to be problematized largely in relation to young people and what has been termed 'sexting'.[2] It was not until the harms caused by intimate image abuse among adults became 'prevalent or entered into public consciousness'[3] and it became clear that existing offences were not adequate to address those harms that jurisdictions began to consider new offences. However, a concern with these early approaches is that offences tended to be created in an ad hoc and patchy way.[4] The result was that offences elements were designed with a specific wrong in mind, which led to a lack of coherency between offences and 'undesirable gaps and limitations and inconsistent application'.[5] Increasing awareness of the extent of wrongful behaviours that new technologies facilitate has prompted a rethink of whether and how criminal law can coherently address the varied ways in which intimate image abuse may be perpetrated.

Criminal law is, of course, not the only means that can be adopted to deter problematic behaviours—and alone it may not be sufficient to help model new ethics around engaging with new and emerging technologies. Furthermore, it may not be able to produce, or provide in a timely fashion, the result that a person subjected to intimate image abuse desires. Nonetheless, the advantage of using criminal law is its deterrent effect. Criminal law aims to prevent conduct that is substantially wrong from occurring through threatening the infliction of criminal

1 Law Commission, *Intimate Image Abuse: A Final Report* (Law Com No 407, 2022) (hereafter Law Commission).

2 See, for instance, Thomas Crofts and others, *Sexting and Young People* (Ashgate 2015) 14, 76 (hereafter Crofts, *Sexting and Young People*).

3 Law Commission, *Intimate Image Abuse: A Consultation Paper* (CP No 253, 2021) [1.29] (hereafter Law Commission, CP).

4 Law Commission (n 1) [1.10].

5 ibid.

sanctions. This threat of punishment of wrongdoers has 'educative, moralizing and habituative' functions.[6] As Andenaes comments, 'with fear or moral influence as an intermediate link, it is possible to create unconscious inhibitions against crime, and perhaps to establish a condition of habitual lawfulness'.[7] The creation of specific offences can then be an important way of communicating, and strengthening, the community's opposition to problematic behaviour.[8] This is particularly important where new technologies present opportunities and challenges which bring about significant social and cultural changes requiring new codes and manners.[9]

However, it is clear that there should be restraints on the use of criminal law to control behaviour 'because it burdens interests not implicated by other modes of social control'.[10] Many scholars are in agreement that criminal law should only be used to censure people for substantial wrongdoing and should only be used as a last resort when other measures are not adequate or appropriate to prevent the behaviour.[11] This means that even if it is decided that certain behaviour amounts to substantial wrongdoing that ought to be prevented it should not be assumed that criminal law must be used and that criminal law is a 'necessarily and effective means of prevention'.[12]

Assessing whether behaviour is substantially wrong involves questions of harm and culpability.[13] Harm focuses primarily on the impact that the behaviour has on individual or collective interests while culpability focuses on the perpetrator and their blameworthiness. Von Hirsch and Jareborg propose that the harmfulness of a behaviour can be assessed based on how much it impacts on the 'living standard' of the individual victim.[14] That is, how much does it adversely effect 'the means and

[6] Gordon Hawkins, 'Punishment and Deterrence: The Educative, Moralizing, and Habituative Effects' (1969) Wisconsin Law Review 550.

[7] Johannes Andenaes, 'The General Preventive Effects of Punishment' (1966) 114 University of Pennsylvania Law Review 950.

[8] See, eg, Commonwealth Parliament of Australia, Senate Legal and Constitutional Affairs Committee, *Phenomenon Colloquially Referred to as 'Revenge Porn'* (Parliamentary Paper No 69, 2016) 50; see also Danielle Keats Citron and Mary Anne Franks, 'Criminalizing Revenge Porn' (2014) 49 Wake Forest Law Review 345, 349 (hereafter Citron and Franks, 'Criminalizing Revenge Porn'); Clare McGlynn and Erika Rackley, 'Image-based Sexual Abuse' (2017) 37(3) Oxford Journal of Legal Studies 534, 553; Thomas Crofts and Tyrone Kirchengast, 'A Ladder Approach to Criminalising Revenge Pornography' (2019) 83 Journal of Criminal Law 87, 94 (hereafter Crofts and Kirchengast, 'ladder Approach'); Gian Marco Caletti, 'Can Affirmative Consent Save "Revenge Porn" Laws? Lessons from the Italian Criminalization of Non-Consensual Pornography' (2021) 25(3) Virginia Journal of Law and Technology 113,162–63.

[9] See Crofts, *Sexting and Young People* (n 2) 11–12.

[10] Douglas Husak, 'The Criminal Law as a Last Resort' (2004) 24 Oxford Journal of Legal Studies 207, 234 (hereafter Husak, 'Last Resort').

[11] See, eg, Andrew von Hirsch, 'Commensurability and Crime Prevention: Evaluating Formal Sentencing Structures and Their Rationale' (1983) 74 Journal of Criminal Law and Criminology 209, 214; Andrew Ashworth, 'Is the Criminal Law a Lost Cause?' (2000) 116 Law Quarterly Review 225, 241, 253 (hereafter Ashworth, 'Lost Cause'); Husak, 'Last Resort' (n 10) 234.

[12] Ashworth, 'Lost Cause' (n 11) 253.

[13] ibid 241.

[14] Andrew von Hirsch and Nils Jareborg, 'Gauging Criminal Harm: A Living-Standard Analysis' (1991) 11 Oxford Journal of Legal Studies 1, 10.

capabilities that would ordinarily help one achieve a good life'.[15] Harms that are 'wrongs that are shared by other members of the community with which the victim is identified and by which her or his identity is partly constituted' can be regarded as a collective harm.[16]

Even when a behaviour is harmful it is generally thought that it should only be subject to criminalization when it is engaged in culpably. Accordingly, offences should usually require proof of some form of subjective mental element before criminal liability is imposed.[17] This is, as pointed out by Hart, because it is only legitimate or fair to convict a person when that person 'has the capacity and a fair opportunity or chance to adjust his behaviour to the law'.[18] Making criminal liability depend on at least advertence to the prohibited behaviour, circumstances, and consequences ensures that criminal law is 'a method of social control that maximises individual freedom within the coercive framework of law'.[19] This is connected to the central idea that criminal law should guide people's behaviour and help them to avoid criminal conduct. Requiring a subjective mental element enhances 'the constitutional values of legality and rule of law' because citizens know that they are only liable to conviction if they intentionally, knowingly, or recklessly cause or risk causing harm.[20] Indeed, as Lacey states, the insistence on subjective fault in criminal law is central to its legitimacy: 'the idea that criminal liability must involve both conduct and responsibility or fault lies at the heart of contemporary criminal law's idea of itself not just as a system of state power and force, but a legitimate—even in some senses a moral—system.'[21]

Despite this general acceptance of the principle that subjective fault should be required to establish liability, it is regarded as a permissive principle.[22] That is, 'depending on the merits in context, it may or may not be right' to apply that principle. This means that there may be contexts where it is acceptable for the evaluation of fault to be made by the judgement of others.[23] In such cases an objective judgement is made that the person can be blamed for their state of mind at the time of the offence, such as failing to think about a circumstance or result when

[15] ibid 33.

[16] Sandra E Marshall and Robin A Duff C 'Criminalization and Sharing Wrongs' (1998) 11 Canadian Journal of Law and Jurisprudence 7, 20–21.

[17] Andrew Ashworth, 'Strict Criminal Liability and Imprisonable Offences' (2010) 45 Irish Jurist 1, 5 (hereafter Ashworth, 'Imprisonable Offences').

[18] Herbert LA Hart, *Punishment and Responsibility* (OUP 1968) 181.

[19] ibid 23.

[20] Jeremy Horder, *Ashworth's Principles of Criminal Law* (9th edn, OUP 2019) 175 (hereafter Horder, *Ashworth's Principles*).

[21] Nicola Lacey, 'In Search of the Responsible Subject: History, Philosophy and Social Sciences in Criminal Law' (2001) 64 Modern Law Review 350, 353.

[22] Horder, *Ashworth's Principles* (n 20) 62.

[23] ibid 175.

the person could and should have done so, or forming a belief based on insufficient consideration of the grounds for that belief.[24]

Without restating the harms associated with intimate image abuse, which has been done elsewhere,[25] it is sufficient here to note that a clear case for criminalization can be made out when applying these principles to a range of forms of intimate image abuse. Non-consensually dealing with intimate images of a person can severely impact on the individual's and collective's ability to lead a good life. In terms of culpability, a perpetrator may deal with an intimate image without thinking about the harm that may be caused to the victim. They may think that they are being playful, or flirty, or they may be driven by their own aims of (sexual, financial, or other) gratification with or without a consideration of the effects of their behaviour on the victim. They may be aware of the harms that can be caused and/or they may intend to cause humiliation, alarm, or distress to the victim. They may act with a further purpose, such as to coerce behaviour or control the subject. A perpetrator may act with none or a combination of these and other beliefs, motivations, or intentions and thus display varying degrees of culpability.

In order to address the serious wrongdoing of intimate abuse, that is, both the harm caused and culpability of the perpetrator, offences must be defined in ways that carefully balance the physical, mental, and defence elements. Overly wide physical elements can extend liability and risk over-criminalization as behaviours may be caught in the offences which are not seriously harmful. This, combined with a low threshold of fault, can lead to relatively inculpable behaviours being subject to criminalization (a wide approach). On the other hand, narrowly defined physical elements combined with a requirement of proof of a high degree of culpability can mean that seriously harmful and culpable behaviours are not criminalized or are difficult to prosecute (a narrow approach). Defences must also be considered in this balance; they can mitigate the criminalizing reach of physical and mental elements and provide specific circumstances in which criminal liability is negated.

The range of offences already created across jurisdictions to address intimate image abuse shows that some have taken a narrow approach, and some have taken a wide approach. Currently, England and Wales take a narrow approach, with a limited definition of the images that fall under the disclosure offence and a requirement for a relatively high degree of subjective fault.[26] Some jurisdictions, particularly in Australia, have taken a broader approach to images that fall within the

[24] Andrew P Simester, 'Can Negligence be Culpable' in Jeremy Horder (ed), *Oxford Essays in Jurisprudence* (4th Series, OUP 2000); Ashworth, 'Imprisonable Offences' (n 17).

[25] See, eg, Clare McGlynn and others, '"It's Torture for the Soul": The Harms of Image-based Sexual Abuse' (2021) 30(4) Social and Legal Studies 541; Samantha Bates, 'Revenge Porn and Mental Health: A Qualitative Analysis of the Mental Health Effects of Revenge Porn on Female Survivors' (2017) 12 Feminist Criminology 22; Nicola Henry and Anastasia Powell, 'Beyond the 'Sext': Technology-facilitated Sexual Violence and Harassment against Women' (2015) 48 ANZ Journal of Criminology 104; Citron and Franks, 'Criminalizing Revenge Porn' (n 8).

[26] Criminal Justice and Courts Act 2015 (UK), s 35 (hereafter CJCA 2015).

scope of intimate image abuse offences and generally have lower fault requirements. Others, such as Hong Kong and Singapore, can be considered to have a more mixed approach, where there is a relatively wide definition of images and behaviours that may fall under the offences combined with a requirement for a relatively high degree of fault.

Based on a comparative review of intimate image abuse offences in various jurisdictions and the reforms proposed by the Law Commission the following explores how offences might be designed and structured to optimally balance offence elements to address the varied harms and states of culpability in relation to intimate image abuse. It begins by examining what sort of images should be covered by intimate image abuse offences and then discusses the element that marks out the core wrong in relation to intimate image abuse—the lack of the subject's consent. This is followed by consideration of the behaviours that should be subject to criminalization and the fault elements that should be required (including whether there should be variations in offences based on fault elements). Finally, there is an examination of what factors should negate liability.

III. What Type of Images Should be Covered by Intimate Image Abuse Offences?

A. Sexual, Nude–Semi-nude, Private

Currently, in England and Wales a relatively narrow range of images fall under the disclosure offence, namely a photograph or film of a private sexual nature.[27] The image must depict something that is not of a kind ordinarily seen in public and show all or part of an individual's exposed genitals or pubic area; something that a reasonable person would consider to be sexual because of its nature; or something that, taken as a whole, has a content that a reasonable person would consider to be sexual.[28] Other jurisdictions, particularly those that have more recently adopted intimate image abuse offences, such as New South Wales (NSW), Western Australia (WA), Singapore, and Hong Kong, generally define an intimate image more broadly to cover not just sexual but also private images. This includes images of a person's private parts (the genital or anal area or the breasts) or images of a person engaged in a private act (in a state of undress, using the toilet, showering or sunbathing, engaged in a sexual act of a kind not ordinarily done in public, or a similar activity).[29]

[27] CJCA 2015 (n 26) s 33.

[28] ibid s 35.

[29] Crimes Act 1900 (NSW), s 91N (hereafter CA 1900); Criminal Code (WA), s 221BA (hereafter CCWA); Penal Code (Sing), ss 377BE(5), 377C(3)(f) (hereafter PC Sing); Crimes Ordinance, Cap 200 (HK), s 159AA (hereafter CO Cap 200).

The Law Commission proposes a broader approach to what should be considered an intimate image, similar to that in the jurisdictions noted above. It would encompass 'an image that is sexual, nude, partially nude, or a toileting image'.[30] Sexual is defined in the same way as above.[31] A nude or partially nude image would include 'images of all or part of a person's genitals, buttocks or breasts,[32] whether exposed, covered with underwear or anything being worn as underwear, or where the victim is similarly or more exposed than if they were wearing only underwear'.[33] A toileting image would be one showing a person using a toilet or engaging in person care related to using a toilet.[34]

There are concerns that such a wide definition of an intimate image could lead to overreach of the criminal law. These concerns can be addressed by adding a condition which excludes images that are not considered inherently intimate. The condition proposed by the Law Commission is that an image will not be regarded as intimate where it shows 'something ordinarily seen on a public street' (except breastfeeding).[35] Other elements which are designed to prevent overreach include a requirement that such image shows a person in circumstances in which a reasonable person would expect to be afforded privacy (eg in NSW).[36] In South Australia (SA), to reduce the possibility of overreach, an image will not be regarded as 'invasive' (the term used in SA) where it 'falls within the standards of morality, decency and propriety generally accepted by reasonable adults in the community'.[37]

B. Altered Images

Technological advancement has made it increasingly easy to amend images, such as manipulating an image of a person's face and mapping it onto a pornographic image or using technology to strip clothing from an image ('sexualized photoshopping', 'nudification, and 'deepfakes').[38] The technology, which is freely available, is now so advanced that it can be impossible or very difficult to detect that the image is not real. The Law Commission found that there is an astonishing and growing prevalence of 'deepfakes' and that there is a high demand for 'deepfake pornography'.[39] In recognition of this, many jurisdictions, especially those that

[30] Law Commission (n 1) Recommendation 9, [3.211].
[31] ibid Recommendation 1, [3.67].
[32] ibid Recommendation 6, [3.161].
[33] ibid Recommendation 6, [3.161].
[34] ibid Recommendation 7, [3.180].
[35] ibid Recommendation 12, [3.300].
[36] CA 1900 (n 29) s 91N(1).
[37] Summary Offences Act 1953 (SA), s 26A(3).
[38] Law Commission, CP (n 3) [3.15]; Alisdair Gillespie, "'Trust Me, It's Only For Me": 'Revenge Porn' and the Criminal Law' (2015) Criminal Law Review 866 (hereafter Gillespie, 'Trust Me, It's Only For Me'); Tyrone Kirchengast, 'Deepfakes and Image Manipulation: Criminalisation and Control' (2020) 29 Information and Communications Technology Law 308.
[39] Law Commission (n 1) [4.222].

have more recently introduced offences, include within the definition of intimate images those images that have been altered so that they appear to show an intimate part or an intimate act of the subject. This is an important extension of the definition of intimate image to address the harm caused, which can be the same as if the image were real. In order to protect victims, but prevent overreach of the criminal law, conditions may be applied, such as in Hong Kong, where the image will be considered an intimate image unless no reasonable person would believe that it shows an intimate part or intimate act of the subject.[40] Similarly, the Law Commission has recommended that the definition includes images 'that are intimate as a result of altering, and that are created (whether by digital or non-digital means) if the altered or created image appears to be an intimate image of a person'.[41]

C. Images Considered Intimate by Certain Groups or because of Circumstances

A more controversial question is whether, and to what extent, images which might be considered intimate within particular religious groups or because of certain circumstances should be included in intimate image abuse offences. Examples of the former are images of a religious person not wearing attire usually worn in public based on religious beliefs to preserve modesty or showing a body part that they would not normally expose in public.[42] Examples of the latter are a not-out gay person kissing or holding hands with someone of the same sex or images of a trans person before transitioning.[43] Such images may harm the subject of those images in similar ways to images more generally understood to be intimate.[44] They may be shared to shame and harass the subject and may lead to the subject being ostracized, harassed, or physically harmed.[45] Threats to share the image may be made with the aim of controlling or coercing the subject.

The question is whether expanding the definition of intimate to bring such images within the proposed offences is appropriate. One approach could be to include a subjective element into the determination of intimate. This, however, raises a number of concerns and questions, primarily that it would make the offence very wide and ambiguous and risk over-criminalization.[46] This is because any image has the potential to be intimate depending on the subject's viewpoint. Other elements, such as combing a subjective assessment with an assessment of the reasonableness

[40] CO Cap 200 (n 29) s159AA.
[41] Law Commission (n 1) Recommendation 21, [4.245]
[42] ibid [3.219].
[43] ibid [3.213].
[44] ibid [3.221].
[45] ibid [3.214], [3.221].
[46] ibid [3.250].

of that assessment, could ameliorate this risk.[47] A specification of the types of matters that can and/or cannot be taken into consideration could address the concern that the objective assessment renders the subjective assessment redundant. Furthermore, the danger of overreach could be addressed through the mental element (discussed below) which could require that the perpetrator intended, knew, or was aware that the image was considered intimate by the subject.

It is possible then to define the elements of intimate image abuse offences in a way that could incorporate such images and address concerns about potential overreach of the criminal law. However, the central question remains whether extending the definition to images which would not generally be understood to be intimate but are regarded as intimate because of the way that they are viewed by certain groups or because of the context of the image would stretch the concept of intimate too far. Such an extension may dilute the core of the offence and would require a deeper discussion of the extent to which invasions of privacy in general should be protected by the criminal law. An alternative approach would be to include such images within a civil penalty regime as is the case under the Commonwealth (federal) law of Australia.[48] It should also be noted that such behaviours could also fall under other offences available,[49] as such, not extending the definition of intimate would not leave those victims without criminal law protection.

IV. What Behaviours Should be Covered?

A. Acting without the Consent of the Subject

The core element that marks out the wrongfulness of intimate image abuse is the subject of the image's lack of consent. Many jurisdictions now provide a definition, in varying degrees of detail, of the meaning of consent and when consent is considered not to have been given. In NSW, for example, the factors which mean that a person does not freely consent to distribution resemble some of the factors which negate consent in relation to sexual activity.[50] These include that the person is under 16 or does not have the cognitive capacity to consent; the person has no opportunity to consent due to unconsciousness or sleep; the person consents because of threats of force or terror; or the person consents because of being unlawfully detained.[51] It is also appropriate to give further clarification to remove ambiguity

47 Such mixed subjective–objective assessments are not unknown to criminal law and can be found, eg, in relation to assessments of provocation, self-defence, and honest and reasonable mistake.

48 Online Safety Act 2021 (Cth), ss 75, 15(4).

49 Such as controlling or coercive behavior in an intimate or family relationship: Serious Crimes Act 2015, s 76.

50 In relation to sexual activity, see CA 1900 (n 29) s 61HJ.

51 ibid s 91O(7).

around what is actually consented to in relation to intimate image abuse. For instance, in NSW, it is stated that consent must be freely given and specific for the particular way in which the image is distributed and to whom it is distributed.[52] Furthermore, consent to recording or distribution on one occasion to a certain person is not to be taken as consent to the distribution of that, or any other, image on another occasion to any other person.

The Law Commission has recommended a similar approach where the consent provisions in relation to sexual offences apply to intimate image abuse offences and that consent relates to a particular instance of taking and sharing and does not extend to additional acts nor to altering an image.[53] Some additional clarification of circumstances indicating that no consent was given, similar to those in relation to sexual activity in NSW, would be appropriate. These might include where the person does not say or do anything to indicate consent; the person gives consent because of coercion, blackmail, or intimidation; or the person gives consent because they are overborne by abuse of a relationship of authority, trust, or dependence.[54]

B. Taking, Making, and Sharing

Intimate image abuse may start with the non-consensual taking of an image. Taking may also occur with the consent of the subject but the image is then dealt with in some way without the consent of the subject, such as sharing. Sharing, sometimes referred to as disclosing or distributing, refers to making an image available to another person.[55] It is relatively uncontroversial that making a subject's intimate image available to another person physically or online without their consent should be subject to criminalization. This applies if the person shows the image to another but does not give up possession of the image. It is the non-consensual showing of the image that causes harm and is thought deserving of criminalization whether or not there is transfer of possession.[56] To add clarity, sharing should also encompass selling, making an image available for access, or entering into an agreement to share the intimate image.[57]

Sharing violates the sexual autonomy and/or dignity of the subject because they have no control over how an intimate image of them is seen and by whom.[58] The Law Commission does not recommend extending the criminal law to secondary

[52] ibid s 91O.
[53] Law Commission (n 1) [8.37], [8.38].
[54] CA 1900 (n 29), s 61HJ.
[55] See, eg, CJCA 2015 (n 26) s 34.
[56] Law Commission (n 1), [4.117].
[57] See, eg, CCWA (n 29) s 221BC.
[58] Law Commission (n 1) [4.117].

sharing, for example sharing information about accessing an intimate image that has already been made available to a third party.[59] This is because, while this amounts to wrongdoing, it is considered less serious than the initial act of making the intimate image available.[60] Furthermore, it was felt that this could extend the reach of the criminal law too far and make it difficult to enforce.[61]

Some other contentious questions discussed by the Law Commission were whether copying, making, and possessing an image should be criminalized.[62] In relation to copying, the Law Commission felt that non-consensually copying an image that had been taken with consent, and so was already in existence, should not be criminalized.[63] This is because in such cases 'the person depicted has control over how they were depicted; they can see the image that was taken and decide, knowing the content, if they want to share it'.[64] Making an image refers to altering an image of a subject without their consent, for example through 'nudification' or 'deepfake technology' to make it appear to be an intimate image of the subject.[65] The Law Commission acknowledged that such behaviours can cause harm to the subject and, indeed, to society in general.[66] Nonetheless, it felt that criminalizing making would not be proportionate to the wrongdoing in the absence of any further behaviours, such as sharing or threatening to share, and without more it would be difficult to prosecute.[67] To an extent, this approach makes sense. Where an image is created the person will usually have done so for some further purpose, such as to share it or threaten to share it, which would found the basis of a sharing or threats to share offence.

C. Possession

There are many ways a person may come into possession of an intimate image, it may have been originally taken with consent, it may have been obtained though hacking a person's device or through downloading from a website (eg a 'revenge pornography site'). The Law Commission acknowledged that non-consensual possession could cause the subject of the image harm. Nonetheless, it recommended against criminalizing possession on the basis that it may be difficult to prosecute

[59] ibid [4.136].
[60] ibid [4.137].
[61] ibid [4.137].
[62] ibid [4.26]-[4.50].
[63] ibid [4.46].
[64] ibid [4.46]. This would be different if the copying (for instance a screenshot from a zoom meeting) created an image that didn't exist before—in which case the Law Commission recommended that it should be classified as taking, [4.50], Recommendation 15.
[65] ibid [4.1]. For background on deepfake technology, see Mika Westerlund, 'The Emergence of Deepfake Technology: A Review' (2019) 9(11) Technology Innovation Management Review 39.
[66] Law Commission (n 1) [4.214].
[67] ibid [4.216].

and without further behaviour it is less harmful and less culpable.[68] In particular, concern was expressed that this could lead to an overreach of the criminal law because of the ease at which the offence might be committed, for example a person can possess an image by doing nothing and could be liable by simply failing to delete an image.[69] It was also noted that when there is further behaviour, such as retaining an image intending to harass threaten, blackmail, or coerce the subject then there are other offences (eg stalking, harassment, or coercive control) or other intimate image abuse offences (eg threatening to share), that could apply.[70]

A model of how to criminalize possession while preventing overreach of the criminal law would be to require a relatively high degree of culpability, such as in Singapore. There it is an offence to possess[71] or gain access to an intimate image of another person knowing or having reason to believe that possessing or accessing the image will or is likely to cause humiliation, alarm, or distress to the person depicted in the image.[72] Such an intention may be difficult to establish where a person merely came into possession of an image and fails to delete it, but may be more readily established where there is an express request to delete the image and a deliberate refusal to do so. This shows the importance of balancing the elements of the offence, where wide physical elements that can be relatively easily satisfied can be combined with a high degree of culpability to ensure that only more egregious behaviours are captured by the offence.

D. Threats

There are a range of situations in which threats to share an intimate image may be made. A threat may be made to force a person to do something they are entitled not to do or prevent them from doing something they are lawfully entitled to do. This may include threats made using an image in the context of an abusive relationship to exert control over the other person, to coerce sexual behaviour or payment (referred to as 'sextortion'), to prevent the person reporting their victimization, or to intimidate or harass the person. Any threat offence should recognize that threats can be made in various ways. They may not always be verbal and explicit, and may also be made conditional on some behaviour by the subject. An example is NSW, where it is an offence to make a threat to distribute an image (even if that image does not exist), which need not be explicitly made but may also be implicit and may be conditional or unconditional.[73] There is no need for proof that the subject of the

[68] ibid [4.275], [4.276].
[69] ibid [4.275].
[70] ibid [4.8].
[71] A person possesses an image in an electronic form if they control access to the image, whether or not they have physical possession: PC Sing (n 29) s 377BD(4).
[72] ibid s 377BD(1)(b).
[73] CA 1900 (n 29), s 91R.

image was put in fear, but rather the offence focuses on the behaviour of the perpetrator and whether they actually intended to cause such fear.

Threat offences tend to balance a wide approach to the physical elements of the offence with a high degree of culpability, such as a requirement that the person intended to cause that other person to fear that the threat will be carried out (as in NSW)[74] or that the threat is knowingly made and the perpetrator knew or ought to have known that the threat will or is likely to cause the other person humiliation, alarm, or distress (as in Singapore).[75] Similar to these approaches, the Law Commission recommends that an offence applies where a threat to share an image is expressly, implicitly, conditionally, or unconditionally made.[76] It includes threats made to the subject or a third party,[77] even if the image does not exist or the threat is impossible to carry out.[78] These relatively wide physical elements are balanced with a requirement for proof of a high degree of culpability (discussed below).[79]

V. What Mental Element Should be Required?

The mental element of an offence focuses on the perpetrator's culpability when engaging in the prohibited behaviour. As noted above, offences which contain wide physical elements can help capture the range of harms that may be caused by intimate image abuse. However, wide physical elements carry the risk of overreach of the criminal law. Conversely, narrow physical elements coupled with a requirement of a high degree of subjective fault can lead to underreach of the criminal law. It is therefore important that all elements of the offences are carefully balanced.

The differences in the harm caused and culpability displayed with intimate image abuse can be reflected in a ladder approach,[80] whereby offences are divided and differentiated based on the gravity of harm caused and degree of culpability of the perpetrator. The Law Commission has noted (in relation to new homicide offences) that this approach ensures 'there is an ascending order of gravity of a clear and just kind'.[81] It is now recommending a similar approach to intimate image abuse with a base offence not requiring any specific intention, a threat offence, and other offences requiring additional fault elements which reflect higher degrees of culpability.

[74] ibid s 91R(2)(b).
[75] PC Sing (n 29), s 377BE(2).
[76] Law Commission (n 1) Recommendation 39, [12.136].
[77] ibid Recommendation 44, [12.193].
[78] ibid Recommendation 39, [12.144]
[79] ibid Recommendation 41, [12.154].
[80] For further discussion, see Crofts and Kirchengast, 'Ladder Approach'.
[81] Law Commission, *A New Homicide Act for England and Wales* (CP No 177, 2005) [2.103].

A. The Base Offence

The Law Commission proposes a base offence to cover a perpetrator intentionally taking or sharing an intimate image of the subject, without the consent of the subject and without reasonably believing that the victim consents.[82] Requiring that the taking or sharing is done intentionally is designed to ensure that the offence only captures culpable behaviour. It recognizes that new technologies mean that it is very easy to complete the physical element with the simple touch or swipe of a button and can be done accidentally, 'for example, by scrolling through a photo album and accidentally sending an intimate image while trying to save it in another location'.[83] Similarly, a person may take or share a photo at a gym or at a beach without realizing that it also depicts someone who is naked.

The proposal that a person would be liable unless they held a reasonable belief that the subject consented would align the offence with the approach to consent in other sexual offences in England and Wales (eg rape, assault by penetration, sexual assault, and causing sexual activity without consent).[84] It is also the approach taken in many Australian jurisdictions. This strikes an appropriate balance in striving to capture harmful and culpable behaviour. Firstly, as stated above, the perpetrator must have intended to take or share an intimate image, thus accidental sharing or sharing without realizing another person is in the image would not lead to liability. Where a person does take or share an intimate image intentionally then in that context not thinking about whether a person consents, or forming a belief in consent that is not based on reasonable grounds, does show a culpable disregard for the sexual autonomy and dignity of the subject that is worthy of criminalization. As the Law Commission notes: '[w]hen sharing an image of someone where there is a connection, even if somewhat remote, between the person sharing and the person depicted, it is right that the person sharing should take steps to ascertain consent.'[85]

Alongside the base offence the Law Commission recommends that there should be a separate offence of threatening to share an intimate image intending to cause, or being reckless as to causing, the subject to fear that the threat will be carried out.[86]

B. Additional Offences Based on Further Intent

Currently, in England and Wales the offence of disclosure requires that the person acts with the intention of causing the subject distress.[87] In Hong Kong and

[82] Law Commission (n 1) Recommendation 23, [6.45].
[83] ibid [5.6].
[84] Sexual Offences Act 2003 (UK), ss 1–4.
[85] Law Commission (n 1) [5.49], Recommendation 23, [6.45].
[86] ibid Recommendation 41, [12.154].
[87] CJCA 2015 (n 26) s 33(1)(b).

Singapore, the offence of publication or threatened publication requires the intention that the publication, or threat thereof, causes humiliation, alarm, or distress to the individual or they know or are reckless about causing such harm.[88] Concern has been expressed that requiring such specific intention can make it difficult to secure a prosecution.[89] A perpetrator can evade liability by asserting that they did not turn their mind to the harm that the victim may suffer or that they had some other intention, such as distributing the intimate image 'for a laugh' or 'to entertain their mates'.[90] Regardless of whether the perpetrator acts with these intentions or no specific intention, harm may be caused to the subject. It is therefore appropriate that a base offence does not require such specific intention. However, where a person does act with an intention to cause harm this reveals a higher level of culpability that deserves marking with a distinct offence.

The Law Commission's proposal is that a separate offence would cover intentionally taking or sharing an intimate image with the intention of causing the subject humiliation, alarm, or distress or with the intention that the person or another person look at the image with the purpose of causing humiliation, alarm, or distress to the subject.[91] The Law Commission also noted that there are websites that 'exist for the purpose of sharing non-consensual intimate images so that people can look at them for the purpose of obtaining sexual gratification'.[92] This is thought to reveal a higher level of culpability which ought to be covered in a further separate offence of intentionally sharing an image with the intention that the perpetrator or another person look at the image for the purposes of sexual gratification.[93]

The Law Commission also considered whether a separate offence should apply to taking or sharing an intimate image with the intention of making a financial gain.[94] The Law Commission recognized the higher degree of culpability (and also increased harm) involved in such cases but recommended against such an offence. One reason for this was the possibility of an overlap between existing offences or other recommended offences (eg where images are taken and shared for pornographic purposes there may be an intention to make a financial gain and acquire sexual gratification).[95] Another reason was that such an intention could be dealt

[88] CO Cap 200 (n 29) s 159AAE(1)(b); PC Sing, ss 377BE(1)(c), 377BE(2)(c).

[89] See Alex Dymock and Charlotte Van Der Westhuizen, 'A Dish Served Cold: Targeting Revenge in Revenge Pornography' (2019) 39 Legal Studies 361; Majid Yar and Jacqueline Drew, 'Image-based Abuse, Non-Consensual Pornography, Revenge Porn: A Study of Criminalization and Crime Prevention in Australia and England & Wales' (2019) 13 International Journal of Cyber Criminology 578; Asher Flynn and Nicola Henry, 'Image-based Sexual Abuse: An Australian Reflection' (2021) 31(4) Women and Criminal Justice 313 (hereafter Flynn and Henry, 'Australian Reflection'); Gillespie, 'Trust Me, It's Only For Me' (n 38).

[90] Commonwealth Parliament of Australia (n 8) [34–35].

[91] Law Commission (n 1) Recommendation 67, [6.67].

[92] ibid [6.70].

[93] ibid Recommendation 25, [6.100].

[94] ibid [10.87].

[95] ibid [6.118].

with as an aggravating factor at sentencing.[96] While this is true, the advantage of a distinct offence is that it clearly labels and packages the particular harm and culpability of the perpetrator.[97] A better approach might therefore make acting with the intention of making a financial gain an alternative mental state to acting for the purposes of sexual gratification.

Another offence considered by the Law Commission would cover taking or sharing an intimate image with the intent to control or coerce the person depicted.[98] This would address 'sextortion', where an image is taken or shared to extort behaviour or money from the subject, and where the image is used to coerce or control in an abusive relationship. While noting that intimate image abuse may often be perpetrated in an abusive relationship and can have a devastating impact,[99] the Law Commission recommended against a distinct offence. This was because existing offences might be better placed to address coercive and controlling behaviours occurring during an abusive relationship.[100] In addition, it was noted that the proposed offences of taking, sharing, or threatening to share an intimate image would cover many such situations.[101] While there is weight to these arguments, there is an educational and communicative advantage in creating offences which specifically mark out and label culpable behaviour,[102] and on this basis it would be preferable to develop a separate offence.

Some are critical of the approach of developing a ladder or hierarchy of offences, with a base offence and offences requiring specific intentions. McGlynn and Rackley argue against this approach on the basis 'there is no evidence that victims suffer more serious harm when the defendant acts with the specific intent'.[103] However, as the Law Commission notes, it is not necessarily the increased harm that is addressed by the specific intent offences but rather the increased culpability of the perpetrator.[104] A further objection expressed by McGlynn and Rackley is that offences requiring specific intentions may quickly become outdated as research identifies new forms of harm,[105] and such offences may not reflect the more prevalent forms of harmful behaviour.[106] Of course, offences should be designed

[96] ibid [6.121].

[97] See Thomas Crofts, 'Criminalization of Voyeurism and "Upskirt Photography" in 'Hong Kong: The Need for a Coherent Approach to Image-based Abuse' (2020) 8(3) Chinese Journal of Comparative Law 505.

[98] Law Commission (n 1), [6.124].

[99] ibid [6.125]

[100] Such as controlling or coercive behaviour or blackmail, ibid [6.165], [6.119].

[101] ibid [6.165].

[102] Crofts (n 97).

[103] Cited in Law Commission (n 1), [6.110]; Clare McGlynn and others, 'Shattering Lives and Myths: A Report on Image-based Sexual Abuse' (July 2019) <https://claremcglynn.files.wordpress.com/2019/06/shattering-lives-and-myths-final.pdf> accessed 10 March 2023.

[104] Law Commission (n 1) [6.110].

[105] ibid [6.58]. The example referred to is 'collector culture' where intimate images of women are collected and traded by men as a means of gaining social status.

[106] ibid [6.58]

to be future proof and able to capture emerging harmful behaviours. However, the fact that new forms of harmful behaviour may emerge that are not within the scope of proposed offences should not prevent the law from specifically addressing those harms that have been identified. In any event, the proposed approach would mean that newly recognized harms could be captured by the base offence. Furthermore, the aim of a hierarchy of offences is to address degrees of harm and or culpability rather than prevalence of the behaviour.[107]

Another argument against a ladder approach is that it would 'create not only a hierarchy of offenses, but a hierarchy of victimization and perpetration based largely on the victim's experience, as opposed to the perpetrator's actions'.[108] Here it should be noted that the additional elements in the higher-level offences relate to the culpability of the perpetrator, not to whether harm is actually caused to the victim. Nonetheless, it is true that requiring proof of any specific intention can make the higher-level offence harder to prosecute. However, where the specific intention cannot be established the prosecution can still rely on the base offence as an alternative. A ladder approach does not mean an all or nothing approach; far from it. Where a higher degree of culpability can be established it is right that this more egregious behaviour is reflected in a higher-level offence. And while higher levels of culpability can be reflected in the sentencing regime, that approach lacks the educative and communicative effect of specifically labelled offences.

Overall then, it is appropriate that there are gradations in the offences in this area. A higher degree of culpability should be reflected in a different, higher level, offence or offences. The importance of this approach has been highlighted by Lord Bingham:

> The interests of justice are not served if a defendant who has committed a lesser offence is either convicted of a greater offence, exposing him to greater punishment than his crime deserves, or acquitted altogether, enabling him to escape the measure of punishment that his crime deserves. The object must be that defendants are neither over-convicted not under-convicted.[109]

VI. What Defences Should be Available?

Defences can mitigate the reach of offences and provide for specific circumstances which should negate liability. This can be particularly important where a wide approach is taken with broadly drawn physical elements and low culpability

[107] Although this may affect deterrent sentencing, see Andrew Ashworth, *Sentencing and Criminal Justice* (6th edn, 2015 Cambridge University Press) 108–09.
[108] Flynn and Henry, 'Australian Reflection' (n 89) 320.
[109] *R v Coutts* [2006] 1 WLR 2154 [12].

requirements. The Law Commission notes that it has proposed a broad base offence which can cover a wide range of behaviours and that this risks capturing non-consensual taking or sharing which, because of the circumstances and nature of the behaviours, is not harmful, causes minimal harm, or is not morally wrong.[110] In such instances the risk of overreach of the criminal law can be mitigated by appropriate defences or exclusion of liability.

Before considering defences it should be noted that there may be physical elements of the offences that can negate liability, for instance, the Law Commission proposes that a 'public element' be included in the base offence to exclude images that were taken in public or previously shared in public.[111]

The Commission proposes that a defence of reasonable excuse should be available to the base offence but not the additional specific intent offences. A similar defence can be found in NSW and WA where a person will not be liable for distributing (or recording in NSW) an intimate image if the image was used for certain listed purposes, or if a reasonable person would consider the conduct of the perpetrator acceptable having regard to factors listed.[112] In NSW and WA, the purposes listed include for a genuine educational, medical, scientific, law enforcement, or legal proceedings purpose, or (in WA) for a media activity purpose without intending harm and with a reasonable belief that distribution was in the public interest.[113] The factors relevant to assessing whether a reasonable person would find the distribution acceptable include the nature and content of the image; the circumstances in which the image was recorded or distributed; the age, intellectual capacity, vulnerability, or other relevant circumstances of the person depicted in the image; the degree to which the accused person's actions affect the privacy of the person depicted in the image; and the relationship between the accused person and the person depicted in the image.[114] Recognizing that there are circumstances in which the distribution of an intimate image is consistent with community standards and should not give rise to criminal liability would be beneficial to guard against overreach of the offence.

After reviewing defences the Law Commission recommended that there should be a non-exhaustive list of the factors to be taken into consideration to determine a reasonable excuse. These are narrower than those in NSW and WA and focus only on the specific purposes rather than providing for a defence based on behaviour that would be considered acceptable by a reasonable person. Such factors include where the perpetrator reasonably believed that the taking or sharing was necessary

[110] Law Commission (n 1) [11.1]

[111] ibid [10.179]. For detail, see Recommendation 32, [10.66]; Recommendation 33, [10.81]; Recommendation 34, [10.178], see also Recommendation 36, [11.219] in relation to images of children of a kind ordinarily shared by family and friends.

[112] CCWA (n 29) s 221BD(3); CA 1900 (n 29) s 91T(1) see also Summary Offences Act 1966 (Vic), s 41DA(3)(b).

[113] CCWA (n 29) s 221BD(3)(a)–(c); CA 1900 (n 29) s 91T(1)(a)–(c).

[114] CCWA (n 29) s 221BD(3)(d); CA 1900 (n 29) s 91T(1)(d).

for the purposes of preventing, detecting, investigating, or prosecuting a crime; the purpose of legal or regulatory proceeding; for the administration of justice; for a genuine medical, scientific, or educational purpose; or was in the public interest.[115] The Law Commission further recommended that the defendant should have the legal burden to establish the defence on the balance of probabilities.[116]

VII. Conclusion

Research continues to bring to public consciousness the range of ways in which intimate images are culpably used which can lead to significant harm to individual and collective interests. The challenge is to create offences that are wide enough to deal with behaviours already identified as harmful and emerging behaviours that may not yet have been recognized as harmful. Offences must also be designed so that they capture behaviours that are sufficiently culpable to be deserving of criminalization without bringing less harmful or less culpable behaviours within the reach of the criminal law. This requires a careful balancing of the physical, mental, and defence elements of any intimate image abuse offences. The ladder approach to offences proposed by the Law Commission largely gets this balance right. The base offence is wide enough to capture the range of situations and scenarios in which a person's sexual autonomy and/or dignity may be violated through the non-consensual taking and sharing of intimate images. A separate threat offence addresses intentionally or recklessly making a person think that an intimate image of them will be shared. The risk of overreach of the criminal law is mitigated by the mental elements, a range of limitations on liability, and a defence of reasonable excuse. Other more serious offences marked by certain specific intentions allow degrees of culpability to be reflected in the offences so that the specific wrongdoing is accurately packaged and labelled. This can enhance the educational and communicative function of the criminal law, which is especially important to help shape manners and ethics around the use of new communication technologies to protect people's sexual autonomy and dignity.

Bibliography

Andenaes J, 'The General Preventive Effects of Punishment' (1966) 114 University of Pennsylvania Law Review 950
Ashworth A, *Sentencing and Criminal Justice* (6th edn, Cambridge University Press 2015)
Ashworth A, 'Strict Criminal Liability and Imprisonable Offences' (2010) 45 Irish Jurist 1
Ashworth A, 'Is the Criminal Law a Lost Cause?' (2000) 116 Law Quarterly Review 225

115 Law Commission (n 1) Recommendation 35, [11.203].
116 ibid [11.204]

Bates S, 'Revenge Porn and Mental Health: A Qualitative Analysis of the Mental Health Effects of Revenge Porn on Female Survivors' (2017) 12 Feminist Criminology 22

Caletti GM, 'Can Affirmative Consent Save "Revenge Porn" Laws? Lessons from the Italian Criminalization of Non-Consensual Pornography' (2021) 25(3) Virginia Journal of Law and Technology 113

Citron DK and Franks MA, 'Criminalizing Revenge Porn' (2014) 49 Wake Forest Law Review 345

Crofts T, 'Criminalization of Voyeurism and "Upskirt Photography" in Hong Kong: The Need for a Coherent Approach to Image-based Abuse' (2020) 8(3) Chinese Journal of Comparative Law 505

Crofts T and Kirchengast T, 'A Ladder Approach to Criminalising Revenge Pornography' (2019) 83 Journal of Criminal Law 87

Crofts, T and others, *Sexting and Young People* (Ashgate 2015)

Dymock A and Van Der Westhuizen C, 'A Dish Served Cold: Targeting Revenge in Revenge Pornography' (2019) 39 Legal Studies 361

Flynn A and Henry N, 'Image-based Sexual Abuse: An Australian Reflection' (2021) 31(4) Women and Criminal Justice 313

Gillespie A, '"Trust Me, It's Only For Me": Revenge Porn' and the Criminal Law' (2015) Criminal Law Review 866

Hart HLA, *Punishment and Responsibility* (OUP, 1968)

Hawkins G, 'Punishment and Deterrence: The Educative, Moralizing, and Habituative Effects' (1969) Wisconsin Law Review 550

Henry N and Powell A, 'Beyond the 'Sext': Technology-facilitated Sexual violence and Harassment against Women' (2015) 48 ANZ Journal of Criminology 104

Horder J, *Ashworth's Principles of Criminal Law* (9th edn, OUP 2019)

Husak D, 'The Criminal Law as a Last Resort' (2004) 24 Oxford Journal of Legal Studies 207

Kirchengast T, 'Deepfakes and Image Manipulation: Criminalisation and Control' (2020) 29 Information and Communications Technology Law 308

Lacey N, 'In Search of the Responsible Subject: History, Philosophy and Social Sciences in Criminal Law' (2001) 64 Modern Law Review 350

Marshall SE and Duff RA, 'Criminalization and Sharing Wrongs' (1998) 11 Canadian Journal of Law and Jurisprudence 7

McGlynn C and others, '"It's Torture for the Soul": The Harms of Image-based Sexual Abuse' (2021) 30(4) Social and Legal Studies 541

McGlynn C and others, 'Shattering Lives and Myths: A Report on Image-based Sexual Abuse' (July 2019) <https://claremcglynn.files.wordpress.com/2019/06/shattering-lives-and-myths-final.pdf> accessed 10 March 2023

McGlynn C and Rackley E, 'Image-based Sexual Abuse' (2017) 37(3) Oxford Journal of Legal Studies 534

Simester AP, 'Can Negligence be Culpable' in J Horder (ed), *Oxford Essays in Jurisprudence* (4th series, OUP 2000)

Von Hirsch and Jareborg N, 'Gauging Criminal Harm: A Living-Standard Analysis' (1991) 11 Oxford Journal of Legal Studies 1

Von Hirsch A, 'Commensurability and Crime Prevention: Evaluating Formal Sentencing Structures and Their Rationale' (1983) 74 Journal of Criminal Law and Criminology 209

Westerlund M, 'The Emergence of Deepfake Technology: A Review' (2019) 9(11) Technology Innovation Management Review 39

Yar M and Drew J, 'Image-based Abuse, Non-Consensual Pornography, Revenge Porn: A Study of Criminalization and Crime Prevention in Australia and England & Wales' (2019) 13 International Journal of Cyber Criminology 578

8

Is This Intimate Image Abuse?

The Harm Principle Delimiting the Criminalization of Virtual Child Pornography and 'Sexting'

Margareth Helfer and Domenico Rosani

I. Introduction

Virtual pornography and self-generated sexual images and videos are clearly pornographic material. Whether virtual or real, they depict a child, or parts thereof, with the aim of stimulating sexual arousal. Objectively, they correspond to the literal definition of child pornography. However, it does not automatically follow from this that they have to be criminally prohibited.

Virtual pornography, for instance, can also be made without resorting in any way to photographs of an existing child. For instance, a drawing stemming completely

Margareth Helfer and Domenico Rosani, *Is This Intimate Image Abuse?* In: *Criminalizing Intimate Image Abuse*. Edited by: Gian Marco Caletti and Kolis Summerer, Oxford University Press. © Oxford University Press 2024. DOI: 10.1093/oso/9780198877813.003.0008

from the imagination of the drawer. Consensual sexual content, on the other hand, is freely generated by the child or by their partner with the child's free consent. Is it reasonable to criminally punish the child for generating or sharing ('sexting') pornographic images of themselves?

This chapter argues that proper respect for the fundamental principles of criminal law, and in particular the harm principle, could challenge the criminalization of fully virtual child pornography and self-generated sexual content. To this end, section II introduces the reader to some cornerstones of the liberal critique to current criminal developments. Section III reflects on Italy's ban on virtual child pornography. Section IV explores the issue of 'sexting', departing from Italian case law and recent international soft law. Section V concludes by discussing the theoretical and practical implications of a strict deference to the harm principle in the field of child pornography.[1]

II. A Liberal Critique against Current Tendencies in Criminal Law

A. Abandoning the Harm Principle

A strong tendency to anticipate criminal protection can be seen in many continental European countries as regards sexually motivated crimes. The protection of the important legal interests at stake—such as personal freedom, sexual self-determination, healthy development—is called to justify a broad variety of criminal law measures. While this may be necessary to efficiently protect these values, each regulatory intervention should be carefully assessed to properly balance the competing interests. In this field, European legislatures have not always complied with fundamental rights and freedoms, as well as criminal and procedural safeguards. In particular, the principle of *ultima ratio*, which calls for penal redress to be used as a measure of last resort, and the systemic coherence of the criminal justice system seem to be at risk.

This tendency has long been the subject of critical remarks by liberally oriented criminal law scholars. Everybody agrees with the need to adequately protect a person from sexual abuse, especially when it comes to children. However, one can clearly see a strong inclination to incriminate acts not directly offensive to the legal interests at stake. In too many cases, legislature merely requires establishing that a person, in carrying out such a conduct, was motivated by a morally despicable attitude.

This approach is dangerous. Abandoning a strict deference to the harm principle, a legislature might end up punishing a conduct as symptomatic of a mere vicious

[1] Margareth Helfer had the main responsibility for drafting sections II and III, and Domenico Rosani for drafting section IV.

behaviour, also disregarding the *ultima ratio* canon. In turn, this may legitimize the punishment of a person for their dangerousness even before a harmful act has actually been committed. Thus, a legislature would adopt a prognostic, rather than retrospective, approach to crime, basing criminal intervention on what might possibly happen in the future rather than on what happened.[2] This hardly seems compatible with a liberal criminal law, fully respecting constitutional rights and safeguards.

B. Towards a *Feindstrafrecht*?

Such an approach can be traced back to subjectivist criminal models (in the German-speaking analysis known as '*personale Unrechtslehre*'). As opposed to an objectivist model ('*klassische Unrechtslehre*'), a subjectivist criminal model conceives the offence as a violation of duties of loyalty on the part of the perpetrator towards state authority and the social community. The focus is not on the repression of a conduct, but instead on the incrimination of dangerous subjects.[3] Only through the 'marginalization' of those who do not obey, would it be possible to effectively protect individuals and society.

This approach reveals a tendency towards a '*Feindstrafrecht*', a criminal law of the enemy.[4] In short, criminal law would cease to be guided by the harm principle, focusing instead on the neutralization of potentially dangerous people and thus on the prevention of possible future criminal acts even before any is committed.[5]

While it is clearly necessary to criminally punish harmful conducts, some hints of a re-moralization of criminal law in the area of sexual offences can also be identified.[6] Germany was an interesting case in point and was later followed by other European countries. Starting in the 1970s, the reform of German sexual offences was imbued with the objective of enhancing the individual interests and marginalizing the focus on public morality and decency. From the 1990s onwards, however,

[2] Manuel Cancio Meliá, '"Diritto penale" del nemico?' in Massimo Donini and Michele Papa (eds), *Diritto penale del nemico. Un dibattito internazionale* (Giuffrè 2007) 80–81 .

[3] See Thomas Würtenberger, *Die geistige Situation der deutschen Strafrechtswissenschaft* (Müller 1957) 48 ff; Franco Bricola, 'Teoria generale del reato' [1973] Novissimo Digesto Italiano 29.

[4] The concept of the 'criminal law of the enemy' was introduced into the German scientific debate by Günther Jakobs, 'Kriminalisierung im Vorfeld einer Rechtsgutsverletzung' [1985] Zeitschrift für die gesamte Strafrechtswissenschaft 753 ff. See also Günther Jakobs, 'Das Selbstverständnis der Strafrechtswissenschaft vor den Herausforderungen der Gegenwart' in Albin Eser, Winfried Hassemer, and Björn Burkhardt (eds), *Die Deutsche Strafrechtswissenschaft vor der Jahrtausendwende* (De Gruyter 2000) 51 ff.

[5] Anna M Maugeri, 'Diritto penale del nemico e reati sessualmente connotati' [2020] Rivista italiana di diritto e procedura penale 911 (hereafter Maugeri, 'Diritto penale del nemico').

[6] Friedrich-Christian Schröder, 'Die Revolution des Sexualstrafrechts 1992-1998' [1999] Juristenzeitung 833; Joachim Renzikowski, 'Vor § 174' in *Münchner Kommentar des StGB* (Beck 2021) 6, 80; Elisa Hoven, 'Der Einfluss der Medienberichterstattung auf die Reform des Sexualstrafrechts' [2017] MschrKrim 163 (hereafter Hoven, 'Der Einfluss der Medienberichterstattung'); Massimo Donini, '"Danno" e "offesa" nella c.d. tutela penale dei sentimenti' [2008] Rivista italiana di diritto e procedura penale 1579 ff.

scholarly analysis has observed an *ex novo* tendency towards the protection of public interests in the field of sexual crimes.[7]

C. International and European Union Law Contributing to This Evolution

The evolution of criminal law in the field of child sexual abuse material seems to have been importantly conditioned by two factors: on the one hand, the security policies of international and European Union (EU) bodies; on the other hand, the focus of the media on this type of crime.[8]

In relation to the first factor, the European Union has sometimes endorsed a 'combating understanding' of criminal law.[9] Expressions of this are some components of the two main key acts on child sexual abuse, namely Council Framework Decision 2004/68/JHA on combating the sexual exploitation of children and child pornography,[10] and Directive 2011/93/EU on combating the sexual abuse and sexual exploitation of children and child pornography, and replacing the first Framework Decision.[11] A similar approach can sometimes be detected within the Council of Europe too. Its two cornerstone treaties in this regard are the 2001 Convention on Cybercrime (hereinafter: Budapest Convention)[12] and the 2007 Convention on the Protection of Children against Sexual Exploitation and Sexual Abuse (hereinafter: Lanzarote Convention).[13] All these interventions have called for a strengthened role for criminal law in fighting child sexual abuse and, in particular, child pornography. Frequently, this has happened anticipating the intervention of criminal law, punishing acts which are 'only' preparatory of actual crimes. Moreover, national legislatures have often opted for the toughest approach. Between the granted minimum and maximum levels of compliance with international and EU law, European countries have usually opted for the latter. In

[7] Hoven, 'Der Einfluss der Medienberichterstattung' (n 6) 163. On the reasons for this countertendency, see, from a criminological point of view, Daniela Klimke and Rüdiger Lautmann, 'Die neoliberale Ethik und der Geist des Sexualstrafrechts' (2006) 19(2) Zeitschrift für Sexualforschung 97 (hereafter Klimke and Lautmann, 'Die neoliberale Ethik').

[8] See Maugeri, 'Diritto penale del nemico' (n 5) 914; Carlo Enrico Paliero, 'Pragmatica e paradigmatica della clausola di "extrema ratio"' [2018] Rivista italiana di diritto e procedura penale 1456; Cornelius Prittwitz, 'Feindstrafrecht' in Arno Pilgram and Cornelius Prittwitz (eds), *Kriminologie. Akteurin und Kritikerin gesellschaftlicher Entwicklung* (Nomos 2004) 218–19.

[9] See Massimo Donini, 'Diritto penale di lotta. Ciò che il dibattito sul diritto penale del nemico non deve limitarsi a esorcizzare' [2007] Studi sulla questione criminale 57.

[10] Council Framework Decision 2004/68/JHA on combating the sexual exploitation of children and child pornography [2003] OJ L13/44.

[11] Directive (EU) 2011/93 on combating the sexual abuse and sexual exploitation of children and child pornography (Child Sexual Abuse Directive) [2011] OJ L335/1.

[12] Council of Europe Convention on Cybercrime [2001] ETS 185.

[13] Council of Europe Convention on the Protection of Children against Sexual Exploitation and Sexual Abuse [2007] CETS 201.

particular, many countries do not seem to have adequately considered the introduction of the various exemption clauses provided by the different acts, which allowed for not criminalizing scenarios only limitedly (or completely not) offending the interests at stake. Similar exemption clauses would have allowed to better comply with the fundamental principles of a liberal criminal law, fully respecting human rights and freedoms and limiting the criminal intervention to the most serious conducts.[14]

D. The Role of Emphatic Media Reports

In relation to the second factor, the media seems to particularly focus on crimes of a sexual nature, more than on other crimes. In addition, the news on sexual crimes is often characterized by alarmist and emphatic expressions. This qualitative distortion is even more serious if one considers that sexual offences are 'signal crimes', likely to change the public's beliefs about security.[15] Actually, these incidents are the object of numerous media reports exactly because they trigger sensitive emotions. In turn, however, these media reports profoundly influence the population, arousing widespread social alarm and generating a need for enhanced security.[16]

The fight for a severe punishment is also increasingly declined as a sign of solidarity with the victims. In recent years, the victim has correctly undergone a considerable social revaluation.[17] Whereas victimization used to be associated with a sensitive and tendentially negative stigma for the person affected, today the status of victim has been noticeably enhanced. In the media, the victim of sexual crimes seems to occupy a more prominent position than victims of other crime groups. This 'victim narration' is not without consequence for the legislature, calling for a more severe punishment for the perpetrators of these crimes.[18]

Some aspects of the current Italian legal framework on child sexual abuse fit into this description. We have highlighted two of them, namely the issue of virtual child pornography and the criminal relevance of self-generated content.

[14] See Malaika Bianchi, *I confini della repressione penale della pornografia minorile. La tutela dell'immagine sessuale del minore fra esigenze di protezione e istanze di autonomia* (Giappichelli 2019) 87, 198 ff (hereafter Bianchi, *I confini della repressione penale*).

[15] Maugeri, 'Diritto penale del nemico' (n 5) 915.

[16] Massimo Donini, 'Sicurezza e diritto penale' [2008] Cassazione penale 3558; Antonio Cavaliere, 'Può la "sicurezza" costituire un bene giuridico o una funzione del diritto penale?' in Winfried Hassemer (ed), *In dubio pro libertate: Festschrift für Klaus Volk zum 65. Geburtstag* (Beck 2009) 111 ff; Josef Isensee, *Das Grundrecht auf Sicherheit* (De Gruyter 1983); Winfried Hassemer, 'Sicherheit durch Strafrecht' [2006] Strafverteidiger 321 ff; Hoven 'Der Einfluss der Medienberichterstattung' (n 6) 163.

[17] Hoven, 'Der Einfluss der Medienberichterstattung' (n 6) 164, with reference to Tobias Kunz and Karl-Ludwig Singelnstein, Kriminologie (utb 2016) 18; Klimke and Lautmann, 'Die neoliberale Ethik' (n 7) 18.

[18] Daniela Klimke and Rüdiger Lautmann, 'Opferorientierungen im Bereich Kriminalität und Strafe' in Roland Anhorn and Marcus Balzereit (eds), *Handbuch Therapeutisierung und Soziale Arbeit* (Springer 2016) 562.

III. A First Case in Point: Virtual Child Pornography

A. Early Developments: International Law Calling on Italy to Criminalize Child Sexual Abuse Material

The current Italian legal framework on child sexual abuse material is, as in many other countries, the result of a series of separate legislative interventions. Most of them were promoted by the need to comply with international and EU legal acts.

The first legislative intervention, in 1998, had become necessary by virtue of the commitment made by Italy in 1991 with the ratification of the UN Convention on the Rights of the Child (hereinafter: CRC),[19] and the final declaration of the 1996 First World Congress against Commercial Sexual Exploitation of Children.[20] Child sexual abuse, and in particular the creation of pornographic material, had to be combated in an effective manner. Consequently, a criminal offence of child pornography was introduced into Italy's Criminal Code (hereinafter: CC). The new provision faithfully followed the international recommendations with regard to both the qualification of child pornography as a modern form of enslavement and the identification of the conduct. In addition to the production of child pornography, the new Articles 600-ter and 600-quater CC also punished a variety of related conducts, such as disseminating, advertising, offering, and possessing child pornography. The different criminal gravity of the conducts was considered in the graduation of the penalty.

B. Following Up: The Criminalization of Virtual Child Pornography

A second legislative intervention was prompted by the 2000 Optional Protocol to the CRC, devoted to the sale of children, child prostitution, and child pornography;[21] the 2001 Council of Europe Budapest Convention; and Council Framework Decision 2004/68/JHA. The latter act especially played a key role for the Italian legislature. With the intention of combating child sexual abuse more efficiently, the Framework Decision laid down minimum provisions to which the Member States were called to conform. Among the innovations, the most debated one at European and national level was the extension of the notion of child pornography to what is now known as 'virtual child pornography'. In defining 'child pornography', Article 1(b)(iii) of the Framework Decision also includes 'realistic images

[19] UN Convention on the Rights of the Child [1989] UNTS 1577, 3.

[20] See Law No 269/1998.

[21] UN Optional Protocol to the Convention on the Rights of the Child on the sale of children, child prostitution and child pornography [2000] UNTS 2171, 227.

of a non-existent child' involved or engaged in sexually explicit conduct, including lascivious exhibition of the genitals or the pubic area. With this, the EU intended to react to a trend reported by judicial authorities. The child abuse 'marketplace' was no longer only fuelled by real material, but also by images created by software capable of generating new content from scratch, or of transforming existing pictures, even harmless ones, into child pornography. Highly debated was also the reference to 'apparent child pornography' in Article 600-quarter.1(b)(ii), calling on states to criminalize the depiction of adults appearing to be children.

Italy reacted to this development in 2006, inserting into the Criminal Code a new provision devoted to virtual child pornography.[22] Article 600-quater.1 CC (*pornografia virtuale*) has extended the scope of the provisions on child sexual abuse materials (the mentioned Articles 600-ter and quater CC). As a consequence, the reform also required the punishment of the production, dissemination, possession, etc, of 'virtual images' created on the basis of depictions of real children or parts thereof. The second paragraph of 600-quater.1 CC specifies that virtual images are 'images produced by means of graphic processing techniques not associated in whole or in part with real situations, the quality of the representation of which makes non-real situations appear to be real'.

Finally, in 2012 Italy ratified the Council of Europe Lanzarote Convention.[23] A number of changes were made to the existing legal framework. In particular, Italy introduced a legal definition of 'child pornography' in Article 600-ter CC. No changes were made to the provision on virtual child pornography.

C. The Partial Implementation by Italy

The mentioned international and EU legal acts provided states with a certain margin of discretion as regards the conducts to be criminalized. In particular, they allowed states not to punish 'apparent' child pornography (depicting adults appearing to be children) as well as, to a lesser extent, 'virtual' child pornography. However, the Italian legislature has only partly made use of this possibility.

Firstly, Italy has refused to criminalize apparent child pornography. This is a choice to be welcomed, fully respecting the harm principle. If one sees the psycho-physical integrity of children as the interest protected by the relevant offences, the production, dissemination, or possession of images of adults appearing to be children is not offensive. Arguably, it is a conduct reprehensible from an ethical point of view, but not justifying a criminal sanction.

Secondly, the notion of 'virtual child pornography' adopted in the Italian Criminal Code does not completely correspond to the European model. The

[22] See Law No 38/2006.
[23] See Law No 172/2012.

definition of virtual pornography provided by the Italian legislature considered as such every picture which does not fully or partly depict real situations. One could wonder, for instance, how to define a picture representing a naked child surrounded by a fictional environment. Indeed, the depiction of (parts of) a real child in a foreign context falls within the notion of virtual child pornography. One could think of an image placing a (real) child next to an adult in such a way as to give the impression that the two have sexual relations. Is this virtual pornography or 'real' pornography? The Italian provision could allow it to be considered as virtual pornography (and therefore punish it less harshly). However, this is hardly in line with the spirit of the Framework Decision and the subsequent Directive.

Indeed, the EU legal framework has changed over the years. Framework Decision 2004/68/JHA covered *totally* virtual child pornography, namely images produced without using even parts of images of real children. The Directive 2011/93/EU has changed this formulation. Deleting the reference to the 'non-existent child', the European legislator has opted—according to some scholars—for a more limited interpretation of virtual child pornography, excluding the criminal relevance of entirely virtual images. However, not everybody agrees. Other scholarly opinions rather consider the current formulation as implicitly encompassing both 'real' children and 'non-existent' ones.[24]

In Italy, totally virtual images cannot be punished. Article 600-quater.1 CC requires the virtual pictures to be based on depictions of real children or parts thereof. Consequently, totally virtual images are excluded from any criminal relevance, despite a single judgment of the Supreme Court referring the offence also to drawings.[25]

D. Italy and the Harm Principle: Still Not Enough

As seen, the Italian legislature has refused to adopt some key features of the European regulation on child sexual abuse materials. Firstly, it has excluded from the outset the criminal relevance of apparent child pornographic images. Secondly, it has also opposed attaching criminal relevance to totally virtual child pornography. Correctly, Italy has rejected a 'hard-core' approach, which—beyond any *ultima ratio* consideration—delegates to criminal law the repression of a conduct without assessing whether it is really offensive to a protected interest.

Nonetheless, the Italian approach is still too cautious. Analysing in more detail the provision on virtual pornography, one realizes that only in a few cases does this

[24] Malaika Bianchi, 'Pornografia virtuale e la recente normativa europea' in Alberto Cadoppi and others (eds), *Trattato di diritto penale. Parte generale e Parte speciale, Riforme 2008–2015* (Giappichelli 2015) 783 (hereafter Bianchi, 'Pornografia virtuale').

[25] Cass pen (III) 9 May 2017, No 22265.

crime result in an offence of the personality of a child. In many hypotheses, the Italian legislature has provided for an incrimination irrespective of the actual offensiveness of the conduct.

Arguably, only images depicting a child in full, or parts of the child's body that make them recognizable, are likely to offend the child's personality.[26] In this case, the individual interests of the child are clearly compromised for children who end up represented as the object of others' sexual instinct. Such a reification of children, which is highly offensive to their personhood and their right to harmonious development, must rightly be criminally repressed. On the contrary, the use of images of (parts of) children that do not allow for their identification does not harm the child's personality.

According to the legislator, however, there is also another reason to criminalize the use of images which do not allow the child to be identified. A person who sees this kind of image might search for real child pornography or produce similar child sexual abuse images. Thus, criminal prosecution would be justified precisely because the conduct could induce criminogenic effects in the population and thus generate delinquent tendencies in some people. Additionally, the offence would aim to protect other values too, in particular the dignity of children in collective terms.

This approach to criminal law cannot be shared. So far, the existence of a causal link between the viewing of child pornography and the perpetration of sexual abuse has not been ascertained.[27] A concentration on collective interests, in addition, is at risk of endorsing neomoralistic tendencies disregarding the constitutionally required focus on the harm principle.

The Italian provision is an example of a criminal law that is not sufficiently anchored to the harm principle.[28] Looking carefully, it highlights a tendency towards a *Feindstrafrecht*, focused on the neutralization of the dangerous person and, thus,

[26] Bianchi, *I confini della repressione penale* (n 14) 102 ff, 116 ff; Bianchi, 'Pornografia virtuale' (n 24) 772; Giovanni Cocco, 'Può costituire reato la detenzione di pornografia minorile?' [2006] Rivista italiana di diritto e procedura penale 889; Bartolomeo Romano, *Delitti contro la sfera sessuale della persona* (Giuffrè 2022) 223 ff. The protected interest has been identified in the individual personality of the child since the criminal offence was introduced in the Italian Criminal Code: Margareth Helfer, 'Davvero indeterminato il concetto di pornografia, specie minorile?' [2004] Diritto penale e processo 622 ff. The importance of focusing on the protection of the child's individual personality, in particular on sexual self-determination, is also emphasized by Tatjana Hörnle, '§ 184b StGB' in *Münchner Kommentar zum StGB* (Beck 2021) 5; Joachim Renzikowski and Anja Schmidt, 'Nach der Reform ist vor der Reform. Zum Abschlussbericht der Reformkommission zum Sexualstrafrecht' [2018] Kriminalpolitische Zeitschrift 333; Alisdair A Gillespie, *Child pornography. Law and Policy* (Routledge 2011) 104 ff (hereafter Gillespie, *Child pornography*).

[27] On this point, see more extensively, Gillespie, *Child pornography* (n 26) 112 ff.

[28] The dangerous lack of determination of the Italian notion of 'virtual child pornography', as provided for by Article 600-quater.1 CC, is demonstrated by a—previously mentioned—judgment of the Supreme Court, whereby even totally virtual child pornographic images (the case concerned child pornographic comics) were brought under the scope of the provision. See Cass pen (III) 9 May 2017, No 22265. For a critique of this case law, see Bianchi, *I confini della repressione penale* (n 14) 488 ff.

on the prevention of possible future criminal acts.[29] People end up being punished not because they have engaged in a harmful *conduct*, but because they have manifested a reprehensible *attitude*. The actual conduct is not relevant for the effect it produces, harming a specific right or interest, but as the expression of its author's antisocial attitude. The latter would be punished not for what they do, but for their way of being, of which the conduct is a symptom.[30] Recourse to the criminal law is no longer a last resort, justified by a harmful act. Rather, it ends up constituting a set of 'educational' measures aim at preventing future harmful acts. In sum, the Italian legislator was excessively guided by the hard-liner approach adopted by the international and EU acts. Moved by an understandable concern for the protection of children, Italy seems to have excessively lowered the threshold of criminal intervention.

It is not only about virtual pornography. With regard to consensually generated sexual images the current criminal approach also needs to be profoundly reconsidered.

IV. A Second Case in Point: Consensually Generated Sexual Content

A. Distinguishing Self-generated Sexual Content from Child Sexual Abuse Material

A second case in point is represented by the creation and sharing of consensually generated images and videos.

Consensual sexual images and videos need to be carefully distinguished from child sexual abuse material. While the latter necessarily denotes an abuse of the child, this is not necessarily true for consensually created content. In fact, in this case, it is the child who freely takes pornographic pictures or videos of themselves and, potentially, shares them with other people (so-called 'sexting'). For this reason, the term 'child sexual abuse material', vastly used in policy discussions, cannot properly apply on self-generated content. A child *freely* taking pornographic pictures of themselves cannot at the same time be abusing themselves.

A word of caution is appropriate. Indeed, one immediately thinks of abusive scenarios, where the child is surreptitiously forced to create or share pornographic

[29] Among the first to identify this tendency was Alberto Cadoppi, 'L'assenza delle cause di non punibilità mette a rischio le buone intenzioni' [2006] Guida al diritto 43–44.

[30] A degenerated form of such a subjectivist conception of criminal law, which ended up abandoning any reference to the harm committed, is known as '*Täterstrafrecht*'. The subject was not punished for what he had done, but instead for corresponding, in the eyes of the state, to a certain criminal image.

content. For instance, minors may be compelled to create pornographic content by threatening them to disseminate private information or other compromising pictures they may have previously sent. Lacking free will, these cases do not however constitute freely generated or consensual content.[31]

In the understanding adopted here, a necessary condition for speaking of 'consensual (sexual) content' is the child's genuine will and consent. Thus, the term is used to refer to two types of content. On one hand, properly self-generated content, freely and autonomously created by the child. On the other hand, pornographic content created by a person with the genuine consent of the child, provided no abuse was involved and the child was above the age of consent. As an example, one could think of a 16-year-old boy taking some 'nudes' and sharing them with his significant other; or of a 17-year-old girl asking her partner to record a video of their sexual intercourse.

Although the phenomenon still needs more empirical analysis, it is probably fair to say that many minors self-generate pornographic content. Scientific evidence collected over the past decade clearly shows this.[32] In view of the sensitivity of the issue, this data may even under-represent the actual extent of consensual content. According to authoritative studies, the creation or sharing of such a content seems particularly widespread among older children, males, LGBTQ + persons, and children coming from economically more modest backgrounds.[33]

[31] This example shows why the term 'consensual sexual content' could be more advantageous than the mainstream 'self-generated sexual material'. In fact, the latter notion could also be used to address materials which the child created as a consequence of other people's threat or coercion. Objectively, they would also be self-generated by the child, even if their will was not free. There is also a second reason for preferring the term 'consensual sexual content'. Following international human rights advice, this contribution also advocates for not criminalizing pornographic content which has been generated by the child's partner, provided no abuse was involved, the child freely consented, they were above the age of sexual consent, and the content was for their private use. In this scenario, the material would not be 'self-generated' (since it was the partner who created it) but still 'consensual'.

[32] See Mariya Stoilova, Sonia Livingstone, and Rana Khazbak, *Investigating Risks and Opportunities for Children in a Digital World*, Unicef Office of Research – Innocenti (Evidence Report, 2021) 45 ff (hereafter Stoilova, Livingstone, Khazbak, *Investigating Risks and Opportunities*). Arguably, 'teenagers increasingly consider sexting to be "normal"': see UN Committee on the Rights of the Child, *Guidelines regarding the implementation of the Optional Protocol to the Convention on the Rights of the Child on the sale of children, child prostitution and child pornography* (Guidelines, CRC/C/156, 2019) para 42 (hereafter UN Committee on the Rights of the Child). See also Andy Phippen and Maggie Brennan, *Sexting and Revenge Pornography* (Routledge 2021) 20 ff; Shaheen Shariff, *Sexting and Cyberbullying. Defining the Line for Digitally Empowered Kids* (Cambridge University Press 2015) 62 (hereafter Shariff, *Sexting and Cyberbullying*); Clay Calvert, 'Youth-Produced Sexual Images, "Sexting," and the Cellphone' in Fabian M. Saleh, Albert Grudzinskas, and Abigail Judge (eds), *Adolescent Sexual Behavior in the Digital Age* (OUP 2014) 96 ff; Alisdair A Gillespie, 'Adolescents, Sexting and Human Rights' (2013) 13(4) Human Rights Law Review 624 ff (hereafter Gillespie, 'Adolescent, Sexting').

[33] Stoilova, Livingstone, and Khazbak, *Investigating Risks and Opportunities* (n 32) 45 ff. Particularly with regards to sexting among sexual minorities, see Michele L Ybarra and Kimberly J Mitchell, 'A National Study of Lesbian, Gay, Bisexual (LGB), and Non-LGB Youth Sexual Behavior in Online and in Person' (2015) 45 Archives of Sexual Behavior 1358, 1363–64; José A Bauermeister and others, 'Sexting among Young Men Who Have Sex With Men' (2014) 54 Journal of Adolescent Health 610.

B. The Need for Effective Protection

There is no doubt that generating pornographic content is a dangerous activity. There is consequently a need to efficiently protect children. Different protective perspectives must be considered separately.

Firstly, the child needs to be protected with regard to the original choice of creating pornographic material. As said, should the child be threatened or coerced to generate images or videos it would not be possible to speak of consensual content anyway. Beyond such a clearly abusive scenario, however, there is a vast array of borderline situations. Did our 16-year-old boy actually decide of his own free will to take nude photos if his partner said that they expected him to do so as proof of their love? Did our 17-year-old girl freely agree to record her sexual intercourse if it was her partner who vigorously asked for it? How free a child's consent actually was is open to speculation. Furthermore, one should not overlook social pressures to share intimate images that children, especially females, seem to feel.[34] How such social pressure may reflect on the freedom of a child's consent is still under-researched. It is unlikely that it can be answered on a theoretical note either, making it necessary to assess the actual circumstances.

Secondly, the child must also be efficiently protected against any unlawful dissemination of the content they have generated. To avoid blatant risks, the pornographic material needs to stay within the intimacy of the child and their partner. Any further dissemination needs to be prevented and repressed. Arguably, it might be appropriate to prohibit such a dissemination even if the child consented. However, it is open to debate whether the child should be punished for sending their own pornographic material to a third person, and, if so, how.

In this regard, one should also consider the gender component of intimate image abuse. In fact, it has been empirically noted that the victims of illicit dissemination of self-generated material are mainly young women. Even the damaging charge of such a dissemination could depend on the gender of the victim. In more traditional or religious societies, a girl might suffer greater damage to her reputation than her male peers if her intimate images were to be disseminated.[35]

[34] 'Sexting often appears to be a product of youth peer pressure': UN Committee on the Rights of the Child (n 32) para 42. As regards to the social pressure and its gender component, see Michel Walrave, Joris Van Ouytsel, and Koen Ponnet, 'A Nuanced Account: Why Do Individuals Engage in Sexting?' in Michel Walrave and others (eds), *Sexting. Motives and Risk in Online Sexual Self-presentation* (Palgrave Macmillan 2018) 41; Stoilova, Livingstone, and Khazbak, *Investigating Risks and Opportunities* (n 32) 45; Sonia Livingstone and Jessica Mason, *Sexual Rights and Sexual Risks among Youth Online*, eNACSO/ London School of Economics and Political Science (Evidence Review 2015) 40; Thomas Crofts and others, *Sexting and Young People* (Palgrave Macmillan 2015) 138; Shariff, *Sexting and Cyberbullying* (n 32) 45 ff. In critical terms, see Anne-Marie McAlinden, *Children as 'Risk'. Sexual Exploitation and Abuse by Children and Young People* (Cambridge University Press 2018) 202 ff.

[35] A study cites as an example an Italian boy (Carlo, 17) interviewed during a qualitative survey: 'If a naked picture of mine goes around the web, no problem ... for a girl it is different ... her reputation would be in trouble ...': Nicky Stanley and others, 'Pornography, Sexual Coercion and Abuse and Sexting in Young People's Intimate Relationships' (2016) 33 Journal of Interpersonal Violence 2935.

Arguably, protecting children from sexual abuse is not only a domestic matter. In ratifying the Convention on the Rights of the Child, UN States Parties—with the notable exception of the United States—agreed to fully 'respect and ensure' its provisions, undertaking 'all appropriate legislative, administrative, and other measures' for implementing them. Notoriously, Articles 19 and 34 CRC require states to protect minors from all forms of abuse and (sexual) exploitation. The Convention's second Optional Protocol, devoted to the sale of children, child prostitution, and child pornography, elaborates further on the protection to be provided to children in this regard. Similar obligations can be found in further international treaties, especially in the Council of Europe's Lanzarote Convention.

Before examining what international and European law provide for in the area of consensually generated material, it must be noted that the legislator cannot fulfil these obligations through criminal law alone. In fact, a purely criminal response is not only unlikely to efficiently protect children but also bears conspicuous risks.

C. The Risks of Resorting to Criminal Law Only

To efficiently protect a child, legislatures need to adopt a holistic approach, applying a variety of preventive and restorative strategies. Resorting to criminal instruments alone is not likely to adequately protect children.

The use of criminal law to address consensual content raises serious questions about the harm principle and the *ultima ratio* canon. Is it justified to punish a child for self-generating pornographic material depicting themselves? Or to punish the child's partner, if they have created pornographic content with the free consent of a child close to adulthood without any abuse? In addition, is it justified to incriminate the child for sharing the self-generated content with other people? In all these cases, one could deliberate what interests have been harmed, and if they have been harmed in such a serious way to justify a criminal intervention. However, in many European countries, children can be prosecuted for freely producing or sharing own pornographic images.[36]

About such 'double standards' between genders, see Jessica Ringrose and others, 'Teen Girls, Sexual Double Standards, and "Sexting": Gendered Value in Digital Image Exchange' (2013) 14 Feminist Theory 305.

[36] According to the Lanzarote Committee, 'a significant minority of [States Parties to the Lanzarote Convention] has rules allowing for the criminalisation of the production of sexually explicit images by children themselves'. Additionally, '[i]n the vast majority of Parties, children are potentially criminally liable for the distribution or transmission of their own self-generated sexually explicit images/videos'. Lanzarote Committee, *The protection of children against sexual exploitation and sexual abuse facilitated by information and communication technologies: addressing the challenges raised by child self-generated sexual images and/or videos* (Implementation Report, 2022) paras 67, 78.

As it has been argued, the consensual production of sexual images and videos bears considerable risk. For instance, the content could be disseminated without the consent of the child. A person could illegally obtain access to the child's phone, or their (former) partner could decide to disseminate the pornographic pictures. As defined above, these scenarios do not actually constitute consensual content, but rather conducts of intimate image abuse. Nonetheless, a purely criminal response also seems inadequate for protecting minors from such risks.[37]

Firstly, if the perpetrator of intimate image abuse is a child, it is widely accepted that a criminal intervention should be used merely as a last resort.[38] This means that a legislature should resort to criminal prosecution only if the child's behaviour cannot be addressed through other means. In fact, there may be alternative ways to address the harm caused that do not involve prosecuting the child, such as education measures, counselling, social intervention, and restorative approaches. In addition, a child could engage in such abusive conduct before the minimum age of criminal responsibility. In most European countries, this is set between 14 and 16 years of age.[39] Resorting to criminal law alone (or mostly) would preclude efficiently intervening in respect of younger children.

Secondly, because of its retrospective nature, criminal law seems hardly adequate to efficiently protect a child. Criminal law is designed to punish individuals for actions which have already occurred. This means that criminal law can only address the harm which has already been done to the child, rather than preventing the harm from occurring in the first place. In addition, the criminal justice system can be slow and cumbersome, making it difficult to bring perpetrators to justice in a timely manner. It is true that a conviction could also deter others from engaging in similar abusive acts. However, it is not evident that such a general preventative effect will efficiently influence the behaviour of a person in their developmental years.

In fact, focusing on criminal law in this field may do more harm than good, as it may drive intimate image abuse among children underground and make it harder to address the underlying issues. Moreover, providing for criminal prosecution may be too easy a way for legislatures to show concern for children without addressing their situation in an effective and beneficial manner. A 'sexting panic' narrative could prompt the politics to 'do something'—which, however, does not equate to 'doing the right thing'.[40]

[37] See Gillespie, 'Adolescent, Sexting' (n 32) 641 ff.

[38] See Lanzarote Committee, *Opinion on child sexually suggestive or explicit images and/or videos generated, shared and received by children* (Opinion 2019) para 7.

[39] See European Commission, *Summary of contextual overviews on children's involvement in criminal judicial proceedings in the 28 Member States of the European Union* (Report 2014) 6 ff; Child Rights International Network, 'Minimum ages of criminal responsibility in Europe' <http://archive.crin.org> accessed 28 February 2023.

[40] See Amy A Hasinoff, *Sexting Panic: Rethinking Criminalization, Privacy and Consent* (University of Illinois Press 2015). On 'moral panic', see also Carolina Villacampa, 'Teen Sexting: Prevalence, Characteristics and Legal Treatment' (2017) 49 International Journal of Law, Crime and Justice 11;

D. International and European Regulation on Consensually Generated Sexual Content

1. International and EU legal acts openly allowing for not criminalizing consensual sexual content

Various international and European legal acts on child sexual abuse leave it up to national legislatures to (or not to) criminalize consensual sexual content. The requirements are, however, different.[41]

As regards the European Union, Council Framework Decision 2004/68/JHA already allowed the Member States to provide for a special regulation for consensual sexual content. According to its Article 3(2)(b), States could have stipulated that the production and possession of child pornography did not constitute a criminal offence as long as the children depicted had reached the age of sexual consent, had given their consent, and the materials were intended solely for their own private use. Consent should have not been considered valid, however, if, 'for example[,] superior age, maturity, position, status, experience or the victim's dependency on the perpetrator has been abused in achieving the consent'.

A similar exception clause was provided for by Directive 2011/93/EU on combating the sexual abuse and sexual exploitation of children and child pornography, which has replaced the Framework Decision. According to its Article 8(3), it shall be at the discretion of Member States not to apply the offences of acquisition, production, and possession of child pornography, if the material involves children who 'have reached the age of sexual consent', the material is 'produced and possessed with the consent of those children', and only 'for the private use of the persons involved', as long as the act 'did not involve any abuse'. Recital No 20 already emphasizes that the Directive does not govern policies with regard to 'consensual sexual activities' which can be regarded as the normal discovery of sexuality, taking account 'of new forms of establishing and maintaining relations among children and adolescents, including through information and communication technologies'.

Eva Lievens, 'Bullying and Sexting in Social Networks: Protecting Minors from Criminal Acts or Empowering Minors to Cope with Risky Behaviour?' (2014) 42 International Journal of Law, Crime and Justice 253.

[41] In the following, this chapter deals only with international and EU legal acts which openly recognize an exception clause for consensual sexual content. In fact, the UN Convention on the Rights of the Child, its second Optional Protocol, and the Budapest Convention did not take a clear stance in this regard. According to authoritative scholarly analysis, however, at least the Convention on the Rights of the Child implicitly allowed states not to incriminate consensual sexual content. See John Tobin and Florence Seow, 'Article 34' in John Tobin (ed), *The UN Convention on the Rights of the Child. A Commentary* (OUP 2019) 1327–28, 1354; Stefanie Schmahl, *United Nations Convention on the Rights of the Child* (Beck, Nomos, Hart 2021) 447. On the relevance of international and European acts for the criminalization of sexting see, in more detail, Domenico Rosani, 'The Increasing Recognition of Child Rights by European Constitutions and its Relevance for the Criminal Regulation of Sexting', in Philip Czech and others (eds), *European Yearbook on Human Rights 2020* (Intersentia 2020) 377 ff.

Concerning the Council of Europe, the 2007 Lanzarote Convention, which has broadly enhanced the protection of children from sexual abuse, provides for a similar exception. According to its Article 20(3), States can opt not to apply the offences of production and possession of child pornography if the depicted children are above the age of sexual consent and the material is 'produced and possessed by them with their consent and solely for their own private use'.

In short, all three provisions allow states to decide not to criminalize the production and possession of consensual child pornography, provided that some criteria are met. These are only partly common criteria. All of the acts require the child depicted to be above the age of sexual consent set by national legislation, and—clearly—to have consented to the production or possession of the material. In the Framework Decision and the Lanzarote Convention, the pictures or videos of the children need additionally to be meant 'for their own private use', therefore for a child's private use. The Directive's provision is more far-reaching, requiring the content to be 'for the private use of the persons involved'. Thus, the Directive also allows these materials to be produced and possessed in order to be used by the person who made them. Additionally, however, the Directive requires that the acts 'did not involve any abuse'. Under these conditions, the Directive also allows—beyond production and possession—the acquisition of consensual sexual content not to be criminalized.

It is important to note that none of these acts openly allow states to decriminalize the consensual *sharing* of sexual content. All of them refer the clause exclusively to the offences of production and possession of child pornography. Only the Directive, with its reference to the 'acquisition' of the content, may hint at a limited tolerance in this regard. In recent years, however, a request not to criminalize some forms of sharing is increasingly being voiced in international soft law.

2. Soft law encouraging states not to criminalize consensual sexual content

In recent years, several international bodies have encouraged states to introduce an exception clause for consensual sexual content. This position has been adopted, in particular, by the UN Committee on the Rights of the Child and the Lanzarote Committee.

In its 2021 General Comment No 25, devoted to children's rights in the digital environment, the UN Committee on the Rights of the Child openly required states to refrain from applying child pornography rules on self-generated contents:

> Self-generated sexual material by children that they possess and/or share with their consent and solely for their own private use should not be criminalized. Child-friendly channels should be created to allow children to safely seek advice and assistance where it relates to self-generated sexually explicit content.[42]

[42] UN Committee on the Rights of the Child, *General comment No. 25 on children's rights in relation to the digital environment* (General Comment 2021), para 118.

This very brief passage does not elaborate further on the requirements for allowing the possession and sharing of child pornography. Moreover, it could be questioned whether the reference to 'self-generated' material was meant to embrace only content created by the very same child depicted in it, or also content produced by a partner with the free consent of the child. A teleological interpretation of the General Comment suggests in favour of the latter position.

The Council of Europe's Lanzarote Committee, monitoring the homonymous Convention, also repeatedly took a position in the matter. Already in 2019, it had called for not criminalizing children where the material generated and exchanged between them was intended solely for their private use, and their participation was 'voluntary and consensual':

> The self-generation of sexually suggestive or explicit images and/or videos by children does not amount to 'the production of child pornography' when it is intended solely for their own private use; ... The voluntary and consensual sharing by children among each other of the sexually suggestive or explicit images and/or videos of themselves does not amount to 'offering or making available, distributing or transmitting, procuring, or knowingly obtaining access to child pornography' when it is intended solely for their own private use.[43]

This opinion seems to go beyond the letter of the Lanzarote Convention, which allowed the mere *production* and *possession* of pornographic material not to be considered as an offence. The Lanzarote Committee, following the UN Committee on the Rights of the Child, also proposes to tolerate its *sharing*. However, a careful reading of the opinion limits the scope of this statement. Indeed, the Lanzarote Committee invites states to not criminalize the conduct of children who share *among each other* the pornographic content of themselves *after having produced it*. In other words, it primarily refers to children who have photographed each other in intimate poses, and then shared the pictures amongst each other.[44]

Nonetheless, in 2022 the Lanzarote Committee called for child sexting to be more broadly tolerated. In the context of an implementation report devoted to the 'challenges raised by child self-generated sexual images and/or videos', the Committee has advised states not to prosecute children for sharing self-generated sexual material with peers as long as the conduct is free, consensual, and the content is aimed at personal use.[45] At the same time, the (child) recipient should also

[43] Lanzarote Committee, *Opinion on child sexually suggestive or explicit images and/or videos generated, shared and received by children* (Opinion 2019) paras 3, 5.

[44] This fact allows the notion of 'self-generated' content to be interpreted in a broader way, also encompassing material which was created by a partner with the informed and free consent of the child. In fact, the notion adopted by the Lanzarote Committee corresponds to that of 'consensual sexual content', as defined earlier in this chapter.

[45] Lanzarote Committee, *The protection of children against sexual exploitation and sexual abuse facilitated by information and communication technologies: addressing the challenges raised by child*

not be punished if they possess the material with the 'informed consent' of the child.[46]

At the present time, the Committee's recommendations only cover children sharing pictures and videos *with other children*. The report postponed a more in-depth discussion of the issue to a future document.[47] This could also be the chance to analyse carefully the case of children sharing their self-generated content with adults. It is hard to disagree that, in this case, particular caution is required. However, it may also sometimes be appropriate to refer the exception clause to relationships between (older) children and (young) adults. To illustrate this, one could think of two classmates, one of 17 years old, and therefore still a child, and the other one already 18, and therefore an adult. At present, the implementation report only addresses the issue of adults *possessing* consensually generated child pornography. In this regard, the Committee has called on states not to incriminate the adult possessing the picture, if the child depicted has reached the age of consent, has given their consent, the act did not involve any abuse, and—importantly—the child and the adult are of similar ages and maturity.[48]

E. Italy: Over-protecting or Under-protecting?

1. The undifferentiated treatment of consensually generated sexual content and child sexual abuse material

During the drafting of the 2006 bill reforming the offences on child sexual abuse, the Italian government had proposed the introduction of an ad hoc regulation for consensual sexual content.[49] However, such an exception clause was deleted in the final version of the bill due to the numerous objections raised. Some objections were of a purely moralistic nature, others affirmed the legal irrelevance of the child's consent, and others were motivated by the aim to protect children from an illegal dissemination of the material produced.[50]

Consequently, scholarly analysis has noted that the conscious decision of the Italian legislature not to introduce an exception would make the consensual production and possession of child pornography criminally relevant.[51] This view is

self-generated sexual images and/or videos (Implementation Report, 2022) recommendation II-8. See also paras 43, 78 ff.

[46] ibid recommendation II-6.
[47] ibid para 79.
[48] ibid recommendation II-5.
[49] See bill (d.d.l.) No 4599/XIV, Article 3.
[50] See Bianchi, *I confini della repressione penale* (n 14) 201 ff. On the 2006 bill, see Margareth Helfer, *Sulla repressione della prostituzione e pornografia minorile. Una ricerca comparatistica* (Cedam 2007) 132 ff.
[51] Annalisa Verza, 'Sexting e pedopornografia: i paradossi' [2013] Ragion pratica 575–76.

also shared by part of the jurisprudence. The case law of the Supreme Court, however, does not provide useful guidance: while some judgments have endorsed the criminal relevance of consensually produced content, others have argued that the legislature did not actually take a position, leaving the issue to the courts.[52]

Lacking a specific regulation on consensual sexual content, Italian courts have been asked to evaluate consensually created content and sexting in the light of the general offences on child sexual abuse. Although most cases do not reach a tribunal, and the Italian juvenile justice system provides for a wide range of instruments to avoid a conviction,[53] the issue has been referred to the Supreme Court several times over the last years.[54] In fact, the lack of a specific provision has led to several challenges in the interpretation of the whole provision.[55]

2. Italian case law introducing an exception clause for consensually generated sexual content

From at least 2016 onwards, it has been clear that children could not be incriminated for self-generating pornography depicting themselves. In Italy, the offence of producing child sexual abuse material is provided for in Article 600-ter (1) CC. Precisely, this paragraph punishes whoever, 'using minors under eighteen years of age … produces pornographic material'. The question was: is a child who freely self-generates pornography 'using', that is, exploiting, themselves? Already in 2016, Italy's Supreme Court replied 'no'. Children who autonomously depict themselves cannot be at the same time exploiting themselves.[56]

However, two capital questions arose. Even if a child cannot be incriminated for self-generating pornographic material, one could wonder if this child could consent to such material being created by another person. Moreover, could this child lawfully decide to send these pictures or videos to other people? On these questions, Italy's Supreme Court was compelled to take an authoritative stance in Spring 2022.

[52] As an example, the following Supreme Court's decisions have hinted at the criminal relevance of consensually generated sexual content: Cass pen (III) 1 July 2021, No 25334, para 2.3, 4.1; Cass pen (III) 6 December 2012, No 47239, para 2. Contrarily, the Court's Grand Chamber has found that the fact that the legislature has not introduced an exemption clause does not hinder the judiciary from interpreting statutory law in order to exclude the criminal relevance of consensual sexual content: Cass pen (sez un) 15 November 2018, No 51815, para 4.1.3. This is exactly what happened a few years later, through Cass pen (sez un) 9 February 2022, No 4616.

[53] See Law No 448/1988, *Disposizioni sul processo penale a carico di imputati minorenni.*

[54] In the case law of the Supreme Court, see in particular Cass pen (III) 21 March 2016, No 11675; Cass pen (sez un) 15 November 2018, No 51815; Cass pen (sez un) 9 February 2022, No 4616

[55] In particular, Italy's Supreme Court deliberated on whether the provisions on disseminating child sexual abuse material could also apply to self-generated content having been non-consensually disseminated. On this stance, the Court took different positions in 2016 and 2020: Cass pen (III) 21 March 2016, No 11675; Cass pen (III) 12 February 2020, No 5522. See Domenico Rosani, 'Sexting mit Minderjährigen—Jüngste Entwicklungen in der höchstgerichtlichen Rechtsprechung Italiens' (2022) 3 Zeitschrift für die gesamte Strafrechtswissenschaft 862 ff.

[56] See Cass pen (III) 21 March 2016, No 11675.

As the Court's Grand Chamber had already pointed out in a 2018 *obiter dictum*, there was a risk of an overly broad application of criminal law.[57] In this context, the judges called for the production and possession of consensual sexual content not to be criminalized provided that the material had been created with the assent of the child above the age of sexual consent and exclusively for the private use of the persons involved.[58] However, this (non-binding) statement could not help appease the different positions within the Supreme Court itself.

The Grand Chamber's new ruling, issued in February 2022, marks a milestone in the Italian debate on consensual sexual content.[59] In short, the Court has found that consensual child pornography might not amount to a criminal offence as long as the child is above the age of consent and they have not been exploited. To this end, however, the content has to stay with the persons involved. It is actually not the consent of the child that makes the production of pornography lawful, but rather the lack of any exploitation of the child. In order to exclude that the child has been exploited, the specific circumstances need to be carefully examined, paying particular attention to the child's age and maturity.[60]

The material created has to remain between the persons involved. Therefore, only sharing the material amongst one another is lawful. Should the material be disseminated or made available to another person, the Court distinguishes between two scenarios.[61] If the dissemination of the material was already intended when the recordings were made, the Court sees the child as exploited from the beginning, already making the production of the content unlawful. If a person depicts a child in pornographic poses with the intention of disseminating the images, this act amounts to the offence of producing child pornography. It is irrelevant whether the child had consented to it. The situation, however, is different if the dissemination is due to a later decision. If the material should have remained private and only at a later date it was decided to pass it on to other people, the act would constitute 'only' unlawful dissemination of child pornography. In this respect, too, any agreement on the part of the child is irrelevant.

The ruling also seems to grant criminal relevance to child sexting. Indeed, the Grand Chamber states that if the dissemination of the material is undertaken by the child, it is the child themselves who is liable to criminal prosecution.[62] Since the provisions on child sexual abuse material do not differentiate according to the age of the perpetrator, a child could also commit this offence. The fact that the content disseminated depicts the very same child does not play a role, for the offence aims

57 See Cass pen (sez un) 15 November 2018, No 51815, para 4.

58 ibid para 4.1.2.

59 Cass pen (sez un) 9 February 2022, No 4616. The case had been referred to the Grand Chamber by Cass pen (III) 1 July 2021, No 25334.

60 Cass pen (sez un) 9 February 2022, No 4616, para 4.

61 ibid para 9.3.

62 ibid para 9.3.

at protecting a collective interest, too. Arguably, these offences intend to prevent children from being collectively reduced to instruments of sexual satisfaction. In this context, however, a number of critical considerations can be made.

3. Critical remarks

It seems reasonable not to criminalize consensual sexual content, and at the same time fundamentally prohibit the disclosure of the material to third persons. This not only strikes a balance between the need for protection and the autonomy rights of the child, but also reconciles individual interests with collective concerns.[63]

Nevertheless, the question arises whether recourse to criminal law is appropriate. Sanctioning a child with child pornography offences for distributing their own images seems neither compatible (to say the least) with the harm principle nor with the *ultima ratio* canon. As already noted, other prevention and reparation instruments seem more adequate in this regard, being more effective and also taking better account of childhood. Despite aiming to protect children, a focus on criminal law (alone) risks undermining children's rights without actually ensuring effective safeguards. Instead of over-protecting minors, such an approach might end up under-protecting them.

In addition, there may be situations where the sharing of pornographic content should also be reasonably tolerated. One could think of a child who sends their current partner pornographic pictures taken the year before by the child's former partner. That such an act is worthy of punishment seems more than questionable in light of the harm principle. To avoid prosecuting similar conducts, one could suggest interpreting extensively the term 'persons involved' found in EU Directive 2011/93. One could hermeneutically consider as such also those who were not originally involved in the production of the material, but who at the time of the act had a special personal bond to the child. In our example, this would allow the child to share their pictures with the new partner, as long as the act did not involve any abuse and the child was above the age of consent.

Finally, it should be noted that the legal developments outlined here are reprehensible from a democratic perspective. The Italian legislature did not intend to exclude consensual sexual content from criminal relevance. It is true that the Supreme Court grounded its ruling on a literal interpretation of positive law. In essence, however, the Court has introduced an exemption clause for consensual sexual content, very similar to what international and EU law had proposed, but which was not implemented by the Italian legislature. Although the result is to be welcomed, one cannot help but notice that the exclusively judicial origin of the clause is hardly compatible with a strict understanding of the separation of powers

[63] See Lorenzo Picotti, 'Il ristretto ambito di non punibilità della c.d. pedopornografia domestica' [2022] Diritto di internet 587–88.

and the democratic principle.[64] This rule should have been introduced by the legislature and not by the judiciary. Realistically, however, it is highly questionable whether the Italian Parliament would have actually acted on this sensitive issue. In fact, it was easier for it to 'delegate' to the judiciary the task of ensuring consistency in the legal framework.

V. Conclusion

This chapter has attempted to outline how certain trends in the field of child sexual abuse material are at risk of neglecting fundamental principles of criminal law. The harm principle and the *ultima ratio* canon especially need to be more rigorously honoured by domestic legislatures as well as European and international decision makers. As two emblematic cases, the chapter explored the issues of virtual child pornography and self-generated sexual content. Both illustrate well how current criminal provisions require a critical review to reconcile them with key principles of criminal law, and—in the case of consensually created content—with the recognition of children's agency.

This is not to say that virtual pornography never deserves criminal prosecution, nor that consensually generated sexual content should be 'liberalized' without regard of its overt risks. However, a rhetorical use of criminal law needs to be carefully averted. It is too easy for political decision makers to resort to criminal intervention to show their concern regarding intimate image abuse. Being the most compelling instrument available to a state, such an intervention is meant to reassure the population that politics is delivering. Criminal law, however, is not necessarily the right response.

Firstly, criminal law does not ensure an efficient protection of rights and values. Other instruments—whether they belong to civil law or administrative law; or provide for prevention or restorative measures—are often likely to bear more fruit than the mere criminalization of a conduct.

Secondly, criminal law is a risky instrument. By definition, it empowers the state to restrict individual liberties in the name of maintaining overriding interests. For this, a meticulous balance of the competing values is essential. An overly permissive recourse to criminal law could lead to over-criminalization whereby minor offences are punished in a disproportionately severe fashion. In addition, the criminal justice system may unreasonably target persons exercising their rights and freedoms, or further contribute to the victimization of a person affected by crime.

64 See Malaika Bianchi, 'Per una tipizzazione della produzione e diffusione di "pedo-pornografia domestica"' (2023) 1 Archivio penale 1 ff; Domenico Rosani, 'La pornografia minorile domestica. Prospettive comparate per una disciplina normativa' (2022) 4 Rivista italiana di diritto e procedura penale 1672.

Fundamental principles exist to remind us of the 'shadows' of criminal law, when too many people focus on its 'lights'. Criminal intervention is manifestly necessary to crack down on child sexual abuse material. To be effective and legitimate, however, criminal law needs to aim precisely at its target—sparing everything outside of it.

Bibliography

Bauermeister JA and others (2014) 54 Journal of Adolescent Health 606

Bianchi M, 'Per una tipizzazione della produzione e diffusione di "pedo-pornografia domestica"' (2023) 1 Archivio penale 1

Bianchi M, 'Pornografia virtuale e la recente normativa europea' in A Cadoppi and others (eds), *Trattato di diritto penale. Parte generale e Parte speciale, Riforme 2008–2015* (Giappichelli 2015)

Bianchi M, *I confini della repressione penale della pornografia minorile. La tutela dell'immagine sessuale del minore fra esigenze di protezione e istanze di autonomia* (Giappichelli 2019)

Bricola F, 'Teoria generale del reato' (1973) Novissimo Digesto Italiano 29

Cadoppi A, 'L'assenza delle cause di non punibilità mette a rischio le buone intenzioni' [2006] Guida al diritto 37

Calvert C, 'Youth-Produced Sexual Images, "Sexting," and the Cellphone' in FM Saleh, A Grudzinskas, and A Judge (eds), *Adolescent Sexual Behavior in the Digital Age* (OUP 2014)

Cancio Meliá M, '"Diritto penale" del nemico?' in M Donini and M Papa (eds), *Diritto penale del nemico. Un dibattito internazionale* (Giuffrè 2007)

Cavaliere A, 'Può la "sicurezza" costituire un bene giuridico o una funzione del diritto penale?' in W Hassemer (ed), *In dubio pro libertate: Festschrift für Klaus Volk zum 65. Geburtstag* (Beck 2009)

Cocco G, 'Può costituire reato la detenzione di pornografia minorile?' [2006] Rivista italiana di diritto e procedura penale 863

Crofts T and others, *Sexting and Young People* (Palgrave Macmillan 2015)

Donini M, 'Diritto penale di lotta. Ciò che il dibattito sul diritto penale del nemico non deve limitarsi a esorcizzare' [2007] Studi sulla questione criminale 57

Donini M, 'Sicurezza e diritto penale' [2008] Cassazione penale 3558

Donini M, "Danno" e "offesa" nella c.d. tutela penale dei sentimenti' [2008] Rivista italiana di diritto e procedura penale 1579

Gillespie AA, *Child pornography. Law and Policy* (Routledge 2011)

Gillespie AA, 'Adolescents, Sexting and Human Rights' (2013) 13(4) Human Rights Law Review 623

Hasinoff AA, *Sexting Panic: Rethinking Criminalization, Privacy and Consent* (University of Illinois Press 2015)

Hassemer, W, 'Sicherheit durch Strafrecht' [2006] Strafverteidiger 321

Helfer M, 'Davvero indeterminato il concetto di pornografia, specie minorile?' [2004] Diritto penale e processo 622

Helfer M, *Sulla repressione della prostituzione e pornografia minorile. Una ricerca comparatistica* (Cedam 2007)

Hörnle T, '§ 184b StGB' in V Erb and J Schäfer (eds), *Münchner Kommentar zum StGB* (Beck 2021)

Hörnle T, 'Kriminalisierung im Vorfeld einer Rechtsgutsverletzung' [1985] Zeitschrift für die gesamte Strafrechtswissenschaft 753

Hoven E, 'Der Einfluss der Medienberichterstattung auf die Reform des Sexualstrafrechts' [2017] Monatsschrift für Kriminologie und Strafrechtsreform 163

Isensee J, *Das Grundrecht auf Sicherheit* (De Gruyter 1983)

Jakobs G, 'Das Selbstverständnis der Strafrechtswissenschaft vor den Herausforderungen der Gegenwart' in A Eser, W Hassemer, and B Burkhardt (eds), *Die Deutsche Strafrechtswissenschaft vor der Jahrtausendwende* (De Gruyter 2000)

Klimke D and Lautmann R, 'Die neoliberale Ethik und der Geist des Sexualstrafrechts' (2006) 19(2) Zeitschrift für Sexualforschung 97

Klimke D, 'Opferorientierungen im Bereich Kriminalität und Strafe' in R Anhorn and M Balzereit (eds), *Handbuch Therapeutisierung und Soziale Arbeit* (Springer 2016)

Kunz T and Singelnstein K-L, *Kriminologie* (utb 2016)

Lievens E, 'Bullying and Sexting in Social Networks: Protecting Minors from Criminal Acts or Empowering Minors to Cope with Risky Behaviour?' (2014) 42 International Journal of Law, Crime and Justice 251

Livingstone S and Mason J, *Sexual Rights and Sexual Risks among Youth Online*, eNACSO/ London School of Economics and Political Science (Evidence review 2015)

Maugeri AM, 'Diritto penale del nemico e reati sessualmente connotati' [2020] Rivista italiana di diritto e procedura penale 911

McAlinden A-M, *Children as 'Risk'. Sexual Exploitation and Abuse by Children and Young People* (Cambridge University Press 2018)

Paliero CE, 'Pragmatica e paradigmatica della clausola di "extrema ratio"' [2018] Rivista italiana di diritto e procedura penale 1456

Phippen A and Brennan M, *Sexting and Revenge Pornography* (Routledge 2021)

Picotti L, 'Il ristretto ambito di non punibilità della c.d. pedopornografia domestica e l'inefficacia del consenso del minore alla diffusione di materiale pornografico con lui realizzato' [2022] Diritto di internet 585

Prittwitz C, 'Feindstrafrecht' in A Pilgram and C Prittwitz (eds), *Kriminologie. Akteurin und Kritikerin gesellschaftlicher Entwicklung* (Nomos 2004)

Renzikowski J and Schmidt A, 'Nach der Reform ist vor der Reform. Zum Abschlussbericht der Reformkommission zum Sexualstrafrecht' [2018] Kriminalpolitische Zeitschrift 333

Renzikowski J, 'Vor § 174' in V Erb and J Schäfer (eds), *Münchner Kommentar des StGB* (Beck 2021)

Ringrose J and others, 'Teen Girls, Sexual double Standards, and "Sexting": Gendered Value in Digital Image Exchange' (2013) 14 Feminist Theory 305

Romano B, *Delitti contro la sfera sessuale della persona* (Giuffrè 2022)

Rosani D, 'La pornografia minorile domestica. Prospettive comparate per una disciplina normativa' (2022) 4 Rivista italiana di diritto e procedura penale 1631

Rosani D, 'Sexting mit Minderjährigen – Jüngste Entwicklungen in der höchstgerichtlichen Rechtsprechung Italiens' (2022) 3 Zeitschrift für die gesamte Strafrechtswissenschaft 852

Rosani D, 'The Increasing Recognition of Child Rights by European Constitutions and its Relevance for the Criminal Regulation of Sexting' in P Czech and others (eds), *European Yearbook on Human Rights* 2020 (Intersentia 2020)

Schmahl S, *United Nations Convention on the Rights of the Child* (Beck, Nomos, Hart 2021)

Schröder F-C, 'Die Revolution des Sexualstrafrechts 1992-1998' [1999] Juristenzeitung 833

Shariff S, *Sexting and Cyberbullying. Defining the Line for Digitally Empowered Kids* (Cambridge University Press 2015)

Stanley N and others, 'Pornography, Sexual Coercion and Abuse and Sexting in Young People's Intimate Relationships' (2016) 33 Journal of Interpersonal Violence 2919

Stoilova M, Sonia Livingstone S, and Rana Khazbak R, *Investigating Risks and Opportunities for Children in a Digital World*, Unicef Office of Research – Innocenti (Evidence Report 2021)

Tobin J and Seow F, 'Article 34' in J Tobin (ed), *The UN Convention on the Rights of the Child. A Commentary* (OUP 2019)

Verza A, 'Sexting e pedopornografia: i paradossi' [2013] Ragion pratica 569

Villacampa C, 'Teen Sexting: Prevalence, Characteristics and Legal Treatment' (2017) 49 International Journal of Law, Crime and Justice 10

Walrave M, Van Ouytsel J, and Ponnet K, 'A Nuanced Account: Why Do Individuals Engage in Sexting?' in M Walrave and others (eds), *Sexting. Motives and Risk in Online Sexual Self-presentation* (Palgrave Macmillan 2018)

Würtenberger T, *Die geistige Situation der deutschen Strafrechtswissenschaft* (Müller 1957)

Ybarra ML and Mitchell KJ, 'A National Study of Lesbian, Gay, Bisexual (LGB), and Non-LGB Youth Sexual Behavior in Online and in Person' (2015) 45 Archives of Sexual Behavior 1357

PART III

PATTERNS OF CRIMINALIZATION OF INTIMATE IMAGE ABUSE IN EUROPE AND ANGLO-AMERICAN SYSTEMS

9

The Criminalization of Non-consensual Pornography in the United States

*Mary Anne Franks**

I. Introduction: A David v Goliath Story

The legal, technological, and social landscape of non-consensual pornography, sometimes referred to as 'revenge porn', in the United States has changed dramatically over the last decade.[1] This transformation is largely attributable to the efforts of courageous victims of this abuse and the civil society advocacy organizations that support them, in particular Dr Holly Jacobs and the Cyber Civil Rights Initiative (CCRI), the organization she founded in 2013. Before 2013, only three US states criminalized the unauthorized disclosure of sexually explicit images of adults; social media platforms and search engines had no policies addressing the abuse; and the public was largely either unaware of or unsympathetic to the phenomenon. Ten

* Special thanks to Madeline Medoff for research assistance.

[1] For a detailed account of the progress made up until 2017, see Mary Anne Franks, 'Revenge Porn Reform: A View from the Front Lines' (2018) 69 Florida Law Review 1251.

Mary Anne Franks, *The Criminalization of Non-consensual Pornography in the United States* In: *Criminalizing Intimate Image Abuse*. Edited by: Gian Marco Caletti and Kolis Summerer, Oxford University Press.
DOI: 10.1093/oso/9780198877813.003.0009

years later, forty-eight states, Washington, DC, the territories of Guam and Puerto Rico, and the US military have criminalized the conduct; major social media and internet companies, including Google, Meta (previously Facebook), Reddit, and X (previously Twitter), have banned non-consensual pornography from their platforms and services; and non-consensual pornography, now also commonly referred to as 'non-consensually distributed intimate imagery' or 'image-based sexual abuse', is widely recognized as a form of abuse. Non-criminal remedies, including civil provisions created specifically to address non-consensual pornography, have also been implemented in multiple jurisdictions.

However, challenges remain. The majority of enacted US state criminal laws wrongly focus on the perpetrator's intent rather than the victim's lack of consent. That is, they apply only to situations in which the perpetrator is motivated by a desire to harm the victim. But many perpetrators of this abuse—the majority, in fact, according to CCRI's research—have other motives: voyeurism, profit, a desire for social status, or some other motive that disregards the humanity of the victim. Requiring an intent to harm treats non-consensual pornography as a form of harassment, which it only sometimes is, rather than a privacy violation, which it always is. This fundamental error, along with many states' decisions to classify the crime as a minor misdemeanour, leaves many victims without a realistic path to justice and undermines the vital deterrence potential of the criminal law. Congress's continued failure to pass federal criminal legislation on the issue as of September 2023, despite multiple introductions of what is currently known as the Stopping Harmful Image Exploitation and Limiting Distribution (SHIELD) Act, means that there is as yet no clear, consistent definition of the crime that applies throughout the United States. The lack of a federal law forces victims to engage with an inconsistent patchwork of protections for what is often a multi-jurisdictional crime, and contributes to the United States' status as a haven for 'revenge porn' sites that target women all around the world.

Just as the remarkable progress towards comprehensive and effective criminalization of non-consensual pornography in the United States is attributable to the concerted efforts of individuals and organizations, so too is the resistance to that project. Unsurprisingly, perpetrators of 'revenge porn' have challenged legislation that would hold them accountable, but their attempts have been greatly aided by powerful organizations and entities such as the American Civil Liberties Union (ACLU), the Electronic Frontier Foundation (EFF), the Media Coalition, the Motion Picture Association (MPA), and tech companies like Google. Unlike the survivors and civil society organizations pushing for criminalization of non-consensual pornography, the groups fighting against criminalization have both deep pockets and broad influence. This dramatic asymmetry in power and resources makes it all the more remarkable that survivors and advocates have made as much progress as they have, but also underscores the significance of the obstacles ahead.

Fortunately, the anti-criminalization lobby's most insidious argument against strong laws against non-consensual pornography—namely, that such laws violate the First Amendment—has been decisively repudiated by the courts. Many First Amendment scholars, including myself, rejected from the start the assertion that non-consensual pornography is a form of free speech protected by the US Constitution, but in the early years of the reform movement, groups like the ACLU were able to exploit uncertainty about whether courts would agree. That uncertainty no longer exists. As of September 2023, every constitutional challenge to a non-consensual pornography law that has achieved a final disposition has been defeated. This includes challenges to half a dozen laws that properly define the crime without reference to the perpetrator's motive, and cases that defendants have appealed all the way to the Supreme Court—and been rejected.

States that passed weak laws based on the anti-criminalization lobby's now-debunked representations about free speech should not hesitate now to amend them, and the two states that have failed to pass laws at all—Massachusetts and South Carolina—should waste no time in enacting strong legislation to protect victims. Similarly, Congress should heed the clear message from the courts and finally enact the federal criminal legislation that advocates began calling for a decade ago. The immediate and irreparable harm of non-consensual pornography, inflicted not only on individual victims but on society as a whole, requires the maximum deterrence potential and moral force of criminal prohibitions at the state and at the federal level.

II. The Rise of 'Revenge Porn' and the Founding of the Cyber Civil Rights Initiative

Non-consensual pornography existed long before a name existed for it. When Marilyn Monroe was a struggling actress known as Norma Jeane Baker, she posed 'out of desperation' for a nude photo shoot, reportedly telling the photographer: 'You must promise to never tell anyone about my posing for you in the nude. I want you to promise me that you will take the pictures so that I wouldn't be recognisable in them.'[2] She signed a false name on the release for the photos, 'hoping that they wouldn't come back to haunt her'.[3] After Monroe became famous, ACLU benefactor and Playboy founder Hugh Hefner paid $500 for the photos and published them without Monroe's consent on the cover of the magazine's inaugural issue in 1953.[4]

2 Megan C Hills, 'How Hugh Hefner Built an Entire Empire without Marilyn Monroe's Consent' *Marie Claire UK* (London, 2 October 2017) <http://www.marieclaire.co.uk/news/celebrity-news/hugh-hefner-marilyn-monroe-541688> accessed 22 November 2017.

3 ibid.

4 ibid.

Another pornographic magazine, Hustler, began running a feature called 'Beaver Hunt' in the 1980s.[5] This displayed sexually explicit photographs submitted by readers, often without the consent or even the knowledge of the women depicted in them.[6] In this sense, it was a precursor to the 'amateur porn' that became ubiquitous with the advent of the Internet, which often depicts individuals who are not aware that they are being filmed or that the material would be made public.

All the same, before 2003, no law in the United States directly addressed the unauthorized disclosure of sexually explicit images of another adult person. Between 2003 and 2013, only three states enacted criminal laws that potentially applied to the abuse. This was despite high-profile cases like that of Hunter Moore, who in 2010 created a website featuring stolen or user-submitted sexually explicit imagery of people, mostly women, without their consent, along with detailed personal, contact, and other identifying information about them.[7] It was around this time that the term 'revenge porn' began to be used to refer to this kind of material. Victims frequently suffered in silence for fear of greater exposure, and those who did seek help from law enforcement were often blamed for the abuse or subjected to further objectification. Even sympathetic police officers and lawyers told victims, not inaccurately, that what happened to them was 'not against the law'.

In 2011, Holly Jacobs—not the name she was born with—was completing her doctorate in Industrial/Organizational Psychology at Florida International University. She had moved on from what she thought had been an amicable break up with a long-time, long-distance boyfriend.[8] She was happy in a new relationship, so much so that she posted a picture of herself with her new boyfriend on Facebook to announce their relationship. Soon after, she received an email that would change her life: 'It's 8:15 where you are. You have until 8:37 to reply. Then I start the distribution'.[9]

Jacobs immediately realized what the emailer was threatening to distribute.[10] She and her ex-boyfriend exchanged intimate photos throughout their three-year, often long-distance relationship.[11] Within a few days of receiving the email,

[5] Emily Poole, 'Fighting Back against Non-consensual Pornography' (2015) 49 University of San Francisco Law Review 181, 186.

[6] While the feature was controversial and led to numerous lawsuits against Hustler, it continues to this day.

[7] See Connor Simpson, 'Revenge Porn King Hunter Moore Arrested for Hacking Email Accounts' *Atlantic* (Washington, 23 January 2014) <https://www.theatlantic.com/national/archive/2014/01/revenge-porn-king-hunter-moore-arrested-conspiracy-hack-email-accounts/357321/> accessed 2 February 2016.

[8] Holly Jacobs, 'Being a Victim of Revenge Porn Forced Me to Change My Name' *Thought Catalog* (27 November 2013) <https://thoughtcatalog.com/dr-holly-jacobs/2013/11/being-a-victim-of-revenge-porn-forced-me-to-change-my-name/> accessed 17 July 2021 (hereafter Jacobs, 'Change My Name').

[9] ibid.

[10] ibid.

[11] ibid.

Jacobs learned that those photos had been posted to more than 200 websites, and she was deluged with sexual propositions from strange men who had seen them.[12] The photos had also been sent to her employer and a co-worker.[13] Jacobs spent the next months trying to explain the situation to her employer, family, friends, and colleagues, and plead with porn sites and search engines to remove the material.[14] After a month of trying to write her dissertation by day and sending takedown notices at night, Jacobs thought she had finally scrubbed the photos from the Internet.[15] But within two weeks, they were online again—this time on 300 websites.[16] At that point, Jacobs gave up trying to change her search results, and began the process of changing her name.[17]

After being told repeatedly by police that what had been done to her was not a crime in Florida, Jacobs began to try to fight back on her own.[18] In 2012, she started an online campaign called End Revenge Porn, which included a petition to ban the practice.[19] That same year, she came across a law review article I had written about the online harassment of women,[20] and emailed me to request a meeting. Jacobs brought a three-ring binder filled with documentation about the numerous sites where her photos and videos had appeared, along with pages of threatening emails and comments.

As horrified as I was by Jacobs's story, I did not know what I could offer her except sympathy. Her response was unforgettable: 'If what happened to me isn't against the law, then the law has to change, and I want you to help me change it.'

I had never received a request like this. While I had taught criminal and constitutional law for several years, I had never drafted a law and had no experience advocating for legislative reform. Jacobs was undeterred by this, and her resolve — and the personal sacrifices she was willing to make to become the public face of this abuse—convinced me that I had to at least try to help. At the time, I was guest blogging for a legal site called Concurring Opinions,[21] and I used that opportunity to get feedback on the model statute I had drafted. In September 2013, I posted an updated draft of this statute to Jacobs' End Revenge Porn website. That same month, the *New York Times* ran an article on the subject of revenge porn that referred to

[12] ibid.
[13] ibid.
[14] ibid.
[15] ibid.
[16] ibid.
[17] ibid.
[18] ibid.
[19] ibid.
[20] ibid; see also Mary Anne Franks, 'Unwilling Avatars: Idealism and Discrimination in Cyberspace' (2011) 20 Columbia Journal of Gender and Law 224.
[21] See Mary Anne Franks, 'Why We Need a Federal Criminal Law Response to Revenge Porn' *Concurring Opinions* (15 February 2013) <https://web.archive.org/web/20130223025746/http://www.concurringopinions.com:80/archives/2013/02/why-we-need-a-federal-criminal-law-response-to-revenge-porn.html/comment-page-1> accessed 30 March 2020.

my model statute,[22] and soon after, a New York Assemblyman contacted me about using the model statute as the basis for their law.

After our first meeting, I introduced Jacobs to my friend and colleague Professor Danielle Keats Citron, an expert in online harassment, and the three of us began collaborating on Jacobs' vision to turn the End Revenge Porn online campaign into a non-profit organization that would provide legal, technological, and social resources to victims of online abuse. In 2013, we launched the Cyber Civil Rights Initiative, after the title of one of Citron's groundbreaking law review articles.[23] I became CCRI's Legislative and Tech Policy Director, and stepped into the additional role of President when Jacobs stepped down in 2018. Today, CCRI is the nation's leading organization focused on image-based sexual abuse. The organization seeks to protect the online civil rights and civil liberties of all people, with a particular focus on women, racial and sexual minorities, and other vulnerable groups. CCRI's three-pronged approach to the problem of non-consensual pornography—change laws, change technology, and change society—has proven remarkably successful.

On the legislative front, my model state statute became the template for the wave of legislative reform that swept the US between 2013 and 2023. As of September 2023, all but two US states have criminalized non-consensual pornography. My model federal statute served as the template for bipartisan Congressional efforts to criminalize the abuse, beginning with the Intimate Privacy Protection Act, introduced in 2016 by Congresswoman Jackie Speier (D-CA). The bill was renamed the ENOUGH Act in 2017 and renamed again to the SHIELD Act in 2019. The SHIELD Act passed the House of Representatives as part of the Violence against Women Reauthorization Act of 2022, but was omitted from the Senate version. The VAWA Reauthorization Act did, however, include a federal civil remedy for non-consensual pornography, based on the Uniform Law Commission's 2018 Uniform Civil Remedies for the Unauthorized Disclosure of Intimate Images Act, for which I served as reporter. The latest update at the time of this writing was that the SHIELD Act had been introduced once again in February 2023 by Senators Amy Klobuchar and John Cornyn.

CCRI has also filed nearly a dozen amicus briefs in support of state laws protecting online privacy and in other cases implicating the privacy, safety, and free expression of vulnerable groups. Our briefs, along with the scholarship of CCRI board members and advisers, are frequently cited by courts. CCRI leadership have testified to Congress on section 230 reform, synthetic media (also known as 'deepfakes'), and other related subject areas. Beginning in 2022, CCRI leader have served as expert advisers to the White House Task Force to Address Online Harassment and Abuse.

[22] See Erica Goode, 'Victims Push Laws to End Online Revenge Porn Posts' *New York Times* (New York, 23 September 2013).

[23] Danielle Keats Citron, 'Cyber Civil Rights' (2009) 89 Boston University Law Review 61, 63.

On the technological front, CCRI successfully helped convince tech industry leaders to ban non-consensual pornography from their platforms and services and to implement procedures for its removal. Following a February 2015 cross-industry summit on non-consensual pornography that featured Jacobs, every major tech company, including Google, Microsoft, Facebook, and Twitter, announced that they were banning this abuse and began implementing takedown procedures for victims. CCRI and its members have served on many companies' Trust and Safety boards and continue to advise major social media and internet platforms on their policies regarding intimate imagery, privacy, and harassment.

On the social front, CCRI maintains a twenty-four-hour Image Abuse Helpline, the only US-based helpline dedicated to supporting victims of image-based sexual abuse. The helpline has provided emotional support, information, and referrals to over 19,000 callers to date. CCRI also provides critical resources through the CCRI Safety Center, including a content removal guide, a roster of pro and low bono attorneys, international resources, and safety bulletins on new and evolving threats such as sextortion and digitally manipulated imagery (also known as 'deepfakes'). CCRI provides training on image-based sexual abuse to educators, employers, law enforcement personnel, direct service providers, judges, legislators, military groups, and attorneys.

In addition, CCRI publishes groundbreaking research on the subject of image-based sexual abuse, including the first peer-reviewed study of non-consensual pornography and sextortion in the US as well as the first peer-reviewed US research related to sextortion during the COVID-19 pandemic. CCRI also collaborates with experts and advocates on these issues across the globe, including in Australia, Canada, Iceland, South Korea, and the United Kingdom.

III. Defining the Harm: Terminology, Scope, and Impact

A. What's in a Name?

It was engagement with UK experts Clare McGlynn and Erika Rackley[24] that led CCRI to adopt 'image-based sexual abuse' as an umbrella term for conduct that includes what CCRI typically refers to as non-consensual pornography as well as sexual image extortion and digitally manipulated sexually explicit imagery. CCRI has always been critical of the term 'revenge porn', not only because it appears to have been created by perpetrators but because the term wrongly implies that perpetrators are primarily motivated by personal vengeance. While some certainly are (especially in the case of ex-partners), other perpetrators are motivated by greed, a

[24] Clare McGlynn and Erika Rackley, 'Not "Revenge Porn" but Abuse: Let's Call it Image-based Sexual Abuse' (2017) Oxford Journal of Legal Studies 1–28.

desire for notoriety, or voyeuristic impulses. In many cases, the perpetrators do not know the victims at all; in others, the perpetrators may go to great lengths to hide the fact that they are distributing the material.

In addition to erasing victims who have been targeted by strangers with a range of motives, the word 'revenge' also arguably normalizes retaliatory behaviour by intimate partners, reinforcing the idea that aggression stemming from the inability to control a partner is a normal and acceptable impulse. This concern is heightened by the fact that 'revenge porn', like domestic violence, sexual assault, and sexual harassment, is a form of abuse that disproportionately involves male perpetrators and female victims.

CCRI uses the term 'non-consensual pornography' to emphasize that the harm flows from the victim's lack of consent, not the perpetrator's intent. It is not a perfect term; some survivors and advocates express concern about the retention of the word 'pornography', which is ambiguous, morally charged, and potentially stigmatizing. One specific concern is that 'porn' conveys a negative moral judgement about sexual imagery generally, or of self-created and shared sexual imagery in particular, leading in turn to the denigration of the people who appear in it. CCRI wholeheartedly rejects any such judgement of consensually created or distributed sexually explicit imagery; the rationale for keeping the term is that 'pornography' is one of the few English words that succinctly describes sexually explicit content aimed at prurient interests, and that it is used in this context to describe not the creation of the content but the transformation of private, intimate images into public sexual entertainment without consent. Accordingly, CCRI defines non-consensual pornography as 'the distribution of sexually graphic images of individuals without their consent'.[25] This term includes not only images consensually exchanged within a confidential relationship, but also images originally obtained without consent, such as surreptitious recordings, hacked images, and images depicting involuntary sexual acts or nudity, such as sexual assaults. In April 2023, CCRI announced that it was shifting to new terminology to 'reflect the evolving nature of our work and to center victim-survivors', including the adoption of the term 'non-consensually distributed intimate images' as an alternative to 'non-consensual pornography'.[26]

B. Scope of the Problem

According to a nationally representative study conducted by CCRI in 2017, more than one in eight adult social media users has been victimized or threatened with

[25] Danielle Keats Citron and Mary Anne Franks, 'Criminalizing Revenge Porn' (2014) 49 Wake Forest Law Review 345, 346 (hereafter Citron and Franks, 'Criminalizing Revenge Porn').

[26] Cyber Civil Rights Initiative (24 April 2023) <https://twitter.com/CCRInitiative/status/1650564326556676099> accessed 8 October 2023.

the unauthorized distribution of private, sexually explicit images or videos, and over one in twenty adult social media users have engaged in such distribution.[27] Experts conducting empirical research on non-consensual pornography emphasize that victimization figures are likely a low estimate, as they only capture victims who are aware that they have been victimized. Many victims, especially those whose images are shared in restricted online communities, may never discover that they have been victimized.

Non-consensual pornography is distributed via social media, blogs, emails, texts, DVDs, hard copies, and websites. One victim's images were posted to nearly 10,000 websites.[28] In May 2017, it was revealed that Facebook disabled more than 14,000 accounts related to non-consensual pornography sexual extortion and handled nearly 54,000 cases of suspected non-consensual pornography in a single month.[29]

Non-consensual pornography is not an equal opportunity form of abuse. The likelihood of being victimized by non-consensual pornography is higher for women and sexual minorities. The 2017 CCRI study revealed that women were about 1.7 times more likely to be victimized than men, and men were by far the primary perpetrators of the abuse.[30] Revenge porn sites are far more likely to feature women than men.[31] The majority of court cases and news stories to date involve female victims and male perpetrators. A 2016 Data & Society Research Institute study found that young women were the most likely group to be threatened with the conduct: one in ten women under the age of thirty had been threatened with disclosure of intimate images.[32] The same study also found that individuals who

[27] Asia Eaton and others, 'National Online Study of Nonconsensual Porn Victimization and Perpetration' (CCRI 2017) 608 (hereafter Eaton and others, 'Victimization and Perpetration'). A previous nationwide study by the Data & Society Research Institute indicated a somewhat lower level of prevalence, finding that one in twenty-five American Internet users—around 10 million people—had been a victim of or threatened with the disclosure of intimate images. The discrepancy appears to be largely due to the latter study's narrower definition of the abuse and differences in methodology. The Data and Society study was limited to nude or nearly nude depictions disclosed without consent with the intention to hurt or embarrass the victim and was conducted via telephone survey. Data and Society, 5. The CCRI study addressed all non-consensual, sexually explicit disclosures and was conducted through Facebook polling.

[28] Victim takedown request list made available to the Cyber Civil Rights Initiative (on file with author). This number is a considerable increase from 2014, when around 3,000 websites were believed to feature non-consensual pornography (*Economist* 2014).

[29] Nick Hopkins and Olivia Solon, 'Facebook Flooded with "Sextortion" and Revenge Porn, Files Reveal, *The Guardian* (London, 22 May 2017) accessed 29 April 2020.

[30] Eaton and others, 'Victimization and Perpetration' (n 27).

[31] Carolyn A Uhl and others 'An Examination of Nonconsensual Pornography Websites' (2018) 28(1) Feminism and Psychology 50–68 (finding that nearly 92 per cent of individuals featured on 'revenge porn' sites are women); Abby Whitmarsh, 'Analysis of 28 Days of Data Scraped from a Revenge Pornography Website' *WordPress.com* (13 April 2015) <https://everlastingstudent.wordpress.com/2015/04/13/analysis-of-28-days-of-data-scraped-from-a-revenge-pornography-website/> accessed 12 January 2017 (finding that of 396 posts to a revenge porn website, 378 depicted women versus 18 men).

[32] Data & Society Research Institute, 'Nonconsensual Image Sharing: One in 25 Americans Has Been a Victim of "Revenge Porn"' (2016) 4. The Data and Research study did find that men and women were roughly equally likely to have their intimate material posted, as opposed to being threatened with posting—an intriguing finding. ibid. However, this study does not appear to have distinguished

identify as gay or bisexual are more than seven times more likely as those who identify as straight to have been threatened with or victimized by non-consensual pornography.[33]

C. Impact

The harm caused by non-consensual pornography is often immediate and irreversible. Once an explicit image of a victim is made available on a website or social media platform, it becomes accessible to a virtually unlimited number of people who can download, forward, share, and copy it within seconds. Within days or even hours, that image can dominate a victim's search engine results and be transmitted to the victim's entire personal, social, and professional circle: family, employers, co-workers, and peers.[34] Victims have been stalked,[35] harassed, threatened with sexual assault,[36] defamed as sexual predators, terminated by their employers,[37] forced to change schools,[38] and forced to change their names.[39] Some have committed suicide.[40] According to researcher Samantha Bates,

> The negative mental health consequences of revenge porn for female survivors are similar in nature to the negative mental health outcomes that rape survivors experience. Rape survivors frequently experience PTSD, anxiety, and depression, all of which participants in this study experienced. In terms of coping mechanisms,

between unsolicited and solicited images, and does not provide information about where, how, and with what information these postings were made. This may be relevant, as some studies have shown that men send more sexually explicit images than women do, and many of these images are what are commonly referred to as 'dick pics', are often unsolicited, and often do not include identifying information about the sender. Many recipients of such images consider them to be a form of harassment. It is not uncommon for women uncomfortable with such unsolicited images to publicize these images in an effort to shame or deter the sender, often without revealing identifying details about the sender. I take the position that the publication of nude or sexually explicit photos in which the sender cannot be identified should not be considered non-consensual pornography for purposes of legal prohibition. The sending of unsolicited nude photos should, in many cases, be considered a form of harassment and, in some cases, a form of public exposure in which the sender does not retain an expectation of privacy.

[33] ibid.

[34] Annmarie Chiarini, 'I Was a Victim of Revenge Porn' *The Guardian* (London, 19 November 2013) (hereafter Chiarini, 'I was a victim').

[35] For detailed cases, see *United States v Osinger* 753 F3d 939 (9th Cir 2014); *United States v Petrovic* 701 F3d 849 (8th Cir 2012); *US v Sayer* 748 F3d 425 (1st Cir 2014).

[36] Jan-Lim, Clarissa, 'Meet the Women Waging War on Revenge Porn' *A Plus* (22 February 2017). <https://medium.com/@aplusapp/meet-the-women-waging-war-on-revenge-porn-8d0323fdd4e1#:~:text=Much%20of%20that%20progress%20can,were%20plastered%20on%20the%20internet> accessed 8 October 2023.

[37] See Ariel Ronneburger, 'Sex, Privacy, and Webpages: Creating a Legal Remedy for Victims of Porn 2.0' (2009) 21 Syracuse Science and Technology Law Reporter 1, 9.

[38] Citron and Franks, 'Criminalizing Revenge Porn' (n 25).

[39] Jacobs, 'Change My Name' (n 8).

[40] Emily Bazelon, 'Another Sexting Tragedy' *Slate* (12 April 2013).

> participants engaged in avoidance/denial and self-medication in attempt to avoid feelings of despair and distress regarding their victimization.[41]

Victims suffer each time a person views or shares their intimate images, and the traffic in such images increases the demand and the pervasiveness of those images. As one victim expressed it: 'I am not victimized one time. I am victimized every time someone types my name into the computer. The crime scene is right before everyone's eyes, played out again and again.'[42] Victims report that one of the worst aspects of non-consensual pornography is the 'unending uncertainty about who has viewed the material'.[43]

A previous survey conducted by CCRI in 2013 produced suggestive findings about the negative impact of non-consensual pornography on victims.[44] In nearly half of all cases, respondents said that identifying information about them was posted along with the private material, including details such as their full name, social network information, email address, phone number, home address, work address, and even, in some cases, social security number. The publication of these details helps explain why half of all victims reported being stalked or harassed online by people who viewed their material, and a third reported offline stalking or harassment. In light of this, it is unsurprising that victims often limited their use of social media in the wake of their experience. Nearly all victims reported suffering significant emotional distress as a consequence of victimization, including significant impairment in social, occupational, or other functioning; serious effects on their professional, educational, and intimate relationships; and suicidal thoughts.

While non-consensual pornography affects both male and female individuals, available evidence to date indicates not only that the majority of victims are women and girls, but that women and girls often face more serious consequences as a result of their victimization.[45] Non-consensual pornography often plays a role in crimes that disproportionately affect women, including intimate partner violence, sexual assault, and sex trafficking. Domestic abusers use the threat of disclosure as a way to keep their partners from leaving or reporting their abuse to law enforcement.[46] Rapists have recorded their attacks not only to further humiliate their victims, but

[41] Samantha Bates, 'Revenge Porn and Mental Health: A Qualitative Analysis of the Mental Health Effects of Revenge Porn on Female Survivors' (2017) 12(1) Feminist Criminology 22–42, especially 34 (hereafter Bates, 'Revenge Porn and Mental Health').

[42] Carissima Mathen, 'Crowdsourcing Sexual Objectification' (2014) 3 Laws 529–52, especially 531.

[43] Bates, 'Revenge Porn and Mental Health' (n 41).

[44] Cyber Civil Rights Initiative (2013) NCP Study Results <https://web.archive.org/web/20170210173952/https://www.cybercivilrights.org/ncpstats//> accessed 8 October 2023.

[45] Citron and Franks, 'Criminalizing Revenge Porn' (n 25) 353–54; Jill Filipovic, '"Revenge Porn" is About Degrading Women Sexually and Professionally' *The Guardian* (London, 28 January 2013) <https://www.theguardian.com/commentisfree/2013/jan/28/revenge-porn-degrades-women> accessed 8 October 2023.

[46] Chiarini, 'I was a victim' (n 34).

also to discourage them from reporting sexual assaults.[47] Traffickers and pimps have used non-consensual pornography to coerce unwilling individuals into the sex trade or to prevent them from exiting it.[48] The disclosure of intimate images—or the threat of such disclosure—is often used to punish and discourage outspoken or successful women.[49]

These points demonstrate how non-consensual pornography harms not only individual victims, but also imposes larger expressive harms on society as a whole.[50] Non-consensual pornography is *disciplinary*: it warns women, in particular, that the cost of displeasing men—whether by exiting a relationship, being sexually unattainable, or simply acting with autonomy—may be sexual exposure against their will. It sends the message that sexual exploitation is an acceptable way to punish or intimidate women. It is no coincidence that many female targets of non-consensual pornography are successful women, from Hollywood celebrities to judges to PhD students to politicians.[51] Along with other gender-based violence such as rape, sexual harassment, and voyeurism, non-consensual pornography reinforces the pernicious belief that men have the right to use women and girls sexually without their consent. Like those forms of abuse, non-consensual pornography is rarely punished, frequently trivialized, and often celebrated.

IV. The Case for Criminalization

Criminal laws are appropriate against conduct that causes severe and irreversible harm to both individuals and society. As the previous section detailed, the unauthorized disclosure of private, sexually explicit images harms not only individual victims but society as a whole. The abuse violates multiple democratic values: privacy, freedom of expression, bodily autonomy, and gender equality. While non-criminal remedies can also be useful to victims, the immediate and often irreparable nature of the harm of 'revenge porn' requires the maximum deterrence potential and moral force of criminal law. Criminal prohibition is one of the most powerful and effective ways for society to acknowledge and condemn serious wrongdoing.[52] Laws prohibiting non-consensual pornography reinforce the

[47] Tara Culp-Ressler, '16-Year-Old's Rape Goes Viral on Social Media: 'No Human Being Deserved This' *ThinkProgress* (10 July 2014).

[48] See Ann Bartow, 'Pornography, Coercion, and Copyright Law 2.0' (2008) 10(4) Vanderbilt Journal of Entertainment and Technology Law 799, 818; Marion Brooks, 'The World of Human Trafficking: One Woman's Story' *NBC Chicago* (Chicago, 22 February 2013).

[49] Emma Gray, 'The Emma Watson Threats Were a Hoax, But Women Face Similar Intimidation Online Every Day' *The Huffington Post* (26 September 2014).

[50] Elizabeth S Anderson and Richard H Pildes, 'Expressive Theories of Law: A General Restatement' (2000) 148 University of Pennsylvania Law Review 1503–75, especially 1527.

[51] Scott Mendelson, 'Jennifer Lawrence Nude Photo Leak Isn't a 'Scandal.' It's a Sex Crime' *Forbes* (1 September 2014)

[52] Citron and Franks, 'Criminalizing Revenge Porn' (n 25) 349.

importance of sexual privacy to individual dignity and autonomy. They serve to ensure that all individuals retain the fundamental right to control who is allowed to view their naked bodies, a right recognized by long-standing prohibitions against trespass, voyeurism, and surveillance.

A. Protecting Privacy

The criminalization of privacy invasions has a distinguished pedigree. In their groundbreaking 1890 article *The Right to Privacy*, Samuel Warren and Louis Brandeis maintained that 'the privacy of the individual should receive the added protection of the criminal law ... [T]hat the community has an interest in preventing such invasions of privacy, sufficiently strong to justify the introduction of such a remedy, cannot be doubted'.[53] Over the past hundred years, state and federal legislators have taken Warren and Brandeis's admonitions seriously.[54] The Privacy Act of 1974 includes criminal penalties for the disclosure of agency records containing individually identifiable information to any person or agency not entitled to receive it. Federal laws against identity theft criminalize, among other things, the transfer or use of another person's means of identification in connection with any state felony or violation of federal law. Federal laws also prohibit the wrongful disclosure of individually identifiable health information.

A year after the publication of Warren and Brandeis's *Right to Privacy*, Supreme Court Justice Horace Gray wrote that '[t]he inviolability of the person is as much invaded by a compulsory stripping and exposure as by a blow. To compel any one ... to lay bare the body, or to submit it to the touch of a stranger, without lawful authority, is an indignity, an assault, and a trespass.'[55] Federal and state criminal laws regarding voyeurism demonstrate that physical contact is not necessary to for sexual exposure to cause harm. The federal Video Voyeurism Prevention Act of 2004 bans intentionally recording or broadcasting an image of another person in a state of undress without that person's consent under circumstances in which the person enjoys a reasonable expectation of privacy. Many state voyeurism laws criminalize the viewing or recording of a person's intimate parts without permission. Video voyeurism laws punish the non-consensual recording of a person in a state of undress in places where individuals enjoy a reasonable expectation of privacy. Criminal laws prohibiting voyeurism rest on the commonly accepted assumption that observing a person in a state of undress or engaged in sexual activity without that person's consent not only inflicts dignitary harms upon the individual

[53] Samuel Warren and Louis Brandeis, 'The Right to Privacy' (1890) 4 Harvard Law Review 193–220 (hereafter Warren and Brandeis, 'The Right to Privacy').

[54] Citron and Franks, 'Criminalizing Revenge Porn' (n 25) 346–47.

[55] *Union Pacific Railway Co v Botsford* 141 US 250, 252 (1891).

observed, but also inflicts a social harm serious enough to warrant criminal prohibition and punishment.

B. Gender Equality

In the United States, sexual privacy has not been protected to the same extent as other forms of privacy. Laws protecting victims from unauthorized disclosures of their financial, legal, or medical information have a much longer, and mostly uncontroversial, history than laws protecting sexual privacy. A combination of factors is at work in this disparity: in addition to misunderstandings of First Amendment doctrine, there is also a lack of understanding about the gravity, scope, and dynamics of sexual privacy violations; historical indifference and hostility to women's autonomy; and inconsistent conceptions of contextual privacy.

As Professor Citron and I detailed in our 2014 law review article, our society has a poor track record in addressing harms that disproportionately burden women and girls.[56] Though great strides have been made towards gender equality in recent years, most social, legal, and political power still remains in the hands of men. The fight to recognize domestic violence, sexual assault, and sexual harassment as serious issues has been long and difficult, and the tendency to tolerate, trivialize, or dismiss these harms persists. It is not surprising that non-consensual pornography, which affects women and girls more frequently than men and boys and often creates more serious consequences for them, is treated similarly.

At the heart of not only non-consensual pornography, but other forms of non-consensual sexual activity, is a tendency to treat sexual consent as different from other kinds of consent, especially women's consent. The commonly expressed belief that a woman who consensually shares sexually explicit photos with one trusted partner has effectively given consent for those images to be shared with a wider audience exposes troubling attitudes about women's sexual autonomy and contextual consent. It is the same attitude that underlies much sexual harassment and sexual assault: the notion that women who have voluntarily participated in some form of sexual activity loses her right to set boundaries about forms of sexual activity.

Outside of sexual practices, however, most people easily understand that consent is context-specific. Privacy regulations, affecting everything from medical records to drivers' licences, make clear that permission to disclose information to one person in one context does not equate to granting permission to all for use in all contexts. The non-consensual sharing of an individual's intimate photos should be no different.

[56] Citron and Franks, 'Criminalizing Revenge Porn' (n 25).

It is sometimes argued that the criminalization of non-consensual pornography *undermines* gender equality, by reinforcing the perception that women should be ashamed of their bodies or of sexual activity. But this criticism is without merit. Firstly, non-consensual pornography laws are not gender-specific: they protect every person's right not to have their bodies exposed without consent. Secondly, this protection has nothing to do with shame, and everything to do with autonomy and bodily integrity. Non-consensual pornography laws do not prohibit voluntary exposure of one's body any more than rape laws prohibit voluntary sexual activity.

C. Drying Up the Market

The market for private nude photos is unlike the market for other private information. We do not (yet) live in a world where thousands of websites are devoted to revealing private medical records, credit card numbers, or even love letters. By contrast, 'revenge porn' is featured on thousands of websites, in addition to being distributed through social media, blogs, emails, and texts. There is a demand for private nude photos that is unlike the demand for any other form of private information. While non-consensual pornography is not a new phenomenon, its prevalence, reach, and impact have increased in recent years in part because technology and social media make it possible to 'crowdsource' abuse, as well as make it possible for unscrupulous individuals to profit from it. Dedicated 'revenge porn' sites and other forums openly solicit private intimate images and expose them to millions of viewers, while allowing the posters themselves to hide in the shadows.[57]

The trafficking of this material increases the demand for images and videos that exploit the individuals portrayed. As the Supreme Court has held in the context of child pornography: 'The most expeditious if not the only practical method of law enforcement may be to dry up the market for this material by imposing severe criminal penalties on persons selling, advertising, or otherwise promoting the product.'[58]

V. Deterrence

Given the nature and severity of the harm caused by non-consensual pornography, legal intervention must focus primarily on deterrence. Unlike, for example, victims of property crimes, victims of non-consensual pornography can never truly be compensated or made whole. There is no undoing a violation of privacy; there

57 Dylan Love, 'It Will Be Hard to Stop the Rise of Revenge Porn.' *Business Insider* <http://www.businessinsider.com/revenge-porn-2013-2> accessed 8 February 2013.

58 *New York v Ferber* 458 US 747, 760 (1982).

is only damage control. Accordingly, legal intervention should seek to prevent the harm from occurring in the first place.

One of the merits of criminalization is that the fear of jail time is far more salient to the average would-be perpetrator than the remote possibility of being sued. The ideal effect of a criminal law is to discourage perpetrators from becoming perpetrators in the first place. Solid empirical evidence of the deterrent effect of criminalization is admittedly hard to come by. It is always hard to discern why people do not engage in crime. But we do know that certainty, more so than severity, of punishment does factor into deterrence, and it is generally acknowledged that most people fear jail more than lawsuits.[59] CCRI's 2017 national study on victimization and perpetration of non-consensual pornography also provides useful insight here. The survey asked respondents who admitted to having engaged in non-consensual pornography what might have stopped them from doing so. Out of more than a dozen possible factors, the majority of respondents (60 per cent) indicated that harsh criminal penalties would have been the most effective deterrent.[60]

VI. Defining the Crime

To advocate for criminalizing non-consensual pornography is not to blindly support any and all efforts to make it illegal. Laws should be clear, specific, and narrowly drawn to protect the right to privacy without unduly interfering with freedom of expression. This section summarizes the specific features an effective law should include, as well as features to avoid.

It is a basic principle of US criminal law that crimes include three basic components: an *actus reus* ('guilty act'), *mens rea* ('guilty mind), and social harm. The social harm of non-consensual pornography is, as has been detailed in the foregoing sections, the invasion of sexual privacy. The following discussion offers a description of what the other components of the crime should look like.[61]

A. *Actus Reus*

The elements of the crime should clearly reflect the fundamental social harm of the conduct, namely, the violation of privacy. Non-consensual pornography *can* involve harassment, extortion, or identity theft; the harm it inflicts *can* be psychological, physical, financial, reputational, professional, educational, or

[59] Valerie Wright, 'Deterrence in Criminal Justice: Evaluating Certainty vs. Severity of Punishment' (The Sentencing Project 2010) 1.

[60] Eaton and others, 'Victimization and Perpetration' (n 27) 22.

[61] See Mary Anne Franks, 'Drafting an Effective "Revenge Porn" Law: A Guide for Legislators' (17 August 2015) available at <http://ssrn.com/abstract=2468823> accessed 19 August 2015.

discriminatory. But what non-consensual pornography *always* involves is an invasion of privacy, and the harm it *always* inflicts is a loss of privacy. Accordingly, the basic elements of the crime should be (1) the disclosure of private, sexually explicit photos or videos of an identifiable person, (2) without the consent of the person depicted.

B. *Mens Rea*

The law should also clearly state the requisite *mens rea* for each element of the crime. It is an axiom of criminal law that a person cannot be guilty 'unless the mind be guilty; that is unless the intention be criminal'.[62] *Mens rea*, or 'guilty mind', refers to the mental state the defendant must have had with regard to the 'social harm' elements set out in the definition of the offence. At common law, the terms for *mens rea* were numerous and often ill-defined. The Model Penal Code (MPC), by contrast, uses just four terms for *mens rea*: purpose, knowledge, recklessness, and negligence.[63] Many states have adopted the MPC approach to *mens rea*.[64]

The *mens rea* for the element of disclosure should be purpose or knowledge. The distinction between the two is not bright in most circumstances, and in the context of disclosures amount effectively to the same thing. The primary point is to ensure that purely accidental disclosures would not be punishable.

The *mens rea* for lack of consent should be no higher than recklessness. In some non-consensual pornography cases, the perpetrator is explicitly aware that the depicted individual did not consent. Imposing liability on such perpetrators is relatively uncontroversial. However, to restrict liability to actors who act knowingly is too narrow. In many cases, the perpetrator has not been expressly informed that the depicted individual does not consent to disclosure of the image. Many intimate partners never have a specific conversation in which they set the boundaries of who has access to intimate photos; they instead presume that the images will be kept private between them. A discloser who is not in a relationship with the depicted individual—say, a hacker of celebrity photos—will likely not have been expressly told that they do not have consent to distribute images, and they may even think that it is possible that the depicted individual did consent.

If a discloser truly has no idea that the person in the image did not consent, then arguably punishing them is too harsh a response. But in many cases, disclosers have, to use the Model Penal Code's language in defining recklessness, 'consciously

62 *Mens Rea*, Black's Law Dictionary (4th edn, 1951).

63 Model Penal Code § 2.02(2) (American Law Institute 2016).

64 Joshua Dressler and Stephen Garvey, *Criminal Law: Cases and Materials* (7th edn, West Academic Publishing 2016) 168–69.

disregarded a substantial and unjustifiable risk';[65] namely, the risk that the depicted individual has not consented. When their uncertainty is weighed against the potentially catastrophic consequences of non-consensual disclosure, it is clear that such individuals should also face liability.

Under a recklessness analysis, only 'substantial and unjustifiable' risks are punishable. The 'substantial' prong indicates that the risk must be weighty in both a quantitative and qualitative sense: risks that are extremely unlikely to result in harm, or risks that are likely only to result in trivial harms, are not 'substantial'. The first prong is moreover informed by the second, 'unjustifiable' prong. The analysis of justification requires a calculation of the social utility of the risk. Speeding on a busy highway involves substantial risk both in terms of the probability and severity of the harm; car accidents are common and pose a grave risk of serious injury or death. But the analysis of the risk is affected by the reason for speeding. If a person speeds to get home in time to watch a favourite TV show, there is little social utility and thus little to justify the taking of that risk; if a person speeds to get a seriously ill child to the hospital, there is much greater social utility and thus justification in the taking of that risk. It is appropriate to criminally punish actors who act recklessly, in addition to those who act purposely or knowingly, when they know that the social utility of the risk they take is far outweighed by the social harm that is likely to result.

With regard to non-consensual pornography, the potential social harm is both highly likely and highly destructive. The likelihood of negative consequences resulting from the public disclosure of personal photos and videos depicting nudity or sexual conduct, especially for women and girls, is extremely high. As discussed above, these consequences include psychological trauma severe enough to lead many to contemplate, and some to commit, suicide; threats of sexual assault; harassment; stalking; loss of employment; loss of educational opportunities; loss of intimate and family relationships; and many other harms. The social utility of the risky activity—disclosing a sexually explicit photo or video of a person without verifying consent—is extremely low. Refraining from such disclosures absent clear consent cannot be a burden in the way that refraining from other risky but socially useful activities, such as driving, would.

This is not only because the social utility of disclosing sexually explicit images is so much lower, but also because the elimination of the risk in most cases will be minimally burdensome. All that is required to avoid the risk of non-consensual disclosure is to confirm consent when there is doubt, or refrain from disclosure when consent cannot be ascertained. The decision to disclose sexually explicit images rarely, if ever, requires split-second decision-making that would make verification impossible or impractical. Contemporary communication technology makes it possible for confirmation to be both easy and quick.

[65] Model Penal Code § 2.02(2)(c) (American Law Institute 2016).

C. Exceptions

The law should include exceptions for sexually explicit images voluntarily exposed in public or commercial settings. These exceptions are important to ensure that recording and reporting unlawful activity in public places (such as indecent exposure), reporting on newsworthy public events (such as topless protests), or forwarding or linking to consensually created commercial pornography are not criminalized.

The law should also include narrow exceptions for disclosures made in the public interest, including the lawful and common practices of law enforcement or medical treatment. As Warren and Brandeis wrote: 'The right to privacy does not prohibit any publication of matter which is of public or general interest.'[66] Law enforcement officers and medical professionals often have to deal with intimate materials, such as visual records of injuries from domestic violence or rape. While it is vital that such materials be kept out of the public eye, the law should not burden the necessary flow of evidence or medical records that takes place in professional settings. Outside of law enforcement and medical practices, the public interest exception might apply, for example to situations in which a concerned partner or parent of a victim of non-consensual pornography contacts an advocacy organization or social media platform and includes links to or copies of the content in the hope of having it removed or otherwise obtaining assistance, without getting express permission from the victim to do so. While the term 'public interest' is not without ambiguity, the dictionary definition of the term— 'the welfare or well-being of the general public'[67]—provides considerable guidance, as does the case law illustrating its boundaries, discussed in more detail below.

D. Other Issues

The law should not be so narrowly drafted as to only apply to disclosures made online or through social media, as non-consensual pornography can also take 'low-tech' forms such as printed photographs and DVDs.[68] State laws should also reflect an awareness, though not necessarily an endorsement and certainly not an expansion, of section 230 of the Communications Decency Act. As currently written, section 230 protects online intermediaries from liability when for content posted by third-party users. Given that section 230 trumps state laws that conflict with

66 Warren and Brandeis 'The Right to Privacy' (n 53) 214.

67 *Public Interest*, Dictionary.com, <http://www.dictionary.com/browse/public-interest> accessed 19 August 2019.

68 Nicholas Phillips, 'Sext Fiend: Jovica Petrovic Tried to Embarrass His Ex-Wife to Death, and Revenge Porn Was the Name of the Game' *Riverfront Times* (18 April 2013).

it,[69] state laws should not be drafted in a way that creates unnecessary confusion about this fact.[70] However, state legislators should also take care not to broaden immunity beyond what is provided by section 230 or assume that section 230 cannot or will not be amended or reinterpreted.

VII. The Unfinished Project of Criminalization

As noted in the introduction, all but two US states now criminalize non-consensual pornography. However, these laws vary widely in terms of definitions, scope, effectiveness, remedies, categorization, and constitutional implications. Only a dozen or so jurisdictions define the abuse as detailed in the previous section. Even though as many as eight out of ten perpetrators engage in this abuse for some reason other than a desire to harm the victim—including to make money, to obtain social status, to provide 'entertainment'—the majority of state laws make intent to harm a required element of the crime. This allows the majority of perpetrators to act with impunity, including some of the worst of the worst: revenge porn site operators; celebrity hackers; and creators of secret distribution networks that trade nude or sexually explicit images of women in the military, female college students, and high school girls without their knowledge, to say nothing of their consent.

Mischaracterizing the harm of non-consensual pornography as a form of harassment rather than a privacy violation renders the majority of US laws underinclusive and largely ineffective.

What is more, most jurisdictions classify non-consensual pornography as a minor misdemeanour, punishable by no more than a fine or a few days in jail. Prosecutors in such jurisdictions maintain that this effectively strips the laws of their practical use.[71] Law enforcement officers will rarely be willing or able to devote significant resources to crimes that are treated so lightly, and search warrants for personal electronic devices, often necessary in non-consensual pornography cases, are hard to obtain when the crime is not classified as a serious one.

The weaknesses and inconsistency of the majority of state laws, combined with the continuing failure of Congress to pass a federal law prohibiting non-consensual pornography, leaves victims at the mercy and discretion of local law enforcement authorities—both inside and outside the US. Advocates in countries such as Australia and South Korea have noted that the majority of 'revenge porn' sites

[69] § 230(e)(3) ('No cause of action may be brought and no liability may be imposed under any State or local law that is inconsistent with this section.').

[70] By the same token, criticisms to the effect that a state 'revenge porn' law can deprive Internet entities of their section 230 immunity are unfounded.

[71] See Tal Kopan and Megan Cassidy, 'Should Revenge Porn be a Federal Crime? Here's What the 190 Bay Area Cases Reveal' *San Francisco Chronicle* (San Francisco, 7 May 2022) accessed 13 June 2022.

exploiting their citizens are hosted in the US, beyond the reach of their national authorities.

The mixed progress on this issue may be attributable in part to political and social ambivalence regarding criminalization of the conduct. The relatively rapid shift towards criminalization of non-consensual pornography has, perhaps predictably, been met with praise in some quarters and criticism in others. The grounds for criticism are diverse, including the belief that non-consensual pornography is best addressed through other means, including intellectual property claims, self-help, civil remedies, or existing criminal law. Others raise concerns about over-criminalization, mass incarceration, and disproportionate impact of criminalization on minorities and teenagers.

Many of these concerns are valid and merit discussion. But the criticism that has been most effective in diluting state laws and blocking federal legislation is the one advanced by deep-pocketed and influential civil libertarian groups as well as lobbyists from the tech and entertainment industry: that effective laws against non-consensual pornography violate the First Amendment right to free speech. The ACLU in particular has led the effort to defeat or dilute criminal legislation against non-consensual pornography, often joined by the Electronic Frontier Foundation (EFF), the Media Coalition, the Motion Picture Association (MPA), and in some cases, tech companies such as Google. The collaboration between civil liberties groups and the film, technology, and bookselling industries means that considerable financial and political resources have been poured into thwarting the movement by grassroots victims' rights organizations and legal scholars to criminalize non-consensual pornography. While the coalition has not been able to stop the wave of legislative reform that led to nearly every state passing a criminal law on the issue, it has been able to render a majority of these laws practically useless by pressuring states to include 'intent to harass' requirements and to categorize the crime as a minor misdemeanour.

In 2013, when the criminalization movement was just beginning, the ACLU attempted to claim that *any* law criminalizing non-consensual pornography would violate the First Amendment.[72] A year later, but without acknowledging or explaining why, the ACLU shifted tactics, insisting on an arbitrarily narrow definition of the crime. The ACLU's preferred definition required not only that perpetrators be motivated by the intent to harm their victims, but that they must be current or former intimate partners. In one of the notable illustrations of its influence, the ACLU sued over Arizona's non-consensual pornography law in 2014, leading the state to withdraw the law and replace it with one drafted to meet the ACLU's much narrower specifications. This early episode in many ways set the stage for the national debate over criminalization, as the ACLU successfully convinced state after

[72] For a fuller account of these events, see Mary Anne Franks, *The Cult of the Constitution* (Stanford University Press 2019) 131–35.

state that an intent to harm requirement was essential to survive First Amendment challenge.

This position directly contradicted the ACLU's own stance on many other privacy laws. The ACLU supports laws that protect many forms of private information, such as social security numbers, genetic information, geolocation data, and biometric data. It has not attempted to argue that state and federal criminal laws prohibiting the unauthorized disclosure of material such as medical records,[73] financial data,[74] and cell phone usage information[75] are unconstitutional, even though none of these statutes require that perpetrators act with the intent to harass their victims (and certainly not that they be intimate partners of the people whose privacy they invade). With regard to these forms of sensitive personal data, the ACLU seems to recognize, in the words of Warren and Brandeis, 'the absence of "malice" in the publisher does not afford a defence' to privacy violations; '[p]ersonal ill-will is not an ingredient of the offence, any more than in an ordinary case of trespass to person or to property'.[76]

There are many First Amendment scholars, including myself, who never considered the claim that non-consensual pornography is a form of free speech protected by the US Constitution to be credible. But the accusation of censorship is a powerful one, and it is understandable that legislators felt they were in uncharted territory with the new crime of non-consensual pornography. It takes a bold legislature to recognize a new crime, and an even bolder one to not be swayed by the confident proclamations of the ACLU regarding free speech. But some states were that bold. In 2015, Illinois enacted the nation's strongest non-consensual pornography law, correctly omitting any requirement of a particular motive and classifying the offence as a felony. The law was challenged on First Amendment grounds, but the Illinois Supreme Court upheld it. The Court held that the statute was 'narrowly tailored to further the important governmental interest identified by the legislature', namely, the protection of privacy. To invalidate this law, the Court found, 'would cast doubt on the constitutionality of ... other statutes that protect the privacy rights of Illinois residents',[77] including those that regulate the distribution of medical records, biometric data, and social security numbers.[78] The Court noted that non-consensual pornography is not speech on a matter of public concern, and therefore does not receive the special protection of such speech: the public has 'no legitimate interest in the private sexual activities of the victim'.[79]

73 42 USC § 1320d-6 (2012).
74 Texas Penal Code § 31.17 (2015).
75 47 USC § 222 (2012).
76 Warren and Brandeis, 'The Right to Privacy' (n 53) 217.
77 *People v Austin* 155 NE 3d 439, 458 (2019).
78 ibid.
79 ibid 459.

The defendant sought review by the US Supreme Court, supported by an array of powerful interest groups including the American Booksellers Association, the Association of American Publishers, Inc, Authors Guild, Inc, the Cato Institute, the First Amendment Lawyers Association, Media Coalition Foundation, Inc, the National Press Photographers Association, and the Woodhull Freedom Foundation. In October 2020, the Supreme Court declined the petition for certiorari, leaving the Illinois Supreme Court ruling in place.

As of September 2023, the non-consensual pornography laws of seven states have been challenged on First Amendment grounds, including six that do not include the intent to harass as an element of the crime. Every single one of these state laws has been found constitutional. In other words, the revenge-porn-as-protected-free-speech argument has been decisively repudiated by the courts, as has the ACLU's claim that the crime must be defined in terms of the perpetrator's motive. States that diluted their laws on the basis of now-debunked First Amendment claims should immediately seek to revise them so that they can actually be of service to the majority of victims, and the remaining two holdouts, Massachusetts and South Carolina, have no reason to repeat the mistakes of other jurisdictions—they can pass strong, effective legislation the first time around. Congress should take note of how similar the SHIELD Act is to the thoroughly constitutionally vetted Illinois state law and pass it as quickly as possible.

VIII. Conclusion

The legislative, technological, and social landscape of non-consensual pornography in the US has undergone a dramatic transformation over the last ten years. The efforts of the courageous survivors and grassroots advocacy organizations in bringing about this revolution should be celebrated, as should the courts' vindication of the importance and constitutionality of strong non-consensual pornography laws. What is left now is for every US jurisdiction to ensure that its law properly recognizes non-consensual pornography as an egregious, life-destroying violation of privacy and classifies it accordingly, and for the US Congress to finally enact strong federal legislation to condemn and deter this abuse.

Bibliography

Anderson ES and Pildes RH, 'Expressive Theories of Law: A General Restatement' (2000) 148 University of Pennsylvania Law Review 1503

Bartow A, 'Pornography, Coercion, and Copyright Law 2.0' (2008)10(4) Vanderbilt Journal of Entertainment and Technology Law 799, 818

Bates S, 'Revenge Porn and Mental Health: A Qualitative Analysis of the Mental Health Effects of Revenge Porn on Female Survivors' (2017) 12(1) Feminist Criminology 22

Citron DK, 'Cyber Civil Rights' (2009) 89 Boston University Law Review 61

Citron DK and Franks MA, 'Criminalizing Revenge Porn' (2014) 49 Wake Forest Law Review 345

Dressler J and Garvey S, *Criminal Law: Cases and Materials* (7th edn, West Academic Publishing 2016)

Franks MA, 'Unwilling Avatars: Idealism and Discrimination in Cyberspace' (2011) 20 Columbia Journal of Gender and Law 224

Franks MA, 'Drafting an Effective "Revenge Porn" Law: A Guide for Legislators' (17 August 2015) <https://ssrn.com/abstract=2468823> accessed 19 July 2020 xx

Franks MA, 'Revenge Porn Reform: A View from the Front Lines' (2018) 69 Florida Law Review 1251

Franks MA, *The Cult of the Constitution* (Stanford University Press 2019)

Mathen C, 'Crowdsourcing Sexual Objectification' (2014) 3 Laws 529

Poole E, 'Fighting Back against Non-consensual Pornography' (2015) 49 University of San Francisco Law Review 181

Ronneburger A, 'Sex, Privacy, and Webpages: Creating a Legal Remedy for Victims of Porn 2.0' (2009) 21 Syracuse Science and Technology Law Reporter 1

Uhl CA and others (2018) 'An Examination of Nonconsensual Pornography Websites' (2018) 28(1) Feminism and Psychology (2018) 50

Warren S and Brandeis L, 'The Right to Privacy' (1890) 4 Harvard Law Review 193

Wright V, 'Deterrence in Criminal Justice: Evaluating Certainty vs. Severity of Punishment' (The Sentencing Project 2010)

10

Patterns of Criminalization of Intimate Image Abuse

Continental Approaches and Foundations

Manuel Cancio Meliá

I. Introduction

It is an understatement to say that the Internet and its ubiquity, especially via smartphones, and the enormous simplification of the production of audiovisual material through these tools, has changed our lives. Practised sexuality is also exposed to these changes as many people, especially younger individuals, are incorporating new technical possibilities into their sexual lives. This includes, in particular, the use of the technical possibilities to produce images and audiovisual materials with sexual content and to potentially spread them spatially and temporally ('viralization').

Manuel Cancio Meliá, Patterns of Criminalization of Intimate Image Abuse In: *Criminalizing Intimate Image Abuse.*
Edited by: Gian Marco Caletti and Kolis Summerer, Oxford University Press. © Oxford University Press 2024.
DOI: 10.1093/oso/9780198877813.003.0010

As has happened so often in the history of criminal law, new technological possibilities bring new opportunities to harm others, and the challenge for criminal law to adapt to the new reality through criminalization. In our age of postmodern acceleration, this challenge forces navigation between the Scylla of an ossification of criminal law and the Charybdis of an ill-considered, instrumentally managed ('penal populism') reformulation of new offences. The emergence of ubiquitous digital sexual material presents, in particular, the phenomenon of obtaining exposure of such content against the will of the people depicted. A veritable flood of spectacularly publicized cases—in which, according to traditional patriarchal patterns, especially women are virtually assaulted with consequences up to and including suicide—has brought legislators to the scene in many different legal systems.[1]

Even a cursory examination of the legal situation in continental European jurisdictions shows that there is no uniform 'continental approach'.[2] Rather, very different approaches can be observed, especially with regard to the coordination of specific criminalizations based on the newer digital phenomenology and the older privacy protection offences. Since a simple listing of various legal descriptions without considering the corresponding case law and scholarly interpretation does not promise any gain in knowledge (very often the real scope of application of the regulations cannot be measured in this way), three representative regulations will be examined a little more closely in order to try to identify the decisive questions for criminalization.

To this end, first (section II), the possible factual scenarios of possibly relevant behaviour will be briefly described without fixating on the cases highlighted in the media and their narrative. Then (section III), an attempt will be made to establish some starting points for criminalization, in order to then (section IV), outline the legal situation in the representative legal systems of Germany, Italy and Spain. Finally (section V), an attempt is made to identify the decisive problems of criminalization in the European-continental tradition.

[1] For updated lists of jurisdictions which have created new offences in this context in recent years, see Gian Marco Caletti, 'Modelos de criminalización de la pornografía no consentida. Reflexiones sobre los diversos enfoques político-criminales de los sistemas angloamericanos y de los países de la Europa continental a la luz de la ley italiana' (2023) 139 Cuadernos de Política Criminal 119 (hereafter Caletti, 'Modelos de criminalización'); see also Carlotta Rigotti and Clare McGlynn, 'Towards an EU Criminal law on Violence against Women: The Ambitions and Limitations of the Commission's Proposal to Criminalise Image-based Sexual Abuse' (2022) 13(4) New Journal of European Criminal Law 460 (hereafter Rigotti and McGlynn, 'Towards an EU Criminal Law'); Miha Šepec, 'Revenge Pornography or Non-Consensual Dissemination of Sexually Explicit Material as a Sexual Offence or as a Privacy Violation Offence' (2019) 13(2) International Journal of Cyber Criminology 429 (hereafter Šepec, 'Revenge Pornography').

[2] Rigotti and McGlynn, 'Towards an EU Criminal Law' (n 1) 467, rightly describe the situation in the EU Member States as 'divergent, piecemeal and confusing'.

II. Possible Factual Scenarios and Scope of Analysis

A. Scenarios

The *factual* scenarios relevant to possible criminalization[3] can be outlined as follows:

1. Seeing (hearing?) and recording (A)

Case area A is about *access to* intimate audiovisual material. Here, it is a matter of simply gaining sight (or hearing) of actions or objects in the intimate area of the victim. Access can be obtained with or without technical aids: through merely seeing with unaided eyes, or through technology-enhanced aids (microphones, binoculars, cameras, drones, etc) directly on the event/object. Access can also be obtained through various storage media (writing, digital audiovisual archives, etc). In the area of the socially mediated cases, the relevant topoi range from direct or technology-enhanced eavesdropping or viewing of the intimate sphere (voyeurism including 'upskirting' or 'downblousing'), to unauthorized digital access (to a storage medium or through remote hacking).

2. Disclosure to others and dissemination of recordings (B)

Case area B, the production of an image or a copy of the relevant material, situation or behaviour, is about the unauthorized *making accessible* or, more or less massive *dissemination of*, this material (images, sound recordings). In the relevant social topicality, this encompasses 'revenge porn' in the narrower sense and other cases of displaying the obtained or produced material for alternative purposes (to make victims, especially women, look bad ('slut shaming'); for economic interest in connection with the online pornography industry).

3. (Fictional) creation (C)

Case area C, the technological amplification through digital media, is particularly relevant when it is not a matter of depicting/reproducing material relevant to the intimacy of the reproduced person, but of *creating* it *ex novo*. The technological evolution from the more or less 'successful' traditional photomontage to the possibility of producing video recordings completely artificially, that is, purely fictitiously ('deepfake'), is astonishing.

[3] See also Chapter 7 in this volume.

B. Areas not to be Treated

The following three areas will remain outside the considerations of this chapter due to their specificity: first, the specific questions that arise when possible victims and/or possible perpetrators are not of age.[4] Secondly, the possibly criminally relevant conduct in order to achieve a certain behaviour by the person depicted ('sextortion'). Depending on the legal system, these can be offences against free will (eg threat of harm, coercion) or direct sexual offences.[5] Finally, the question of the apparently widespread (non-corporeal) mere imposition of sexually relevant content or representations. Whether through verbal means of sexual harassment ('catcalling'); unwanted sexually relevant displays through physical actions (eg 'indecent exposure', 'obscene exhibition'); or unwanted transmission of digital sexually relevant content ('dick pics'), it will be left aside. The issues of assessment that arise here belong in a different context.

III. Starting Points

Before explaining the legal regulations to be examined (section IV), and discussing and partially answering the decisive questions regarding a criminalization model (section V), some considerations must be briefly presented.

A. Comprehensive-Systematic, not Topic Approach: No Media-Friendly Monikers

In view of the genesis of many national criminal law regulations, it seems appropriate to point out that a scholarly analysis, which is to become a useful tool for possible criminalization, must not be the slave of media-mediated social monikers. The chasing of the media-hyped emergence of various new harmful and potentially criminalizable case constellations, often on the basis of particularly striking individual cases reported salaciously or sensationalistically, leads the law maker (and theoretical discussion) to fragmentary consideration on the possible scope of regulation so often encountered in this area, and sometimes to a downright

[4] See Chapter 8 in this volume.

[5] The conduct of making intimate material available or disseminating it to others, or obtaining it from the victim, is specifically regulated as a criminal offence against minors in several legal systems. However, a sexual offence can also be committed online among adults, as this offence does not require physical contact between the perpetrator and the victim; see Manuel Cancio Meliá, 'Commentary to the sexual offences' in Fernando Molina Fernández (ed), *Memento Penal 2023* (7th edn, Lefebvre 2022) 9287 (hereafter Cancio Meliá, 'Commentary'); Clare McGlynn, Erika Rackley, and Ruth Houghton, 'Beyond 'Revenge Porn': The Continuum of Image-based Sexual Abuse' (2017) 25 Feminist Legal Studies 37 (hereafter McGlynn, Rackley and Houghton, 'Beyond 'Revenge Porn'').

counterproductive criminal law coverage of relevant behaviour from various perspectives. As is well known, the rapid reaction to (real or supposed) problem areas that appear in the media, especially in extreme cases, is a main characteristic of penal populism or purely symbolic criminal law, up to and including the non-reflective creation of so-called 'enemy criminal law'.[6]

In particular, it should be noted that there now seems to be a scholarly consensus on the inappropriate use of the label 'revenge porn'.[7] This term refers, in its nuclear meaning, to the typically patriarchally biased male use of sexually intimate images as a weapon to take revenge for what is perceived as female 'misbehaviour'. First of all, it should be noted that this definition does not even begin to describe the whole field at stake when considering possible issues of criminalization.[8]

The use of these weaponized images, which may be relevant under criminal law, not only concern revenge, but also concern other gendered disciplinary strategies towards women (committed by men but also by women) outside of an existing or past (love) relationship; jealousy scenarios; attempts made independently of gender to harm the persons concerned; commercially motivated behaviour (for use in the pornography industry); economically motivated blackmail of the depicted person; simple mischief to gain sexual or other social status especially among adolescents in peer groups; etc.[9] The use of the term, thus, makes it difficult to even gauge the entire factual range of possible relevant behaviours. Secondly, the term also encourages blaming the victim in various respects.[10] If the term 'revenge' is used, it is obvious to think that something has been done by the person concerned. On the other hand, the very use of the term 'pornography' is a hint that a knowing and voluntary display has taken place by the person depicted. Therefore,

[6] On this, with references to German- and Spanish-language scholarship, see Manuel Cancio Meliá, '*Feindstrafrecht*?' (2005) 117 Zeitschrift für die gesamte Strafrechtswissenschaft 267; Manuel Cancio Meliá, 'De nuevo: ¿'Derecho penal' del enemigo?' in Günther Jakobs and Manuel Cancio Meliá, *Derecho penal del enemigo* (2nd edn, Civitas 2006) 85.

[7] For all the arguments, see Clare McGlynn and Erika Rackley, 'Image-based Sexual Abuse' (2017) 37(3) Oxford Journal of Legal Studies 535 (hereafter McGlynn and Rackley, 'Image-based Sexual Abuse'); McGlynn, Rackley and Houghton, 'Beyond 'Revenge Porn'' (n 5) 28, 30, 38: 'too narrow and applied too widely'; Gian Marco Caletti, '"Revenge Porn" e tutela penale. Prime riflessioni sulla criminalizzazione specifica della pornografia non consensuale alla luce delle esperienze angloamericane' (2018) 3 Diritto Penale Contemporaneo 71 f (hereafter Caletti, 'Revenge Porn').

[8] And in particular obscures the view of other variants of the 'continuum' of sexualized aggression against women; see McGlynn, Rackley, and Houghton, 'Beyond 'Revenge Porn'' (n 5) 25. The fact that the term exists socially is normally, of course, a positive element in matters of legislation. However, in this case we should avoid a term that is in many respects inappropriate and counterproductive; it is certainly not an 'advantage' (see Šepec, 'Revenge Pornography' (n 1) 420).

[9] This indicates that, as will be explained later, the legal establishment of special subjective characteristics beyond the requirement of mere intent, that is, knowledge of the objective elements of the offence, is a mistake that pre-programmes regulatory gaps (on this, see McGlynn, Rackley and Houghton, 'Beyond 'Revenge Porn'' (n 5) 31). This is also because, in general for sexual offences, the requirement of a sexual motivation ('lustful intent') traditionally read into the law in doctrine and jurisprudence is not appropriate (and is also rejected by a large majority of more recent jurisprudence); for the Spanish regulation, see, Cancio Meliá, 'Commentary' (n 5) 9288.

[10] See, for instance, Tahlee Mckinlay and Tiffany Lavis, 'Why Did She Send it in the First Place? Victim Blame in the Context of 'Revenge Porn'' (2020) 27(3) Psychiatry, Psychology and Law 386.

the terminology of 'non-consensual pornography' or 'involuntary pornography' is also to be avoided: it unduly shifts the attention to the behaviour of the possible victim.[11]

All in all, an analysis on the question of the possible criminalization of the behaviours of interest here should strive to develop its own objective terminology avoiding the entailing of preliminary decisions on criminalization.

B. Wrong and Harm—and 'Expressive' Function of Criminal Law?

It should also be noted, at the outset, that the complexity of the abovementioned issues is not only relevant from a moral or socio-pedagogical perspective. The enormous systemic importance of the legal interests involved indicates that both criminal wrong and harm could be present. As is obvious, depending on the design of the cases, privacy and sexual self-determination are being attacked. Both the empirical and normative perspectives indicate that fundamental elements of our social order are at stake, not only from a personal-individual perspective, but also institutionally normatively.

Indeed, normatively, the right to privacy is systemically essential. The legal position of a citizen must be defined normatively from the outset, through the attribution of a sphere free from state control and from harmful intervention of other people. It becomes clear that the inner sphere attributed to citizens is not limited to neuronal impulses (as the act requirement—*cogitationis nemo poenam patitur*—for a liberal criminal law emphasizes). In our society there is not only a limited space reserved for thought, but a wider personal sphere. Criminalization is only legitimate if it respects the sphere of inner freedom, the private sphere of the citizen, and correspondingly, harmful penetration into this sphere by others can be legitimately criminalized. The citizen leaves this sphere through an actual, externalized arrogation of the organization of others (as for criminally relevant behaviour), and it is obvious that penetrating into this sphere not only by the state, but also by intrusions of other people must be deemed an important wrong:

> . . . in an order of liberties, a subject is not only an animated body, but also a citizen, i.e. a system of whose internal sphere also includes property, his dwelling, agreed social contacts, etc. A control of what happens in this inner sphere would destroy the civil person; for without a private sphere there is no such thing as a citizen'.[12]

[11] For further arguments, see McGlynn, Rackley and Houghton, 'Beyond 'Revenge Porn'' (n 5) 38.

[12] Günther Jakobs, *Strafrecht. Allgemeiner Teil. Die Grundlagen und die Zurechnungslehre* (2nd edn, de Gruyter 1991) 25/1a. For the implications for the definition of the 'act requirement' for criminalization, see Manuel Cancio Meliá, 'Principios del Derecho penal' in Juan Antonio Lascurain Sánchez (ed) and others, *Introducción al Derecho penal* (Civitas-Thompson Reuters 2011) 81.

The legal interest of sexual self-determination,[13] a somewhat essential part of privacy,[14] is quite obviously also a central element of every citizen's fundamental rights fund. These two dimensions are clearly affected by the conduct at issue.[15]

On the other hand, the social position of sexual intimacy and of sexuality in general, as it is generally known, has recently undergone almost Copernican upheavals, connected to the recognition of women as citizens in this field.[16] A situation in which, in Gramsci's well-known formulation, 'the crisis consists precisely in the fact that the old dies and the new cannot be born. In this interregnum, the most diverse morbid phenomena occur'.[17]

The empirical research available on the effects on concrete victims, moreover, confirms the outstanding significance of the behavioural pattern under discussion. It can range from suicide to social ostracism or social disappearance.[18] In particular, it should be emphasized that a significant vector of these dimensions of harm is gendered, and affects women as the victim is blamed of being morally depraved.

In summary, the harm caused cannot be dismissed wholesale as irrelevant under criminal law, as expressed in some of the scholarly debates in connection with the introduction of specific new offences, especially for the dissemination of consensually obtained relevant image content, previously not punishable in many jurisdictions.[19] Rather, the task of a penal-criminal policy enquiry must be to determine how far and in what form criminalization should take place.

[13] From the perspective of criminal law, the negative manifestation, that is, the right to exclude others from one's own sexual sphere—see Stuart P Green, *Criminalizing Sex. A Unified Liberal Theory* (OUP 2021) 19 (hereafter Green, *Criminalizing Sex*); Tatjana Hörnle, 'Preliminary Commentary before § 174' in Gabriele Cirener and others (eds), *Strafgesetzbuch. Leipziger Kommentar* vol 10(34) (13th edn, De Gruyter 2023) (hereafter Hörnle, 'Preliminary Commentary'); Cancio Meliá, 'Commentary' (n 5) 9216.

[14] As is well known, the European Court of Human Rights (ECtHR) classifies this legal interest as a component of the fundamental right under Article 8.1 of the European Convention on Human Rights (ECHR): the right to defend oneself against sexual interference is part of the right to respect for private life (*MC v Bulgaria* App no 39272/98, paras 148–53 (ECHR, 4 December 2003); Hörnle, 'Preliminary Commentary' (n 13) 35–36 with references). This is at a time when sexuality is much more present in the public sphere and, in the course of the expansion of autonomy and gender equality, much more versatile than in earlier times.

[15] For a careful account of wrong and harm, see Green, *Criminalizing Sex* (n 13) 201, regarding invasion of privacy and dissemination of image content obtained in this sphere.

[16] See Boris Burghardt, Anja Schmidt and Leonie Steinl, 'Der strafrechtliche Schutz der sexuellen Selbstbestimmung vor nicht körperlichen Beeinträchtigungen' (2022) (10) Juristenzeitung 502 (hereafter Burghardt, Schmidt, and Steinl, 'Der strafrechtliche Schutz').

[17] Antonio Gramsci, *Quaderni dal carcere* vol 1 (Enaudi 1975) 311.

[18] On the harm dimensions for victims, see the detailed accounts in McGlynn, Rackley and Houghton, 'Beyond 'Revenge Porn'' (n 5) 29; McGlynn and Rackley, 'Image-based Sexual Abuse' (n 7) 534, 544; Caletti, 'Revenge Porn' (n 7) 65 ff, 78 ff. It is repeatedly pointed out that victims very often experience the event as being just as serious as physical assault—see McGlynn and Rackley, 'Image-based Sexual Abuse' (n 7) 542; Gloria Berghäuser, 'Commentary to § 184k' in Gabriele Cirener and others (eds), *Strafgesetzbuch. Leipziger Kommentar* vol 10(2) (13th edn, De Gruyter 2023) (hereafter Berghäuser, 'Commentary to § 184k'). All victims naturally react very differently; while some victims are driven to the point of suicide by the publication and 'viralization' of appropriate content, as mentioned (Caletti, 'Revenge Porn' (n 7) 65), others are much more resilient.

[19] On this, see Burghardt, Schmidt, and Steinl, 'Der strafrechtliche Schutz' (n 16) 507.

It is not about creating a new social reality with the means of criminal law. However, in this sense, there is talk of an 'expressive' function of criminal legislation in terms of an 'education' for a new sexual morality.[20] Such thinking, with regard to penal norms, is a danger to the rule of law and harm principle. Criminal law is a social event which has the function of stabilizing a certain configuration of the social reality of this society.[21] This means an approach to the collective, to the social function. However, it is about the current society, not a future one.[22] Naming the right values will not solve the problem; rather, we have to work out what the 'spirit of the times' and the evolutionary state of society actually are.[23] This ensures no possible theoretical-jurisprudential solipsism. This grounding in actual social conditions further allows for the examination of (present or past) discourses on criminal law and their real content. If the reference to society is not maintained, criminal law can have no influence on its development, thus is without any effect, mere discourse. Criminalization must be compatible with the conditions of evolutionary progress. Neither the social system nor the legal system can jump over their own shadow.[24]

For our concerns, we can simply assume that, at the present time, there is a social situation in which the relevant dimensions of protection do not represent a future programme, but at least partially correspond to our reality (including gender equality). This is what is at stake, not the creation of a new culture through criminal law.

C. Consent and Assumption of Risk

A third starting point is the question of how the event is shaped by the autonomy of the possible 'victim', who, if the event is attributed to them, is not a 'victim', hence no crime has been committed. This goes far beyond the clear cases of consent (eg a person who knowingly participates in pornographic productions, or someone who knowingly shows themself naked in the middle of the street, in front of millions of people on a playing field, or in the context of a protest against the fur industry).

[20] See, eg, McGlynn, Rackley, and Houghton, 'Beyond 'Revenge Porn'' (n 5) 31, 40; Caletti, 'Revenge Porn' (n 7) 87, both with references.

[21] Günther Jakobs, 'Das Strafrecht zwischen Funktionalismus und "alteuropäischem" Prinzipiendenken' (1995) 107 Zeitschrift für die gesamte Strafrechtswissenschaft 843 (hereafter Jakobs, 'Das Strafrecht').

[22] For the following, see Manuel Cancio Meliá, 'Non licet? Überlegungen zum Status der Kriminalpolitik in der Strafrechtslehre Günther Jakobs' in Urs Kindhäuser and others (ed), *Strafrecht und Gesellschaft. Ein kritischer Kommentar zum Werk von Günther Jakobs* (Mohr Siebeck 2019) 697.

[23] Günther Jakobs, 'Sozialschaden' in Martin Böse and Detlev Sternberg-Lieben (eds), *Grundlagen des Straf- und Strafverfahrensrechts. Festschrift für Knut Amelung zum 70. Geburtstag* (Duncker & Humblot 2009) 47.

[24] Jakobs, 'Das Strafrecht' (n 21) 136–37.

The central position of victim behaviour is addressed in another chapter in this anthology.[25]

It should be noted here that there can be no general, pre-formulated guidelines, but rather in each concrete factual universe of the forms of conduct of interest here, it is the criminal law (and its interpretation) in its orientation that must determine the possible effects of the 'victim's' behaviour on the responsibility of the possible offender, as entirely new social relations and factual circumstances could be involved. Thus, as is well known, several jurisdictions have ruled that the dissemination of consensually produced sexually relevant material without the consent of the victim constitutes a criminal offence and has been explicitly criminalized, even if the risk of disclosure was present for them.[26]

In the case of voyeurism, the criminal law (and its interpretation in case law) must decide, for example, when access to the view of a naked person, or the taking of pictures of them, belongs to the area of responsibility of the person seen or depicted, and therefore cannot constitute a criminal offence, and when this access does amount to a criminal offence. These decisions must or can partly be made by the legal text formulation. For instance, some jurisdictions explicitly protect against the invasion of privacy through voyeurism only considering the *taking of* images (ie not mere viewing), and only in certain spaces such as one's own home or other 'protected' spaces. However, even in these jurisdictions, the concrete framework has to be decided: is a shared shower room in a sports centre a protected area? In other jurisdictions, no explicit limitation of the protection of the intimate sphere to specific spaces is provided for by law. If someone stands behind a bush to urinate, are they entitled not to have this behaviour viewed/recorded? Other jurisdictions specifically criminalize photographing under a woman's skirt, or her cleavage, even if undergarments are present. Again: from simple cases where the exercise of autonomy-consent is obvious (eg a woman, as is sometimes the fashion, wears a brassiere directly as outerwear with no clothes over it) to borderline cases: does this apply to the moment when a skirt-clad woman gets out of a car, revealing her pants? Or: even without technical aids designed to see what is not visible (concealed camera in a shoe to be able to see/record the pelvic area of a skirt-clad woman), could the use of the zoom function of a phone camera to see relevant parts of the body be prosecuted?[27]

The penal law is unable to cover all the possible circumstances in its wording. Rather, the interpretation must take place within a theoretical framework. The

[25] See Chapter 14 in this volume.

[26] In this regard, the Spanish Supreme Court held in its ruling (*Sentencia del Tribunal Supremo*) no 492/2020—ECLI:ES:TS:2020:492 that the defence's argument that the victim had put himself in danger could not succeed, given the legislature's decision to introduce Article 197.7 SCC (see section IV.C in this chapter).

[27] In the Anglo-Saxon literature on this, see the convincing expositions of Green in *Criminalizing Sex* (n 13) 221.

formulation of the scope of the relevant offences via infinitely long and meticulous lists of facts (as in the continental criminal codes of the nineteenth century) leads to gaps in punishability when technological progress brings new forms of action. A normative justification of general patterns of attribution (the demarcation of areas of responsibility between 'victim' and 'perpetrator') is needed.

In continental scholarship of the last decades (and in jurisprudence), numerous solution concepts have been proposed in this area, primarily aimed at cases of 'contributive negligence' of the 'victim' in possible negligent homicides or bodily injuries, or in the offence of fraud. In particular, one line of thought can be noted. In fact, an attempt is made to establish a 'victimological principle' as a teleological maxim of interpretation, according to which '... all those forms of conduct are to be eliminated from the scope of criminal liability within the framework of a permissible interpretation of the offence against which the victim ... is neither worthy nor in need of protection.'[28] This principle of interpretation is justified deductively, because it is to be derived from the principle of subsidiarity. Since state intervention can only be legitimized if no other social instruments for conflict resolution are available, the self-protection of the victim is to be understood as a non-state mechanism.

The obvious criticism to this construction brings criminal policy or even the self-understanding of criminal law onto the scene. The consequence of such a general principle of interpretation would be a tendency for criminal law to retreat, a privatization of conflicts, not implying any kind of 'restitution' to society,[29] rather a mere lack of protection of the victims, a partial establishment of a state of nature, an institutionalized blaming of the victim.[30] Indeed, such a conclusion from the factual possibilities of self-protection to the exclusion of criminal liability[31] is wrong. This is because, firstly, subsidiarity of criminal law is a maxim to the legislator (and not to the interpretation); and secondly, because it is necessary to establish a normatively founded starting point.[32]

[28] Bernd Schünemann, 'Das System des strafrechtlichen Unrechts: Rechtsgutsbegriff und Viktimodogmatik als Brücke zwischen dem *System des* Allgemeinen Teils und dem Besonderen Teil' in Bernd Schünemann (ed), *Strafrechtssystem und Betrug* (Centaurus 2002) 62; see also Bernd Schünemann, 'Die Zukunft der Viktimo-Dogmatik: die viktimologische Maxime als umfassendes regulatives Prinzip zur Tatbestandseingrenzung im Strafrecht' in Wolfgang Zeidler (ed), *Festschrift für Hans Joachim Faller* (Beck 1984) 356, 362.

[29] In the well-known abolitionist terminology of Nils Christie, 'Conflicts as Property' (1977) 17 British Journal of Criminology 1, 10.

[30] See, with various nuances Thomas Hillenkamp, *Vorsatztat und Opferverhalten* (Schwartz 1981) 178, 206; Winfried Hassemer, *Einführung in die Grundlagen des Strafrechts* (2nd edn, Beck 1990) 77; Juan Bustos Ramírez and Elena Larrauri Pijoan, *Victimología: presente y futuro (hacia un sistema penal de alternativas)* (Promociones y Publicaciones Universitarias 1993) 27.

[31] For similar arguments against criminalizing the dissemination of at least consensually obtained relevant material in Anglo-Saxon literature, see Caletti, 'Revenge Porn' (n 7) 88.

[32] For criticism, see Manuel Cancio Meliá, 'Viktimologischer Ansatz vs. Selbstverantwortungsgrundsatz (zugleich: Allgemeiner Teil vs. Besonderer Teil)?' in Tatjana Hörnle and others (eds), *Festschrift für Bernd Schünemann zum 70. Geburtstag* (Walter de Gruyter 2014) 313; Manuel Cancio Meliá, *Conducta de la víctima e imputación objetiva en Derecho penal* (3rd edn, Bdf 2022) 285 with references (hereafter Cancio Meliá, *Conducta de la víctima*).

This normative starting point must be based on the definition of the citizen in our society as a person oriented towards self-realization and the synnalagma of responsibility for it. However, consent must be seen as only one phenomenologically particularly clear manifestation of the principle of autonomy, and therefore a global concept of the assumption of risk is necessary.[33]

IV. Three Regulatory Examples and the Proposal of a Directive by the EU Commission

As previously mentioned, the regulations for the spectrum of cases of interest in three jurisdictions in continental Europe will be presented very briefly (in the absence of something like a uniform 'continental approach'), in addition to the relevant contents of the recently formulated proposal of the Commission of the European Union. The three jurisdictions represent three different models that might, through comparison, offer insights into the fundamental conditions of criminalization.

A. Germany

In the German *Criminal* Code (GCC[34]), the areas of interest identified above in section II. A (seeing and recording) and B (disclosure and dissemination) are partially regulated in three different sections: as an offence against sexual self-determination only the production and dissemination of intimacy-relevant images with the help of technical aids in public in section 183 k (Division 18) GCC; as offences against privacy (Division 15: Violation of privacy of personal and private sphere) in sections 201, 201a, the access to, and the recording and dissemination of relevant audio elements and images, and corresponding recordings; and finally, as an offence against 'personal liberty' (Division 18), specifically, as stalking, some cases of repeated access via data processing systems, or repeated dissemination of relevant data or images in section 238(1) 6 GCC.[35]

[33] I have tried to develop adjudication criteria based on the notion of autonomy and beyond consent for cases in the parallel ambit of joint risk enterprises that end up harming one of the persons involved (treated in Anglo-American literature as 'comparative fault' or 'contributory negligence' problems) in Manuel Cancio Meliá, *Conducta de la víctima* (n 32) 341, 347; Manuel Cancio Meliá, 'Opferverhalten und objektive Zurechnung' (1999) 111 Zeitschrift für die gesamte Strafrechtswissenschaft 357; in English, see Manuel Cancio Meliá, 'Victim Behaviour and Offender Liability: A European Perspective' (2004) 7(2) Buffalo Criminal Law Review 513; Manuel Cancio Meliá, 'Victims and Self-liability in Criminal Law: Beyond Contributive Negligence and Foreseeability (Without Blaming the Victim)' (2008) 28(4) Pace Law Review 739.

[34] The legal texts that follow are taken from the official translation by Michael Bohlander available at <https://www.gesetze-im-internet.de/englisch_stgb/> accessed 1 February 2023.

[35] Sections 201 and 238 are not reproduced here, but are available online in the official translation referred to in the previous footnote.

Section 184k
Violation of intimate parts of body by taking photographs or other images

(1) Whoever
1. intentionally or knowingly, without being authorized to do so, creates or transmits a photograph or other image of the genitals, buttocks, female breast of another person, or of underwear which is covering those parts of the body, insofar as those parts are protected from view,
2. uses or makes available to a third party a photograph or other image created through an act of the type set out in no. 1 or
3. makes available to a third party, in the awareness of lacking the authorization to do so, a photograph or other image of the type set out in no. 1 which was produced with authorization incurs a penalty of imprisonment not exceeding two years or a fine.

...

Section 201a
Violation of intimate privacy and of rights of personality by taking photographs or other images

(1) Whoever
1. without being authorized to do so creates or transmits photographs or other images of another person in private premises or in a room which is specially protected from view, and thereby violates the intimate privacy of the person depicted,

...

4. uses a photograph or other image produced by an offence under no. 1 to no. 3 or makes it available to a third party or
5. makes available to a third party, in the awareness of lacking authorization to do so, a photograph or other image of the type set out in no. 1 to no. 3 which was produced with authorization, and, in the cases under no. 1 and no. 2, thereby violates the intimate privacy of the person depicted, incurs a penalty of imprisonment for a term not exceeding two years or a fine.

(2) Whoever, without being authorized to do so, makes available to a third party a photograph or other image of another person which is of such a nature as to significantly damage the reputation of the person depicted incurs the same penalty.

...

As can be observed, only section 184k GCC is specific to the matters of interest here. This provision is, moreover, rather recent: it was introduced in 2020 on the petition of two women.[36] Originally, the draft bill defined conduct as an offence against privacy. In the course of the legislative process, it was decided to introduce it as an offence against sexual self-determination, as this was the primary legal interest due to the 'sexual connotation'.[37]

The older layers of criminal legislation are very obviously only partially and fragmentarily applicable to cases of intimate image related abuse.[38] Indeed, the lack of coverage of facts is very broad. To highlight just a few: under section 201a GCC, pure voyeurism without making an image is excluded, as the conduct (whether with or without technical aids) of merely viewing is not covered by the wording. Additionally, even if the features of the 'private premises'[39] and 'protected space'[40] can be interpreted in a reasonable and normative way in scholarship,[41] in practice, the scope of this interpretation is not clear,[42] and precisely because of this physical limitation requirement, many possible relevant cases outside such 'spaces' remain excluded from criminal liability, such as urinating in a public space or having sexual intercourse on a beach or in a park, even if the victims in question have withdrawn before being seen by others.

Section 201 GCC, moreover, only covers 'words' with regard to audio recordings,[43] so that an intimacy-relevant sexualized conversation, for example,

[36] Prior to this, the conduct was unpunished (there was therefore a loophole), as section 201a GCC—see below—only protects certain 'areas of retreat': Berghäuser, 'Commentary to § 184k' (n 18) 7.

[37] Berghäuser, 'Commentary to § 184k' (n 18) 2.

[38] For general critical assessment of the state of the German system, see, eg, Burghardt, Schmidt, and Steinl, 'Der strafrechtliche Schutz' (n 16) 503.

[39] Brian Valerius, 'Commentary to § 201a' in Gabriele Cirener and others (eds), *Strafgesetzbuch. Leipziger Kommentar* vol 10(34) (13th edn, De Gruyter 2023) (hereafter Valerius, 'Commentary to § 201a'): private premises in a normative sense: hotel room, caravan, prisoner's room.

[40] Karsten Altenhain, 'Commentary to § 201a' in Holger Matt and Joachim Renzikowski (eds) *Strafgesetzbuch Kommentar* (2nd edn, Franz Wahlen 2020) 6 (hereafter Altenhain, 'Commentary to § 201a'): protected space: private premises as physical manifestation of privacy, as 'private sphere of personal intimacy', 'höchstpersönlicher Privatbereich', and in the terminology of the German Federal Constitutional Court understood as 'area of retreat', 'Rückzugsbereich', ruling *Entscheidung des Bundesverfassungsgerichts* BVerfGE 101, 361, 382 f (1999), ie as 'nuclear area of private life'. See Altenhain, 'Commentary to § 201a' (n 40) 18.

[41] Altenhain, 'Commentary to § 201a' (n 40) 8: shower cabin or locker room, toilets, medical treatment room, solaria; Valerius, 'Commentary to § 201a' (n 39) 38: also confessional, closed psychiatric ward. Protection by a 'visual barrier' is a 'recognisable manifestation of will' n 2, 24 ff; Valerius, 'Commentary to § 201a' (n 39) 36: also covered are other areas of privacy, beyond living quarters: what matters is protection from visual penetration. Visual protection also matters, eg on the beach by towels or privacy racks in hospitals around a patient's bed. The question of when protection is given should be solved according to the recognizable will of the possible victim, precisely in order to avoid neutralization techniques of the perpetrator and the corresponding secondary victimization by blaming the victim (see Valerius, 'Commentary to § 201a' (n 39) 27): perfect, gapless protection is not necessary, rather sight needs only to be objectively impeded.

[42] Burghardt, Schmidt and Steinl, 'Der strafrechtliche Schutz' (n 16) 506.

[43] Christopher Wietz and Jutta Zoblinski, 'Commentary to § 201' in Holger Matt and Joachim Renzikowski (eds) *Strafgesetzbuch Kommentar* (2nd edn, Franz Wahlen 2020) 2; Walter Kargl, 'Commentary to § 201' in Kindhäuser Neumann and Hans-Ullrich Paeffgen (eds) *Nomos Kommentar zum Strafgesetzbuch* vol 2 (5th edn, Nomos 2017) 5.

is covered, but not other equally intimacy-relevant audio content (moaning, screaming) without words.

Finally, the applicable scope of section 238.1 GCC is quasi-random and very fragmentary: the requirement of 'repeated' commission of the conduct excludes a large part of the relevant cases of dissemination of sexually relevant recordings (even a single dissemination plus viralization can obviously cause relevant harm).

In general, the legislative coverage in the GCC does not reveal an overall approach to responding to the issue and is rightly described as a 'legislative patchwork'.[44]

B. Italy

In Italy, too, a new ad hoc offence can be found in addition to already existing offences which might be relevant to the phenomena in case areas A and B. This concerns the offence considered by Article 612-ter of the Criminal Code (*Codice Penale*, Italian Criminal Code, ICC), hastily introduced as a consequence to the media build up in 2019 mainly on the occasion of a tragic case in which the dissemination of consensually produced audiovisual sexual video victimized a woman member of the Parliament. Further to this specific offence, the offences most applicable to the area of interest are as follows:[45]

> Article 612-ter ICC
> Unless the act constitutes a more serious offence, any person who, after having taken or removed them, sends, delivers, assigns, publishes or disseminates sexually explicit images or videos intended to remain private, without the consent of the persons represented, shall be punished by imprisonment of from one to six years and a fine ranging from € 5000 to € 15000.
>
> The same punishment shall apply to any person who, having received or in any case acquired the images or videos referred to in the first paragraph, sends, delivers, assigns, publishes or disseminates them without the consent of the persons represented for the purpose of causing them harm.
>
> The penalty shall be increased if the acts are committed by a spouse, including a separated or divorced spouse, or by a person who is or has been linked by emotional relationship to the offended person, or if the acts are committed by means of computer or telematic tools.

[44] Berghäuser, 'Commentary to § 184k' (n 18) 10.

[45] On other offences perhaps peripherally applicable in some cases (defamation, unauthorized obtaining of data), see Caletti, 'Revenge Porn' (n 7) 82.

> The penalty is increased by between a third and a half if the acts are committed to the detriment of a person in a condition of physical or mental inferiority or to the detriment of a pregnant woman.
>
> ...
>
> Article 615-bis ICC
>
> Whoever, by means of visual or sound recording instruments, unlawfully obtains news or images pertaining to private life taking place in the places indicated in Article 614, shall be punished by imprisonment of from six months to four years.
>
> The same punishment shall apply, unless the act constitutes a more serious offence, to anyone who discloses or disseminates, by any means of information to the public, news or images obtained in the manner indicated in the first part of this Article.
>
> ...
>
> Article 617-septies ICC
>
> Whoever, in order to damage the reputation or image of others, uses any means whatsoever to disseminate audio or video recordings, fraudulently made, of private meetings or recordings, also fraudulent, of conversations, including telephone or telematic conversations, carried out in his/her presence or with his/her participation, shall be punished with imprisonment of up to four years.
>
> ...

Italian legislation is, furthermore, characterized by fragmentary coverage and a hasty legislative process, especially with regard to the novel offence in Article 612-ter ICC.[46]

Article 615-bis ICC covers both audio and video recordings, but is limited to cases of recording (not viewing/listening). The conduct covered is limited to the disclosure with certain media ('means of information'), not the accessing per se, and is also limited to the home and home-like premises. Therefore, obtaining relevant images of a victim's body in public is not covered.[47] The offence of dissemination of relevant material, introduced in 2017 and contained in Article 617-septies ICC, seems to have a very limited scope of application: only video recordings are covered, but not simple images. Moreover, there is a limitation to 'fraudulently' obtained recordings: it seems from the wording that only the person who made the recordings can be the offender. The presence of a specific intent to 'harm' the

[46] Paolo Beccari, 'Le prime difficoltà applicative della nuova fattispecie di "revenge porn" in caso di diffusione del materiale da parte di soggetti estranei al rapporto sessuale' (2022) 6 Sistema penale 5 <https://sistemapenale.it/it/sentenza/tribunale-reggio-emilia-2021-528-revenge-porn-video-bagni-discoteca> accessed 1 February 2023 (hereafter Beccari, 'Le prime difficoltà applicative'); Caletti, 'Modelos de criminalización' (n 1) 136.

[47] Caletti, 'Revenge Porn' (n 7) 85.

depicted person's reputation brings a clear narrowing of the conduct covered,[48] and in a first ruling established interpretation, a recording of others cannot be included in the scope of the offence for lack of common intimacy.[49] All in all, it is a 'very fragmented' coverage by the 'old' regulations, that is, those centred on intimacy.[50]

The 'new' offence in Article 612-ter ICC, introduced in 2019 and specifically relevant to the phenomenon of images received by consent but disseminated without it, has the advantage of including second distributors in the second paragraph. It covers all unauthorized forms of dissemination without distinguishing between different penalty ranges. However, it must also be noted that the offence provides for a very high custodial sentence, which may—under certain circumstances—counteract its actual enforcement. The option for a specific criminalization limited to sexually relevant ('explicit') images in cases of consensually created or received images, in addition to the comparatively very high prison sentence, brings the Italian solution close to the forms of criminalization prevailing in Anglo-Saxon countries.[51] On closer inspection, however, the description of the offence is full of loopholes. First of all, as in many other legal systems, only images are covered, not audio recordings. Moreover, it seems that mere disclosure, that is, making the material accessible by simply showing it to third parties, is not covered.[52] This also seems to imply an unjustified restriction: simply showing the relevant material to people in the victim's immediate circle, or to a large number of people, is presumably no less relevant and harmful than sending it. Unjustified is, moreover, the fragmentary description in the first paragraph, which requires the perpetrator to have made the recordings themselves, that is, to have taken part in the depicted acts, or unjustifiably 'removed' the recordings or files. Does this mean that material voluntarily sent by the victim without the intervention of the subsequent perpetrator is not covered? As is well known, this is one of the phenomenologically relevant factual variants. Finally, it is incomprehensible that a discrepancy in the description of the subjective side of the offence is established for first and second distributors, since an intention to harm the victim is established for the latter. The advantage of explicitly covering second distributors can be thwarted by the unjustified limitation resulting from this requirement.[53] The specific coverage by the new offence seems to be a bluff, at least in some areas. If one scratches under the surface, there are many logical explosives in the description of the offence, which undoubtedly limit the scope of the offence.

[48] Caletti, 'Revenge Porn' (n 7) 84; Paolo Furlotti, 'Art. *617-septies*' in Alberto Cadoppi and others (eds), *Codice penale commentato* (Giappichelli 2018) 2669.

[49] Beccari, 'Le prime difficoltà applicative' (n 46).

[50] Caletti, 'Revenge Porn' (n 7) 87.

[51] Caletti, 'Modelos de criminalización' (n 1) 125.

[52] ibid 20.

[53] ibid 18, 34; on other problematic elements of the offence ('sexually explicit', 'intended to remain private'), see ibid 23 ff; see also Beccari, 'Le prime difficoltà applicative' (n 46).

C. Spain

In the case of the Spanish Penal Code (Código Penal, SCC), the areas of interest of intimacy-related content case areas A and B are uniformly regulated in the general offence against attacks on privacy in Article 197. In this legal system, too, the dissemination of consensually obtained material was regulated ad hoc in 2015 on the basis of a media-relevant case in a new paragraph (Article 197.7 SCC) with a lower range of punishment, as previously the basic form of the offence in Article 197.1 SCC only covered viewing, receiving, and disseminating material obtained without consent and it was difficult to apply other pre-existing offences.[54]

Recently (in 2022), this new offence was also reformed to cover second distributors in a specific offence with a lesser penalty range, as the original wording only provided for the perpetration of the person who had consensually received or participated in the production of the material.

Article 197 SCC

1. whoever, in order to discover the secrets or to breach the privacy of another, without his consent, seizes his papers, letters, electronic mail messages or any other documents or personal belongings, or intercepts his telecommunications or uses technical devices for listening, transmitting, recording or to play sound or image, or any other communication signal, shall be punished with imprisonment of one to four years and a fine of twelve to twenty-four months.

...

3. a prison sentence of two to five years shall be imposed if the data or facts discovered or the images captured referred to in the previous numbers are disseminated, disclosed or transferred to third parties.

   A term of imprisonment of one to three years and a fine of twelve to twenty-four months shall be imposed on anyone who, with knowledge of their unlawful origin and without having taken part in their discovery, engages in the conduct described in the previous paragraph.

...

5. Likewise, when the facts described in the previous sections affect personal data revealing ideology, religion, beliefs, health, racial origin or sexual life, or when the victim is a minor or a disabled person in need of special protection, the penalties provided for in the upper half of the sentence shall be imposed.
6. if the acts are carried out for financial gain, the penalties provided for in paragraphs 1 to 4 of this Article shall be imposed in their upper half. If they also

[54] See María del Mar Carrasco Andrino, 'Descubrimiento y revelación de secretos' in Francisco Javier Álvarez García (ed), *Tratado de Derecho penal. Parte Especial I. Delitos contra las personas* (Tirant lo Blanch 2021) 1463 (hereafter Carrasco Andrino, 'Descubrimiento').

affect data mentioned in the previous section, the penalty to be imposed shall be imprisonment for a term of four to seven years.

7. a prison sentence of three months to one year or a fine of six to twelve months shall be imposed on anyone who, without the authorization of the person concerned, disseminates, discloses or transfers to third parties images or audiovisual recordings of that person which they have obtained with their consent in a home or any other place out of sight of third parties, when the disclosure seriously undermines the personal privacy of that person.

   A fine of one to three months shall be imposed on anyone who, having received the images or audiovisual recordings referred to in the previous paragraph, disseminates, discloses or transfers them to third parties without the consent of the person concerned.

   In the cases of the preceding paragraphs, the penalty shall be imposed in its upper half when the acts have been committed by the spouse or by a person who is or has been united to him/her by an analogous relationship of affectivity, even without cohabitation, the victim is a minor or a disabled person in need of special protection, or the acts have been committed with a lucrative purpose.

The 'older' offence forms in section 1 are formulated in a very abstract way, allowing for the coverage of all relevant modalities summarized above in case areas A and B, regardless of whether they happen off- or online.

As to area A, merely viewing fits into the described behaviour[55] or merely listening (as far as it is done with any technical aids: only unaided eyes or ears are excluded) to relevant content. Furthermore, there is no restriction to a certain spatial area, so the interpretation of which public situations are covered is to be taken from the understanding of the element of 'breach of privacy' in the case law/interpretation. The cases of technically assisted viewing of sexually relevant body parts in public (in particular, shots of the pelvic area of women under their skirts) are also covered by the general formulation of conduct in Article 197.1 SCC.[56] The specific intent included in the description of the offence ('in order to discover the secrets or to breach the privacy of another') is actually not that specific, and only confirms that the perpetrator is aware of the privacy relevant content (to exclude 'accidental discoveries').[57] The behaviours in case area B, disclosure and dissemination,

[55] 'Seize' is understood here by case law in a broader sense as 'notice'; see María Teresa Castiñeira Palou and Albert Estrada i Cuadras, 'Descubrimiento de secretos' in Jesús-María Silva Sánchez (ed) *Lecciones de Derecho penal. Parte Especial* (7th edn, Atelier 2021) 159 (hereafter Palou and Estrada I Cuadras, 'Descubrimiento de secretos').

[56] Several proceedings are already underway in this regard; see *El País*, 22 August 2019, <https://elpais.com/sociedad/2019/08/22/actualidad/1566464180_921588.html> accessed 1 February 2023.

[57] For example, urinating in public in a way that is protected from view is covered by the legal description in Article 197 SCC; the claim by Rigotti and McGlynn, 'Towards an EU Criminal Law' (n 1) 462 that this is not the case is based on a misunderstanding. Indeed, in a case relevant to the media (where the offender had positioned cameras to record the women who he knew were in the habit of urinating in a particular place in the open air at a public festival), the investigating judge responsible had

are, moreover, covered in a very broad way in number 3: merely showing the relevant material, even to a single person[58], is included in the description. The material of interest here must make it possible to identify the person concerned so that the legal interest of privacy is affected.[59] Furthermore, the more serious case in number 5 should be pointed out. It punishes sexually significant facts, primarily relevant in practice here, with a higher penalty, together with other variants of 'hard core' privacy. Here too, second disseminators who have knowledge of the unlawful origin of the material are also punished in the aggravated case of number 3. The specific intent included in the offence description ('in order to discover the secrets or to breach the privacy of another') is actually not that specific, and only confirms that the perpetrator is aware of the privacy-relevant content (to exclude 'accidental discoveries').

The specific coverage of the core area in gendered cases of 'punishment' of an ex-partner by dissemination of relevant content in number 7[60] (with a lesser penalty to take account of the fact that the victim had opened their intimacy area to the offender) finally covers those cases where the material was sent by the victim, that is, the offender was not involved in the material's production.[61] The clause 'in a home or any other place out of sight of third parties' does not preclude relevant conduct undertaken in a public place (eg in a sheltered place in a public park) from being

initially closed the case on the grounds that there was no privacy here. This is an obviously legally erroneous interpretation: there is no restriction in the wording of the law to certain spaces, and if someone withdraws from view to perform this act, which is private in our culture (see Green, *Criminalizing Sex* (n 13) 230, 266), there is undoubtedly privacy worth protecting (the decisive factor is the 'expectation of privacy' on the part of the victim; see Carrasco Andrino, 'Descubrimiento' (n 54) 167). The erroneous interpretation was corrected by the competent Provincial Court and the investigating judge was ordered to continue the investigation; see *El País*, 11 November 2021, <https://elpais.com/sociedad/2021-11-11/la-audiencia-de-lugo-reabre-el-caso-de-las-grabaciones-vejatorias-a-mujeres-en-la-romeria-de-a-maruxaina.html> accessed 1 February 2023.

[58] See, eg, Joan Josep Queralt Jiménez, *Derecho penal. Parte Especial* (7th edn, Tirant lo Blanch 2015) 337 (hereafter Queralt Jiménez, *Derecho penal).*

[59] The mere image of a woman's breasts does not allow this and must therefore be excluded; see, eg, Ruling of the Provincial Court (*Audiencia Provincial*) Madrid, section 26, 372/2017.

[60] Which parts of scholarship have met with harsh criticism that it is a case of media-mediated penal populism based on an individual case, and that it has unduly expanded the scope of punishability to the point of establishing a global 'duty of silence' (see María Asunción Colás Turégano, 'Nuevas conductas contra la intimidad (arts. 197; 197 bis; 197 ter)' in José Luis González Cussac (ed), *Comentarios a la Reforma del Código Penal de 2015* (Tirant lo Blanch 2015) 663; Fermín Morales Prats, 'Delitos contra la intimidad, el derecho a la propria imagen y la inviolabilidad del domicilio', in Fermín Morales Prats and Gonzalo Quintero Olivares *Comentarios al Código Penal Español* vol 1 (7th edn, Thomson Reuters Aranzadi 2016) 1468); Queralt Jiménez, *Derecho penal* (n 58) 337 about 'opportunistic punitivism'; but for the justification of the provision, probably the majority of scholarship, see Carrasco Andrino, 'Descubrimiento' (n 54) 1464.

[61] In its *Sentencia del Tribunal Supremo* decision no 492/2020—ECLI:ES:TS:2020:492, the Supreme Court clarified that 'obtain' in Article 197.7 SCC includes not only participation in the recording but also receipt, eg by mailing; against this, for reasons of legal certainty, see Palou and Estrada I Cuadras, 'Descubrimiento de secretos' (n 55) 167.

included within the scope of the offence.[62] The question of whether the characteristic 'audiovisual recordings' covers only audio material is still controversial.[63] The offence explicitly covers second distributors after the reform in 2022,[64] and differentiates in the penalty ranges upwards according to the lucrative motivation of the perpetrator and due to the specific trust association in love relationships. The (actually unnecessary, given the wording in point 1) clause 'when the disclosure seriously undermines the personal privacy of that person' has so far been understood rather broadly, and covers, for example, mere nude photos.[65] In case law, cases of sexual content predominate, but the offence is not limited to this, covering generally relevant privacy content too.[66]

D. The EU Commission's Proposal for a Directive

On 8 March 2022, the EU Commission finally adopted a proposal for a directive on combating violence against women and domestic violence,[67] directly related to the conduct of interest here. The proposal is based on the competences of the EU in harmonizing the criminal laws of the Member States regarding the 'sexual exploitation of women' and regarding 'computer crime'.[68]

The provision of the proposal that is of interest here is Article 7:

> Non-consensual sharing of intimate or manipulated material
> Member States shall ensure that the following intentional conduct is punishable as a criminal offence:

[62] See Francisco Muñoz Conde, *Derecho penal. Parte Especial* (24th edn, Tirant lo Blanch 2022) 298.

[63] Denying this possibility, see Carrasco Andrino, 'Descubrimiento' (n 54) 1467; Muñoz Conde, *Derecho penal* (n 62) 298.

[64] Muñoz Conde, *Derecho penal* (n 62) 299, points out the practical difficulties of enforcements in cases of massive dissemination.

[65] Criticism of the indeterminacy of the clause, eg in Carrasco Andrino, 'Descubrimiento' (n 54) 1468.

[66] See Carrasco Andrino, 'Descubrimiento' (n 54) 1469; eg the consensual recording of a person using cocaine, which is then forwarded to the person's father, also falls within the description: ruling of the Provincial Court of Madrid s 27 no 772/2019; not covered are, eg, photographs from which the existence of a love relationship is inferred; see ruling of the Provincial Court of Barcelona no 302/2017. In general, the Supreme Court has mentioned marital status, income, and disability as examples of typical elements of privacy-relevant data; see ruling 968/2017.

[67] See <https://eur-lex.europa.eu/legal-content/EN/TXT/?uri=CELEX%3A52022PC0105> accessed 1 February 2023.

[68] See Explanatory Memorandum, 2: 'Article 83(1) TFEU provides the legal basis for minimum rules on the definition of criminal offences and sanctions in relation to the sexual exploitation of women and children and computer crimes'.... 'The term "sexual exploitation" in Article 83(1) TFEU can be understood as any actual or attempted abuse of a position of vulnerability' ... 'Cyber violence against women ... has emerged as a new form of such violence, spreading and amplifying beyond individual Member States via the internet. Given cyber violence's inherent cross-border dimension, action by Member States acting individually will be insufficient to solve this problem.'

(a) making intimate images, or videos or other material depicting sexual activities, of another person without that person's consent accessible to a multitude of end-users by means of information and communication technologies;

(b) producing or manipulating and subsequently making accessible to a multitude of end-users, by means of information and communication technologies, images, videos or other material, making it appear as though another person is engaged in sexual activities, without that person's consent;

...

Irrespective of the Commission's obvious shoehorning of the competence base (and the uncertainty this creates for the effective adoption of such a directive), the following observations can be made. Firstly, it must be remembered that it is not a question of a textual regulation proposal, even if many Member States often simply copy and paste corresponding EU instruments and incorporate them directly into their legal systems, just like that. Rather, national parliaments have to analyse their own legal systems in order to determine whether the mentioned facts are covered by their existing criminal laws. Secondly, the wording of the competence base on which the proposal is grounded is limited exclusively to conduct involving digital dissemination. Thirdly, in (b) the proposal takes the step of naming the fictional creation of relevant content (section II.C above) as the target of criminal law regulation.

V. Issues of and Insights into Criminalization

It is now possible to identify some issues to be addressed in the criminalization of the case areas of interest by the continental jurisdictions, as well as some insights into what starting points should certainly be considered in doing so.

A. Issues

First of all, the question must be addressed in which regulatory context the corresponding provisions are to be placed: in the protection of privacy or as part of the offences against sexual self-determination, that is, intimate or sexual abuse?

This question, which has occupied scholarship intensively, should not be overrated from the perspective adopted here. Most continental jurisdictions seem to place the issue in the regulatory context of privacy protection. However, it seems clear that most of the conduct of interest here relates to sexually relevant material. On the other hand, there are also privacy attacks of a different kind. It is clear that sexual self-determination and the right to control the display and dissemination of elements of one's sexuality are crucial elements of the right to privacy. A contrast to such close objects of protection[69] cannot therefore exist, therefore the debate seems partly artificial.[70] Consequently, the main issue is how to effectively coordinate the grounds relevant to the legal interest of sexual autonomy with other attacks on privacy through the same means of commission. This could be more realistically possible when general rules against these behaviours are linked to the specifically sexual ones in the same regulatory context (eg by using grounds of aggravation of punishment for the cases of the sexually relevant forms of assault).[71]

Here, too, depending on the system of the respective legal system, the introduction of a specific ground for aggravation of punishment may mean adequate coverage.

Thirdly, it must be considered to what extent the recording of the acts of second distributors, decisive for viralization, is feasible at all, and does not remain merely symbolic. Perhaps a decisive policy towards service providers[72] is needed instead of symbolic criminalization.

Fourthly, it needs to be determined whether it is appropriate to limit it, as most jurisdictions have done so far, to images only; or whether it is appropriate to include audio content as well.

B. Insights

First of all, it is essential to devise a global design of criminalization with the necessary reflection. In all three jursidictions examined here, individual case-controlled, piecemeal legislation has led to some serious regulatory gaps and internal contradictions in the legal regulation. Rather, general, flexible formulations of the corresponding offences are necessary, in compliance with the principle of legal certainty, in order to react to changes in the behaviour and technological possibilities of the attacks.

[69] See Chapter 2 in this volume; in any case, it does not seem appropriate to start from the *petitio principii* that recording as a privacy offence means 'not taking the conduct seriously'; but see Šepec, 'Revenge Pornography' (n 1) 418, 422. See also Green, *Criminalizing Sex* (n 13) 206; Berghäuser, 'Commentary to § 184k' (n 18) 10; Rigotti and McGlynn, 'Towards an EU criminal law' (n 1) 462; Caletti, 'Modelos de criminalización' (n 1) 126.

[70] It is not clear what it means for the criminal law to be 'more than a breach of privacy' (McGlynn, Rackley and Houghton, 'Beyond 'Revenge Porn'' (n 5) 29, 39): given the close relationship between sexual self-expression and self-determination and privacy, it is more appropriate to assume a particularly serious breach of privacy.

[71] See the very impressive account of Canadian case law made and the arguments developed in Alexia Dodge, 'Trading Nudes Like Hockey Cards: Exploring the Diversity of 'Revenge Porn' Cases Responded to in Law' (2021) 30(3) Social & Legal Studies 448, with references to empirical research; see also McGlynn, Rackley and Houghton, 'Beyond 'Revenge Porn'' (n 5) 28; Rigotti and McGlynn, 'Towards an EU criminal law' (n 1) 462.

[72] See Chapter 18 in this volume.

Secondly, it is clear that the introduction of special intent forms on the subjective side of the offence in the corresponding offences is not appropriate and leads to regulatory gaps and legal uncertainty.

Thirdly, it also seems obvious that in view of the rapid development of technology, the criminal law coverage of the completely fictional creation of relevant image content—as envisaged in the proposal of the EU Commission—must be planned and promoted. As far as can be seen, with the exception of the Netherlands (Article 138 h of the Criminal Code), none of the continental European jurisdictions has yet taken this step, and it is high time to do so.

Bibliography

Altenhain K, 'Commentary to § 201a' in H Matt and J Renzikowski (eds) *Strafgesetzbuch Kommentar* (2nd edn, Franz Wahlen 2020)

Asunción Colás Turégano M, 'Nuevas conductas contra la intimidad (arts. 197; 197 bis; 197 ter)' in JL González Cussac (ed), *Comentarios a la Reforma del Código Penal de 2015* (Tirant lo Blanch 2015)

Beccari P, 'Le prime difficoltà applicative della nuova fattispecie di "revenge porn" in caso di diffusione del materiale da parte di soggetti estranei al rapporto sessuale' (2022) 6 Sistema penale 5 <https://sistemapenale.it/it/sentenza/tribunale-reggio-emilia-2021-528-revenge-porn-video-bagni-discoteca> accessed 1 February 2023

Berghäuser G, 'Commentary to § 184k' in G Cirener and others (eds), *Strafgesetzbuch. Leipziger Kommentar* vol 10(2) (13th edn, De Gruyter 2023)

Burghardt B, Schmidt A, and Steinl L, 'Der strafrechtliche Schutz der sexuellen Selbstbestimmung vor nicht körperlichen Beeinträchtigungen' 2022 (10) Juristenzeitung 502

Bustos Ramírez J and Larrauri Pijoan E, *Victimología: presente y futuro (hacia un sistema penal de alternativas)* (Promociones y Publicaciones Universitarias 1993)

Caletti GM, '"Revenge Porn" e tutela penale. Prime riflessioni sulla criminalizzazione specifica della pornografia non consensuale alla luce delle esperienze angloamericane' (2018) 3 Diritto Penale Contemporaneo 71

Caletti GM, 'Modelos de criminalización de la pornografía no consentida. Reflexiones sobre los diversos enfoques político-criminales de los sistemas angloamericanos y de los países de la Europa continental a la luz de la ley italiana' (2023) 139 Cuadernos de Política Criminal 119

Cancio Meliá M, 'Opferverhalten und objektive Zurechnung' (1999) 111 Zeitschrift für die gesamte Strafrechtswissenschaft 357

Cancio Meliá M, 'Victim Behaviour and Offender Liability: A European Perspective' (2004) 7(2) Buffalo Criminal Law Review 513

Cancio Meliá M, '*Feindstrafrecht?*' (2005) 117 Zeitschrift für die gesamte Strafrechtswissenschaft 267

Cancio Meliá M, 'De nuevo: ¿'Derecho penal' del enemigo?' in G Jakobs and M Cancio Meliá (eds), *Derecho penal del enemigo* (2nd edn, Civitas 2006)

Cancio Meliá, M, 'Victims and Self-liability in Criminal Law: Beyond Contributive Negligence and Foreseeability (Without Blaming the Victim)' (2008) 28(4) Pace Law Review 739

Cancio Meliá M, 'Principios del Derecho penal' in JA Lascurain Sánchez (ed), *Introducción al Derecho penal* (Civitas-Thompson Reuters 2011)

Cancio Meliá M, 'Viktimologischer Ansatz vs. Selbstverantwortungsgrundsatz (zugleich: Allgemeiner Teil vs. Besonderer Teil)?' in R Hefendehl, T Hörnle, and L Greco (eds), *Festschrift für Bernd Schünemann zum 70. Geburtstag* (Walter de Gruyter 2014)

Cancio Meliá M, 'Non licet? Überlegungen zum Status der Kriminalpolitik in der Strafrechtslehre Günther Jakobs' in U Kindhäuser and others (eds), *Strafrecht und Gesellschaft. Kritischer Kommentar zum Werk von Günther Jakobs* (Mohr Siebeck 2019)

Cancio Meliá M, 'Commentary to the Sexual Offences' in F Molina Fernández (ed), *Memento Penal 2023* (7th edn, Lefebvre 2022)

Cancio Meliá M, *Conducta de la víctima e imputación objetiva en Derecho penal* (3rd edn, Bdf 2022)

Castiñeira Palou MT and Estrada i Cuadras A, 'Descubrimiento de secretos' in JM Silva Sánchez (ed), *Lecciones de Derecho penal. Parte Especial* (7th edn, Atelier 2021)

Christie N, 'Conflicts as Property' (1977) 17 British Journal of Criminology 1, 10

del Mar Carrasco Andrino M, 'Descubrimiento y revelación de secretos' in FJ Álvarez García (ed), *Tratado de Derecho penal. Parte Especial I. Delitos contra las personas* (Tirant lo Blanch 2021)

Dodge A, 'Trading Nudes Like Hockey Cards: Exploring the Diversity of 'Revenge Porn' Cases Responded to in Law' (2021) 30(3) Social & Legal Studies 448

Furlotti P, 'Art. *617-septies*' in A Cadoppi, S Canestrari, and P Veneziani (eds), *Codice penale commentato* (Giappichelli 2018)

Gramsci A, *Quaderni dal carcere* vol I (Enaudi 1975)

Green SP, *Criminalizing Sex. A Unified Liberal Theory* (OUP 2021)

Hassemer W, *Einführung in die Grundlagen des Strafrechts* (2nd edn, Beck 1990)

Hillenkamp T, *Vorsatztat und Opferverhalten* (Schwartz 1981)

Hörnle T, 'Preliminary commentary before § 174' in G Cirener and others (eds), *Strafgesetzbuch. Leipziger Kommentar* vol 10(34) (13th edn, De Gruyter 2023)

Jakobs G, *Strafrecht. Allgemeiner Teil. Die Grundlagen und die Zurechnungslehre* (2nd ed, De Gruyter 1991) 25/1°

Jakobs G, 'Das Strafrecht zwischen Funktionalismus und "alteuropäischem" Prinzipiendenken' (1995) 107 Zeitschrift für die gesamte Strafrechtswissenschaft 843

Jakobs G, 'Sozialschaden' in M Böse and D Sternberg-Lieben (eds), *Grundlagen des Straf- und Strafverfahrensrechts. Festschrift für Knut Amelung zum 70. Geburtstag* (Duncker & Humblot 2009)

Kargl W, 'Commentary to § 201' in K Neumann and HU Paeffgen (eds), *Nomos Kommentar zum Strafgesetzbuch* vol 2 (5th edn, Nomos 2017)

McGlynn C and Rackley E, 'Image-based Sexual Abuse' (2017) 37(3) Oxford Journal of Legal Studies 535

McGlynn C, Rackley E, and Houghton R, 'Beyond 'Revenge Porn': The Continuum of Image-based Sexual Abuse' (2017) 25 Feminist Legal Studies 37

Mckinlay T and Lavis T, 'Why Did She Send it in the First Place? Victim Blame in the Context of "Revenge Porn" ' (2020) 27(3) Psychiatry, Psychology and Law 386

Morales Prats F, 'Delitos contra la intimidad, el derecho a la propria imagen y la inviolabilidad del domicilio', in F Morales Prats and G Quintero Olivares, *Comentarios al Código Penal Español* vol 1 (7th edn, Thomson Reuters Aranzadi 2016)

Muñoz Conde F, *Derecho penal. Parte Especial* (24th edn, Tirant lo Blanch 2022)

Queralt Jiménez JJ, *Derecho penal. Parte Especial* (7th edn, Tirant lo Blanch 2015)

Rigotti C and McGlynn, C, 'Towards an EU Criminal Law on Violence against Women: The Ambitions and Limitations of the Commission's Proposal to Criminalise Image-based Sexual Abuse' (2022) 13(4) New Journal of European Criminal Law 460

Schünemann B, 'Das System des strafrechtlichen Unrechts: Rechtsgutsbegriff und Viktimodogmatik als Brücke zwischen dem *System des* Allgemeinen Teils und dem Besonderen Teil' in B Schünemann (ed), *Strafrechtssystem und Betrug* (Centaurus 2002)

Schünemann B, 'Die Zukunft der Viktimo-Dogmatik: die viktimologische Maxime als umfassendes regulatives Prinzip zur Tatbestandseingrenzung im Strafrecht' in W Zeidler (ed), *Festschrift für Hans Joachim Faller* (Beck 1984)

Šepec M, 'Revenge Pornography or Non-Consensual Dissemination of Sexually Explicit Material as a Sexual Offence or as a Privacy Violation Offence' (2019) 13(2) International Journal of Cyber Criminology 429

Valerius B, 'Commentary to § 201a' in G Cirener and others (eds), *Strafgesetzbuch. Leipziger Kommentar* vol 10(34) (13th edn, De Gruyter 2023)

Wietz C and Zoblinski J, 'Commentary to § 201' in H Matt and J Renzikowski (eds), *Strafgesetzbuch Kommentar* (2nd edn, Franz Wahlen 2020)

PART IV

REGIONAL REPORTS ON INTIMATE IMAGE ABUSE FROM LATIN AMERICA AND ASIA

11

Criminalization of Intimate Image Abuse in Latin America

*María Camila Correa Flórez**

I. Introduction

Intimate image abuse is a phenomenon that has become endemic around the world. Latin America has been no exception as several intimate image abuse cases have been reported in the region. Moreover, while it can affect anyone, reported cases indicate that women are often the primary victims of this phenomenon. For instance, in Argentina, in 2015, Emmanuel Ioselli, also known as 'Camus Hacker', posted naked pictures of some famous actresses on Twitter.

* I would like to thank María José García (Law student at Universidad del Rosario) and Carol Natalia Parra (Law student at Universidad de los Andes) for their help in finding the information to write this chapter.

María Camila Correa Flórez, *Criminalization of Intimate Image Abuse in Latin America* In: *Criminalizing Intimate Image Abuse*. Edited by: Gian Marco Caletti and Kolis Summerer, Oxford University Press. © Oxford University Press 2024.
DOI: 10.1093/oso/9780198877813.003.0011

As there is no legal framework that criminalizes intimate image abuse, 'Camus Hacker' was convicted for extortion and other charges.[1] In Chile, a boy filmed a girl having oral sex with another underage boy and shared the video. The girl was expelled from her school and was the victim of bullying, which caused her to become depressed and attempt suicide.[2] In Colombia, in 2018, a group of male college students created a WhatsApp group called 'FEDEGAN', in which they shared, without consent, personal intimate images they had received from women.[3]

The number of reported cases and the damage that has been done has forced countries in the region to take criminal legislative action. In addition, the fact that most victims are women and girls has drawn the attention of Inter-American human rights institutions responsible for monitoring women's rights.

This chapter aims to expose and analyse the patterns of criminalization of intimate image abuse in some Countries of Latin America. It also aims to conceptualize intimate image abuse as a manifestation of violence against women from a theoretical approach. The legal framework in Latin America is then set out. This includes not only the manner in which some Latin American countries have (or have not) responded from a legal perspective to intimate image abuse, but also the regional instruments, such as the Belém Do Pará Convention and the Follow-up Mechanism recommendation on cyberviolence against women in Latin America. The foregoing leads to the conclusion that prevention, punishment, and eradication of violence against women, including intimate image abuse, is an international obligation of the Latin American states that are party to the Belém do Pará Convention.

The chapter concludes by analysing the patterns of criminalizing intimate image abuse in Latin American legal frameworks. Three patterns were identified: (a) countries where there is no autonomous criminalization of intimate image abuse; (b) countries where intimate image abuse can be considered as an offence against privacy; and (c) countries that prohibit intimate image abuse as an offence of sexual and/or gender content.

However, in some cases where the phenomenon is criminalized, the forms of criminalization do not fully comply with the international obligation of states or do not fully penalize the harm caused by intimate image abuse.

[1] 'El "hacker de las famosas" condenado por extorsión' *Periódico la Nación* (Argentina, 4 January 2017).

[2] Paz Peña Ochoa, *Reporte de la situación de América Latina sobre la violencia de género ejercida por medios electrónicos* (2017) 18.

[3] Camilo Andrés Delgado Gómez, 'El Fedegan de la Nacional: una historia de acoso sexual' *La línea del medio* (Bogotá, 13 August 2020) (hereafter Delgado Gómez, 'El Fedegan de la Nacional').

II. Intimate Image Abuse as Violence against Women: Theoretical Approach

Technological advancements, such as having live conversations and sharing photos, videos, audio, smartphones, and social media, have made people comfortable sharing aspects of their lives, work, and private matters. It has also changed the way people relate to each other. These technologies have changed interpersonal relationships, including romantic, dating, and sexual relationships. In this context of 'digitalization' of interpersonal contacts, sexting has emerged. Sexting is a modern digital phenomenon consisting of 'the exchange of pictures, videos or personal images of sexual content'[4] and is one of the risk factors for intimate image abuse.

Adult persons voluntarily engage in sexting with partners, acquaintances, or strangers, who abusively share them in chat groups, social media, or websites without consent.[5] Usually those who share these photos are ex-partners seeking revenge for infidelity, abandonment, or simply exposing their former romantic or sexual partner on social media. Therefore, this phenomenon has been called *revenge porn*. However, experts have criticized this neologism. For instance, Henry, McGlynn, Flynn, Johnson, Powell, and Scott in *Imaged-based Sexual Abuse. A Study on the Causes and consequences of Non-consensual Nude or Sexual Imagery*[6] present some of the criticisms that have been made regarding the term. Firstly, the term is inaccurate because revenge is not always an intimate image abuse motivation.[7] Secondly, the term 'ignores other forms of image-based sexual abuse by known and unknown persons'[8] such as 'upskirting' or 'downblousing'. Thirdly, the term *revenge porn* 'has victim-blaming connotations because it implies that the victim has done something to provoke the ire of the offender'. At this point, it is essential to clarify that the actual victim blaming component of the term is that it insinuates that the victim not only did something that aroused the offender's anger but also that what the victim did authorizes the offender to exercise revenge against them.

The fourth criticism raised by Henry and others is that linking the phenomenon to pornography ignores the harm caused by intimate image abuse and that not all images shared are pornographic or sexually explicit.[9] Finally, the term emphasizes

[4] Laura Cruz Gómez and Encarnación Soriano Ayala, 'Psychological Aspects, Attitudes and Behaviour Related to the Practice of Sexting: A Systematic Review of the Existent Literature' (2014) 115 Social and Behavioral Sciences 132 (hereafter Cruz and Soriano, 'Psychological Aspects').

[5] Matthew Hall and Jeff Hearn, *Revenge Pornography: Gender, Sexuality and Motivations* (Routledge 2018) 5 (hereafter Hall and Hearn, *Revenge Pornography*).

[6] Nicola Henry and others, *Imaged-based Sexual Abuse. A Study on the causes and consequences of non-consensual nude or sexual imagery* (Routledge 2021) (hereafter Henry and others, *Imaged-based Sexual Abuse*).

[7] ibid 3–4. See also Hall and Hearn, *Revenge Pornography* (n 5) 15.

[8] Henry and others, *Imaged-based Sexual Abuse* (n 6) 4.

[9] ibid.

the content of the images and not the fact that sharing them is abusive behaviour on the perpetrator's part.[10]

These criticisms show that the term *revenge porn* is a misnomer and highlight that there are many ways to obtain the images that are shared abusively. Not only are they obtained when the victim sends them to the perpetrator voluntarily, but also when the victim's devices are hacked or when the images are taken without the consent of the person depicted, including situations where the victim is forced to send them or take them.

For all the above reasons, in this chapter intimate image abuse shall be understood as 'the online and offline non-consensual distribution or sharing of genuine or fake explicit images of someone else by former or current partners, others, or hackers in order to seek revenge, for entertainment or for political motives'.[11] This definition also includes different motives such as, for example, profiting from images or videos.

How the images are obtained does not change the fact that using them without consent constitutes intimate image abuse. However, if the images are also obtained without the victim's consent, another possible criminal conduct may be involved. The same is true in cases where images are shared or sold. In these cases, other offences relating to pornography, sexual exploitation, or extortion may be invoked.

Intimate image abuse manifests as cyberviolence or violence exercised using technology.[12] It is a form of violence because the non-consensual sharing of intimate images constitutes an attempt against people's autonomy, privacy, and sexual freedom. Any action that assaults people's rights is *violence*.[13]

Intimate image abuse is not only a form of violence but also a form of violence against women. Violence against women is a kind of prejudice-based violence,[14] which targets bodies perceived to be different and is intended to eradicate or mark these differences.[15] When violence seeks to mark these differences, it is called 'hierarchical violence', which is used to reaffirm the inferior place that this person (perceived as different) must occupy or to punish them for trying to step out of that social place.[16]

[10] ibid.

[11] Hall and Hearn, *Revenge Pornography* (n 5) 14.

[12] On this point, see Chapter 3 in this volume.

[13] Günther Jakobs, *Coacciones. Explicación de la raíz de los delitos* (Universidad Externado de Colombia 2017) 33 (hereafter Jakobs, *Coacciones*).

[14] María Mercedes Gómez, "Violencia por prejuicio" in C Motta and M Sáez (eds), *Sexualidades diversas en la jurisprudencia latinoamericana* vol 2 (Siglo del hombre Editores 2008) (hereafter Gómez, 'Violencia por prejuicio').

[15] María Camila Correa Flórez, 'La violencia contra las mujeres en la legislación penal colombiana' (2018) 15 Nuevo Foro Penal 90 (hereafter Correa Flórez, 'La violencia contra las mujeres').

[16] Gómez, 'Violencia por prejuicio' (n 14) 90.

In this context, violence against women exhibits hierarchical violence because it is used to remind women that they have specific roles based on historical gender stereotypes such as motherhood, care, beauty, virginity, and being a source of pleasure for men, among others. Likewise, this violence punishes women who choose not to fulfil these socially imposed roles[17, 18] and constitutes a form of domination, oppression, and an exercise of power by men.[19] Therefore, it is a form of discrimination that violates human dignity.[20]

Throughout time, the female body has been perceived as an object. When someone shares an intimate image of a female body, without consent, they treat her body as an object to achieve revenge or pleasure, to punish the body's owner for not being a 'good woman', or to shame or humiliate her. That is why intimate image abuse has a gender component: as Hall and Hearn affirm, 'it is largely the practices of men and masculinities'.[21] The use of women's bodies as objects reflects and expresses the power that men have over women in society.[22]

This can be illustrated by the Colombian case described in the introduction to this chapter, where male students shared intimate photos of women through a WhatsApp group called 'FEDEGAN'. In Colombia, FEDEGAN is the National Federation of Livestock Farmers responsible for supporting the competitive development of the country's livestock sector. The name of the WhatsApp group is an allusion to the Federation that deals with livestock and compares women to traded animals.

In conclusion, intimate image abuse is a form of violence against women because it reaffirms the prejudice that the female body is objectifiable. When intimate photos of a woman are shared without consent, it is assumed there is a privacy infringement in exposing her body. In this way, women are reminded of their role in the social structure. This practice is also used to punish those women who step out of the imposed role, 'misbehaving' and sending nude photos. This is no different from punishing them for exercising their sexuality for non-reproductive purposes. Alternatively, they are punished for leaving a partner, and the images are published as a form of revenge and humiliation.

[17] Thus, eg, femicide out of jealousy is a form of hierarchical violence: the woman is killed for leaving home or getting a new partner. In other words, she is punished for not being the woman she should be.

[18] Correa Flórez, 'La violencia contra las mujeres' (n 15) 17–18.

[19] Catharine Mackinnon, 'Sexuality, Pornography and Method: Pleasure under Patriarchy' (1989) 99(2) Ethics 315 (hereafter Mackinnon, 'Sexuality, Pornography and Method').

[20] Committee on the Elimination of Discrimination against Women, General Recommendation 19.

[21] Hall and Hearn, *Revenge Pornography* (n 5) 7.

[22] Mackinnon, 'Sexuality, Pornography and Method' (n 19) 315.

III. The Legal Framework of Intimate Image Abuse in Latin America

A. Regional Legal Framework: The Belém do Pará Convention and the Recommendations of the Committee of Experts of the Follow-up Mechanism

The Inter-American Convention on the Prevention, Punishment, and Eradication of Violence against Women, also known as the 'Belem do Pará Convention', is an Inter-American human rights treaty establishing women's right to live free of violence. Thirty-two American countries have ratified it. In doing so, they undertook certain obligations,[23] such as enacting general laws to prevent, punish, and eradicate violence against women, which create rules or modify domestic legislation. Most countries have enacted general laws that contain criminal, civil, procedural, and administrative rules and public policy provisions.

The Follow-up Mechanism (MESECVI) was created to effectively enforce the Convention. The Mechanism consists of a technical body that analyses and evaluates the implementation of the Convention by the state parties. This technical body is the Committee of Experts that issues recommendations and regional and national reports on the implementation of the Convention and specific topics.

While the Convention does not contain a clear definition of cyberviolence, it does state that violence against women 'shall be understood as any act or conduct, based on gender, which causes death or physical, sexual or psychological harm or suffering to women, whether in the public or the private sphere'.[24] The MESECVI stated that this broad definition includes all forms of violence against women, and is a framework for understanding, for example, cyberviolence.[25] Consequently, intimate image abuse, as seen earlier, is a manifestation of violence against women, and its prevention, penalization, and eradication are obligations of the state parties of the Convention. In 2022 the MESECVI published a report about cyberviolence and cyberharassment against women and girls.[26]

According to the report, cyberviolence against women is 'any action or conduct against women, based on their gender, that causes death, physical, sexual or psychological, economic or symbolic harm or suffering, in any area of their lives, which is committed, instigated or aggravated, in whole or in part, with the assistance of information and communication technologies'.[27] This kind of violence can

[23] Belém do Pará Convention, Articles 7, 8, and 9.

[24] ibid Article 1.

[25] Guía para la aplicación de la convención de Belém do Pará (Mecanismo de Seguimiento de la Convención Belém do Pará) 2014, 21 (hereafter MESECVI, Guía, 2014).

[26] Informe sobre ciber violencia y ciberacoso contra las mujeres y las niñas en el marco de la Convención Belém do Pará (Mecanismo de Seguimiento de la Convención Belém do Pará) 2022, 74 (hereafter MESECVI, Informe 2022).

[27] ibid 13.

occur in the context of an interpersonal relationship or in the community, such as in educational settings. It also can be perpetrated by any person in the context of any social interaction or can be committed by the state or its agents or tolerated by them.[28]

The report defines intimate image abuse manifestations as cyberviolence against women. It consists of 'the non-consensual online dissemination of intimate images obtained with or without the person's consent for embarrassing, stigmatizing or harming the victim'.[29]

This kind of violence includes but is not limited to the real-time creation, distribution, or publication of intimate images of sexual assault or rape through platforms such as Facebook Live. It also includes creating and publishing online pictures or videos of intimate body parts taken in public spaces (*creepshots*), 'including *upskirting* pictures or *downblousing* ones'.[30] This violence also occurs when someone creates or edits sexual images or *deepfake* videos or if someone sends audio-visual intimate or sexual images without the victim's authorization in closed Facebook, WhatsApp, or similar groups. Finally, the report notes that the publication of pornographic images or videos on websites such as OnlyFans or websites specifically intended for revenge publications is also a manifestation of intimate image abuse.[31]

Regarding the lack of the victim's consent, the report establishes that there are two possible scenarios which can be configured: that there is consent for the obtainment and subsequent publication of the material or that the victim shared the material with the perpetrator but did not consent to its publication or distribution.[32]

Among the recommendations contained in the report, there is one concerning the creation or modification of criminal offences to punish all forms of cyberviolence against women.[33]

The report also outlines the legal treatment it has received in the different state parties.[34]

B. National Legal Framework: General Overview

This section will outline the legal framework for the abusive use of intimate images in some Latin American countries. The exposition focuses on two aspects: (1) whether the country's legislation contains any connection between

[28] ibid 13–14.
[29] ibid 39.
[30] ibid 41.
[31] ibid.
[32] ibid 40.
[33] ibid 136.
[34] ibid 73–83.

digital or cyberviolence and violence against women, such as a legal definition or similar provisions; (2) whether the country's criminal code enshrines digital or cyberviolence, including intimate image abuse, as a crime.

1. Argentina

Currently, intimate image abuse is not a crime in Argentina. There is no reference to cyberviolence against women or similar concepts in the Argentine legal framework, not even in Act 26.485, which seeks to prevent, penalize, and eradicate violence against women. Although Article 6 of Act 26.485 refers to 'media violence', this definition does not include other modalities of cyberviolence against women, such as intimate image abuse.

In 2016, Bill 2119/2016 was proposed to reform the Penal Code and criminalize intimate image abuse. In 2019, within a bill for a new Penal Code, intimate image abuse was included as an autonomous offence. However, none of these bills have entered into force. The 'Olimpia' and 'Belen' bills, which seek to criminalize digital violence against women, including the abusive use of intimate images, are currently being debated in Argentina.

2. Bolivia

In July 2020, the Bolivian Senate approved Bill no 237/2019-2020 (Act to Criminalize Cyberviolence against Women). Article 2 of Bill no 237/2019-2020 amends Article 7 of Bolivia's Act to Guarantee Women a Life Free of Violence by including a definition of cyberviolence against women as follows:

> Any action carried out through Information and Communication Technologies (ICT), internet platforms, social networks or email or any other digital space, that violates the psychological integrity, dignity, intimacy or private life of women; manifested through the dissemination of sexual content in texts, photographs, videos or other graphic or audio prints, without the consent of the victim when these correspond to her or linked to her'

In addition, Article 3 of Bill no 237/2019-2020 amends the Bolivian criminal code and includes the crime of cyberviolence against women. This crime sentences with imprisonment anyone who, without the consent of the victim, disseminates, shares, distributes, or publishes texts, photographs, videos, or other graphic or audio elements with sexual content.

The Bill is expected to be approved in 2023.

3. Brazil

The 'Maria da Penha Law' (Act 11340/2006) is the Brazilian Act on violence against women that contains provisions to penalize, eradicate, and prevent violence against women.[35] Like other countries with this Act, Brazil transposes the Belém do Pará Convention into its legal system. Nevertheless, this Act does not contain any definition of cyberviolence.

However, in September 2018 Act 13.718 was approved. This Act amended the Brazilian Penal Code and introduced Article 218 C, which criminalizes the disclosure of rape, sex, or pornographic-related images or videos. In other words, it establishes that:

> [I]t is a crime to offer, exchange, make available, transmit, sell or exhibit for sale, distribute, publish or disseminate, by any means, including through mass communication or computer or telematics system, photography, video or other audio-visual records that contains a scene of rape or rape of a vulnerable person or that makes incitement or induces its practice, or, without the consent of the victim, sex scene, nudity or pornography.[36]

The fact that the perpetrator had or has an intimate relationship with the victim increases the penalty as does the fact that the conduct is committed with the intention of revenge or humiliation of the victim.[37]

4. Chile

Intimate image abuse is not a crime in Chile. There are some criminal offences that may punish similar behaviours, but not intimate image abuse specifically. The Chilean criminal legislation punishes anyone who 'captures, records, films or photographs images or events of a private character' and anyone who discloses those films, pictures, or events.[38] However, this criminal provision does not apply to cases of unauthorized dissemination of images, videos, or photographs taken with the consent of the victim.[39]

Some bills aimed at criminalizing intimate image abuse as a specific offence have been presented; however none have been approved.[40]

5. Colombia

As in Argentina and Chile, intimate image abuse is not a crime in Colombia, and there is no mention of cyberviolence in the legal framework. Act 1257/2008 (Act to

35 For a complete analysis of the treatment of intimate image abuse in Brazil, see Lima Machado Rocha, Roberta Duboc Pedrinha, and Maria Helena Barros de Oliveira, 'The Treatment of Revenge Pornography by the Brazilian Legal System' (2019) 4 Saúde debate 43 (hereafter Machado Rocha and others, 'The Treatment').

36 Machado Rocha and others, 'The Treatment' (n 35) 183.

37 Brazilian Criminal Code, Article 218-C §1.

38 Chilean Criminal Code, Articles 161-A and 161-C.

39 MECSEVI, Informe 2022 (n 26) 16.

40 ibid 16–17.

Prevent and Penalize Violence against Women) defines all the forms of this kind of violence except for cyberviolence.

As no cases have reached the criminal courts, intimate image abuse has not been penalized by means of other offences. However, Article 269 F of the Colombian Penal Code punishes the violation of personal data. This rule penalizes whoever 'without being authorised to do so, obtains, compiles, subtracts, offers, sells, exchanges, sends, buys, intercepts, discloses, modifies or uses personal codes, personal data contained in files, archives, databases or similar media' making a profit for themselves or someone else. As is evident, this rule only penalizes those cases in which a benefit is obtained by sharing or disseminating intimate images, leaving out other cases of intimate image abuse in which either there is no intention to obtain a benefit, or the benefit is not obtained.

There are currently several proposals, such as bill 241/2022S, to criminalize cyberviolence against women; however, the Colombian Congress has not processed them.

6. Ecuador

Ecuador does not have a specific criminal offence related to intimate image abuse. Nevertheless, a general offence in the Criminal Code can be utilized to prosecute the conduct. Article 178 of the Ecuadorian Code criminalizes the violation of privacy. The conducts of the *actus reus* include dissemination of personal data (including videos and images) without the consent of the person depicted. Some authors criticized the use of this standard in cases of intimate image abuse because it simplifies the phenomenon and does not penalize the full extent of the harm caused by intimate image abuse.[41]

In 2020 the bill to 'Prevent Violence, Digital Harassment, and Violations of Privacy', which amends the Criminal Code, and the 'Act to Prevent and Eradicate Violence against Women' by including digital sexual violence as a manifestation of violence, were presented.[42] Despite this, the reform of the Code proposed in the bill does not include the criminalization of intimate image abuse.[43]

7. Guatemala

Article 190 of the Guatemalan Penal Code penalizes the 'violation of sexual intimacy' which occurs when a person seizes or captures 'messages, conversations, sounds, any type of images of the victim's body' to affect the victim's dignity by violating their sexual intimacy. Likewise, this rule punishes the person who seizes,

[41] Sofia Recalde Salazar, 'Criminalización de la porno venganza en Ecuador' (2020) unpublished.

[42] MECSEVI, Informe 2022 (n 26) 77.

[43] See <https://www.asambleanacional.gob.ec/sites/default/files/private/asambleanacional/filesasambleanacionalnameuid-29/Leyes%202013-2017/1272-mmontañov/ro-4s-526-de-30-08-2021.pdf> accessed 15 JAnuary 2023. The General Assembly of Ecuador is currently analysing this bill.

captures, uses, or modifies communications made by any physical or electronic means, or reserved data of sexual content, without consent and to the detriment of the victim or another person.

This rule penalizes intimate image abuse because 'use' is broad enough to cover the conduct, given that intimate image abuse involves the non-consensual use of images, videos, and communications (as stipulated in the rule) of intimate content without the consent of the person depicted.

8. Mexico

In 2019 the 'Olimpia Act' was enacted in Mexico. This Act contains a 'set of legislative reforms aimed at recognizing digital violence and punishing crimes that violate people's sexual privacy through digital media, also known as cyberviolence'.[44]

One of the legislative reforms is the creation of criminal offences in the Federal Criminal Code and in the Criminal Codes of the different Mexican states that prohibit intimate image abuse. The Federal Criminal Code was modified in 2021 when a decree-law introduced Article 199 Octies. This article penalizes the crime of violation of sexual privacy, which is executed when a person discloses, shares, distributes, or publishes 'sexually intimate images, video or audio of a person without that person's consent, approval or authorisation'. The victim must be over 18 years of age.

The criminal codes of the following states have been amended by including similar provisions: Aguascalientes, Baja California, Baja California Sur, Campeche, Chiapas, Chihuahua, Ciudad de México, Coahuila, Colima, Durango, Estado de México, Guanajuato, Guerrero, Hidalgo, Jalisco, Michoacán, Morelos, Nuevo León, Oxaca, Puebla, Querétaro, Quintana Roo, Sinaloa, Sonora, Tamaulipas, Tlaxcala, Veracruz, Yucatán, and Zacatecas.

Conversely, the Olimpia Act amends the Mexican 'Law on women's access to a life free of violence' by recognizing cyberviolence as a form of violence against women and introducing its definition.[45]

9. Nicaragua

Some provisions of Nicaragua's legal framework permit the prosecution of intimate image abuse. On the one hand, Article 195 of the Criminal Code enshrines the conduct of 'propagation' as follows: 'Whoever, being lawfully in possession of communications, documents, or recordings of a private nature, makes them public without due authorisation, shall be punished with sixty to one hundred and eighty-days imprisonment.' If the recordings, images, communications, or public

[44] Ficha técnica 'Ley Olimpia' <http://ordenjuridico.gob.mx/violenciagenero/LEY%20OLIMPIA.pdf> accessed 15 January 2023 (hereafter Ficha Ley Olimpia).

[45] Mexican 'Law on women's access to a life free of violence', Article 20 Quárter.

documents contain sexual or erotic content even if the perpetrator obtained them with consent, the penalty increases.

On the other hand, Article 26 of the Special Act of Cybercrimes punishes anyone who discloses, disseminates, or transfers personal (including sexual-related) information, data (videos, images, texts, audios) without the consent of the owner of the information or data and which are obtained through ICTs.

The Nicaraguan legal framework does not associate these conducts with cyberviolence against women or cyberviolence in general.

10. Paraguay

Act 5777/2016 'for the protection of women against all forms of violence', defines cyberviolence as: 'The act of disseminating or publishing messages, photos, audio, videos or others that affect the dignity or privacy of women through ICTs.' As is evident, the law defines intimate image abuse as a form of violence against women. However, as in most Latin American countries, the Paraguayan legal framework does not enshrine intimate image abuse as a specific offence. Nevertheless, as in other countries, the Paraguayan Penal Code contains provisions that allow for the penalization of this practice, such as those in Articles 143 and 144.

Article 143 penalizes the violation of a person's privacy, among other cases, when private information, including sexual information, is publicly disclosed. In the same way, Article 144 of the Paraguayan Penal Code prohibits disclosing another person's images without that person's consent. This disclosure infringes the victim's right to privacy. One might think that this article penalizes intimate image abuse, and, to some extent, this is true. However, discriminatory and/or revenge motives are not penalized by the criminal offence, although it comes very close to penalizing the conduct addressed in this chapter.

11. Peru

In 2018, the Peruvian Criminal Code was amended, enshrining, among other conducts, the dissemination of images, audio visual materials or audio with sexual content: 'Whoever, without authorisation, disseminates, discloses, publishes, transfers or markets images, audio visual materials or audio with sexual content of any person, which he or she obtained with the victim's consent, shall be punished by law.'[46] The fact that the victim has or had a relationship with the perpetrator and that the images are disseminated using social networks or mass media increases the penalty.

[46] Peruvian Criminal Code, Article 154 B.

12. Uruguay

Article 92 of the Uruguayan 'Act on Violence against Women'[47] punishes with six months to two years imprisonment anyone who discloses images or videos with intimate content of another person without their authorization. The offence is also committed if the person who discloses the images or videos has participated in them.

13. Venezuela

The Venezuelan Criminal Code does not criminalize intimate image abuse specifically. Nevertheless, the 'Act against Cybercrimes' punishes the disclosure of personal data or information. Article 22 imposes a penalty of imprisonment of two to six years on anyone who discloses, disseminates, or transfers images. This audio or personal data must be obtained in violation of the privacy of such data or information or in violation of the privacy of communications.

The Venezuelan criminal framework punishes one form of intimate image abuse, but not all. It is only an offence to disclose the material when it has been obtained through the commission of other offences, but not when it has been obtained, for example, with the victim's consent. In addition, it treats intimate image abuse as cybercrime, not as an attack on the right to intimacy through sexual content.

IV. Patterns of Criminalization of Intimate Image Abuse in Latin America

As is evident, the penalization of intimate image abuse is an international obligation of the states that are party to the Belém do Pará Convention. Some have complied with this obligation by criminalizing the conduct, while others have not. This last part of the chapter will identify and analyse some patterns of criminalization of intimate image abuse.

Before doing so, it is essential to highlight that in most Latin American countries there are comprehensive laws that respond to the obligations of the Belém do Pará Convention. Nevertheless, not all of these legal systems define cyberviolence. Therefore, it does not seem to be recognized, at least legislatively, as a form of violence against women.

Concerning this specific criminalization, and after reviewing the legal-criminal systems of thirteen Latin American countries, it seems possible to identify three different patterns: (a) countries where there is no autonomous criminalization of intimate image abuse; (b) countries where intimate image abuse can be addressed

[47] Act no 19580/2018.

with an offence against privacy; and (c) countries that introduced an intimate image abuse offence based on sexual and/or gender content.

A. Countries Where There is no Autonomous Criminalization of Intimate Image Abuse

In Argentina, Colombia, and Venezuela, intimate image abuse is not criminalized as a violation of privacy, a crime with a sexual component, or as violence against women. In some cases, the conduct is nevertheless criminally relevant because of the application of other criminal offences, such as extortion or cybercrimes.

This legal framework creates at least two problems. The first concerns the principle of legality. Criminalizing conduct through criminal offences with a different target may violate this central principle of criminal law because expansive interpretations which go beyond the limits of the criminal offence itself are made.

While it is true that this is not the case in any of the countries analysed, the absence of regulation can indeed lead to the need for such interpretations of existing rules. These interpretations can be risky precisely because of their possible antagonism with the principle of legality.

The second is that only some conducts are penalized, for example offences against property, as in the case of Argentina described in the introduction to this chapter. However, the actual damage to privacy, sexual autonomy, and dignity caused by intimate image abuse is not prosecuted.

As explained above, in countries such as Colombia and Venezuela, cybercrimes are the only resort in order to criminalize this conduct. Criminalizing intimate image abuse using a cybercrime conceals the fact that it is a conduct that infringes privacy and sexual autonomy and is a form of violence against women. For instance, the Colombian legal framework criminalizes intimate image abuse through Article 269 F, implying that what is being punished is the obtainment of the profit instead of intimate image abuse as an autonomous conduct. Furthermore, as explained above, the Venezuelan legal framework only contemplates one form of intimate image abuse.

This criminalization option is perhaps the most problematic because it completely ignores the harm done by intimate image abuse and prioritizes the harm caused in cyberspace.

The patterns of criminalization outlined above are intended to address the lack of regulation that leads to a loophole in protecting victims. However, such lack of protection is not solved by this strategy because the actual harm or harms caused by intimate image abuse are not penalized. This shows that, on top of everything else, these countries are in breach of the international obligations contained in the Belém do Pará Convention.

B. Countries Where Intimate Image Abuse can be Addressed with an Offence against Privacy

The legal systems of Chile, Ecuador, and Paraguay contain general rules that allow criminalization of some cases of intimate image abuse. For instance, in Chile, cases in which the images are obtained with the victim's consent cannot be prosecuted. Obviously these cases are the most common, since they include situations in which the victim voluntarily shares their intimate pictures with the aggressor, and the aggressor shares them with others without their consent.

In Ecuador, on the other hand, the law is extremely general and does not penalize the violation of sexual autonomy that comes with intimate image abuse, nor does it penalize the discriminatory content of this conduct when it manifests as violence against women.

The same happens in Paraguay, where the existing criminal law does not address motives that usually guide intimate image abuse, such as revenge or discrimination.

Intimate image abuse is indeed a violation of intimacy or privacy. However, this conduct also infringes sexual freedom when it involves images of sexual content and can be considered in many cases a form of violence against women.

This pattern of criminalization responds to only one of the many harms of intimate image abuse. It does not penalize, for example, the violation of sexual autonomy. In addition, it does not recognize the explicit component of violence against women that intimate image abuse contains.

This necessarily leads to the conclusion that this pattern of criminalization does not sufficiently protect the victims of intimate image abuse. Therefore, the legislation of these countries does not comply with the international obligations acquired by signing the Belém do Pará Convention.

C. Countries That Introduced a Specific Offence of Intimate Image Abuse Based on Sexual and/or Gender Content

Six[48] of the thirteen Latin American legal systems analysed consider intimate image abuse as a crime against sexual autonomy or intimacy. Thus, the legal systems of Brazil, Guatemala, Mexico, and Peru punish intimate image abuse as a crime against intimacy or sexual privacy. The criminal laws of these countries are specific in stating that images or material shared without consent must have sexual content. These laws encompass all or most hypotheses or scenarios where intimate image abuse occurs.

[48] This section will not refer to the Bolivian legal system, as the Bolivian Senate has not approved the legal reforms.

In contrast, Uruguayan criminal law is slightly broader because it refers to images or material shared without consent that must have intimate content. One might think that the criminalization of intimate image abuse in this country would correspond to the previous pattern; however, there are two reasons to include it in this group. The first is that the offence is included in the Violence against Women Act, which clearly recognizes the gendered content of the *actus reus*. The second is that, precisely because of its breadth, the Uruguayan law is perhaps the one that better addresses the phenomenon of intimate image abuse. Not only does it recognize the harm caused, but it also punishes all the hypotheses of intimate image abuse presented above.

The Nicaraguan case is similar because criminal law penalizes intimate image abuse as an attack against privacy in general but aggravates the sentence when the content of the material that is shared without consent is of a sexual or erotic nature and is obtained by the perpetrator with the consent of the victim. This is perhaps the most common case of intimate image abuse.

The fact that the legal systems of these countries give intimate image abuse the connotation of sexual assault implicitly recognizes that these are, on many occasions, situations of violence against women as it is precisely this sexual content that objectifies the female body. Therefore, this pattern of criminalization is the most appropriate way to respond to this phenomenon. For the same reason, it fulfils the international obligations undertaken by signing the Belém do Pará Convention.

V. Conclusions

Several conclusions can be drawn from what has been set out in this chapter. Intimate image abuse is a recurrent form of digital violence primarily affecting women and girls. Because of its sexual content and the motives that encourage it, it is usually a form of violence against women that should be investigated and sanctioned by all countries. In the case of Latin American countries, this obligation is established in the Belém do Pará Convention.

After analysing the legislation of thirteen Latin American countries, it was pointed out that there are three patterns of criminalization of intimate image abuse. In countries with an autonomous criminal offence for intimate image abuse, the law is sufficient to address all the damages it entails and all the modalities of this phenomenon. In other countries, where it is dealt with through other offences, an evident lack of protection is generated, or it is punished as an invasion of privacy and, usually, in an incomplete manner.

However, the fact that in most of the countries analysed, intimate image abuse is penalized either as an invasion of privacy or as a conduct with sexual and/or gender-based violence content indicates that in Latin America there are legal responses to this phenomenon in criminal law. It also shows that intimate image abuse is recognized as violence against women, or at least as a form of violence with gendered content.

In addition, in most legal systems, it appears that these laws are, in one way or another, an attempt to comply with the international obligations contained in the Belém do Pará Convention. It is also evident that some countries still need to update their legal framework to comply, or completely comply, with them.

Finally, it seems that the third pattern of criminalization identified is the most appropriate one for addressing intimate image abuse from a criminal perspective. This is because conceptualizing the phenomenon as an attack on intimacy or sexual privacy provides a complete assessment of the harmful conduct.

Bibliography

Correa Flórez MC, 'La violencia contra las mujeres en la legislación penal colombiana' (2018) 15 Nuevo Foro Penal 90

Cruz Gómez L and Soriano Ayala E, 'Psychological Aspects, Attitudes and Behaviour Related to the Practice of Sexting: A Systematic Review of the Existent Literature' (2014) 115 Social and Behavioral Sciences 132

Delgado Gómez CA, 'El Fedegan de la Nacional: una historia de acoso sexual' *La línea del medio* (Bogotá, 13 August 2020)

Gómez MM, 'Violencia por prejuicio' in C Motta and M Sáez (eds), *Sexualidades diversas en la jurisprudencia latinoamericana* vol 2 (Siglo del hombre Editores 2008)

Hall M and Hearn J, *Revenge Pornography: Gender, Sexuality and Motivations* (Routledge 2018)

Henry N and others, *Imaged-based Sexual Abuse. A Study on the causes and consequences of non-consensual nude or sexual imagery* (Routledge 2021)

Jakobs G, *Coacciones. Explicación de la raíz de los delitos* (Universidad Externado de Colombia 2017)

Machado Rocha L, Duboc Pedrinha R, and Barros de Oliveira MH, 'The Treatment of Revenge Pornography by the Brazilian Legal System' (2019) 4 Saúde debate 43

Mackinnon C, 'Sexuality, Pornography and Method: Pleasure under Patriarchy' (1989) 99(2) Ethics 315

Peña Ochoa P, *Reporte de la situación de América Latina sobre la violencia de género ejercida por medios electrónicos* (2017) <https://adc.org.ar/wp-content/uploads/2019/06/Latin-American-Report-on-Online-Gender-Violence-final_v2.pdf> accessed 9 October 2023

Recalde Salazar S, 'Criminalización de la porno venganza en Ecuador' (2020) unpublished

12
Criminalization of Intimate Image Abuse in Japan

Yoshifumi Okada

I. Introduction

The spread of camera-equipped mobile phones and the rapid progress in information and communication technology have made it easier for anyone to publish images they have taken. In Japan, as in other countries, revenge pornography, voyeurism, child pornography, sexting, sextortion, and other forms of harm related to sexual images have become social problems.

This chapter first outlines the criminal legal response to so-called 'non-consensual pornography' in Japan. Then, the legislation that deals with the prevention of so-called revenge pornography (the Act Concerning the Prevention of Damage Caused by the Provision of Private Sexual Image Records, hereafter referred to as the Revenge Pornography Prevention Act) is described. Finally, the problems surrounding the Act are examined.

Yoshifumi Okada, *Criminalization of Intimate Image Abuse in Japan* In: *Criminalizing Intimate Image Abuse.* Edited by: Gian Marco Caletti and Kolis Summerer, Oxford University Press. © Oxford University Press 2024. DOI: 10.1093/oso/9780198877813.003.0012

II. History of Criminalization in Japan

In Japan, there was no law to directly regulate so-called 'revenge pornography'. However, this does not mean that existing laws have not been used. Even in the past, in the Penal Code, Breaking into a Residence (section 130), Intimidation (section 222), Compulsion (section 223), Defamation (section 230), and Distribution of Obscene Objects (section 175) were applied to some cases of intimate image abuse. Furthermore, as special laws, the Minor Offence Act (section 1, chapter 23), Child pornography-related crimes (section 7 of the Act on Regulation and Punishment of Acts Relating to Child Prostitution and Child Pornography, and the Protection of Children: Child Pornography Prohibition Act), Stalking (section 2, chapter 7, sections 18–20 of the Anti-Stalking Act) and so-called nuisance prevention ordinances established by local governments have been applied.

However, it must be emphasized that the existing laws encountered significant limitations. For example, in case of publication without permission of an image depicting a naked body obtained through sexting, it is not always possible to affirm that the subject's personal reputation has been adversely affected. For example, according to a victim blaming logic, the person depicted may be labelled as a 'sexually loose person'. Nevertheless, the person's sexual dignity is deeply hurt, and they may be restricted in their social activities. However, the offence of defamation requires that the act is sufficient to lower the social reputation of the subject.[1] Therefore, if only revenge pornography images were published, it may not be easy to prove whether the social reputation has been lowered.

To charge a perpetrator with a crime[2] related to 'child pornography', it must fall under the definition of 'child pornography'[3] under the Child Pornography

[1] Defamation shall be established if 'a person who defames another person by making allegations in public, regardless of whether such facts are true or false' (translated by Ministry of Justice). 'In public' means 'unspecified or in a state that many people can recognize' (Supreme Court Judgment, 13 October 1961, Keishu 15-9-1586). 'Making allegations' means that it is sufficient to show the facts were enough to lower a person's social reputation, and it is not necessary that they are actually harmed (Supreme Court Judgment, 11 July 1932, Keishu 11-1250). In addition, it is sufficient that there is a *mens rea* to defame, and it is not necessary to have an intention to defame or any other purpose (Supreme Court Judgment, 14 July 1938, Keishu 17-608).

[2] Article 7 of the Child Pornography Prohibition Act provides for penalties. The Act regulates the following: 'Possession of child pornography for the purpose of satisfying one's sexual curiosity' (subsection 1), 'provision of child pornography' (subsection 2), 'production, possession, transportation, import to or export from Japan of child pornography for the purpose of provision of child pornography' (subsection 3), 'production of child pornography' (subsections 4, 5), 'the provision or display in public of child pornography to many or unspecified people' (subsection 6), 'the production, possession, transportation, import to or export from Japan of child pornography for the purpose of the provision to many or unspecified people or display in public' (subsection 7).

[3] Child Pornography Prohibition Act, section 2, subsection 1 defines that a 'child' is a person under 18 and subsection 3 defines child pornography as follows (translated by the Ministry of Justice): 'The term "Child Pornography" as used in this Act means photographs recording media containing electronic or magnetic records (meaning a record used in computerized information processing which is created in electronic form, magnetic form, or any other form that cannot be perceived by the human senses; the same applies hereinafter) or any of the following media which depicts the image of a child, in a form recognizable by the sense of sight: (i) any image of sexual intercourse or any conduct similar to

Prohibition Act, but many cases of publication of images do not meet the definition of 'child pornography' even if the subject's sexual privacy is infringed.

Therefore, it cannot be said that the existing penalties covered every harmful conduct. Given that there are many cases in which victims of revenge pornography have suffered from great mental distress over a long period, have been socially driven into a corner, have attempted suicide, etc, it has been said that new legislation is necessary to prevent the occurrence or expansion of damages caused by this form of privacy violation.

In Japan, in around 2013, the term revenge pornography began to appear in reports. A stalker murder case in Mitaka, Tokyo, in October of 2013[4] is considered the catalyst for enacting the 'Act on Prevention of Damage Caused by the Provision of Private Sexual Image Records' (the so-called Revenge Pornography[5] Prevention Act). This incident was brought up in Parliament, and the pros and cons of enacting a law to combat revenge pornography were debated. The Minister of Justice at the time was cautious about this new criminalization, stating that '[revenge pornography] can be dealt with under the current law'.[6] However, regarding the spread of 'revenge pornography', the law in force at the time was inadequate, and there had been a strong movement calling for new legislation. As a result, in November 2014, to prevent the occurrence and spread of damage caused by such new phenomenon, a bill was submitted by lawmakers to Parliament. The House of Representatives and the House of Councillors unanimously passed this bill (Act no 126 of 2014). Section 3 of the same law, which stipulates penalties, came into effect on 17 December 2014. The Act on the Limitation of Liability for Damages of Specified Telecommunications Service Providers and the Right to Demand Disclosure of Identification Information of the Sender (the so-called 'Provider Liability Limitation Act') section 4, which stipulated notable exceptions, came into effect on 27 December. Other sections came into effect on promulgation (27 November).

Revenge pornography is a form of sexual violence in which the perpetrator exposes the sexual image of the victim to public curiosity. Given the fact that, as

sexual intercourse with a child or between children; (ii) any image of a child having the genital organs, etc. touched by another person or of a child touching another person's genital organs, etc. which arouses or stimulates sexual desire; or (iii) any image of a child wholly or partially naked, in which sexual body parts of the child (genital organs or the parts around them, buttocks or chest) are exhibited or emphasized and arouses or stimulates sexual desire.' Therefore, sexting images among teenagers fall under the concept of child pornography of this Act.

[4] The defendant was charged with murder and publishing child pornography after murdering a girlfriend of a high school student whom he met on social media and making naked images of the victim available for viewing and downloading on the Internet, and he was found guilty. See, Tokyo District Court Tachikawa Branch Judgment 15 March 2016 Hanreihisho Document no L07130064).

[5] The term 'revenge porn' is understood to give the false impression that it is motivated by personal hatred and malice towards the other party. In Japan, as in other countries, the term 'revenge porn' is not legally used.

[6] House of Councillors Budget Committee Proceedings 2013 s 1(34).

already mentioned, defamation, child pornography, and displays in public of obscene objects were unable to fully capture the core of the problem, it is significant that a new specific crime was introduced.

III. Overview of the So-called 'Revenge Pornography Prevention Act'

A. Purpose of the Act (Section 1)

This Act aims to prevent the occurrence or spread of damages caused by revenge porn that infringes personal honour[7] and the tranquillity of private lives. This Act also provides exceptions to the Provider Liability Limitation Act in cases where the distribution of sexual images violates the victim's reputation or peace of mind. The Act also stipulates the establishment of a support system for victims.

B. Definition of Terms Utilized in the Act (Section 2)

The Act defines the object of the *actus reus* of so-called revenge porn as 'private sexual image records'. Recording media (photographs, CD-ROMs, USB memory, etc) on which 'private sexual image records' are recorded are called 'private sexual image recording objects'. A definition is provided in section 2(1)[8]. The contents are as follows (translated by the author):

> The term 'Private Sexual Image Record' as used in this Act means recording media containing electronic or magnetic records (meaning a record used in computerized information processing which is created in electronic form, magnetic form, or any other form that cannot be perceived by the human senses; the same applies hereinafter) or any of the following records which depict the filmed image of a person: (i) any image of sexual intercourse or any conduct similar to sexual intercourse; (ii) any image of a person having the genital organs, etc. (meaning genitals, anus, or nipples; hereinafter, the same shall apply in this item and the next item) touched by another person or of a person touching another person's genital organs, etc. which arouses or stimulates sexual desire; or (iii) any image of a person wholly or partially naked, in which sexual body parts of the person

[7] Like the concept of honour in defamation crimes, it is understood to refer to victim's social reputation. See Takeo Mizukoshi, 'Summary of the Act on Prevention of Damage Caused by the Provision of Private Sexual Image Records (Act No. 126 of 2014)' (2015) 68(3) Houritu no hiroba 23 (hereafter Mizukoshi, 'Summary').

[8] Under this definition, it is unclear whether penalties can be applied to abusing personal sexual images using photo collages and deepfakes.

(genital organs or the parts around them, buttocks or chest) are exhibited or emphasized and arouses or stimulates sexual desire.

One of the purposes of this Act is to protect the sexual privacy of individuals. 'Private' is also affirmed by taking sexual images with the promise not to show them to a third party, selfie images by so-called sexting, and voyeur images. 'Private' is not affirmed in the following cases: so-called pornographic movies and gravure photographs, and so on, which are taken on the premise that they will be disclosed to a third party.

Since the subject's privacy is a requirement that becomes an issue at the time of the filming of the filmed person, as long as the filmed person consented to publication of the images at the time of the filming, even if consent was withdrawn after that, 'private' is denied.

Points i to iii above are stipulated with reference to the definition of 'child pornography' in the Child Pornography Prohibition Act, and only change the subject of the term from 'child' to 'person'. If it is both child pornography and revenge pornography, then that is fine. Still, when it comes to adults, there seems to be room for reconsideration of whether this definition is acceptable. In addition, unlike the Penal Code, this Act uses the definition 'arouses or stimulates sexual desire'. Therefore, it should be noted that images that do not necessarily reach the level of obscenity in the Penal Code are also deemed a 'private sexual image record'.

C. Penalties (Section 3)

Penalties are stipulated in Article 3. Provision of private sexual image records (subsection 1), provision of private sexual image recording objects (first part of subsection 2), displays in public of private sexual image recording objects (second part of subsection 2), provision of private sexual image records or private sexual image recording objects for the purpose of subsection 1 or 2 (subsection 3) are punishable.

These are intended to protect the subject's sexual privacy.[9] All require *mens rea*. As to the content of *mens rea*, the offender is required to be aware that the

[9] Katsuei Hirasawa and others, *Yokuwakaru Revenge Porn Boushiho [Understand Well Revenge Pornography Prevention Act]* (Tachibana Shobo 2016) 66 (hereafter Hirawasa and others, *Revenge Porn*). Although this Act aims to protect an individual's honour and sexual privacy (section 1), as for penalties, since there is defamation under the Penal Code that protects honour as a legal interest, the penalties of this Act are construed as protecting only sexual privacy. There is still some debate as to how the contents should be interpreted. Mizukoshi sees it as 'The right not to disclose information about sexuality in private life without good reason': Mizukoshi, 'Summary' (n 7) 23. On the other hand, Sonoda sees it as 'the right to voluntarily block other people's interest in one's sexual information'. Cf Hisashi Sonoda, 'About Revenge Pornography Prevention Act' (2015) 44 Keijiho Journal 50 (hereafter Sonoda, 'Prevention Act'). Therefore, there is a dispute over who is the subject of private sexual image records. I understand 'sexual privacy' as the right to decide about sexual information in my private life. See Yoshifumi Okada, 'Consideration on New Issues Related to Revenge Porn' (2020) 138 Senshu Hogaku Ronshu 37.

image is a private sexual image record or a private sexual image recording object. Therefore, if there is no recognition of 'private', *mens rea* is denied. Also, it is not a crime under this Act if the image records were leaked due to negligence or hacking.

Penalties are as follows (translation by the author):

> Provision of private sexual image records is punished by imprisonment for not more than 3 years or a fine of not more than 500,000 yen against a person who provides private sexual image records to many or unspecified people through telecommunication lines in a way that allows a third party to identify the filmed subject.
>
> Provision of private sexual image recording objects is punished by imprisonment for not more than 3 years or a fine of not more than 500,000 yen against a person who provides private sexual image recording objects to many or unspecified persons through telecommunication lines in a way that allows a third party to identify the filmed subject.
>
> Display in public of private sexual image recording objects is punished by imprisonment for not more than 3 years or a fine of not more than 500,000 yen against a person who displays in public private sexual image recording objects to many or unspecified persons through telecommunication lines in a way that allows a third party to identify the filmed subject.
>
> A person who provides private sexual image records or private sexual image recording objects through telecommunication lines for the purpose of provision of private sexual image records or private sexual image recording objects or displays in public private sexual image recording objects is punished by imprisonment for not more than 10 years or a fine of not more than 300,000 yen.

D. Prosecution

These offences are crimes indictable upon a complaint (subsection 4). If the perpetrator is prosecuted, it is treated as a crime indictable upon a complaint because facts about the victim's sexual privacy may become public. Investigative authorities must conduct investigations with due consideration for the concerned person's privacy. The scope of crimes indictable upon a complaint is stipulated in the Code of Criminal Procedure (Articles 230 –232 and 234). Based on its provisions, the scope of the complainant in the Revenge Pornography Prevention Act consists, in principle, of the victim (the filmed subject) and their legal representative.

These offences apply, by section 3 of the Penal Code, to any Japanese national who commits one of these crimes outside the territory of Japan (subsection 5).

E. Controversial Elements of the Offence and Case Law

The perpetrator of the act of these offences is not limited. These offences can apply not only to those who filmed the private sexual image records or received them directly from the filmed subject, but also to those who acquired them secondarily. For example, suppose someone unrelated to the person who took the picture discovers a private sexual image record already posted on social media. When the discoverer recognizes that it is a private sexual image record and reposts the image, the provision of private sexual image recordings may apply.

These offences are intended to protect the sexual privacy of the victim and are only applicable if a third party can identify them. Even if it is impossible for a third party to identify the victim, if the depicted subject can identify themselves in the image record, the sexual privacy of the victim is considered compromised. However, the degree of infringement in such cases is considered to be less serious than in cases where identification by a third party is possible. Therefore, legislators decided to make identification of the filmed subject by a third party a requirement for punishment.

'In a way that allows a third party to identify the filmed subject' means, in addition to cases in which the victim can be identified from the published image itself, such as the face or an object appearing in the background, also cases where they can be identified from parts other than the image, such as the accompanying text and location information (for instance, so-called doxing).

'Displays in public' is understood in the same way as section 175, subsection 1 of the Penal Code (Display in public of obscene objects).[10] According to the Japanese Supreme Court Judgment regarding the interpretation of section 175 of the Penal Code, 'displays in public' means being in a state that can be recognized by many or unspecified people.[11] 'Display in public' also applies when a record is stored on the hard disk of a server computer and placed in a situation where an unspecified number of people can access and recognize the image.

The 30 June 2017 judgment of the Osaka High Court is an example of a dispute over 'display in public' under the Revenge Pornography Prevention Act.[12] The defendant uploaded images and video data of the victim's naked body to an online storage service. Then, impersonating a third party, the defendant sent the victim an email threatening to distribute the image and video data on the Internet if the victim did not reply, and attaching a URL for accessing the uploaded data. Prosecutors insisted on 'display in public'. In response, the defendant argued that although the data was set to be 'display in public', the URL was sent only by one email addressed to the victim and not disclosed to third parties, so it was not 'display in

[10] Hirasawa and others, *Revenge Porn* (n 9) 77.
[11] Supreme Court Decision 16 July 2001, Keishu 55-5-31.
[12] Hanreihisho Document no L07220271.

public'. The Osaka District Court of the first instance considered that at the stage of uploading the data and receiving the public email, the content of the data could be recognized by many or unspecified people. The Court acknowledged the application of display in public of private sexual image recording objects. On the other hand, the Osaka High Court ruled that, at this stage, it still did not fall under the category of 'display in public', that the crime of display in public was inapplicable, and that only attempted coercion would be applied. The central part of the reason stated by the Osaka High Court is as follows (translated by the author): 'When setting "display in public", the public URL is only issued to the user. To enable third parties to view the data set to be public, in addition to the public setting, another action by the user is required in order for it to become public.' 'The defendant only set the data to be public; the contents of the Data do not yet constitute a state that can be recognized by many or unspecified people. In addition, sending the public URL of the data to the victim by e-mail is merely addressed to a specific individual. Therefore, it cannot be acknowledged that the content of the data has been placed in a state where many or unspecified people can recognize it.' It can be understood that the Osaka High Court's denial of the crime of public display was based on the decision of the Supreme Court on 16 July 2001. In other words, it indicates the understanding that many or unspecified people must be able to easily access image records in order for them to be recognized as 'public'.

It is controversial whether penalties can be applied if a private sexual image record is made public after the person depicted has died. Some argue that if the person depicted is dead, the penalties cannot be applied because the subject does not exist.[13] In this view, for example, defamation of the dead person (section 230, subsection 2 of the Penal Code) requires the presentation of false facts, so unless that requirement is met, the perpetrator will not be punished. In this case, there could be a loophole. However, unless there are exceptional circumstances in which the filmed subject has consented to the publication of a private sexual image record, the right to decide about private sexual information should be respected posthumously. Given that section 3 does not require the person who is the filmed subject to be alive, I interpret that in such cases a crime against private sexual image recordings can be applied.

F. Providers' Liability

When the person who manages and operates the computer network server (hereinafter referred to as 'the provider') neglects information online that infringes on the rights of others, the provider may be sued for damages by the victim. On the

[13] Hirasawa and others, *Revenge Porn* (n 9) 90; Sonoda, 'Prevention Act' (n 9) 52.

other hand, when the provider deletes information that does not infringe on the rights of others, the provider may be sued for damages by the sender. Therefore, in 2001 the Provider Liability Limitation Act was enacted to enable providers to delete infringing information while maintaining a balance between 'relief for victims' and 'freedom of expression'.[14] The Provider Liability Limitation Act grants victims of violated rights the right to demand disclosure of sender information.[15] The Act stipulates the judicial proceedings regarding the case of the sender's information disclosure order and clarifies the requirements for exemption from responsibility for damages of the provider.

Section 3 of the Provider Liability Limitation Act stipulates that the provider shall not be liable for damages. Subsection 2 is a provision for damages caused to the originator of information whose transmission is prevented. It applies when the provider's measures to prevent transmission of information are taken to the extent necessary to prevent transmission of such information to unspecified persons and any of the following apply (translated by the author):

> (1) When there are reasonable grounds for believing that the rights of others have been unfairly violated; (2) When a person who claims that his rights have been infringed has requested that the provider take measures to prevent the transmission of information, the provider shall contact the sender and when the sender has no objection within 7 days.

When a private sexual image is shared through the Internet, it may spread quickly and cause severe and irreparable damage to the sexual privacy of the person depicted. The provider urgently needs to take measures to prevent transmission at the request of a person whose honour or private life has been violated by the distribution of information related to private sexual image records. For that reason, section 4 of the Revenge Porn Prevention Act provides an exception to the Provider Liability Limitation Act. Providers are exempted from liability for damages in the following cases (translated by the author):

[14] The Act was amended in April 2021, triggered by the suicide of a famous female professional wrestler who was heavily slandered on social media. See Yoshifumi Okada 'Trends in Legal Revisions against Online Insults' (2022) 76 Senshu University Imamura Institute of Legal Studies Report 1.

[15] An ordinance of the Ministry of Internal Affairs and Communications stipulates the content to disclose by requesting the disclosure of sender information. According to the ordinance, the victim can request the provider to disclose, eg, the sender's name, address, telephone number, email address, IP address, etc. Under the Provider Liability Limitation Act, providers are obligated to hear opinions from senders who are believed to have made infringing posts on whether to disclose information. This is because the disclosure of sender information is a matter of privacy and freedom of expression for the sender, and it is the sender and not the provider who has a substantial interest. When the sender does not consent to the disclosure during the opinion hearing, the provider must also ask why (section 6, subsection 1). This obligation to hear opinions ensures the privacy and freedom of expression of the sender. At the same time, if the sender does not agree to the disclosure, the provider is required to ask why and encouraged to take appropriate action.

(1) When the person depicted (if the person depicted is dead, their spouse, lineal relative or brother or sister) indicates information about the private sexual image, the facts and reasons for the infringement of honour and so on and the fact that the information about the private sexual image is related to the private sexual image record, and requests the provider to take measures to prevent the transmission of private sexual image information; (2) When the provider inquires whether the sender of the information agrees to take measures to prevent the transmission of information by showing the private sexual image information; (3) When the sender has not indicated his or her disapproval of taking measures to prevent information transmission within 2 days from the inquiry date.

G. Responsibilities of the National and Local Governments

Section 5 establishes that the national government and local governments shall develop systems necessary for appropriate response in order to contribute to the appropriate and prompt protection of victims and the reduction of their burden. The following three points are listed as measures to be taken by the national and local governments: '(1) Enhancement of the system of Investigative agency necessary to make it easier for the victim to report; (2) Enhancement of publicity of the contact and application method when applying to take measures to prevent the transmission of private sexual image information; (3) Development of the necessary system for governments to respond to consultation from the victim in a centralized manner and respond appropriately.'

In addition, it is stipulated that the national and local governments should enhance educational and enlightenment activities required to deepen the public's understanding and interest in matters necessary to prevent damage from occurring (section 6).[16] To prevent damages due to the provision of private sexual image records, etc, it is essential to conduct educational and enlightenment activities in schools and other places to avoid becoming victims or perpetrators.

The supplementary provision of the Act stipulates that after the law comes into effect, it will be reviewed, and necessary measures will be taken based on the results of that review. Nonetheless, there have been almost no reviews in relation to the Revenge Pornography Prevention Act.

[16] eg the Ministry of Education, Culture, Sports, Science and Technology and the National Police Agency are creating and distributing an educational leaflet. In addition, the Ministry of Internal Affairs and Communications has published 'Internet Trouble Case Examples' and its 'guidance plan' <https://www.soumu.go.jp/use_the_internet_wisely/trouble/> accessed 26 December 2022. These include raising awareness about sexting and sextortion damage prevention.

IV. Crime Applications and Statistics

The first case in which the Revenge Pornography Prevention Act was applied was an incident in January 2015 when a person scattered sexual photographs of a former partner in a shopping centre parking lot.[17] It was in January of the same year that the law was first applied to a case involving the publication of revenge pornography online.[18] In this case, the perpetrator posted a sexual photograph on social media without the consent of the former lover. In addition, the Revenge Pornography Prevention Act is also applied to cases in which a third party other than the poster posts sexual images on social media without consent[19] and to cases where videos of victims secretly filmed in the bathroom are uploaded to a voyeur site.[20]

The breakdown of consultations, etc related to the Revenge Pornography Prevention Act as seen in the statistics of the National Police Agency is shown in Tables 12.1–12.6.[21]

Observing the above data collectively yields the following. Most of the perpetrators are men under the age of 50 or younger. Most of the victims are women under the age of 40 or younger. Most of both are dating partners or former dating partners or friends relationships or former friends relationships. In the case of child victimization there are many cases involving the production of child pornography and the publication of revenge pornography. In cases other than child victimization, there are many cases involving threats and the publication of revenge pornography based on images that have been taken or that have come into possession in some way.

Table 12.1 Number of consultations

	2014	2015	2016	2017	2018	2019	2020	2021
Total	110	1,143	1,063	1,243	1,347	1,479	1,570	1,845
Male	11	102	84	105	90	97	142	195
Female	99	1,041	979	1,138	1,257	1,382	1,427	1,432

[17] Yokohama District Court Judgment 12-6-2015 (Hanreihisho Document no L07050319).

[18] Yokohama District Court Judgment 12-6-2015 (Hanreihisho Document no L07050319).

[19] 'Spreading naked women on LINE . . . Revenge porn first caught, two men arrested' <https://bit.ly/3Rb4OBP> accessed 26 December 2022

[20] Fukuoka District Court Judgment 16-11-2016 (Hanreihisho Document no L07150950)

[21] <https://www.npa.go.jp/publications/statistics/safetylife/dv.html> accessed 26 December 2022. Note that 2014 is after the date of enforcement of the Revenge Pornography Prevention Act.

Table 12.2 Victim's gender and age

	2014	2015	2016	2017	2018	2019	2020	2021
Male	11	102	84	105	90	97	142	195
Female	99	1,041	979	1,138	1,257	1,382	1,427	1,432
Under 19	24	223	236	307	352	376	429	429
20's	41	434	442	468	515	637	660	647
30's	16	257	194	214	254	235	247	268
40's	16	170	140	183	158	145	149	168
50's	7	42	40	60	54	65	54	76
60's	1	7	6	6	4	9	13	12
Over 70	0	3	2	2	3	0	3	4
unknown	5	7	3	3	7	12	15	24

Table 12.3 Perpetrator's gender and age

	2014	2015	2016	2017	2018	2019	2020	2021
Male	88	1,019	949	1,039	1,181	1,249	1,310	1,285
Female	8	53	57	103	62	88	89	119
unknown	14	71	57	101	104	142	171	224
Under 19	4	116	117	130	171	182	189	172
20's	20	251	256	294	334	393	435	428
30's	25	264	249	238	251	289	239	254
40's	14	208	187	227	220	192	201	189
50's	8	94	82	99	123	95	89	100
60's	5	30	28	33	29	28	30	36
Over 70	3	11	13	15	10	16	15	11
unknown	31	169	131	207	209	284	372	438

Table 12.4 Relationship between victim and perpetrator

	2014	2015	2016	2017	2018	2019	2020	2021
Spouse (including ex)	2	53	32	36	45	60	51	60
Dating partner (including ex)	68	725	736	765	830	912	848	821
Acquaintances and friends (Online-related only)	14	130	118	164	149	182	258	326
Acquaintances and friends (other than that)	10	113	105	136	177	154	208	226
people in the workplace	1	21	13	34	24	27	29	31
Unknown	12	44	33	57	63	84	79	101
Others	3	57	26	51	59	60	97	63

Table 12.5 Contents of consultations[a]

	2014	2015	2016	2017	2018	2019	2020	2021
Published the image	18	188	196	236	234	272	286	329
Threatened to publish images	42	502	451	514	498	584	567	580
Image was sent	22	245	229	255	231	239	254	313
Image is in possession, was taken	33	343	297	362	512	494	559	582
Others[b]	6	28	20	24	8	24	24	41

[a] If more than one applies, each is accounted for.

[b] Including 'the image may be possessed by the perpetrator'.

V. Issues Concerning Non-consensual Creation of Private Sexual Images

A. Voyeurism

When a third party distributes voyeur images to many or unspecified people in a way that allows them to identify the person depicted, the perpetrator will be charged with the offence of providing private sexual image records. However, as of 2022, there is no provision in the Japanese Penal Code to address so-called 'voyeurism'. Until now, we have dealt with voyeurism entirely by using existing laws.

Table 12.6 Breakdown by type of crime

	2014	2015	2016	2017	2018	2019	2020	2021
Penal Code/Special Act Arrests[a]	7	250	238	226	217	227	198	242
Intimidation	1	69	69	56	46	47	43	40
Violation of Child Pornography Prohibition Act	1	56	35	39	42	44	34	47
Compulsion	3	25	33	37	22	39	27	33
Violation of Anti-stalking Act	0	18	27	26	28	22	20	18
Defamation	0	15	13	4	9	11	10	10
Distribution of obscene objects	0	6	7	5	5	8	5	8
Others[b]	2	61	54	59	65	56	59	86
Violation of Revenge Pornography Prevention Act	0	53	48	57	36	34	47	47

[a] If a person is arrested for multiple offences, the statutory sentence is counted for the most severe offence.
[b] Includes crimes such as forcible sexual intercourse and extortion.

Regarding the regulation of voyeurism, currently, 'nuisance prevention ordinances' stipulated for each prefecture are often used. However, since 'ordinances' are established for each municipality, there was a problem: unless it was possible to specify in which region the act of voyeurism occurred, punishment could not be carried out.[22] In addition, although ordinances initially regulated voyeurism in 'public places or public vehicles', many have revised the controlled locations as the damage caused by voyeurism expanded. This is because it was pointed out that it was impossible to prosecute voyeurism in company changing rooms, restaurant toilets, and private rooms in chiropractic clinics. However, some ordinances still limit the areas subject to regulation, and currently there are regional differences.[23] Moreover, penalties are mild and differ from region to region.[24] For example, in the

[22] eg when a perpetrator secretly takes a picture of a flight attendant's underwear on a domestic flight, it is impossible to pinpoint the picture's location because the plane moves at high speed. In that case, law enforcement may not know which ordinance to apply to the perpetrator, so the perpetrator may not be arrested and punished.

[23] eg in the Chiba Prefecture's ordinance amended in 2020, in addition to 'public places or vehicles', the following places or vehicles are also subject to regulation: (1) places and dwellings where people usually do not wear all or part of their clothes; and (2) places or vehicles that can be used or accessed by unspecified or many people. On the other hand, the Aomori Prefecture's ordinance still limits voyeurism to 'public places or vehicles'.

[24] The Constitution of Japan section 94 stipulates 'Local public entities shall have the right to enact their own regulations within law' (translated by Ministry of Justice), and Local Autonomy Act, section 14, subsection defines that ordinances must not violate laws and regulations. Among the crimes stipulated the Penal Code, section 9, according to the provisions of Local Autonomy Act, section 14, subsection 3, the punishment imposed by the ordinance is limited imprisonment for not more than two years, a fine of not more than one million yen, penal detention and petty fine, with confiscation. The Supreme

Chiba Prefecture and in Tokyo's nuisance prevention ordinance, penalties are imprisonment for not more than one year or a fine of not more than one million yen (for habitual practice, imprisonment for not more than two years or a fine of not more than one million yen), while in the Aomori Prefecture, penalties are imprisonment for not more than six months or a fine of not more than 500,000 yen (for habitual practice, imprisonment for not more than one year or a fine of not more than one million yen).

Japan adopts the principle of prosecution expediency (Code of Criminal Procedure, section 248). Where the public prosecutor finds that prosecution is deemed unnecessary owing to the character, age, and environment of the offender, the seriousness of the offence, and the circumstances or situation after the offence, prosecution need not be instituted.

Suspension of prosecution is an attempt by public prosecutors to avoid unnecessary punishment as much as possible from the standpoint of criminal policy and to try to rehabilitate offenders. Therefore, even if the perpetrator is arrested for voyeurism, in many cases, if it is the first offence, the prosecution will be suspended by basically settling with the victim. Moreover, it is said that even if a settlement cannot be reached, the final punishment will consist only of a fine of around 300,000 yen. It is challenging to detect voyeurism because the victim does not notice it. Perpetrators also tend to be less aware that they are infringing the sexual privacy of victims, resulting in a high recidivism rate and many additional offences.

Nowadays, anyone can practice voyeurism with a smartphone, and it is necessary to curb this phenomenon. Therefore, on 24 October 2022, while the Legislative Council, an advisory body to the Minister of Justice, was considering a review of the sex crimes regulations, a written opinion was created regarding the introduction of a new crime of voyeurism in the Penal Code. The written statement indicates that the statutory penalty for voyeurism should be imprisonment for up to three years or a fine of up to three million yen. Compared to local ordinances and minor offence laws, this is a relatively drastic and severe punishment and can be expected to have a deterrent effect. In addition to this, there was no law in Japan to discard or delete copies of voyeur photographs and videos. The draft proposed a mechanism for discarding or deleting seized items kept by public prosecutors. Until now, it had to be a tangible item and be the original in order to be confiscated (Penal Code, section 19). Copies could not be confiscated.[25] It was always said that

Court has held that the authorization of laws must be sufficiently specific and limited to determine punishment (Supreme Court Grand Bench Judgment 30 May 1962, Keishu 16-5-577).

[25] Section 19, subsection 1 of the Penal Code states that the following objects can be confiscated (translated by Ministry of Justice): (i) an object which is used as a key component of a criminal act; (ii) an object used or intended for use in the commission of a criminal act; (iii) an object produced or acquired by means of a criminal act or an object acquired as reward for a criminal act; and (iv) an object received in exchange for the object set forth in the preceding item. In a case where a defendant raped

confiscating only the original is meaningless, because copying is now commonplace, but this is about to be revised.

The written opinion issued by the Legislative Council is a draft, and it is likely that discussions will continue after this. If the offence of voyeurism is newly established, it is expected that crackdowns on voyeurism will become even stricter in the future. The number of cases where even first-time offenders are arrested or prosecuted is likely to increase.

Discussions continue regarding the criminalization of voyeurism and the introduction of a mechanism that allows the confiscation and deletion of copy images. When the problem of voyeurism becomes widely known as a social issue, the people around voyeurs will be more critical of the filming, and it will become difficult to carry out. Widespread coverage of this issue may have a deterrent effect. The hope is that the newly established offence of voyeurism will lead to the deterrence of sexual violations. Attention will be paid to the discussion on establishing the crime of voyeurism in the future.

B. Photo Collage, Computer Graphics, and Deepfake Images

It is unclear from Japanese legislation whether the Revenge Pornography Prevention Act penalties can be applied to the abuse of private sexual images using photo collages, sophisticated computer graphics that look like photographs, and deepfakes, given that the above do not seem to fall under the requirement of 'filmed'.

Let us consider the case of a composite image of the victim's headshot with an elaborate naked body made by means of computer graphics or an elaborate photo collage of images of the victim's face and someone else's naked parts. Should it be said that such images do not constitute private sexual image records since the victim's nude body has not been filmed?

Some argue that persons whose faces only are shown in such images are not acceptable subjects for private sexual image records.[26] In this view, in the case of photo collages, the subject of the private sexual image record is the person whose nude photographs are used.

a victim and secretly filmed a digital video, the Supreme Court allowed the confiscation of the filmed videocassette as an object used to commit a criminal act (Supreme Court Decision 26 June 2018 Keishu 72-2-209). For that reason, when the perpetrator has copied the data to another recording medium, it would be difficult to confiscate it based on the requirement that it has been 'used in the commission of a criminal act'.

[26] Mizuhoshi, 'Summary' (n 7) 24; Hirasawa, *Revenge Porn* (n 8) 56; Sonoda, 'Prevention Act' (n 8) 24.

The penalties of section 3 are valid only in a way that allows a third party to identify the person depicted. When it is possible to identify the person whose nude body alone was photographed from the background etc, it may be possible to affirm private sexual image recording for the person who used the image of the nude part. However, it generally seems difficult to identify the subject only from the nude body. Furthermore, identification will be very difficult if a collage image is created by merging a plurality of body parts. The degree of violation of sexual privacy is much smaller than the case where the person being filmed can be identified. Therefore, an image of a person with nude parts that a third party cannot identify should not be considered a private sexual image record.

In photo collages that combine photographs, computer graphics that look like photographs at first glance, and images made with deepfakes, the naked body of the subject is not directly filmed. However, just by looking at an elaborate collage of images of the victim's face and somebody's nude body parts, it is almost impossible to tell if it is a composite image. As the image as a whole involves the reality of the person being portrayed, there is a risk that the person who sees the image may think that the victim had the perpetrator depict them. Anyone who is unable to recognize it as a collage would mistakenly believe that the victim took a selfie of a sexual image or had the perpetrator take it. The victim is then assessed as if they were sexting and is deemed to have published photos that should not have been published. When a person who sees this fake image thinks that the victim may have had the perpetrator actually take it, it should be understood that the victim's honour has been violated.

As mentioned earlier, the Revenge Pornography Prevention Act protects sexual privacy. The images made using photo collages, sophisticated computer graphics images, and deepfakes, when it can be understood that they infringe on the subject's sexual privacy as a whole, in the author's opinion can be deemed private sexual image recordings.

The identity of the model of the image and the person depicted in the image need not rely on mechanical matching.

A realistic depiction may be recognized as a description of the filmed person, so whether or not the figure depicted in the fake image can be admitted as applicable to the images falling under each item of section 2 should be evaluated as a whole.

VI. Concluding Thoughts

The criminalization of revenge pornography has tremendous significance in enabling agencies such as the police to take various systematic measures against this kind of conduct. In this sense, lofty expectations are placed on law enforcement authorities and educators to implement the Revenge Pornography Prevention Act's purpose thoroughly.

Creating private sexual images is a form of (sexual) expression. Regulating revenge porn is also regulating expression. Freedom of expression is an important human right that underpins democracy and must be protected. Legal, primarily criminal, restrictions on expression should be kept to a minimum as much as possible. On the other hand, the personal rights of victims of revenge pornography must also be protected. We must continue to discuss balancing freedom of expression with protecting personal rights. Regulations must be grounded not on protecting society from the harm of revenge pornography but on safeguarding those depicted from damage caused by the publication and distribution of revenge pornography. Investigative authorities must conduct investigations carefully so as not to overly restrict expression. We must monitor whether investigative agencies are conducting arbitrary investigations.

In Japan, many people are becoming aware that filming non-consensual pornography has become a problem. Widespread recognition of this issue may have a deterrent effect.

Deliberations have just begun in Japan. Attention will be paid to the discussion on establishing criminalization in the future.

Bibliography

Fujimoto T, 'About So-called Revenge Pornography Damage Prevention Act' (2015) 727 Koseki Jiho 82–85

Hirasawa K and others, *Yokuwakaru Revenge Porn Boushiho* [*Understand Well Revenge Pornography Prevention Act*] (Tachibana Shobo 2016) 66

Matsui S, 'Revenge Pornography and Freedom of Expression' (2015) 91(3) Juchi Kenkyu 52–80, 91(4) 44–66

Mizukoshi T, 'Summary of the Act on Prevention of Damage Caused by the Provision of Private Sexual Image Records (Act No. 126 of 2014)' (2015) 68(3) Houritu no hiroba 23

Okada Y, 'Consideration on New Issues Related to Revenge Porn' (2020) 138 Senshu Hogaku Ronshu 37

Okada Y, 'Trends in Legal Revisions against Online Insults' (2022) 76 Senshu University Imamura Institute of Legal Studies Report 1

Sonoda H, 'About Revenge Pornography Prevention Act' (2015) 44 Keijiho Journal 50

PART V
CHANGING THE CULTURE OF CONSENT

13

Consent

Making the Difference between Pleasure and Crime

Thomas Weigend

I. Introduction

In a seminal article, legal philosopher Heidi M Hurd wrote that consent can transform 'trespasses into dinner parties ... and rape into lovemaking ...'[1] This statement succinctly captures the power of consent[2] (and non-consent) in sexual relations. Conversely, an act that creates bliss, happiness, and fulfilment between consenting adults can become sheer horror for one (usually the female[3]) participant if consent is lacking.

[1] Heidi M Hurd, 'Was the Frog Prince Sexually Molested?' (2005) 103 University of Michigan Law Review 1329.

[2] An earlier article by Heidi M Hurd is entitled 'The Moral Magic of Consent' (1996) 2 Legal Theory 121.

[3] The fact that the great majority of sexual offences are committed by men makes the use of gender pronouns difficult in this chapter. Especially when referring to rape and similar violent offences, I use male pronouns so as to reflect empirical reality. To avoid stereotyping gender roles, however, in the hypotheticals I use in the text I sometimes refer to the active person in a sexual encounter (called 'A') by a female pronoun and to the more passive person (B) by a male pronoun.

Thomas Weigend, *Consent* In: *Criminalizing Intimate Image Abuse*. Edited by: Gian Marco Caletti and Kolis Summerer, Oxford University Press. © Oxford University Press 2024. DOI: 10.1093/oso/9780198877813.003.0013

The criminal law has always reflected this fact, although for a long time it lay hidden under additional requirements for a conviction for rape. In many jurisdictions, a defendant could be found guilty of rape only if he had used force, threats, or a similar kind of pressure to make the victim comply with his sexual wishes. However, it was understood that a woman cannot be raped, regardless of any force used, if she genuinely and voluntarily agreed to the sexual acts involved. The primordial sexual offence of rape thus always contained an element of overbearing the will of the other person—an element which is necessarily missing when that person's will encompasses the sexual acts in question.

The issue of consent has become even more important as the definitions of core sexual offences have moved from requiring force or threats to describing the relevant act as the sexual touching of a person without his or her consent.[4] This shift is due to many legislatures' effort to provide better protection of sexual autonomy. If the law is to guarantee every person the right to autonomously decide when, with whom and to what extent he or she engages in sex, it makes no sense to limit criminal liability to extreme cases in which the perpetrator uses particularly invidious means to force the other party to comply with his wishes. Knowingly or perhaps even just recklessly neglecting the other person's opposition to having sex has thus become the core element of the crime of sexual assault.[5]

Criminal law theorists have long debated the question of whether consent negates the *actus reus* of a criminal offence or should be regarded as a ground of justification. Although the practical impact of that issue is negligible, it is worth noting that both partners' valid consent in a sexual act makes it impossible to commit the *actus reus* of rape or a similar offence[6] and thus completely removes this act from the sphere of the criminal law.[7]

If lack of consent has become the key element of sexual offences, one would expect that the preconditions and limits of legally valid consent are beyond doubt, thus enabling courts to determine without difficulty whether B had, in any given situation, consented to A's sexual advances. But on closer inspection, the concept of consent in sexual relations is anything but simple. Does B consent to sexual acts, for example, if she is mistaken about A's identity? At what age can a young person

[4] A typical example is Swedish Penal Code, Ch 6, s 1, which defines as rape the performance of sexual intercourse (or a similar act) 'with a person who is not participating voluntarily'. German Penal Code § 177, ss 1 makes punishable the performance of a sexual act 'against the recognizable will' of the person involved.

[5] Some legal systems, such as Austria and Germany, have turned the former crime of rape by force or threats into an aggravated form of sexual assault.

[6] It should be noted that this effect is brought about only by legally *valid* consent. If, eg, a child expresses her 'consent' to a sexual act, that act can nevertheless be punished as a serious crime.

[7] For a slightly different view, see Michelle M Dempsey, 'The Normative Force of Consent in Moral, Political, and Legal Perspective' in Tatjana Hörnle (ed), *Sexual Assault. Law Reform in a Comparative Perspective* (OUP 2023), at note 17, claiming that 'penetration involves forcible entry through B's sphincteric musculature (in cases of vaginal or anal penetration), and risks physical and psychological harm to B', so that A needs consent as a ground of justification for the physical intrusion involved.

give valid consent to sex? If B agrees to having his penis touched by A, does that mean that A may also penetrate B's body?

In this chapter, I will try to unravel some of these issues, relying on information from various jurisdictions.[8] In the following section II, I will discuss the preconditions of valid consent, such as age and mental capacity, freedom from pressure, and the absence of a personal dependence of B on A. Section III will present issues concerning the expression and the scope of consent, and section IV will deal with an offender's *mens rea* concerning absence of consent. Finally, I will discuss issues of consent in the more specialized area of 'revenge porn', in particular the question of whether consent for having intimate pictures taken includes consent for the distribution of such images (section V).

II. Preconditions of Valid Consent

Section 74 of the Sexual Offences Act 2003 of England and Wales provides: 'For the purposes of this Part, a person consents if he agrees by choice, and has the freedom and capacity to make that choice.' This definition captures the necessary elements of valid consent: the person must be mature and of sound mind, must know the relevant circumstances, and must be free from constraint. The English definition does not, however, explain when these conditions are deemed to be fulfilled. We therefore need to take a closer look at each of them.

A. Age

Children are generally deemed incapable of giving valid consent to sexual acts because they lack sufficient insight into the meaning of sexuality and because they are often mentally and physically unable to resist an adult's advances. Yet, there exists a surprisingly broad range of legal rules as to the 'legal age' of giving consent to sexual acts. Some jurisdictions recognize consent by 14-year-old teenagers, others set the age limit at 16 years old. A growing trend in legislation is to differentiate according to the age of the other party. The law seeks to avoid criminalizing sexual experimentation among teenagers—which to some extent is to be welcomed—but on the other hand intends to protect young persons from adult predators who seek to exploit young persons' gullibility and lack of experience. The laws of the various states of the United States present a patchwork of different regulations in

[8] For a more extensive treatment of these issues and several national reports, see Elisa Hoven and Thomas Weigend (eds), *Consent and Sexual Offenses* (Nomos 2023) (hereafter Hoven and Weigend, *Consent*).

this regard.[9] For example, in Delaware a 12-year-old child can give valid consent to sexual acts of a person no more than four years older than the child but a 30-year-old person can be sentenced to fifteen years imprisonment if he has intercourse with a consenting person of 17 years old.[10] Some jurisdictions distinguish between sexual intercourse and other sexual acts; for example, in Turkey a teenager aged at least 15 can give valid consent to sexual acts; but for vaginal or anal intercourse, the age of consent has been fixed at 18 years, so that two 17-year-olds who have consensual intercourse will both be punishable.[11] In the Netherlands, even children younger than 12 years old can give valid consent to sexual acts not involving penetration, if such acts are age-adequate and the partner is roughly in the same age group.[12]

B. Mental Handicaps and Intoxication

Many legal systems seek to protect people with severe mental handicaps from being exploited by others for sexual purposes. Relevant criminal provisions declare any consent expressed by such persons to be legally invalid. For example, § 177, s 2, no 1 of the German Penal Code makes it a crime for A to perform a sexual act on B if A exploits the fact that B is incapable of forming or expressing his will in opposition to A's intention. Any acts or words on B's part seemingly expressing his consent, thus, remain irrelevant. One problem of such legal provisions lies in drawing the line between a mere impairment of B's intellectual capacity or willpower on the one hand and his incapacity to comprehend sexuality or to resist A's advances on the other. Section 243 of the Dutch Penal Code presents rather than resolves this problem:

> Any person who engages in acts comprising or including sexual penetration of the body with a person whom he knows to be unconscious, to have diminished consciousness or to be physically unable to resist, or to be suffering from such a degree of mental disease or defect that such person is incapable or not sufficiently capable of exercising or expressing his will in the matter or of offering resistance, shall be liable to a term of imprisonment . . .

Prosecutors and courts applying this provision—and indeed any person who wishes to engage in sex with a mentally challenged person—must make the difficult

[9] For an overview, see Aya Gruber, 'United States' in Hoven and Weigend, *Consent* (n 8) 303, 312–15.

[10] See Delaware Code, Title 11, §§ 761(l), 770(2).

[11] For a critical discussion, see Baris Atladi, 'Turkey' in Hoven and Weigend, *Consent* (n 8) 289, 295–99.

[12] Dutch Penal Code, s 244 and s 247. For a discussion, see Kai Lindenberg, 'Netherlands' in Hoven and Weigend, *Consent* (n 8) 215, 224–25.

determination of whether B is 'sufficiently capable of exercising or expressing his will in the matter', the word 'sufficiently' obviously referring to some value judgement without any clear contours. Another problem of such formulations lies in the fact that the blanket criminalization of sex with mentally impaired persons practically excludes them from the enjoyment of sex. Even a person not 'sufficiently' able to express his will may like to be touched sexually, especially by his spouse or permanent partner. The criminal law should not interfere with such pleasures.[13] Some legal systems have therefore wisely limited criminal liability to persons who 'exploit' or 'abuse' the mentally handicapped person's inability to understand the meaning of consenting to sexual acts, thus leaving open a legal path to sexual relations embedded in a personal relationship.[14]

Intoxication by alcohol or drugs can temporarily have similar effects as permanent mental impairment. A person who is so drunk that he or she is unconscious or close to that state cannot give valid consent to sexual acts. However, between the extremes of sobriety and drunken unconsciousness there lies a grey area of inebriation in which a determination of the validity of consent is difficult. Even drunkenness of a moderate degree can suppress normal inhibitions and can cause B to consent to sexual acts with a partner whom B would not find acceptable if she were sober. Some jurisdictions make the absence of valid consent depend on vague formulations such as a 'substantial impairment' of a person's ability to resist or to control her actions.[15] Typical signs of loss of control, such as tripping over one's own feet, sitting down on a dirty street, or being too uncoordinated to undress indicate such disabling impairment.[16] German law[17] generally accepts B's consent even if her ability to form or express her will is significantly impaired, but in that instance requires A to ascertain B's consent to each sexual act.

C. Power Differentials

Verbal consent to sex given by B can be invalid if there exists a strong power differential between A and B. Typical examples are relationships between a psychotherapist and his client, a teacher and her student, or a prison warden and a prisoner. Some jurisdictions declare sexual relations in such relationships generally taboo and make it a crime for A to have sex with B. Other systems, such as Germany, leave

[13] Cf Gruber, 'United States' (n 9) 318–19.

[14] See, eg, German Penal Code, § 177, s 2, no. 1 ('exploiting' incapacity); Swiss Criminal Code, Art 191 ('abusing' incapacity).

[15] For a discussion of 'substantial impairment' and a broad range of other standards on intoxication in various states of the United States, see Gruber, 'United States' (n 9) 315–16.

[16] See Swiss Federal Court, Judgment of 20 August 2015—BGer 6B_96/2015, para 2.3; Nora Scheidegger, 'Switzerland' in Hoven and Weigend, *Consent* (n 8) 275, 281.

[17] German Penal Code, §177, ss 2, no. 2.

some room for genuine loving relationships and provide for criminal liability only if the person in the superior position 'abuses' his or her authority for performing sexual acts on B.[18] In some states of the United States in relationships with power differentials there exists a rebuttable presumption that B did not genuinely consent, so that the burden of proof is on A to show that there was no 'coercion by status'.[19] Sex between an employer and his or her employee is not generally criminalized, hence it must be determined in each case whether employer A used implied threats (for example, of firing B) for making B comply with his sexual wishes.

D. Consent Brought about by Unfair Means

In the instances discussed above, the lack of valid consent is related to B's personal status: age, mental capacity, or powerlessness in relation to A. But there also exist situational factors which can negate the legal recognition of an expression of consent.

1. Threats

Threats are a typical means of rape, but in that context, they are mostly limited to threats of imminent violence. There is, however, a growing recognition in various jurisdictions that other threats can also vitiate consent because the fear of negative consequences may make it psychologically difficult or impossible for B to resist A's demands. On the other hand, there are many situations in daily life where B submits to A's 'request' because B fears some negative consequences if he refuses. Such consequences can consist of A getting into a bad mood or A refusing to talk to B for a few hours. Such routine compromises to accommodate differing interests should not lead to criminal consequences, even if it is true that B's expressed consent in such a situation is not 'enthusiastic' and based on an entirely free decision.

On a more serious level, there are threats like 'I will leave you if you don't have sex with me'. Clearly, it is not unlawful to leave one's long-time partner, but on the other hand threatening him with breaking up can have a much stronger psychological impact than threatening him with a criminal offence[20] such as destroying his favourite wristwatch. Relevant legal provisions struggle with drawing the line between acceptable persuasion and unlawful threats. According to Austrian and German laws, B's consent is invalid if A had threatened to harm any important interest of B.[21] The latest draft of the American Model Penal Code makes it a crime

[18] German Penal Code, §§ 174a, 174b, 174c.

[19] Gruber, 'United States' (n 9) 320.

[20] According to Swedish Criminal Code, Ch 6, s 1, participation in a sexual act is deemed involuntary whenever it is the result of a threat of a criminal act.

[21] Austrian Penal Code, § 202; German Penal Code, § 177, s 2, no. 5.

to have sex with a person after threatening 'to take any action or cause any consequence that would cause submission to or performance of the act of sexual penetration or oral sex by someone of ordinary resolution in that person's situation under all the circumstances'.[22] This, of course, leaves the decision on whether A committed a sexual offence almost entirely to the prosecutor and court in each case. A preferable solution might be to conclusively list the consequences that A must not threaten B with—even if this means that someone may escape punishment if he uses more individualized but equally effective threats.

2. Deceit

Persuading another person to engage in sexual relations often involves the manipulation of facts. To appear more attractive to B as a potential sexual partner, A may inflate his wealth, may lie about his marital status, or may claim—against his better knowledge—that B is the love of his life. If such lies result in B's willingness to agree to sexual relations, the question arises whether B's consent is still legally valid or whether A commits 'rape by deception'.

Legal systems differ greatly in their approach to this issue. Some penal codes tellingly list threats, force, and lack of consciousness as grounds for vitiating consent, but do not mention deceit, thereby implying *e contrario* that the criminal law does not sanction the introduction of 'alternative facts' for making a person agree to a sexual encounter.[23] But the tide may be turning. Due to an increasing emphasis on the need for full autonomy in decision-making on sexual relations, some countries[24] explicitly list deceit (along with violence and threats) as one form of committing rape.[25]

Regardless of these differing starting points, there is widespread agreement on the rule that valid consent presupposes that B is aware that a sexual act is involved. If, for example, a doctor tells his female patient that his manipulation of her vagina is a necessary part of medical diagnosis or treatment, whereas its real purpose is to give him sexual gratification, the patient's consent to his acts is invalid.[26] Some—but not all—jurisdictions assume that consent is vitiated by deceit about A's

[22] American Law Institute (ed), *Model Penal Code, Sexual Assault and Related Offenses, Tentative Draft no 5* (American Law Institute 2021) Art 213.4 (1)(b).

[23] See, eg, German Penal Code, § 177, s 2, nos 4 and 5; s 5, nos 1 and no 2; Swiss Penal Code, Arts 189, 190; Swedish Penal Code, Ch 6, s 1 (see Linnea Wegerstad, 'Sweden' in Hoven and Weigend, *Consent* (n 8) 255, 266); for Italy, see Gian Marco Caletti, 'Italy' in Hoven and Weigend, *Consent* (n 8) 199, 207.

[24] For a review of relevant case law in England and Commonwealth jurisdictions, see Tom O'Malley and Elisa Hoven, 'Consent in the Law Relating to Sexual Offences' in Kai Ambos and others (eds), *Core Concepts in Criminal Law and Criminal Justice* vol 1, (Cambridge University Press 2020) 135, 155–60.

[25] See Polish Criminal Code, Art 197. See also the discussion of the divergent laws in Australian states and territories by Andrew Dyer, 'Australia' in Hoven and Weigend, *Consent* (n 8) 131, 139–40.

[26] On Austrian law, see Sebastian Mayr and Kurt Schmoller, 'Austria' in Hoven and Weigend, *Consent* (n 8) 151, 164; on England, see Lyndon Harris and Hannah Quirk, 'England and Wales' in Hoven and Weigend, *Consent* (n 8) 173, 181 (criminal deceit about the 'nature and purpose of the act'); on US law, see Gruber, 'United States' (n 9) 321.

identity, if A manages to make B believe that she is having sex not with A but with her regular partner X.[27] Other lies about one's identity may well leave B's consent intact, for example if A and B meet for the first time in a bar and A presents himself as Jim Roe whereas his real name is John Doe.

In social interactions, we necessarily face the risk of being deceived. The criminal law wisely refrains from penalizing every deception but leaves it to the individuals to check on the truth of what they are being told. This means that some lies leave consent to sexual acts intact, even though they may in fact have a great impact on B's decision whether to engage in sexual relations with A. For example, misinformation on one's religious affiliation, ethnic background, or occupation is in most jurisdictions regarded as legally irrelevant in the context of sexual offences. This rule is partly due to the consideration that the law would support invidious discrimination if it penalized A for preventing B from rejecting him as a partner, for example because of his nationality or religion.[28] Moreover, if, for example, B is determined to have sex only with Catholics, the responsibility for checking on A's religious affiliation may well be put on B. The same applies to false promises: if A persuades B to have sex with him by telling her that he will marry her or give her money, B acts on her own risk if she gives her consent based on the expectation that A will be true to his word.[29]

Borderline cases concern misinformation about health-related issues. The laws of several states of the United States have criminalized falsely denying one's HIV-positive status before having sex.[30] This rule can be based on the serious health risk involved in unprotected sexual intercourse with an HIV-positive partner. However, criminalization becomes questionable if A uses a condom and thus minimizes B's risk of infection.[31] Similar considerations apply to other sexually transmissible diseases. Deceit about measures to avoid pregnancy (eg B falsely claims to be on the pill, or A pretends that he has been sterilized) are not covered by rules on increased health risks; lies in these matters therefore do not invalidate the partner's consent to sexual intercourse.[32]

The international trend seems to favour an extension of criminal liability in cases of deceiving another person into consenting to sex. This trend dovetails with the generally increased emphasis on the protection of sexual autonomy. Yet,

[27] Such impersonation is criminal, eg, under Italian Penal Code, Art 609-*bis*, s 2.

[28] Cf Dyer, 'Australia' (n 25) 146.

[29] See, eg, Thomas Weigend, 'Germany' in Hoven and Weigend, *Consent* (n 8) 193–94; Wojciech Jasinski and Karolina Kremens, 'Poland' in Hoven and Weigend, *Consent* (n 8) 235, 250. But for a different approach in some Australian states, see Dyer, 'Australia' (n 25) 139. If A promises B money in exchange for her sexual services and does not intend to pay her, A does not commit a sexual offence but may well be punishable for fraud. This surprising result is due to the extensive protection of economic interests against deceit.

[30] Gruber, 'United States' (n 9) 321–22. England, by contrast, does not regard deceit about one's HIV status as relevant for the legal validity of consent; see Harris and Quirk, 'England and Wales' (n 26) 181.

[31] Mayr and Schmoller, 'Austria' (n 26) 167.

[32] See, eg, Wegerstad, 'Sweden' (n 23) 266.

although an effective protection of personal autonomy in sexual matters is an important interest, legislatures and courts should beware of over-using the sharp tool of criminal law for regulating verbal interactions between persons in the process of establishing their personal relationship.

III. Expression and Scope of Consent

A. Expression of Consent

In situations where sex may be at issue, communication can be a problem. Many people find it difficult or embarrassing to verbalize sexual desires or the lack of them, and non-verbal conduct may be contradictory or at least open to different interpretations. In many cases, the issue is whether B's passivity amounted to consent. Social role expectations can exacerbate this problem: in societies that assign women a role subservient to men, it may be that a woman says 'yes' although she does not want sex; or she may say 'no' even when she desires sex because that is what is expected of a 'decent' woman. The criminal law, entering the scene long after the fact, is an inadequate tool for resolving such problems of communication. But the law must determine which of the persons involved bears the burden if ambiguous conduct has led to a hidden dissent.

Under traditional rape laws, it is B who must clearly communicate to A that she does not wish to engage in sex. If rape by definition requires the use of force or threats, the crime is unlikely to be committed if A thinks that B agrees to having sex, because A will then see no need to resort to such means. Traditionally, B is therefore assumed to consent unless she shows some resistance to A's advances, and B's silence and passivity are regarded as equalling consent.[33]

The opposite approach has been taken, for example, by some states in Australia and in the U.S.[34] Under the laws of these states, A is guilty of sexual assault if she sexually touches B unless B has previously made a clear verbal or non-verbal statement of consent to A's acts.[35] These laws seek to protect B's sexual autonomy by

[33] See, eg, Polish Penal Code, Art. 197 (cf. Jasinski and Kremens, 'Poland' (n 29) 237–38); Swiss Penal Code, Arts. 189, 190 (cf. Scheidegger, 'Switzerland' (n 16) 276–77).

[34] For an extensive discussion, see Aya Gruber, 'Affirmative Consent' in Hoven and Weigend, *Consent* (n 8) 59. See also Stephen J Schulhofer, 'Consent: What It Means and Why It's Time to Require It' (2016) 47 University of the Pacific Law Review 665.

[35] See, eg, Tasmania Criminal Code Act 1924, s 2A(2): '. . . a person does not freely agree to an act if the person—(a) does not say or do anything to communicate consent'. For a critical discussion of this and similar provisions in Australia, see Dyer, 'Australia' (n 25) 141–42. For the United States, see, eg, Wisconsin Statutes, s 940.225(4): 'Consent, as used in this section, means words or overt actions by a person who is competent to give informed consent indicating a freely given agreement to have sexual intercourse or sexual contact.' Vermont Statutes, § 3251(3) has this definition for consent in sexual acts: '"Consent" means the affirmative, unambiguous, and voluntary agreement to engage in a sexual act, which can be revoked at any time.'

placing the burden of any misunderstanding on A: 'If in doubt', the rule tells A, 'ask before you act!'. The idea is thus to encourage active communication before any sexual interaction takes place. But such laws have been criticized for (at least theoretically) criminalizing conduct that is perfectly normal between long-term partners, as where A initiates sexual contact without first asking for B's permission, because A knows from experience that B does not mind such contact. Seen in context with the participants' earlier interactions, even B's express 'no' may not be intended to stop A from going ahead with sexual acts.[36] Since highly individualized sexual relations defy the rules of contract law, their over-formalization extends criminal liability too far and may even expose the criminal law to ridicule.

Matters are even more complicated in systems which define rape as sexual intercourse without consent but do not require 'affirmative' consent. Some of these jurisdictions require B to 'recognizably' express her opposition to sexual acts; if she does not do so, B will be assumed to have consented.[37] The 'recognizability' standard in these jurisdictions is an objective one—it is not what A understood B to say that is determinative, but how an objective observer would have interpreted B's words or conduct.[38] This approach puts much of the burden of possible misunderstandings on B—it is B's responsibility to clearly communicate her unwillingness to enter into sexual relations with A. Other jurisdictions that recognize B's consent as negating the *actus reus* of sexual assault focus on B's 'true' (internal) attitude. If B did not adequately express her opposition to A's advances, this is not regarded as a substitute for B's consent, but may only have an impact on A's intention. These jurisdictions require the finder of fact to determine the existence of consent on the basis of all the circumstances of the case, including prior interactions between A and B.[39]

B. Timing of Consent

Consent must be present at the time when the sexual acts are performed. That means that a declaration of consent made some time before the sexual interaction does not automatically remain in effect unless the circumstances clearly indicate that B still adheres to his earlier statement. In fact, B may withdraw

[36] See Dyer, 'Australia' (n 25) 118–19; Gruber, 'United States' (n 9) 325.

[37] See German Penal Code, § 177, s 1. For a similar conclusion as to the meaning of Austrian Penal Code § 205a, see Mayr and Schmoller, 'Austria' (n 26) 163.

[38] Joachim Renzikowski, '§ 177 Marginal Note 48' in Jürgen Schäfer (ed), *Münchener Kommentar zum Strafgesetzbuch* vol 3 (4th edn, Beck 2021).

[39] See England and Wales Sexual Offences Act 2003, s 1(2): 'Whether a belief is reasonable is to be determined having regard to all the circumstances, including any steps A has taken to ascertain whether B consents.' See also Swedish Penal Code, Ch 6, s 1: 'When assessing whether participation is voluntary or not, particular consideration is given to whether voluntariness was expressed by word or deed or in some other way.' On the similar situation under Dutch law, see Lindenberg, 'Netherlands' (n 12) 228–29.

his prior consent at any time, even while the sexual interaction takes place. If B does so, A must immediately desist from any sexual act no longer covered by consent.[40]

Since A cannot be made to guess at his own risk about possible changes in B's attitude as to the continuation of sexual acts, B must communicate her change of mind to make it legally relevant. This is true even in jurisdictions that follow the 'only yes means yes' maxim. Otherwise, A would have to continually ask B to confirm her consent while the sexual interaction is going on.[41] Withdrawal of consent need not, however, be indicated verbally; it is sufficient that B's conduct (eg crying, turning away from A) clearly indicates to A that his sexual acts are no longer welcome.[42]

A denial or withdrawal of consent need not be B's last word on the matter. If B, at a later time, (again) shows her willingness to engage in sexual relations with A, neither of them is bound by B's earlier statement.[43] It is an open question, however, for how long and how insistently A may try to persuade B to give up her negative attitude towards having sex with A. This may amount to psychological pressure approaching illicit threats, and the criminalization of 'nagging sex' has indeed been discussed in Sweden but has not (yet) been established as a variant of sexual assault.[44]

C. Scope of Consent

Since verbal or non-verbal agreements to have sex rarely contain itemized statements as to what sexual acts are consented by both parties, misunderstandings may occur about how far A may go, and B may subsequently feel violated in her sexual autonomy by A's acts that B had not even thought about when she agreed to have 'sex' with A. Even if there is agreement between A and B that they wish to 'have sex', that does not mean that they mutually consent to any conceivable sexual act. A good guideline is to ask what B could have expected to happen, given the circumstances—which, of course, can differ greatly, as between teenagers on their third date and a couple after ten years of marriage. If the persons involved know each other well and

[40] For Italy, see Caletti, 'Italy' (n 23) 208–09. In countries that require the use of force or threats for the commission of rape, a verbal withdrawal of consent is valid, but A commits rape or sexual assault only if he then uses force or threats to overcome B's unwillingness to continue with the sexual interaction. See Jasinski and Kremens, 'Poland' (n 29) 250; Scheidegger, 'Switzerland' (n 16) 283–84.

[41] Cf Gruber, 'United States' (n 9) 327.

[42] For Austria, see Mayr and Schmoller, 'Austria' (n 26) 165.

[43] Gruber, 'United States' (n 9) 327.

[44] Wegerstad, 'Sweden' (n 23) 266. For a thorough discussion of this issue, see Nora Scheidegger, 'Of Nagging and Guilt-Tripping' in Hoven and Weigend, *Consent* (n 8) 35. In Switzerland, the definition of rape in Penal Code, Art 190 includes 'psychological pressure' as a forbidden means of forcing another person to submit to sexual intercourse. But it is questionable whether persistent 'nagging' amounts to such psychological pressure; cf Scheidegger, 'Switzerland' (n 16) 282–83.

have had sex many times before, it is fair to say that their consent extends to 'the usual'; for new practices that involve more intense forms of penetration (eg anal sex), a particularized agreement would be necessary. By contrast, if A and B have not had sex with each other before, the best way for them to proceed would be to explore the scope of consent gradually, unless there is a clear verbal agreement as to particular acts. In other words, A cannot assume that B agrees to every sexual practice if she lets him kiss her or touch her intimate sphere. If A respects these limitations of consent, he is unlikely to risk criminal punishment for sexual assault; but he may well commit that offence if he knowingly goes beyond the limit that he must reasonably expect to exist for B without waiting for B's reaction.[45]

In recent years, the scope of consent has been discussed with regard to a practice called stealthing, that is, the secret removal of a condom during sexual intercourse.[46] Courts and scholars have taken different approaches toward this practice. Some authors regard B's consent to intercourse as void due to deceit if A withheld the information that he planned to remove the condom.[47] Others treat intercourse without a condom as a sexual act that is distinct from the intercourse with a condom, hence that new sexual act is not covered by B's original consent.[48] In jurisdictions that treat non-consensual intercourse as rape even where the actor uses neither force nor threats, A can then be convicted of rape. As a matter of criminal policy, stealthing should be punishable because A, by removing the condom, creates an increased risk of transmitting diseases and (in vaginal intercourse) causing pregnancy, which goes beyond any risk connected with the protected intercourse B had consented to. Both approaches mentioned above lead to similar results. An element of deceit is difficult to establish, however, if A spontaneously removes the condom in the course of the sexual interaction. It is thus preferable to view unprotected intercourse as a different (and more risky) sexual act, which is permissible only with B's informed consent.

IV. *Mens Rea* as to Lack of Consent

In most jurisdictions, rape, sexual assault, and similar offences can be committed only if the perpetrator acts intentionally. Since lack of consent is an element of the *actus reus*, intent requires that the actor knows about the absence of consent.

[45] Jasinski and Kremens, 'Poland' (n 29) 251.

[46] For a comprehensive treatment of this topic, see Sebastian Mayr and Kurt Schmoller, 'Particularized Consent and Non-consensual Condom Removal' in Hoven and Weigend, *Consent* (n 8) 97. See also the seminal article by Alexandra Brodsky, 'Rape-Adjacent: Imagining Legal Responses to Nonconsensual Condom Removal' (2017) 32 Columbia Journal of Gender and Law 183.

[47] See, eg, Harris and Quirk, 'England and Wales' (n 26) 181; Jasinski and Kremens, 'Poland' (n 29) 251; Mayr and Schmoller, 'Austria' (n 26) 166.

[48] See, eg, Scheidegger, 'Switzerland' (n 16) 248 (citing a decision of the Swiss Federal Court holding that 'stealthing' is not rape under present Swiss law); Wegerstad, 'Sweden' (n 23) 269; Weigend, 'Germany' (n 29) 196 (citing German court decisions which held defendants responsible for sexual abuse in stealthing cases).

However, since sexual interactions normally take place without eyewitnesses, proof of A's awareness of B's non-consent will often be difficult. Unless the use of force on B left visible traces, A's claim that B agreed to have sex with him or that at least he thought that she had agreed, will be hard to refute by objective evidence. The court is then constrained to determining A's state of mind as to B's non-consent based on the objective circumstances presented at the trial. Judges are likely to find the defendant guilty of intentional rape if they think that a reasonable person in A's position would not have thought that B is consenting.

Some jurisdictions apply the concept of 'conditional intent' (*dolus eventualis*) according to which it is sufficient for a finding of intent that A is aware of the *possibility* that B does not consent and still goes ahead with his plan, accepting the possibility that he acts against B's wishes.[49] Other jurisdictions, for example Sweden and some states of the United States, recognize offences of 'reckless' rape. This offence is perpetrated if the actor performs a sexual act while consciously taking the risk that the victim does not consent to it.[50] Yet other legal systems have taken or are about to take the step of criminalizing 'negligent rape', that is, engaging in a sexual interaction against the other person's will while being grossly negligent about determining that person's true wishes.[51] Under these laws, A's inadvertent negligence can be established if he did not make any effort to ensure that B is participating voluntarily although there were strong reasons to do so. Negligent rape in these legal systems carries a lesser sentence than intentional rape.

This last step towards a comprehensive protection of B's sexual autonomy may be the most consistent approach to dealing with the problem of proving the actor's *mens rea*. It is more honest to punish a person for negligent rape than to over-extend the concept of intent to avoid impunity if full and convincing proof of the defendant's knowledge is not available, or to shift the burden of proof to the defendant.

V. Consent with Regard to the Dissemination of Sexual Images

The illicit dissemination of private images with sexual content can have grave consequences for the victim. It is not so much a crime against the victim's honour but against his or her sexual privacy, a highly vulnerable and important interest. Similarly to the sexual offences considered above, it is the issue of consent (or its absence) which determines the social meaning of the act. If, for example, B asks A to place nude pictures of her along with contact data on social media in the

[49] This is the case in Austria (see Austrian Penal Code, § 5, s 1); Germany (see Weigend, 'Germany' (n 29) 197); and Switzerland (Swiss Penal Code Art, 12, s 2).

[50] See Wegerstad, 'Sweden' (n 23) 270–71; Gruber, 'United States' (n 9) 329.

[51] Sweden has already passed such legislation (Wegerstad, 'Sweden' (n 23) 271–72), and the Netherlands are contemplating its introduction (Lindenberg, 'Netherlands' (n 12) 232).

hope of attracting customers for her commercial sale of such pictures, no harm is done if A complies with B's wishes. But if B is unaware of the same act, it can lead to the complete destruction of her private sphere and her reputation among her acquaintances.[52]

Consent of the person whose image is distributed is needed at two stages: at the level of production and at the level of distribution. It is important to realize that normally consent at the first level does not also imply consent at the second level. The fact that B allows A to make photographic images of her in sexually connoted situations thus does not mean that B authorizes A (or anyone else) to distribute these images to others.[53]

Making photos of other persons in private surroundings without their consent is, as such, a criminal offence in many jurisdictions. For example, German Penal Code, § 201a, s 1, no 1 prohibits making photographic images of persons who are in a home or in a place that is protected from viewing, if making the image violates the personal sphere of the person. More specifically, German Penal Code, § 184k defines as a criminal offence the act of producing a photographic image of another person's genitals, buttocks, or female breast if these parts are hidden from view.[54] In both instances, the making of photographs is prohibited only if it is 'unauthorized' (*unbefugt*), which means that the affected person's consent negates the *actus reus*.[55] Consent is, of course, subject to the same preconditions and limitations (concerning age, absence of threats, etc) as discussed earlier for consent to sexual acts.

Distributing sexual images is a separate crime. German Penal Code, § 184k, s 1 provides for two variants: displaying or distributing images of the intimate sphere produced without authorization (no. 2) and distributing without proper consent images produced in an 'authorized' way, that is, with the consent of the person photographed (no. 3). This statutory scheme demonstrates that specific consent is needed for the dissemination of images even if they were produced consensually. If, for example, B asks A to make photographs of her naked breast, A commits a criminal offence if he later shows these photographs to a friend without special authorization from B. If B is less than 18 years old, the production and dissemination of sexually connoted photographs can be separately punishable under the heading of juvenile pornography. German Penal Code, § 184c defines as juvenile pornography, inter alia, images showing a totally or partly naked person between

[52] For an excellent discussion of the relevant issues of punishing 'revenge porn', see Gian Marco Caletti, 'Can Affirmative Consent Save "Revenge Porn" Laws? Lessons from the Italian Criminalization of Non-Consensual Pornography' (2021) 25 Virginia Journal of Law and Technology 112 (hereafter Caletti, 'Affirmative Consent'). See also Danielle Keats Citron and Mary Anne Franks, 'Criminalizing Revenge Porn' (2014) 49 Wake Forest Law Review 345.

[53] Caletti, 'Affirmative Consent' (n 52) 144 speaks of 'contextuality of any form of consent'.

[54] A similar provision is Austrian Penal Code, § 120a.

[55] Joachim Renzikowski, '§ 184k Marginal Note 21' in Jürgen Schäfer (ed), *Münchener Kommentar zum Strafgesetzbuch* vol 3 (4th edn, Beck 2021).

14 and 18 years old in a sexually stimulating position, and images of the naked genitals or buttocks of a person of that age (German Penal Code, § 184c, s 1, no 1(b) and (c)). The consent of the juvenile whose image has been taken does not justify the distribution of these images; consent does, however, negate the punishability of producing such images exclusively for the private use of the person who made the photographs (German Penal Code, § 184c s 4). This exception is meant to decriminalize the consensual creation and mutual exchange of sexual images for the private use of young couples.[56]

Other jurisdictions recognize further exceptions to the prohibition of distributing other persons' sexual images. One potential exception exists when the affected person had himself posted sexual images. Since autonomy with regard to sex is the overarching legal interest at stake here, one can argue that there is nothing left to protect if the affected person has already given up privacy with respect to an image.[57] But the concept of autonomy should also include the determination as to where and when one's intimate images are posted. B may, for example, regret having posted an image of herself and may seek to have it deleted; her efforts would be undermined if A could with impunity re-post this same image on other platforms, which may have a much larger number of users than the platform B had originally used.

Both English[58] and Italian[59] law limit punishability of the unauthorized dissemination of intimate images to instances in which the actor intends to cause distress to the victim. It is difficult, however, to find a good reason for this limitation. In typical cases of 'revenge porn', the perpetrator will indeed be driven by a wish to do harm to the victim. But other instances of unauthorized distribution of intimate images may be just as harmful to the victim, for example if the perpetrator wishes to make a profit, wants to please friends, or derives sexual gratification from distributing the images. In many cases, it will even be impossible to prove the actor's intention. If a legislature wishes (unnecessarily) to put a subjective limit on the incrimination of the distribution of such images, it should be sufficient that the actor knows that his act is likely to cause distress to the person depicted if he or she becomes aware of the dissemination of the images.[60]

[56] See Tatjana Hörnle, '§ 184c Marginal Note 17' in Jürgen Schäfer (ed), *Münchener Kommentar zum Strafgesetzbuch* vol 3 (4th edn, Beck 2021).

[57] Criminal Justice and Courts Act (England and Wales), s 33(5) provides that A is not punishable for distributing B's sexual image if A reasonably believed that the photograph or film had previously been disclosed for reward with B's consent.

[58] Criminal Justice and Courts Act 2015, s 33(1)(b).

[59] Italian Penal Code, Art. 612-ter, s 2.

[60] By contrast, the English Criminal Justice and Courts Act 2015, s 33(8) states that: 'A person charged with an offence under this section is not to be taken to have disclosed a photograph or film with the intention of causing distress merely because that was a natural and probable consequence of the disclosure.' This means that the prosecution must prove the defendant's specific intention beyond showing his knowledge of the probable consequences of his conduct.

A final issue concerns the subjective element of the offence with regard to the victim's non-consent. Since distributing images with the consent of the person depicted is not a crime,[61] a defendant charged with unauthorized distribution is likely to claim that he had thought that B had consented. If the maxim *in dubio pro reo* applies to a mistake of fact in that regard, it will be difficult to convict A unless there is proof that B explicitly asked A not to show or distribute the images to others.

We have seen above, however, that in sexual offences there is growing support for the 'Only yes means yes' model, which would require A—if he wishes to avoid criminal liability—to take affirmative steps to ascertain that B consents to sexual relations with him. This rule may in some cases be inapposite, especially where A and B are married or have known each other for a long time. But with regard to the dissemination of sexual images, there exist two strong arguments in favour of demanding that A explicitly ask for B's consent. First, the potential harm for B of an emergence of her sexual images on social media or even their distribution among acquaintances can be grave and long-lasting, whereas the social benefit of the act is negligible.[62] Second, it may for many people be difficult to verbally discuss possible sexual practices in the fraught situation of an initial sexual encounter, but asking an acquaintance whether she agrees to have certain images posted or disseminated is neither embarrassing nor difficult.[63] The law should therefore exonerate A of the charge of unauthorized distribution only if he had discussed the matter with B and on the basis of their communication reasonably believed that B consented.

VI. Conclusion

In the course of the above discussion, consent has lost some of its magic. Although it remains true that consent in sexual relations (including the distribution of sexual images) is the key to harmless pleasure, the legal concept of consent has turned out to be fraught with preconditions and exceptions. The basic reason for the fragility of consent in this area is the sensitivity of sexual autonomy. If autonomy is to reflect what a person 'really' wants under conditions of freedom of will, autonomy is bound to be jeopardized by various interior and exterior factors. The criminal law is too blunt a tool to be able to do justice to each situation in which B may have felt that A violated his sexual autonomy. But there are some ground rules that need to be adhered to: B must be mature and mentally alert enough to understand what it means to consent to sexual acts; his decision must not be influenced by threats of

[61] Caletti, 'Affirmative Consent' (n 52) 143 points out that in any event 'no harm arises' if the depicted person consents to the distribution of the image. It is an open but immaterial question whether the person's consent negates the *actus reus* of unauthorized distribution or works as a ground of justification.

[62] Caletti, 'Affirmative Consent' (n 52) 166.

[63] ibid.

violence or other serious harm, and he must know that a sexual act (and not, eg, a medical examination) is at stake. If these conditions are fulfilled, A should make sure that B actually consents before A proceeds with sexual acts. It is still an open question, however, in what way consent needs to be expressed in order to foreclose A's criminal liability. There can be little doubt, however, that only B's express authorization is sufficient to permit A to distribute sexual images of B.

Sexual relations between human beings are complicated, and they will continue to present challenges to the criminal law. But the international trend toward greater sensitivity to the protection of sexual autonomy, especially of women, is certainly to be welcomed.

Bibliography

American Law Institute (ed), *Model Penal Code. Sexual Assault and Related Offenses, Tentative Draft no 5* (American Law Institute 2021)

Atladi B, 'Turkey' in E Hoven and T Weigend (eds), *Consent and Sexual Offenses* (Nomos 2023)

Brodsky A, 'Rape-Adjacent: Imagining Legal Responses to Nonconsensual Condom Removal' (2017) 32 Columbia Journal of Gender and Law 183

Caletti GM, 'Can Affirmative Consent Save "Revenge Porn" Laws? Lessons from the Italian Criminalization of Non-Consensual Pornography' (2021) 25 Virginia Journal of Law and Technology 112

Caletti GM, 'Italy' in E Hoven and T Weigend (eds), *Consent and Sexual Offenses* (Nomos 2023)

Citron DK and Franks M, 'Criminalizing Revenge Porn' (2014) 49 Wake Forest Law Review 345

Dempsey MM, 'The Normative Force of Consent in Moral, Political, and Legal Perspective' in T Hörnle (ed), *Sexual Assault. Law Reform in a Comparative Perspective* (OUP 2023)

Dyer A, 'Australia' in E Hoven and T Weigend (eds), *Consent and Sexual Offenses* (Nomos 2023)

Gruber A, 'Affirmative Consent' in E Hoven and T Weigend (eds), *Consent and Sexual Offenses* (Nomos 2023)

Gruber A, 'United States' in E Hoven and T Weigend (eds), *Consent and Sexual Offenses* (Nomos 2023)

Harris Land Quirk H, 'England and Wales' in E Hoven and T Weigend (eds), *Consent and Sexual Offenses* (Nomos 2023)

Hoven E and Weigend T (eds), *Consent and Sexual Offenses* (Nomos 2023)

Hurd HM, 'The Moral Magic of Consent' (1996) 2 Legal Theory 121

Hurd HM, 'Was the Frog Prince Sexually Molested?' (2005) 103 University of Michigan Law Review 1329

Jasinski W and Kremens K, 'Poland' in E Hoven and T Weigend (eds), *Consent and Sexual Offenses* (Nomos 2023)

Lindenberg K, 'Netherlands' in E Hoven and T Weigend (eds), *Consent and Sexual Offenses* (Nomos 2023)

Mayr S and Schmoller K, 'Austria' in E Hoven and T Weigend (eds), *Consent and Sexual Offenses* (Nomos 2023)

Mayr S and Schmoller K, 'Particularized Consent and Non-consensual Condom Removal' in E Hoven and T Weigend (eds), *Consent and Sexual Offenses* (Nomos 2023)

O'Malley T and Hoven E, 'Consent in the Law Relating to Sexual Offences' in K Ambos and others (eds), *Core Concepts in Criminal Law and Criminal Justice* vol 1 (Cambridge University Press 2020)

Schäfer J (ed), *Münchener Kommentar zum Strafgesetzbuch* vol 3 (4th edn, Beck 2021)

Scheidegger N, 'Of Nagging and Guilt-Tripping' in E Hoven and T Weigend (eds), *Consent and Sexual Offenses* (Nomos 2023)

Scheidegger N, 'Switzerland' in E Hoven and T Weigend (eds), *Consent and Sexual Offenses* (Nomos 2023)

Schulhofer SJ, 'Consent: What It Means and Why It's Time to Require It' (2016) 47 University of the Pacific Law Review 665

Wegerstad L, 'Sweden' in E Hoven and T Weigend (eds), *Consent and Sexual Offenses* (Nomos 2023)

Weigend T, 'Germany' in E Hoven and T Weigend (eds), *Consent and Sexual Offenses* (Nomos 2023)

14

Victims of Intimate Image Abuse and Other Crimes

Is It Right to Blame Them?

*Michael Vitiello**

I. Introduction

A young woman sends her boyfriend an erotic picture or an explicitly sexual message.[1] Or a man convinces his girlfriend to engage in intercourse with other men and films it. After the films' dissemination on social media, the woman's mental health deteriorates, leading to her suicide.[2]

On occasion, judges or commentators argue that the victim's conduct is relevant, perhaps in a personal injury or criminal case brought against someone for spreading intimate information.[3]

* I would like to thank my research assistants Mikayla Anderson, Sierra Horton, Vivian Lee, and Marcie Murtha for their excellent work on this chapter. I am also very appreciative of Professors Gian Marco Caletti and Kolis Summerer for their invitation to participate in the Bolzano symposium that gave rise to this chapter.

[1] See Tahlee McKinlay and Tiffany Lavis, 'Why Did She Send it in the First Place? Victim Blame in the Context of "Revenge Porn"' (2020) 27 Psychiatry, Psychology and Law 386 (discussing revenge porn more generally).

[2] Gian Marco Caletti, 'Can Affirmative Consent Save "Revenge Porn" Laws? Lessons From the Italian Criminalization of Non-Consensual Pornography' (2021) 25 Virginia Journal of Law and Technology 112, 117 (hereafter Caletti, 'Affirmative Consent').

[3] See eg John L Diamond, Lawrence C Levine, and Anita Bernstein, *Understanding Torts* (6th edn, Carolina Academic Press 2018) 35–36, 219–21 (hereafter Diamond and others, *Understanding Torts*).

Michael Vitiello, *Victims of Intimate Image Abuse and Other Crimes* In: *Criminalizing Intimate Image Abuse*. Edited by: Gian Marco Caletti and Kolis Summerer, Oxford University Press. © Oxford University Press 2024. DOI: 10.1093/oso/9780198877813.003.0014

Yet another example comes from a California case that generated international headlines.[4] A Stanford University athlete sexually assaulted an intoxicated woman whom he had met at a fraternity party. One of the defendant's friends attempted to defend him by raising concerns that the university encouraged, and the victim was part of, a culture of excessive alcohol consumption.[5]

In such cases, critics claim that questioning the victim's conduct amounts to victim blaming, with the clear implication that a victim's conduct is legally irrelevant.[6] Such arguments are compelling. What person with any compassion could suggest that a victim's conduct excuses or justifies an offender's conduct? In effect, this chapter explores that question in the American legal context. Contrary to widely held views, focusing on a victim's conduct is often consistent with fundamental principles of the criminal law.[7]

A threshold issue involves defining who qualifies as a victim. One also needs to understand why critics suggest that blaming victims is inappropriate. Section II of this chapter takes up those questions.[8]

Section III examines instances in which the criminal law makes a victim's conduct legally relevant. Notably, traditional rules of homicide may make victim blaming relevant to reduce an offender's degree of homicide. The law does so despite the risk that the evidence will result in the jury finding for the defendant because the jurors believe that the victim was a bad person.[9] That section also focuses on well-established principles of self-defence where the law routinely allows a defendant to introduce evidence about the victim's conduct to determine the validity of a claim of self-defence.[10] Not only does the criminal law allow the defendant to turn the jury's attention to the victim's conduct, but the criminal law is correct in doing so when a victim's conduct is relevant and if it relates to an offender's culpability.[11]

[4] See, eg, Mariah Tiffany, 'Chanel Miller, Who was Sexually Assaulted by Brock Turner, Reveals Her Identity' (*ABC News*, 4 September 2019) <https://www.abc.net.au/news/2019-09-05/brock-turner-sexual-assault-survivor-reveals-her-name/11480278> accessed 10 September 2022; Sam Levin and Julia Carrie Wong, 'Brock Turner's Statement Blames Sexual Assault on Stanford "Party Culture"' (*The Guardian*, 7 June 2016). <https://www.theguardian.com/us-news/2016/jun/07/brock-turner-statement-stanford-rape-case-campus-culture> accessed 10 September 2022; Marina Koren, 'Telling the Story of the Stanford Rape Case' (*The Atlantic*, 6 June 2016) <https://www.theatlantic.com/news/archive/2016/06/stanford-sexual-assault-letters/485837> accessed 10 September 2022 (hereafter Koren, 'Stanford Rape').

[5] Alex Zielinski, 'Friend of Stanford Rapist Blamed Victim, Urged Judge not to be "Politically Correct"' (*ThinkProgress*, 6 June 2016) <https://archive.thinkprogress.org/friend-of-stanford-rapist-blamed-victim-urged-judge-not-to-be-politically-correct-a2b114fafc07/> accessed 10 September 2022 (hereafter Zielinski, 'Friend of Stanford').

[6] Amy Morin, 'Sexual Assault and Victim Blaming: The Reason behind the Blame' (*VeryWell Mind*, 11 October 2021) <https://www.verywellmind.com/sexual-assault-and-victim-blaming-4802707> accessed 10 September 2022 (stating that victim blaming comments are 'often seen in courtrooms where defense attorneys insist that victims are at fault. Victims are often blamed in the media as well.').

[7] See sections II, III, IV, and V of this chapter.

[8] See section II of this chapter.

[9] See section III of this chapter.

[10] See ibid.

[11] See ibid.

Section IV tackles more difficult examples of when a victim's conduct may have legal relevance.[12] This section examines instances when critics blame revenge porn victims for their conduct to assess whether such blame is appropriate.[13] Despite the widely held view that the victims in such cases should not have their conduct examined at trial, focus on the victim's conduct is often relevant to an offender's culpability.[14] As argued in this chapter, sadly members of the public too easily adopt the mantra that a bona fide defence is an inappropriate form of victim blaming.[15]

II. Victim Blaming

Who qualifies as a victim? And what is wrong with 'victim blaming?'

In some cases, the definition of 'victim' is obvious: for example, if the defendant kills another person and now claims the partial defence of provocation, the decedent is a victim, even if they are partially to blame for provoking the defendant.[16] The victim did not forfeit the full protection of the law by provoking the defendant.[17]

More complex is whether a complaining witness is a victim when the defendant interposes a claim of self-defence.[18] The defendant may want to show that the complaining witness was the aggressor or used excessive force.[19] If the defendant prevails, the complaining witness is the perpetrator. Nonetheless, self-defence involves victim blaming.[20] This is because, initially, the prosecution had probable cause that the complaining witness was the victim.[21]

A similar situation occurs in sexual assault cases. There, a defendant charged with assault may offer evidence about the complaining witness's conduct.[22] Whether the complaining witness is a victim presents complex questions. The

[12] See Part IV of this chapter.

[13] See ibid.

[14] See ibid.

[15] See ibid.

[16] See, eg, *Girouard v State* 583 A 2d 718 (MD 1991) (limiting the defence only to established fixed categories) (hereafter *Girouard v State*); *State v Mauricio* 568 A 2d 879 (NJ 1990) (adopting a more flexible standard focused on whether a reasonable person would be provoked).

[17] Joshua Dressler, *Understanding Criminal Law* (8th edn, Carolina Academic Press 2018) 507–10 (hereafter Dressler, *Understanding*).

[18] Dressler, *Understanding* (n 17) 210–11.

[19] See, eg, *United States v Peterson* 483 F 2d 1222 (1973); *State v Norman* 378 SE 2d 8 (NC 1989).

[20] See section III of this chapter.

[21] Tamara Aparton, 'Veteran Acquitted in Self-Defense Case—Jurors Speak Out against Injustice' (*San Francisco Bay View*, 18 December 2017) <https://sfbayview.com/2017/12/veteran-acquitted-in-self-defense-case-jurors-speak-out-against-injustice> accessed 11 September 2022.

[22] See *Commonwealth v Lopez* 745 NE 2d 961 (MA 2001) 966–67 ('Other jurisdictions have held that a mistake of fact instruction is necessary to prevent injustice. New Jersey, for instance, does not require the force necessary for rape to be anything more than what is needed to accomplish penetration . . . Thus, an instruction as to a defendant's honest and reasonable belief as to consent is available in New Jersey to mitigate the undesirable and unforeseen consequences that may flow from this construction.').

complaining witness may have engaged in unconsented to sexual conduct, but the defendant may not be guilty of sexual assault.[23] For example, a woman may not have consented to intercourse, but the man lacks the *mens rea* required to prove the crime.[24] In one sense, the woman is not a victim of a crime, and yet, is a victim of unwanted sexual contact.[25] I treat the complaining witness in such a case as a crime victim because probable cause must have existed to justify a trial.[26]

What then is 'victim blaming?' Typically, it occurs when the person who is blaming a victim uses attributes of the 'victim' to reduce or eliminate legal consequences for another person.[27] 'He had it coming to him' captures the idea.

Researchers offer several reasons why we may blame a victim. We may do so when we view what happened to the victim in hindsight. For example, we may blame a person who suffered a heart attack because they did not exercise regularly. Or it seems reasonable to blame a victim of a burglary if they left their garage door unlocked.[28] Closely related is our tendency to engage in 'attribution error', the tendency to explain events occurring to others by reference to internal attributes.[29] We may explain our own performance by reference to external factors, but believe others suffer because of personal attributes.[30]

Blaming victims may help us believe that we live in a just world. Explaining why bad things happen to others by insisting that the victim must have done something wrong may relieve one's anxiety. As one psychologist explains, we have a 'really strong need to believe we all deserve our outcomes and consequences'.[31]

23 See section IV of this chapter.

24 See ibid. *People v Sojka* 196 Cal App 4th 733, 736 (2011) ('[O]ur Supreme Court held that a defendant who entertains a reasonable and good faith, but mistaken, belief that a victim voluntarily consented to intercourse does not have the wrongful intent necessary to be convicted of rape by force').

25 *Commonwealth v Berkowitz* 609 A 2d 1338 (PA 1992); *People v Mayberry* 15 Cal 3d 143, 155 (1975) ('If a defendant entertains a reasonable and bona fide belief that a prosecutrix voluntarily consented to accompany him and to engage in sexual intercourse, it is apparent he does not possess the wrongful intent that is a prerequisite ... to a conviction'); *Laseter v State* 684 P2d 139, 142 (Alaska Ct App 1984) (finding reversible error when trial court erroneously required the jury to find that the defendant actually knew the victim did not consent when the standard for conviction was 'recklessly disregarded victim's lack of consent'); *People v Sojka* 196 Cal App 4th 733, 739–40 (2011) (reversing conviction because trial court failed to instruct on defence of defendant's good faith but mistaken belief that victim consented in view of prosecution's erroneous argument—'whether he thinks she is consenting is irrelevant ... It is actual consent involved here. Did [she] consent is the issue. Not whether he imagined that she did.')

26 See section IV of this chapter.

27 The Canadian Resource Centre for Victims of Crime, 'Victim Blaming' (*The Canadian Resource Centre for Victims of Crime*, 2009) <https://crcvc.ca/docs/victim_blaming.pdf> accessed 11 September 2022 (hereafter Canadian Resource Centre, 'Victim Blaming'); See also Anne M Coughlin, 'Interrogation Stories' (2009) 95 Virginia Law Review 1599, 1605.

28 Kendra Cherry, 'Why do People Blame the Victim?' (*VeryWell Mind*, 23 July 2020) <https://www.verywellmind.com/why-do-people-blame-the-victim-2795911> accessed 11 September 2022 ('When we look at an event that happened in the past, we have a tendency to believe that we should have been able to see the signs and predict the outcome.') (hereafter Cherry, 'Why Do People Blame').

29 ibid.

30 ibid.

31 See Kayleigh Roberts, 'The Psychology of Victim Blaming' (*The Atlantic*, 5 October 2016) <https://www.theatlantic.com/science/archive/2016/10/the-psychology-of-victim-blaming/502661> accessed 11 September 2022.

Today, when we hear about 'victim blaming', the message is that it is wrong.[32] That may be the case. For example, in his important article on revenge pornography, Gian Marco Caletti offers an example from Italy: a 14-year-old girl passed out from drinking too much. Several boys at the party surrounded her and simulated sexual acts. After the footage went viral, she committed suicide.[33]

Shaming the victim can distract attention from the harm done by the perpetrator. It may make victims unwilling to report criminal conduct for fear of being made to feel ashamed.[34] If a case goes to trial, blaming the victim may result in an acquittal of a guilty defendant because the fact finder decided that the victim was not worthy of the protection of the law.[35]

But as often is the case, the questions surrounding victim blaming are far more complicated than may appear when we first hear about them. Headline cases generate outrage, resulting in little space for nuanced discussions of difficult policy questions.[36] This chapter attempts to look carefully at victim blaming to ask when victim blaming is justified in the criminal law.[37]

III. Clear Relevance of Victim Blaming in the Criminal Law

Self-defence and voluntary manslaughter present classic examples where the defendant may want to put the victim on trial.

Self-defence cases often involve a defendant and a victim who have a history of conflict.[38] Charged with assault or homicide, the defendant wants to introduce evidence of the victim's reputation for violence. That often includes prior bad acts. *State v Bass*, a state court decision from North Carolina, demonstrates the point.[39] The defendant killed a man named Fogg. Over time, the two men had had various unpleasant confrontations. At his trial for murder, the defendant sought to introduce evidence of Fogg's prior acts of violence, evidence excluded by the trial court.[40] A sample of that evidence is as follows:

> Williford, Fogg's ex-girlfriend, would have testified that Fogg had, without provocation and in front of Williford's three-year-old daughter, pulled a gun on Williford and choked her until she passed out. She also would have testified that

[32] Canadian Resource Centre, 'Victim Blaming' (n 27).
[33] Caletti, 'Affirmative Consent' (n 2) 120.
[34] JoAnne Sweeney, 'Brock Turner is not a Rapist': The Danger of Rape Myths in Character Letters in Sexual Assault Cases (2020) 89 UMKC Law Review 121, 122 (hereafter Sweeney, 'Brock Turner').
[35] Sweeney, 'Brock Turner' (n 34).
[36] See section IV of this chapter.
[37] See sections III and IV of this chapter.
[38] See Dressler, *Understanding* (n 17) 229–35; *State v Bass* 819 SE 2d 322 (NC 2018) (hereafter *State v Bass*).
[39] *State v Bass* (n 38) 323.
[40] ibid.

> Fogg beat her so badly that her eyes were swollen shut and she was left with a bruise reflecting an imprint of Fogg's shoe on her back. Michael Bauman would have testified that, on one occasion, he witnessed Fogg punch his own dog in the face because it approached another individual for attention.[41]

There was more evidence too.[42]

Rules of evidence in the United States make character evidence inadmissible.[43] Thus, evidence that a defendant has committed frequent acts of violence in the past is inadmissible to show a propensity to act violently even if they are charged with a crime of violence.[44] The fear is that a jury might convict the defendant because of their bad character, not because they committed the crime charged.[45] Self-defence cases create the same risk: the jury may find a defendant not guilty because the evidence of the victim's bad character distracts the jury from the truth.[46] A jury might find that a victim like Fogg 'had it coming to him'.[47] But on balance, such evidence is admissible to explain whether the defendant, in fact, acted in self-defence.[48] Thus, the general rule of evidence does not apply when the prior acts of violence are relevant to an issue other than a person's propensity to act violently.

Voluntary manslaughter presents similar issues. American jurisdictions vary on their approaches to voluntary manslaughter.[49] Some jurisdictions allow the partial defence only if the case is within a narrow set of criteria.[50] Thus, a defendant must show that their killing resulted after they and the victim engaged in mutual combat; the victim committed a serious crime against one of defendant's close relatives; or the defendant discovered one's spouse in an act of adultery.[51]

41 ibid 328.

42 ibid.

43 Federal r Evidence 404.

44 ibid. See also *People v Zackowitz* 172 NE 466 (NY 1930) (hereafter *People v Zackowitz*).

45 *People v Zackowitz* (n 44) 468.

46 See Federal r Evidence 404(2)(B) (stating that, subject to limitations and stipulations, 'a defendant [in a criminal case] may offer evidence of an alleged victim's pertinent trait').

47 *State v Bass* (n 38) 323.

48 ibid.

49 Dressler, *Understanding* (n 17) 477–78.

50 Joshua Dressler and Stephen P Garvey, *Criminal Law Cases and Materials* (8th edn, West Academic Publishing 2019) 285–86 (hereafter Dressler and Garvey, *Criminal Law Cases*); *Girouard v State* (n 16).

51 Dressler and Garvey, *Criminal Law Cases* (n 50) 285. Some jurisdictions in the United States have changed this kind of partial defence through legislation. Maryland Crim L s 2-207 ('The discovery of one's spouse engaged in sexual intercourse with another does not constitute legally adequate provocation for the purpose of mitigating a killing from the crime of murder to voluntary manslaughter even though the killing was provoked by that discovery.')

Scholars in the United States debate whether the abandonment of such a partial defence is good policy. Dressler, 'Provocation Defense' (n 69) 1001 ('Nonetheless, the provocation defense plays an important role in homicide law. Particularly with serious felonies like criminal homicide, the law is well-served by partial excuses that permit juries to finely tune levels of criminal responsibility on the basis of differential culpability. As long as people get angry and that anger affects their capacity for self-control, there will be a need for a partial legal excuse that recognizes the fact that even people who possess normal levels of self-control sometimes "lose it." ') Similarly, in Europe, some countries still allow 'honour killings', while other countries have abolished such a kind of homicide. Anna Momigliano, 'Italy's views on violence against women are finally changing. The national discourse on 'crimes of

Other jurisdictions take a more flexible approach. If the trial court determines that a reasonable person would be provoked,[52] the jury decides whether the provocation was sufficient.[53] In either jurisdiction, the victim's conduct often becomes a focal point of the litigation.[54]

While many provocation cases involve men who have killed a spouse found in bed with another man, modern case law includes cases where women have killed abusive spouses. They have sought to put the victim on trial as well.[55] *State v Norman* provides such an example. Judy Norman shot her husband when he was asleep.[56] That prevented her from succeeding on a claim of self-defence: a person may not use deadly force unless faced with the imminent use of deadly force.[57] Nonetheless, the facts demonstrate how the victim's character may be central to the defendant's claim.

Consider a few details of Judy's relationship with her husband. During their twenty-five-year marriage, John Norman often beat his wife when he was drunk.[58] At trial '[t]he defendant described other instances of abuse, such as her husband putting her cigarettes out on her, throwing hot coffee on her, breaking glass against her face and crushing food on her face'.[59] John made Judy engage in prostitution.[60] He would beat her if she resisted in engaging in such acts or if she failed to bring home enough money.[61] John 'routinely called [Judy] "dog," "bitch" and "whore,"

passion' is exploding precisely when the phenomenon is in decline' (*The Washington Post*, 2 November 2016) <https://www.washingtonpost.com/world/europe/how-italy-has-changed-its-view-on-murdering-women/2016/11/02/8f22d42a-930b-11e6-bc00-1a9756d4111b_story.html> accessed 26 February 2023 ('Until 1981 the country's penal code granted a special status to the so-called delitto d'onore, or 'honor killing'—mandating extreme leniency in judging the killing of 'spouses, daughters and sisters caught in illicit sex'. Only in 2007 did the Supreme Court rule that "honor" was an "obsolete" concept.'); CETS 210, 'Violence against women and domestic violence', 11V2011, Art 42 (Council of Europe Treaty ratified in 2014 required parties bar 'honour' justification for crimes).

[52] Dressler, *Understanding* (n 17) 502–04. See also *Maher v State* 10 Mich 212, 219 (1862) ('But if the act of killing, though intentional, be committed under the influence of passion or in heat of blood, produced by an adequate or reasonable provocation, and before a reasonable time has elapsed for the blood to cool and reason to resume its habitual control, and is the result of the temporary excitement, by which the control of reason was disturbed, rather than of any wickedness of heart or cruelty or recklessness of disposition; then the law, out of indulgence to the frailty of human nature, or rather, in recognition of the laws upon which human nature is constituted, very properly regards the offense as of a less heinous character than murder, and gives it the designation of manslaughter.')

[53] Dressler, *Understanding* (n 17) 505.

[54] ibid 502–03.

[55] *State v Norman* (n 19); *State v Leidholm*, 334 NW 2d 811 (ND 1983); Erin Blakemore, 'Francine Hughes Killed Her Abusive Husband—And Changed U.S. Views on Domestic Violence' (*History*, 21 Mar 2019) <https://www.history.com/news/burning-bed-syndrome-francine-hughes-domestic-abuse> accessed 17 September 2022.

[56] *State v Norman* (n 19) 9.

[57] ibid 12 ('The right to kill in self-defense is based on the necessity, real or reasonably apparent, of killing an unlawful aggressor to save oneself from *imminent* death or great bodily harm at his hands.')

[58] ibid.

[59] ibid 10.

[60] ibid.

[61] ibid.

and on a few occasions made her eat pet food out of the pets' bowls and bark like a dog'.[62] The record included more of the same kind of abuse.[63]

Because the law allows the use of deadly force only if a defendant is faced with an imminent deadly force, Judy could not interpose her claim of self-defence. But the facts provide a springboard to discuss victim blaming.[64]

Assume the same facts, except for one: that Judy killed her husband when he was awake. Without doubt, John's conduct would be relevant to key issues in the case. His history of violence would be relevant to whether Judy had a reasonable fear of imminent serious bodily injury or death.[65] In addition, regardless of whether the victim represented a threat on that particular occasion, the defendant would be able to prevail on self-defence grounds if her belief that she needed to use force was reasonable.[66] Also at issue would be the defendant's subjective state of mind, that is, did she really believe that she needed to use force to repel force?[67] The prior history of violence would support that claim.

Judy's case also easily fits within the rules governing the partial defence of voluntary manslaughter in all jurisdictions following the more modern rule, where the issue would be whether a reasonable jury could find that a defendant's claim of provocation was sufficient.[68]

Relevant to my thesis is an examination of why American law routinely allows the victim to be put on trial in such cases. At times, courts and commentators have viewed the provocation defence as a partial justification.[69] That is, the victim's misconduct results in the forfeiture of the full protection of the law.[70]

[62] ibid.

[63] ibid 10–11.

[64] ibid.

[65] Dressler, *Understanding* (n 17) 229–31.

[66] ibid 231–32 ('A decedent's prior aggressive and violent behavior is relevant to show that the actor reasonably feared deadly force at the decedent's hands on the present occasion. A reasonable person in the abused victim's shoes would surely take into consideration an abuser's prior violence against her, as well as other actions that have been a regular precursor to violence, in determining whether he represents a deadly threat on the present occasion.') Another reason that the victim's conduct may be relevant is to show that the defendant's use of force was proportionate to the force the defendant needed to repel or reasonably believed that he needed to repel.

[67] Dressler, *Understanding* (n 17) 231.

[68] See *State v Mauricio* (n 16); *Girouard v State* (n 16).

[69] Joshua Dressler, 'Rethinking Heat of Passion: A Defense in Search of a Rationale' (1982) 73 Journal of Criminal Law and Criminology 421, 436–43 (hereafter Dressler, 'Heat of Passion'); Joshua Dressler, 'Why Keep the Provocation Defense?: Some Reflections on a Difficult Subject' (2002) 86 Minnesota Law Review 959, 971–75 (hereafter Dressler, 'Provocation Defense').

[70] See Dressler, 'Heat of Passion' (n 69) 436–37 ('With a justification, society indicates its approval of the actors conduct. With homicide, for example, the existence of a justification implies that under the circumstances society does not believe that the death of the human being was undesirable, or that it at least represents a lesser harm than if the defendant had not acted as he did ... A defendant asserting an excuse admits to wrongdoing, but asserts that he should not be punished because he is not morally blameworthy for harm.').

The better explanation is that the defence is an excuse, not a justification, defence.[71] As one court has stated, the heat of passion defence is 'the legal system's recognition of the weaknesses or infirmity of human nature and that those who kill [in the sudden heat of passion] … are less morally blameworthy than those who kill in the absence of such influence'.[72] The defence is grounded in the view that the extraordinary circumstances, not the person's normal character, contributes to the killing.[73]

The latter view, that provocation is an excuse, not a justification, is consistent with modern criminal law. Talk of the victim's loss of full protection of the law is more consonant with the tort system.[74] The recognition that the defence is an excuse allows a lesser punishment based on the defendant's culpability.[75] Indeed, a fact pattern that tests the difference has arisen in the case law: a defendant acting in the heat of passion kills not the provoker, but someone in the vicinity.[76] Thus, a defendant who shoots and misses the provoker, but who kills a bystander receives the partial defence if it is an excuse, but not a justification, defence.[77]

These cases underscore when the law recognizes victim blaming as legitimate.[78] Victim blaming is appropriate when the conduct is relevant to offender culpability.[79] While victim blaming in these instances may not be controversial, the next section turns to some examples where commentators contend that victim blaming is illegitimate.[80]

[71] See Dressler, 'Provocation Defense' (n 69) 971 ('The provocation defense is an excuse defense, albeit a partial one, but one that may (but need not) have a justification-like component.'). As indicated, jurisdictions within the United States differ on whether provocation is a partial justification or an excuse. The Model Penal Code's provision §210.3(1)(b) makes clear that the American Law Institute's view was that some killings should be excused based on an offender's emotional disturbance and that the jury should be given a great deal of discretion in determining when an intentional killer should not be condemned as the most culpable murderer. The result in a given case can turn on that jurisdiction's view of the partial defence. If an offender kills someone other than the provoking actor, presumably the partial defence is not available because in lay terms, the victim did not have it coming to them.

[72] *Simpson v United States* 632 A 2d 374, 377 fn 8 (District of Columbia 1993).

[73] Dressler, *Understanding* (n 17) 225–26.

[74] See, eg, Diamond and others, *Understanding Torts* (n 3) 249–50.

[75] See Dressler, *Understanding* (n 17) 509–10 (discussing the legal system's recognition that those who kill in the heat of passion are less morally blameworthy).

[76] ibid 875 (explaining the misdirected retaliation rule as applied in *Rex v Scriva*).

[77] ibid.

[78] Reid Griffith Fontaine, 'An Attack on Self-Defense' (2010) 47 American Criminal Law Review 57, 69 (hereafter Fontaine, 'Self-Defense' ('Historically, self-defense has referred to cases by which the killer reasonably believes that his victim is about to wrongfully takes his life. Anglo-American criminal law has long viewed these killings as justified.').

[79] Joan L Brown, 'Blaming the Victim: The Admissibility of Sexual History in Homicides' (1987) 16 Fordham Urban Law Journal 263, 263–64 ('Just as some people once believed that "women who get raped are 'asking for it'", a morbid twist has some people blaming [the victim] for her own death.').

[80] See, eg, Kimberly Peterson, 'Victim or Villain?: The Effects of Rape Culture and Rape Myths on Justice for Rape Victims' (2019) 53 Valparaiso University Law Review 467 (hereafter Peterson, 'Victim or Villain?').

IV. Harder Cases Involving Victim Blaming

Often, claims about victim blaming come about through lack of accurate information about why defendants, their lawyers, or judges focus on a victim's conduct.[81] Critics suggest that such efforts are cruel to victims, aimed merely at shaming them for things that are not their fault or that detract from an offender's criminality.[82] This section examines a case that made headlines in the United States and beyond,[83] and also cases of revenge porn.[84] These instances offer the opportunity to examine legitimate instances where defendants might invite the jury to scrutinize the victim's behaviour.

Until charges against movie mogul Harvey Weinstein and once-admired actor Bill Cosby pushed the Brock Turner case off the front page,[85] Turner's case generated international headlines.[86] Despite strong evidence to the contrary, some commentators continue to call Turner 'the Stanford Rapist'.[87]

At first blush, Turner seemed to represent everything wrong with the rape culture in the United States. The case seemed to involve 'white privilege', 'special treatment for an elite college athlete', and perhaps, an 'illegal sentence'.[88] Efforts to defend Turner were often met with claims that the commentator was victim blaming.[89]

I am getting ahead of the story. For readers unfamiliar with the case, here are some of the details: in the early morning hours, two students saw Turner lying on top of a woman who seemed to be unconscious.[90] He ran when they confronted

[81] See, eg, Michael Vitiello, 'Brock Turner: Sorting through the Noise' (2018) 49 University of the Pacific Law Review 631, 634–49 (hereafter Vitiello, 'Sorting Through the Noise') (providing the full record of Brock Turner's sexual assault and the Probation Report to dispute Turner's misleading reference as a 'rapist'). See also Sonnen Andrea Michele and Joedeman Brown, 'Rape and Victim-Blaming: A Critical Examination of the Tendency to Blame Victims and Exonerate Perpetrators in Cases of Rape' [2011–2012] University of California Davis Prized Writing 75.

[82] Catharine A MacKinnon, 'Reflections on Sex Equality Under Law' (1991) 100 Yale Law Journal 1281, 1294 (comparing the focus on a rape victim's conduct as '[making] pornography in court' to illustrate humiliation a rape victim suffers from such scrutiny).

[83] Koren, 'Stanford Rape' (n 4) (providing a synopsis of the *Brock Turner* case).

[84] Suzanne Downing, 'Breaking: Berkowitz Resigns' (*Must Read Alaska*, 13 October 2020) <https://mustreadalaska.com/breaking-berkowitz-resigns> accessed 18 September 2022 (reporting on the resignation of the Mayor of Anchorage, Alaska over Berkowitz's admission of engaging in an extramarital sexting relationship with TV news reporter Maria Athens).

[85] Colin Dwyer, 'The Harvey Weinstein Trial: A Brief Timeline of How We Got Here' (*NPR*, 22 January 2020) <https://www.npr.org/2020/01/22/798222176/the-harvey-weinstein-trial-a-brief-timeline-of-how-we-got-here> accessed 18 September 2022; 'Timeline: Bill Cosby: A 50-year Chronicle of Accusations and Accomplishments' (*Los Angeles Times*, 25 September 2018) <https://www.latimes.com/entertainment/la-et-bill-cosby-timeline-htmlstory.html> accessed 18 September 2022.

[86] Sweeney, 'Brock Turner' (n 34) 122.

[87] ibid.

[88] Vitiello, 'Sorting Through the Noise' (n 81) 631, 645 (outlining the consequences Turner faced at the outset of his trial: 'expulsion from [one of the most] elite college[s] [in the United States and the world], loss of a scholarship, death threats, and public contempt.').

[89] ibid 644 ('The recommended sentence made a "mockery of the seriousness of [Turner's] assaults" ').

[90] ibid 635.

him. They caught him and detained him until campus police arrived.[91] A deputy sheriff believed that the woman was unconscious; she was unable to speak coherently for three hours after police found her.[92]

Some details of how Turner and the woman ended up on the ground near a dumpster are uncontested.[93] The victim and her sister attended a fraternity party at the university.[94] They and Turner consumed large quantities of alcohol over the course of the evening.[95]

Also uncontested is the fact that Turner and the victim left the party together.[96] Less clear was what occurred next. I have described some of the inconsistencies in Turner's accounts elsewhere:

> ... At first [Turner] indicated that he met the victim outside the fraternity house and then left with her. He acknowledged that he did not know her name. After his arrest, he said that he and the victim met at the party, drank beer together, and left holding hands. He claimed that he and the victim engaged in some foreplay, at which point he got sick and left to vomit. Turner claimed that he heard someone speaking to him at that point, but was not able to understand what the person was saying. That person turned out to be one of the Swedish graduate students. Still, Turner's trial testimony varied further. At trial, he said that he and the victim agreed to go back to his room and ended up on the ground when she fell. He got down on the ground and received permission to engage in sexual activity. According to Turner, '[a]t no time did I see that she was not responding. If at any time I thought that she was not responding, I would have stopped immediately'.[97]

While Turner's testimony may have been clouded by intoxication, the victim was severely intoxicated. Turner's blood alcohol exceeded .17 per cent, over two times the legal limit for, say drunk driving.[98] Worse, the victim's blood alcohol when measured several hours later was .12 per cent, leading experts to conclude that at the time of the incident, it was about .220–.249 per cent, about three times the legal limit.[99]

[91] ibid.

[92] ibid.

[93] ibid. See also Kayla Lombardo, 'How a Rape Case Involving a Stanford Swimmer Became National News' (*Sports Illustrated*, 9 June 2018) <https://www.si.com/more-sports/2016/06/09/brock-turner-stanford-swimming-sexual-assault-rape-case> accessed 18 September 2022.

[94] Vitiello, 'Sorting Through the Noise' (n 81).

[95] ibid.

[96] ibid.

[97] ibid 635–36.

[98] Maia Szalavitz, 'The Story of the Stanford Rape is Also the Story of a Drug Overdose' (*Vice*, 16 June 2016) <https://www.vice.com/en/article/ppve78/the-story-of-the-stanford-rape-is-also-the-story-of-a-drug-overdose> accessed 18 September 2022 ('Turner's BAC was estimated to be .171 at the time—far less than that of his victim.').

[99] Emily Bazelon, 'Why the Stanford Rape Trial Actually Represents Progress' (*New York Times*, 9 June 2016) <https://www.nytimes.com/2016/06/09/magazine/why-the-stanford-rape-convict

The prosecutor charged Turner with two counts of rape as well as with assault with attempt to rape and two counts of sexual assault.[100] The prosecutor dropped the rape charges because of a lack of any evidence of penile penetration.[101] The controversy about the Turner case emerged after the jury convicted him of the three remaining charges and Judge Aaron Persky, the trial judge, sentenced him.[102]

Consistent with California law, a probation officer prepared a pre-sentencing report, taking into consideration factors prescribed by the California Penal Code.[103] Typical today, courts rely on risk-assessment measurements to right-size criminal sentences.[104] Turner's youth and lack of a criminal record contributed to a low score, predicting a low chance of recidivism.[105] The probation report included Turner's statements of remorse for the harm to the victim.[106] The probation officer also relied on the victim's initial statement in recommending that a short sentence be imposed.[107] Notably, the victim stated: 'I want him to know it hurt me, but I don't want his life to be over. I want him to be punished, but as a human, I just want him to get better. I don't want him to feel like his life is over and I don't want him to rot away in jail; he doesn't need to be behind bars.'[108] The judge's sentence tracked the probation report's recommendations.[109]

Turner's sentence included a six-month sentence, which meant that he could be released after three months.[110] He was also sentenced to a term of probation.[111] He will remain on a sexual offender registry for the rest of his life.[112]

ion-actually-represents-progress.html> accessed 18 September 2022 ('The victim's blood-alcohol level was about three times the legal limit when it was tested.').

[100] Callie Marie Rennison, 'I'm the Professor Who Made Brock Turner the "Textbook Definition" of a Rapist' (*Vox*, 17 November 2017) <https://www.vox.com/first-person/2017/11/17/16666290/brock-turner-rape> accessed 18 September 2022 (hereafter Rennison, 'Textbook Definition') ('The two dropped charges were rape of an intoxicated person and rape of an unconscious person.')

[101] Rennison, 'Textbook Definition') (n 100).

[102] Liam Stack, 'Light Sentence for Brock Turner in Stanford Rape Case Draws Outrage' (*New York Times*, 6 June 2016) <https://www.nytimes.com/2016/06/07/us/outrage-in-stanford-rape-case-over-dueling-statements-of-victim-and-attackers-father.html> accessed 18 September 2022 ('A recall effort ... was announced ... in a sexual assault case ... that ignited public outrage after the defendant was sentenced to a mere six months in jail and his father complained that his son's life had been ruined for "20 minutes of action" fueled by alcohol and promiscuity.').

[103] See California r Court 4.411.5.

[104] Brandon Garrett and John Monahan, 'Assessing Risk: The Use of Risk Assessment in Sentencing' (2019) 103(2) Judicature 43.

[105] Vitiello, 'Sorting Through the Noise'(n 81) 642.

[106] *Probation Report: People v Turner, Case number B1577162* (*CA Superior Court*, 2 June 2016) 8 <https://www.documentcloud.org/documents/2858997-Probation-officer-s-report-in-Brock-Turner-case.html> accessed 18 September 2022 (hereafter *Probation Report*).

[107] Vitiello, 'Sorting Through the Noise' (n 81).

[108] ibid (quoting *Probation Report* (n 106) 6).

[109] ibid 641.

[110] ibid 637.

[111] ibid 637.

[112] Ellie Kaufman, 'Brock Turner Registers as Sex Offender in Ohio' (*CNN*, 6 September 2016) <https://www.cnn.com/2016/09/06/us/brock-turner-sex-offender-registry/index.html> accessed 18 September 2022.

The judge's sentence began a firestorm. As allowed in most states in the United States and encouraged by victims' rights supporters, the victim made an additional victim impact statement at the sentencing hearing.[113] The victim's 7,000-word statement included a powerful attack on Turner.[114] Here are a few of the most dramatic statements: 'You don't know me, but you've been inside me, and that's why we are here today.'[115] She targeted criticism at the defence team and Turner's decision to testify in his own defence: she asserted that Turner's testimony revictimized her.[116]

The victim, now identified as Chanel Miller, clearly had a change of heart between her statement to the probation officer and her victim impact statement.[117] As Professor Aya Gruber has stated, now she 'sought retribution, not restraint. [Miller] attributed the change of heart to Turner's lack of remorse in his probation statement, but some believe she was influenced by the heady publicity surrounding the case.'[118]

Turner and Judge Persky became pariahs and Miller a social media celebrity through the efforts of one of her family friends.[119] Stanford Law Professor Michele Dauber orchestrated a social media campaign that resulted in an outpouring of criticism of Judge Persky. Through Dauber's connections, *BuzzFeed* published a story about the case, resulting in eleven million hits in four days.[120] At a time of increased concern about sexual assault, an articulate victim, backed by celebrities and a prominent academic, became emblematic of America's rape culture.[121] Starting with that kind of publicity and what appeared to be a good victim–monster

[113] Katie JM Baker, 'Here's the Powerful Letter the Stanford Victim Read to Her Attacker' (*Buzzfeed News*, 3 June 2016) <https://www.buzzfeednews.com/article/katiejmbaker/heres-the-powerful-letter-the-stanford-victim-read-to-her-ra> accessed 18 September 2022 (hereafter Baker, 'Powerful Letter').

[114] ibid.

[115] Aya Gruber, *The Feminist War on Crime: The Unexpected Role of Women's Liberation in Mass Incarceration* (University of California Press Books 2021) 179 (hereafter Gruber, *Feminist War*).

[116] Baker, 'Powerful Letter' (n 113) ('And then it came time for him to testify and I learned what it meant to be revictimized.').

[117] Gruber, *Feminist War* (n 115) 180.

[118] ibid 180.

[119] Maura Dolan, 'Vandalism, Threats, Broken Friendships: The Heated Campaign to Recall Judge in Brock Turner Case' (*Los Angeles Times*, 3 June 2018) <https://www.latimes.com/local/lanow/la-me-ln-recall-judge-20180601-story.html> accessed 21 September 2022 (reporting on Dauber's leadership in the recall of Judge Persky); Wiemond Wu, 'Crocodiles in the Judge's Bathtub: Why California Should End Unregulated Judicial Recall' (2018) 49 University of the Pacific Law Review 699, 716 (hereafter Wu, 'Crocodiles') (Michele Dauber stated that the 'recall is the only realistic way to remove Judge Persky from office') (emphasis added).

[120] See Aishwarya Kumar, 'From Survivor to Activist, Chanel Miller is Taking Toxic Sports Culture to Task' (*ESPN*, 30 March 2020) <https://www.espn.com/espnw/story/_/id/28962824/from-survivor-activist-chanel-miller-taking-toxic-sports-culture-task> accessed 22 September 2022.

[121] See, eg, Amanda Holpuch, 'Stanford Students Launch Tribute to Sexual Assault Survivor Chanel Miller' (*The Guardian*, 27 September 2019) <https://www.theguardian.com/us-news/2019/sep/27/stanford-students-launch-tribute-to-sexual-assault-survivor-chanel-miller> accessed 25 September 2022 (hereafter Holpuch, 'Chanel Miller') (launching the Dear Visitor project, which would project excerpts of Miller's victim impact statement near the site where the assault occurred, in recognition of Miller's newfound status as the poster child of American rape culture).

defendant story, subsequent efforts to recall Judge Persky from the bench was a foregone conclusion.[122]

Even today, many news stories refer to Turner as the 'Stanford rapist', even though he did not commit rape.[123] In recent years, after years of increasing prison sentences for criminal defendants, California had begun to reverse the trends that led to mass incarceration.[124] But, in the aftermath of the Turner case, the California legislature changed its criminal law to require a mandatory minimum sentence for someone convicted of the same crimes as Turner was.[125] It also changed the definition of rape to include digital penetration.[126]

Efforts to challenge the orthodoxy about the Turner case led to claims of victim blaming. Leslie Rasmussen, one of Turner's friends, submitted a letter on his behalf at the time of his sentencing. She raised concerns about the way in which Stanford encouraged excessive drinking, and saw Miller's intoxication as a contributing factor to Turner's conduct. She described the drinking culture's effect on young people: 'These are idiot boys and girls having too much to drink … and having clouded judgment.'[127]

Rasmussen, a member of a 'girl' band, faced immediate retaliation for her support of Turner. Organizers of one music festival, for example, removed the band from the festival. A representative wrote: 'We have been informed of the situation regarding a member of Good English and a letter written in support of Brock Turner, convicted rapist.… We do not support any such action, and will be removing them from the festival.'[128]

Serious scholars have also added their support for Turner's critics. Some have accused Judge Persky of being influenced by 'rape myths' in imposing such a short sentence. For example, Professor JoAnne Sweeny argued that one myth about rape

[122] See generally Wu, 'Crocodiles' (n 119) (explaining that the media attention enabled California voters to utilize the judicial recall process against Judge Persky).

[123] See, eg, Alex Johnson, 'After Months of Requests, Mugshots of Stanford Rapist Brock Turner Finally Emerge' (*NBC News*, 6 June 2016) <https://www.nbcnews.com/news/us-news/after-months-requests-mugshots-stanford-rapist-brock-turner-finally-emerge-n586936> accessed 24 September 2022; Ruth Styles, 'EXCLUSIVE: Pictured—Stanford Rapist Brock Turner, Working in a Factory for $12 an Hour and Living with His Mom and Dad Who Begged for His Freedom, While His Victim Writes a Tell-All Memoir about Her Ordeal' (*Daily Mail*, 6 June 2019) <https://www.dailymail.co.uk/news/article-7112587/Pictured-Stanford-rapist-Brock-Turner-working-factory-12-hour.html> accessed 24 September 2022; Kory Grow, 'Stanford Rapist Brock Turner Registers as Sex Offender' (*Rolling Stone*, 6 September 2016) <https://www.rollingstone.com/culture/culture-news/stanford-rapist-brock-turner-registers-as-sex-offender-105931/> accessed 25 September 2022.

[124] Christina L Woods, 'Proposition 47: The Unintended Consequence' (2016) 38 University of La Verne Law Review 83, 93 ('Prop 47 was designed to ensure law enforcement agencies prioritize serious and violent offenders instead of sending people to state prison for drug use.').

[125] See Gruber, *Feminist War* (n 115) 188 (discussing the passage of AB 2888).

[126] ibid 189.

[127] Zielinski, 'Friend of Stanford' (n 5).

[128] Lindsey Bever, 'Girl Band Faces Backlash over Drummer's Support for Stanford Sex Offender' (*The Washington Post*, 9 June 2016) <https://www.washingtonpost.com/news/morning-mix/wp/2016/06/09/girl-band-faces-backlash-over-drummers-support-for-stanford-sex-offender/> accessed 25 September 2022.

is that it is a crime committed by a stranger, through an act of violence.[129] Another myth that Sweeny identifies is that in a case like Turner's, observers, including the judge,

> 'blame the victim for their rape, express a disbelief in claims of rape, exonerate the perpetrator, and allude that only certain kinds of women are raped'. These myths serve to comfort us that we live in a just world where people are not raped at random. However, they also cause us to disbelieve or discount the suffering of rape victims, or even blame them for their own suffering, leading to systemic injustice.[130]

Her article '"Brock Turner is Not a Rapist": The Danger of Rape Myths in Character Letters in Sexual Assault Cases' identifies other 'myths' as well, including what she calls the '"miscommunication" myth'.[131] That is, she sees a claim that a man misperceived the woman's willingness to engage in intercourse, especially when they have been drinking together, as a myth often perpetuated by people who urge leniency in cases like Turner's.[132]

Sweeny's article, in effect, summarizes the victim blaming position. Questioning a woman who has engaged in sex under circumstances like those involved in the *Turner* case is inappropriate. But is it?

Many accounts about the *Turner* case suggest that discussing the victim's intoxication is putting her on trial inappropriately.[133] Such accounts seem to assume that anyone suggesting that the victim's intoxication is relevant believes that somehow, a woman who gets drunk gets what she deserves or, at least, was at fault for not knowing better than leaving herself vulnerable. That is not what thoughtful commentators mean when they raise questions about the victim's intoxication.[134]

Two charges against Turner involved sexual assault of an unconscious person.[135] The jury found him guilty on both counts.[136] Headlines about the *Turner* case focused on Turner's sexual assault of an unconscious woman.[137] The media accounts

129 Sweeney, 'Brock Turner' (n 34) 140.

130 ibid 138.

131 ibid 144–46.

132 ibid.

133 Peterson, 'Victim or Villain?' (n 80) 468 (discussing victims' feelings of being put on trial for their own victimization within the context of Chanel Miller's victim impact statement).

134 See Gruber, *Feminist War* (n 115) 164–65 (discussing how college administrators should reflect further on the carceral effects of blindly advocating for sexual assault victims' rights).

135 Enjoli Francis, 'Victim in Brock Turner Stanford Sexual Assault Goes Public With Her Name and Memoir' (*ABC News*, 4 September 2019) <https://abcnews.go.com/US/victim-brock-turner-stanford-sexual-assault-case-public/story?id=65385613> accessed 25 September 2022 (hereafter Francis, 'Name and Memoir') ('A Santa Clara County jury convicted Turner in March 2016 of three felony charges: assault with intent to commit rape of an intoxicated/unconscious person, penetration of an intoxicated person and penetration of an unconscious person.') (emphasis added).

136 ibid.

137 Holpuch, 'Chanel Miller' (n 121).

made the case seem like the defendant engaged in various sexual acts with a person incapable of responding.[138] As described by one source, an unconscious person does not respond to sounds or to being shaken; the person may stop breathing.[139] Or as another source describes unconsciousness, the person is 'passed out'.[140]

If the widely publicized narrative was accurate, Turner could not plausibly claim that he believed he had his victim's consent.[141] Even if the law allowed a man to introduce evidence of his own intoxication as relevant to his belief, one would have trouble believing someone who claimed that a person who had passed out was consenting. But the record was more complicated than was widely reported.[142] Initially, the prosecutor needed to demonstrate the severity of Miller's intoxication to prove that she was unconscious.[143]

To make a plausible defence, Turner's attorney needed to demonstrate[144] that a person whose blood alcohol was as high as Miller's was nonetheless able to appear to give consent. The prosecutor's evidence about the victim's level of intoxication certainly left the impression that Turner or any sapient being could not believe that she consented. She was out cold, in the vernacular. Or was she?

A defence psychologist's testimony undercut the popular perception that someone legally unconscious could not appear to give consent. Such testimony had to highlight the victim's behaviour because her behaviour was essential to determine what the defendant could have believed as he sought to engage in sexual conduct.[145] His testimony that he believed that the victim consented would be dismissed out of hand without careful examination of her behaviour.[146]

To some degree, as with cases of provocation and self-defence, allowing such extensive examination of the victim's conduct may invite the jury to decide the case based on prejudice.[147] In the case of a drunken victim, the jury might conclude

[138] ibid.

[139] Rod Brouhard, 'Unconsciousness First Aid and Treatment' (*VeryWell Health*, 13 December 2021) <https://www.verywellhealth.com/what-is-unconscious-1298695> accessed 25 September 2022.

[140] Ellen Tan, 'Syncope: What Really Happened When You Fainted' (*OrthoNeuro*). <https://orthoneuro.com/syncope-what-really-happened-when-you-fainted/> accessed 25 September 2022

[141] Typically, a man's intoxication is irrelevant in sexual assault cases. In classic terms, 'rape' is a 'general intent' crime. As a result, intoxication is not a defence. The exception is for 'specific intent' crimes, where intoxication may negate the *mens rea*. See Dressler, *Understanding* (n 17) 306–07.

[142] Vitiello, 'Sorting Through the Noise' (n 81).

[143] That is obviously the case: a crime of sexual assault of an unconscious person makes 'unconsciousness' a material element of the offence, which the prosecutor must, therefore, prove beyond a reasonable doubt.

[144] Even if the burden of proof remained on the prosecutor, a defence attorney in a case like Turner's must give the jury a strong reason to reject the prosecution's case.

[145] Vitiello, 'Sorting Through the Noise' (n 81) 643–44 (discussing how the psychologist's testimony, along with other relevant information about the night of the incident, were instrumental in demonstrating Turner's reliance on Miller's purported ability to give consent).

[146] Elena Kadvany, 'Prosecution Questions Integrity of Witnesses in Turner Trial' (*Palo Alto Online*, 22 March 2016) <https://www.paloaltoonline.com/news/2016/03/22/prosecution-questions-integrity-of-witness-in-turner-trial> accessed 24 September 2022 (testifying that the only way to confirm someone had blacked out is if the person later says they lost memory while drinking).

[147] Peterson, 'Victim or Villain?' (n 80).

that, 'she had it coming to her'.[148] But again, as with provocation and self-defence, the American criminal justice system tolerates that risk when the evidence relates to the defendant's culpability.[149] No doubt, the victim, as in the *Turner* case, may feel that she is being shamed in public for her misconduct.[150] But unless society is willing to tolerate forms of strict criminal liability, the relevance of the evidence outweighs the potential for prejudice.[151]

What about some of the widely reported intimate image abuse cases? Is it possible that a focus on the victim's conduct might be appropriate? An example highlighted by Caletti provides fertile grounds to discuss the issue.[152]

Consider Tiziana Cantone's situation. Her boyfriend pressured her into having sex with other men and asked her to film those acts. He sent the videos to four friends, probably in agreement with Tiziana.[153] Apparently, those four friends shared the videos without her consent.[154] Devastated and unable to regain her privacy, she committed suicide.[155]

If the men involved were charged with crimes based on their dissemination of the videos, could they realistically ask the fact finder to consider the victim's conduct as legally relevant? The answer is, maybe. The starting point is to ask how the crime charged defines the elements of the offence. Almost certainly, an offence would include a non-consent element.[156] Examples that Caletti has highlighted appear to be ones in which the prosecutor would be able to prove the absence of consent.[157] But as he notes, sex crimes are *mala in se*. Consistent with a core principle of the criminal law, legislatures typically include a *mens rea* term, and a prosecutor must prove the culpable state of mind beyond a reasonable doubt.[158] Thus, even in a case like Tiziana's, her decision to engage in the sexual conduct and to allow it to be videoed may become relevant if the defendants argued that her conduct led them to believe that she consented not only to the acts of intercourse but to

[148] Mary Wood, 'City Attorney Shares Reality of Prosecuting Sexual Assault Cases' (*U Virginia: News & Media*) <https://www.law.virginia.edu/news/2001_02/zug.htm> accessed 24 September 2022 ('in cases where the victim had something to drink (and was drunk or not), older women jurors feel that "she was putting herself in that position" while they excuse the defendant's drinking').

[149] Fontaine, 'Self-Defense' (n 78).

[150] Emma Brockes, 'Chanel Miller on Why She Refuses to be Reduced to the "Brock Turner Sexual Assault Victim"' (*The Guardian*, 25 September 2019) <https://www.theguardian.com/us-news/2019/sep/25/stanford-sexual-assault-victim-chanel-miller-interview> accessed 24 September 2022 ('You have trolls, then you have very sophisticated way [of writing] ... It's so easy for someone to copy and paste these sections from the transcript ... but it's so difficult to live with.').

[151] See Michael Vitiello, 'The Expanding Use of Genetic and Psychological Evidence: Finding Coherence in the Criminal Law' (2014) 14 Nevada Law Journal 897, 916 (explaining that American criminal law still demonstrates a preference for basing punishment on offender culpability).

[152] See Caletti, 'Affirmative Consent' (n 2).

[153] ibid 117.

[154] ibid.

[155] ibid 118.

[156] See Italian Penal Code, Art 612-*ter*. Compare with California Penal Code 2021, s 647(j)(4). Also compare with Florida Statute, s 784.049(3).

[157] Caletti, 'Affirmative Consent' (n 2) 117–22.

[158] See Dressler, *Understanding* (n 17) 133.

their dissemination.[159] Such a claim may be plausible given that pornography is so widely disseminated online today with many participants doing so for financial gain.[160]

Caletti's article focused on the need for legislatures to spell out elements in any 'revenge porn' statute.[161] Indeed, in crafting a meaningful 'revenge porn' law, a legislature might include a high bar for the consent-to-disseminate element.[162] Given the extent of the harm caused once such videos go viral, a legislature might make the consent-to-disseminate element and correlative *mens rea* an affirmative defence.[163] Nonetheless, commentators like Caletti do not argue in favour of strict liability offences, even when such material goes viral.

As long as criminal offences include *mens rea* as an essential element of an offence, attention to the victim's conduct will remain relevant.[164] Even if, as Caletti suggests, the legislature makes the consent element an affirmative defence, the fact finder must find a defendant to have had some culpable state of mind.[165] For example, criminal law routinely allows a defendant to interpose a mistake-of-fact defence to show that the actor lacks the culpable mindset that makes the actor blameworthy. Thus, if a statute requires a prosecutor to prove that a defendant knew that the actor received stolen property, the prosecutor cannot prevail if the

[159] Cf Sweeney, 'Brock Turner' (n 34) 121–23 (providing a summary of the *Brock Turner* case). A legislature would have to choose the appropriate level of culpability and might set the *mens rea* at recklessness or even some form of negligence. Jurisdictions in the United States seldom criminalize conduct based on ordinary negligence but require some heightened level of blameworthiness. See Model Penal Code, s 2.02, comment 3.

[160] See, eg, Tiffany Alberty, 'The New Ponzi Scheme: BitTorrent & Hardcore Pornography' (2016) 15 John Marshall Review of Intellectual Property Law 799, 817 (discussing the lucrative business of claiming copyright infringement on online pornography videos); Hannah Frishberg, 'OnlyFans Stars Make 270 Times More Than the Average Worker: Report' (*New York Post*, 9 August 2021) <https://nypost.com/2021/08/09/onlyfans-stars-make-270-times-more-than-the-average-worker/> accessed 25 February 2023.

[161] Caletti, 'Affirmative Consent' (n 2) 147–50.

[162] ibid 166 (arguing that the requirement of affirmative consent is appropriate in non-consensual pornography statutes provides a stronger deterrent than current Italian legislation). See, eg, Idaho Code 2020, s 18-6609 (requiring the defendant to have known or should have known that the person depicted in the explicit images did not consent to dissemination of such images); Vermont Statute Annotated 2019, Title 13, s 2606(b)(1) (stating that consent to recording the visual image does not constitute consent to disseminate the image)

[163] See US Department of Justice, 'Criminal Resource Manual 1732' (2020) <https://www.justice.gov/archives/jm/criminal-resource-manual-1732-protection-government-processes-constitutionality-18-usc-1512d> accessed 25 September 2022.

[164] Eleanor Murphy, 'No Means No: A Critical Examination of the Effectiveness of the Yes Means Yes Law' (2017) 39 Thomas Jefferson Law Review 93, 106–107 (comparing the definitions of consent in Pomona College's Title IX policy to that of the University of La Verne's to show that the 'yes means yes' standard requires a victim to show that they indicated an unwillingness to participate and also that the perpetrator misinterpreted the victim's conduct).

[165] Dressler, *Understanding* (n 17) 148–49 ('A defendant is not guilty of an offense if his mistake of fact negates the specific intent portion of the crime i.e., he lacks the intent required in the definition of the offense. Thus … [i]f D2 truly believed that V2 was consenting to intercourse, then D2 did not *intend* to rape V2 … Acquittal follows inextricably from that fact that a person may not be convicted of an of an offense unless every element thereof … is proved, which did not occur here assuming the defendants were genuinely mistaken').

defendant made a mistake that negated the *mens rea* of knowledge. In the United States, one might be liable for committing a tort even without a culpable state of mind. But the goals of the two systems are different: tort law is about allocating risk between parties and compensating innocent injured parties. Criminal law is blaming culpable actors.

Worth considering before concluding is whether counterarguments weigh against allowing the kind of evidence described above.

Especially when policy makers consider low reporting rates among sexual assault victims, one might argue that the cost to the victim of having their behaviour put on public display is too great.[166] In fact, anyone with a modicum of compassion must understand the humiliation of having the jury hear facts about sexual assault. But one must ask what the alternatives are to assure adequate protection for those who report sexual assault.

Some advocates argue for what amounts to strict liability for men who commit sexual assault. As quoted above, Professor Sweeny comes close to contending for such a position when she argues about mistaken consent in acquaintance rape cases:

> [I]t is unlikely that miscommunication about consent is a major contributing factor to acquaintance rape. It is more likely that sexually aggressive men selectively ignore or reinterpret what women say to fit what they want to hear, using miscommunication as an excuse for raping. These men 'benefit from the misconception that consent is a murky, complicated thing'.[167]

The implication seems to be that, in such cases, men should be denied the defence of mistake as to consent.

Some jurisdictions include a form of sexual assault that denies a man a defence of mistake, at least in instances in which a woman says 'no', and does not thereafter affirmatively consent.[168] Such provisions usually include relatively minor sentences.[169] One ought to be clear: even in such a case, a woman must testify as to the act of sexual assault, forcing her to take the stand in a public trial.[170] Hence, some

[166] Sweeney, 'Brock Turner' (n 34) 138 (discussing how the under-reporting of sexual assault, along with other issues, such as judges falling for 'rape myths', creates extraordinarily emotional tolls on victims in the criminal justice system).

[167] ibid 145.

[168] See Model Penal Code, s 2.04(1) (American Law Institute 2022); Rosanna Cavallaro, 'Eroding the Defense of Mistake of Fact' (1996) 86 Journal of Criminal Law and Criminology 315, 818–19 (explaining the application of the defence of mistake in rape).

[169] See, eg, New York Penal Law 2001, s 130.25 (denying the use of the defence of consent for rape in the third degree, which is punishable by no more than four years of imprisonment). See New York Penal Law 2019, s 70.00.

[170] See *People v Shaulov* 29 NE 3d 227, 228 (NY 2015) (requiring the victim/complainant to testify about the night of the sexual assault if the prosecution sought to present expert testimony about rape trauma syndrome)

of the trauma or retraumatizing of a victim is inevitable in any fair criminal justice system.

Beyond the reality that a victim must testify in open court, such proposals, amounting to a form of strict liability, fly in the face of the basic norm of criminal justice. Men generally may ignore signals in sexual assault cases, whereby they hear what they want to hear.[171] But guilt is individual: as long as criminal justice is about culpable conduct of individual defendants, not groups, a man who may have legitimately misunderstood his sexual partner's signals about consent has not committed a culpable act.[172]

V. Concluding Thoughts

Sexual assault cases arouse passions, often rightly so. For years, powerful men have got away with outrageous exploitation.[173] Many jurisdictions in the United States have responded with expanded definitions of sexual assault and increased efforts to provide protection for victims.[174]

The tension remains between the goal of supporting victims and fundamental goals of the criminal law.[175] That conflict can be seen in cases where a criminal defendant attempts to highlight the victim's conduct.

In some areas, such a focus on the victim's conduct is widely accepted. Thus, self-defence cases may inevitably require focusing the jury's attention on the victim's behaviour. Somewhat more controversial, but widely accepted nonetheless, are cases involving legally sufficient provocation, resulting in a reduction from murder to manslaughter.

Those rules are accepted as part of the criminal law because wide consensus exists that the victim's conduct may eliminate or reduce the defendant's culpability.

[171] Sweeney, 'Brock Turner' (n 34).

[172] Kenneth W Simmons, 'The Crime/Tort Distinction: Legal Doctrine and Normative Perspectives' (2008) 17 Widener Law Journal 719, 719.

[173] Constance Grady, 'Some Say the Me Too Movement Has Gone Too Far. The Harvey Weinstein Verdict Proves That's False' (*Vox*, 24 February 2020) <https://www.vox.com/culture/2020/2/24/21150966/harvey-weinstein-rape-conviction-sexual-predatory-assault-me-too-too-far> accessed 25 September 2022; Holly Yan, 'What Legal Consequences Could Bill Cosby Face Now?' (*CNN*, 9 July 2015) <https://www.cnn.com/2015/07/08/us/bill-cosby-whats-next/index.html> accessed 23 September 2022; Phil McCausland and Nicole Acevedo, 'Epstein's Alleged Victims "Angry" and Frustrated He Won't Be Alive to Face Justice' (*NBC News*, 10 August 2019) <https://www.nbcnews.com/news/us-news/epstein-s-accusers-continue-demand-justice-after-his-death-suicide-n1041096> accessed 25 September 2022; Eli Yokley, 'Allegations of Sexual Misconduct against Trump Largely Fall on Deaf Ears' (*Morning Consult*, 8 July 2019) <https://morningconsult.com/2019/07/08/allegations-of-sexual-misconduct-against-trump-largely-fall-on-deaf-ears/> accessed 25 September 2022.

[174] Wayne R LaFave, *Criminal Law* (6th edn, West Academic Publishing 2017) 1122–23 (describing the modern trend expanding definitions of sexual assault).

[175] Michael Vitiello, 'Expanding Statutes of Limitations for Sex Crimes: Bad Public Policy' (2022) 49 DPCE Online 4093, 4109 ('Victims may experience harm; but, absent a culpable criminal mind, society should not punish the offender.').

This chapter has argued that many critics of victim blaming ignore that core assumption of the criminal law in many sensationalized cases. This is unfortunate: punishing a defendant, even when harm occurs, is unacceptable when the defendant lacks a culpable mind. Abandoning that commitment risks violating the most fundamental principle of the criminal law.

Bibliography

Alberty T, 'The New Ponzi Scheme: BitTorrent & Hardcore Pornography' (2016) 15 John Marshall Review of Intellectual Property Law 799

Brown JL, 'Blaming the Victim: The Admissibility of Sexual History in Homicides' (1987) 16 Fordham Urban Law Journal 263

Caletti GM, 'Can Affirmative Consent Save "Revenge Porn" Laws? Lessons From the Italian Criminalization of Non-Consensual Pornography' (2021) 25(3) Virginia Journal of Law and Technology 112

Cavallaro R, 'Eroding the Defense of Mistake of Fact' (1996) 86 Journal of Criminal Law and Criminology 815

Coughlin A, 'Interrogation Stories' (2009) 95 Virginia Law Review 1599

Diamond JL, Levine LC, and Bernstein A, *Understanding Torts* (6th edn, Carolina Academic Press 2018)

Dressler J, 'Rethinking Heat of Passion: A Defense in Search of a Rationale' (1982) 73 Journal of Criminal Law and Criminology 421

Dressler J, 'Why Keep the Provocation Defense?: Some Reflections on a Difficult Subject' (2002) 86 Minnesota Law Review 959

Dressler J, *Understanding Criminal Law* (8th edn, Carolina Academic Press 2018)

Dressler J, and Garvey S, *Criminal Law Cases and Materials* (8th edn, West Academic Publishing 2019)

Fontaine RG, 'An Attack on Self-Defense' (2010) 47 American Criminal Law Review 57

Garrett B and Monahan J, 'Assessing Risk: The Use of Risk Assessment in Sentencing' (2019) 103(2) Judicature

Gruber A, *The Feminist War on Crime: The Unexpected Role of Women's Liberation in Mass Incarceration* (University of California Press Books 2021)

LaFave W, *Criminal Law* (6th edn, West Academic Publishing 2017)

MacKinnon CA, 'Reflections on Sex Equality Under Law' (1991) 100 Yale Law Journal 1281

McKinlay T and Lavis T, 'Why Did She Send it in the First Place? Victim Blame in the Context of "Revenge Porn"' (2020) 27 Psychiatry, Psychology and Law 386

Michele SA and Brown J, 'Rape and Victim-Blaming: A Critical Examination of the Tendency to Blame Victims and Exonerate Perpetrators in Cases of Rape' [2011–2012] University of California Davis Prized Writing 75

Murphy E, 'No Means No: A Critical Examination of the Effectiveness of the Yes Means Yes Law' (2017) 39 Thomas Jefferson Law Review 93

Peterson K, 'Victim or Villain?: The Effects of Rape Culture and Rape Myths on Justice for Rape Victims' (2019) 53 Valparaiso University Law Review 467

Simmons KW, 'The Crime/Tort Distinction: Legal Doctrine and Normative Perspectives' (2008) 17 Widener Law Journal 719

Sweeney J, 'Brock Turner Is Not a Rapist': The Danger of Rape Myths in Character Letters in Sexual Assault Cases (2020) 89 UMKC Law Review 121

Vitiello M, 'The Expanding Use of Genetic and Psychological Evidence: Finding Coherence in the Criminal Law' (2014) 14 Nevada Law Journal 897

Vitiello M, 'Brock Turner: Sorting Through the Noise' (2018) 49 University of the Pacific Law Review 631

Vitiello M, 'Expanding Statutes of Limitations for Sex Crimes: Bad Public Policy' (2022) 49 DPCE Online 4093

Woods CL, 'Proposition 47: The Unintended Consequence' (2016) 38 University of La Verne Law Review 83

Wu W, 'Crocodiles in the Judge's Bathtub: Why California Should End Unregulated Judicial Recall' (2018) 49 University of the Pacific Law Review 699

PART VI

THE LAW IN PRACTICE FROM THE VICTIM'S PERSPECTIVE

15

'It Wasn't Worth the Pain to Me to Pursue It'

Justice for Australian Victim-Survivors of Image-based Sexual Abuse

*Nicola Henry**

I. Introduction

Image-based sexual abuse refers to the non-consensual taking, creating, or sharing of intimate images, including threats to share intimate images.[1] In Australia over the past decade, most states and territories have introduced new offences to criminalize the taking, creating, or sharing of intimate images without consent, including making threats to share intimate images. Despite the significant changes to

* This work was supported by an Australian Research Council Discovery grant (DP170101433). The author would like to express her sincere gratitude to the participants who spoke about their experiences of image-based sexual abuse, as well as stakeholders who generously gave their time and invaluable perspectives. She is also grateful to Magdalena Furgalska, Jessamy Gleeson, Sarah McCook, and Stefani Vasil for their excellent research assistance. The author acknowledges the research funding provided by the Australian Research Council (DP170101433) 'Revenge Pornography: The Implications for Law Reform', and the contributions of the Chief Investigators, Asher Flynn, and Anastasia Powell, and Partner Investigators, Clare McGlynn, Erika Rackley, Nicola Gavey, Adrian Scott, as well as Kelly Johnson, in providing ideas, data and/or underpinning conceptualization.

[1] Nicola Henry and others, *Image-based Sexual Abuse: The Causes and Consequences of Non-consensual Nude or Sexual Imagery* (Routledge 2020) (hereafter Henry and others, *Image-based Sexual Abuse*).

Nicola Henry, *'It Wasn't Worth the Pain to Me to Pursue It'* In: *Criminalizing Intimate Image Abuse*.
Edited by: Gian Marco Caletti and Kolis Summerer, Oxford University Press.
DOI: 10.1093/oso/9780198877813.003.0015

Australian image-based sexual abuse laws, as well sustained public attention to this issue over the past decade, little is known about the experiences of victim-survivors and how they navigate complex reporting pathways and justice processes.

Drawing on data from a larger project that examined the pervasiveness, nature, and impacts of image-based sexual abuse in Australia, New Zealand, and the UK,[2] this chapter discusses the key findings from qualitative interviews conducted with twenty-five Australian adults who had experienced image-based sexual abuse. The chapter proceeds as follows: first, it provides a brief review of the research literature on justice responses to image-based sexual abuse; second, it summarizes legislative responses to image-based sexual abuse in Australia; third, the chapter outlines the methodology for the study; and fourth, it reports on the key findings of the study, including the experiences and impacts of image-based sexual abuse, and the justice experiences and needs of victim-survivors. The chapter concludes with a call for comprehensive civil and criminal legal responses, wider community education, and prevention initiatives, as well as increased resourcing for online tools, support organizations, and law enforcement.

II. Literature Review

Image-based sexual abuse is a persistent problem in many countries around the world, affecting a significant proportion of the population.[3] In a 2019 Australian study with 2,054 respondents aged 16–64 years, Henry and others found that one in three respondents reported that someone had taken a nude or sexual image of them without their consent (33.2 per cent); one in five reported that someone had shared a nude or sexual image of them without their consent (20.9 per cent); and almost one in five reported that someone had threatened to share a nude or sexual image of them (18.7 per cent).[4] The study also found that one in three (35.9 per cent) Indigenous respondents, one in two (56.4 per cent) LGB + (lesbian, gay, bisexual) respondents, and one in two young people (aged 16–39) (47.2 per cent) had experienced one or more forms of image-based sexual abuse. While women and men were equally likely to report experiencing image-based sexual abuse (38.1

[2] ibid.

[3] Kathryn Branch and others, 'Revenge Porn Victimization of College Students in the United States: An Exploratory Analysis' (2017) 11(1) International Journal for Cyber Criminology 128; Asia A Eaton, Holly Jacobs, and Yanet Ruvalcaba, '2017 Nationwide Online Study of Non-Consensual Porn Victimization and Perpetration: A Summary Report' (2017) <https://www.cybercivilrights.org/wp-content/uploads/2017/06/CCRI-2017-Research-Report.pdf> accessed 14 March 2023; Manuel Gámez-Guadix and others, 'Prevalence and Association of Sexting and Online Sexual Victimization among Spanish Adults (2015) 12(2) Sexuality Research and Social Policy 145; Henry and others, *Image-based Sexual Abuse* (n 1); Amanda Lenhart, Michelle Ybarra, and Myeshia Price-Feeney, 'Nonconsensual Image Sharing: One in 25 Americans Has been a Victim of "Revenge Porn"' (2016) <https://apo.org.au/node/2666206> accessed 5 October 2023.

[4] Henry and others, *Image-based Sexual Abuse* (n 1).

per cent women and 37.4 per cent men), women respondents (11.7 per cent) were significantly more likely than men (4.8 per cent) to report feeling afraid for their safety following their experience.[5]

While much of the focus of the scholarly literature has been on the prevalence of image-based sexual abuse, several studies have focused qualitatively on victim-survivor experiences and impacts. For instance, Samantha Bates conducted interviews with eighteen US and Canadian victim-survivors of 'revenge porn' who reported serious mental health effects, including post-traumatic stress, suicidality, anxiety, and depression.[6] Similarly, Richard Abayomi Aborisade undertook interviews with twenty-seven Nigerian women, finding that self-blame, anxiety, depression, and other mental health effects were common among victim-survivors who typically experienced victim-blaming, stigmatization, and social isolation.[7] In another multicultural study by Henry and others and McGlynn and others, semi-structured interviews with seventy-five victim-survivors in Australia, New Zealand, and the UK were undertaken, exploring the 'all-encompassing, ongoing and often devastating harms' which are often not recognized, validated, or acted upon by friends, family, community, and criminal justice personnel.[8]

Within the academic literature, there has also been significant attention to legislative responses to image-based sexual abuse in multiple countries, including (but not limited to): Australia,[9] Canada,[10] Hong Kong,[11] Indonesia,[12] Italy,[13] New

[5] ibid.

[6] Samantha Bates, 'Revenge Porn and Mental Health: A Qualitative Analysis of the Mental Health Effects of Revenge Porn on Female Survivors' (2017) 12(1) Feminist Criminology 22

[7] Richard A Aborisade, 'Image-based Sexual Abuse in a Culturally Conservative Nigerian Society: Female Victims' Narratives of Psychosocial Costs (2021) 19(1) Sexuality Research and Social Policy 220.

[8] Clare McGlynn and others, '"It's Torture for the Soul": The Harms of Image-based Sexual Abuse' (2020) 30(4) Social and Legal Studies 541. For other qualitative studies reporting similar findings in relation to mental health and social isolation, see Julia K Campbell and others, 'Social Anxiety as a Consequence of Non-Consensually Disseminated Sexually Explicit Media Victimization (2022) 37(9–10) Journal of Interpersonal Violence NP7268; Antoinette Huber, "A Shadow of Me Old Self": The Impact of Image-based Sexual Abuse in a Digital Society' (2022) 29(2) International Review of Victimology 199; Morten Birk Hansen Mandau, '"Snaps", "Screenshots", and Self-Blame: A Qualitative Study of Image-based Sexual Abuse Victimization among Adolescent Danish Girls' (2021) 15(3) Journal of Children and Media 431.

[9] Asher Flynn and Nicola Henry, 'Image-based Sexual Abuse: An Australian Reflection' (2021) 31(4) Women and Criminal Justice 313.

[10] Alexa Dodge, 'Trading Nudes Like Hockey Cards: Exploring the Diversity of "Revenge Porn" Cases Responded to in Law' (2021) 30(3) Social and Legal Studies 448.

[11] Thomas Crofts, 'Criminalization of Voyeurism and "Upskirt Photography" in Hong Kong: The Need for a Coherent Approach to Image-based Abuse (2021) 8(3) Chinese Journal of Comparative Law 505.

[12] Aulia Shifa Hamida, 'Moral Disagreement of Revenge Porn Law in Indonesia: In Comparison with Israel' (2021) Asian Journal of Legal Studies 1.

[13] Gian Marco Caletti, 'Can Affirmative Consent Save "Revenge Porn" Laws? Lessons from the Italian Criminalization of Non-Consensual Pornography' (2021) 25(3) Virginia Journal of Law and Technology 112.

Zealand,[14] Nigeria,[15] the United Kingdom,[16] and the United States.[17] With the exception of Noelle Martin[18] (discussing her own experiences of seeking justice for image-based sexual abuse), Rackley and others[19] (discussing victim-survivor experiences of justice in the United Kingdom), and Henry and others[20] (discussing victim-survivor experiences of justice in New Zealand), there have been very few studies examining victim-survivors' experiences of the criminal justice system in Australia or elsewhere.

III. Australian Legislative Responses to Image-based Sexual Abuse

Multiple international jurisdictions have created or amended their criminal or civil laws in response to the growing problem of image-based sexual abuse. Some jurisdictions have focused exclusively on criminalizing the non-consensual distribution of intimate images and have not introduced criminal offences for the non-consensual *taking* or *creating* of intimate images, or making *threats to share* intimate images. Some jurisdictions require the prosecution to prove that the accused intended to cause harm or distress, while others do not define 'intimate images' or 'private sexual material' as encompassing images that have been digitally altered.[21]

In Australia, all states and territories, except Tasmania, have introduced specific criminal offences to address the non-consensual taking, creating, or sharing of intimate images, including threats to share intimate images. In 2018, the federal *Criminal Code Act 1995* (Cth) (the telecommunications legislation) was amended to introduce special aggravated offences involving private sexual material of a person over the age of 18 for using a carriage service to menace, harass, or cause

[14] Nicola Henry and others, '"Devastating, Like it Broke Me": Responding to Image-based Sexual Abuse in Aotearoa New Zealand' (2022) Criminology and Criminal Justice (hereafter Henry and others, 'Devastating, Like it Broke Me').

[15] Ifeoma E Nwafor, Ndubuisi Nwafor, and Josiah Alozie, 'Revenge Pornography in Nigeria: A Call for Legal Response and Cyber-Censorship of Content by Internet Service Providers' (2020) 13(2) African Journal of Legal Studies 103.

[16] Clare McGlynn and Erika Rackley, 'Image-based Sexual Abuse' (2017) 37(3) Oxford Journal of Legal Studies 534; Erika Rackley and others, 'Seeking Justice and Redress: Victim-Survivors' Experiences of Image-based Sexual Abuse' (2021) 29 Feminist Legal Studies 293 (hereafter Rackley and others, 'Seeking Justice').

[17] Danielle Keats Citron and Mary-Anne Franks, 'Criminalizing Revenge Porn' (2014) 49 Wake Forest Law Review 345.

[18] Noelle Martin, 'Image-based Sexual Abuse and Deepfakes: A Survivor Turned Activist's Perspective' in Asher Flynn, Anastasia Powell, and Lisa Sugiura (eds), *The Palgrave Handbook on Gendered Violence and Technology* (Palgrave Macmillan 2021).

[19] Rackley and others, 'Seeking Justice' (n 16).

[20] Henry and others, 'Devastating, Like it Broke Me' (n 14).

[21] Henry and others, *Image-based Sexual Abuse* (n 1).

offence. In 2021, the Australian Government introduced a civil Image-based Abuse Scheme, which sits under the federal *Online Safety Act 2021* (Cth). Under this civil scheme, people who post, or threaten to post, intimate images of another person without their consent can face a range of consequences, including takedown orders and civil penalties.

Overall, Australia has some of the most advanced legislative responses to image-based sexual abuse globally. No Australian jurisdiction requires the prosecution to prove the victim suffered distress or harm, or that the perpetrator intended to cause the victim distress or harm. For example, the only requirement under New South Wales law is that the accused intentionally distributed an intimate image of another person without their consent and either knew that they did not consent or were reckless as to whether they consented.

Most Australian jurisdictions have criminal penalties in place for threats made to distribute intimate images. Significantly, in these Australian jurisdictions, the law makes it clear that it is irrelevant whether the image actually exists. This is important because domestic abusers will often tell the victim that they have images in their possession and use them as a threat when those images do not even exist. Furthermore, more recently introduced criminal offences in various Australian jurisdictions, including Victoria, New South Wales, and the Australian Capital Territory, include wording that makes it clear that digitally altered material is covered, which is in contrast to many other countries.[22]

The laws, however, are not consistent across Australian states and territories, and separate laws cover the different forms of image-based sexual abuse—for instance, in some Australian jurisdictions, the non-consensual distribution of intimate images is a separate law from voyeurism or 'upskirting' offences. In some states and territories, image-based sexual abuse falls under summary offences legislation, which poses significant challenges for police investigations, leading the police to only charge offenders for image-based abuse crimes when they can be attached to other offences, such as rape or stalking.[23]

Legal remedies to the problem of image-based sexual abuse are important because they have a deterrent effect and can play an important expressive role in condemning the harms of image-based sexual abuse, yet the law is largely reactive *after* the damage has been done (ie the non-consensual nude or sexual images have been taken, created, shared, or threatened to be shared). The law can do little to prevent the further dissemination of non-consensual nude or sexual images, nor ensure that such images are removed altogether from Internet sites or digital devices. The law is thus only part of the solution to image-based sexual abuse.

22 Rackley and others, 'Seeking Justice' (n 16).

23 Anna Chalton and Paul Schollum, 'Sentencing Image-based Sexual Abuse Offences in Victoria'. Sentencing Advisory Council (Vic); Nicola Henry, Asher Flynn, and Anastasia Powell, 'Policing Image-based Sexual Abuse: Stakeholder Perspectives' (2018) 19(6) Police Practice and Research 565.

Although legislative responses to image-based sexual abuse in Australia have been comprehensive and in many ways exemplary, at least from a global perspective, little is known about how these laws are working in practice. In particular, there is a lack of knowledge about victim-survivors' experiences of reporting to the police or going through the court process. There is also a lack of understanding about victim-survivor 'justice needs'. The study described below responds to this gap.

IV. The Current Study

The aim of the study was to examine the experiences, impacts, and help-seeking pathways of Australian victim-survivors of image-based sexual abuse. In 2017, ethics approval was granted by the RMIT University Human Ethics Committee to conduct interviews with victim-survivors, as well as key stakeholders. Interviews were conducted in 2017 and 2018.

Victim-survivor participants were recruited through a range of methods, including paid Facebook advertising; social media postings; electronic and hard-copy distribution of recruitment flyers; and snowball sampling through victim-support organizations and networks. Participants were required to be 18 years old or older, living in Australia, and have had intimate images (photos or videos) taken or shared of them without their consent, or had experienced someone threatening to share their intimate images. Participants were given a store voucher of $50 AUD to compensate for their time and any travel costs.

The interview schedule centred on the following themes: experiences; harms and impacts; causes or underlying drivers; the availability of support services and resources; police responses; and legal and non-legal forms of justice. The interviews were audio-recorded with participants' permission and later transcribed by an external transcription company and then de-identified. The de-identified data were thematically coded by the research team using the NVivo 12 software program. To protect participants' identities and their confidentiality, pseudonyms were used for all participants.

In total, twenty-five participants were recruited, and interviews were conducted either in person or by telephone. Most participants (60 per cent) were younger adults at the time of the interview, aged between 18 and 29 years, followed by 24 per cent between the ages of 30 and 39 years, and 20 per cent between 40 and 50 years. Most participants were cisgender women (88 per cent), followed by cisgender men (8 per cent), with only one participant identifying as transgender (4 per cent). In relation to sexuality, 60 per cent identified as heterosexual, 24 per cent identified as bisexual, and the remaining 16 per cent either identified as lesbian, gay, pansexual, or 'other'. In relation to race and ethnicity, 92 per cent identified as Australian Caucasian, while only 8 per cent identified as a different race or ethnicity. Given the small number of participants, and that most participants were either ciswomen or Australian Caucasian, the study was not able to undertake an in-depth exploration of the intersections of disadvantage (eg on the basis of race, gender, sexuality, etc) faced by some participants. The key findings of the interviews with victim-survivors are summarized below according to the following four topics: experiences; impacts; justice experiences; and justice needs.

V. Victim-Survivor Experiences of Image-based Sexual Abuse

Image-based sexual abuse is an umbrella term for a wide range of acts involving non-consensual intimate imagery (photos or videos).[24] It can include: pressure, coercion, or deception to share intimate images; recording a consensual or non-consensual sexual or intimate act or situation without the consent of the person in the photo or video; creating digitally altered images (including 'deepfakes'); sharing intimate images without consent; and making threats to share intimate images.

Australian victim-survivors in the study described a range of experiences of image-based sexual abuse. Most of the time the perpetrators of the abuse were known to the victim-survivor, however several participants said they either did not know the identity of the perpetrator, or had only known them online. For 28 per cent (n = 7) of participants, there was a clear pattern of abusive and controlling behaviour over and above the image-based sexual abuse. Four participants described a one-off experience of image-based sexual abuse by a single perpetrator, while others described experiencing image-based sexual abuse by different people in their lifetime. Several participants said they had multiple experiences that included a typical pattern of being coerced into sharing images or images were taken or recorded without their consent or knowledge. For many participants, these acts were then followed by threats to share images and images being shared without consent.

Most participants in the study described instances of intimate images being shared or distributed without their consent. For instance, Chelsea described sitting next to her boyfriend's friend who was scrolling through his phone when she saw a screenshot of the video that her boyfriend had taken of her after she had got out of the shower. She said that she didn't know how many friends he had sent the video to and when she asked him about it the next morning, he said 'whatever' and he 'didn't really care'.

[24] Henry and others, *Image-based Sexual Abuse* (n 1).

Kyle used the gay-dating app Grindr, and after communicating his lack of interest in a man he met online, the man threatened him, saying 'I've got your pictures, I've got your IP address as well, I'm going to post them up and send them around to people.' Some time later, Kyle's Facebook profile was changed showing a nude picture of him using a sex toy.

Some participants described their intimate images being shared when they were under the age of 18. When Julia was 12 or 13 years old, a man from the US coerced her into sending nude photos which were shared on 'child pornography' sites. Another participant, Tara, was filmed when she was drunk at a party making out with a guy—which was later put on YouTube. When Colleen was at high school, she sent a photo to an older man she had a crush on who then shared the photo around. When she confronted him, he said 'If you don't send me more, I'll send it to the whole school.' Steph also had an experience at high school—she had taken some intimate images of herself and then shared it with a boy and 'he distributed it pretty much to really the whole school'.

Some participants recounted how photos or videos had been taken or recorded without their knowledge and then shared without their consent. For instance, Alana was photographed going to the toilet outside in the bush without her consent and her photo was later posted onto pornography sites. Dee had been in hospital undergoing gynaecological surgery when a nurse took a photo of her genitals without her consent and showed it to other hospital staff. Several other participants in the study spoke about their partners, ex-partners, lovers, or dating partners taking intimate photos or videos of them without their consent. Casey talked about being in an abusive relationship and finding out later that her partner had pulled down her dress while she was asleep and had taken a photo of her, which he later put on her Facebook page. Nicole had a similar experience. A man she had been in a relationship with took a naked photo of her while she was asleep and then sent the photo to a Snapchat group of about fifty men who were part of a sporting group, which included some of her friends.

Others described being filmed without their consent or knowledge while engaged in a sexual act. Alison's partner, for instance, had recorded them having sex. In the interview, she commented that the sex was not consensual as she did not know she was being filmed.

In some cases, the image-based sexual abuse was part of a broader pattern of domestic or family violence or abuse. For instance, Karen described how her then partner forced her into filming when she didn't want to:

> When the marriage ended – we've got lots of drugs, lots of violence and I got to the other side of the country, he was still in phone contact and he started threatening to share the images if I didn't come back. And then after a couple of months of me just not coming back, he started telling me that he was going to sell the images to make money . . .

Similarly, Ellen described being in an abusive relationship, and whenever she tried to break up with her partner, he would make all kinds of threats, including taking his own life and sharing her intimate images. She said that this made her 'feel a bit trapped to stay' in the relationship and the only way the relationship was going to end 'was on his terms'.

There was only one participant in the study, Maya, who did not know the identity of the perpetrators who digitally altered her images to make 'fake porn':

> People had been following me on social media and stealing or lifting those photos—ordinary photos of me and then doctoring them or altering them into pornography and then posting them online. That was involved with a lot of very, very highly explicit sexual commentary with my details, like name, where I lived, where I studied ... so they'd Photoshop my face onto naked women, so adult actresses, they would Photoshop me onto images where I was having sexual intercourse, they Photoshopped me into images where I was being ejaculated on which they would literally have to Photoshop sperm onto my face to make it look like there's sperm on my face and the body of the woman. They would also do this thing where they would ejaculate on ordinary images of me and then post those like tributes which is what they would call it, tributes to her.

VI. The Harms of Image-based Sexual Abuse

Participants in the study had diverse experiences of image-based sexual abuse, as described above, and likewise, the impacts on them were diverse. Tim said he did not suffer severe, life-changing impacts after a woman he knew showed videos of him masturbating to her friends. He said that he did not recall bringing it up with the therapist he was seeing at the time and that he does not feel he has 'too much trauma around it'. In comparison to Tim, most participants in the study spoke about the devastating impacts that the image-based sexual abuse had on them. For instance, Dee said 'I just fell apart'. Two participants said they had attempted suicide. One participant said: 'I'm in a sense recovered now, but there's a degree to which you just never recover. So it's sort of just basically destroyed my life ...' And the other who tried to take her own life described it as a 'massive nightmare' and as socially isolating: '... the impacts are lethal ... it was isolating beyond belief because no one understood or validated the harm'. The feeling of social isolation was also described by Kyle who said the experience was 'mortifying', 'traumatic', and 'scary'. He said that in the first two weeks, he was 'just being totally consumed by it, to try and collect evidence and figure out what's going on and why at the same time as being totally withdrawn and feeling isolated and alone and suspicious of everyone. It was awful.' Nicole too described losing sleep, getting stomach ulcers from stress: '... like I was just sick. I was just so worried all the time. Just living in fear.'

The ever-present possibility of intimate images being shared and reshared was another common concern among participants, leading to hyper-vigilance and an overwhelming sense of anxiety and powerlessness that the images could appear at any time. For instance, Candice said that her photos were posted on the Internet where 'someone could find them anytime', which led to a state of 'heightened anxiety'. Dylan described wondering whether the images were still online and occasionally checking. And Maya felt powerless and that 'nothing can be done' to the perpetrators because 'society doesn't take it seriously ... I just really hate the fact that they feel like they can get away with it and they feel like they have that power over me and I hate that they have the audacity to do that to me, and I can't do anything.'

For many victim-survivors of image-based sexual abuse, it changed how they interact with others both online and offline. Steph ended up leaving her school after her images were shared and she was subjected to peer bullying at both the old and new schools. Nicole described experiencing paranoia with her friends and worrying that when they said they were unavailable, they were 'against her' and were never going to talk to her again.

Some participants described other forms of abuse that they were also experiencing. For instance, Alison said the image-based abuse alongside 'the other thing that happened' had a 'definite emotional impact' and that she was 'crying a lot', 'couldn't sleep with her legs open for a few weeks', felt 'disgusting' and 'vulnerable' and 'pretty shit for a while'. Ainsley, who was in an emotionally abusive relationship, said she felt like 'an absolute train wreck' and that she was 'crying constantly'.

Victim-survivors also described experiencing blame and judgement from others. Steph, for instance, said that 'everyone was talking about it' and they were 'asking me why I'd done something stupid like that'. She could tell by the way people looked at her that they were judging her, including her new friends after changing schools, leading her to feel unsafe at her new school. She said: 'I was left to deal with the situation by myself and I was made to feel like I was the one who did the wrong thing.'

VII. Reporting Image-based Sexual Abuse

Like sexual or domestic violence, there is a significant under-reporting of image-based sexual abuse to the police.[25] The reasons for under-reporting were articulated

[25] Manuel Gámez-Guadix and others, 'Assessing Image-based Sexual Abuse: Measurement, Prevalence, and Temporal Stability of Sextortion and Nonconsensual Sexting ("Revenge Porn") among Adolescents' (2022) 94(5) Journal of Adolescence 789.

by many participants in this study. For instance, Ellen said that she did not consider reporting her abusive partner to the police because he had threatened her and also because she was worried that reporting 'would ruin his reputation and he'd never forgive' her. Linda was worried about her former partner being 'pissed off' with her. Nicole said she was too scared to talk to the police because her former partner was 'very abusive'. Casey said the same thing and that she was too scared of her former partner to take any action.

Some participants downplayed or minimized the abuse perpetrated against them and this influenced their decision about reporting to the police. Karly said that she did not consider reporting because it 'wasn't about physical harm' and she 'wasn't under any sort of direct threats'. Georgia said that she 'did send those images consensually ... [and] it's not like he obtained them; it's more just what he's doing now to make me feel sort of awkward or manipulated'. Candice also mentioned that she had shared her images consensually in the first place and expressed self-blame because of this. She said she didn't think there was anything she could do about it: 'I thought that once you've sent something, it's you that sent it so they deserve to do whatever they want with it after that.' Karen also said: 'I've got to do this on my own. I essentially thought that I created the mess, I've been a part of the mess being created and therefore it was my responsibility and that to tell anybody would make it unbearable.'

In some cases, it was others who put them off reporting. Steph said that the teacher at her school had called her into the office and told her that there could be legal implications on her for sharing the image in the first place. Steph mentioned that this was the reason she decided not to report to the police and that she was worried about getting into trouble as well as feeling 'quite embarrassed'. She 'wanted to forget that I did it and move forward'.

Negative past experiences of reporting to the police also shaped victim-survivors' decisions. Casey had previously tried to report to the police, but the police told her the threats were not 'actual' but 'veiled threats'. They told her she 'couldn't press charges, there was nothing to press charges against ... they didn't even take a report'. Julia also had previous negative experiences with the police after being physically assaulted and said they were 'useless'; 'no one showed up, they were not helpful, nothing happened'. She said: 'I don't feel that the police do anything really other than stand around at train stations and harass people that get off the train. That's all I see them do.' Lisa's negative past experiences with the police similarly led her to believing there wasn't any point in reporting: 'They hadn't been helpful before with previous incidents ... they were completely shit.' Lucy, based on her previous experiences, felt that the police 'can't be bothered, and sometimes it can kind of like make you feel like an idiot, if that makes sense, when you want to be heard and taken seriously'.

Other participants said that they did not know that what had happened to them was a crime, or they were not aware of any legal recourse that they could have taken. Indeed, the most common sentiment amongst nearly all victim-survivor participants interviewed for this study was that there was nothing that could be done and there was little point in reporting. According to Julia: 'I feel like nothing can be done ... I had so little evidence ...'. Alison mentioned that she didn't want to go to the police for two key reasons: first, because she would 'probably have to give the video as evidence', and second 'there probably wouldn't actually be any consequences'. For Karen, it never occurred to her that the police 'actually could do something ... [I] felt like I was on my own'. And Alana also thought that going to the police would make no difference 'because those images are out there and you cannot get them back, that's just it. Like nothing you can do ...'.

For some participants, they didn't know the perpetrator, or the perpetrator was someone from overseas, so they felt there wasn't much they could do. For instance, Dylan said that the only action he felt he could take was contacting the websites to get the images taken down. Maya mentioned that she didn't know who the perpetrators were and because they were using VPNs, they were 'getting away with things'. She said: 'If you're someone who doesn't know the perpetrator there is no justice afforded to you, and there's no laws that can actually be handed down.'

Finally, some participants did not want to report to the police because they just wanted the issue to go away. Julia didn't want to tell another woman who was also depicted in non-consensual images because she previously had a falling out with her and the perpetrator and felt it would be 'two very destructive people back in my sphere again after so much effort to get them out'. Kyle similarly remarked: 'I didn't want to give it more air than it was already getting ... I also didn't want to talk about it as well. So it's like you need other people's help at the same time as also that you want to avoid talking about it and essentially isolate yourself from the situation.' Sarah too wanted to 'forget it' and for it to go away.

Victim-survivors were also concerned about how the police would treat them. Chelsea didn't want the police to say: 'Why were you getting changed in front of him then?' or 'Why didn't you tell him to delete the video before he had the chance to share it?' Nicole did not want to report to the police because she was concerned about having to reveal personal details about her experience, that it would be too hard to prove, that it would not be treated as serious, and that she would be 'slut-shamed':

> ... it was like I'd have to show all the things I'd sent and like I'd have to admit that I had sex with him and like I just, I guess, I felt like I'd just be slut shamed for it. And even though I felt like I was a victim, everything I did would be critiqued and judged and investigated ... So, I just thought like it wasn't worth the pain to me to pursue it ... I kind of felt like I didn't have concrete proof, even though he had admitted to doing it ... and to have to go through that ordeal would just like hurt me more than it would hurt him ... I felt kind of belittled, like I was just this silly girl who was like 'this boy is being mean to me', when really I think it should be just

> as serious as like if somebody hits you, or if somebody rapes you, or if somebody mugs you or whatever.

While most participants in the study did not report to the police, six participants either themselves reported to the police or had someone do it on their behalf. For instance, Dylan contacted his local police station and said that while the police were 'sympathetic', they also said 'Yeah, don't share photos of yourself again with people you don't know'. Kyle tried reporting on three different occasions. He said that the first time he went to the local police station, the officer 'didn't take it at all seriously, he didn't do anything at all'. The third time he reported he finally felt like it was treated seriously by a female officer. Kyle said that after this point, at the start of the investigation phase, it was 'absolutely excellent' and he was 'very impressed'.

Maya also reported her experience to the police, government agencies, and a private investigator. She said that it was a process 'where no one would really know what you could do and there was no help'. She said that when she went to the police, she experienced 'a lot of victim-blaming'. The male police officer said: 'You need to be careful what you put on Facebook, anyone can take anything and if it's public they can do whatever they want.' When she contacted the Australian Federal Police (AFP), they said the same thing. Nicole's experience was similar: 'they pretty much just fobbed me off and said because I'd sent the pictures to him, that it was his, he could keep them or whatever and that I just had to take action after the fact if he did post them or whatever, which I was just super scared that he would'.

There were only two participants in the study who said that the perpetrator went to court to face charges. Kyle, whose social media account was hacked, said that the person was initially charged under both federal and state law, with a plea agreement made on the Victorian charges. Kyle said that the perpetrator called him on the phone and offered him money to drop the charges. He said that he didn't feel like he was 'being kept abreast with what was happening. I felt pretty powerless.' Another participant, Ainsley, made a report to the police. Through this process, she discovered that her former partner had four different identities with the police. He ended up receiving a combined sentence for the abuse as well as for the rape of a 13-year-old girl. Neither case involved any specific image-based abuse charge and neither participant acted as a complainant in the criminal trial process.

VIII. Justice Needs

Although victim-survivors differ in their views on what justice entails, most participants in this study indicated that recognition of the harms was crucial. Casey suggested that there needs to be 'a place to record that kind of thing, even if it's not pressing charges, even if they can't get to it being an offence like that, there needs to be somewhere you can report it so that it's listed somewhere in the very least'. Casey lodged paperwork to Victims of Crime because she 'figured that was the only way I could get it in a system. I didn't care about anything else ... I wanted it written down somewhere for future reference.'

When asked what justice meant to her, Maya said that when the Attorney General in her state in his second reading speech mentioned her name, 'it was so, so powerful ... I'm telling you, when someone in a position of power ... recognizes the harm that's happened to you, recognizes the fight that you've tried to do alone ... that is more powerful I feel than the perpetrator being behind bars'.

Others mentioned the importance of perpetrator punishment or accountability. For some, there were imagined scenarios, such as Alison, who said that she had 'this fantasy about going around to his house ... and getting all of his computers and all of his hard drives and all of his electronic instruments and running this beautiful big bubbly bubble bath with sparkles in it and then just dumping everything in this bubble bath'. Dee said that 'in the early days ... all I wanted to do was go round there and knock on the door and smack her in the face. Or throw eggs, I was going to fill a big tub of yogurt and I was going to go and put it in her mail box, or I'm going to chuck eggs at her door.'

Traditional justice responses were also mentioned as important by some participants, such as Zoe, who said she would like 'people actually to be charged ... so I want like men to be afraid that if they go ahead and do this, that they can be charged'. Candice stated that she would 'like him locked up', as did Lisa who said: 'I hope that he goes to jail.' Alison, on the other hand, expressed disillusionment with traditional forms of punishment. Instead, she suggested, it would have been preferable for the perpetrator to have been made to call up 'every single person he knows and tell them [what he'd done]'. Ellen expressed a similar sentiment: 'I'm not too sure about punishment, but I feel people being aware of what he's like as a person, and more and more people being aware of what he's like as a person.' Nicole said when she confronted the perpetrator, 'he admitted to doing it. He didn't apologize or anything. And then I just told everyone that I knew really, to shame him.'

Some participants said that there was little that could be done for them in terms of justice—for instance, Julia said that 'nothing would resolve it honestly with me' but she did say that 'preventing others from experiencing it ... [would be] ... a form of justice'. Similarly, Tim said that justice means that 'the same person wouldn't repeat that behaviour'.

For many victim-survivors, justice is much broader than perpetrator accountability, involving support and care from the broader community. For instance, Steph said she would have liked more support from her school as she was left to 'deal with the situation by myself'. Maya was concerned that the federal civil penalty scheme that was introduced in Australia in 2018 fails to provide victim-survivors with any recognition payment for acknowledgement of the harm. Maya felt that fines do 'nothing' and that victim-survivors need 'other support rather than counselling', and rather than punishment, 'they also need some sort of compensation for the harm that's caused'.

Dee also mentioned that she would have appreciated support from the hospital where a nurse had taken a photo of her without her consent. She said that she would have liked them to help make a complaint, pay for her psychology bills, which can 'mount up to the tens of thousands', and then just to have rung her in a month's time to see how she was getting on and if there was anything else they could do.

For others, justice was about moving on with one's life. Casey mentioned that for her justice was about the situation 'disappearing' and being 'able to get on with my life ... I just don't want it to take up any more of my brain space ... Justice to me would be just leave me alone.' And for Linda, justice was about breaking up with her abusive boyfriend and achieving 'closure'.

Participants made many suggestions for change. First, better education was frequently mentioned. Colleen said that schools need to take image-based sexual abuse 'more seriously'. Tara felt that awareness of the serious nature of image-based sexual abuse was crucial. Chelsea too felt that strong messaging that image-based sexual abuse was against the law needed to be conveyed at an early age. Ainsley wanted better education about the dangers of sharing intimate images for young women: 'this is what happens if you take those pictures and send the pictures to others', as did Dylan who said there should be some sort of 'internet self-defence' teaching in high school to help people know what to do if image-based abuse happens to them. Tim suggested that it could be less of the 'don't do it sort of vibe' and more of 'the internet images can be shared quite rapidly, quite quickly'.

Some participants felt that education was also crucial for the police. Maya, for instance, remarked: 'the damn police need to be taught in the damn academy ... It is such an issue if the police are not taking this seriously, and they are not.' Others mentioned training and education for counselling and hotline staff. Alana, for instance, said that the people who the victims go to 'don't understand the phenomena that is being presented to them, so they can't adequately provide any support'. Casey said that 'people need to be trained and made aware of the psychological effects ... I don't think lots of people in these positions understand hugely'.[26]

Second, participants discussed how processes could be improved. Kyle, for instance, said that he would have liked to have been kept more abreast of the justice process and to have been at the court hearings. He said he tried to request a copy of the sentencing judgment so he could have understood the judge's reasons for sentencing but it was never sent to him and he 'got sick of chasing them'.

Third, victim-survivors also said they wanted more research, awareness, and accessible information. Chelsea, for instance, wanted to know what her rights were and what kind of avenues were available: '... if a friend said "This is happened", I'd

26 See Emma Bond and Katie Tyrrell, 'Understanding Revenge Pornography: A National Survey of Police Officers and Staff in England and Wales' (2018) 36(5–6) Journal of Interpersonal Violence 2166.

be like "It's against the law. You've got these avenues, let's look them up together"'. Ellen expressed something similar:

> I guess we've got to look at the victims and work on empowering them, or potential victims, work on empowering them, so they're educated to know their rights and know the services and know the supports that they have. Have them easily accessible.

Candice wanted to know that there was something she could do—'... somewhere on the internet would be the best'. Karly too suggested an online resource 'because everyone's first step is Google.... Like, all that stuff in one place, because obviously there are mental health places to go, there's a police thing, but there's not just one site, "if you've experienced this, here's your rights, here's your responsibilities, here's your portal, if you want to take it further", whatever that may be'.

Overall, the victim-survivors in this study had different justice ideals as well as experiences, but collectively they expressed a strong need for broader awareness and recognition of the serious harms of image-based sexual abuse. Their poor perceptions or past experiences of reporting to the police, combined with their own lack of awareness of their rights or of the laws, shaped their decisions about their next steps, fed into internalized self-blame, and overall led them to feeling that nothing could be done. Indeed, only two participants mentioned their case going to trial and neither of them appeared as complainants in those trials.

IX. Conclusion

Victim-survivors in this Australian study described diverse and harmful experiences of image-based sexual abuse. While they had different views on how to respond to this form of abuse, they all spoke about the importance of justice, redress, and support—through formal justice avenues, such as police, or civil or criminal proceedings, as well as through more informal support avenues such as counsellors, family, friends, workplaces, or schools.

The study participants expressed unequivocal agreement that the harms and wrongdoings against them (and others like them) must be appropriately recognized. For some this meant a form of interpersonal justice with perpetrators reflecting on what they had done and why their behaviour was wrong; whereas others wanted perpetrators sent to jail. For many, justice also meant being recognized and appropriately supported by the police, counsellors, teachers, and others.

The experiences of victim-survivors of image-based sexual abuse underscore the importance of a whole-of-community approach, which includes primary prevention education, criminal offences and civil penalty schemes, well-resourced victim support services, police training, as well as greater action and transparency from the digital platforms and mobile applications that encourage, support, or otherwise host non-consensual imagery with little to no consequences.[27]

Despite the introduction of specific criminal offences and greater public attention to image-based sexual abuse in Australia, many participants felt there was no point in reporting to the police and that very little could be done. This was often because the police had advised victim-survivors that there was nothing they could do and provided unhelpful advice, or expressed victim-blaming attitudes, such as admonishing them for sharing their intimate images or even having photos on their social media. This finding of 'institutional betrayal'[28] points strongly to the importance of education and resources for the police, teachers, managers, as well as victim support services. Institutional betrayal is a significant form of injustice which serves to deepen the harms of the experience and inhibit a victim-survivors' recovery journey.

In conclusion, this study provides important insights into the experiences of twenty-five victim-survivors seeking justice for image-based sexual abuse in Australia, yet more research must be undertaken to address further gaps. The limitations of this study included: firstly, only two participants had had an experience of image-based sexual abuse that led to a court case (neither were complainants to those cases); secondly, the majority of participants recruited for the study were white, cisgender women, and so the study does not adequately capture the experiences of other marginalized people, including children, Indigenous people, people living in rural and remote communities, sex workers, migrants and refugees, and those living with a disability; thirdly, as the participants in the study volunteered to take part in an interview, it is possible that most of them had either disclosed or reported their experiences previously, or were sufficiently able and willing to participate and articulate their experiences, which means the study may not have captured people who have told no one about their experiences or who do not have the resources or capacity to speak to an interviewer; and fourthly, the interviews were conducted in 2017 and 2018 and do not capture experiences involving more recent advances in technology, such as 'deepfake' images.

Further research is needed to explore: the lived experiences of victim-survivors as complainants in courtroom settings; the intersections of age, gender, race, sexuality, and disability and how these intersections shape a person's journey of justice and recovery; and how new and emerging forms of image-based sexual abuse shape experiences and help-seeking behaviours.

[27] Henry and others, *Image-based Sexual Abuse* (n 1); Rackley and others, 'Seeking Justice' (n 16).

[28] Delanie Woodlock and others, '"Living in the Darkness": Technology-Facilitated Coercive Control, Disenfranchised Grief, and Institutional Betrayal' (2022) 29(5) Violence against Women 987.

Bibliography

Aborisade RA, 'Image-based Sexual Abuse in a Culturally Conservative Nigerian Society: Female Victims' Narratives of Psychosocial Costs (2021) 19(1) Sexuality Research and Social Policy 220

Bates S, 'Revenge Porn and Mental Health: A Qualitative Analysis of the Mental Health Effects of Revenge Porn on Female Survivors' (2017) 12(1) Feminist Criminology 22

Bond E and Tyrrell K, 'Understanding Revenge Pornography: A National Survey of Police Officers and Staff in England and Wales' (2018) 36(5–6) Journal of Interpersonal Violence 2166

Branch K and others, 'Revenge Porn Victimization of College Students in the United States: An Exploratory Analysis' (2017) 11(1) International Journal for Cyber Criminology 128

Caletti GM, 'Can Affirmative Consent Save "Revenge Porn" Laws? Lessons from the Italian Criminalization of Non-Consensual Pornography' (2021) 25(3) Virginia Journal of Law and Technology 112

Campbell J and others, 'Social Anxiety as a Consequence of Non-Consensually Disseminated Sexually Explicit Media Victimization' (2022) 37(9–10) Journal of Interpersonal Violence, NP7268

Chalton A and Schollum P, 'Sentencing Image-based Sexual Abuse Offences in Victoria'. Sentencing Advisory Council (Vic)

Citron DK and Franks MA, 'Criminalizing Revenge Porn' (2014) 49 Wake Forest Law Review 345

Crofts T, 'Criminalization of Voyeurism and "Upskirt Photography" in Hong Kong: The Need for a Coherent Approach to Image-based Abuse' (2021) 8(3) Chinese Journal of Comparative Law 505

Dodge A, 'Trading Nudes Like Hockey Cards: Exploring the Diversity of "Revenge Porn" Cases Responded to in Law' (2021) 30(3) Social and Legal Studies 448

Eaton AA, Jacobs H, and Ruvalcaba Y, '2017 Nationwide Online Study of Non-Consensual Porn Victimization and Perpetration: A Summary Report' (2017) <https://www.cybercivilrights.org/wp-content/uploads/2017/06/CCRI-2017-Research-Report.pdf> accessed 5 October 2023

Flynn A and Henry N, 'Image-based Sexual Abuse: An Australian Reflection' (2021) 31(4) Women and Criminal Justice 313

Gámez-Guadix M and others, 'Prevalence and Association of Sexting and Online Sexual Victimization among Spanish Adults (2015) 12(2) Sexuality Research and Social Policy 145

Gámez-Guadix M and others, 'Assessing Image-based Sexual Abuse: Measurement, Prevalence, and Temporal Stability of Sextortion and Nonconsensual Sexting ("Revenge Porn") among Adolescents' (2022) 94(5) Journal of Adolescence 789

Hamida AS, 'Moral Disagreement of Revenge Porn Law in Indonesia: In Comparison with Israel' (2021) Asian Journal of Legal Studies

Henry N, Asher F, and Powell A, 'Policing Image-based Sexual Abuse: Stakeholder Perspectives' (2018) 19(6) Police Practice and Research 565

Henry, Nicola and others, *Image-based Sexual Abuse: The Causes and Consequences of Non-Consensual Nude or Sexual Imagery* (Routledge 2020)

Henry N and others, '"Devastating, Like it Broke Me": Responding to Image-based Sexual Abuse in Aotearoa New Zealand' (2022) Criminology and Criminal Justice

Huber A, '"A Shadow of Me Old Self": The Impact of Image-based Sexual Abuse in a Digital Society' (2022) 29(2) International Review of Victimology 199

Lenhart A, Ybarra M, and Price-Feeney M, 'Nonconsensual Image Sharing: One in 25 Americans Has been a Victim of "Revenge Porn"' (2016) <https://apo.org.au/node/2666206> accessed 5 October 2023

Mandau MBH, '"Snaps", "Screenshots", and Self-Blame: A Qualitative Study of Image-based Sexual Abuse Victimization among Adolescent Danish Girls' (2021) 15(3) Journal of Children and Media 431

Martin N, 'Image-based Sexual Abuse and Deepfakes: A Survivor Turned Activist's Perspective' in A Flynn, A Powell, and Lisa Sugiura (eds), *The Palgrave Handbook on Gendered Violence and Technology* (Palgrave Macmillan 2021)

McGlynn C and Rackley E, 'Image-based Sexual Abuse' (2017) 37(3) Oxford Journal of Legal Studies 534

McGlynn C and others, '"It's Torture for the Soul": The Harms of Image-based Sexual Abuse' (2020) 30(4) Social and Legal Studies 541

Nwafor IE, Ndubuisi N, and Alozie J, 'Revenge Pornography in Nigeria: A Call for Legal Response and Cyber-Censorship of Content by Internet Service Providers' (2020) 13(2) African Journal of Legal Studies 103

Rackley E and others, 'Seeking Justice and Redress: Victim-Survivors' Experiences of Image-based Sexual Abuse' (2021) 29 Feminist Legal Studies 293

Woodlock D and others, '"Living in the Darkness": Technology-Facilitated Coercive Control, Disenfranchised Grief, and Institutional Betrayal' (2022) 29(5) Violence against Women 987

16

Image-based Abuse in Intimate Partnerships in Canada

Lessons from the Criminal Case Law

Moira Aikenhead

I. Introduction

Intimate partner violence remains a pressing social problem in Canada. Incidents of police-reported intimate partner violence increased for the seventh consecutive year in 2021, with women and girls making up 79 per cent of victims.[1] Intimate partner violence takes many forms, often occurring within an overarching dynamic of gendered coercive controlling behaviour. Image-based abuse involving the non-consensual creation or distribution of harmful images, or threats to engage in this behaviour, is playing a growing role in abusive relationships. The fact

[1] Statistics Canada, 'Victims of Police-reported Family and Intimate Partner Violence in Canada, 2021' (The Daily, 19 October 2022) <https://www150.statcan.gc.ca/n1/daily-quotidien/221019/dq221019c-eng.htm> accessed 29 December 2022.

Moira Aikenhead, *Image-based Abuse in Intimate Partnerships in Canada* In: *Criminalizing Intimate Image Abuse*. Edited by: Gian Marco Caletti and Kolis Summerer, Oxford University Press. © Oxford University Press 2024.
DOI: 10.1093/oso/9780198877813.003.0016

that harmful images may be digitally captured and potentially disseminated to a wide online audience is being exploited as a powerful tool of dominance and control.

This chapter explores how image-based abuse is manifesting in the Canadian intimate partner violence context through an exploration of three representative criminal cases. These cases provide insight into the lived realities of this violence and point to areas of potential reform within the Canadian criminal justice system to better address the harms of image-based abuse.[2] In Section II, I discuss the phenomenon of image-based abuse in the context of intimate partnerships. In Section III, I describe Canada's criminal justice response to intimate partner violence and image-based abuse, highlighting potentially applicable provisions of the Criminal Code[3] and highlighting certain feminist critique of the application of these provisions in the context of intimate partner violence or technology-facilitated violence. In Section IV, I engage in a feminist legal analysis of three representative criminal cases involving intimate partner image-based abuse, exploring how the facts of these cases relate to broader dynamics of intimate partner violence, and examining how judges are applying Canada's criminal laws to these relatively novel behaviours. In Section V, I reach conclusions about the adequacy of the current criminal justice response to image-based abuse in intimate partnerships and make recommendations for how this response may be improved.

II. Image-based Abuse in Intimate Partnerships

Image-based abuse is a form of technology-facilitated violence. Much of the literature on image-based abuse focuses on the non-consensual creation or distribution of sexual images.[4] These behaviours are often a form of gender violence, involving perpetrators with similar motivations, and survivors experiencing similar harms, to cases of sexual assault.[5] Women and members of marginalized

[2] For a discussion of the value of criminal case law review as methodology, see Scott Phillips and Ryken Grattet, 'Judicial Rhetoric, Meaning-Making, and the Institutionalization of Hate Crime Law' (2000) 34(3) Law and Society Review 567.

[3] Criminal Code, RSC 1970, c C-34.

[4] Clare McGlynn, Erika Rackley, and Ruth Houghton, 'Beyond "Revenge Porn": The Continuum of Image-based Sexual Abuse' (2017) 25(1) Feminist Legal Studies 25 (hereafter McGlynn, Rackley, and Houghton, 'Beyond Revenge Porn'); Anastasia Powell and others, 'Image-based Sexual Abuse: The Extent, Nature, and Predictors of Perpetration in a Community Sample of Australian Residents' (2019) 92 Computers in Human Behavior 393; Anastasia Powell and others, *Image-based Sexual Abuse: An International Study of Victims and Perpetrators* (RMIT University 2020) <https://www.researchgate.net/publication/339488012_Image-based_sexual_abuse_An_international_study_of_victims_and_perpetrators> accessed 29 December 2022 (hereafter Powell and others, *Image-based Sexual Abuse: An International Study*).

[5] Samantha Bates, 'Revenge Porn and Mental Health: A Qualitative Analysis of the Mental Health Effects of Revenge Porn on Female Survivors' (2017) 12(1) Feminist Criminology 22 (hereafter Bates, 'Revenge Porn and Mental Health'); McGlynn, Rackley, and Houghton, 'Beyond Revenge Porn' (n 4); Jane Bailey and Carissima Mathen, 'Technology-facilitated Violence against Women and Girls: Assessing the Canadian Criminal Law Response' (2019) 97 Canadian Bar Review 664.

and equality-deserving groups such as LGBTQ + persons, individuals with disabilities, and newcomer populations are all disproportionately targets of image-based abuse.[6]

The most well-known iteration of image-based abuse is the non-consensual distribution of intimate images (NCDII). While the term 'revenge pornography' is sometimes used interchangeably with NCDII, previous authors have critiqued this term for its inaccurate and euphemistic nature.[7] Non-consensual distribution is not limited to the context of former intimate partnerships, nor is the motive for such behaviour exclusively 'revenge'. Other forms of sexualized image-based abuse apart from NCDII include voyeurism, coercing a person to create or share nude or sexual images, non-consensually filming or livestreaming a person who is nude or engaged in sexual activity without their consent, filming sexual assault, and creating false 'deepfake' sexual images of another person.[8] Individuals may threaten to share the resulting images online, or can use them for other means such as impersonating that person or creating fake online dating or sexual service profiles. All of these behaviours have received attention in the literature in recent years as harmful forms of image-based abuse, and many of these behaviours are becoming increasingly common in the context of intimate relationships.[9]

Image-based abuse can extend beyond the sexual context and include the recording, distribution, or threatened distribution of any harmful digital images of another person. In the intimate partner context, this can include filming the physical assault of a partner, recording arguments with a partner, recording a partner's

[6] Anastasia Powell, Nicola Henry, and Asher Flynn, 'Image-based Sexual Abuse' in Walter DeKeseredy and Molly Dragiewicz (eds), *Handbook of Critical Criminology* (Routledge 2018) 305 (hereafter Powell, Henry, and Flynn, 'Image-based Sexual Abuse'); Anastasia Powell, Adrian J Scott, and Nicola Henry, 'Digital Harassment and Abuse: Experiences of Sexuality and Gender Minority Adults' (2020) 17(2) European Journal of Criminology 199; Nicola Henry, Asher Flynn, and Anastasia Powell, 'Technology-Facilitated Domestic and Sexual Violence: A Review' (2020) 26(15–16) Violence against Women 1828; Nicola Henry and others, 'Technology-Facilitated Domestic Violence against Immigrant and Refugee Women: A Qualitative Study' (2021) 37(13–14) Journal of Interpersonal Violence NP12634.

[7] McGlynn, Rackley, and Houghton, 'Beyond Revenge Porn' (n 4); Sophie Maddocks, 'From Non-consensual Pornography to Image-based Sexual Abuse: Charting the Course of a Problem with Many Names' (2018) 33(97) Australian Feminist Studies 345 (hereafter Maddocks, 'Non-consensual Pornography').

[8] Deepfake sex videos involve individuals' faces and voices being inserted into real pornography using machine learning technology (see Danielle Keats Citron, 'Sexual Privacy' (2019) 128(7) Yale Law Journal 1870, 1921–24 (hereafter Citron, 'Sexual Privacy')). See also McGlynn, Rackley, and Houghton, 'Beyond Revenge Porn' (n 4); Nicola Henry and Anastasia Powell, 'Sexual Violence in the Digital Age: The Scope and Limits of Criminal Law' (2016) 25(4) Social and Legal Studies 397 (hereafter Henry and Powell, 'Sexual Violence in the Digital Age').

[9] Powell, Henry, and Flynn, 'Image-based Sexual Abuse' (n 6); Maddocks, 'Non-consensual Pornography' (n 7); Molly Dragiewicz and others, *Domestic Violence and Communication Technology: Survivor Experiences of Intrusion, Surveillance, and Identity Crime* (Australian Communications Consumer Action Network 2019) (hereafter Dragiewicz and others, *Domestic Violence*); Moira Aikenhead, 'Canada's Criminal Justice Response to Technology-Facilitated Intimate Partner Violence' (PhD dissertation, University of British Columbia 2022) (hereafter Aikenhead, 'Criminal Justice Response').

movements with a hidden camera, or coercing a partner into making incriminating statements or engaging in incriminating behaviour on film. Each of these forms of abuse have been recounted in the literature on technology-facilitated intimate partner violence, often forming part of a broader pattern of coercive control.[10] Coercive control, as theorized by Evan Stark, is a gendered pattern of rules, surveillance, and behavioural regulation within an abusive intimate relationship that erodes women's sense of privacy, personal space, and access to the outside world.[11] Harris and Woodlock define 'digital coercive control' as 'the use of devices and digital media to stalk, harass, threaten and abuse partners or ex-partners (and children)'.[12] Coercive control relies heavily on threats against and surveillance of intimate partners, creating a sense in that person that their abuser is omnipresent, and that they have limited space for choice or ameliorative action, such as ending the relationship.[13]

Image-based abuse may play a key role in coercive control. While the act of recording certain behaviours, such as violence or sexual assault, is an inherently harmful extension of perpetrators' power and entitlement in relation to their partners,[14] the resulting recordings and any explicit or implied threats to distribute

[10] Tammy Hand, Donna Chung, and Margaret Peters, *The Use of Information and Communication Technologies to Coerce and Control in Domestic Violence and Following Separation* (Australian Domestic and Family Violence Clearinghouse 2009); Dragiewicz and others, *Domestic Violence* (n 9); Heather Douglas, Bridget A Harris, and Molly Dragiewicz, 'Technology-facilitated Domestic and Family Violence: Women's Experiences' (2019) 59(3) British Journal of Criminology 551; Aikenhead, 'Criminal Justice Response' (n 9).

[11] Evan Stark, *Coercive Control: How Men Entrap Women in Personal Life* (OUP 2007) (hereafter Stark, *Coercive Control*).

[12] Bridget A Harris and Delanie Woodlock, 'Digital Coercive Control: Insights from Two Landmark Domestic Violence Studies' (2019) 59(3) British Journal of Criminology 530, 533 (hereafter Harris and Woodlock, 'Digital Coercive Control'. See also Molly Dragiewicz and others, 'Technology Facilitated Coercive Control: Domestic Violence and the Competing Roles of Digital Media Platforms' (2018) 18(4) Feminist Media Studies 609 (hereafter Dragiewicz and others, 'Domestic Violence and Competing Roles'); Powell, Henry, and Flynn, 'Image-based Sexual Abuse' (n 6); Delanie Woodlock and others, 'Technology as a Weapon in Domestic Violence: Responding to Digital Coercive Control' (2020) 73(3) Australian Social Work 368; Bridget Harris and Delanie Woodlock, 'Digital Coercive Control and Spatiality: Rural, Regional, and Remote Women's Experience' in Jane Bailey, Asher Flynn, and Nicola Henry (eds), *The Emerald International Handbook of Technology-Facilitated Violence and Abuse* (Emerald Publishing 2021) 387 (hereafter Harris and Woodlock, 'Digital Coercive Control').

[13] Mary Ann Dutton and Lisa A Goodman, 'Coercion in Intimate Partner Violence: Toward a New Conceptualization' (2005) 52(11–12) Sex Roles 743 (hereafter Dutton and Goodman, 'Intimate Partner Violence'); Stark, *Coercive Control* (n 11); Harris and Woodlock, 'Digital Coercive Control' (n 12) 538; Elizabeth Yardley, 'Technology-Facilitated Domestic Abuse in Political Economy: A New Theoretical Framework' (2021) 27(10) Violence against Women 1479 (hereafter Yardley, 'Domestic Abuse in Political Economy').

[14] Andrea Slane, 'Legal Conceptions of Harm Related to Sexual Images Online in the United States and Canada' (2015) 36(4) Child and Youth Services 288 (hereafter Slane, 'Legal Conceptions'); Alexa Dodge, 'Digitizing Rape Culture: Online Sexual Violence and the Power of the Digital Photograph' (2016) 12(1) Crime, Media, Culture: An International Journal 65 (hereafter Dodge, 'Digitizing Rape Culture'); Sveinung Sandberg and Thomas Ugelvik, 'Why do Offenders Tape Their Crimes? Crime and Punishment in the Age of the Selfie" (2017) 57 British Journal of Criminology 1023 (hereafter Sandberg and Ugelvik, 'Offenders Tape').

those recordings can be a significant source of power for abusive partners.[15] The ease with which such recordings may be shared widely online can lend credibility to threats to distribute harmful images, resulting in fear and compliance on the part of the person depicted. Where images are consensually created, such as an agreed-to recording of sexual activity between partners, it is the threat of distribution that can transform a positive form of sexual expression into a harmful tool of abuse and coercion.

Survivors of image-based abuse may experience significant psychological impacts, such as trust issues, post-traumatic stress disorder, anxiety, depression, and damage to their self-esteem, frequently stemming from a sense of loss of control over images of their bodies.[16] They may also experience harm to their physical safety and integrity, or fear of such harm, if their images are posted online and form the basis of a campaign of harassment, or are shared with individuals who may physically harm them, such as current or former partners or family members.[17] Survivors have experienced economic and reputational damage from image-based abuse.[18] Where images or recordings are relied on as leverage in legal battles such as custody proceedings, survivors may lose custody of their children or other legal interests or entitlements. A key harm consistently identified in the literature by survivors of image-based abuse is the potential permanence of harmful images online, and the attendant loss of control over who views them, how they are used, and if and when they might resurface.[19]

The harms of image-based abuse in intimate relationships extends beyond the individual survivors—there is a significant market online for recordings of sexual and physical abuse of women.[20] The ready availability of online audiences for such

[15] Sandberg and Ugelvik, 'Offenders Tape' (n 14) 1036; Powell, Henry, and Flynn, 'Image-based Sexual Abuse' (n 6); Nicola Henry, Asher Flynn, and Anastasia Powell, 'Policing Image-based Sexual Abuse: Stakeholder Perspectives' (2018) 19(6) Police Practice and Research 565 (hereafter Henry, Flynn, and Powell, 'Stakeholder Perspectives'); Dragiewicz and others, *Domestic Violence* (n 9); Aikenhead, 'Criminal Justice Response' (n 9).

[16] Anastasia Powell and Nicola Henry, 'Conceptualising Technosocial Harms' in Anastasia Powell and Nicola Henry (eds), *Sexual Violence in a Digital Age* (Palgrave Macmillan 2017) 94 (hereafter Powell and Henry, 'Technosocial Harms'); Bates, 'Revenge Porn and Mental Health' (n 5); McGlynn, Rackley, and Houghton, 'Beyond Revenge Porn' (n 4); Dragiewicz and others, *Domestic Violence* (n 9).

[17] Carissima Mathen, 'Crowdsourcing Sexual Objectification' (2014) 3(3) Laws 529; Mary Anne Franks, 'Revenge Porn Reform: A View from the Front Lines' (2017) 69(5) Florida Law Review 1251 (hereafter Franks, 'Revenge Porn Reform'); Delanie Woodlock, 'The Abuse of Technology in Domestic Violence and Stalking' (2017) 23(5) Violence against Women 584.

[18] Franks, 'Revenge Porn Reform' (n 17); Powell and Henry, 'Technosocial Harms' (n 16).

[19] Jane Bailey, 'A Perfect Storm: How the Online Environment, Social Norms, and Law Shape Girls' Lives' in Jane Bailey and Valerie Steeves (eds), *eGirls, eCitizens* (University of Ottawa Press 2015); Bates, 'Revenge Porn and Mental Health (n 5); Powell and Henry, 'Technosocial Harms' (n 16); Dragiewicz and others, *Domestic Violence* (n 9); Olga Marques, 'Intimate Image Dissemination and Consent in a Digital Age: Perspectives from the Front Line' in Jane Bailey, Asher Flynn, and Nicola Henry (eds), *The Emerald International Handbook of Technology-Facilitated Violence and Abuse* (Emerald Publishing 2021) 309 (hereafter Marques, 'Image Dissemination').

[20] Walter S DeKeseredy and Martin D Schwartz, 'Thinking Sociologically About Image-based Sexual Abuse: The Contribution of Male Peer Support Theory' (2016) 2(4) Sexualization, Media, and Society 1 (hereafter DeKeseredy and Schwartz, 'Thinking Sociologically'); Dodge, 'Digitizing Rape Culture' (n 14); Sandberg and Ugelvik, 'Offenders Tape' (n 14); Dragiewicz and others, 'Domestic

content can result in a large number of individuals viewing these harmful images, and disseminating them further. Some perpetrators' primary motivation for engaging in image-based abuse is to produce such images and distribute them online.[21] Producing a supply of such harmful recordings to meet this demand not only results in more individuals (usually women) being harmed, but may feed into viewers' sense of the perceived normalcy or desirability of such violent behaviour, increasing the risk of misogynist and patriarchal violence in society more generally.[22]

Image-based abuse is not new, nor is it an entirely novel form of intimate partner violence. Surreptitious recording and threats to distribute harmful images of partners predate the invention of smartphones or even digital recording devices. Dodge has explored a 'pre-digital history' of NCDII in Canadian case law, including cases of ex-partners sharing or threatening to share physical copies of nude images or VHS recordings of their ex-partners.[23] What the proliferation of handheld digital technologies has changed is the ease with which a motivated partner can create surreptitious or otherwise non-consensual recordings, and share these images to a large targeted or random audience online within seconds. Once images have been posted online, the person depicted loses virtually all control over the images, and may live in fear that they could resurface online at any point in the future.[24]

III. The Role of Canada's Criminal Law in Responding to Image-based Abuse in Intimate Relationships

Many of the forms of image-based abuse discussed above can constitute criminal behaviour if certain requisite elements are present. While the Criminal Code does

Violence and Competing Roles' (n 12); Anastasia Powell, Gregory Stratton, and Robin Cameron, 'Liminal Images: Criminality, Victimisation and Voyeurism' in Anastasia Powell, Gregory Stratton, and Robin Cameron (eds), *Digital Criminology: Crime and Justice in Digital Society* (Routledge 2018) 91 (hereafter Powell, Stratton, and Cameron, 'Liminal Images'); Powell and others, *Image-based Sexual Abuse: An International Study* (n 4) 393–94; Jordan Fairbairn and Dale Spencer, 'Virtualized Violence and Anonymous Juries: Unpacking Steubenville's 'Big Red' Sexual Assault Case and the Role of Social Media' (2018) 13(5) Feminist Criminology 477.

21 Powell, Stratton, and Cameron, 'Liminal Images' (n 20). See also Sandberg and Ugelvik, 'Offenders Tape' (n 14); Dodge, 'Digitizing Rape Culture' (n 14); Slane, 'Legal Conceptions' (n 14); Henry and Powell, 'Sexual Violence in the Digital Age' (n 8).

22 DeKeseredy and Schwartz, 'Thinking Sociologically' (n 20).

23 Alexa Dodge, 'Nudes are Forever: Judicial Interpretations of Digital Technology's Impact on "Revenge Porn"' (2019) 34(1) Canadian Journal of Law and Society 121, 123 (hereafter Dodge, 'Nudes Forever'), discussing *LaRose v Yavis* [1993] BCJ No 3050 (QL), *R v Lepore* [2001] OJ No 2053 (QL), *R v JT* [1994] OJ No 3937 (QL), and *R v DKP* (1991) 5 BCAC 308.

24 Dodge acknowledges the impact of digital technologies on the scope and impact of non-consensual distribution, but cautions against placing too much emphasis on these affordances and suggests judges must consider the impacts of digital technologies on a case-by-case basis in cases of non-consensual distribution. See Dodge, 'Nudes Forever'.

not contain any general prohibition against intimate partner violence, sentences may be increased to account for offences occurring within the context of an intimate partnership.

A. Applicable Criminal Code Provisions

1. Image-based abuse

The Canadian Criminal Code prohibits the publication, distribution, transmission, selling, making available, or advertising of an intimate image, knowing that the person depicted did not give their consent or being reckless as to whether they consented.[25] 'Intimate images' are images or recordings depicting nudity or sexual activity, recorded in circumstances giving rise to a reasonable expectation of privacy, and in relation to which the person depicted retains a reasonable expectation of privacy at the time of distribution.[26] These provisions were enacted in response to a number of highly publicized Canadian cases in which young people took their own lives in the wake of online harassment following instances of sexual abuse.[27] These provisions were specifically aimed at addressing novel privacy concerns arising from the proliferation of handheld digital technologies, and the permanence and ease of distribution of harmful images online.[28] To date, the vast majority of reported cases of NCDII involve current or former intimate partners.[29]

The Criminal Code's voyeurism provisions, enacted in 2005, similarly arose out of concerns around the implications of novel digital technologies on Canadians' privacy and sexual integrity.[30] These provisions prohibit the surreptitious observation or recording of a person in circumstances that give rise to a reasonable expectation of privacy, in certain circumstances in which nudity or sexual activity is occurring or expected, or where the observation is done for a sexual purpose.[31] A person's 'reasonable expectation of privacy' is to be assessed based on the totality of the circumstances, rather than turning on the complainant's physical

[25] Criminal Code (n 3) [ss 162.1(1)].

[26] ibid [ss 162.1(2)].

[27] Jane Bailey, 'Time to Unpack the Juggernaut?: Reflections on the Canadian Federal Parliamentary Debates on Cyberbullying' (2014) 37 Dalhousie Law Journal 661.

[28] Government of Canada, *House of Commons Debates*, 41st Parl, 2nd Sess, No 27 (29 May 2014) 1110–15, cited in *R v Ly* [2016] OJ No 7196 (QL) [*Ly*] para 33.

[29] Moira Aikenhead, 'Non-consensual Disclosure of Intimate Images as a Crime of Gender-based Violence' (2018) 30(1) Canadian Journal of Women and the Law 117 (hereafter Aikenhead, 'Non-consensual Disclosure'); Alexa Dodge, 'Trading Nudes Like Hockey Cards: Exploring the Diversity of "Revenge Porn" Cases Responded to in Law' (2020) 30(3) Social and Legal Studies 448; Moira Aikenhead, 'Revenge Pornography and Rape Culture in Canada's Nonconsensual Distribution Case Law' in Jane Bailey, Asher Flynn, and Nicola Henry (eds), *The Emerald International Handbook of Technology-Facilitated Violence and Abuse* (Emerald Publishing 2021) 533.

[30] Moira Aikenhead, 'A "Reasonable" Expectation of Sexual Privacy in the Digital Age' (2018) 41(2) Dalhousie Law Journal 273 (hereafter Aikenhead, 'Reasonable Expectation').

[31] Criminal Code (n 3) [ss 162(1)].

location or factual risk of being recorded.[32] While no official statistics document the prevalence of voyeurism in the context of intimate partnerships, abusive partners may exploit their physical or technological access to their partners by placing hidden cameras around the home, or installing spyware on their partners' camera-equipped devices without their knowledge, in order to capture voyeuristic images.

Another Criminal Code provision potentially applicable in relation to image-based abuse is criminal harassment, which prohibits certain forms of harassing conduct that cause the complainant to reasonably fear for their safety or the safety of anyone known to them.[33] Criminal harassment cases in Canadian courts overwhelmingly involve individuals who are known to one another, often former intimate partners.[34] The Criminal Code's extortion provisions have also been found to apply in the context of offenders threatening to distribute their partners' intimate images.[35] The Criminal Code's uttering threats provisions will typically not apply to threats to distribute intimate images, as these provisions cover threats of physical harm, property damage, or injury to a pet.[36]

There are a number of additional Criminal Code provisions that could potentially apply to certain forms of image-based abuse, but which do not frequently appear in the reported case law involving these behaviours. These include identity fraud,[37] distribution of obscene materials,[38] and harassing communications.[39]

2. Intimate partner violence

As previously noted, there is no criminal offence of 'intimate partner violence' in Canada. However, the fact that an offence was committed against the offender's current or former intimate partner is a mandatory aggravating factor on sentencing.[40] Further, sentencing judges must consider the increased vulnerability of female persons who are victims, giving particular attention to the circumstances of Indigenous female victims, when sentencing offenders in relation to intimate partner violence.[41] If an offender is convicted of an indictable violent offence against an intimate partner, and has previously been convicted of a similar offence,

[32] *R v Jarvis* [2019] SCC 10, 433 DLR (4th) 195, para 30.

[33] Criminal Code (n 3) [ss 264(1), (2)]. See, eg, *R v Myles*, 2017 ONCA 375, [2017] OJ No 2311 (QL); *R v Said*, 2017 ONCJ 124, 137 WCB (2d) 168; *R v JR*, 2018 ONCJ 851, [2018] OJ No 6409 (QL); *R v BS*, 2019 MBPC 26, [2020] 2 WWR 362.

[34] Isabel Grant, 'Intimate Partner Criminal Harassment through a Lens of Responsibilization' (2015) 52(2) Osgoode Hall Law Journal 552.

[35] See, eg, *R v AH*, 2019 ONSC 4849, [2019] OJ No 4328 (QL) [*AH*]; *R v Sobh*, 2018 ONSC 2299, 2018 CarswellOnt 5519 (WL); *R v Khamb*, 2019 BCSC 1822, [2019] BCJ No 2010 (QL).

[36] Criminal Code (n 3) [s 264.1].

[37] ibid [s 403].

[38] ibid [ss 163(1), (2)].

[39] ibid [ss 372(3)].

[40] ibid [ss 718.2(ii)].

[41] ibid [ss 718.201].

the court may impose a penalty higher than the statutory maximum period of imprisonment.[42]

IV. Three Representative Cases of Intimate Partner Image-based Abuse

A. *R v Hirsch*

R v Hirsch[43] involved facts mirroring a 'typical' case of 'revenge pornography'—the offender shared an intimate image of his ex-partner, without her consent, in circumstances indicating an intention to humiliate and degrade her. Hirsch physically and emotionally abused the complainant over the course of their eight-year relationship. Several months after the complainant ended the relationship, Hirsch posted an image of her exposed breasts to his Facebook page with the comment, 'Hirsch is gonna choke a bitch ... and her names [redacted] ... somebody help me cure this disease ... b4 i end it with a shotgun shell ... or 2'.[44] The offender was convicted of a single count of uttering threats in relation to this posting,[45] and sentenced to six months' incarceration followed by twelve months' probation.

While the facts in *Hirsch* are relatively straightforward, the offender's appeal to the Saskatchewan Court of Appeal raised two important legal questions in relation to intimate partner image-based abuse. The first relates to the authentication of digital evidence in the context of technology-facilitated violence, and the second to the relevant considerations in determining whether a social media post is 'threatening' in the context of intimate partner violence.

On appeal, Hirsch argued that the electronic evidence relied on by the Crown, a screen shot depicting the nude image of the complainant and the threatening Facebook post, had not been properly authenticated. Hirsch had blocked the complainant from accessing his Facebook account approximately two months prior to the posting. As a result, the complainant only became aware of the posting after a friend who had viewed it alerted her, and subsequently sent her the screenshot relied upon by the Crown. This evidence was introduced at trial through the complainant, who testified she was familiar with Hirsch's Facebook page, recognized the page depicted in the screenshot as his, recognized the nude photograph as being one which she had taken and had only shared with Hirsch, recognized the page's profile picture as depicting Hirsch and her cat, and testified that the post was consistent with how Hirsch typically communicated. The trial judge had found this

[42] ibid [ss 718.3(8)].
[43] 2017 SKCA 14, [2017] SJ No 59 (hereafter *R v Hirsch*).
[44] ibid para 7.
[45] The offence took place in October 2013, prior to the enactment of the Code's NCDII provisions. As a result the offender was not charged with NCDII.

testimony sufficient to authenticate the screenshots, and to establish that Hirsch was the person who posted the nude image and authored the threatening post.

Hirsch argued on appeal that because the complainant had not had access to his Facebook page, she was not in a position to authenticate the screenshots. The Court of Appeal noted that while it may have been preferable for the Crown to have called the friend who created the screenshots to give evidence, the complainant's testimony, and the speculative nature of any suggestion that the screenshot evidence may have been tampered with, were sufficient to authenticate that evidence.[46]

Hirsch further argued that the trial judge's verdict was unreasonable as the Crown had not proved the essential elements of uttering threats. The offender argued that the Facebook posts involved 'glib banter', and were not intended to be taken seriously.[47] The complainant had testified that she was not concerned by the postings as the offender often spoke in a threatening manner, and she was more concerned with the nude images than the threatening post.[48] The Court of Appeal dismissed this ground of appeal. The trial judge had relied on the broader context in finding the post to be threatening, noting:

> On their face, these words amount to a threat to cause bodily harm or worse. In terms of the context in which the words were uttered, this was a Facebook post that was accompanied by a screen shot of [the complainant's] exposed breast. While a portion of the words uttered may have been borrowed from a comedy sketch, the fact they referenced an ex-domestic partner from a troubled relationship, and juxtapose a copy of her exposed breast, would also support the notion the words uttered were a threat.

The Court of Appeal agreed with the trial judge's analysis and dismissed this ground of appeal.[49]

B. *R v Hunt*

R v Hunt[50] is a sentencing decision involving a fairly common form of intimate partner image-based abuse—a threat to distribute intimate images.[51] The Criminal Code does not expressly prohibit threats to distribute intimate images, though such threats can meet the definition of extortion if made in an attempt to induce the

[46] *R v Hirsch* (n 43) paras 8, 24.
[47] ibid para 42.
[48] ibid para 11.
[49] ibid para 46.
[50] [2017] NJ No 430 (QL) (hereafter *R v Hunt*).
[51] Sandberg and Ugelvik, 'Offenders Tape' (n 14); Powell, Henry, and Flynn, 'Image-based Sexual Abuse' (n 6); Henry, Flynn, and Powell, 'Stakeholder Perspectives' (n 15); Dragiewicz and others, *Domestic violence* (n 9); Aikenhead, 'Criminal Justice Response' (n 9).

complainant to do something.[52] In *R v Hunt*, the offender possessed nude images of his ex-girlfriend, and images in which the two were involved in explicit sexual activity. Hunt threatened to post these images on the complainant's Facebook page if she did not tell her friends that they had not, in fact, separated. To avoid the images being posted online, the complainant complied with this demand. Hunt was charged with extortion under section 346(1) of the Criminal Code. Hunt initially pleaded not guilty, but changed his plea midway through his trial.

After Crown and defence submissions on sentence, Judge Gorman advised he was going to impose a sentence greater than that being sought be either side (six months' incarceration by the Crown, and two to four months' incarceration by the defence). Judge Gorman described the harmful nature of threats to distribute intimate images online and the need for denunciation and deterrence in sentencing these cases as follows:[53]

> The present day access to social media cites [*sic*] has dramatically changed the potential impact of extortion. For instance, a present day threat to release intimate photographs through social media cites [*sic*] allows for the sharing and dissemination of such photographs on a worldwide basis. This technology also makes it impossible for the victim to limit circulation or to retrieve the photographs. This modern day form of extortion is much different and more serious than older forms of extortion. The sentencing for such offences must reflect the changes in the sharing of information and the impact upon victims. General deterrence and denunciation must be the primary principles of sentencing applied.

After reviewing the relevant case law, Judge Gorman noted that Hunt's threat to post the images on Facebook 'adds an element of widespread public access which would not exist in other forms of extortion'.[54] After considering the relevant aggravating and mitigating factors, including the fact that Hunt was a 22-year-old man with no previous criminal record, Judge Gorman imposed a sentence of nine months' imprisonment and two years' probation. The period of probation included an order that Hunt could not access the complainant's Facebook account or post anything about her on social media.

C. *R v NM*

R v NM,[55] is a decision that stands out as a particularly disturbing example of intimate partner image-based abuse. As *NM* is a sentencing decision, it does not

[52] Criminal Code (n 3) [ss 346(1)].
[53] *R v Hunt* (n 50) para 8.
[54] ibid para 45.
[55] [2019] OJ No 6238 (QL) (hereafter *NM*).

provide the level of factual detail or legal analysis that would be present in a trial-level decision. However, the facts explored by Justice Sopinka in her attempt to determine a fit sentence for the first-time offender[56] describe an extremely harmful and sustained example of image-based abuse.

The offender in *NM* pleaded guilty to a number of offences falling into two broad categories. The first related to a sustained pattern of sexual violence against his long-term partner, for which NM was charged with numerous counts of sexual assault, sexual assault with a weapon, voyeurism, and NCDII. The second were charges stemming from his large collection of child pornography. Justice Sopinka described both categories of behaviour as 'depraved and sexually abusive conduct'.[57] The facts of the intimate partner sexual abuse were variously described by Justice Sopinka as 'horrifying',[58] 'vile',[59] and 'abhorrent'.[60] Over a period of just under two years, NM made 195 non-consensual video recordings of the complainant, involving thirty-six separate instances of voyeurism, nineteen sexual assaults, six sexual assaults using a weapon or other object, and eleven incidents 'of non consensual sexual activity involving the family dog'.[61] The offender's behaviour had escalated from filming the complainant naked while she was sleeping, to filming himself sexually touching her while she was unconscious, involving the family dog in this sexual abuse, inserting weapons and other objects into her vagina, and ultimately inserting his penis into her mouth and vagina and ejaculating on her. He filmed all of these incidents, in many cases creating compilations of the recordings, setting them to music, giving them vulgar titles, and in some cases posting them online.

Justice Sopinka reviewed the significant mitigating and aggravating factors in *NM*. The offender's lack of a related criminal record, guilty plea, attempts at and ongoing commitment to rehabilitation, and seemingly genuine remorse, were all considered as mitigating. Justice Sopinka also considered NM's support within the community, but found this factor to be 'tempered by the fact that offences of this nature are committed in private and the trust placed in Mr. N.M. by his partner was the very means by which he was able to commit the heinous acts of sexual violation'.[62] This assessment reflects feminist understandings of violence and critiques of judicial consideration of a person's 'good character' and public reputation as justifying a mitigation in sentence for violent offences committed against

[56] ibid paras 11, 44. While it is unclear whether NM had a previous record, he had no related record and was treated as 'essentially a first time offender'.
[57] ibid para 13.
[58] ibid para 9.
[59] ibid para 40.
[60] ibid para 12.
[61] ibid para 4.
[62] ibid para 11.

their partners in the home, away from public scrutiny.[63] The aggravating factors related to the offender's planned, deliberate, and extreme sexual abuse of his intimate partner over an extended period of time, as well as his choice to record and circulate images of that abuse online.[64]

After weighing the relevant aggravating and mitigating factors, and finding that denunciation and deterrence must be the key sentencing considerations, Justice Sopinka sentenced NM to a global sentence of eight and a half years' incarceration for all of the offences. She also imposed a restriction on the offender's use of the Internet, prohibiting NM from '[u]sing the internet to access content that violates the law or to access social media sites, social network sites, internet discussion forums or chat rooms or maintain a personal profile on any such service or use any file sharing services such as BitTorrent or similar services' for a period of twenty years.[65]

V. Lessons from the Case Law

In each of the cases discussed in the previous section, judges were attentive to abusive relationship dynamics, did not minimize abuse simply because it took place online, and did not blame complainants or disbelieve them, all of which have been identified as concerns by feminist and critical legal scholars in relation to technology-facilitated violence.[66] The seriousness and harmful nature of the offending behaviour was recognized in each case, and denunciation and deterrence were emphasized in the two sentencing decisions. In *NM*, Justice Sopinka noted that voyeurism cases involving the publication of the images may warrant incarceration as a starting point.[67] While there are urgent and significant feminist and other critiques of the use of incarceration as a remedy to gender violence,[68] a serious engagement with these critiques is beyond the scope of this paper. From

[63] Elizabeth M Schneider, 'The Violence of Privacy' (1991) 23 Connecticut Law Review 973; Rosemary Hunter, 'Narratives of Domestic Violence' (2006) 28 Sydney Law Review 733 (hereafter Hunter, 'Narratives').

[64] *NM* (n 55) para 12.

[65] ibid para 46.

[66] Danielle Citron, 'Law's Expressive Value in Combatting Cyber Gender Harassment' (2009) 108(3) Michigan Law Review 373 (hereafter Citron 'Law's Expressive Value'); Jordan Fairbairn, 'Rape Threats and Revenge Porn: Defining Sexual Violence in the Digital Age' in Jane Bailey and Valerie Steeves (eds), *eGirls, eCitizens* (University of Ottawa Press 2015) 229; McGlynn, Rackley, and Houghton, 'Beyond Revenge Porn' (n 4); Citron, 'Sexual Privacy' (n 8).

[67] *NM* (n 55) para 32, citing *R v Jarvis* [2019] OJ No 4371 (SJC).

[68] Sherene Razack, *Looking White People in the Eye: Gender, Race and Culture in the Courtrooms and Classrooms* (University of Toronto Press 1999); Angela P Harris, 'Gender, Violence, Race, and Criminal Justice' (2000) 52(4) Stanford Law Review 777; Angela P Harris, 'Heteropatriarchy Kills: Challenging Gender Violence in a Prison Nation' (2011) 37(13) Journal of Law and Policy 13; Constance Backhouse, 'A Feminist Remedy for Sexual Assault: A Quest for Answers' in Elizabeth A Sheehy (ed), *Sexual Assault in Canada: Law, Legal Practice and Women's Activism* (University of Ottawa Press 2012) 725; Beth Richie, 'The Matrix: A Black Feminist Response to Male Violence and the State' in Beth Richie (ed), *Arrested Justice: Black Women, Violence, and America's Prison Nation* (New York University Press 2012).

a theoretical legal perspective, it is relevant that Canadian judges are recognizing the serious and harmful nature of image-based abuse in the context of intimate partnerships.[69]

There are additional lessons that can be learned from these three cases, directly and indirectly, in relation to Canada's and other countries' judicial and legal responses to intimate partner image-based abuse in the criminal context. Below, I summarize the lessons drawn from each of these decisions and outline relevant recommendations to improve criminal justice responses to intimate partner image-based abuse from a feminist and technology-informed perspective.[70]

A. *Hirsch*—Contested Authorship and Uttering Threats in the Context of Image-based Abuse

Concerns about the authentication of digital evidence, such as those raised by the offender in *R v Hirsch*, are likely to occur with increasing frequency as digital images and evidence gain centrality in many intimate partner violence cases, particularly those involving image-based abuse.[71] As explored by Dunn and Aikenhead, many accused are attempting to cast doubt on their identity as the poster of harmful online content or as the author of abusive or harassing messages in the context of gender violence.[72] Judges must walk a careful line to ensure that doctored digital evidence is not improperly relied on, while not disregarding relevant digital evidence on the basis of speculative claims that it could have been altered or authored by another individual.[73] Crucially, in the context of intimate partner violence, judges should be aware of the prevalence of gendered stereotypes of vengeful female partners who fabricate allegations against their former spouses to punish them or gain other advantages, such as success in custody proceedings.[74] In cases

[69] Citron, 'Law's Expressive Value' (n 66). The finding that many Canadian judges are treating technology-facilitated gender violence as a serious form of criminal offending has been found in previous case law analyses (Aikenhead, 'Non-Consensual Disclosure' (n 29); Dodge, 'Nudes Forever' (n 23); Aikenhead, 'Criminal Justice Response' (n 9)).

[70] Aikenhead, 'Reasonable Expectation' (n 30); Aikenhead, 'Criminal Justice Response' (n 9) 150.

[71] Alexa Dodge, 'The Digital Witness: The Role of Digital Evidence in Criminal Justice Responses to Sexual Violence' (2018) 19(2) Feminist Theory 303 (hereafter Dodge, 'Digital Witness'); Alexa Dodge and others, 'This Isn't Your Father's Police Force: Digital Evidence in Sexual Assault Investigations" (2019) 52(4) Australia and New Zealand Journal of Criminology 488; Suzie Dunn and Moira Aikenhead, 'On the Internet, Nobody Knows You Are a Dog: Contested Authorship of Digital Evidence in Cases of Gender-based Violence' (2022) 19 Canadian Journal of Law and Technology 371 (hereafter Dunn and Aikenhead, 'Nobody Knows').

[72] Dunn and Aikenhead, 'Nobody Knows'.

[73] ibid.

[74] Hunter, 'Narratives' (n 63); Karen Busby, 'Every Breath You Take: Erotic Asphyxiation, Vengeful Wives, and Other Enduring Myths in Spousal Sexual Assault Prosecutions' (2012) 24(2) Canadian Journal of Women and the Law 328 Canada; Ruthy Lowenstein Lazar, 'The 'Vindictive Wife': The Credibility of Complainants in Cases of Wife Rape' (2015) 25(1) Southern California Review of Law and Social Justice 1.

where there is no circumstantial evidence to support a claim of contested authorship or fabrication, judges should be wary of lending too much credence to such claims in their assessment of the evidence.[75]

R v Hirsch is frequently cited as an authority in relation to authentication of digital evidence,[76] however I believe the Court's endorsement of the trial judge's approach to assessing whether or not the Facebook post constituted a legal threat is equally compelling. In order for a statement to meet the Criminal Code's criteria for 'uttering threats', the trier of fact must determine whether the words would convey a threat to a reasonable person, in light of the entire context.[77] This analysis includes an assessment of the complainant's subjective fear, which, in previous cases of intimate partner violence, has raised feminist concerns. In particular, the fact that a complainant may be accustomed to an abusive partner making threats against her has been relied on in finding a claim of uttering threats has not been made out.[78]

In *R v Hirsch*, the trial judge found that the presence of an image of the complainant's exposed breast, alongside a threatening statement by her abusive intimate partner, supported the notion that the words were intended to be taken seriously, a finding which was upheld by the Alberta Court of Appeal.[79] This finding may be relevant in future cases where accused persons post sexual images alongside overt or implied threats, as this choice to juxtapose a partner's nude images with threats of violence can be seen as relevant to the accused's intention to harm their partner.

B. *Hunt*—the Legislative Gap Regarding Threats to Distribute Intimate Images

Threats to distribute intimate images, such as those made by the offender in *R v Hunt*, are not criminalized under the Criminal Code. The Code's NCDII provisions do not prohibit threats to distribute intimate images, and the Criminal Code's 'uttering threats' provisions do not apply to this conduct unless paired with threats of violence.[80] The offender in *R v Hunt* was charged with extortion, as the threats were made in an attempt to induce the complainant to inform her friends they had not, in fact, separated. Other Canadian extortion cases have involved allegations of

[75] Dunn and Aikenhead, 'Nobody Knows' (n 71).

[76] See, eg, *R v Martin* [2021] NLCA 1, 170 WCB (2d) 343; *R v Ball* [2019] BCCA 32, 152 WCB (2d) 371; *R v Durocher* [2019] SKCA 97, 158 WCB (2d) 677.

[77] Joanna Birenbaum and Isabel Grant, 'Taking Threats Seriously: Section 264.1 and Threats as a Form of Domestic Violence' (2012) 59 Criminal Law Quarterly 206 (hereafter Birenbaum and Grant, 'Taking Threats Seriously').

[78] ibid 208–13; Janine Benedet, Annotation of *R v O'Brien* [2013] CarswellMan 3, 2013 SCC 2.

[79] *R v Hirsch* (n 43) para 46.

[80] Code (n 3) [s 264.1(1)].

individuals threatening to distribute their partners' intimate images in an attempt to induce their partners to have sex with them,[81] get back together with them,[82] respond to their communications,[83] or give them money.[84]

Despite not being explicitly prohibited by the Criminal Code, threats to distribute partners' intimate images are a common and harmful form of intimate partner violence.[85] Threats are a key component of coercive control in intimate partnerships.[86] Such threats need not include threats of physical violence, rather the crucial factor in the effectiveness of threats in controlling a partner is whether such threats are credible, that is, whether the person believes that a negative consequence described by their partner will in fact be delivered.[87] Threats to distribute intimate images online may be considered extremely credible—this action is easy to undertake, and such postings can reach a potentially massive audience. The credibility of such threats and the harmful impacts of NCDII may be sufficient to warrant criminalization, without the necessity of any explicit attempt to induce a person to do or refrain from doing something.

This legislative gap also exposes a broader limitation of the criminal law. In the context of an abusive intimate partnership, threats to distribute intimate images need not be explicit in order to constitute a powerful basis for dominance and control. The mere possession of intimate images by an abusive partner may cause some individuals to experience a persistent, implied threat that those images may be distributed online at any time.[88] In their analysis of offenders' varied motivations for creating digital recordings of their crimes, Sandberg and Ugelvik note that modern digital recording technologies create an implication of dissemination, as recordings are 'in their very essence, meant to be communicated, at least potentially'.[89] In the context of a coercive controlling partnership, an abuser's creation or retention of a potentially harmful image of their partner may be understood as creating an implied threat of dissemination, without the abuser needing to explicitly threaten to post that image online. As Canadian criminal law requires a discrete, harmful action be undertaken on the part of the offender, it is likely an inadequate tool to address such subtle dynamics as implied threats to distribute intimate images. However, the harms that can flow from the creation of an abusive recording,

[81] *R v JC*, 2018 ONSC 5547, [2018] OJ No 5047 (QL), rev'd 2021 ONCA 131; *R v AH*, 2019 ONSC 4849, [2019] OJ No 4328 (QL).

[82] *R v Khamb* (n 35).

[83] *R v SLS* [2018] OJ No 4874 (QL).

[84] *R v Sobh* (n 35).

[85] Henry, Flynn, and Powell, 'Stakeholder Perspectives' (n 15); Marques, Image Dissemination' (n 19).

[86] Dutton and Goodman, 'Intimate Partner Violence' (n 13); Stark, *Coercive Control* (n 11); Birenbaum and Grant, 'Taking Threats Seriously' (n 77); Harris and Woodlock,, 'Digital Coercive Control' (n 12); Yardley, 'Domestic Abuse in Political Economy' (n 13).

[87] Dutton and Goodman, 'Intimate Partner Violence' (n 13).

[88] Henry, Flynn, and Powell, 'Stakeholder Perspectives' (n 15).

[89] Sandberg and Ugelvik, 'Offenders Tape' (n 14) 1036.

whether or not it is actually distributed or explicitly threatened to be distributed, should be borne in mind by judges hearing cases involving image-based abuse, as discussed further below.

C. *NM*—the Double-edged Nature of Abusive Recordings

The accused's behaviour in *NM* involved a two-year pattern of escalating sexual abuse and image-based abuse against his wife. Digital technologies have the double-edged impacts of providing abusers with new opportunities and means of harming their partners, while at the same time creating a record of forms of violence and abuse that were previously shielded from public scrutiny, such as intimate partner violence and sexual assault.[90] The double-edged nature of this evidence is abundantly clear in *NM*. The complainant was unconscious for many of the instances of sexual violence committed against her, and at no time consented to any sexual activity being recorded.[91] Had the offender not created a digital record of these assaults, the complainant would likely never have become aware of many of them, nor would the offender have faced any legal or other repercussions. The abusive recordings were only discovered as part of a police investigation into an online child pornography sharing platform, and NM's guilty plea likely emerged from the Crown's 'extremely strong' case based on this digital evidence.[92]

While NM's recordings are the reason his pattern of sexually abusive behaviour was discovered and prosecuted, without digital technology allowing him to easily capture these recordings, it is unclear whether he would have sexually abused his partner in this manner in the first place. The offender's actions in creating and retaining recordings of his increasingly invasive, violent, and harmful sexual assaults of his partner; compiling them; setting them to music; giving them vulgar names; and posting them online indicate that the sexual abuse was at least partly motivated by creating an exploitative visual product 'for him and others to view'.[93] The act of sharing recordings of sexual violence online and participating in collective viewing of such images serves as a primary motivating factor for some men in committing sexual violence.[94] Such sharing of abusive images, on public online pornography websites or in more tailored forums such as the 'manosphere',[95] can have extremely

[90] Dodge, 'Digital Witness' (n 71); Dunn and Aikenhead, 'Nobody Knows' (n 71).

[91] *NM* (n 55) para 7

[92] ibid para 11.

[93] ibid para 12.

[94] DeKeseredy and Schwartz, 'Thinking Sociologically' (n 20). See also Slane, 'Legal Conceptions' (n 14); Dodge, 'Digitizing Rape Culture' (n 14); Sandberg and Ugelvik, 'Offenders Tape' (n 14); Powell, Stratton, and Cameron, 'Liminal Images' (n 20).

[95] The 'manosphere' is a network of blogs, Facebook groups, forums, subreddits, and other online platforms dedicated to 'men's rights activists', 'incels' (involuntarily celibate men), and others who are united by shared resentment or hatred towards women, anti-feminist sentiment, and idolization of a particular form of white masculinity. See Lise Gotell and Emily Dutton, 'Sexual Violence

harmful impacts on survivors. In *NM*, the complainant recounted in her Victim Impact Statement that she was traumatized by the fact the videos were posted online, and that the extent of their distribution would never be known.[96] While there is no information in the sentencing reasons in *NM* as to the offender's motivations in creating the recordings, the fact he edited many of them and posted many online indicates at least some desire to have others participate in the abuse of his partner.

The tailored, twenty-year prohibition on aspects of the offender's use of the Internet ordered in *NM* has some potential as a tool in preventing the offender from engaging in similar behaviour in the future. The widespread use of such prohibitions in cases of image-based abuse may be instrumental in stopping the spread of harmful violent and misogynistic content online. While that order was issued pursuant to section 161 of the Criminal Code, which allows such orders to be made where an offender has been convicted of a sexual offence against a child (as NM was also convicted of a serious of child pornography offences), the judge's restriction on the offender accessing social media, online forums, and file sharing services, would also restrict him from posting harmful and violent content involving sexual abuse of adult women online. Judges may order restrictions on an offender's use of the Internet as conditions of a probation order,[97] a conditional sentence order,[98] or as part of any sentence in relation to a conviction for NCDII.[99] There has been some push-back against broad or blanket Internet prohibitions in the case law, given the current centrality of the Internet to everyday life.[100] While blanket orders restricting a person from using the Internet or possessing or accessing a device capable of accessing the Internet are likely to be overly restrictive in a majority of cases and frequently unenforceable, tailored orders such as those set out in *NM* and *Hunt* that target the specific, harmful behaviour of certain offenders could be effective at preventing further forms of image-based abuse and technology-facilitated violence in the future. An order prohibiting a person from accessing the online forums and platforms where they connect with like-minded individuals to further abuse of women could serve to de-radicalize the offenders and shrink the community of online abusers.

in the 'Manosphere': Antifeminist Men's Rights Discourses on Rape' (2016) 5(2) International Journal for Crime, Justice and Social Democracy 65; Sarah Banet-Weiser and Kate M Miltner, '#MasculinitySoFragile: Culture, Structure, and Networked Misogyny' (2016) 16(1) Feminist Media Studies 171; Anti-Defamation League, *When Women are the Enemy: The Intersection of Misogyny and White Supremacy* (ADL Center on Extremism 2018).

[96] *NM* (n 55) para 12.
[97] Criminal Code (n 3) [ss 732.1(3)(h)].
[98] ibid [ss 742.3(2)(f)].
[99] ibid [ss 162.2(1)].
[100] Meoldy Isadi, 'Do We Need the Court of Appeal to Weigh in About the Importance of Internet Use in Modern Society?' 41(6) Law Now 55; *R v Brar* [2016] ONCA 724, 133 WCB (2d) 413; *R v RJH* [2021] BCCA 54, 170 WCB (2d) 278.

Bibliography

Aikenhead M, 'Non-Consensual Disclosure of Intimate Images as a Crime of Gender-based Violence' (2018) 30(1) Canadian Journal of Women and the Law 117

Aikenhead M, 'A "Reasonable" Expectation of Sexual Privacy in the Digital Age' (2018) 41(2) Dalhousie Law Journal 273

Aikenhead M, 'Revenge Pornography and Rape Culture in Canada's Nonconsensual Distribution Case Law' in J Bailey, A Flynn, and N Henry (eds), *The Emerald International Handbook of Technology-Facilitated Violence and Abuse* (Emerald Publishing 2021)

Aikenhead M, 'Canada's Criminal Justice Response to Technology-Facilitated Intimate Partner Violence' (PhD dissertation, University of British Columbia 2022)

Backhouse C, 'A Feminist Remedy for Sexual Assault: A Quest for Answers' in EA Sheehy (ed), *Sexual Assault in Canada: Law, Legal Practice and Women's Activism* (University of Ottawa Press 2012)

Bailey J, 'Time to Unpack the Juggernaut?: Reflections on the Canadian Federal Parliamentary Debates on Cyberbullying' (2014) 37 Dalhousie Law Journal 661

Bailey J and Mathen C, 'Technology-facilitated Violence against Women and Girls: Assessing the Canadian Criminal Law Response' (2019) 97 Canadian Bar Review 664

Bates S, 'Revenge Porn and Mental Health: A Qualitative Analysis of the Mental Health Effects of Revenge Porn on Female Survivors' (2017) 12(1) Feminist Criminology 22

Birenbaum J and Grant I, 'Taking Threats Seriously: Section 264.1 and Threats as a Form of Domestic Violence' (2012) 59 Criminal Law Quarterly 206

Citron DK, 'Law's Expressive Value in Combatting Cyber Gender Harassment' (2009) 108(3) Michigan Law Review 373

Citron DK, 'Sexual Privacy' (2019) 128(7) Yale Law Journal 1870

DeKeseredy WS and Schwartz MD, 'Thinking Sociologically about Image-based Sexual Abuse: The Contribution of Male Peer Support Theory' (2016) 2(4) Sexualization, Media and Society 1

Dodge A, 'Digitizing Rape Culture: Online Sexual Violence and the Power of the Digital Photograph' (2016) 12(1) Crime, Media, Culture: An International Journal 65.

Dodge A, 'The Digital Witness: The Role of Digital Evidence in Criminal Justice Responses to Sexual Violence' (2018) 19(2) Feminist Theory 303

Dodge A, 'Nudes are Forever: Judicial Interpretations of Digital Technology's Impact on "Revenge Porn"' (2019) 34(1) Canadian Journal of Law and Society 121

Dodge A, 'Trading Nudes Like Hockey Cards: Exploring the Diversity of "Revenge Porn" Cases Responded to in Law' (2020) 30(3) Social and Legal Studies 448

Dragiewicz, M and others, 'Technology Facilitated Coercive Control: Domestic Violence and the Competing Roles of Digital Media Platforms' (2018) 18(4) Feminist Media Studies 609

Dragiewicz M and others, *Domestic Violence and Communication Technology: Survivor Experiences of Intrusion, Surveillance, and Identity Crime* (Australian Communications Consumer Action Network 2019)

Dunn S and Aikenhead M, 'On the Internet, Nobody Knows You Are a Dog: Contested Authorship of Digital Evidence in Cases of Gender-based Violence' (2022) 19 Canadian Journal of Law and Technology 371

Dutton MA and Goodman LA, 'Coercion in Intimate Partner Violence: Toward a New Conceptualization' (2005) 52(11–12) Sex Roles 743

Fairbairn J, 'Rape Threats and Revenge Porn: Defining Sexual Violence in the Digital Age' in J Bailey and V Steeves (eds), *eGirls, eCitizens* (University of Ottawa Press 2015)

Franks MA, 'Revenge Porn Reform: A View from the Front Lines' (2017) 69(5) Florida Law Review 1251

Gotell L and Dutton E, 'Sexual Violence in the "Manosphere": Antifeminist Men's Rights Discourses on Rape' (2016) 5(2) International Journal for Crime, Justice and Social Democracy 65

Grant I, 'Intimate Partner Criminal Harassment Through a Lens of Responsibilization' (2015) 52(2) Osgoode Hall Law Journal 552

Hand T, Chung D and Peters M, *The Use of Information and Communication Technologies to Coerce and Control in Domestic Violence and Following Separation* (Australian Domestic and Family Violence Clearinghouse 2009)

Harris AP, 'Gender, Violence, Race, and Criminal Justice' (2000) 52(4) Stanford Law Review 777

Harris AP, 'Heteropatriarchy Kills: Challenging Gender Violence in a Prison Nation' (2011) 37(13) Journal of Law and Policy 13

Harris BA and Woodlock D, 'Digital Coercive Control: Insights from Two Landmark Domestic Violence Studies' (2019) 59(3) British Journal of Criminology 530

Harris BA and Woodlock D, 'Digital Coercive Control and Spatiality: Rural, Regional, and Remote Women's Experience' in J Bailey, A Flynn, and N Henry (eds), *The Emerald International Handbook of Technology-Facilitated Violence and Abuse* (Emerald Publishing 2021)

Henry N and Powell A, 'Sexual Violence in the Digital Age: The Scope and Limits of Criminal Law' (2016) 25(4) Social and Legal Studies 397

Henry N, Flynn A, and Powell A, 'Policing Image-based Sexual Abuse: Stakeholder Perspectives' (2018) 19(6) Police Practice and Research 565

Henry N and others, 'Technology-Facilitated Domestic Violence against Immigrant and Refugee Women: A Qualitative Study' (2021) 37(13–14) Journal of Interpersonal Violence NP12634

Hunter R, 'Narratives of Domestic Violence' (2006) 28 Sydney Law Review 733

Isadi M, 'Do We Need the Court of Appeal to Weigh in about the Importance of Internet Use in Modern Society?' 41(6) Law Now 55

Lazar RL, 'The "Vindictive Wife": The Credibility of Complainants in Cases of Wife Rape' (2015) 25(1) Southern California Review of Law and Social Justice 1

Maddocks S, 'From Non-consensual Pornography to Image-based Sexual Abuse: Charting the Course of a Problem with Many Names' (2018) 33(97) Australian Feminist Studies 345

Marques O, 'Intimate Image Dissemination and Consent in a Digital Age: Perspectives from the Front Line' in J Bailey, A Flynn, and N Henry (eds), *The Emerald International Handbook of Technology-Facilitated Violence and Abuse* (Emerald Publishing 2021)

McGlynn C, Rackley E, and Ruth H, 'Beyond "Revenge Porn": The Continuum of Image-based Sexual Abuse' (2017) 25(1) Feminist Legal Studies 25

Phillips S and Grattet R, 'Judicial Rhetoric, Meaning-Making, and the Institutionalization of Hate Crime Law' (2000) 34(3) Law and Society Review 567

Powell A and Henry N, 'Conceptualising Technosocial Harms' in A Powell and N Henry (eds), *Sexual Violence in a Digital Age* (Palgrave Macmillan 2017)

Powell A, Henry N, and Flynn A, 'Image-based Sexual Abuse' in W DeKeseredy and M Dragiewicz (eds), *Handbook of Critical Criminology* (Routledge 2018)

Powell A, Stratton G, and Cameron R, 'Liminal Images: Criminality, Victimisation and Voyeurism' in A Powell, G Stratton, and R Cameron (eds), *Digital Criminology: Crime and Justice in Digital Society* (Routledge 2018)

Powell A, Scott AJ, and Henry N, 'Digital Harassment and Abuse: Experiences of Sexuality and Gender Minority Adults' (2020) 17(2) European Journal of Criminology 199

Richie B, 'The Matrix: A Black Feminist Response to Male Violence and the State' in B Richie (ed), *Arrested Justice: Black Women, Violence, and America's Prison Nation* (New York University Press 2012)

Sandberg S and Ugelvik T, 'Why do Offenders Tape Their Crimes? Crime and Punishment in the Age of the Selfie' (2017) 57 British Journal of Criminology 1023

Schneider EM, 'The Violence of Privacy' (1991) 23 Connecticut Law Review 973

Slane A, 'Legal Conceptions of Harm Related to Sexual Images Online in the United States and Canada' (2015) 36(4) Child and Youth Services 288

Stark E, *Coercive Control: How Men Entrap Women in Personal Life* (OUP 2007)

Woodlock D, 'The Abuse of Technology in Domestic Violence and Stalking' (2017) 23(5) Violence against Women 584

Yardley E, 'Technology-Facilitated Domestic Abuse in Political Economy: A New Theoretical Framework' (2021) 27(10) Violence against Women 1479

PART VII

LAW ENFORCEMENT, PREVENTION, AND ALTERNATIVE JUSTICE STRATEGIES

17

Seeking Justice for Image-based Sexual Abuse

Examining the Possibilities of Restorative and Transformative Justice Approaches

Clare McGlynn

I. Introduction

In response to the growing prevalence of image-based sexual abuse, and increasing awareness that it can cause devastating and potentially life-threatening harms, governments around the world have introduced new laws criminalizing many forms of such abuse.[1] While such reforms are welcome, providing a vital foundation from which to challenge intimate image abuse, and offering the option of redress through criminal sanctions, the search for justice goes beyond criminal justice. This is because for some victim-survivors, the traditional criminal justice system is failing, with some police not taking reports seriously and sometimes

[1] The term 'image-based sexual abuse' is used here to include all forms of the non-consensual taking or sharing of intimate images, including threats to share and altered or manipulated images. For a discussion of this terminology and concept, see Clare McGlynn and Erika Rackley, 'Image-based Sexual Abuse' (2017) 37(3) Oxford Journal of Legal Studies 534. The terms image-based sexual abuse and intimate image abuse are used interchangeably in this chapter.

Clare McGlynn, *Seeking Justice for Image-based Sexual Abuse* In: *Criminalizing Intimate Image Abuse*. Edited by: Gian Marco Caletti and Kolis Summerer, Oxford University Press. © Oxford University Press 2024. DOI: 10.1093/oso/9780198877813.003.0017

blaming victims for their experiences.[2] Further, in many countries, the new criminal laws are resulting in few prosecutions or convictions, leaving victims feeling marginalized and not believed.[3] Not surprisingly, therefore, victim-survivors are looking outside of the conventional criminal justice system for redress. In addition, and even if criminal justice systems were working better to meet the interests of victims, some sexual violence survivors, including those who have experienced intimate image abuse, seek justice in a variety of ways and from a range of perspectives, including more innovative and additional processes of restorative and transformative justice. However, there is less legal and policy focus on such alternative or innovative justice mechanisms, giving victim-survivors few options when experiencing intimate image abuse.

The aim of this chapter is to examine the justice perspectives of those who have experienced various forms of intimate image abuse, setting these in the broader context of what we also know about the perceptions of sexual violence survivors more generally. In this light, it is argued that while criminal laws provide a vital foundation for challenging intimate image abuse, and criminal justice systems must be reformed to better meet victim-survivors' needs and interests, alternative and innovative justice mechanisms must be more swiftly and effectively advanced if victim-survivors' wide-ranging justice interests are to be met.

II. Victim-Survivors' Understandings of Justice

In examining justice responses in relation to intimate image abuse, and particularly the perspectives of victim-survivors, there are broadly three overlapping areas of research which can shine a light on this issue and that are the focus of this section. The first is research on the perspectives of sexual violence survivors, a group which may include those who are victims of image-based sexual abuse as many describe their experiences as forms of sexual assault.[4] Secondly, there is a much smaller body of work focusing on the perspectives of those who have specifically

[2] See Erika Rackley and others, 'Seeking Justice and Redress for Victim-Survivors of Image-based Sexual Abuse' (2021) 29 Feminist Legal Studies 293 (hereafter Rackley and others 'Seeking Justice').

[3] Nicola Henry and others, *Image-based Sexual Abuse: A Study on the Causes and Consequences of Non-consensual Nude or Sexual Imagery* (Routledge 2021) (hereafter Henry and others, *Image-based Sexual Abuse*).

[4] See Clare McGlynn and others, 'Shattering Lives and Myths: A Report on Image-based Sexual Abuse' (2019) <https://dro.dur.ac.uk/28683/3/28683.pdf?DDD34+DDD19+> accessed 30 January 2023 (hereafter McGlynn and others, 'Shattering Lives') and Rackley and others 'Seeking Justice' (n 2). In these studies, when explaining the impacts of intimate image abuse, many victim-survivors describe similar harms to those of sexual violence survivors, and often describe their experiences as a form of sexual offence or sexual assault. This understanding of intimate image abuse as a form of sexual offence is reflected in terminology adopted to describe these harms ('image-based *sexual* abuse'), as well as in the legal systems in some countries, such as Singapore.

experienced image-based sexual abuse. Thirdly, the perspectives of those who have been subject to online harassment more generally are considered.

A. Sexual Violence Survivors' Perspectives on Justice

In the broader context of sexual violence, what constitutes justice is most commonly assumed to be convictions and long prison sentences, secured through conventional criminal justice systems.[5] This approach has long represented the dominant understanding of justice in public and policy discourse: it frames debates and is deeply embedded culturally.[6] Nonetheless, the dominance of this approach, and its stranglehold on public discourse, has been challenged in recent years, as more and more studies have emerged where victim-survivors themselves are asked about what justice means to them.

This body of work on sexual violence survivors' perspectives on justice has found that their ideas of justice are complex and varied, beginning with Judith Herman's foundational study in the early 2000s.[7] She found that for sexual violence survivors, their view of justice was 'neither restorative nor retributive in the conventional sense'.[8] Their vision 'combined both elements in the service of healing a damaged relationship, not between the victim and offender but between the victim and his or her community'.[9] Around the same time, Shirley Jülich's study of adult survivors of child sexual abuse found that a common theme was a desire to 'tell their story in a safe forum', address underlying causes of offending, and, while survivors wanted to de-emphasize punishment, they still wanted consequences for the perpetrator.[10]

Subsequent studies have developed this growing recognition of the nuanced nature of justice interests, with Robyn Holder reporting that conventional theories of justice are 'insufficient to capture the complexity' of the 'contextualised thinking' underpinning women survivors' understandings of justice.[11] Justice, she has suggested, is a 'vibrant experience' that is 'layered, nuanced and contingent'.[12]

[5] David Garland, *Punishment and Modern Society: A Study in Social Theory* (University of Chicago Press 2012).

[6] Diane Martin, 'Retribution revisited: A reconsideration of feminist criminal law reform strategies' (1998) 36 Osgoode Hall Law Journal 36.

[7] Judith Herman, 'Justice from the Victim's Perspective' (2005) 11(5) Violence Against Women 571 (hereafter Herman, 'Justice').

[8] ibid 597.

[9] ibid.

[10] Shirley Jülich, 'Views of Justice among Survivors of Historical Child Sexual Abuse—Implications for Restorative Justice in New Zealand' (2006) 10(1) Theoretical Criminology 129.

[11] Robyn Holder, 'Satisfied? Exploring Victims' Justice Judgments' in Dean Wilson and Ross Stuart (eds), *Crime, Victims and Police* (Palgrave Macmillan 2015) 184–213, 205 (hereafter Holder, 'Satisfied?'). See also Robyn Holder, *Just Interests: Victims, Citizens and the Potential for Justice* (Edward Elgar 2018).

[12] Holder, 'Satisfied?' (n 11) 195.

Haley Clark found that the meanings of justice for sexual assault survivors had 'considerable variation',[13] with Kathleen Daly suggesting that this variation included participation, voice, validation, vindication, and 'offender accountability-taking responsibility' as essential components.[14] More recently, Hildur Fjola Antonsdóttir has conceptualized justice for survivors as a pluralistic and deconstructive force, emphasizing the '*continuum*' of injustice experienced by sexual violence survivors.[15] Further, research with black and minority ethnic survivors has emphasized that justice is contingent on survivors' intersecting identities, with Geetanjoli Gangoli and others finding that justice entails recognition and validation, including through formal criminal justice processes, adherence to human rights protections, as well as 'gender justice' through changes within families and communities.[16]

This more expansive notion of survivor-centred justice in cases of sexual violence, as opposed to only equating justice with punitive state actions, is reflected in my own work with Nicole Westmarland.[17] From our work with sexual violence survivors, we developed the concept of 'kaleidoscopic justice' to reflect their perceptions of justice as being a 'continually shifting pattern ... constantly refracted through new circumstances, experiences and understandings ... [with] multiple beginnings and possible endings'.[18] We found that survivors expressed many different ways of understanding a sense of justice, from securing consequences for the perpetrator, developing educational and prevention responses, and treating survivors with dignity and affording them recognition of the harms experienced. Justice also means that survivors feel that their experience is listened to, perceived as true, and recognized, and that victims can speak about their experiences and share them with others.[19]

[13] Haley Clark, 'A Fair Way to Go: Justice for Victim-Survivors of Sexual Violence' in Anastasia Powell, Nicola Henry, and Asher Flynn (eds), *Rape Justice: Beyond the Criminal Law* (Palgrave 2015) 18–35, 32–33.

[14] Kathleen Daly, 'Sexual Violence and Victims' Justice Interests' in Estelle Zinsstag and Marie Keenan (eds), *Restorative Responses to Sexual Violence—Legal, Social and Therapeutic Dimensions* (Routledge 2017) 108–39. See also Kathleen Daly, *Remaking Justice After Sexual Violence: Essays in Conventional, Restorative, and Innovative Justice* (Eleven International Publishing 2022).

[15] Hildur Fjóla Antonsdóttir, 'Injustice Disrupted: Experiences of Just Spaces by Victim-Survivors of Sexual Violence' (2019) 29(5) Social and Legal Studies 718.

[16] Geetanjali Gangoli, Lis Bates, and Marianne Hester, 'What Does Justice Mean to Black and Minority Ethnic (BME) Victims/Survivors of Gender-based Violence?' (2020) 46(15) Journal of Ethnic and Migration Studies 3119.

[17] Clare McGlynn and Nicole Westmarland, 'Kaleidoscopic Justice: Sexual Violence and Victim-Survivors' Perceptions of Justice' (2019) 28(2) Social and Legal Studies 179 (hereafter McGlynn and Westmarland, 'Kaleidoscopic Justice').

[18] ibid 186.

[19] This study drew on other work investigating alternative and innovative justice options. See Clare McGlynn, Nicole Westmarland, and Nikki Godden, '"I Just Wanted Him to Hear Me": Sexual Violence and the Possibilities of Restorative Justice' (2012) 39 Journal of Law and Society 213 (hereafter McGlynn, Westmarland, and Godden, 'I Just Wanted Him to Hear Me') and Nicole Westmarland and others, 'Using Restorative Justice Approaches to Police Domestic Violence and Abuse' (2018) 2(2) Journal of Gender-based Violence 339.

Taken together, these studies reveal that survivors' understandings of justice are neither driven by, nor reflective of, conventional criminal justice.[20] What stands out is the emphasis on complexity and nuance; on the variability of the justice interests, particularly across different intersecting identities; and on the challenge to commonly held assumptions that survivors only seek punitive outcomes. Indeed, it is interests in recognition of the harms experienced, of understanding leading to change, and of having a voice, that mark the justice perspectives of the sexual violence survivors.

B. Survivors of Image-based Sexual Abuse and the Search for Justice

The studies examined above consider the justice perspectives of those who have experienced many different forms of sexual and gender-based violence. As some survivors of intimate image abuse understand their experiences as a form of sexual assault, many of the themes identified above will likely echo the perspectives of intimate image abuse survivors.[21] Indeed, this appears to be borne out by the few studies emerging which address the specific question of what justice means to those who have experienced various forms of image-based sexual abuse.

The largest study to date of the experiences of survivors of intimate image abuse, examining the views of seventy-five survivors across Australia, New Zealand, and the UK, investigated this question of justice perceptions.[22] This study similarly found a complex, nuanced, and varied approach to what constitutes justice. Specifically, while almost all the survivors referred to the criminal justice system when considering what they understood as justice, it was equally evident that for most, this was just one route among many to securing justice, and for some, not an option at all.[23]

For example, Kimberly expressed her concern about the long-term consequences of engaging with the criminal justice system following her experience of intimate image abuse when her former partner took naked photos of her while she was sleeping without her consent. She reported that:

> [The criminal justice system] was never really on my radar.... Because ... he was what 20 at the time. And I thought I don't really know what could happen but

[20] For similar work focusing on intimate partner violence, see Michele Decker and others, 'Defining Justice: Restorative and Retributive Justice Goals among Intimate Partner Violence Survivors' (2022) 37(5–6) Journal of Interpersonal Violence 2844.

[21] As discussed above (n 2).

[22] For more detail on this study, and the justice issues in particular, see Henry and others *Image-based Sexual Abuse* (n 3); Rackley and others, 'Seeking Justice' (n 2); and McGlynn and others, 'Shattering Lives' (n 4).

[23] Rackley and others, 'Seeking Justice' (n 2).

> I just thought he's very young and actually the person who he is when he's 40 or 50 years old is probably not going to be that same person and is it worth ruining so much for him?[24]

Other survivors talked about a sense of justice coming from 'cultural change', identifying the need for widespread and bespoke education on the impact and effects of image-based sexual abuse.[25] Echoing the views of many, Heather commented:

> They're sharing it because they think it's a cool thing to do and [do] not realise the effect that it actually has on the person, and I think if they were more aware [that might change] ... even if it was just one of them that changed their view.[26]

Beyond criminal justice and educational change, what emerged from the survivors was a complex and varying picture of what constitutes justice, at the heart of which was a desire to ensure greater recognition of the wrongfulness of the abuse and the harms caused by their experiences. This often manifested itself as a wish for 'some kind of punishment, but not prison', possibly through more 'restorative' approaches, which were seen by some to be more effective (in terms of attitudinal change) than a prison sentence.[27]

Thus, some survivors spoke of wanting to convey to the perpetrator and others the full impact and harm of what had happened to them, often (but not always) with the hope that the perpetrator would take responsibility for what they had done. Mary, whose images were taken and shared on a group chat without her consent, commented: 'I think, looking back now, an apology would have been nice, or some ownership of, "Okay, I thought you would have been okay with that and I'm sorry, I should have asked." '.[28] Another survivor stated that she wished that 'someone had sat him down and said this is wrong'.[29]

This desire for understanding and recognition, leading to seeking more direct contact with perpetrators, was the action taken by some survivors. For Kimberly, this helped her to obtain 'closure':

> Maybe two years, three years [later], I sent him ... [a] WhatsApp message basically saying 'I know what you did. I want you to know that this is very wrong.... This is the impact it's had on me since.... I hope you haven't done it to anyone else. Don't do it to anyone else in the future.' And then ... [I said] 'I have genuinely

[24] ibid 312.
[25] ibid.
[26] ibid 314.
[27] ibid 313.
[28] ibid.
[29] ibid 312.

> forgiven you.' And it actually was such a release for me to be able to say that as well, which felt really good.... Within about five minutes, probably less than that, he'd sent me a response [in which he admitted it was wrong].[30]

Another survivor said that in retrospect she just wanted the perpetrator to 'realise that what he did was wrong and like have some kind of mediation where I could actually confront him about it and just tell him what he'd done and like how awful it made me feel and just make it clear to him like what he did was wrong and why it was wrong and what the consequences were of it'.[31] This echoes similar sentiments such as: 'An apology and confirmation that he deleted everything he had, would have been good. Some kind of reassurance that I'm not at risk anymore and that he knows he did something wrong.'[32]

In this way, ensuring greater understanding was central to many survivors' understandings of justice, with another stating that:

> I think then the most important thing would be has he actually properly thoroughly understood it and understood how much it affected me, and how gross it is and then that changed his view ... I would like him to have to actually face me ... so I can tell him how it has affected me.[33]

These perspectives, particularly the significance of recognition, as well as a fundamental interest in the perpetrator understanding the nature of the wrong and harm caused, are echoed in research with young people who have experienced intimate image abuse. Alexa Dodge and Dale Spencer found from their research with Canadian police officers that teenage victims were generally not interested in criminal justice responses, but rather were seeking alternatives such as image removal and educational work challenging discriminatory beliefs fuelling victim blaming and shaming.[34] Dodge, with Emily Lockhart, developed this work through an in-depth study with ten young people and some adults who work closely with young people around image-sharing practices.[35] Their study found that, in general, young people were extremely reluctant to engage in any formal responses to intimate image abuse due to a desire to avoid criminalizing their peers and seeing criminal justice interventions as an 'overreaction'.[36] Interestingly, those supporting young

[30] ibid 313.

[31] McGlynn and others, 'Shattering Lives' (n 4) 18.

[32] ibid.

[33] ibid.

[34] Alexa Dodge and Dale Spencer, 'Online Sexual Violence, Child Pornography or Something Else Entirely? Police Responses to Non-Consensual Intimate Image Sharing among Youth' (2018) 27(5) Social and Legal Studies 636.

[35] Alexa Dodge and Emily Lockhart, '"Young People Just Resolve It in Their Own Group": Young People's Perspectives on Responses to Non-consensual Intimate Image Distribution' (2021) 22(3) Youth Justice 304 (hereafter Dodge and Lockhard, 'Young People').

[36] ibid 314.

people were concerned by what they saw as their limited ability to effectively respond to problematic behaviours, favouring alternative responses such as restorative or transformative approaches.[37]

C. Justice and Redress for Online Harassment

While there are only a few studies examining the experiences of survivors of image-based sexual abuse specifically, the perspectives of those who have experienced online harassment more generally, which can include forms of intimate image abuse, can add to our understanding of justice perspectives. For example, a similar distrust by young people in formal legal responses was also evident from a review of a Canadian government agency which provided 'informal' responses to cyberbullying and some forms of intimate image abuse.[38] This study found that a vast majority of young people were not interested in engaging in legal processes, but rather emphasized image-removal and broader support. Actions such as informing offenders of the nature of the harm they have caused and outlining potential legal consequences were rarely sought. Interestingly, in such cases where contact was made with those perpetrating forms of abuse, the matter was resolved to the complainant's satisfaction and legal processes were neither required nor desired. As the report therefore noted, most cases are resolved 'without recourse to legal remedies (and that most complainants do not desire legal remedies) demonstrates the need for alternatives to legal responses'.[39]

Similarly, other research with young people who have experienced online harassment more generally found that, in terms of redress, they prioritized sensemaking, support and validation, and safety, before any retributive or transformative interventions.[40] Another study, while focusing on platform responses to harassment, reported that due to the perceived limitations of criminal justice processes, those who had experienced harassment were seeking alternative approaches that recognized systematic and structural power imbalances.[41] In addition, this study found that perceived desirable responses to online harassment varied considerably according to individuals' intersecting identities, with women,

[37] ibid 313.

[38] Alexa Dodge, *Deleting Digital Harm: A Review of Nova Scotia's CyberScan Unit* (Dalhousie University 2021).

[39] ibid 4.

[40] Sijia Xiao, Coye Cheshire, and Niloufar Salehi, 'Sensemaking, Support, Safety, Retribution, Transformation: A Restorative Justice Approach to Understanding Adolescents' Needs for Addressing Online Harm' (2022) CHI Conference on Human Factors in Computing Systems (CHI '22) 146, 1–15 <https://doi.org/10.1145/3491102.3517614> accessed 26 January 2023 (hereafter Xiao, Cheshire, and Salehi, 'Sensemaking').

[41] Sarita Schoenebeck, Oliver Haimson and Lisa Nakamura, 'Drawing from Justice Theories to Support Targets of Online Harassment' (2021) 23(5) New Media and Society 1278–300 (hereafter Schoenebeck, Haimson, and Nakamura , 'Justice theories').

for example, particularly less favourable towards mediation responses.[42] This complexity was also found in studies examining victims' responses to forms of redress from Internet platforms, finding that women were more inclined towards what the authors described as 'punitive' responses such as banning individuals, rather than more reparative measures.[43]

D. Survivors' Justice Perspectives

Overall, what this body of research suggests is that many of those who have experienced forms of sexual violence, intimate image abuse, and online harassment are seeking a variety of responses to their victimization, with formal, particularly criminal, legal responses generally low down on any priority list. Uppermost is recognition of the nature of the experience, understanding of the significance of the harm caused, as well as prevention and education of perpetrators and society more generally. Finally, while there is little specific naming of redress options such as restorative or transformative justice, many of the values embedded in such processes resonate with the perspectives shared by survivors.

III. Possibilities of Restorative and Transformative Justice

If alternatives to the conventional criminal justice system are being sought by survivors, the focus needs to shift to what such approaches and forms of justice might look like. Starting with the more commonly understood process, 'restorative justice', this may best be understood as a generic term to cover many different processes, all of which revolve around a common core, usefully defined by Tony Marshall as 'a process whereby all parties with a stake in a particular offence come together to resolve collectively how to deal with the aftermath of the offence and its implications for the future'.[44] The 'process' can take many different forms, from victim–offender mediation involving direct or indirect victim contact, as well as a common focus on restorative conferencing where the offender and victim meet face to face, together with other community and/or family supporters, with dialogue managed by a trained restorative justice facilitator. The overall rationale is a shift away from an adversarial process pitting victim against offender, towards a recognition of the harms and impacts on communities and society more generally.[45] The aim is not

42 ibid.

43 Im Jane and others, 'Women's Perspectives on Harm and Justice after Online Harassment' (2022) 6(2) Proceedings of the ACM on Human-Computer Interaction Article No 355, 1–23.

44 Tony Marshall, *Restorative Justice: An Overview* (Home Office 1999) 5.

45 John Braithwaite, *Restorative Justice and Responsive Regulation* (OUP 2002).

punishment, as conventionally understood in the criminal justice system, but reintegration of offenders, rehabilitation, and understanding.[46]

While restorative justice can take place entirely outside of criminal justice systems, it most often runs alongside such conventional processes. It can have a role, for example in sentencing or post-conviction rehabilitation. It is particularly common in youth justice processes, often involving diversion from conventional criminal justice processes. It is such close association with conventional criminal justice processes that led to the development of alternatives entirely outside such contexts, such as transformative justice.

Transformative justice, therefore, is an approach eschewing state-based criminal approaches, operating through grassroots organizations and typically with more radical aims of 'transforming' the community.[47] Transformative justice developed from the social movement aligned with prison abolition and, particularly in the context of gendered violence, abolition feminism, underpinned by the understanding that it is the conventional criminal justice system that is itself responsible for maintaining conditions of 'structural violence' particularly against marginalized communities.[48] Transformative justice responses and interventions, therefore, principally do not rely on the state and 'actively cultivate the things we know prevent violence such as healing, accountability, resilience, and safety for all involved'.[49]

Building on many of the principles and practices of restorative justice, transformative justice moved beyond formal mechanisms, and relationships with the state, to develop more informal, community-based approaches. Mimi Kim explains, for example, that transformative justice responses to gender violence seek resolutions with 'more intimate systems of community or civil society'[50] and rely on the leadership and interests of marginalized communities. The transformation explicitly recognizes that interpersonal violence takes place within the 'structural conditions of poverty, racism, sexism, homophobia, ableism and systemic forms of violence'.[51]

The values underpinning both approaches are similar and in the context of sexual violence and image-based sexual abuse, these mechanisms may provide

[46] Heather Strang and John Braithwaite (eds), *Restorative Justice and Family Violence* (Cambridge University Press 2001) (hereafter Strang and Braithwaite, *Restorative Justice*).

[47] Ejeris Dixon and Leah Lakshmi Piepzna-Samarasinha (eds), *Beyond Survival: Strategies and Stories from the Transformative Justice Movement* (AK Press 2020) (hereafter Dixon and Lakshmi Piepzna-Samarasinha, *Beyond Survival*).

[48] See Beth Richie, *Arrested Justice: Black Women, Violence and America's Prison Nation* (New York University Press 2012) and Angela Davis and others, *Abolition. Feminism. Now.* (Penguin Books 2022).

[49] Mia Mingus, 'Transformative Justice: A Brief Description', Transformharm.org <https://transformharm.org/tj_resource/transformative-justice-a-brief-description/> accessed 26 January 2023.

[50] Mimi Kim, 'From Carceral Feminism to Transformative Justice: Women-of-Color Feminism and Alternatives to Incarceration' (2018) 27(3) Journal of Ethnic and Cultural Diversity in Social Work 219, 226 (hereafter Kim 'Carceral Feminism').

[51] ibid 227.

valuable and meaningful participation for some in a justice process to an extent not possible in the conventional criminal justice system. These approaches may enable recognition and validation, as well as vindication—aspects that are usually absent from formal legal processes.[52] Herman found that survivors' most important objective was to gain validation by a 'denunciation of the crime' which 'transferred the burden of disgrace' to the offender.[53] This may mean that image-based sexual abuse survivors gain the recognition sought of the nature of what happened to them, its seriousness and its impact. These alternatives processes may encourage admissions of offending, offering validation; an acknowledgement of responsibility which, again, few gain through the criminal justice system.[54] For some survivors, this acknowledgement of responsibility can be very significant; for some, more so than levels of punishment measured by imprisonment. We also see this in the responses of those who have experienced intimate image abuse, with many expressing concern over the consequences of criminal interventions, yet seeking some consequences for what happened to them.

Further, restorative and transformative approaches may also enable us to hear survivors' stories more holistically, and to give voice to the real harm experienced, providing a form of hermeneutical justice. Particularly for image-based sexual abuse survivors, there is often a challenge naming what has happened to them as harmful, as their experiences are so often minimized or trivialized. Kathleen Daly and Danielle Wade compared restorative justice conferences with other mechanisms of justice and found that they fostered higher degrees of victim participation and voice.[55] An opportunity, therefore, to tell their story in their way, in an environment where they are heard, may provide a real sense of understanding and justice.

Justice mechanisms outside of the criminal justice process may also afford survivors greater control and decision-making, offering empowerment.[56] While Julie Stubbs reminds us that we must not assume that 'women who have been abused are well equipped to speak in their own interests',[57] for some a restorative process can be about 'taking back personal power' which can be an important part of the

[52] McGlynn, Westmarland, and Godden, 'I Just Wanted Him to Hear Me' (n 19).

[53] ibid 585.

[54] Nonetheless, an offender admission of responsibility is complex in that, as Julie Stubbs discusses, while an offender 'may admit his conduct, those words or behaviours may be minimized, neutralized or their significance may be opaque to others': Julie Stubbs, 'Beyond Apology? Domestic Violence and Critical Questions for Restorative Justice' (2007) 7 Criminology and Criminal Justice 169, 173.

[55] Kathleen Daly and Danielle Wade, 'Sibling Sexual Violence and Victims' Justice Interests: A Comparison of Youth Conferencing and Judicial Sentencing' in Estelle Zinsstag and Marie Keenan (eds), *Restorative Responses to Sexual Violence—Legal, Social and Therapeutic Dimensions* (Routledge 2017) 143–78.

[56] Barbara Hudson, 'Restorative Justice and Gendered Violence—Diversion or Effective Justice' (2002) 42 British Journal of Criminology 616.

[57] Julie Stubbs, 'Shame, Defiance and Violence Against Women' in Judith Bessant and Sandy Cook (eds), *Women's Encounters with Violence—Australian Experiences* (Sage 1997) 109–126, 122.

healing process.[58] Recent studies of intrafamilial abuse found that a restorative process enabled survivors and family members to make themselves 'heard, become empowered and grow towards recovery'.[59] More broadly, in focusing on community responses, rehabilitation, and change, these processes may lead to reduced offending and broader cultural changes.[60] As Kim suggests, transformative and innovative justice processes in 'elevating the voice of the victim or survivor' and addressing the harms caused, may enable better reintegration of 'all parties back into the community'.[61]

For all these reasons, restorative and transformative processes are being used in cases of domestic and sexual violence, as well as other forms of gendered and interpersonal violence.[62] However, this is not without challenge and controversy. Resistance is long-standing and first came from those who argued that it may trivialize violence against women, revictimize the vulnerable, and endanger the safety of victim-survivors. Angela Cameron, for example, has long argued that to introduce restorative justice is to 'gamble' with women's lives.[63] Similarly, Ruth Lewis and others have suggested that restorative conferencing is just another example of an attempt to 'divert' violence against women 'away from the justice system and into the hands of others'.[64] There is, however, often confusion as to the nature of restorative justice which contributes to some misguided criticisms. Sarah Curtis-Fawley and Kathleen Daly trace some of the scepticism over restorative justice for sexual violence back to concerns expressed by feminists in the 1990s over the use of civil mediation, especially in divorce.[65]

There are, however, key differences between civil mediation and restorative justice. Mediation necessarily involves *mediating* facts between individuals seeking to resolve a 'dispute', with the implication that no blame is apportioned. In contrast, restorative justice is predicated on an acknowledgement by the offender that a criminal offence has taken place.[66] The roles of 'victim' and 'offender' are, therefore,

[58] Kay Pranis, 'Restorative Values and Confronting Family Violence' in Strang and Braithwaite, *Restorative Justice* (n 43) 30.

[59] Carmit Klar-Chalamish and Inbal Peleg-Koriat, 'From Trauma to Recovery: Restorative Justice Conferencing in Cases of Adult Survivors of Intrafamilial Sexual Offenses' (2021) 36 Journal of Family Violence 1057.

[60] Kathleen Daly, 'Restorative Justice and Sexual Assault—an Archival Study of Court and Conference Cases' (2006) 46 British Journal of Criminology 334.

[61] Kim, 'Carceral Feminism' (n 50) 226.

[62] For detailed discussion of restorative justice and violence against women, see James Ptacek (ed), *Restorative Justice and Violence against Women* (OUP 2010); Strang and Braithwaite, *Restorative Justice* (n 43); and Marie Keenan and Estelle Zinsstag, *Sexual Violence and Restorative Justice* (OUP 2022) (hereafter Keenan and Zinsstag, *Sexual Violence and Restorative Justice*).

[63] Angela Cameron, 'Stopping the Violence' (2006) 10 Theoretical Criminology 49, 59.

[64] Ruth Lewis and others, 'Law's Progressive Potential: The Value of Engagement with the Law for Domestic Violence' (2001) 10 Social and Legal Studies 105, 123.

[65] Sarah Curtis-Fawley and Kathleen Daly, 'Gendered Violence and Restorative Justice—the Views of Victim Advocates' (2005) 11(5) Violence against Women 603, 607. See also Kathleen Daly and Julie Stubbs, 'Feminist Engagement with Restorative Justice' (2006) 10(1) Theoretical Criminology 9, 17–19.

[66] There will be different understandings of acceptance and understanding of, and responsibility for, the offending behaviour. Nonetheless, it can be argued that one aim of the restorative justice process is

clearly established: there is no fact-finding. In addition, resistance appears to assume that restorative practices only 'divert' cases away from the conventional justice system, thereby foreclosing any possibility of a conviction and conventional punishment. In fact, restorative justice can be used at many different stages of the criminal justice system, including pre-sentence, as part of a sentence and post-conviction, albeit that such links to the criminal justice system are opposed by those advocating transformative justice. Further, while restorative processes can also be used entirely separately from the criminal justice system, for example where there has been no police report,[67] the development of an extensive range of transformative justice projects and processes are operating entirely outside of the state justice system.

While controversy remains, Kim notes that dialogues between restorative justice, transformative justice, and 'mainstream anti-violence advocates' have begun to build alliances and understandings to identify areas of collaboration, resolution, and redress beyond conventional criminal justice systems.[68] As Leigh Goodmark comments, a victim-centred process attentive to the particular challenges posed by gender-based harms, such as restorative practices, can provide those who have been harmed with a sense of justice.[69]

Therefore, more projects are emerging with restorative processes and principles at their heart, including in areas of intimate partner violence.[70] There is a growing body of work, for example, investigating the use of restorative justice processes for domestic and sexual violence with the aim of shifting perceptions away from conventional justice approaches.[71] Further work emphasizes transformative justice processes providing the accountability and vindication survivors seek, but without the potentially harmful and traumatizing effects of criminal justice systems.[72]

to deepen the offender's understanding of the harm that they caused and therefore of the offender's responsibility: Shirley Jülich and others, 'Project Restore: An Exploratory Study of Restorative Justice and Sexual Violence' (2010) 38, <https://www.academia.edu/324795/Project_Restore_An_Exploratory_Study_of_Restorative_Justice_and_Sexual_Violence> accessed 26 January 2023

[67] eg Project Restore in New Zealand takes referrals from the community and individuals where there has been no police report. An evaluation of the project notes that in some cases this may be because of a reluctance to report family members to the police, but at the same time victim-survivors' having a strong need for a voice and a desire for some form of justice: ibid, 17 and 26. In non-report cases, offenders are urged to seek legal advice, and are reminded that while the process is confidential this cannot necessarily be guaranteed.

[68] Kim, 'Carceral Feminism' (n 50) 229.

[69] Leigh Goodmark, 'Restorative Justice as Feminist Practice' (2018) 1(3) International Journal of Restorative Justice 372.

[70] Joan Pennell and others, 'Family and Community Approaches to Intimate Partner Violence: Restorative Programs in the United States' (2021) 27(10) Violence against Women 1608.

[71] Keenan and Zinsstag, *Sexual Violence and Restorative Justice* (n 62); Kim, 'Carceral feminism' (n 50); Dixon and Lakshmi Piepzna-Samarasinha, *Beyond Survival* (n 47); Angela Davis and others, *Abolition. Feminism. Now.* (Hamish Hamilton 2022); and Eunilda Pali and Victoria Canning, 'Challenging Co-optive Criminalisation: Feminist-centred Decarceration Strategies for Interpersonal and Sexualised Violence' (2022) 61 Howard Journal of Criminal Justice 68.

[72] ibid.

IV. Conclusions

In relation to image-based sexual abuse, a growing body of work recognizing the limits of criminal justice responses, and the potential of more restorative and transformative approaches, is emerging. Dodge, for example, has written powerfully that, particularly from the perspective of young people, restorative processes may enable greater awareness and responses to victim-blaming and shaming among youth, peers, and families, helping both victims and communities to address these harms.[73] In canvassing such options, Dodge and Lockhart suggest nonetheless that 'much groundwork is needed to create a cultural context in which young people feel that they can seek adult support without being exposed to victim blaming and shaming or inciting a response that they perceive as an unhelpful overreaction'.[74] Rackley and others found that victims speak of an interest in 'some kind of punishment, but not prison', with the search continuing for what that might mean in practice.[75] McGlynn and others found that survivors, in seeking justice, typically focus on the need for greater recognition—from perpetrators and society more generally—possibly through more 'restorative' approaches which were seen by some to be more effective in terms of attitudinal change.[76] Similarly, Ashlee Hamilton suggests that transformative approaches may better deal with the cultural causes of image-based sexual abuse and therefore reduce harm more generally.[77]

Such possibilities are also being canvassed in relation to online harassment more broadly. Harder and Hasinoff suggest that studies of online abuse should pay greater attention to shame management, including how people blame digital technology for harmful behaviour, with restorative justice processes potentially being more productive in rehabilitating offenders and therefore repairing the harm.[78] In relation to online moderation processes specifically, Hasinoff, Gibson, and Salehi have proposed that restorative justice approaches focusing on repairing harms rather than punishment can improve content moderation.[79] Further, research by

[73] Alexa Dodge, 'Restorative Responses to the Rhizomatic Harm of Nonconsensual Pornography' in Anastasia Powell, Asher Flynn, and Lisa Sugiura (eds), *The Palgrave Handbook of Gendered Violence and Technology* (Palgrave Macmillan 2021). See also Alexa Dodge, 'Trading Nudes Like Hockey Cards: Exploring the Diversity of "Revenge Porn" Cases Responded to in Law' (2021) 30(3) Social and Legal Studies 448.

[74] Dodge and Lockhard, 'Young People' (n 35) 313.

[75] Rackley and others, 'Seeking Justice' (n 2) 313.

[76] McGlynn and others, 'Shattering Lives' (n 4) 18.

[77] Ashlee Hamilton, 'Is Justice Best Served Cold? A Transformative Approach to Revenge Porn' (2018) 25(1) UCLA Women's Law Journal 1.

[78] Sidsel Harder and Amy Hasinoff, 'Ashamed of Shaming? Stories of Managing, Deflecting, and Acknowledging Shame after Committing Image-based Sexual Abuse' (2021) 26(4) First Monday <https://doi.org/10.5210/fm.v26i4.11671> accessed 26 January 2023.

[79] Amy Hasinoff, Anna Gibson, and Niloufar Salekhi, 'The Promise of Restorative Justice in Addressing Online Harm' (27 July 2020) <https://www.brookings.edu/techstream/the-promise-of-restorative-justice-in-addressing-online-harm/> accessed 26 January 2023.

Xiao and others identified many actions Internet platforms could take to tackle online harassment and abuse that could potentially embed restorative justice values.[80]

Nonetheless, in responding to survivors' interests and examining alternatives, we must not pit restorative and transformative justice against conventional criminal justice in some sort of mirror of the adversarial process itself. Each process has its role; each has limitations. There are many survivors seeking criminal justice interventions and redress for the harm they have experienced. Others are seeking recognition and validation beyond criminal processes. Being attentive to the interests and voices of survivors means listening and acting on their varied, complex, kaleidoscopic justice interests. Indeed, there will be a role for working towards hybrid processes which may afford survivors the greatest opportunities and choices.

New processes to respond to image-based sexual abuse therefore need to be developed with survivors perspectives and interests to the fore. This includes reforming criminal justice systems so that they recognize the harms experienced, without causing further harm. It means helping survivors to 'reclaim control' of their images, bodies, lives, relationships, careers, physical, and mental health.[81] For many, reclaiming control, as well as understanding and recognition of their experiences, rather than punishment are primary concerns. As Rackley and others argue, therefore, what is required is an approach which provides a multi-stranded, multi-institutional, and multi-agency response that allows survivors to pursue simultaneously or consecutively one or more of a number of options within and beyond the criminal justice system.[82]

Bibliography

Antonsdóttir HF, 'Injustice Disrupted: Experiences of Just Spaces by Victim-Survivors of Sexual Violence' (2019) 29(5) Social and Legal Studies 78

Braithwaite J and Strang H (eds), *Restorative Justice and Family Violence* (Cambridge University Press 2001)

Braithwaite J, *Restorative Justice and Responsive Regulation* (OUP 2002)

Cameron A, 'Stopping the Violence' (2006) 10 Theoretical Criminology 49

Clark H, 'A Fair Way to Go: Justice for Victim-Survivors of Sexual Violence' in A Flynn, N Henry, and A Powell (eds), *Rape Justice: Beyond the Criminal Law* (Palgrave 2015)

Curtis-Fawley S and Daly K, 'Gendered Violence and Restorative Justice—the Views of Victim Advocates' (2005) 11(5) Violence against Women 603

Daly K, 'Restorative Justice and Sexual Assault—an Archival Study of Court and Conference Cases' (2006) 46 British Journal of Criminology 334

Daly K, 'Sexual Violence and Victims' Justice Interests' in M Keenan and E Zinsstag (eds), *Restorative Responses to Sexual Violence—Legal, Social and Therapeutic Dimensions* (Routledge 2017)

80 Xiao, Cheshire, and Salehi, 'Sensemaking' (n 40).
81 Rackley and others, 'Seeking Justice' (n 2).
82 ibid.

Daly K and Stubbs J, 'Feminist Engagement with Restorative Justice' (2006) 10(1) Theoretical Criminology 9

Daly K and Wade D, 'Sibling Sexual Violence and Victims' Justice Interests: A Comparison of Youth Conferencing and Judicial Sentencing' in M Keenan and E Zinsstag (eds), *Restorative Responses to Sexual Violence—Legal, Social and Therapeutic Dimensions* (Routledge 2017)

Daly K, *Remaking Justice After Sexual Violence: Essays in Conventional, Restorative, and Innovative Justice* (Eleven International Publishing 2022)

Davis A and others, *Abolition. Feminism. Now* (Penguin Books 2022)

Decker M and others, 'Defining Justice: Restorative and Retributive Justice Goals among Intimate Partner Violence Survivors' (2022) 37(5–6) Journal of Interpersonal Violence 2844

Dixon E and Piepzna-Samarasinha L (eds), *Beyond Survival: Strategies and Stories from the Transformative Justice Movement* (AK Press 2020)

Dodge A, 'Restorative Responses to the Rhizomatic Harm of Nonconsensual Pornography' in A Flynn, A Powell, and L Sugiura (eds), *The Palgrave Handbook of Gendered Violence and Technology* (Palgrave Macmillan 2021)

Dodge A, 'Trading Nudes Like Hockey Cards: Exploring the Diversity of "Revenge Porn" Cases Responded to in Law' (2021) 30(3) Social and Legal Studies 448

Dodge A and Spencer D, 'Online Sexual Violence, Child Pornography or Something Else Entirely? Police Responses to Non-Consensual Intimate Image Sharing among Youth' (2018) 27(5) Social and Legal Studies 448

Dodge A, *Deleting Digital Harm: A Review of Nova Scotia's CyberScan Unit* (Dalhousie University 2021).

Dodge A and Lockhart E, 'Young People Just Resolve It in Their Own Group': Young People's Perspectives on Responses to Non-Consensual Intimate Image Distribution' (2021) 22(3) Youth Justice 304

Flynn A and others, *Image-based Sexual Abuse: A Study on the Causes and Consequences of Non-consensual Nude or Sexual Imagery* (Routledge 2021)

Gangoli G, Bates L, and Hester M, 'What Does Justice Mean to Black and Minority Ethnic (BME) Victims/Survivors of Gender-based Violence?' (2020) 46(15) Journal of Ethnic and Migration Studies 3119

Garland D, *Punishment and Modern Society: A Study in Social Theory* (University of Chicago Press 2012)

Gibson A, Hasinoff A, and Salekhi N, 'The Promise of Restorative Justice in Addressing Online Harm' (27 July 2020) <https://www.brookings.edu/techstream/the-promise-of-restorative-justice-in-addressing-online-harm/> accessed 26 January 2023

Goodmark L, 'Restorative Justice as Feminist Practice' (2018) 1(3) International Journal of Restorative Justice 372–84

Hamilton A, 'Is Justice Best Served Cold? A Transformative Approach to Revenge Porn' (2018) 25(1) UCLA Women's Law Journal 1–45

Harder S and Hasinoff A, 'Ashamed of Shaming? Stories of Managing, Deflecting, and Acknowledging Shame after Committing Image-based Sexual Abuse' (2021) 26(4) First Monday <https://doi.org/10.5210/fm.v26i4.11671> accessed 26 January 2023

Herman J, 'Justice from the Victim's Perspective' (2005) 11(5) Violence against Women 571

Holder R, 'Satisfied? Exploring Victims' Justice Judgments' in R Stuart and D Wilson (eds), *Crime, Victims and Police* (Palgrave Macmillan 2015)

Holder R, *Just Interests: Victims, Citizens and the Potential for Justice* (Edward Elgar 2018)

Hudson B, 'Restorative Justice and Gendered Violence—Diversion or Effective Justice' (2002) 42 British Journal of Criminology 616

Im J and others, 'Women's Perspectives on Harm and Justice after Online Harassment' (2022) 6(2) Proceedings of the ACM on Human-Computer Interaction Article No 355, 1–23

Jülich S, 'Views of Justice among Survivors of Historical Child Sexual Abuse—Implications for Restorative Justice in New Zealand' (2006) 10(1) Theoretical Criminology 129

Jülich S and others, 'Project Restore: An Exploratory Study of Restorative Justice and Sexual Violence' (2010) <https://www.academia.edu/324795/Project_Restore_An_Exploratory_Study_of_Restorative_Justice_and_Sexual_Violence> accessed 26 January 2023

Keenan M and Zinsstag E, *Sexual Violence and Restorative Justice* (OUP 2022)

Kim M, 'From Carceral Feminism to Transformative Justice: Women-of-Color Feminism and Alternatives to Incarceration' (2018) 27(3) Journal of Ethnic and Cultural Diversity in Social Work 219

Klar-Chalamish C and Peleg-Koriat I, 'From Trauma to Recovery: Restorative Justice Conferencing in Cases of Adult Survivors of Intrafamilial Sexual Offenses' (2021) 36 Journal of Family Violence 1057–68

Lewis R and others, 'Law's Progressive Potential: The Value of Engagement with the Law for Domestic Violence' (2001) 10 Social and Legal Studies 105

Marshall T, *Restorative Justice: An Overview* (Home Office 1999)

Martin D, 'Retribution Revisited: A Reconsideration of Feminist Criminal Law Reform Strategies' (1998) 36 Osgoode Hall Law Journal 36

McGlynn C and Rackley E, 'Image-based Sexual Abuse' (2017) 37(3) Oxford Journal of Legal Studies 534

McGlynn C, and Westmarland N, 'Kaleidoscopic Justice: Sexual Violence and Victim-Survivors' Perceptions of Justice' (2019) 28(2) Social and Legal Studies 179

McGlynn C and others, 'Shattering Lives and Myths: A Report on Image-based Sexual Abuse (2019) <https://dro.dur.ac.uk/28683/3/28683.pdf?DDD34+DDD19+> accessed 30 January 2023

McGlynn C, Westmarland N, and Godden N, '"I Just Wanted Him to Hear Me": Sexual Violence and the Possibilities of Restorative Justice' (2012) 39 Journal of Law and Society 213

Mingus M, 'Transformative Justice: A brief Description', Transformharm.org <https://transformharm.org/tj_resource/transformative-justice-a-brief-description/> accessed 26 January 2023

Pali B and Canning V, 'Challenging Co-optive Criminalisation: Feminist-centred Decarceration Strategies for Interpersonal and Sexualised Violence' (2022) 61 Howard Journal of Criminal Justice 68

Pennell J and others, 'Family and Community Approaches to Intimate Partner Violence: Restorative Programs in the United States' (2021) 27(10) Violence against Women 1608

Pranis K, 'Restorative Values and Confronting Family Violence' in J Braithwaite and H Strang, *Restorative Justice* (Cambridge University Press 2002) 23

Ptacek J (ed), *Restorative Justice and Violence against Women* (Oxford University Press 2010)

Rackley E and others, 'Seeking Justice and Redress for Victim-Survivors of Image-based Sexual Abuse' (2021) 29 Feminist Legal Studies 293

Richie B, *Arrested Justice: Black Women, Violence and America's Prison Nation* (New York University Press 2012)

Schoenebeck S, Haimson O, and Nakamura L, 'Drawing from Justice Theories to Support Targets of Online Harassment' (2021) 23(5) New Media and Society 1278

Stubbs J, 'Beyond Apology? Domestic Violence and Critical Questions for Restorative Justice' (2007) 7 Criminology and Criminal Justice 169

Stubbs J, 'Shame, Defiance and Violence against Women' in J Bessant and S Cook (eds), *Women's Encounters with Violence—Australian Experiences* (Sage 1997)

Westmarland N, McGlynn C, and Humphreys C, 'Using Restorative Justice Approaches to Police Domestic Violence and Abuse' (2018) 2(2) Journal of Gender-based Violence 339

Xiao S, Cheshire C, and Salehi N, 'Sensemaking, Support, Safety, Retribution, Transformation: A Restorative Justice Approach to Understanding Adolescents' Needs for Addressing Online Harm' (2022) CHI Conference on Human Factors in Computing Systems (CHI '22)

18

The Changing Role of Internet Service Providers

Governing Cyberviolence and Online 'Hate Speech' against Women

Johanna Rinceanu

I. Introduction

The proliferation of high-speed broadband networks and the affordability of technical devices, such as computers, tablets, and smartphones, make it simple for users to own new technologies and access the Internet.[1] The twenty-first digital media century thus offers numerous outstanding opportunities for the protection and enforcement of human rights in this regard. It has never been easier for women to access the Internet at any time and become part of the new digital world order. One prominent example is the hashtag #MeToo movement, which started online on X (formerly, Twitter) and went viral instantly, in so doing sparking significant social and legal changes for millions of women around the world. The impact of social media has also recently been demonstrated by the current protest movement in Iran. In mid-2022,

[1] Europäisches Parlament, Generaldirektion Interne Politikbereiche der Union, Adriane van der Wilk, 'Cyber Violence and Hate Speech Online against Women' (European Parliament 2018), <https://data.europa.eu/doi/10.2861/738618> accessed 15 March 2023 (hereafter Wilk, 'Cyber Violence and Hate Speech Online against Women').

Johanna Rinceanu, *The Changing Role of Internet Service Providers* In: *Criminalizing Intimate Image Abuse*. Edited by: Gian Marco Caletti and Kolis Summerer, Oxford University Press.
DOI: 10.1093/oso/9780198877813.003.0018

numerous women joined an online campaign with the hashtag #No2Hijab—a response to the Islamic Republic's newly introduced 'National Day of Hijab and Chastity'. As an expression of their resistance, Iranian women posted photos and videos of themselves without headscarves in public under the hashtag #No2Hijab. The Iranian protest movement and its spread through social media was amplified after the death of a 22-year-old Iranian Kurdish woman in Tehran. She died in police custody after having been arrested and detained by the so-called morality police in mid-September 2022 because her headscarf apparently did not cover her hair according to regulations. Since then, people in Iran have been marching in the streets and spreading these images on the Internet. At the risk of their lives, they are raising their voices on social media against an oppressive regime and in support of human rights. There is no doubt that digital media has an inherent transformative power.

Despite a multitude of possibilities, however, the Internet harbours plenty of dangers. The distinction between reality and virtuality is becoming blurred, as '[we] no longer live online or offline but *onlife*'.[2] This newly created '... special space, or infosphere',[3] has changed our self-perception and the perception of others, which in turn impacts how we communicate with each other. Communication in the digital sphere has become noticeably harsher. Hardly a day goes by without reports of online 'hate speech', hate crime, so-called fake news, and disinformation. Abysses of prejudice, resentment, and fanaticism are emerging on the Internet, which spill over into the real world and possibly—although this has not yet been proven by studies—cause an initially verbal escalation to lead to racist, anti-Semitic, and right-wing extremist attacks.[4] Women, children, and the elderly, as well as politicians, human rights lawyers, human rights activists, and minorities, are affected by verbal escalations that mostly take place on social media. Women are particularly exposed to online hate and incitement, cyberviolence, doxing, sexist humiliation, revenge porn,[5] digital voyeurism, upskirting and downblousing,[6] and even rape

[2] See Luciano Floridi, 'Soft Ethics and the Governance of the Digital' (2018) 31 Philosophy and Technology 1.

[3] ibid.

[4] Jasper von Altenbockum, 'Die Gefahr von rechts' *Frankfurter Allgemeine Zeitung* (Frankfurt, 21 February 2020) 1. The violent terrorist act in Hanau (Germany), in which nine people with an immigration background were murdered, joins a series of racially motivated crimes, such as the National Socialist Underground murders, the assassination of Christian Democratic Union of Germany politician Walter Lübcke, and the attack on the Halle synagogue.

[5] This refers to cases in which a partner or former sexual partner publishes intimate videos or image files on social media. Usually these are pictures or videos that were taken or sent with consent during the relationship and intended exclusively for the eyes of the respective partner. For whatever reason, the intimate recordings are then published online. For an overview of the Italian criminalization of revenge porn in a comparative perspective, see Gian Marco Caletti, 'Can Affirmative Consent Save "Revenge Porn" Laws? Lessons from the Italian Criminalization of Non-Consensual Pornography' (2021) 25 Virginia Journal of Law and Technology 113.

[6] Upskirting and downblousing refer to the intentional and unauthorized filming or photographing of women under their skirts or other clothing or down their necklines. Section 184k of the German Criminal Code (StGB) criminalizes upskirting and downblousing as a violation of intimate body parts by taking photographs or other images. StGB s 184k determines that '(1) [w]hoever 1. intentionally

and death threats. In Europe, one in ten women has experienced some form of digital violence after the age of 15.[7]

Efforts by Internet Service Providers to combat hate crime and other unlawful online content against women by means of self-imposed Community Guidelines or Terms of Use have been underpinned by a plethora of legal frameworks, with a special focus on cyberviolence and online 'hate speech'—including non-consensual nudity sharing (revenge porn).

After a brief introduction to the phenomenon of an 'aggressive online debate culture' and the delineation of 'hate speech' as a striking example of it, this chapter provides an overview of key international and supranational action plans and conventions, recommendations, resolutions, on EU directives, guidelines, and regulations--particularly the recent enactment of the EU's DSA[8]--as well as on Germany's NetzDG,[9] which serves as an example of a national regulatory model. The chapter further reveals how the role of private Internet Service Providers has changed—against their will—as a result of current digital media regulations, which impose on them a role of gatekeeper at the threshold of fundamental and human rights.

II. Aggressive Online Debate Culture

An aggressive tone often characterizes the new debate culture taking place online ('*Verrohung der Debattenkultur*'[10]). This emerging online tone has numerous facets, ranging from intimidation, humiliation, degradation, and defamation to insults, harassment, threats of violence, and explicit killing and rape scenarios,[11]

or knowingly, without being authorised to do so, creates or transmits a photograph or other image of the genitals, buttocks, female breast of another person, or of underwear which is covering those parts of the body, insofar as those parts are protected from view, 2. uses or makes available to a third party a photograph or other image created through an act of the type set out in no. 1, or 3. makes available to a third party, in the awareness of lacking the authorization to do so, a photograph or other image of the type set out in no. 1 which was produced with authorization incurs a penalty of imprisonment not exceeding two years or a fine. (2) The offence is only prosecuted upon request, unless the prosecuting authority deems there to be a special public interest in prosecution which calls for ex officio intervention. (3) Subsection (1) does not apply to activities done by way of exercising overriding legitimate interests, namely those serving the arts or science, research or teaching, to report about current or historical events, or for similar purposes....'

[7] Wilk, 'Cyber Violence and Hate Speech Online against Women' (n 2) 10.

[8] See Regulation (EU) 2022/2065 of the European Parliament and of the Council of 19 October 2022 on a Single Market for Digital Services and amending Directive 2000/31/EC (Digital Services Act) [2022] OJ LI277/1 (Digital Services Act), available at <https://eur-lex.europa.eu/legal-content/EN/TXT/PDF/?uri=CELEX:32022R2065> accessed 15 March 2023 (hereafter DSA).

[9] Gesetz zur Verbesserung der Rechtsdurchsetzung in sozialen Netzwerken (Netzwerkdurchsetzungsgesetz--NetzDG) from 1 September 2017 (BGBl I p 3352), available at <https://www.gesetze-im-internet.de/netzdg/BJNR335210017.html> accessed 15 March 2023.

[10] BT-Drucks 18/12356, 13.

[11] Julia Fleischhack, 'Der "Hass" der vielen Formen' in Kai Kaspar, Lars Gräßler, and Aycha Riffi (eds), *Online Hate Speech—Perspektiven auf eine neue Form des Hasses* (kopaed verlagsGmbH 2017) 24.

especially against women. Women experience image-based sexual exploitation and are exposed and shamed by having private information researched, manipulated, and published without their consent (doxing[12]). Some women affected by doxing experience follow-up attacks in the real world.

A debate culture marked by aggressive, hurtful, and often hateful or unlawful online content together with a dramatic increase in online fake news, disinformation, and conspiracy narratives has led to an overall change in public discourse on social media. Under the semblance of anonymity, digital self-expression deteriorates into digital self-disentanglement.[13] The portrayal of violence combined with vulgar and demeaning language on social media contributes to a hazardous online environment and allows hate, particularly against women, to creep insidiously into the mainstream.

III. Cyberviolence and Online 'Hate Speech' against Women

'Hate speech' has become a global phenomenon. Yet, a legally binding international definition of 'hate speech' still does not exist. The lack of a legal definition is primarily due to the difficulty of distinguishing statements protected by the freedom of expression (free speech) from statements that fall under punishable 'hate speech'. The German Federal Constitutional Court (*Bundesverfassungsgericht*) has consistently emphasized that even sharp, exaggerated, polemical, hurtfully worded, and harmful statements, and even offensive and insulting speech, fall under the protection of freedom of expression.[14] The European Court of Human Rights likewise emphasizes that the human right to freedom of expression safeguards not only friendly, harmless, and positive statements but equally protects speech that 'offend[s], shock[s] or disturb[s] the State or any sector of the population'.[15] The Court highlights that '[f]reedom of expression constitutes one of the essential foundations of [a democratic] society'[16] and is one of the elementary 'conditions for its progress and for each individual's self-fulfillment'.[17] At the same time, the

[12] Doxing or doxxing comes from the English abbreviation *dox* and stands for documents. Doxing refers to the Internet-based collection and subsequent publication of personal data, usually with malicious intentions towards those affected.

[13] Barbara Kolany-Raiser and Lucas Werner, 'Fake News und Hate Speech' [2018] *ABIDA-Dossier* 1, note that the Internet 'lowers the threshold given the low risk of prosecution'. At the same time, however, they emphasize that anonymity on the Internet can also be stimulating for the exchange of opinions.

[14] Sebastian Müller-Franken, 'Netzwerkdurchsetzungsgesetz: Selbstbehauptung des Rechts oder erster Schritt in die selbstregulierte Vorzensur? – Verfassungsrechtliche Fragen' [2018] *AfP Zeitschrift für das gesamte Medienrecht* 2.

[15] *Handyside v United Kingdom* App no 5493/72 (ECHR, 7 December 1976) § 49. For recent commentary on this point, see Jacob Mchangama and Natalie Alkiviadou, 'Hate Speech and the European Court of Human Rights: Whatever Happened to the Right to Offend, Shock or Disturb?' (2021) 21 Human Rights Law Review 1008.

[16] *Handyside v United Kingdom* (n 16) § 49.

[17] *Gündüz v Turkey* App no 35071/97 (ECHR, 4 December 2003) § 37.

European Court of Human Rights stresses that, in democratic societies, it may nevertheless be deemed necessary to sanction or even prevent certain forms of expression that spread hatred based on intolerance, incite hatred, promote hatred, or justify hatred based on intolerance.[18]

It is commonly understood that online 'hate speech' of criminal relevance is derogatory, inhuman, and contains language of an inciting nature directed against *population groups* with certain characteristics. Perpetrators and victims do not usually know each other personally. Through 'hate speech', groups of people experience racism, anti-Semitism, anti-Muslim racism, sexism, homo-transphobia, antiziganism, ableism,[19] classism, lookism,[20] and ageism.[21] The list is not exhaustive, as there is virtually no human characteristic that cannot be made the object of hate.[22] Moreover, 'hate speech' also affects those groups that stand up for minorities and against misanthropy, such as journalists,[23] politicians, and human rights lawyers. 'Hate speech' as a *group-based* form of misanthropy and incitement to hatred on the Internet has an inherent message that aims to polarize society and can lead to attacks in the real world.[24]

Digital violence and online 'hate speech' against women as a population group is a gendered form of online violence that includes online harassment, cyberstalking, image abuse, and the aforementioned revenge porn and doxing, to name but a few examples. Online platforms where these various forms of 'hate speech' occur include social media platforms such as Facebook, X (formerly, Twitter), Instagram, LinkedIn; web content and discussion sites such as Reddit; search engines such as Google; messaging services such as WhatsApp, Facebook, Messenger, Snapchat, WeChat, and Skype; blogs; dating websites and dating apps; online forums such as 4chan; and online video game chat rooms.

Another form of digital violence—which should not be confounded with online 'hate speech'—is cyberbullying.[25] The latter refers to insulting, harassing, or humiliating comments against a *single person*, for instance against a *particular woman*.[26]

[18] *Erbakan v Turkey* App no 59405/00 (ECHR, 6 July 2006) § 56.

[19] 'Ableism' refers to discrimination against people with a physical or mental disability.

[20] For the different forms of 'hate speech', see, eg, Bundeszentrale für politische Bildung, 'Hate Speech—Gruppenbezoge Menschenfeindlichket im Netz' <https://www.bpb.de/shop/materialien/themenblaetter/270493/hate-speech-gruppenbezogene-menschenfeindlichkeit-im-netz/> accessed 15 March 2023 (hereafter Bundeszentrale für politische Bildung, 'Hate Speech').

[21] 'Ageism' refers to hostility towards the elderly as a form of social and economic discrimination.

[22] Jörg Meibauer, 'Hassrede—von der Sprache zur Politik' in Jörg Meibauer (ed), *Hassrede/Hate Speech—Interdisziplinäre Beiträge zu einer aktuellen Diskussion* (Gießener Elektronische Bibliothek 2013) 2.

[23] See Magdalena Obermaier, Michaela Hofbauer, and Carsten Reinemann, 'Journalists as Targets of Hate Speech: How German Journalists Perceive the Consequences for Themselves and How They Cope with it' [2018] Studies in Communication and Media 499.

[24] Bundeszentrale für politische Bildung, 'Hate Speech' (n 21).

[25] Matthias Felling, 'Cyber-Mobbing & Hate Speech—vom Umgang mit Online-Konflikten' [2017] JMS-Report 7.

[26] See Shreyas Mishra, 'Cyberbullying of Women' [2022] 2 Jus Corpus Law Journal 627.

Bullying in general is characterized by the prolonged, targeted harm of a specific person in the context of an imbalance of power between the perpetrator(s) and the victim. Bullying scenarios involve the perpetrator(s), the victim, and so-called bystanders, that is, individuals who support perpetrators as spectators or as actors themselves. Bullying becomes cyberbullying when the action takes place by means of digital media. Cyberbullying is thus understood to be any action by a person or group using digital media over a longer period of time to systematically cause harm or discomfort to another weaker person.[27] Specific characteristics of cyberbullying are the high degree of anonymity on the Internet combined with a high degree of publicity and seemingly endless victimization.[28] Two forms of cyberbullying are differentiated: verbal cyberbullying and psychological cyberbullying. The first category includes teasing, insults, and verbal abuse, while the second category refers to the spreading of rumours and lies online or the isolation and exclusion of a particular person from digital spaces, as well as the online dissemination of intimate photos and videos.[29]

Unlike 'hate speech', cyberbullying involves insults, harassment, and humiliation that are always directed at specific individuals and not at entire groups of people. Rather than humiliating specific groups of women, a specific woman is targeted. In the digital media age, cyberbullying has reached a new dimension—in terms of both quality and quantity—especially among young people.

In order to counter online hatred and incitement, racism, and xenophobia particularly against women—especially on social media platforms—international action plans have been drawn up, conventions concluded, and framework resolutions and guidelines adopted. In the following, some of the key international, supranational, and national regulations are illustrated in more detail.

IV. International and Supranational Regulations to Combat Online Hate and Incitement

In 2019, the United Nations (UN) developed a Strategy and Plan of Action on Hate Speech[30] in response to the currently alarming global trends towards xenophobia, racism, and intolerance, violent misogyny, anti-Semitism, and anti-Muslim hatred. The Plan of Action further strengthens efforts on the part of the United Nations and its 193 Member States to address the root causes and drivers of criminalized 'hate speech'. In doing so, the UN emphasizes that addressing 'hate speech' does

[27] See Catarina Katzer, *Cybermobbing—Wenn das Internet zur W@ffe wird* (Springer 2014) 58.

[28] ibid 60–61.

[29] ibid 62.

[30] See United Nations Strategy and Plan of Action on Hate Speech, available at <https://www.un.org/en/genocideprevention/documents/advising-and-mobilizing/Action_plan_on_hate_speech_EN.pdf> accessed 15 March 2023.

not mean restricting or banning free speech. 'It means keeping hate speech from escalating into something more dangerous, particularly incitement to discrimination, hostility and violence, which is prohibited under international law.'[31] In addition, there are several UN resolutions that address the issue of gender-based digital violence against women, such as the UN Human Rights Council resolution on accelerating efforts to eliminate violence against women and girls: preventing and responding to violence against women and girls in digital contexts adopted in 2018[32] and the UN Human Rights Council resolution on the promotion, protection and enjoyment of human rights on the Internet adopted in 2016.[33]

The Council of Europe has created a body of rules that enables its forty-seven Member States to act against digital violence and online 'hate speech' against women: the Budapest Convention on Cybercrime of 2001[34] and its Additional Protocol on the criminalization of acts of a racist and xenophobic nature committed through computer systems adopted in 2003, the Lanzarote Convention of 2007 on the protection of children against sexual exploitation and sexual abuse,[35] and the Istanbul Convention of 2011 on preventing and combating violence against women and domestic violence.[36]

The European Union, in its 2008 Council Framework Decision on combating certain forms and expressions of racism and xenophobia through criminal law, has ensured that certain serious manifestations of racism and xenophobia can be subject to effective, proportionate, and dissuasive criminal sanctions throughout the European Union. The Framework Decision also aims to improve and promote judicial cooperation in this area. In addition, in 2016, the European Union joined forces with four major Internet Service Providers (ie Facebook, Microsoft, X (formerly, Twitter), and YouTube) to introduce a code of conduct in order to effectively combat the spread of racist and xenophobic incitement online. The Internet Service Providers thereby committed to review requests to remove online content deemed unlawful within twenty-four hours and to, where necessary, remove the content, while always upholding the principle of freedom of expression. Other major Internet Service Providers have since also committed to this code of conduct, namely Instagram, Dailymotion, Snapchat, jeuxvideos.com, and TikTok.[37]

[31] ibid 1.

[32] See UN Human Rights Council resolution on accelerating efforts to eliminate violence against women and girls: preventing and responding to violence against women and girls in digital contexts (2018) <https://digitallibrary.un.org/record/1640463?ln=en> accessed 15 March 2023.

[33] See UN Human Rights Council resolution on the promotion, protection and enjoyment of human rights on the Internet (2016) <https://digitallibrary.un.org/record/845728> accessed 15 March 2023

[34] See Budapest Convention on Cybercrime of the Council of Europe [2001], available at <https://rm.coe.int/1680081561> accessed 15 March 2023.

[35] See the Council of Europe Convention on the Protection of Children against Sexual Exploitation and Sexual Abuse [2007], available at <https://rm.coe.int/1680084822> accessed 15 March 2023.

[36] See Council of Europe Convention on preventing and combating violence against women and domestic violence [2011], available at <https://rm.coe.int/168008482e> accessed 15 March 2023.

[37] For more information provided by Internet Service Providers about measures taken to counter 'hate speech', including their actions to automatically detect content, see <https://commission.eur

In December 2020, the European Commission delivered a proposal for a regulation of the European Parliament and of the Council on a Single Market for Digital Services (Digital Services Act, DSA) and amending Directive 2000/31/EC. The DSA entered into force on 16 November 2022 as Regulation (EU) 2022/2065.[38] Designed as a cornerstone by which to shape Europe's digital future, the DSA's overall aim is to create a safer digital environment in which the fundamental rights of all users are protected while simultaneously fostering innovation, growth, and competitiveness. These aims shall be achieved by establishing clear responsibilities and accountability for all private digital intermediaries providing services in the European Union. All such intermediaries have to comply with new transparency obligations, including, '... at least once a year, clear, easily comprehensible [online] reports on any content moderation'.[39] In addition, special requirements are introduced for a number of so-called very large online platforms and very large online search engines (with more than 45 million monthly active users in the European Union), such as a comprehensive annual risk assessment in relation to online harms caused by their services, for example related to illegal goods or content or the spread of disinformation. Under the DSA, very large online platforms and very large online search engines must also implement appropriate risk mitigation measures and subject their services and risk mitigation measures to independent review each year.

In order to better counter harmful online content, the DSA introduces a 'notice-and-action' mechanism[40] that requires private Internet Service Providers to offer an accessible and user-friendly procedure for users (ie any individual or entity) who wish to complain about illegal online content. What is considered illegal content, however, is not defined in detail. Rather, 'illegal content' is, according to Article 3 of the DSA, 'any information that, in itself or in relation to an activity, including the sale of products or the provision of services, is not in compliance with Union law or the law of any Member State which is in compliance with Union law, irrespective of the precise subject matter or nature of that law'. Notices of illegal content submitted by so-called trusted flaggers, '... acting within their designated area of expertise, ... are given priority and are processed and decided upon without undue delay'.[41] Internet Service Providers shall process any complaint that they

opa.eu/system/files/2022-12/Information%20provided%20by%20the%20IT%20companies%20about%20measures%20taken%20to%20counter%20hate%20speech%20%E2%80%93%202022.pdf> accessed 15 March 2023.

[38] DSA (n 9). According to Art 93(2), DSA shall apply from 17 February 2024.

[39] DSA (n 9) Art 15.

[40] ibid Art 16.

[41] ibid Art 22. 'Trusted flagger' status is awarded to (public, semi-public, non-governmental, or private) entities--not individuals--'... that have demonstrated ... that they have particular expertise and competence in tackling illegal content and that they work in a diligent, accurate and objective manner' (eg Europol, INHOPE). See ibid Preamble 61.

receive under the 'notice-and-action' mechanism in a timely, diligent, and non-arbitrary manner and decide whether to block, delete, or otherwise act with regard to the indicated content. Non-compliance of obligations enshrined in the DSA attracts fines.[42] In case of '... a suspicion that a criminal offence involving a threat to the life or safety of a person or persons has taken place, is taking place or is likely to take place' online, Internet Service Providers have to notify the law enforcement or judicial authorities of one or more Member States.[43]

In response to the rise of online 'hate speech' and hate crime across Europe, in December 2021, the European Commission additionally proposed extending the list of 'EU crimes' in Article 83(1) TFEU to 'hate speech' and hate crime as a new, distinct area of crime in its own right.[44] By extending the list of areas of 'EU crimes', the European Commission expects a common and coordinated criminal law approach against 'hate speech' and hate crime within the twenty-seven Member States of the European Union. The Member States currently tend to take a divergent and fragmented criminal law approach.

In March 2022, the European Commission proposed a directive which, for the first time, sets clear guidelines for the criminalization of acts categorized under the term digital violence.[45] This includes non-consensual dissemination of intimate recordings, cyberstalking, and online harassment. Among other things, it requires the twenty-seven Member States of the European Union to uniformly criminalize image-based violence (so-called revenge porn). The dissemination of intimate recordings without the consent of those shown is to be punished with at least one year of imprisonment. It is thereby irrelevant whether the persons concerned consented to the recordings at one point in time or even made and sent the images themselves. The decisive factor is whether they were disseminated against their will. This means that the directive would also cover cases in which the persons concerned have themselves sent images depicting nudity that are subsequently published on the Internet. The directive also covers the dissemination of manipulated images intended to make it appear as though someone is in a pornographic photograph. These so-called deepfakes[46] involve realistic-looking media content (photo, audio, and video content) that has been altered and distorted with the help of artificial intelligence. Lastly, the proposal provides for a takedown procedure, that is, a procedure that regulates when and how quickly potentially unlawful content must

[42] ibid Art 74, Preamble 117.

[43] ibid Art 18.

[44] See the Communication from the Commission to the European Parliament and the Council <https://commission.europa.eu/strategy-and-policy/policies/justice-and-fundamental-rights/combatting-discrimination/racism-and-xenophobia/extending-eu-crimes-hate-speech-and-hate-crime_en> accessed 15 March 2023

[45] See European Commission Proposal for a Directive of the European Parliament and of the Council on combating violence against women and domestic violence [2022] COM(2022) 105 final <https://eur-lex.europa.eu/legal-content/EN/TXT/PDF/?uri=CELEX:52022PC0105&from=EN> accessed 15 March 2023.

[46] The term 'deepfake' is a compound word made up of the terms 'deep learning' and 'fake'.

be deleted from the Internet, for example on social media or on pornography platforms. The directive still has to go through the legislative process in the European Union. Once the directive comes into force, the Member States have two years to implement the rules into national law.

Independently of the various above-mentioned regulations, national legislative initiatives already exist to combat racism and xenophobia, hatred, and incitement to hatred on the Internet. The digital world is not a lawless space. Laws that apply offline are equally applicable online.

In Germany, for instance, criminal offences that currently apply to 'hate speech' are Incitement of masses (Section 130 StGB), Insult (Section 185 StGB), Malicious gossip (Section 186 StGB), Defamation (Section 187 StGB), Malicious gossip and defamation in relation to persons in political life (Section 188 StGB), and Public incitement to commit offences (Section 111 StGB). Criminal offences applicable to cyberbullying include Coercion (Section 240 StGB), Threatening commission of serious criminal offence (Section 241 StGB), Stalking (Section 238 StGB), Bodily harm (Section 223 StGB), Violation of intimate privacy by taking photographs or other images (Section 201a StGB), Depictions of violence (Section 131 StGB), and violation of the right to one's own image (Sections 22, 23 KunstUrhG).

In October 2017, the German legislator also adopted an Act to Improve Enforcement of the Law in Social Networks (Network Enforcement Act, NetzDG) in order to more effectively combat hate and incitement as well as right-wing extremism on the Internet and in addition to independent efforts already undertaken by Internet Service Providers with self-imposed communication rules.

V. Germany's Network Enforcement Act (NetzDG)

The regulatory framework of NetzDG[47] makes the previously autonomous fight against online hate crime, 'hate speech', and fake news by providers of social networks and their self-imposed Community Guidelines or Terms of Use subject to legal provisions. NetzDG has been controversial since its coming into force.[48]

NetzDG is applicable to Internet Service Providers with more than two million registered users in Germany that operate, '. . . for profit-making purposes, . . . internet

[47] For a first introduction to the NetzDG, see Heidi Tworek and Paddy Leerssen, 'An Analysis of Germany's NetzDG Law' (2019) 1 Transatlantic Working Group <https://www.ivir.nl/publicaties/download/NetzDG_Tworek_Leerssen_April_2019.pdf> accessed 15 March 2023.

[48] For a critical review of the NetzDG, see Jacob Mchangama, 'The War on Free Speech: Censorship's Global Rise' (2022) 101 Foreign Affairs 117, 123–24; Johanna Rinceanu, 'Menschenrechte in der digitalen Krise' in Marc Engelhart, Hans Kudlich, and Benjamin Vogel (eds), Digitalisierung, Globalisierung und Risikoprävention: Festschrift für Ulrich Sieber zum 70. Geburtstag (Duncker & Humblot 2021) 831; Johanna Rinceanu, 'Verso una forma di polizia privata nello spazio digitale? L'inedito ruolo dei provider nella disciplina tedesca dei social network' in Mauro Cantenacci, Vincenzo Nico D'Ascola, and Roberto Rampioni (eds), *Studi in onore di Antonio Fiorella* (Roma Tre press 2021) 333.

platforms which are designed to enable users to share any content with other users or to make such content available to the public (social networks)'.[49] Internet Service providers having the size of Google, Facebook, YouTube, X (formerly, Twitter), and Instagram are affected, to name just a few. These Internet Service Providers are now legally obliged, as private stakeholders, to act against hate crime, fake news, and other unlawful content on their platforms. NetzDG sets binding standards for an effective and transparent complaint management system. Providers of social networks are required to offer users an easily identifiable, directly accessible procedure that is available at all times to submit complaints about unlawful content.[50] What is considered illegal content in this regard is strictly listed in NetzDG's catalogue of criminal offences.[51]

Individual user complaints must be noted by the Internet Service Providers immediately and checked for unlawfulness. Content that is manifestly unlawful must be deleted or blocked within twenty-four hours of receipt of the complaint. Other unlawful content (ie content that is not manifestly unlawful) must generally be deleted or blocked within seven days of receipt of the complaint or handed over to a recognized 'regulated self-regulation' institution[52] and subjected to its decision. Users must be informed of the outcome of their complaints.

The complaints management systems of the individual Internet Service Providers ensure transparency by complying with the obligation to regularly publish a report in German on the handling of complaints about unlawful content on their platforms, both in the German Federal Gazette and on their own homepages, every six months. If an Internet Service Provider violates its complaint management and reporting obligations by intentionally or negligently failing to set up a complaints management system, or by setting it up inadequately, by failing to eliminate organizational deficiencies, or by failing to comply with the legal requirements for complaint management over a considerable period of time,[53] it becomes subject to a fine. Fines for systematic non-compliance under NetzDG are severe and can reach up to 50 million Euros for corporate entities, and 5 million Euros for corporate officials.[54]

[49] See NetzDG s 1(1).
[50] See ibid s 3.
[51] See ibid s 1(3).
[52] See ibid s 3(6).
[53] See BT-Drucks 18/12356, 12.
[54] See NetzDG s 4. Prosecution of the owner of the company operating the social network is possible through the parallel application of OWiG s 130, provided that 'the infringement of the obligation to maintain an effective complaints management system or of the reporting obligation could have been prevented or made significantly more difficult by proper supervision'. Ultimately, a fine can be imposed on legal entities and associations of persons pursuant to OWiG s 30. Due to the reference to s 30(2) sentence 3 OWiG in NetzDG s 4(2), 'the maximum fine ... is increased tenfold for the offenses specified in the Act'. Since operators are usually legal entities, the fine range is thus de facto extended up to 50 million Euros. Guidelines on fines are intended to lead to greater transparency, based on the size of the network and the circumstances and consequences of the offence, but this is not done adequately.

Lastly, NetzDG imposes on Internet Service Providers the obligation to name a national person authorized to receive service (*inländischer Zustellungsbevollmächtigter*) and a national information officer (*inländische Auskunftsperson*) to deal with requests for information from a domestic law enforcement agency. Each Internet Service Provider must point these authorized contact persons out on its own platform in an easily recognizable and directly accessible manner. Violations of these obligations are also subject to fines.

Internet Service Providers must likewise provide information about the identity of the user to a person whose personal rights have been violated. NetzDG has created regulations to ensure that this right to information can also be enforced. Internet Service Providers are given the authority under data protection law to hand over the infringer's login data to the infringed party. However, the handover of data by the Internet Service Provider must be ordered by a judge at the competent civil court (*Richtervorbehalt*).

Since its entry into force, NetzDG has been further substantiated—and at the same time tightened—by two amendments in 2021. First, in April 2021, the Act to Combat Right-Wing Extremism and Hate Crime came into force. It introduced a proactive reporting obligation for Internet Service Providers. According to the reporting obligation, Internet Service Providers must transmit content reported to them in a complaint concerning unlawful content, and which has been removed or blocked by them, to the Federal Criminal Police Office (*Bundeskriminalamt, BKA*), in order to enable the prosecution of criminal offences. This transmission to the Federal Criminal Police Office must include the content and, if available, to facilitate a rapid identification of potential offenders, the IP address (including the port number) used by a certain user to share the content with other users or make it available to the public. The BKA subsequently identifies potential perpetrators and forwards the data to the relevant law enforcement authorities.

Second, the Act Amending the Network Enforcement Act (*NetzDGÄndG*), which came into force in June 2021, strengthened the rights of users on social networks. Users are able to take more effective action against decisions made by Internet Service Providers if there are differences of opinion regarding the deletion or retention of individual posts. In addition, in the future those affected by punishable posts, such as insults or threats, will be able to more easily assert their claims to obtain information against Internet Service Providers. Transparency about the practices of Internet Service Providers is achieved by making their reporting obligations more specific.

Germany's NetzDG is being superseded by the entry into force of the EU's Digital Service Act, which determines that EU Member States 'should not . . . maintain additional national requirements relating to the matters falling within [its] scope' in order not to undermine the harmonization of EU Internet regulation.[55]

[55] See DSA (n 9) Preamble 9.

However, NetzDG's concept of imposing on private digital platforms the primary responsibility for handling illegal online content ('notice-and-takedown' model) has inspired over twenty-five countries--and the European Union as well--to propose or adopt legislative acts that directly or indirectly follow NetzDG's example.[56]

VI. Concluding Remarks

As a global communication platform, the Internet offers a unique opportunity to instantly connect with people from all over the world and to attract attention. The vast majority of people use the digital space for legitimate purposes, but anti-human rights statements by groups and individuals also abound.

Digital violence, 'hate speech'--especially against women--fake news, and propaganda have become a steadily growing social problem. The last five years have presented Europe and the world with new challenges: migration crises, political upheavals, a rapid rise of populism--which is not only part of the problem but also a symptom--disinformation, the COVID-19 pandemic, and the war in Ukraine. These challenges have added to the increased sense of global insecurity and made the future even more unpredictable.

Unlawful online content must be countered resolutely, but, at the same time, adequately. In Germany, it is possible to act against unlawful online content with the help of the Criminal Code. Even before NetzDG or the DSA were enacted, Internet Service Providers were obliged to remove unlawful content as soon as they became aware of it, that is, without culpable hesitation. In addition, the providers have been acting against racism and xenophobia, hatred, and incitement to hatred on the Internet for some time by means of self-imposed communication rules, most recently by means of a code of conduct--in close cooperation with the European Commission, civil society organizations, and national authorities.

Whether NetzDG and its successor DSA represent further adequate means of combating hate and incitement on the Internet is, however, highly questionable. The human rights of various actors in the digital space are at risk. Users must fear for their freedom of expression, freedom of information, and freedom of artistic expression if Internet Service Providers block their content locally or delete it globally. In most cases this happens without first hearing out the authors of a deleted post or the owner of a blocked account or without providing them with suitable legal remedies. In addition, Internet Service Providers have been responsible for numerous encroachments on the right to informational self-determination as regards deletion, storage, and transmission obligations. These proceedings are not only to the detriment of content providers. Complainants, who are not necessarily

[56] See Jacob Mchangama and Natalie Alkiviadou, The Digital Berlin Wall: How Germany (Accidentally) Created a Prototype for Global Online Censorship—Act Two (Justitia 2020) 21.

the same as the violated person, must fear not only for their personal rights and privacy but also, for example, for their right to justice. Internet Service Providers, in turn, have cause to worry primarily about their professional freedom.

NetzDG and DSA largely transfer law enforcement to private stakeholders. In this way, the constitutional state circumvents its primary responsibility and alters the role of Internet Service Providers at the same time. In a domain in which the exact demarcation between permitted expression and prohibited or unlawful expression is unclear, and a careful weighing of constitutional interests is required, any legal assessment should not be carried out by private stakeholders, who pursue their own financial interests, but should be left to judges and thus to the rule of law. NetzDG and DSA push Internet Service Providers towards 'over-blocking' and 'over-filtering', and to some extent towards 'over-reporting'--phenomena that are to the detriment especially of freedom of expression. Internet Service Providers are made private guardians of opinion against their will.

In closing, the many conventional regulatory approaches have so far been lacking a coherent policy concept or a functioning strategy, as the root causes and drivers of cyberviolence, in general, and 'hate speech', in particular, are still obscure. Cyberviolence and 'hate speech' are symptoms of a serious societal disease.[57] We must first identify the disease before continuing to treat only its symptoms inadequately and before shifting law enforcement--and ultimately surveillance and censorship--to private stakeholders.

Bibliography

Caletti GM, 'Can Affirmative Consent Save "Revenge Porn" Laws? Lessons from the Italian Criminalization of Non-Consensual Pornography' (2021) 25 Virginia Journal of Law and Technology 113

Felling M, 'Cyber-Mobbing & Hate Speech—vom Umgang mit Online-Konflikten' [2017] JMS-Report 7

Fleischhack J, 'Der "Hass" der vielen Formen' in K Kaspar, L Gräßler, and A Riffi (eds), Online Hate Speech—Perspektiven auf eine neue Form des Hasses (kopaed verlagsGmbH 2017)

Floridi L, 'Soft Ethics and the Governance of the Digital' (2018) 31 Philosophy and Technology 1

Katzer C, *Cybermobbing—Wenn das Internet zur W@ffe wird* (Springer 2014)

Kolany-Raiser B and Werner L, 'Fake News und Hate Speech' [2018] ABIDA-Dossier 1–10

Mchangama J, 'The War on Free Speech: Censorship's Global Rise' (2022) 101 Foreign Affairs 117, 123

Mchangama J and Alkiviadou N, 'Hate Speech and the European Court of Human Rights: Whatever Happened to the Right to Offend, Shock or Disturb?' (2021) 21 Human Rights Law Review 1008

[57] Randall Stephenson and Johanna Rinceanu, 'Digital Iatrogenesis—Towards an Integrative Model of Internet Regulation' (2023) 1 eucrim 73; Johanna Rinceanu and Randall Stephenson, 'Diagnosing Digital Disease' [2022] MaxPlanckResearch 14.

Mchangama J and Alkiviadou N, *The Digital Berlin Wall: How Germany (Accidentally) Created a Prototype for Global Online Censorship—Act Two* (Justitia 2020)

Meibauer J, 'Hassrede—von der Sprache zur Politik' in J Meibauer (ed), *Hassrede/Hate Speech - Interdisziplinäre Beiträge zu einer aktuellen Diskussion* (Gießener Elektronische Bibliothek 2013)

Mishra S, 'Cyberbullying of Women' (2022) 2 Jus Corpus Law Journal 627

Müller-Franken S, 'Netzwerkdurchsetzungsgesetz: Selbstbehauptung des Rechts oder erster Schritt in die selbstregulierte Vorzensur?—Verfassungsrechtliche Fragen' [2018] AfP Zeitschrift für das gesamte Medienrecht 2

Rinceanu J, 'Menschenrechte in der digitalen Krise' in M Engelhart, H Kudlich, and B Vogel (eds), *Digitalisierung, Globalisierung und Risikoprävention: Festschrift für Ulrich Sieber zum 70. Geburtstag* (Duncker & Humblot 2021)

Rinceanu J, 'Verso una forma di polizia privata nello spazio digitale? L inedito ruolo dei provider nella disciplina tedesca dei social network' in M Catenacci, V Nino D'Ascola, and R Rampioni (eds), *Studi in onore di Antonio Fiorella* (Roma Tre press 2021)

Rinceanu J and Stephenson R, 'Diagnosing Digital Disease' (2022) MaxPlanckResearch 14–19

Obermaier M, Hofbauer M, and Reinemann C, 'Journalists as Targets of Hate speech: How German Journalists Perceive the Consequences for Themselves and How They Cope with it' [2018] Studies in Communication and Media 499

Stephenson, R and Rinceanu, J, 'Digital Iatrogenesis—Towards an Integrative Model of Internet Regulation' (2023) 1 eucrim 73

Tworek H and Leerssen P, 'An Analysis of Germany's NetzDG Law' (2019) Transatlantic Working Group 1–11

von Altenbockum J, 'Die Gefahr von rechts' *Frankfurter Allgemeine Zeitung* (Frankfurt, 21 February 2020)

van der Wilk A, 'Cyber Violence and Hate speech Online against Women' (European Parliament 2018) <https://data.europa.eu/doi/10.2861/738618> accessed 15 March 2023

19

An Empirical Research Study on Barriers, Facilitators, and Strategies to Promote Bystander Intervention in Intimate Image Abuse Contexts

Asher Flynn, Adrian J. Scott, and Elena Cama

I. Introduction

The increased accessibility of technologies has had many positive outcomes, including alleviating social isolation during COVID-19. However, the expansion of such technologies has also had unintended adverse outcomes, such as extending the reach and impacts of abusive behaviours.[1, 2, 3, 4] Intimate image abuse (IIA),

[1] Jane Bailey, Asher Flynn, and Nicola Henry (eds), *The Emerald International Handbook of Technology-Facilitated Violence and Abuse* (Emerald Publishing 2021).

[2] Elena Cama, 'Understanding Experiences of Sexual Harms Facilitated through Dating and Hook Up Apps among Women and Girls' in Jane Bailey, Asher Flynn, and Nicola Henry (eds), *The Emerald International Handbook of Technology-Facilitated Violence and Abuse* (Emerald Publishing 2021).

[3] Asher Flynn and others, 'Deepfakes and Digitally Altered Imagery Abuse: A Cross-Country Exploration of an Emerging Form of Image-based Sexual Abuse' (2022) 62(6) British Journal of Criminology 1341.

[4] Anastasia Powell and others, 'A Multi-country Study of Image-based Sexual Abuse: Extent, Relational Nature and Correlates of Victimisation Experiences' (2022) Journal of Sexual Aggression (hereafter Powell and others, 'A Multi-country Study of Image-based Sexual Abuse').

Asher Flynn, Adrian J. Scott, and Elena Cama, *An Empirical Research Study on Barriers, Facilitators, and Strategies to Promote Bystander Intervention in Intimate Image Abuse Contexts* In: *Criminalizing Intimate Image Abuse*.
Edited by: Gian Marco Caletti and Kolis Summerer, Oxford University Press. © Oxford University Press 2024.
DOI: 10.1093/oso/9780198877813.003.0019

also known as 'revenge pornography',[5] 'non-consensual pornography',[6] and image-based sexual abuse,[7] is one example of this harmful behaviour. We consider IIA to involve three main behaviours: the non-consensual taking or creation of nude or sexual images (taking/creating); the non-consensual sharing or distribution of nude or sexual images (sharing/distributing); and/or the threat to share or distribute nude or sexual images (threatening).

Research on IIA suggests that experiences of these behaviours are common and increasing.[8] In their survey of respondents aged 16 to 64 years across Australia ($n = 2{,}054$), New Zealand ($n = 2{,}027$), and the United Kingdom ($n = 2{,}028$), Powell and others reported that 38 per cent of respondents had experienced at least one form of IIA victimization, with the figures being comparable across the three countries (Australia, 35 per cent; New Zealand, 39 per cent; UK, 39 per cent).[9] Research has also shown that IIA disproportionately impacts gender and sexuality-diverse people, people with a disability, young people, and Indigenous and First Nations' people.[10, 11, 12]

Over the past decade, there has been greater attention paid to IIA in legal reforms, academic research, public discourse, and through the creation of new authorities to respond to IIA, such as the eSafety Commissioner in Australia, the Online Safety Commission in Fiji, and NetSafe in New Zealand. In Australia, specific offences to criminalize IIA have been introduced in all but one of eight state and territory jurisdictions,[13] and the Commonwealth government introduced laws to criminalize IIA at a federal level in 2018.[14] While the introduction of specific IIA

[5] Emma Bond and Katie Tyrrell, 'Understanding Revenge Pornography: A National Survey of Police Officers and Staff in England and Wales' (2021) 36(5–6) Journal of Interpersonal Violence 2166.

[6] Mary Anne Franks, '"Revenge Porn" Reform: A View from the Front Lines' (2017) 69 Florida Law Review 1252.

[7] Nicola Henry and others, *Image-based Sexual Abuse: A Study on the Causes and Consequences of Nonconsensual Nude or Sexual Imagery* (Routledge 2021) (hereafter Henry and others, *Image-based Sexual Abuse: A Study*).

[8] Anastasia Powell and others, 'Image-based Sexual Abuse: An International Study of Victims and Perpetrators' (RMIT University 2020) (hereafter Powell and others, 'Image-based Sexual Abuse: An International Study').

[9] Anastasia Powell and others, 'Image-based Sexual Abuse: Gendered Nature and Correlates of Victimisation in a Multi-Country Survey' (2022) Journal of Sexual Aggression <https://doi.org/10.1080/13552600.2022.2119292> accessed 3 March 2023 (hereafter Powell and others, 'Image-based Sexual Abuse: Gendered Nature').

[10] Asia A Eaton, Holly Jacobs, and Yanet Ruvalcaba, '2017 Nationwide Online Study of Non-consensual Porn Victimization and Perpetration: A Summary Report' (Cyber Civil Rights Initiative 2017) <https://www.cybercivilrights.org/wp-content/uploads/2017/06/CCRI-2017-Research-Report.pdf> accessed 3 March 2023.

[11] eSafety, 'Image-based Abuse: National Survey—Summary Report' (eSafety 2017) <https://www.esafety.gov.au/about-us/research/image-based-abuse> accessed 3 March 2023 (hereafter eSafety, 'Image-based Abuse').

[12] Powell and others, 'Image-based Sexual Abuse: An International Study' (n 8).

[13] Asher Flynn, 'Image-based Sexual Abuse' in Henry N Pontell (ed), *Oxford Research Encyclopedia of Criminology and Criminal Justice* (OUP 2022).

[14] Asher Flynn and Nicola Henry, 'Image-based Sexual Abuse: An Australian Reflection' (2021) 31(4) Women and Criminal Justice 313 (hereafter Flynn and Henry, 'Image-based Sexual Abuse').

laws is a positive step towards recognizing the impacts on victims, there remains limited understanding among Australians of the harms of IIA, the existence and scope of IIA laws, and where to find help.[15, 16, 17]

Support for, and intervention by, people who witness abusive behaviours—referred to as bystanders—may have the potential to reduce the extent and impacts of IIA behaviours, attitudes, and harms.[18, 19, 20, 21, 22] Research suggests that engaging bystanders to take action when they witness violence and discrimination can be an effective prevention tool.[23, 24, 25, 26] In this regard, bystanders could play a greater role in preventing IIA. Despite this, bystander intervention remains a relatively untapped area in IIA research and prevention.[27]

The aim of this chapter is to build on the existing bystander intervention theory and literature base[28, 29, 30] to better understand bystander intervention in relation to intimate image abuse. Utilizing data from thirty-five in-person focus groups with 219 participants in four Australian states/territories, this chapter explores barriers and facilitators to bystander intervention in intimate image abuse contexts, and

[15] Asher Flynn, Elena Cama, and Adrian J. Scott, 'Image-based Abuse: Gender Differences in Bystander Experiences and Responses' (2022) 656 Trends & Issues in Crime and Criminal Justice <https://doi.org/10.52922/ti78672> accessed 2 October 2023; eSafety, 'Image-based Abuse' (n 11).

[16] Nicola Henry, Asher Flynn, and Anastasia Powell, 'Responding to 'Revenge Pornography': Prevalence, Nature and Impacts. Report to the Criminology Research Council' (CRG 08/15–16, Australian Institute of Criminology 2019) <https://www.aic.gov.au/crg/reports/crg-0815-16> accessed 3 March 2023.

[17] Henry and others, *Image-based Sexual Abuse: A Study* (n 7).

[18] Asher Flynn, Elena Cama, and Adrian J. Scott, *Preventing Image-based Cybercrime in Australia: The Role of Bystanders. A Report to the Criminology Research Council* (AIC 2022) (hereafter Flynn, Cama, and Scott, *Preventing Image-based Cybercrime in Australia*); Julia Barlińska, Anna Szuster, and Mikołaj Winiewski, 'Cyberbullying among Adolescent Bystanders: Role of the Communication Medium, Form of Violence, and Empathy' (2013) 23(1) Journal of Community and Applied Social Psychology 37.

[19] Sandra Brochado, Sara Soares, and Sílvia Fraga, 'A Scoping Review on Studies of Cyberbullying Prevalence among Adolescents' (2017) 18(5) Trauma, Violence, and Abuse 523.

[20] Robin M Kowalski and others, 'Bullying in the Digital Age: A Critical Review and Meta-Analysis of Cyberbullying Research among Youth' (2014) 140(4) Psychological Bulletin 1073.

[21] Angeles Rebollo-Catalan and Virginia Mayor-Buzon, 'Adolescent Bystanders Witnessing Cyber Violence against Women and Girls: What They Observe and How They Respond' (2020) 26(15–16) Violence against Women 2024.

[22] Jiyeon Song and Insoo Oh, 'Factors Influencing Bystanders' Behavioral Reactions in Cyberbullying Situations' (2018) 78 Computers in Human Behavior 273.

[23] John Darley and Bibb Latané, 'Bystander Intervention in Emergencies: Diffusion of Responsibility' (1968) 8(4 Pt 1) Journal of Personality and Social Psychology 377 (hereafter Darley and Latané, 'Bystander intervention').

[24] John F Dovidio and others, *The Social Psychology of Prosocial Behavior* (Erlbaum 2006) (hereafter Dovidio and others, *The Social Psychology of Prosocial Behavior*).

[25] Deborah Gordon-Messer and others, 'Sexting among Young Adults' (2013) 52(3) Journal of Adolescent Health 301.

[26] Bibb Latané and John Darley, *The Unresponsive Bystander: Why Doesn't He Help?* (AppletonCentury-Croft 1970) (hereafter Lantané and Darley, *The Unresponsive Bystander*).

[27] See Flynn, Cama, and Scott, *Preventing Image-based Cybercrime in Australia* (n 18) for an exception.

[28] Darley and Latané, 'Bystander Intervention' (n 23).

[29] Latané and Darley, *The Unresponsive Bystander* (n 26).

[30] Dividio and others, *The Social Psychology of Prosocial Behavior* (n 24).

how messaging could be improved to promote safe and effective bystander intervention. We begin by briefly reflecting on relevant literature relating to bystander intervention and intimate image abuse, before outlining the methodology. We then discuss the main barriers and facilitators to intervention arising from focus group discussions of two hypothetical scenarios involving intimate image abuse incidents. One of the key findings from this research related to the role that gender plays in creating barriers and facilitators to intervention. Therefore, we present a section on the role of gender in facilitating and impeding bystander intervention, before concluding the chapter by discussing what mechanisms participants identified as potential ways to improve bystander intervention when witnessing intimate image abuse.

II. Bystander Research

Bystanders are people who witness an emergency or critical event, such as the perpetration of harmful behaviour against another person.[31] When bystanders take action to disrupt or prevent the critical event from occurring, this is known as bystander intervention. Bystander intervention has its theoretical origins in social psychology, and became a key research focus following World War II, when researchers sought to examine why people remained passive or did not intervene to prevent the Holocaust.[32] Researchers have since been interested in how bystanders respond in emergency situations, how their behaviours are influenced by the actions of other bystanders, the barriers and facilitators of intervention, and programmes that may help encourage intervention.

One theory on barriers to bystander intervention is known as the 'bystander effect',[33] which suggests that a person's likelihood of intervening when witnessing a critical event decreases when other bystanders are present. Darley and Latané[34] suggested that if an individual is alone and notices an emergency situation, they will feel a greater sense of responsibility to intervene than if there are other people present who could intervene in their place.[35, 36] These authors found three elements fuelling this effect: diffusion of responsibility, whereby the greater the number of bystanders present, the less personal responsibility a bystander will feel

[31] Ann Taket and Beth R Crisp, *Bystanders for Primary Prevention: A Rapid Review* (VicHealth 2017).

[32] Anastasia Powell, *Review of Bystander Approaches in Support of Preventing Violence against Women* (Victorian Health Promotion Foundation 2011).

[33] Darley and Latané, 'Bystander Intervention' (n 23).

[34] ibid.

[35] ibid.

[36] Bibb Latané and John Darley, 'Group Inhibition of Bystander Intervention in Emergencies' (1968) 10(3) Journal of Personality and Social Psychology 215 (hereafter Latané and Darley, 'Group Inhibition').

to intervene; evaluation apprehension, or fears of being judged or viewed negatively when intervening; and social influence, regarding how other bystanders will likely react.

In 1970, Latané and Darley introduced the five-step situational model of bystander intervention, whereby the bystander:[37] (1) notices a critical situation; (2) construes the situation as an emergency; (3) develops a feeling of personal responsibility; (4) believes they have the skills to successfully intervene; and (5) reaches a conscious decision to take action.[38, 39] Situational barriers at each of the five steps can prevent the bystander from intervening. Other researchers have suggested that bystanders will be more motivated to intervene if the situation arouses an emotional response, such as empathy, with the bystander intervening to alleviate these feelings by relieving the distress of the person/s directly impacted by the event.[40, 41, 42, 43] To do so, they may weigh the potential rewards (eg praise, compensation) against the potential costs of intervening (eg guilt if they do not intervene, personal harm, embarrassment).[44, 45, 46] Researchers suggest that bystanders will look to maximize the potential rewards and minimize the personal costs of intervening.[47]

There is limited evidence on the extent to which people witness or are bystanders to intimate image abuse, or the extent to which people take action to intervene when witnessing intimate image abuse.[48] In a representative survey of 4,248 US adults, the Pew Research Center found that 66 per cent of respondents had witnessed online harassment directed at others, and this was highest (86 per cent) among respondents aged 18 to 29 years.[49] Although 60 per cent of respondents felt that people who witness online harassment should step in, only 30 per cent said they had personally engaged in bystander intervention. In a nationally representative survey of 4,122 Australians, the eSafety Commissioner found almost one-fifth of respondents had been bystanders to intimate image abuse (19 per cent), but very few had taken action, with 44 per cent reporting that they did not say or do

[37] Latané and Darley, *The Unresponsive Bystander* (n 26).

[38] ibid.

[39] Latané and Darley, 'Group Inhibition' (n 36).

[40] Dividio and others, *The Social Psychology of Prosocial Behavior* (n 24).

[41] Jane A Piliavin and others, *Emergency Intervention* (Academic Press 1981) (hereafter Pilavin and others, *Emergency Intervention*).

[42] Sven C Voelpel, Robert A Eckhoff, and Jens Förster, 'David against Goliath? Group Size and Bystander Effects in Virtual Knowledge Sharing' (2008) 61(2) Human Relations 271.

[43] Sai Wang, 'Standing Up or Standing By: Bystander Intervention in Cyberbullying on Social Media' (2021) 23(6) New Media and Society 1379 (hereafter Wang, 'Standing Up').

[44] Dividio and others, *The Social Psychology of Prosocial Behavior* (n 24).

[45] Piliavin and others, *Emergency Intervention* (n 41).

[46] Wang, 'Standing Up' (n 43).

[47] ibid.

[48] See Flynn, Cama, and Scott, *Preventing Image-based Cybercrime in Australia* (n 18) for an exception.

[49] Maeve Duggan, 'Online Harassment' (Pew Research Center 2017) <https://www.pewresearch.org/internet/2017/07/11/online-harassment-2017/> accessed 3 March 2023.

anything, and 7 per cent reporting that they did not know what to say or do.[50] This corresponds with research that has examined people's perceptions of whether they would intervene in hypothetical scenarios, in comparison with actual bystander behaviour. Powell and others surveyed 6,109 respondents across Australia, New Zealand, and the United Kingdom about experiences and perpetration of intimate image abuse.[51] Respondents were asked a series of questions about bystander intervention, with 68 per cent reporting that they would say or do something to indicate their disapproval, or would like to say or do something (but did not know how), if another person showed or sent them a nude or sexual image of a third person without that person's consent. Among respondents who had witnessed intimate image abuse and reported having the opportunity to intervene, only 46 per cent said that they did so. Women were more likely than men to report that they would hypothetically intervene, and that they had actually intervened when witnessing intimate image abuse.

It is evident from these findings that more information, support, and guidance is needed on the available options for bystanders, and more research is needed to understand the barriers and facilitators to intervention.

III. Study Methodology

Focus groups (n = 35) were conducted in-person with a cohort of Australians aged 18 to 71 years across four locations: Adelaide (South Australia), Canberra (Australian Capital Territory), Melbourne (Victoria), and Sydney (New South Wales). Ethics approval was received from the Monash University Human Research Ethics Committee (project number: 17905). Funding for the project was received through a Criminology Research Council Grant (CRG02/19-20).

A. Recruitment

Flyers were created to advertise the research and direct interested parties to a project Facebook page and website. Members of the team sent the digital flyers to their professional contacts, including stakeholders, community leaders, academics, and community organizations. The team also distributed digital and hard copies of the flyer across university campuses, Facebook group pages and community noticeboards (eg local libraries, shopping centres), and advertised the project on their professional Twitter accounts. Finally, paid Facebook advertising was used to target potential participants who lived in the four focus group locations.

50 eSafety, 'Image-based Abuse' (n 11).
51 Powell and others, 'Image-based Sexual Abuse: An International Study' (n 8).

A project website was created providing study details; participation requirements; focus group dates, times and locations; and a link to register interest in participating. When a potential participant registered their interest, this information was sent to the project email, and a team member responded to confirm their preferred date, time, and location.

B. Sample

Thirty-five focus groups were conducted in-person between May and June 2019 across Adelaide (n = 60 participants), Canberra (n = 30 participants), Melbourne (n = 64 participants), and Sydney (n = 65 participants). These locations were selected as they had introduced specific intimate image abuse laws at the time the study was conducted.

All focus groups were conducted face-to-face in a central location (a university campus or public events space) and facilitated by two researchers. They had an average duration of sixty minutes, with no more than eight participants per focus group. Participants were provided with food and drink, and were compensated for their time with a $50 voucher.

C. Procedure

Each focus group included a discussion of two scenarios depicting different types of intimate image abuse, and questions pertaining to bystander information and resources (outlined below). There were two versions of each scenario: 1(a) and 2(a) were presented to eighteen focus groups, 1(b) and 2(b) were presented to seventeen focus groups.

Scenario 1a: Maryam (female, aged 21) has been seeing your friend Kai (male, aged 25) for about a week. Without any prior discussion, Maryam sends Kai a photo of herself completely naked. The next day, Kai shows the photo to a group of his friends (including you) during a broad discussion about sex.

Scenario 1b: Arjun (male, aged 25) has been seeing your friend Sarah (female, aged 21) for about a week. Without any prior discussion, Arjun sends Sarah a photo of himself completely naked. The next day, Sarah shows the photo to a group of her friends (including you) during a broad discussion about sex.

Scenario 2a: You are on a train sitting near a trans woman named Alex (who you don't know). She is wearing a t-shirt and a skirt and is 20 years old. A 30-year-old man named Lou (who you also don't know) is sitting opposite Alex. He tries to engage Alex in conversation, but it is clear she doesn't know him, so she ignores him.

Later, you see Lou using his iPhone to secretly take a photo up Alex's skirt. Alex doesn't know Lou has done this.

Scenario 2b: You are on a train sitting near a trans woman named Alex (who you don't know). She is wearing a t-shirt and a skirt and is 20 years old. A 30-year-old woman named Lou (who you also don't know) is sitting opposite Alex. She tries to engage Alex in conversation, but it is clear Alex doesn't know the woman, so she ignores her. Later, you see Lou using her iPhone to secretly take a photo up Alex's skirt. Alex doesn't know Lou has done this.

The variations were developed to explore whether participants' views differed according to the gender identity and/or the perceived racial, ethnic, and religious background of those depicted in the scenario. These decisions were made to respond to the clear gap in the literature on intimate image abuse involving trans and non-binary people,[52, 53, 54] and to explore some of the intersections of marginalization that have emerged as relevant in studies of intimate image abuse prevalence.[55, 56]

After reflecting on the scenarios, participants were asked four sets of questions divided into *action questions* (eg would you say or do anything in this situation? What would make you more/less likely to do something?); *context/intent questions* (eg would the relationship between or the intent of the perpetrator and/or victim affect whether you would say or do anything?); *responsibility questions* (eg to what extent is the victim responsible? Is the behaviour against the law?); and *gender-based questions* (eg would you feel differently if the perpetrator and/or victim were of the opposite gender?).

D. Analysis

The focus groups were audio-recorded and transcribed verbatim by an external transcription company, then checked for accuracy, and all identifying information was removed. The transcripts were then uploaded into NVivo version 12 (qualitative data analysis software) and analysed thematically. Participants were assigned a pseudonym based on the focus group number (eg FG1) and location attended (ie Adelaide [ADE], Canberra [CAN], Melbourne [MEL], Sydney [SYD]), their gender, if identified (ie Male [M], Female [F], Intersex [I]) and participant number (eg 1). For example, male participant one in the third focus group in Adelaide

52 Flynn and Henry, 'Image-based Sexual Abuse' (n 14).
53 Leah Juliett, 'Youth and LGBTQ Communities Disproportionately Victimized by Revenge Porn and Cyber Crimes' (Glaad 2017).
54 Powell and others, 'Image-based Sexual Abuse: Gendered Nature' (n 9)
55 ibid.
56 Powell and others, 'A Multi-country Study of Image-based Sexual Abuse' (n 4).

became FG3ADEM1, and female participant four in the fourth focus group in Sydney became FG4SYDF4.

IV. Results and Discussion

A. Barriers

When presented with the two scenarios, participants identified several barriers to bystander intervention. Primarily, these related to the nature of the relationship between parties; the perceived risk of intervening; the gender of all parties; and the perceived likelihood of receiving support from other bystanders. In scenario 2, several additional barriers were identified, including ambiguity around what had occurred, the victim's feelings, and power imbalances between the perpetrator and bystander, such as age and physicality.

1. Relationships

The 'nature of the friendship' (FG4ADEM2) between all parties was described by participants as impacting whether they would intervene. This was particularly so in scenario 1, where several participants felt that if there were people in the group who were closer friends with the person showing the image, then the responsibility for intervention should shift to them:

> If it was someone I wasn't as close to, I'd probably be a bit not sure what the boundaries were within that relationship. (FG10ADEF1)

> If I wasn't as close of a friend . . . I feel like it would be another person who's closer to that person—it would be their responsibility. (FG10ADEM2)

In addition to the relationship with the person showing the image, some participants said their relationship with the broader social group or the 'group dynamics' could impact their decision whether to intervene. In particular, participants felt it would be difficult to intervene if the group was largely supportive of the person showing the image:

> It's going to be dependent on the group dynamic as well, isn't it? So, if everyone is shocked and it seems like no-one knew what to do, or if everyone's just in the pub and having a laugh, then it's a bit confronting to say something. (FG5ADEM3)

In scenario 2, participants primarily discussed the nature of the relationship between the victim and perpetrator as impacting whether they would intervene. Participants were less likely to intervene if the victim and perpetrator knew each other or were friends. This was linked to the perceived ambiguity of the situation, where participants expressed confusion as to whether the incident might be normative to the friendship of the two people. As FG3ADEF2 reflected:

> If they were friends, it's sort of like, I'm going to ruin their friendship—even though he's already ruined it, because he took the photo. I think I'd find it a little harder to stand up to him, or even just pull her aside once she gets off the train, and be like, hey did you know he just did this? Or like, is this a thing, a friendship thing that you do? . . . Because she might take his side.

Receiving support from friends and other bystanders was also a key factor influencing intervention. Participants described that it might be 'daunting' (FG5ADEF5) to intervene if they were alone in scenario 2, whereas they might be more likely to take action if they were with friends or if there were other people present:

> If I'm on the train and I'm with my friends, I'll definitely say something because I know I'll have that support and they'll back me. But if you're on your own and it's just you against someone else, that's a bit more daunting. (FG5ADEF5)

> If there was anyone else around in the carriage, yes. If I was by myself, I would be less inclined to step up. (FG10SYDF1)

This reliance on others for support links with the next section exploring perceptions of safety and risk.

2. Safety and risk

In line with much research on bystander intervention,[57, 58, 59] participants recognized the potential cost of 'putting yourself in a position of risk' (FG1ADEM1) as a key barrier to intervention in both scenarios. However, the perceived risks varied between scenarios, with participants primarily identifying the social risks of intervening in scenario 1, and the potential personal or physical safety risks in scenario 2. In scenario 1, participants were conscious of how intervention might be perceived by their friendship group and any negative perceptions or consequences: being 'the one that deviates from the herd' or acts like the 'black sheep' (FG2CANF2) by intervening. The social risks included potentially negative reactions from the perpetrator, as well as from the broader social group if they supported the victim. Participants felt that intervening could result in being perceived

[57] Peter Fischer and others, 'The Bystander-Effect: A Meta-Analytic Review on Bystander Intervention in Dangerous and Non-dangerous Emergencies' (2011) 137(4) Psychological Bulletin 517.

[58] Sherry L Hamby and others, 'What Difference do Bystanders Make? The Association of Bystander Involvement with Victim Outcomes in a Community Sample' (2016) 6(1) Psychology of Violence 91.

[59] Jodie Lodge and Erica Frydenberg, 'The Role of Peer Bystanders in School Bullying: Positive Steps toward Promoting Peaceful Schools' (2005) 44(4) Theory into Practice 329.

as a 'killjoy' (FG5ADEF2) or 'the morality police' (FG3ADEF1). Participants also described the potential to lose the friendship, if the perpetrator was their friend, as a possible barrier.

Physical safety was not a dominant concern in scenario 1, as participants noted there would be a greater level of comfort from being in a group situation surrounded by friends. However, as the following comment reflects, some participants raised the issue of safety in relation to being surrounded by the perpetrator's friends, rather than their own:

> If I felt threatened or couldn't guarantee my safety for confronting Kai or even Kai's friends, if it was in a situation that I didn't feel [safe]—then that would be a big barrier. (FG7MELF3)

Personal or physical safety was repeatedly identified as a barrier in scenario 2. Many participants described needing to assess their own safety before intervening. These feelings were strongly influenced by participants' perceptions of the perpetrator. For example, where the perpetrator was perceived to be physically intimidating:

> I would say safety, I don't know if they're going to attack me.... I don't know if they're going to bash me.... You just don't know, so I'd be a bit worried about that. (FG1MELF1)

Perceptions of intimidation were largely linked to Lou's—the perpetrator's—physical appearance and age: 'It would depend on how big and threatening Lou looked' (FG2CNM1) and 'the fact that he's 30, and I'm 19, that's pretty scary' (FG3ADEF2). Others pointed to age as an indicator of authority and a clear power imbalance that would be difficult to overcome:

> The fact that Lou is so much older than me—like, I really quite struggle with standing up to authority, and people being my senior is a big thing for me: oh, they're older, they're the boss of you. I don't think I could have the strength to go up to a 30-year-old woman and say, 'Hey, what you're doing is wrong', as a 20-year-old girl. (FG6ADEF4)

B. Facilitators

When presented with the two scenarios, participants identified several facilitators to intervention related to the relationship between parties and the perceived likelihood of receiving support from other bystanders.

1. Relationships

Although participants commented on how the nature of the relationship between the bystander and perpetrator may create a barrier for intervention in scenario 1, they also commented on this as a potential facilitator. Participants were more likely to intervene if the perpetrator was a close friend due to a perceived reduction in risk to personal safety in the likelihood of a negative outcome:

> Friends are friends. You can say whatever and life is good. Like, there's that level of, like, trust or, like, unconditional love, friendship, a level, makes sense. With an acquaintance, it's kind of like you're kind of expendable. (F1FG7SYD)

Further, the perpetrator's attitude in scenario 1 was identified as a key facilitator, for example if they were making fun of the victim or overtly sexualizing them. Even where participants believed they would intervene, the type of intervention proposed differed according to the perpetrator's tone and attitude:

> If she's sort of like, maybe distressed about it or kind of in shock, like, 'Someone sent me this, I don't want to deal with it', she's sort of already upset about everything, I'd be a lot more gentle with my words.... But if she's sort of like laughing about it, like, 'Ha! Look at this dick pic! What a joke!', it's easier for me to be like, 'Hey, hey. Calm down. That's not really cool'. (FG2ADEF2)

In scenario 2, participants were asked whether their preparedness to intervene would change if Alex (the victim) was their friend. Overwhelmingly, participants said it would, with all participants indicating that it would increase their preparedness to intervene, whether that involved telling Alex the incident occurred or confronting the perpetrator. This was largely because participants believed they would need to defend their friend. Further, participants felt that knowing the victim would remove any uncertainty or ambiguity over whether the victim would want another person to intervene:

> I'd be more willing to, like, approach him [Lou] if it was, like, my friend that I was trying to defend and then if she didn't want me to, like, because then I could—because I would know her, I'd know how she would react and then I'd be, like, how much do you want me to be involved? (FG2SYDF1)

2. Support from others

Having support or potential backup from other bystanders was a key facilitator:

> If it's a pretty busy train and there's other people noticing as well, so it's not just me, that would give me more incentive to actually do something. (FG10ADEM1)

> If it was on a public train as well and others heard the conversation, I would hope that people with good morals would interject as well. (FG3MELF1)

Participants also described how having other people present would act as a deterrent for the perpetrator in continuing their behaviour or escalating the situation:

> I would say to someone else, if I was alone, another passenger, I'd be, like, 'Hey, this guy's being real[ly] creepy. Can you help me to intervene?' Because then it's kind of like the psychological thing for him, where there's more than one person confronting him, so then he feels uncomfortable and stops. (FG2ADEM2)

Others suggested that having other people present would be useful, as they may be compelled or feel pressured to intervene if another bystander took action:

> If it's a very quiet train, there's more risk that that person could snap or do something bad. But if it's packed, I think there would be pressure from other people who would help to stand up against them. (FG8SYDF2)

C. Gender Identity

Throughout the discussions, we sought to test whether the gender of bystanders, victims, and perpetrators was a consideration in intervention and the role it may play in a person's willingness to intervene. When explicitly asked about gender, participants consistently stated it would not change their response. However, in the broader discussions, gender was evidently a key barrier and facilitator to intervention. Gender influenced whether participants would feel comfortable or safe intervening, indicating that they would have greater safety concerns, and would be less likely to intervene, if the perpetrator was a man. As FG2SYDF2 explained, 'if [the perpetrator] was a man, I would not say a damn thing'. Others observed that 'you'd be more worried about Lou's reaction if it was a man' (FG10ADEF2), compared to 'if she's, like, a little woman, I wouldn't be so scared' (FG9ADEF3). In one focus group, there was universal agreement among the female participants that if the perpetrator was a man, it would prevent them from intervening:

> F1: For women, I don't want to generalise here though, but there are different issues with physical safety.
>
> F3: Yeah. We're more vulnerable, no matter what you say.
>
> F1: I certainly carry with me a fear of confronting men, because being a woman in a public space, and trying to take up any kind of public space, and to challenge men, can be incredibly risky. (FG3ADE)

These participants were less prepared to intervene if the perpetrator was a man because of their personal or physical safety concerns and having been socially conditioned to avoid risk with regard to men. This supports bystander research both offline and in cyberbullying incidents whereby bystanders report reacting differently according to their own gender.[60, 61, 62, 63]

In our study, male participants who were prepared to intervene generally said that they would do so regardless of Lou's gender. However, several male participants commented they would be less likely to intervene or would take a different action if Lou was a woman. As FG5ADEM5 observed, 'If it's a woman taking a photograph of another woman, I wouldn't intervene'. FG7SYDM2 similarly stated: 'I really don't think I would step in there. If it looked like it was a more aggressive dude taking a photo of a woman, I would be more concerned. But, like, two chicks, I'm, like, do whatever.' This shift in reaction according to gender reflects two main gendered assumptions. First, that it would be more challenging for a man to intervene effectively if the act was committed by a woman (based on a lack of confidence in having the appropriate skills to intervene), either because the intervention may become physical or that it was not the man's place to intervene:

> I would feel more confident confronting a guy, personally, because I know I can—I feel more confident being physical. (FG9ADEM3)

Second, there was disbelief among some participants that a woman would commit this type of behaviour, leading to a sense of ambiguity around the nature of the incident. As FG3CANM1 described:

> I'd be shocked, probably, because I would just not think it would be [done by a woman]. It's a thing that creepy men do.... That would be really strange if it was a case of that.

This view was not restricted to male participants, with several female participants expressing 'shock' over the switching of the perpetrator's gender in scenario 2:

60 Sara Bastiaensens and others, 'Cyberbullying on Social Network Sites: An Experimental Study into Bystanders' Behavioural Intentions to Help the Victim or Reinforce the Bully' (2014) 31 Computers in Human Behavior 259.

61 Marie-Louise Obermann, 'Moral Disengagement among Bystanders to School Bullying' (2011) 10(3) Journal of School Violence 239.

62 Insoo Oh and Richard J Hazler, 'Contributions of Personal and Situational Factors to Bystanders' Reactions to School Bullying' (2009) 30(3) School Psychology International 291.

63 Virpi Pöyhönen, Jaana Juvonen, and Christina Salmivalli, 'Standing Up for the Victim, Siding with the Bully or Standing by? Bystander Responses in Bullying Situations' (2012) 21(4) Social Development 722.

> It's a woman? That's the other thing that I was shocked at, that it was actually a female taking photographs. I'm used to men [doing this], but not women. (FG8SYDF4)

One group (FG1MEL) reflected on how the gender of the perpetrator might affect the support they would receive from other bystanders:

M1: You'd get more support if there were people on the train if it was a male taking a photo of a female.... You know, asking for that help from bystanders or eyeballing people, I think you'd get a lot more support if it was a male taking the picture.
M2: Yeah, correct.

Similarly, gender was a barrier to intervention in scenario 1, however, this was connected to the gendered make-up of the group, as well as of the perpetrator. FG7ADEF2 reflected:

> If it was a group of female friends, you might be a little bit more inclined to pipe up and say something. Whereas if it's a bunch of guys going, 'Ha ha, look at this!' you feel a bit awkward.

FG9ADEM1 observed:

> If it's a group of really kind of, like, alpha males, I would definitely not say anything because I myself would feel threatened.

The perceived difference in how male versus female friends would react to being shown a non-consensual nude image was a strong theme to emerge across all focus groups.

Gendered perceptions also impacted participant responses in scenario 1 regarding the perceived motivations of the perpetrator for taking or sharing the image. Overwhelmingly, when the perpetrator was a man, participants felt the motivation was to sexualize the victim, to boost the perpetrator's standing among their peers, and to 'brag' about their dating conquest. When the perpetrator was a woman, the motivation was to laugh at or humiliate the victim, or to indicate distress at receiving the image.

Several participants reflected on the 'vulnerability of being a woman' (FG1ADEF1), in terms of either receiving an unsolicited nude image from a man or being the subject of that image, as a factor that would influence their decision-making:

M1: Maybe it's more of a bragging thing or something if a guy's sharing the image. I tend to see the woman as the more vulnerable person in that scenario.
F1: You can't ignore the wider context of culture and things, and I think the woman probably, even if she sent it unsolicited herself ... I think she probably is more vulnerable having her naked photo out there than a man is. (FG4ADEF2)

Similar findings have emerged in the small number of studies that have explored attitudes towards non-consensual image sharing.[64, 65, 66, 67] In Scott and Gavin's study, for example, when presented with two hypothetical scenarios—one with a male perpetrator and female victim and one with a female perpetrator and male victim—participants perceived the scenario involving the male perpetrator and female victim to be more serious.[68]

Across the focus groups, very few participants believed that a man would share a non-consensual image because they were distressed or seeking support, or that a woman would be bragging or sexualizing the person in the image. This contrasts with recent research among perpetrators of intimate image abuse which shows little difference in motivations between genders. In their study of 1,070 respondents who reported engaging in intimate image abuse, Powell and others found no significant difference between men and women, with the most common motivation for intimate image abuse behaviours being for 'fun' or to be 'sexy'.[69] Similarly, despite focus group participants in our study suggesting men would be motivated by impressing their friendship group or sexualizing the person and women would be motivated by distress, Powell and others found no significant difference between the motivations of male and female perpetrators with regard to wanting to impress friends.[70]

In scenario 2, the victim's gender identity was a barrier and facilitator. Some participants felt they would be more likely to confront the perpetrator because of the challenges and discrimination experienced by trans women:

[64] Sarah Bothamley and Ruth J Tully, 'Understanding Revenge Pornography: Public Perceptions of Revenge Pornography and Victim Blaming' (2018) 10(1) Journal of Aggression, Conflict and Peace Research 1.

[65] Heather K Hudson, Joyce V Fetro, and Roberta Ogletree, 'Behavioral Indicators and Behaviors Related to Sexting among Undergraduate Students' (2014) 45(3) American Journal of Health Education 183.

[66] Afroditi Pina, James Holland, and Mark James, 'The Malevolent Side of Revenge Porn Proclivity: Dark Personality Traits and Sexist Ideology' (2017) 8(1) International Journal of Technoethics 30.

[67] Adrian J Scott and Jeff Gavin, 'Revenge Pornography: The Influence of Perpetrator–Victim Sex, Observer Sex and Observer Sexting Experience on Perceptions of Seriousness and Responsibility' (2018) 8(2) Journal of Criminal Psychology 162.

[68] ibid.

[69] Anastasia Powell and others, 'Perpetration of Image-based Sexual Abuse: Extent, Nature and Correlates in a Multi-Country Sample' (2022) 37(23–24) Journal of Interpersonal Violence 22864.

[70] ibid.

> I'd do something. My instinct would be to give a loud dressing down of his behaviour because it's fucking disgusting, and particularly just the dynamics of the genders and stuff, and all the oppression against transwomen in particular would just make me think, that is so not on. You'd try to intervene in that situation to stop him doing that immediately. (FG3CANM1)

> Being transgender too, because they cop enough harassment, enough stigma, enough everything—that's so completely inappropriate. If I saw anything like that, I'd call it out. (FG1SYDM1)

There was also a common concern raised around the motivation for this abuse being fuelled by discrimination:

> Another part of the issue is that she is transgender. So, knowing a lot of people who are trans who have experienced a lot of this stuff, it's not so much just sexual, it's also pointing out that someone is different. (FG4SYDF2).

For others, reflecting on the marginalization and discrimination the victim may have experienced in her life was a reason not to tell them what had happened:

> Alex is a transwoman. As a member of that community, as a minority, I feel like she already experiences—or would be struggling enough. So, I would want to spare her that extra burden [of telling her]. (FG3SYDF2)

Participants often responded that they would prefer to find a way to tell the victim, as opposed to confronting Lou, and to ask 'her [the victim] how she wanted it handled' (FG8MELF2). Participants described wanting to tell the victim so they could make a decision about intervention:

> A transperson can already feel incredibly visible, and may not want to be seen in the way of you yelling that this creeper is taking a photo of them. So, I might try to get to them first, and just say, because it's great being an ally, but it's not always the case that other people want you to speak for them. So, to just say, 'I have observed this, would you like me to do anything?' I will do something, I will do what you want though. (FG3ADEF1)

> You might not want to create a bigger scene. It's up to Alex, because it's quite humiliating already, and being a transwoman would be difficult anyway.... She might not necessarily want more attention drawn to her. (FG8MELF2)

Gender identity was also recognized as a key reason why participants would not contact the police, or encourage the victim to contact the police, unless they wanted to. In the latter case, several participants noted that they would 'definitely go with Alex to the police, because sending a trans woman alone to the police is potentially dangerous' (FG10MELM1). Others expanded on this view, stating that 'police can be pretty violent against transpeople and wouldn't necessarily believe her.... The police might be more likely to harass [her]' (FG10SYDM2). FG3CANM1 similarly commented on this potential discrimination:

> I would not tell a police officer or a ticket inspector or something, but that's mainly based on my opinion about them being awful people that abuse lots of minorities, in particular transpeople. So, I would think that getting them involved wouldn't be something I would be [up] for. I think the decision's up to Alex, but it wouldn't be something that I would jump to do.

These comments are reflective of much of the literature on trans people's experiences with police.[71, 72, 73, 74, 75] For example, Langenderfer-Magruder and others found that transgender people were significantly less likely to report experiences of intimate partner violence to police than cisgender persons because of doubts that they would be treated fairly or taken seriously.[76] Fear and mistrust of police have also been identified as key factors that impact on trans and gender-diverse people's likelihood to report to police.[77, 78, 79] Serpe and Nadal's study of 266 participants (n = 66 cisgender male, n = 147 cisgender female, n = 53 transgender) found that transgender people reported lower levels of comfort interacting with police; higher levels of police victimization, discrimination and bias; and more negative perceptions of police than cisgender persons.[80]

[71] Alliance for a Safe & Diverse DC, *Move Along: Policing Sex Work in Washington, D.C.—A Report by the Alliance for a Safe & Diverse DC* (Different Avenues 2008).

[72] Alan Berman and Shirlee Robinson, *Speaking Out: Stopping Homophobic and Transphobic Abuse in Queensland* (Australian Academic Press 2010).

[73] Jaime M Grant and others, *Injustice at Every Turn: A Report of the National Transgender Discrimination Survey* (National Center for Transgender Equality and National Gay and Lesbian Task Force 2011).

[74] Tania Israel and others, 'Evaluation of Police Training on LGBTQ Issues: Knowledge, Interpersonal Apprehension, and Self-Efficacy' (2013) 29(2) Journal of Police and Criminal Psychology 1.

[75] Toby Miles-Johnson, 'Policing Diversity: Examining Police Resistance to Training Reforms for Transgender People in Australia' (2016) 63(1) Journal of Homosexuality 103.

[76] Lisa Langenderfer-Magruder and others, 'Experiences of Intimate Partner Violence and Subsequent Police Reporting among Lesbian, Gay, Bisexual, Transgender, and Queer Adults in Colorado: Comparing Rates of Cisgender and Transgender Victimization' (2016) 31(5) Journal of Interpersonal Violence 855.

[77] Rebecca Campbell and Sheela Raja, 'Secondary Victimization of Rape Victims: Insights from Mental Health Professionals Who Treat Survivors of Violence' (1999) 14(3) Violence and Victim 261.

[78] Eric Silver and Lisa L Miller, 'Sources of Informal Social Control in Chicago Neighborhoods' (2004) 42(3) Criminology 551.

[79] Barbara D Warner, 'Directly Intervene or Call the Authorities? A study of Forms of Neighborhood Social Control within a Social Disorganization Framework' (2007) 45(1) Criminology 99.

[80] Christine R Serpe and Kevin L Nadal, 'Perceptions of Police: Experience in the Trans* Community' (2017) 29(3) Journal of Gay and Lesbian Social Services 280.

D. Improving Bystander Intervention Messages

Participants discussed the ways in which messaging could be improved to increase the likelihood of bystander intervention in intimate image abuse contexts and better inform the actions people take when witnessing intimate image abuse. Participants felt messages should be readily accessible, and not, as FG1ADEF2 described them, 'something you have to search for'. This view was common: 'It's about putting it in people's heads in case they're a bystander one day' (FG1ADEM2). Participants also highlighted the need for messages to be clear, 'concise', and 'something everyone could see at different places.... It needs to say, this is illegal, you can't do it, it can happen, this is where you can go or where you can tell people to go if it happens' (FG1ADEM1). FG6ADEF2 similarly noted the benefits of 'having a universal message spread around about the behaviour never being okay and that you can do something'.

Participants were strongly of the view that any messaging directed towards bystanders should provide guidance on what to do. This reflected some of the concerns that participants discussed in the scenarios, in that they were often unsure what types of action would be appropriate and what sources of support were available.

> It has to help them to understand that it is the right thing to do, to do something and here's what you can do. Because sometimes in a situation that you see something wrong is happening, it's very hard to quickly figure out what to do. So, if you've seen a video or something, it can come into your mind and you can be like, 'Oh, I'll do this'. (FG2ADEM3)

> It should show you what to do in the moment when it's happening, and then what to do after it's happened, like who to report it to. (FG3CANF4)

Some participants identified the need for clear messages around responsibility, and the idea that harms should be addressed and responded to by everyone:

> It's everyone's responsibility. It isn't just about empowering victims, it isn't just about letting perpetrators know that it's not okay. It is about this idea that it's everyone's problem. The behaviour you walk by is the behaviour you accept. (FG1ADEM2)

This idea of a shared social responsibility for harms caused to individuals was also reflected in some of the ideas proposed for the content of educational messaging:

You could just have something for people that would show what would happen if they intervene when something happened, but then if they didn't and ... show [the] adverse consequences. (FG3CANF2)

M1: It could have bystanders just standing there doing nothing, while something would happen. And then it would show the consequences of that. And then it would say some kind of tagline or something about helping out.
M2: Yeah, 'It's a dick move to share someone's dick pics'. (FG2ADE)

It was evident from the discussions that participants wanted guidance on how to respond, what to say and how to act, and needed this to be communicated concisely both online and in other public settings. Participants felt strongly that such messaging should be presented in a format that you 'can't just skip through' (FG1ADEM2), citing how most people skip through advertisements on platforms like YouTube. Participants also suggested that any messaging should be presented across multiple platforms.

At the conclusion of the discussion, many participants reflected that they would now be more likely to intervene in intimate image abuse contexts, should the environment be safe, because they felt better equipped with the necessary skills:

> I feel like I know what to do and how to respond if someone is a victim of it. And like, I have a guide for acceptable behaviour, like, 'This is what should be done, when you're in this position' (FG2ADEM5).

These findings highlight the importance of clear, effective awareness messaging that aims to empower bystanders to safely intervene when and where appropriate, by providing the requisite tools and information to do so. Further, effective educational messaging on intimate image abuse, particularly messaging that responds to the barriers to bystander intervention, will not only increase awareness, but will help challenge the cultural attitudes that normalize and downplay its seriousness.

V. Conclusion

Overall, we found that bystander intervention was affected by perceptions of safety and the potential risks of intervening; gender; perceptions of how the intervention would be perceived by the perpetrator and other bystanders; relationships; the age, physicality, and mental state of the perpetrator; and the presence of others. In this regard, Latané and Darley's[81] and Piliavin and others'[82] psychological process models were useful in understanding participant responses, as there were clear crossovers with their findings around the diffusion of responsibility, evaluation apprehension, and social influence, as well as cost-benefit assessments of intervention. However, there were some clear deviations, particularly in scenario 2, where

[81] Piliavin and others, *Emergency Intervention* (n 41).
[82] Latané and Darley, *The Unresponsive Bystander* (n 26).

more bystanders being present increased the preparedness and perceived likelihood of participants intervening.

When asked explicitly about gender, participants consistently stated it would not change their response. However, throughout discussions, gender was frequently discussed as influencing the likelihood of intervention. Participants, particularly female participants, generally indicated that they would have greater safety concerns and would be less likely to intervene if the perpetrator was a man. However, some male participants commented that they would be less likely to intervene or would intervene differently if the perpetrator was a woman, reflecting two main gendered assumptions. First, that men perceived it to be more challenging to intervene effectively if the act is committed by a woman, and second, that participants found it harder to believe that a woman would commit this type of offending behaviour, despite evidence that women do indeed perpetrate intimate image abuse.[83] Gendered assumptions also influenced perceived motivations for the non-consensual sharing of an intimate image, with participants suggesting men were motivated by the desire to brag or sexualize the person in the image, and women were motivated because they were distressed or seeking support. Participants found it more challenging to believe that a man might be distressed or seeking support, even though research indicates that men experience and are impacted by intimate image abuse.[84] Further, participants discussed how they would be more likely to confront the perpetrator when the victim is a trans woman, as well as the need to ask them how they would like the situation to be handled, because of the challenges and discrimination they may experience. These challenges also impacted on the likelihood of contacting the police as there was a perception that going to the police is potentially dangerous, because they may aggravate rather than assuage the situation.

Regarding the provision of appropriate messaging, some common suggestions emerged, namely that any messaging needs to make clear that intimate image abuse is a crime and that is not tolerated in society, together with examples of appropriate types of intervention to help guide bystanders. It was also argued that messaging must move away from blaming the victim to holding the perpetrator accountable for their behaviour,[85] and shifting more of the responsibility to avoid, diffuse, or control the situation to bystanders. These shifts are vital in both confirming the importance of bystander intervention and challenging problematic cultural attitudes within society that minimize the harms of intimate image abuse or attribute responsibility to victims.

[83] Powell and others, 'A Multi-country Study of Image-based Sexual Abuse' (n 4).

[84] Powell and others, 'Image-based sexual abuse: An International Study' (n 8).

[85] Asher Flynn and others, 'Victim-blaming and Image-based Sexual Abuse' (2023) 56(1) Journal of Criminology 7.

Intimate image abuse is a serious problem that requires a multifaceted response. Part of this response must be the development of education campaigns around the laws, supports, and remedies available for those who experience intimate image abuse and those who witness it. It is vital that any campaigns include prevention education for perpetrators to actively discourage intimate image abuse and highlight its harms and consequences, alongside education on how bystanders can safely and effectively intervene and/or support victims when witnessing intimate image abuse.

Bibliography

Bailey J, Flynn A, and Henry N (eds), *The Emerald International Handbook of Technology-facilitated Violence and Abuse* (Emerald Publishing 2021)

Barlińska J, Szuster A, and Winiewski M, 'Cyberbullying among Adolescent Bystanders: Role of the Communication Medium, Form of Violence, and Empathy' (2013) 23(1) Journal of Community and Applied Social Psychology 37

Bastiaensens B and others, 'Cyberbullying on Social Network Sites: An Experimental Study into Bystanders' Behavioural Intentions to Help the Victim or Reinforce the Bully' (2014) 31 Computers in Human Behavior 259

Berman A and Robinson S, *Speaking out: Stopping Homophobic and Transphobic Abuse in Queensland* (Australian Academic Press 2010)

Bond E and Tyrrell K, 'Understanding Revenge Pornography: A National Survey of Police Officers and Staff in England and Wales' (2021) 36(5–6) Journal of Interpersonal Violence 2166

Bothamley S and Tully RJ, 'Understanding Revenge Pornography: Public Perceptions of Revenge Pornography and Victim Blaming' (2018) 10(1) Journal of Aggression, Conflict and Peace Research 1

Brochado S, Soares S, and Fraga S, 'A Scoping Review on Studies of Cyberbullying Prevalence among adolescents' (2017) 18(5) Trauma, Violence, and Abuse 523

Cama E, 'Understanding Experiences of Sexual Harms Facilitated through Dating and Hook Up Apps among Women and Girls' in J Bailey, A Flynn, and N Henry (eds), *The Emerald International Handbook of Technology-facilitated Violence and Abuse* (Emerald Publishing 2021)

Campbell R and Raja S, 'Secondary Victimization of Rape Victims: Insights from Mental Health Professionals Who Treat Survivors of Violence' (1999) 14(3) Violence and Victim 261

Darley J and Latané B, 'Bystander Intervention in Emergencies: Diffusion of Responsibility' (1968) 8(4 Pt 1) Journal of Personality and Social Psychology 377

Dovidio JF and others, *The Social Psychology of Prosocial Behavior* (Erlbaum 2006)

Fischer P and others, 'The Bystander-Effect: A Meta-Analytic Review on Bystander Intervention in Dangerous and Non-dangerous Emergencies' (2011) 137(4) Psychological Bulletin 517

Flynn A, 'Image-based Sexual Abuse' in Pontell HN (ed), *Oxford Research Encyclopedia of Criminology and Criminal Justice* (OUP 2022)

Flynn A and Henry N, 'Image-based Sexual Abuse: An Australian Reflection (2021) 31(4) Women and Criminal Justice 313

Flynn A, Cama E, and Scott AJ, 'Image-based Abuse: Gender Differences in Bystander Experiences and Responses' (2022) 656 Trends & Issues in Crime and Criminal Justice <https://doi.org/10.52922/ti78672> accessed 2 October 2023

Flynn A, Cama E, and Scott AJ, *Preventing Image-based Cybercrime in Australia: The Role of Bystanders. A Report to the Criminology Research Council* (AIC 2022)

Flynn A and others, 'Deepfakes and Digitally Altered Imagery Abuse: A Cross-Country Exploration of an Emerging Form of Image-based Sexual Abuse' (2022) 62(6) British Journal of Criminology 1341

Flynn and others, 'Victim-blaming and Image-based Sexual Abuse' (2023) 56(1) Journal of Criminology 7

Franks MA, '"Revenge Porn" Reform: A View from the Front Lines' (2017) 69 Florida Law Review 1252

Gordon-Messer D and others, 'Sexting Among Young Adults' (2013) 52(3) Journal of Adolescent Health 301

Grant JM and others, *Injustice at Every Turn: A Report of the National Transgender Discrimination Survey* (National Center for Transgender Equality and National Gay and Lesbian Task Force 2011)

Hamby SL and others, 'What Difference do Bystanders Make? The Association of Bystander Involvement with Victim Outcomes in a Community Sample' (2016) 6(1) Psychology of Violence 91

Henry N, Flynn A, and Powell A, 'Responding to "Revenge Pornography": Prevalence, Nature and Impacts. Report to the Criminology Research Council' (CRG 08/15–16, Australian Institute of Criminology 2019) <https://www.aic.gov.au/crg/reports/crg-0815-16> accessed 3 March 2023

Henry N and others, *Image-based Sexual Abuse: A Study on the Causes and Consequences of Nonconsensual Nude or Sexual Imagery* (Routledge 2021)

Hudson HK, Fetro JV, and Ogletree R, 'Behavioral Indicators and Behaviors Related to Sexting among Undergraduate Students' (2014) 45(3) American Journal of Health Education 183

Israel T and others, 'Evaluation of Police Training on LGBTQ Issues: Knowledge, Interpersonal Apprehension, and Self-efficacy' (2013) 29(2) Journal of Police and Criminal Psychology 1

Kowalski and others, 'Bullying in the Digital Age: A Critical Review and Meta-Analysis of Cyberbullying Research among Youth' (2014) 140(4) Psychological Bulletin 1073

Langenderfer-Magruder L and others, 'Experiences of Intimate Partner Violence and Subsequent Police Reporting among Lesbian, Gay, Bisexual, Transgender, and Queer Adults in Colorado: Comparing Rates of Cisgender and Transgender Victimization' (2016) 31(5) Journal of Interpersonal Violence 855

Latané B and Darley J, 'Group Inhibition of Bystander Intervention in Emergencies' (1968) 10(3) Journal of Personality and Social Psychology 215

Latané B and Darley J, *The Unresponsive Bystander: Why Doesn't He Help?* (AppletonCentury-Croft 1970)

Lodge J and Frydenberg E, 'The Role of Peer Bystanders in School Bullying: Positive Steps Toward Promoting Peaceful Schools' (2005) 44(4) Theory into Practice 329

Miles-Johnson T, 'Policing Diversity: Examining Police Resistance to Training Reforms for Transgender People in Australia' (2016) 63(1) Journal of Homosexuality 103

Obermann M, 'Moral Disengagement among Bystanders to School Bullying' (2011) 10(3) Journal of School Violence 239

Oh M and Hazler RJ, 'Contributions of Personal and Situational Factors to Bystanders' Reactions to School Bullying' (2009) 30(3) School Psychology International 291

Piliavin JA and others, *Emergency Intervention* (Academic Press 1981)

Pina A, Holland J, and James M, 'The Malevolent Side of Revenge Porn Proclivity: Dark Personality Traits and Sexist Ideology' (2017) 8(1) International Journal of Technoethics 30

Powell A, *Review of Bystander Approaches in Support of Preventing Violence against Women* (Victorian Health Promotion Foundation 2011)

Powell A and others, 'Image-based Sexual Abuse: An International Study of Victims and Perpetrators' (RMIT University 2020)

Powell A and others, 'Image-based Sexual Abuse: Gendered Nature and Correlates of Victimisation in a Multi-Country Survey' (2022) Journal of Sexual Aggression, <https://doi.org/10.1080/13552600.2022.2119292> accessed 3 March 2023

Powell A and others, 'Perpetration of Image-based Sexual Abuse: Extent, Nature and Correlates in a Multi-Country Sample' (2022) 37(23–24) Journal of Interpersonal Violence 22864

Powell A and others, 'A Multi-country Study of Image-based Sexual Abuse' (2022) Journal of Sexual Aggression

Pöyhönen V, Juvonen J, and Salmivalli C, 'Standing Up for the Victim, Siding with the Bully or Standing By? Bystander Responses in Bullying Situations' (2012) 21(4) Social Development 722

Rebollo-Catalan A and Mayor-Buzon V, 'Adolescent Bystanders Witnessing Cyber Violence against Women and Girls: What They Observe and How They Respond' (2020) 26(15–16) Violence against Women 2024

Scott AJ and Gavin J, 'Revenge Pornography: The Influence of Perpetrator–Victim sex, Observer Sex and Observer Sexting Experience on Perceptions of Seriousness and Responsibility' (2018) 8(2) Journal of Criminal Psychology 162

Serpe CR and Nadal KL, 'Perceptions of Police: Experience in the Trans* Community' (2017) 29(3) Journal of Gay and Lesbian Social Services 280

Silver E and Miller LL, 'Sources of Informal Social Control in Chicago Neighborhoods' (2004) 42(3) Criminology 551

Song J and Oh I, 'Factors Influencing Bystanders' Behavioral Reactions in Cyberbullying Situations' (2018) 78 Computers in Human Behavior 273

Taket A and Crisp BR, *Bystanders for Primary Prevention: A Rapid Review* (VicHealth 2017)

Voelpel SC, Eckhoff RA, and Förster J, 'David against Goliath? Group Size and Bystander Effects in Virtual Knowledge Sharing' (2008) 61(2) Human Relations 271

Wang S, 'Standing Up or Standing By: Bystander Intervention in Cyberbullying on Social Media' (2021) 23(6) New Media and Society 1379

Warner BD, 'Directly Intervene or Call the Authorities? A Study of Forms of Neighborhood Social Control within a Social Disorganization Framework' (2007) 45(1) Criminology 99

Index

For the benefit of digital users, indexed terms that span two pages (e.g., 52–53) may, on occasion, appear on only one of those pages.

The manufacturer's authorised representative in the EU for product safety is Oxford University Press España S.A. of el Parque Empresarial San Fernando de Henares, Avenida de Castilla, 2 – 28830 Madrid (www.oup.es/en or product.safety@oup.com). OUP España S.A. also acts as importer into Spain of products made by the manufacturer.

www.ingramcontent.com/pod-product-compliance
Lightning Source LLC
LaVergne TN
LVHW011904200926
848484LV00002B/521

9780198877813